Elmira Prison Camp Roster

Volume II

Elmira Prison Camp Roster

Volume II, G-N

By

Richard H. Triebe

ISBN—13: 978-0-9798965-8-3

ISBN—10: 0-9798965-8-4

Cover photograph: This photograph shows the tents where 5,000 Confederate prisoners lived until early January 1865. The photograph was taken in November or early December of 1864 as evidenced by the lack of leaves on the tree in the foreground. Note the hills, which had been heavily forested before the war, are now nearly devoid of trees. *Photograph courtesy of the North Carolina Museum of History.*

All photographs in this book are from the author's collection unless otherwise noted.

Other books by this author:

Confederate Fort Fisher, ISBN 1484032497

Elmira Prisoner of War Camp ISBN 1539496791

Fort Fisher to Elmira, ISBN 1530023238

On A Rising Tide, ISBN 1-4208-7849-2

Point Lookout Prison Camp and Hospital, ISBN 1495310140

Port Royal, ISBN 0-9798-9650-9

Printed in the United States of America

This book is printed on acid-free paper.

Coastal Books

Acknowledgments

I owe a debt of gratitude to these people and institutions. I wish to thank Tom Fagart for his help in furnishing important Elmira Prison documents. Also, I want to thank Joe Beasley for helping me with the Excel Spreadsheet regarding the prisoners. I also wish to commend the Federal Army for its meticulous record keeping. Without the prisoners records this book would not have been possible. I also owe a debt of gratitude to the National Archives for storing these records in such an organized manner.

Table of Contents

Roster of Prisoners Volume II, G-N
July 6, 1864-July 5, 1865

All prisoners who died are buried in Woodlawn National Cemetery,
Elmira, New York, unless otherwise noted.

Name & Rank	Age	Enlisted	Regiment and State	Where Captured	Prison	Remarks
Gable, James H. Sergeant	Unk	February 11, 1862, Apalachicola, Florida	Co F, 6th Florida Infantry	September 29, 1864, Near Vernon, Florida	New Orleans, Louisiana transferred to Elmira November 19, 1864.	Exchanged February 13, 1865 at Boulware's Wharf on the James River, Virginia
Gabriel, Andrew J. Private	Unk	February 11, 1862, Apalachicola, Florida	Co. F, 6th Florida Infantry	September 29, 1864, Near Vernon, Louisiana	New Orleans, Louisiana transferred to Elmira November 19, 1864.	Died January 4, 1865 of Pneumonia, Grave No. 1269
Gaddy, Richard M. Private	Unk	March 17, 1864, Fayetteville, North Carolina	Co. A, 5th North Carolina Cavalry	May 27, 1864, Hanover, Virginia	Point Lookout, Maryland, transferred to Elmira Prison, NY, July 12, 1864	Exchanged March 10, 1865 at Boulware's Wharf on the James River, Virginia
Gafney, John Sergeant	Unk	March 20, 1862, Memphis, Tennessee	Co. D, Jackson's 1st Regiment, Tennessee Heavy Artillery	August 23, 1864, Fort Morgan, Alabama	New Orleans, Louisiana transferred to Elmira Prison, NY, December 4, 1864.	Exchanged February 13, 1865 at Boulware's wharf on the James River, Virginia
Gaggans, T. F. Private	Unk	Unknown	Co. K, 53rd Virginia Infantry	June 1, 1864, Gaines Mill, Cold Harbor, Virginia	Point Lookout, Maryland, transferred to Elmira Prison, NY, July 17,1864	Oath of Allegiance June 21, 1865
Gaines, E. P. Private	Unk	August 1, 1861, Cobb County, Georgia	Co. C, Phillips Legion, Georgia	June 2, 1864, Gaines Farm, Virginia	Point Lookout, Maryland, transferred to Elmira Prison, NY, July 17,1864	Exchanged October 29, 1864 at Venus Point, Savannah River, GA.

Name & Rank	Age	Enlisted	Regiment and State	Where Captured	Prison	Remarks
Gaines, G. W. Private	Unk	Unknown	Co. A, 16th Georgia Infantry	June 1, 1864, Gaines Farm, Virginia	Point Lookout, Maryland, transferred to Elmira Prison, NY, July 17,1864	Oath of Allegiance May 19, 1865
Gaines, John Private	Unk	Unknown	Co. A, 15th Louisiana Infantry	May 20, 1864, Spotsylvania Court House, Virginia	Point Lookout, Maryland, transferred to Elmira Prison, NY, July 12,1864	Oath of Allegiance May 29, 1865
Gaines, Samuel B. Private	28	July 23, 1861, Matthews Court House, Virginia	Co. F, 5th Virginia Cavalry	May 11, 1864, Yellow Tavern, Hanover County, Virginia	Point Lookout, Maryland, transferred to Elmira Prison, NY, August 17, 1864	Oath of Allegiance June 27, 1865
Gainey, George W. Private	16	December 20, 1861, Chesterfield, South Carolina	Co. E, 21st South Carolina Infantry	June 18, 1864, Near Petersburg, Virginia	Point Lookout, Maryland, transferred to Elmira Prison, NY, July 25, 1864	Died September 4, 1864 of Chronic Diarrhea, Grave No. 74
Gainey, Thomas W. Private	Unk	March 22, 1863, Darlington District, South Carolina	Co. G, 21st South Carolina Infantry	January 15, 1865, Fort Fisher, North Carolina	January 30, 1865, Elmira Prison Camp, New York	Oath of Allegiance July 11, 1865
Gainor, William T. Private	Unk	May 14, 1862, Greenville, North Carolina	Co. K, 10th Regiment, 1st North Carolina Artillery	January 15, 1865, Fort Fisher, North Carolina	January 30, 1865, Elmira Prison Camp, New York	Died March 4, 1865 of Chronic Diarrhea, Grave No. 2001. Headstone has Gaines W. J.
Gaither, John R. Private	Unk	July 6, 1861, Harrisonburg, Virginia	Co. B, 10th Virginia Infantry	May 12, 1864, Spotsylvania Court House, Virginia	Point Lookout, Maryland, transferred to Elmira Prison, NY, August 2, 1864	Died September 16, 1864 of Chronic Diarrhea, Grave No. 301
Galbreath, Malcom Private	Unk	January 23, 1863, Camp Whiting, North Carolina	Co. D, 51st North Carolina Infantry	June 1, 1864, Cold Harbor, Virginia	Point Lookout, Maryland, transferred to Elmira Prison, NY, July 17,1864	Died September 2, 1864 of Chronic Diarrhea, Grave No. 70

Name & Rank	Age	Enlisted	Regiment and State	Where Captured	Prison	Remarks
Gallagher, James Private	27	April 28, 1861, New Orleans, Louisiana	Co. D, 1st Louisiana Infantry	May 20, 1864, Spotsylvania Court House, Virginia	Point Lookout, Maryland, transferred to Elmira Prison, NY, July 6,1864	Oath of Allegiance June 16, 1865
Gallagher, William C. Sergeant	Unk	September 1, 1862, Montgomery, Alabama	Co. M, 6th Alabama Infantry	May 5, 1864, Wilderness, Virginia	Point Lookout, Maryland, transferred to Elmira Prison, NY, August 17, 1864	Oath of Allegiance June 19, 1865
Gallaher, Charles Frank Private	18	April 18, 1861, Jefferson Court House, Virginia	Co. A, 2nd Virginia Infantry	May 12, 1864, Near Spotsylvania Court House, Virginia	Point Lookout, Maryland, transferred to Elmira Prison, NY, August 6, 1864	Exchanged March 2, 1865 at Akins Landing on the James River, Virginia
Gallaher, John Private	Unk	February 11, 1863, Abingdon, Virginia	Co. L, 26th Battalion Virginia Infantry	June 3, 1864, Gaines Farm Cold Harbor, Virginia	Point Lookout, Maryland, transferred to Elmira Prison, NY, July 17,1864	Exchanged 2/20/65 on the James River, VA, Died 3/12/65 of Phthisis Pulmonalis at Chimborazo Hospital No. 2, Richmond, VA
Gallaway, G. Civilian	Unk	Unknown	Citizen of Chesterfield, Virginia	May 12, 1864, Bermuda Hundred, Virginia	Point Lookout, Maryland, transferred to Elmira Prison, NY, July 23, 1864	Exchanged March 14, 1865 at Boulware's Wharf on the James River, Virginia
Gallaway, Joseph E. Private	Unk	June 27, 1861, Wytheville, Virginia	Co. H, 50th Virginia Infantry	May 12, 1864, Spotsylvania Court House, Virginia	Point Lookout, Maryland, transferred to Elmira Prison, NY, August 2, 1864	Transferred For Exchange October 11, 1864 to Point Lookout Prison Camp, MD. Nothing Further.
Gallimore, Roby Private	18	July 11, 1861, Salisbury, North Carolina	Co. K, 8th North Carolina Infantry	May 31, 1864, Cold Harbor, Virginia	Point Lookout, Maryland, transferred to Elmira Prison, NY, July 12, 1864	Exchanged October 29, 1864 at Venus Point, Savannah River, GA.
Galloway, Abram M. Private	Unk	April 15, 1861, Darlington, South Carolina	Co. H, 21st South Carolina Infantry	January 15, 1865, Fort Fisher, North Carolina	January 30, 1865, Elmira Prison Camp, New York	Oath of Allegiance August 7, 1865

Name & Rank	Age	Enlisted	Regiment and State	Where Captured	Prison	Remarks
Galloway, Charles W. Private	Unk	Unknown	Co. C, 26th Virginia Infantry	Unknown	Point Lookout Prison Camp, Maryland. Transferred to Elmira Prison Camp, New York August 14, 1864	Died September 12, 1864 of Chronic Diarrhea, Grave No. 190
Galloway, John Private	Unk	April 28, 1862, Richmond County, North Carolina	Co. E, 52nd North Carolina Infantry	May 12, 1864, Spotsylvania Court House, Virginia	Point Lookout, Maryland, transferred to Elmira Prison, NY, August 12, 1864	Died February 13, 1865 of Variola (Smallpox), Grave No. 2042. Name Gallaway on Headstone.
Galloway, L. Chappel Private	24	January 20, 1862, Darlington District, South Carolina	Co. H, 21st South Carolina Infantry	January 15, 1865, Fort Fisher, North Carolina	January 30, 1865, Elmira Prison Camp, New York	Died April 25, 1865 of Chronic Diarrhea, Grave No. 1417
Galloway, Pipkin Private	Unk	March 1, 1864, James Island, South Carolina	Co. H, 21st South Carolina Infantry	January 15, 1865, Fort Fisher, North Carolina	January 30, 1865, Elmira Prison Camp, New York	Died March 7, 1865 of Gangrene of Feet, Grave No. 2397. Headstone has Gallaway.
Gamble, James C. Sergeant	Unk	August 2, 1861, Moorefield, Hardy County, Virginia	Co. E, 25th Virginia Infantry	May 12, 1864, Spotsylvania Court House, Virginia	Point Lookout, Maryland, transferred to Elmira Prison, NY, August 12, 1864	Oath of Allegiance June 16, 1865
Gamble, John F. Private	Unk	December 20, 1862, Sumter District, South Carolina	Co. H, 26th South Carolina Infantry	July 30, 1864, Petersburg, Virginia	Point Lookout, Maryland, transferred to Elmira Prison, NY, August 12, 1864	Exchanged 3/14/65. Died 4/3/65 of Chronic Diarrhea at Confederate States Army Hospital, Danville, VA.
Gamble, Joseph W. Private	37	December 29, 1861, Williamsburg, South Carolina	Co. K, 25th South Carolina Infantry	January 15, 1865, Fort Fisher, North Carolina	January 30, 1865 Elmira Prison Camp, New York	Oath of Allegiance July 3, 1865

Name & Rank	Age	Enlisted	Regiment and State	Where Captured	Prison	Remarks
Gamble, Thomas E. Private	27	May 16, 1862, Charleston, South Carolina	Co. K, 25th South Carolina Infantry	January 15, 1865, Fort Fisher, North Carolina	January 30, 1865 Elmira Prison Camp, New York	Died April 7, 1865 of chronic Diarrhea, Grave No. 2645
Gambrel, Stephen A. Corporal	Unk	August 24, 1861, Clayton, Georgia	Co. E, 24th Georgia Infantry	August 16, 1864, Front Royal, Virginia	Old Capital Prison, Washington, DC transferred to Elmira Prison, NY, August 29, 1864	Oath of Allegiance July 11, 1865
Gammon, William A. Private	Unk	March 24, 1862, Louisa Court House, Virginia	Co. A, 23rd Virginia Infantry	May 20, 1864, Spotsylvania Court House, Virginia	Point Lookout, Maryland, transferred to Elmira Prison, NY, July 6, 1864	Died April 27, 1865 of Chronic Diarrhea, Grave No. 2722
Gandy, Ephraim Private	21	January 1, 1864, Darlington District, South Carolina	Co. E, 21st South Carolina Infantry	June 17, 1864, Petersburg, Virginia	Point Lookout, Maryland, transferred to Elmira Prison, NY, July 30, 1864	Exchanged February 13, 1865 at Boulware's wharf on the James River, Virginia
Gann, Bethel Private	37	September 1, 1863, Valley Town, North Carolina	Co. D, 25th North Carolina Infantry	July 29, 1864, Petersburg, Virginia	Point Lookout, Maryland, transferred to Elmira Prison, NY, August 12, 1864	Exchanged October 29, 1864 at Venus Point, Savannah River, GA.
Gann, Samuel T. Private	24	October 17, 1864, Rockingham, North Carolina	Co. F, 45th North Carolina Infantry	April 1, 1865, Petersburg, Virginia. Gunshot Wound left Hand.	Old Capital Prison, Washington D. C. Transferred to Elmira Prison, NY, May 2, 1865.	Oath of Allegiance July 7, 1865
Gannon, Andrew J. Private	Unk	June 11, 1861, Pickens County, Alabama	Co. H, 11th Alabama Infantry	May 10, 1864, Spotsylvania Court House, Virginia	Point Lookout, Maryland, transferred to Elmira Prison, NY, August 17, 1864	Oath of Allegiance May 29, 1865
Gannon, James Private	Unk	July 22, 1861, Camp Moore, Louisiana	Co. C, 10th Louisiana Infantry	May 12, 1864, Spotsylvania Court House, Virginia	Point Lookout, Maryland, transferred to Elmira Prison, NY, July 25, 1864	Exchanged February 25, 1865 at Boulware's or Cox Wharf on the James River, Virginia

Name & Rank	Age	Enlisted	Regiment and State	Where Captured	Prison	Remarks
Ganns, Wiley Private	Unk	October 20, 1863, Fort Caswell, North Carolina	Co. D, 36th Regiment, 2nd North Carolina Artillery	January 15, 1865, Fort Fisher, North Carolina	February 1, 1865 Elmira Prison Camp, New York	Oath of Allegiance July 7, 1865
Gant, John S. Private	Unk	September 19, 1861, Dalton, Georgia	Co. C, 60th Georgia Infantry	August 11, 1864, Newton, Virginia	Old Capital Prison, Washington, DC transferred to Elmira Prison, NY, August 27, 1864	Oath of Allegiance May 29, 1865
Gant, William T. Private	25	December 9, 1861, Camp Trousdale, Tennessee	Co. D, 44th Tennessee Infantry	June 12, 1864, Petersburg, Virginia	Point Lookout, Maryland, transferred to Elmira Prison, NY, July 23, 1864	Oath of Allegiance March 10, 1865
Gantz, Emil Private	22	June 27, 1861, Cedar Town, Polk County, Georgia	Co. D, 21st Georgia Infantry	July 8, 1864, Near Harper's Ferry, Virginia	Old Capital Prison, Washington, DC, transferred to Elmira July 23, 1864	Oath of Allegiance January 24, 1865
Ganus, Stephen D. Private	21	July 3, 1861, Wilmington, North Carolina	Co. C, 8th North Carolina Infantry	June 1, 1864, Cold Harbor, Virginia	Point Lookout, Maryland, transferred to Elmira Prison, NY, July 17, 1864	Oath of Allegiance May 19, 1865
Gardener, David W. Private	24	July 19, 1861, Columbus, Mississippi	Co. C, 48th Mississippi Infantry	May 12, 1864, Spotsylvania Court House, Virginia. Gunshot Wound Thigh.	Old Capital Prison, Washington, DC transferred to Elmira Prison, NY, August 27, 1864	Exchanged February 25, 1865 at Boulware's or Cox Wharf on the James River, Virginia
Gardener, E. T. Private	Unk	April 11, 1864, Montgomery, Alabama	Co. A, 1st Alabama Artillery	August 23, 1864, Fort Morgan, Alabama	New Orleans, Louisiana transferred to Elmira Prison, NY, December 4, 1864.	Exchanged February 20, 1865 at Boulware's or Cox Wharf on the James River, Virginia
Gardener, J. B. Private	Unk	May 11, 1861 New Orleans, Louisiana	Co. F, 2nd Louisiana Infantry	May 20, 1864, Spotsylvania Court House, Virginia	Point Lookout, Maryland, transferred to Elmira Prison, NY, July 3, 1864	Exchanged February 25, 1865 at Boulware's or Cox Wharf on the James River, Virginia

Name & Rank	Age	Enlisted	Regiment and State	Where Captured	Prison	Remarks
Gardner, A. M. Private	Unk	June 15, 1863, M. Bluff, Virginia	Co. F, 26th Virginia Infantry	May 31, 1864, Cold Harbor, Virginia	Point Lookout, Maryland, transferred to Elmira Prison, NY, July 17,1864	Died August 2, 1864 of Rubeola (Measles), Grave No. 3
Gardner, Benjamin W. Private	Unk	May 15, 1864, Smithville, North Carolina	Co. F, 10th Regiment, 1st North Carolina Artillery	January 15, 1865, Fort Fisher, North Carolina	January 30, 1865, Elmira Prison Camp, New York	Died March 5, 1865 of Intermittent Fever, Grave No. 2375
Gardner, Bartlett G. Private	17	April 30, 1861, Corinth, Mississippi	Co. A, 12th Mississippi Infantry	July 29, 1864, Petersburg, Virginia. Deserted while on Picket near Petersburg.	Point Lookout, Maryland, transferred to Elmira Prison, NY, August 12, 1864	Oath of Allegiance June 23, 1865
Gardner, Harvel N. Private	Unk	February 1, 1863, Camden, South Carolina	Co. G, 7th Battalion South Carolina Infantry	May 16, 1864, Near Drury's Bluff, Virginia	Point Lookout, Maryland, transferred to Elmira Prison, NY, August 17, 1864	Exchanged March 14, 1865. Died April 27, 1865 of Chronic Diarrhea at CSA General Hospital, No. 11, Charlotte, NC.
Gardner, J. B. Private	35	January 20, 1862, Darlington, South Carolina	Co. H, 21st South Carolina Infantry	June 18, 1864, Near Petersburg, Virginia	Point Lookout, Maryland, transferred to Elmira Prison, NY, July 12, 1864	Exchange 10/11/1864. Exchanged 11/15/1864 at Venus Point, Savannah River, GA
Gardner, J. M. Private	Unk	July 9, 1863, Marion, South Carolina	Co. I, 6th South Carolina Cavalry	July 30, 1864, Lee's Mill, Petersburg, Virginia	Point Lookout, Maryland, transferred to Elmira Prison, NY, August 12, 1864	Oath of Allegiance June 19, 1865
Gardner, James F. Sergeant	Unk	July 2, 1861, Bethel, Virginia	Co. F, 50th Virginia Infantry	May 12, 1864, Spotsylvania Court House, Virginia	Point Lookout, Maryland, transferred to Elmira Prison, NY, July 30, 1864	Exchanged March 14, 1865 at Boulware's Wharf on the James River, Virginia
Gardner, Robinson Private	16	October 19, 1861, Elizabethtown, Bladen County, North Carolina	Co. E, 36th Regiment, 2nd North Carolina Artillery	January 15, 1865, Fort Fisher, North Carolina	February 1, 1865 Elmira Prison Camp, New York	Died March 2, 1865 of Variola (Smallpox), Grave No. 2018

Name & Rank	Age	Enlisted	Regiment and State	Where Captured	Prison	Remarks
Gardner, T. W. Private	Unk	July 1, 1861, Lafayette, Alabama	Co. G, 14th Alabama Infantry	May 31, 1864 Mechanicsville, Virginia	Point Lookout, Maryland, transferred to Elmira Prison, NY, July 11, 1864	Oath of Allegiance June 14, 1865
Gardner, William C. Private	22	April 18, 1862, Greenville, North Carolina	Co. E, 55th North Carolina Infantry	May 5, 1864, Wilderness, Virginia. Gunshot Right Thigh.	Old Capital Prison, Washington D. C. Transferred to Elmira, NY, August 12, 1864	Died January 1, 1865 of Chronic Diarrhea, Grave No. 1329
Gardner, William R. Private	20	July 5, 1861, Murfreesboro, North Carolina	Co. F, 1st North Carolina Infantry	May 12, 1864, Wilderness, Spotsylvania Court House, Virginia	Point Lookout, Maryland, transferred to Elmira Prison, NY, August 6, 1864	Exchanged March 14, 1865 at Boulware's Wharf on the James River, Virginia
Garen, Michael Sailor	Unk	Unknown	Confederate States Navy	April 6, 1865, Sailor's Creek, Virginia	Old Capital Prison, Washington D. C. Transferred to Elmira, NY, May 12, 1865.	Oath of Allegiance July 11, 1865
Garner, Addison Private	32	July 15, 1862, Raleigh, North Carolina	Co. E, 1st North Carolina Infantry	May 12, 1864, Wilderness, Spotsylvania Court House, Virginia	Point Lookout, Maryland, transferred to Elmira Prison, NY, August 6, 1864	Died March 23, 1865 of Pneumonia, Grave No. 1513. Name Gerner on Headstone.
Garner, Alex G. Private	Unk	May 14, 1862, Sandersville, Georgia	Co. E, 12th Georgia Light Artillery	July 8, 1864, Near Harper's Ferry, Virginia	Old Capital Prison, Washington, DC, transferred to Elmira July 23, 1864	Died April 27, 1865 of Chronic Diarrhea, Grave No. 2723
Garner, David F. Private	21	July 20, 1861, Shephards-ville, North Carolina	Co. F, 10th Regiment, 1st North Carolina Artillery	January 15, 1865, Fort Fisher, North Carolina	January 30, 1865, Elmira Prison Camp, New York	Died May 8, 1865 of Chronic Diarrhea, Grave No. 2778
Garner, Francis A. Private	24	February 15, 1863, Yadkinville, North Carolina	Co. B, 38th North Carolina Infantry	May 6, 1864, Wilderness, Virginia	Point Lookout, Maryland, transferred to Elmira Prison, NY, August 14, 1864	Oath of Allegiance June 16, 1865

Name & Rank	Age	Enlisted	Regiment and State	Where Captured	Prison	Remarks
Garner, H. S. Private	Unk	April 12, 1862, Battery Island, South Carolina	Co. C, 25th South Carolina Infantry	May 14, 1864, Near Fort Darling, Virginia	Point Lookout, Maryland, transferred to Elmira Prison, NY, August 17, 1864	Exchanged October 29, 1864 at Venus Point, Savannah River, GA.
Garner, J. William Private	Unk	January 25, 1864, James Island, South Carolina	Co. C, 25th South Carolina Infantry	January 15, 1865, Fort Fisher, North Carolina	January 30, 1865 Elmira Prison Camp, New York	Exchanged February 20, 1865. Died Of Unknown Disease 3/9/1865 In Howard's Grove Hospital, Richmond, VA
Garner, John J. Private	20	March 7, 1861, Texas, Alabama	Co. A, 1st Battalion Alabama Artillery	August 23, 1864, Fort Morgan, Alabama	Steam Press No. 4 New Orleans, Louisiana transferred to Elmira October 8, 1864.	Oath of Allegiance May 15, 1865
Garner, Washington W. Private	Unk	April 29, 1861, Calhoun, Georgia	Co. F, 4th Georgia Infantry	July 13, 1864, Near Washington, DC	Old Capital Prison, Washington, DC, transferred to Elmira July 23, 1864	Exchanged October 29, 1864 at Venus Point, Savannah River, GA.
Garner, William Private	Unk	February 17, 1864, Richmond, Virginia	Co. G, 27th Virginia Infantry	May 20, 1864, Spotsylvania Court House, Virginia	Point Lookout, Maryland, transferred to Elmira Prison, NY, July 3, 1864	Died July 26, 1864 of Rubeola (Measles) and Pneumonia, Grave No. 1
Garrell, W. H. Private	28	March 6, 1862, Fort Johnson, Brunswick County, North Carolina	Co. D, 20th North Carolina Infantry	May 12, 1864, Near Spotsylvania Court House, Virginia	Point Lookout Prison, Maryland. Transferred to Elmira Prison Camp New York August 14, 1864.	Died March 30, 1865 of Diarrhea, Grave No. 2531. Headstone has Garrett.
Garretson, Napoleon B. Private	Unk	February 14, 1864, Lewisburg, Virginia	Co. D, 26th Battalion, Virginia Infantry	May 31, 1864, Cold Harbor, Virginia	Point Lookout, Maryland, transferred to Elmira Prison, NY, July 12, 1864	Exchanged October 29, 1864 at Venus Point, Savannah River, GA.

Name & Rank	Age	Enlisted	Regiment and State	Where Captured	Prison	Remarks
Garrett, G. F. Private	Unk	Unknown	Co. C, 23rd North Carolina Infantry	May 12, 1864, Near Spotsylvania Court House, Virginia	Point Lookout Prison, Maryland. Transferred to Elmira Prison Camp New York August 14, 1864.	Oath of Allegiance June 19, 1865
Garrett, George W. Private	Unk	May 6, 1862, Lafayette, Georgia	Co. J, 60th Georgia Infantry	September 22, 1864, Fishers Hill, Virginia	November 11, 1864, Old Capital Prison, Washington, DC. February 4, 1865 Elmira, Prison Camp, NY	Oath of Allegiance July 11, 1865
Garrett, George W. Private	20	July 15, 1862, Raleigh, North Carolina	Co. E, 1st North Carolina Infantry	May 12, 1864, Spotsylvania Court House, Virginia	Point Lookout, Maryland, transferred to Elmira Prison, NY, August 6, 1864	Oath of Allegiance June 30, 1865
Garrett, Henry W. Corporal	24	July 15, 1862, Raleigh, North Carolina	Co. C, 1st North Carolina Infantry	May 12, 1864, Spotsylvania Court House, Virginia	Point Lookout, Maryland, transferred to Elmira Prison, NY, August 6, 1864	Oath of Allegiance June 30, 1865
Garrett, J. S. Sergeant	Unk	July 19, 1861, Montgomery, Alabama	Co. D, 3rd Alabama Infantry	May 12, 1864, Spotsylvania Court House, Virginia	Point Lookout, Maryland, transferred to Elmira Prison, NY, August 12, 1864	Oath of Allegiance June 19, 1865
Garrett, Lemuel Private	33	August 12, 1861, Campbellton, Campbell County, Georgia	Co. B, 35th Georgia Infantry	May 6, 1864, Smith Ford, Virginia	Point Lookout, Maryland, transferred to Elmira Prison, NY, July 26, 1864	Exchanged October 29, 1864 at Venus Point, Savannah River, GA.
Garrett, Richard C. Private	40	June 2, 1861, Little Plymouth, Virginia	Co. G, 26th Virginia Infantry	June 15, 1864, Petersburg, Virginia	Point Lookout, Maryland, transferred to Elmira Prison, NY, July 30, 1864	Died March 8, 1865 of Typhoid Fever, Grave No. 2362. Name Richard Garnett on Headstone.

Name & Rank	Age	Enlisted	Regiment and State	Where Captured	Prison	Remarks
Garrett, Thomas C. Private	28	June 2, 1861, Little Plymouth, Virginia	Co. G, 26th Virginia Infantry	August 31, 1863, Big Black, Mississippi	Point Lookout, Maryland, transferred to Elmira Prison, NY, August 18, 1864	Exchanged March 10, 1865 at Boulware's wharf on the James River, Virginia
Garrett, W. B. Private	Unk	May 28, 1863, Wilmington, North Carolina	Co. D, 18th South Carolina Infantry	July 30, 1864, Petersburg, Virginia	Point Lookout, Maryland, transferred to Elmira Prison, NY, August 12, 1864	Transferred for Exchange 10/11/64. Died 10/14/64 of Unknown Causes at US Army Hospital, Baltimore, MD.
Garrett, William H. Private	Unk	August 15, 1863, Montgomery, Alabama	Co. G, 3rd Alabama Infantry	May 12, 1864, Spotsylvania Court House, Virginia	Point Lookout, Maryland, transferred to Elmira Prison, NY, August 12, 1864	Oath of Allegiance June 16, 1865
Garrigan, Robert Private	23	May 4, 1861, Orleans Barracks, New Orleans, Louisiana	Co. K, Nelligan's 1st Louisiana Infantry	May 23, 1864, North Anna, Virginia	Point Lookout, Maryland, transferred to Elmira Prison, NY, July 28,1864	Oath of Allegiance March 2, 1865. Early Release per Lincoln's Proclamation, 12/8/1863.
Garris, Blount Private	46	October 27, 1862, Pitt County, North Carolina	Co. G, 8th North Carolina Infantry	June 1, 1864, Cold Harbor, Virginia	Point Lookout, Maryland, transferred to Elmira Prison, NY, July 17,1864	Died September April 9, 1865 of Chronic Diarrhea, Grave No. 2620
Garris, James R. Private	23	June 1, 1861, Dogwood Grove, North Carolina	Co. K, 3rd North Carolina Infantry	May 12, 1864, Near Spotsylvania Court House, Virginia	Point Lookout Prison, Maryland. Transferred to Elmira Prison Camp New York August 14, 1864.	Oath of Allegiance June 12, 1865
Garrison, J. T. Private	Unk	January 1, 1862, Camp Hampton, Columbia, South Carolina	Co. H, 18th South Carolina Infantry	July 30, 1864, Petersburg, Virginia	Point Lookout, Maryland, transferred to Elmira Prison, NY, August 12, 1864	Oath of Allegiance June 19, 1865

Name & Rank	Age	Enlisted	Regiment and State	Where Captured	Prison	Remarks
Garrison, Samuel Private	Unk	Unknown	Captain Cooper's Battery Virginia Light Artillery	May 12, 1864, Spotsylvania, Virginia	Point Lookout, Maryland, transferred to Elmira Prison, NY, July 23, 1864	Oath of Allegiance June 21, 1865
Garrison, William S. Private	Unk	January 1, 1862, Charlottes-ville, Virginia	Co. D, 46th Virginia Infantry	June 17, 1864, Near Petersburg, Virginia	Point Lookout, Maryland, transferred to Elmira Prison, NY, July 30, 1864	Oath of Allegiance July 3, 1865
Garriss, George W. Private	20	July 14, 1862, Wilmington, North Carolina	Co. A, 51st North Carolina Infantry	June 1, 1864, Gaines Mill, Virginia	Point Lookout, Maryland, transferred to Elmira Prison, NY, July 17,1864	Exchanged February 20, 1865 at Boulware's or Cox Wharf on the James River, Virginia
Garritt, Durill Private	17	July 20, 1862, Raleigh, North Carolina	Co. E, 35th North Carolina Infantry	June 17, 1864, Petersburg, Virginia	Point Lookout, Maryland, transferred to Elmira Prison, NY, July 30, 1864	Exchanged October 29, 1864 at Venus Point, Savannah River, GA.
Garrity, James Sergeant	Unk	July 9, 1861, New Orleans, Louisiana	Co. C, 15th Louisiana Infantry	May 20, 1864, Spotsylvania Court House, Virginia	Point Lookout, Maryland, transferred to Elmira Prison, NY, July 3, 1864	Exchanged February 13, 1865 at Boulware's wharf on the James River, Virginia
Garver, S. H. Private	Unk	Unknown	Co. H, 31st North Carolina Infantry	June 1, 1864, Gaines Mill, Virginia	Point Lookout, Maryland, transferred to Elmira Prison, NY, July 17,1864	Exchanged October 29, 1864 at Venus Point, Savannah River, GA.
Garvey, James Private	23	May 27, 1861, Wilmington, North Carolina	Co. D, 3rd North Carolina Infantry	May 10, 1864, Spotsylvania, Virginia	Point Lookout, Maryland, transferred to Elmira Prison, NY, August 17, 1864	Exchanged October 29, 1864 at Venus Point, Savannah River, GA.
Garvey, Peter Private	23	June 7, 1861, Camp Moore, Louisiana	Co. D, 7th Louisiana Infantry	May 5, 1864, Wilderness, Virginia	Point Lookout, Maryland, transferred to Elmira Prison, NY, August 17, 1864	Oath of Allegiance May 17, 1865
Gasque, J. M. Corporal	18	January 14, 1862, Marion District, South Carolina	Co. L, 21st South Carolina Infantry	January 15, 1865, Fort Fisher, North Carolina	January 30, 1865, Elmira Prison Camp, New York	Oath of Allegiance July 11, 1865

Name & Rank	Age	Enlisted	Regiment and State	Where Captured	Prison	Remarks
Gasque, Samuel O. Private	18	May 14, 1862, Marion District, South Carolina	Co. L, 21st South Carolina Infantry	January 15, 1865, Fort Fisher, North Carolina	January 30, 1865, Elmira Prison Camp, New York	Died March 28, 1865 of Diarrhea, Grave No. 2503. Headstone has Glasque.
Gasque, Wilson H. Sergeant	Unk	September 1, 1862, New Road, Louisiana	Co. J, 2nd Louisiana Cavalry	October 10, 1864, Atchafalia, Louisiana	New Orleans, Louisiana transferred to Elmira November 19, 1864.	Died January 19, 1865 of Typhoid Fever, Grave No. 1586
Gaster, Joseph Private		September 20, 1862, Charleston, Virginia	Co. A, 26th Virginia Infantry	May 11, 1864, Hanover Court House, Virginia	Point Lookout, Maryland, transferred to Elmira Prison, NY, August 17, 1864	Oath of Allegiance May 29, 1865
Gatchell, John G. Private	30	May 1, 1863, Richmond, Virginia	2nd Battery Maryland Artillery	September 14, 1863, Near Culpepper, Virginia	Point Lookout, Maryland, transferred to Elmira Prison, NY, August 18, 1864	Exchanged February 25, 1865 at Boulware's or Cox Wharf on the James River, Virginia
Gates, H. W. Private	Unk	Unknown	Co. B, 1st Jackson's Tennessee Heavy Artillery	August 23, 1864, Fort Morgan, Alabama.	New Orleans, Louisiana transferred to Elmira Prison, NY, December 4, 1864.	Oath of Allegiance March 16, 1865
Gates, Joseph J. Private	Unk	June 8, 1861, Isbell's Store, Virginia	Co. D, 44th Virginia Infantry	May 12, 1864, Spotsylvania Court House, Virginia	Point Lookout, Maryland, transferred to Elmira Prison, NY, August 12, 1864	Died September 29, 1864 of Chronic Diarrhea, Grave No. 435
Gates, Marcus W. Private	25	August 15, 1862, Iredell County, North Carolina	Co. C, 37th North Carolina Infantry	May 24, 1864, Hanover Junction, Virginia	Point Lookout, Maryland, transferred to Elmira Prison, NY, July 11, 1864	Oath of Allegiance May 13, 1865
Gatewood, A. Llewellyn Private	Unk	August 16, 1864, Fort Davis, Virginia	Co. A, 10th Virginia Artillery	April 3, 1865, Henrico County, Virginia	Old Capital Prison, Washington D. C. Transferred to Elmira, NY, May 12, 1865.	Oath of Allegiance July 7, 1865

Name & Rank	Age	Enlisted	Regiment and State	Where Captured	Prison	Remarks
Gatewood, William Henry Private	Unk	June 13, 1861, Clarkson, Virginia	Co. J, 26th Virginia Infantry	June 17, 1864, Near Petersburg, Virginia	Point Lookout, Maryland, transferred to Elmira Prison, NY, July 30, 1864	Exchanged September 18, 1864 at Akins Landing on the James River, Virginia
Gatewood, Wyatt Private	Unk	July 2, 1861, Bethel Am., Virginia	Co. F, 50th Virginia Infantry	May 12, 1864, Spotsylvania Court House, Virginia	Point Lookout, Maryland, transferred to Elmira Prison, NY, August 2, 1864	Exchanged March 2, 1865 at Akins Landing on the James River, Virginia
Gathin, Isaac T. Private	27	January 21, 1862, Bowling Green, Tennessee	Co. F, 44th Tennessee Infantry	June 17, 1864, Petersburg, Virginia	Point Lookout, Maryland, transferred to Elmira Prison, NY, July 23, 1864	Oath of Allegiance May 2, 1865
Gats, Randolph Private	Unk	Unknown	Co. E, 50th Virginia Infantry	May 12, 1864, Spotsylvania Court House, Virginia	Point Lookout, Maryland, transferred to Elmira Prison, NY, August 2, 1864	Exchanged March 14, 1865 at Boulware's Wharf on the James River, Virginia
Gatton, William F. Private	Unk	Unknown	Co. B, 35th Battalion Virginia Cavalry	June 3, 1864, Gaines Mill, Virginia	Transferred From Point Lookout Prison, MD, July 12, 1864. Train Never Arrived at Elmira Prison Camp, NY.	Died July 15, 1864 in Train Wreck at Shohola, Pennsylvania.
Gause, William Q. Private	18	February 26, 1863, Brunswick County, North Carolina	Co. H, 36th Regiment, 2nd North Carolina Artillery	January 15, 1865, Fort Fisher, North Carolina	February 1, 1865 Elmira Prison Camp, New York	Oath of Allegiance July 7, 1865
Gauze, D. Private	Unk	Unknown	Co. B, Donaldson's Battalion Infantry	October 7, 1864, Near Greensburg, Louisiana	New Orleans, Louisiana transferred to Elmira November 19, 1864.	Died February 13, 1865 of General Debility, Grave No. 2062. Headstone has D. Ganae.
Gawthrop, James W. Private	Unk	May 27, 1861, Buckhannon, Virginia	Co. B, 25th Virginia Infantry	May 12, 1864, Spotsylvania Court House, Virginia	Point Lookout, Maryland, transferred to Elmira Prison, NY, July 30, 1864	Exchanged October 29, 1864 at Venus Point, Savannah River, GA.

Name & Rank	Age	Enlisted	Regiment and State	Where Captured	Prison	Remarks
Gay, James B. Private	28	May 3, 1862, Dublin, Georgia	Co. H, 14th Georgia Infantry	May 12, 1864, Spotsylvania, Virginia	Old Capital Prison, Washington, DC, transferred to Elmira July 23, 1864	Exchanged February 13, 1865 at Boulware's wharf on the James River, Virginia
Gay, P. W. Private	Unk	January 15, 1864, Bennettsville, South Carolina	Co. F, 21st South Carolina Infantry	January 15, 1865, Fort Fisher, North Carolina	January 30, 1865, Elmira Prison Camp, New York	Died February 13, 1865 of Pneumonia, Grave No. 2063. Headstone has Gray.
Gay, William Private	20	July 15, 1862, Raleigh, North Carolina	Co. K, 1st North Carolina Infantry	May 12, 1864, Spotsylvania Court House, Virginia	Point Lookout, Maryland, transferred to Elmira Prison, NY, August 6, 1864	Exchanged March 14, 1865 at Boulware's Wharf on the James River, Virginia
Gaylor, Gum M. Sergeant	Unk	November 11, 1863, Bath County, Virginia	Co. E, 46th Battalion Virginia Cavalry	July 17,1864, Near Washington, DC	Old Capital Prison, Washington, DC, transferred to Elmira Prison July 25, 1864	Exchanged October 29, 1864 at Venus Point, Savannah River, GA.
Geddis, Hiram J. Private	Unk	April 22, 1861, Greensboro, Alabama	Co. D, 5th Alabama Infantry	May 12, 1864, Spotsylvania Court House, Virginia	Point Lookout, Maryland, transferred to Elmira Prison, NY, July 6, 1864	Exchanged October 29, 1864 at Venus Point, Savannah River, GA.
Geer, Frederick S. Private	22	March 8, 1862, Lake City, Florida	Co. B, 5th Florida Infantry	May 12, 1864, Spotsylvania Court House, Virginia	Point Lookout, Maryland, transferred to Elmira Prison, NY, August 12, 1864	Oath of Allegiance June 19, 1865
Geer, Thomas Private	Unk	Unknown	Co. B, 48th Virginia Infantry	May 12, 1864, Spotsylvania Court House, Virginia	Point Lookout, Maryland, transferred to Elmira Prison, NY, August 2, 1864	Oath of Allegiance June 14, 1865
Gellespie, David Private	Unk	September 4, 1862, Jefferson County, Alabama	Co. A, 21st Alabama Infantry	August 23, 1864, Fort Morgan, Alabama	Steam Press No. 4 New Orleans, Louisiana transferred to Elmira October 8, 1864.	Oath of Allegiance July 7, 1865

Name & Rank	Age	Enlisted	Regiment and State	Where Captured	Prison	Remarks
Gennotte, Raphael Private	31	May 9, 1861, Lewisburg, Virginia	Co. F, 27th Virginia Infantry	May 20, 1864, Spotsylvania Court House, Virginia	Point Lookout, Maryland, transferred to Elmira Prison, NY, July 3, 1864	Oath of Allegiance May 13, 1865
Gent, Luther Private	Unk	Unknown	Co. A, 23rd Virginia Cavalry	July 16, 1864, Loudoun County, Virginia	Old Capital Prison, Washington, DC, transferred to Elmira July 23, 1864	Oath of Allegiance July 11, 1865
Gentry, David R. Private	Unk	June 8, 1861, Isbell's Store, Virginia	Co. D, 44th Virginia Infantry	May 12, 1864, Spotsylvania Court House, Virginia	Point Lookout, Maryland, transferred to Elmira Prison, NY, August 2,1864	Oath of Allegiance June 14, 1865
George, Charles C. Private	Unk	Unknown	Co. C, 12th Georgia Infantry	July 4, 1864 Alexander County, Virginia	Old Capital Prison, Washington, DC, transferred to Elmira July 23, 1864	Joined Federal Army and deserted. Captured and ordered for trial by Major General Dix August 30, 1864
George, Francis M. Private	Unk	June 22, 1861, Richmond, Virginia	Co. C, 46th Virginia Infantry	June 16, 1864, Petersburg, Virginia	Point Lookout, Maryland, transferred to Elmira Prison, NY, August 18, 1864	Exchanged February 20, 1865 at Boulware's or Cox Wharf on the James River, Virginia
George, Jefferson Private	24	June 1, 1861, Valley Town, North Carolina	Co. D, 25th North Carolina Infantry	July 30, 1864, Petersburg, Virginia	Point Lookout, Maryland, transferred to Elmira Prison, NY, August 12, 1864	Oath of Allegiance July 3, 1865
George, Thomas Seaman	Unk	Unknown	Confederate States Navy	May 5, 1864, Albemarle Sound on Steamer CSS Bombshell	Point Lookout, Maryland, transferred to Elmira Prison, NY, August 17, 1864	Transferred For Exchange October 11, 1864 to Point Lookout Prison Camp, MD. Nothing Further.
George, Thomas N. Private	Unk	March 1, 1862, Heathsville, Virginia	Co. A, 40th Virginia Infantry	May 5, 1864, Wilderness, Virginia	Point Lookout, Maryland, transferred to Elmira Prison, NY, July 23, 1864	Died November 25, 1864 of Pneumonia, Grave No. 916

Name & Rank	Age	Enlisted	Regiment and State	Where Captured	Prison	Remarks
George, Zamuth W. Civilian	Unk	Unknown	Citizen of Lancaster County, Virginia	August 10, 1863, Lancaster County, Virginia	Point Lookout, Maryland, transferred to Elmira Prison, NY, July 25, 1864	Exchanged March 20, 1865 at Boulware's Wharf on the James River, Virginia
Gerard, Joseph Private	Unk	Unknown	Captain Hutton's Co. A, Crescent Louisiana Artillery	March 14, 1864, Fort DeRussy, Louisiana	New Orleans, LA, Transferred to Elmira Prison, NY, November 19, 1864	Oath of Allegiance May 15, 1865
Gerken, E. F. Henry Musician Private	38	February 22, 1862, Charleston, South Carolina	Co. E, 25th South Carolina Infantry	January 15, 1865, Fort Fisher, North Carolina	January 30, 1865 Elmira Prison Camp, New York	Oath of Allegiance May 15, 1865
Gerry, James Private	Unk	June 19, 1861, New Orleans, Louisiana	Co. A, 21st Louisiana Infantry	October 8, 1864, Near St. Joseph, Louisiana	New Orleans, Louisiana transferred to Elmira November 19, 1864.	Exchanged February 25, 1865 at Boulware's or Cox Wharf on the James River, Virginia
Gholson, John E. Private	Unk	June 15, 1861, Eatonton, Georgia	Co. G, 12th Georgia Infantry	May 10, 1864, Spotsylvania Court House, Virginia	Point Lookout, Maryland, transferred to Elmira Prison, NY, July 25, 1864	Oath of Allegiance June 16, 1865
Gholston, William J. Private	Unk	July 10, 1861, Danielsville, Georgia	Co. A, 16th Georgia Infantry	August 16, 1864, Front Royal, Virginia	Old Capital Prison, Washington, DC transferred to Elmira Prison, NY, August 29, 1864	Oath of Allegiance May 17, 1865
Gholston, Willis W. Private	Unk	February 1, 1862, Yorktown, Virginia	Co. C, 3rd Battalion Georgia Sharp Shooters	August 16, 1864, Front Royal, Virginia	Old Capital Prison, Washington, DC transferred to Elmira Prison, NY, August 29, 1864	Oath of Allegiance June 16, 1865
Gibbes, J. Perouneau Private	Unk	March 24, 1863, Charleston, South Carolina	Co. A, 27th South Carolina Infantry	June 24, 1864, Near Petersburg, Virginia	Point Lookout, Maryland, transferred to Elmira Prison, NY, August 18, 1864	Exchanged October 29, 1864 at Venus Point, Savannah River, GA.

Name & Rank	Age	Enlisted	Regiment and State	Where Captured	Prison	Remarks
Gibbs, Benjamin Private	28	May 20, 1862, Richmond, Virginia	Co. K, 13th Alabama Infantry	May 6, 1864, Wilderness, Virginia	Point Lookout, Maryland, transferred to Elmira Prison, NY, August 14, 1864	Oath of Allegiance June 16, 1865
Gibbs, William B. Private	25	September 9, 1861, Middleton, North Carolina	Co. F, 33rd North Carolina Infantry	May 6, 1864, Wilderness, Virginia	Old Capital Prison, Washington, DC, transferred to Elmira July 14, 1864	Oath of Allegiance July 7, 1865
Gibbs, William B. Private	Unk	Unknown	Co. A, 30th Battalion Virginia Sharp Shooters	June 1, 1864, Ashland, Virginia	Point Lookout, Maryland, transferred to Elmira Prison, NY, July 17,1864	Died February 28, 1865 of Variola (Smallpox), Grave No. 2113
Gibbs, William C. Private	Unk	April 10, 1862, Yorktown, Virginia	Co. K, 13th Alabama Infantry	May 8, 1864, Wilderness, Virginia	Point Lookout, Maryland, transferred to Elmira Prison, NY, August 14, 1864	Exchanged February 20, 1865 at Boulware's or Cox Wharf on the James River, Virginia
Gibbs, William F. Private	27	July 8, 1861, Marion, North Carolina	Co. B, 22nd North Carolina Infantry	May 5, 1864, Wilderness, Virginia	Point Lookout, Maryland, transferred to Elmira Prison, NY, July 23, 1864	Died September 12, 1864 of Chronic Diarrhea, Grave No. 188
Gibbs, William H. Private	19	July 23, 1861, Manassas, Virginia	Co. A, 12th Mississippi Infantry	May 12, 1864, Spotsylvania, Virginia	Old Capital Prison, Washington, DC, transferred to Elmira December 17, 1864	Exchanged February 13, 1865 at Boulware's Wharf on the James River, Virginia
Gibson, Albert Sergeant	23	January 26, 1862, Marion District, South Carolina	Co. L, 21st South Carolina Infantry	January 15, 1865, Fort Fisher, North Carolina. Wounded in Hip.	January 30, 1865, Elmira Prison Camp, New York	Oath of Allegiance June 23, 1865
Gibson, Charles Private	Unk	June 8, 1861, Mobile County, Alabama	Co. J, 12th Alabama Infantry	July 8, 1864, Near Harper's Ferry, Virginia	Old Capital Prison, Washington, DC, transferred to Elmira July 23, 1864	Oath of Allegiance June 21, 1865

Name & Rank	Age	Enlisted	Regiment and State	Where Captured	Prison	Remarks
Gibson, Ebenezer B. Private	18	August 17, 1863, Laurinburg, Richmond County, North Carolina	Co. E, 40th Regiment, 3rd North Carolina Artillery	January 15, 1865, Fort Fisher, North Carolina	February 1, 1865 Elmira Prison Camp, New York	Died May 10, 1865 of Chronic Diarrhea, Grave No. 1883
Gibson, George K. Corporal	19	March 18, 1862, Richmond, Virginia	Co. G, 12th Virginia Infantry	August 18, 1864, Weldon Railroad, Virginia. Gunshot Wound Left Thigh.	Old Capital Prison, Washington, DC transferred to Elmira Prison, NY, August 27, 1864	Exchanged February 25, 1865 at Boulware's or Cox Wharf on the James River, Virginia
Gibson, George P. Private	19	August 15, 1862, Flat Creek, Tennessee	Co. D, 63rd Tennessee Infantry	June 17, 1864, Petersburg, Virginia	Point Lookout, Maryland, transferred to Elmira Prison, NY, July 30, 1864	Exchanged February 25, 1865 at Boulware's or Cox Wharf on the James River, Virginia
Gibson, Henry Private	26	November 15. 1861, Portsmouth, Virginia	Co. A, 32nd North Carolina Infantry	May 10, 1864, Near Mine Run, Spotsylvania, Virginia	Point Lookout, Maryland, transferred to Elmira Prison, NY, August 6, 1864	Died November 5, 1864 of Scorbutus (Scurvy), Grave No. 764
Gibson, Hiram A. Sergeant	Unk	June 15, 1861, Columbus, Georgia	Co. E, 12th Georgia Infantry	May 10, 1864, Spotsylvania Court House, Virginia	Point Lookout, Maryland, transferred to Elmira Prison, NY, July 25, 1864	Oath of Allegiance June 16, 1865
Gibson, J. J. Private	Unk	May 9, 1862, Morris Island, South Carolina	Co. D, 4th South Carolina Cavalry	June 11, 1864, Trevilian Station, Louisa Court House, Virginia	Point Lookout, Maryland, transferred to Elmira Prison, NY, July 25, 1864	Exchanged October 29, 1864 at Venus Point, Savannah River, GA.
Gibson, J. M. Private	34	May 7, 1863, Mecklenburg County, North Carolina	Co. H, 35th North Carolina Infantry	June 17, 1864, Petersburg, Virginia	Point Lookout, Maryland, transferred to Elmira Prison, NY, July 30, 1864	Died March 19, 1865 of Chronic Diarrhea, Grave No. 1732
Gibson, James Private	Unk	Unknown	Co. A, 2nd Virginia Cavalry	August 8, 1864, Maryland Heights, Maryland	Old Capital Prison, Washington, DC, transferred to Elmira, NY August 12, 1864	Exchanged October 29, 1864 at Venus Point, Savannah River, GA.

Name & Rank	Age	Enlisted	Regiment and State	Where Captured	Prison	Remarks
Gibson, James Private	Unk	April 29, 1862, Gloucester Point, Virginia	Co. E, 5th Virginia Cavalry	May 31, 1864, Cold Harbor, Virginia	Point Lookout, Maryland, transferred to Elmira Prison, NY, July 11, 1864	Oath of Allegiance June 16, 1865
Gibson, John B. Sergeant	Unk	April 21, 1861, Memphis, Tennessee	Co. L, Jackson's 1st Regiment, Tennessee Heavy Artillery	August 23, 1864, Fort Morgan, Alabama	New Orleans, Louisiana transferred to Elmira Prison, NY, December 4, 1864.	Exchanged February 25, 1865 at Boulware's or Cox Wharf on the James River, Virginia
Gibson, John B. Corporal	24	July 1, 1862, Rockingham, North Carolina	Co. E, 33rd North Carolina Infantry	May 6, 1864, Wilderness, Virginia	Point Lookout, Maryland, transferred to Elmira Prison, NY, August 14, 1864	Oath of Allegiance June 14, 1865
Gibson, John P. Private	Unk	February 16, 1863, Giles County, Tennessee	Co. J, 3rd Tennessee Infantry	May 12, 1863, Raymond, Mississippi	Point Lookout, Maryland, transferred to Elmira Prison, NY, August 18, 1864	Oath of Allegiance July 11, 1865
Gibson, Nicholas Private	22	March 11, 1862, Spring Garden, Grogansville, North Carolina	Co. A, 45th North Carolina Infantry	May 10, 1864, Spotsylvania Court House, Virginia	Point Lookout, Maryland, transferred to Elmira Prison, NY, August 6, 1864	Died March 14, 1865 of Typhoid Fever, Grave No. 1662. Name Gipson on Headstone.
Gibson, Philip Private	33	April 1, 1864, Ashland, Virginia	Co. E, 5th Virginia Cavalry	May 11, 1864, Yellow Tavern, Hanover County, Virginia	Point Lookout, Maryland, transferred to Elmira Prison, NY, August 17, 1864	Exchanged October 29, 1864 at Venus Point, Savannah River, GA.
Gibson, Raiford Private	16	1224 1864, Fort Holmes, Brunswick County, North Carolina	Co. E, 40th Regiment, 3rd North Carolina Artillery	January 15, 1865, Fort Fisher, North Carolina	February 1, 1865 Elmira Prison Camp, New York	Oath of Allegiance June 12, 1865
Gibson, Raymond Private	31	July 4, 1862, Winston, North Carolina	Co. D, 57th North Carolina Infantry	August 22, 1864, Charlestown, Virginia	Old Capital Prison, Washington, DC transferred to Elmira Prison, NY, August 29, 1864	Oath of Allegiance June 16, 1865

Name & Rank	Age	Enlisted	Regiment and State	Where Captured	Prison	Remarks
Gibson, Richard Private	24	June 29, 1861, Wytheville, Virginia	Co. B, 50th Virginia Infantry	May 12, 1864, Spotsylvania Court House, Virginia	Point Lookout, Maryland, transferred to Elmira Prison, NY, August 2, 1864	Oath of Allegiance June 30, 1865
Gibson, Robert W. Private	Unk	May 11, 1862, Marion, South Carolina	Co. L, 21st South Carolina Infantry	May 9, 1864, Near Petersburg, Virginia	Point Lookout, Maryland, transferred to Elmira Prison, NY, August 17, 1864	Transferred For Exchange October 11, 1864 to Point Lookout Prison Camp, MD. Died October 16, 1864 at US Army Hospital, Baltimore, MD.
Gibson, Thomas P. Private	Unk	February 24, 1863, Bennett, South Carolina	Co. D, 4th South Carolina Cavalry	June 11, 1864, Trevilian Station, Louisa Court House, Virginia	Point Lookout, Maryland, transferred to Elmira Prison, NY, July 25, 1864	Oath of Allegiance June 14, 1865
Gibson, Wesley Private	28	March 18, 1862, Valley Town, North Carolina	Co. D, 25th North Carolina Infantry	July 30, 1864, Petersburg, Virginia	Point Lookout, Maryland, transferred to Elmira Prison, NY, August 12, 1864	Oath of Allegiance May 29, 1865
Gibson, William J. Private	Unk	September 5, 1862, Montgomery, Alabama	Co. F, 3rd Alabama Infantry	May 13, 1864, Spotsylvania Court House, Virginia	Point Lookout Prison Camp, Maryland. Transferred to Elmira Prison, NY, August 17, 1864	Died November 26, 1864 of Typhoid-Pneumonia, Grave No. 979
Gilbert, Henry Private	Unk	October 5, 1863, Conecuh County, Alabama	Co. G, 61st Alabama Infantry	July 23, 1864, Windsor, Maryland. Deserted to Union Lines.	Old Capital Prison, Washington, DC, transferred to Elmira Prison, NY, August 12, 1864	Oath of Allegiance January 30, 1865. Early Release per Lincoln's Proclamation, 12/8/1863.
Gilbert, James E. Private	21	March 26, 1862, Huntsville, Texas	Co. D, 5th Texas Infantry	May 6, 1864, Wilderness, Virginia. Gunshot Right Thigh and Left Shoulder.	Old Capital Prison, Washington, DC, transferred to Elmira Prison, NY, August 12, 1864	Exchanged October 29, 1864 at Venus Point, Savannah River, GA.

Name & Rank	Age	Enlisted	Regiment and State	Where Captured	Prison	Remarks
Gilbert, T. F. Private	Unk	July 26, 1861, Union Mills, Virginia	Co. A, 6th Louisiana Infantry	May 20, 1864, Spotsylvania Court House, Virginia	Point Lookout, Maryland, transferred to Elmira Prison, NY, July 6, 1864	Exchanged February 25, 1864 on the James River, Virginia
Gilbert, Timothy B. Private	28	March 12, 1862, Norfolk County, Virginia	Co. F, 15th Virginia Cavalry	September 14, 1863, Near Culpepper, Virginia	Point Lookout, Maryland, transferred to Elmira Prison, NY, August 18, 1864	Exchanged March 10, 1865 at Boulware's Wharf on the James River, Virginia
Gilchrist, John R. Private	Unk	May 16, 1861, Montgomery, Alabama	Co. M, 6th Alabama Infantry	May 5, 1864, Wilderness, Virginia	Point Lookout, Maryland, transferred to Elmira Prison, NY, August 17, 1864	Oath of Allegiance June 10, 1865
Gilcott, George H. Private	Unk	July 1, 1862, St. Johns, Hertford County, North Carolina	Co. C, 40th Regiment, 3rd Battalion North Carolina Light Artillery	January 15, 1865, Fort Fisher, North Carolina	February 1, 1865 Elmira Prison Camp, New York	Oath of Allegiance June 12, 1865
Giles, Alexander Private	19	September 25, 1862, Camp Holmes, North Carolina	Co. E, 8th North Carolina Infantry	June 1, 1864, Gaines Mill, Cold Harbor, Virginia	Point Lookout, Maryland, transferred to Elmira Prison, NY, July 17, 1864	Exchanged October 29, 1864 at Venus Point, Savannah River, GA.
Giles, John N. Private	20	March 26, 1861, Union Springs, Alabama	Co. E, 1st Battalion Alabama Artillery	August 23, 1864, Fort Morgan, Alabama	New Orleans, Louisiana transferred to Elmira Prison, NY, December 4, 1864.	Oath of Allegiance July 7, 1865
Giles, Richard S. Private	Unk	Unknown	Co. K, 21st Virginia Cavalry	July 8, 1864, Near Harper's Ferry, Virginia	Old Capital Prison, Washington, DC, transferred to Elmira July 23, 1864	Oath of Allegiance July 3, 1865
Giles, William Private	26	June 1, 1861, Lock's Creek, North Carolina	Co. E, 8th North Carolina Infantry	May 31, 1864, Cold Harbor, Virginia	Point Lookout, Maryland, transferred to Elmira Prison, NY, July 12, 1864	Transferred for Exchange 10/11/64. Died 4/29/65 of Debility at Baltimore U. S. Army Hospital, MD.

Name & Rank	Age	Enlisted	Regiment and State	Where Captured	Prison	Remarks
Gilkeson, Thomas E. Private	27	February 14, 1864, Lewisburg, Virginia	Co. D, 26th Virginia Infantry	May 31, 1864, Cold Harbor, Virginia	Point Lookout, Maryland, transferred to Elmira Prison, NY, July 12, 1864	Oath of Allegiance May 12, 1865
Gill, John L. Sergeant	Unk	May 9, 1861, New Orleans, Louisiana	Co. H, 2nd Louisiana Infantry	May 12, 1864, Spotsylvania Court House, Virginia	Point Lookout, Maryland, transferred to Elmira Prison, NY, August 17, 1864	Exchanged October 29, 1864 at Venus Point, Savannah River, GA.
Gill, Samuel Private	Unk	July 8, 1862, Hillsboro, North Carolina	Co. F, 33rd North Carolina Infantry	May 12, 1864, Near Spotsylvania Court House, Virginia	Point Lookout, Maryland, transferred to Elmira Prison, NY, August 14, 1864	Oath of Allegiance June 23, 1865
Gillam, Robert Private	24	August 1, 1862, Raleigh, North Carolina	Co. D, 32nd North Carolina Infantry	May 10, 1864, Near Mine Run, Spotsylvania, Virginia	Point Lookout, Maryland, transferred to Elmira Prison, NY, August 6, 1864	Exchanged March 14, 1865 at Boulware's Wharf on the James River, Virginia
Gillam, William H. Private	Unk	March 4, 1862, Macon, Georgia	Co. A, 45th Georgia Infantry	July 14, 1863, Falling Waters, Maryland	Point Lookout, Maryland, transferred to Elmira Prison, NY, August 18, 1864	Exchanged March 10, 1865 at Boulware's Wharf on the James River, Virginia
Gillespie, Thomas Private	23	December 27, 1861, Camp Trousdale, Tennessee	Co. H, 44th Tennessee Infantry	May 16, 1864, Near Drury's Bluff, Virginia	Point Lookout, Maryland, transferred to Elmira Prison, NY, August 17, 1864	Oath of Allegiance March 10, 1865 Early Release per Lincoln's Proclamation, 12/8/1863.
Gillespie, Wiatt Private	Unk	July 2, 1861, Bethel Am., Virginia	Co. F, 50th Virginia Infantry	May 12, 1864, Spotsylvania Court House, Virginia	Point Lookout, Maryland, transferred to Elmira Prison, NY, August 2, 1864	Died May 8, 1865 of Chronic Diarrhea, Grave No. 2776. Headstone has Galaspy.
Gillespie, William A. Private	Unk	July 2, 1861, Bethel, Virginia	Co. F, 50th Virginia Infantry	May 12, 1864, Spotsylvania Court House, Virginia	Point Lookout, Maryland, transferred to Elmira Prison, NY, July 30, 1864	Oath of Allegiance May 29, 1865

Name & Rank	Age	Enlisted	Regiment and State	Where Captured	Prison	Remarks
Gillespie, William J. Corporal	Unk	Unknown	Co. E, 50th Virginia Infantry	May 12, 1864, Spotsylvania Court House, Virginia	Point Lookout, Maryland, transferred to Elmira Prison, NY, August 2, 1864	Died October 4, 1864 of Chronic Diarrhea, Grave No. 635
Gillett, Colquitt Private	26	July 15, 1862, Onslow County, North Carolina	Co. K, 61st North Carolina Infantry	June 17, 1864, Petersburg, Virginia	Point Lookout, Maryland, transferred to Elmira Prison, NY, July 25, 1864	Exchanged October 29, 1864 at Venus Point, Savannah River, GA.
Gilliam, William H. Private	Unk	August 1, 1861, Manassas, Virginia	Co. D, 6th Alabama Infantry	May 20, 1864, Spotsylvania Court House, Virginia	Point Lookout, Maryland, transferred to Elmira Prison, New York, July 6, 1864	Oath of Allegiance May 29, 1865
Gilliam, William M. Private	Unk	March 1, 1862, Coushatte Chute, Louisiana	Co. A, 12th Louisiana Infantry	May 16, 1863, Baker's Creek, Champion Hill, Mississippi	Point Lookout, Maryland, transferred to Elmira Prison, NY, August 18, 1864	Exchanged October 29, 1864 at Venus Point, Savannah River, GA.
Gillis, C. Private	Unk	December 4, 1862, Charleston, South Carolina	Co. B, 7th Georgia Cavalry	June 11, 1864, Trevilian Station, Louisa Court House, Virginia	Point Lookout, Maryland, transferred to Elmira Prison, NY, July 25, 1864	Exchanged 2/20/65. Died 5/11/65 of Variola (Smallpox) at Jackson Hospital, Richmond, VA.
Gillis, William D. Private	Unk	March 4, 1862, Isabella, Worth County, Georgia	Co. G, 14th Georgia Infantry	May 12, 1864, Spotsylvania Court House, Virginia	Point Lookout, Maryland, transferred to Elmira Prison, NY, July 30, 1864	Oath of Allegiance June 19, 1865
Gillispie, Theo Y. Private	Unk	May 11, 1861, New Orleans, Louisiana	Co. D, 2nd Louisiana Infantry	May 12, 1864, Spotsylvania Court House, Virginia	Point Lookout, Maryland, transferred to Elmira Prison, NY, August 17, 1864	Exchanged February 13, 1865 at Boulware's wharf on the James River, Virginia
Gilly, Marshall Private	Unk	March 10, 1864, Camp Holmes, Raleigh, North Carolina	Co. B, 32nd North Carolina Infantry	May 10, 1864, Near Mine Run, Spotsylvania, Virginia	Point Lookout, Maryland, transferred to Elmira Prison, NY, August 6, 1864	Oath of Allegiance June 16, 1865

Name & Rank	Age	Enlisted	Regiment and State	Where Captured	Prison	Remarks
Gilmer, James M. Corporal	20	May 13, 1861, Lynchburg, Virginia	Co. J, 11th Mississippi Infantry	May 30, 1864, Cold Harbor, Virginia	Point Lookout, Maryland, transferred to Elmira Prison, NY, July 11, 1864	Oath of Allegiance June 14, 1865
Gilmer, Richard Private	Unk	April 16, 1862, Rudes Hill, Virginia	Co. F, 2nd Virginia Infantry	May 12, 1864, Near Spotsylvania Court House, Virginia	Point Lookout, Maryland, transferred to Elmira Prison, NY, August 6, 1864	Died January 13, 1865 of Pneumonia, Grave No. 1466. Name Gilmore on Headstone.
Gilmore, John J. Private	19	August 31, 1861, Green Mountain, North Carolina	Co. E, 8th North Carolina Infantry	June 1, 1864, Gaines Mill, Cold Harbor, Virginia	Point Lookout, Maryland, transferred to Elmira Prison, NY, July 17, 1864	Exchanged March 2, 1865 at Akins Landing on the James River, Virginia
Gilmore, Uriah S. Private	Unk	July 1, 1863, Butler County, Alabama	Co. E, 61st Alabama Infantry	May 12, 1864, Spotsylvania Court House, Virginia	Point Lookout, Maryland, transferred to Elmira Prison, NY, July 30, 1864	Exchanged October 29, 1864 at Venus Point, Savannah River, GA.
Gilpin, John Private	Unk	August 8, 1863, Tazewell County, Virginia	Co. B, 22nd Virginia Cavalry	July 16, 1864, Loudoun County, Virginia	Old Capital Prison, Washington, DC, transferred to Elmira July 23, 1864	Transferred for Exchange 10/11/64. Died 10/13/64 at US Army General Hospital, Baltimore, MA.
Ginnett, Matthew Private	19	July 22, 1861, Goldsboro, North Carolina	Co. F, 10th Regiment, 1st North Carolina Artillery	January 15, 1865, Fort Fisher, North Carolina	January 30, 1865, Elmira Prison Camp, New York	Oath of Allegiance July 11, 1865
Ginnett, Needham Private	Unk	January 10, 1864, Fort Holmes, North Carolina	Co. F, 40th Regiment, 3rd North Carolina Artillery	January 15, 1865, Fort Fisher, North Carolina	January 30, 1865 Elmira Prison Camp, New York	Exchanged February 20, 1865 at Boulware's or Cox Wharf on the James River, Virginia
Ginobles, Rufus B. Private	Unk	March 1, 1863, Sullivan's Island, South Carolina	Co. G, 20th South Carolina Infantry	July 29, 1864, Petersburg, Virginia	Point Lookout, Maryland, transferred to Elmira Prison, NY, August 12, 1864	Died September 8, 1864 of Typhoid-Pneumonia, Grave No. 215. Grenables on Headstone.

Name & Rank	Age	Enlisted	Regiment and State	Where Captured	Prison	Remarks
Girardean, Charles Private		June 13, 1862, Camp Millen, Georgia	Co. B, 20th Battalion, Georgia Cavalry	May 30, 1864, Old Church, Cold Harbor, Virginia	Point Lookout, Maryland, transferred to Elmira Prison, NY, July 17, 1864	Died February 20, 1865 of Fever, Grave No. 2306.
Githins, Jackson D. Private	25	December 31, 1861, Springfield, Missouri	Co. F, 1st Missouri Cavalry	May 17, 1863, Big Black Bridge, Champion Hill, Mississippi	Point Lookout, Maryland, transferred to Elmira Prison, NY, August 18, 1864	Exchanged February 13, 1865 at Boulware's wharf on the James River, Virginia
Gladden, Silas Private	32	November 13, 1861, Winnsboro, South Carolina	Co. B, 7th South Carolina Infantry	August 21, 1864, Weldon Railroad, Near Petersburg, Virginia. Grapeshot Wound Right Side of Abdomen.	Old Capital Prison, Washington, DC transferred to Elmira Prison, NY, August 27, 1864	Died February 15, 1865 of Variola (Smallpox), Grave No. 2176
Gladden, William T. Private	Unk	March 20, 1864, Green Pond, South Carolina	Co. D, 17th South Carolina Infantry	July 30, 1864, Petersburg, Virginia	Point Lookout, Maryland, transferred to Elmira Prison, NY, August 12, 1864	Oath of Allegiance June 19, 1865
Gladney, J. F. Private	Unk	June 1, 1864, Winnsboro, South Carolina	Co. F, 6th South Carolina Cavalry	July 30, 1864, Lee's Mill, Petersburg, Virginia	Point Lookout, Maryland, transferred to Elmira Prison, NY, August 12, 1864	Oath of Allegiance June 19, 1865
Glass, Benjamin P. Private	Unk	July 5, 1861, Buffalo Gap, Virginia	Co. D, 44th Virginia Infantry	May 12, 1864, Spotsylvania Court House, Virginia	Point Lookout, Maryland, transferred to Elmira Prison, NY, August 2, 1864	Oath of Allegiance July 16, 1865
Glass, Charles E. Private	27	May 20, 1861, Palmyra, Virginia	Co. F, 44th Virginia Infantry	May 12, 1864, Spotsylvania Court House, Virginia. Gunshot Wound Upper Left Arm and Chest.	Old Capital Prison, Washington, DC, transferred to Elmira Prison, NY, August 12, 1864	Exchanged October 29, 1864 at Venus Point, Savannah River, GA.
Glass, David D. Sergeant	Unk	October 19, 1861, Richmond, Virginia	Co. G, 59th Virginia Infantry	May 7, 1864, Nottoway Bridge, Virginia	Point Lookout, Maryland, transferred to Elmira Prison, NY, August 17, 1864	Died September 21, 1864 of Chronic Diarrhea, Grave No. 335

Name & Rank	Age	Enlisted	Regiment and State	Where Captured	Prison	Remarks
Glass, Greenbury B. Private	Unk	October 7, 1863, Moreton's Ford, Virginia	Co. D, 2nd Virginia Infantry	August 15, 1864, Winchester, Virginia	Old Capital Prison, Washington, DC transferred to Elmira Prison, NY, August 27, 1864	Oath of Allegiance May 29, 1865
Glass, John C. Private	22	April 28, 1862, Jonesboro, Tennessee	Co. D, 63rd Tennessee Infantry	June 17, 1864, Near Petersburg, Virginia	Point Lookout, Maryland, transferred to Elmira Prison, NY, July 30, 1864	Died November 14, 1864 of Pneumonia, Grave No. 801
Glasscock, Richard T. Private	Unk	November 8, 1863, Camp Wappoo, South Carolina	Co. G, 59th Virginia Infantry	May 8, 1864, Nottoway Bridge, Virginia	Point Lookout, Maryland, transferred to Elmira Prison, NY, August 17, 1864	Exchanged March 2, 1865 at Akins Landing on the James River, Virginia
Glausier, William F. Private	Unk	February 20, 1863, Albany, Georgia	Co. D, 64th Georgia Infantry	June 17, 1864, Petersburg, Virginia	Point Lookout, Maryland, transferred to Elmira Prison, NY, July 30, 1864	Died March 24, 1865 of Diarrhea, Grave No. 2454
Gleaton, Joseph T. S. Private	Unk	August 4, 1863, Quincy, Florida	Co. D, 64th Georgia Infantry	August 16, 1864, New Market, Virginia	Old Capital Prison, Washington, DC transferred to Elmira Prison, NY, August 27, 1864	Died March 28, 1865 of Remittent Fever, Grave No. 2490
Glenn, Alonzo M. Sergeant	Unk	June 8, 1861, Isbell's Store, Virginia	Co. D, 44th Virginia Infantry	May 12, 1864, Spotsylvania Court House, Virginia	Point Lookout, Maryland, transferred to Elmira Prison, NY, August 12, 1864	Escaped October 7, 1864 by Tunneling Under Fence.
Glenn, John F. Private	28	July 20, 1861, Camp Pickens, Sandy Springs, South Carolina	Co. D, 1st South Carolina Infantry	July 28, 1864, Malvern Hill, Virginia. Gunshot Wound Right Side.	Old Capital Prison, Washington, DC transferred to Elmira Prison, NY, August 27, 1864	Exchanged February 13, 1865 at Boulware's wharf on the James River, Virginia

Name & Rank	Age	Enlisted	Regiment and State	Where Captured	Prison	Remarks
Glenn, Joseph K. Private	18	May 1, 1861, Tippah County, Mississippi	Co. B, 2nd Mississippi Infantry	July 14, 1863, Falling Waters, Maryland	Point Lookout, Maryland, transferred to Elmira Prison, NY, August 18, 1864	Exchanged March 10, 1865 at Boulware's Wharf on the James River, Virginia
Glenn, Michael Private	Unk	May 16, 1862, Charleston, South Carolina	Co. C, 27th South Carolina Infantry	June 24, 1864, Near Petersburg, Virginia	Point Lookout, Maryland, transferred to Elmira Prison, NY, July 23, 1864	Died January 31, 1865 of Pneumonia, Grave No. 1772
Glenn, Wade M. Private	24	May 14, 1861, Camp Duncan, Tennessee	Co. A, 14th Tennessee Infantry	April 2, 1865, Near Petersburg, Virginia. Gunshot Wound of Scalp.	Old Capital Prison, Washington, DC, transferred to Elmira Prison, NY, May 2, 1865.	Oath of Allegiance July 7, 1865
Glenn, Walker T. Private	Unk	January 10, 1862, Columbia, South Carolina	Co. C, 22nd South Carolina Infantry	July 30, 1864, Petersburg, Virginia	Point Lookout, Maryland, transferred to Elmira Prison, NY, August 12, 1864	Oath of Allegiance July 3, 1865
Glimps, James L. Private	Unk	Unknown	Co. C, 6th North Carolina Infantry	July 13, 1864, Rockville, Maryland	Old Capital Prison, Washington, DC, transferred to Elmira July 23, 1864	Died March 29, 1865 of Chronic Diarrhea, Grave No. 2516
Glover, Eli S. Private	Unk	August 21, 1863, Henry County, Alabama	Co. F, 1st Battalion Alabama Artillery	August 23, 1864, Fort Morgan, Alabama	Steam Press No. 4 New Orleans, Louisiana transferred to Elmira October 8, 1864.	Died February 16, 1865 of Chronic Bronchitis, Grave No. 2215
Glover, James J. Sergeant	Unk	July 16, 1861, Lawrenceville, Georgia	Co. C, 16th Georgia Infantry	June 1, 1864, Gaines Farm, Virginia	Point Lookout, Maryland, transferred to Elmira Prison, NY, July 17, 1864	Oath of Allegiance July 7, 1865
Glover, John Private	33	January 17, 1862, Raleigh, North Carolina	Co. 47th North Carolina Infantry	October 14, 1864, Bristow Station, Virginia. Gunshot Wounds Right Leg and Left Arm.	Old Capital Prison, Washington, DC transferred to Elmira Prison, NY, August 27, 1864	Oath of Allegiance May 17, 1865

Name & Rank	Age	Enlisted	Regiment and State	Where Captured	Prison	Remarks
Glover, John B. Private	25	February 24, 1862, Charleston, South Carolina	Co. B, 25th South Carolina Infantry	January 15, 1865, Fort Fisher, North Carolina	January 30, 1865 Elmira Prison Camp, New York	Oath of Allegiance July 26, 1865
Glover, Laurens H. Private	Unk	Unknown	Co. J, 27th South Carolina Infantry	June 24, 1864, Petersburg, Virginia	Point Lookout, Maryland, transferred to Elmira Prison, NY, July 23, 1864	Exchanged October 29, 1864 at Venus Point, Savannah River, GA.
Glover, Thornton Kirk Private	26	April 21, 1861, Harper's Ferry, Virginia	Co. J, 2nd Virginia Infantry	May 12, 1864, Near Spotsylvania Court House, Virginia	Point Lookout, Maryland, transferred to Elmira Prison, NY, August 2, 1864	Exchanged March 2, 1865 at Akins Landing on the James River, Virginia
Glover, William R. Private	30	March 31, 1862, Cumberland County, North Carolina	Co. I, 51st North Carolina Infantry	June 1, 1864, Cold Harbor, Virginia	Point Lookout, Maryland, transferred to Elmira Prison, NY, July 17,1864	Exchanged October 29, 1864 at Venus Point, Savannah River, GA.
Gobble, Emory A. Private	19	July 15, 1861, Lee County, Virginia	Co. G, 42nd Virginia Infantry	May 12, 1864, Near Spotsylvania Court House, Virginia	Point Lookout, Maryland, transferred to Elmira Prison, NY, August 6, 1864	Oath of Allegiance June 27, 1865
Gochagen, D. B. Private	17	July 13, 1861, Bay Point, South Carolina	Co. E, 11th South Carolina Infantry	June 24, 1864, Near Petersburg, Virginia	Point Lookout, Maryland, transferred to Elmira Prison, NY, August 18, 1864	Oath of Allegiance June 16, 1865
Godbee, William W. Private	Unk	May 9, 1862, Reidsville, Tattnall County, Georgia	Co. H, 61st Georgia Infantry	May 12, 1864, Spotsylvania Court House, Virginia	Point Lookout, Maryland, transferred to Elmira Prison, NY, July 30, 1864	Oath of Allegiance June 30, 1865
Godley, William S. Private	22	September 7, 1861, Colleton, South Carolina	Co. K, 11th South Carolina Infantry	August 21, 1864, Weldon Railroad, Near Petersburg, Virginia. Gunshot Wound Right Thigh.	Old Capital Prison, Washington, DC transferred to Elmira Prison, NY, August 27, 1864	Exchanged February 13, 1865 at Boulware's wharf on the James River, Virginia

Name & Rank	Age	Enlisted	Regiment and State	Where Captured	Prison	Remarks
Godsey, John G. Private	18	February 1, 1864, Zollicoffer, Tennessee	Co. F, 63rd Tennessee Infantry	May 16, 1864, Near Drury's Bluff, Virginia	Point Lookout, Maryland, transferred to Elmira Prison, NY, August 17, 1864	Exchanged February 25, 1865 at Boulware's or Cox Wharf on the James River, Virginia
Godwin, Ichabod Private	17	March 1, 1862, Wilmington, North Carolina	Co. E, 36th Regiment, 2nd North Carolina Artillery	January 15, 1865, Fort Fisher, North Carolina	February 1, 1865 Elmira Prison Camp, New York	Oath of Allegiance July 11, 1865
Godwin, Joel G. Private	Unk	May 1, 1862, Fayetteville, Georgia	Co. C, 53rd Georgia Infantry	June 1, 1864, Gaines Mill, Cold Harbor, Virginia	Point Lookout, Maryland, transferred to Elmira Prison, NY, July 17,1864	Exchanged 3/2/65. Died 5/3/65 at Jackson Hospital, Richmond, VA.
Godwin, Leonard Private	Unk	June 10, 1861, Camp Holmes, Sampson County, North Carolina	Co. F, 25th North Carolina Infantry	July 30, 1864, Petersburg, Virginia	Point Lookout, Maryland, transferred to Elmira Prison, NY, August 12, 1864	Exchanged October 29, 1864 at Venus Point, Savannah River, GA.
Godwin, Reaves M. Private	21	April 23, 1861, Fair Bluff, North Carolina	Co. C, 20th North Carolina Infantry	May 20, 1864, Spotsylvania Court House, Virginia	Point Lookout, Maryland, transferred to Elmira Prison, NY, July 6, 1864	Oath of Allegiance June 30, 1865
Godwin, Robert Corporal	Unk	May 18, 1861, Meadowville, Virginia	Co. K, 31st Virginia Infantry	May 5, 1864, Wilderness, Virginia	Point Lookout, Maryland, transferred to Elmira Prison, NY, August 2, 1864	Oath of Allegiance June 27, 1865
Goen, F. Private	Unk	Unknown	Co. H, 5th Virginia Infantry	May 12, 1864, Spotsylvania Court House, Virginia	Point Lookout, Maryland, transferred to Elmira Prison, NY, August 2, 1864	Exchanged March 2, 1865 at Akins Landing on the James River, Virginia
Goff, George A. Private	Unk	May 15, 1863, Gilmer County, Virginia	Co. E, 19th Virginia Cavalry	July 15, 1864, Near Harper's Ferry, Loudoun County, Virginia	Old Capital Prison, Washington, DC, transferred to Elmira July 23, 1864. Ward No. 9	Died August 7, 1864 of Pyaemia from gunshot wound of foot. Grave No. 12

Name & Rank	Age	Enlisted	Regiment and State	Where Captured	Prison	Remarks
Goff, James L. Private	Unk	January 18, 1864, Orange County, Virginia	Co. C, 42nd Virginia Infantry	May 12, 1864, Spotsylvania Court House, Virginia	Point Lookout, Maryland, transferred to Elmira Prison, NY, August 2,1864	Oath of Allegiance June 30, 1865
Goff, John H. Private	Unk	May 18, 1861, Lisbon, Virginia	Co. C, 42nd Virginia Infantry	May 12, 1864, Spotsylvania Court House, Virginia	Point Lookout, Maryland, transferred to Elmira Prison, NY, August 2,1864	Oath of Allegiance June 30, 1865
Goff, William A. Private	Unk	May 18, 1861, Lisbon, Virginia	Co. C, 42nd Virginia Infantry	May 12, 1864, Spotsylvania Court House, Virginia	Point Lookout, Maryland, transferred to Elmira Prison, NY, August 2,1864	Exchanged October 29, 1864 at Venus Point, Savannah River, GA.
Gogan, Thomas Private	Unk	May 29, 1863, Macon County, Alabama	Co. E, 61st Alabama Infantry	May 12, 1864, Spotsylvania Court House, Virginia	Point Lookout, Maryland, transferred to Elmira Prison, NY, July 30, 1864	Oath of Allegiance May 17, 1865
Going, William Private	17	March 8, 1862, Amherst Court House, Virginia	Co. J, 49th Virginia Infantry	May 30, 1864, Cold Harbor, Virginia. Gunshot Wound Right Thigh.	Old Capital Prison, Washington, DC transferred to Elmira Prison, NY, August 27, 1864	Exchanged February 13, 1865 at Boulware's Wharf on the James River, Virginia
Goins, William H. Private	Unk	March 20, 1862, Elk Creek, Virginia	Co. F, 4th Virginia Infantry	May 12, 1864 Spotsylvania Court House, Virginia	Point Lookout, Maryland, transferred to Elmira Prison, NY, August 2, 1864	Oath of Allegiance June 27, 1865
Golden, Gilly Private	26	April 21, 1862, Buena Vista, Georgia	Co. K, 12th Georgia Infantry	May 10, 1864, Spotsylvania Court House, Virginia	Point Lookout, Maryland, transferred to Elmira Prison, NY, July 25, 1864	Oath of Allegiance June 21, 1865
Goldman, Thomas Private	Unk	March 10, 1863, Montross, Virginia	Co. A, 15th Virginia Cavalry	September 14, 1863, Near Culpepper, Virginia	Point Lookout, Maryland, transferred to Elmira Prison, NY, August 18, 1864	Exchanged March 10, 1865 at Boulware's Wharf on the James River, Virginia

Name & Rank	Age	Enlisted	Regiment and State	Where Captured	Prison	Remarks
Goldon, Benjamin Private	18	March 10, 1864, Fort Morgan, Alabama	Co. F, 1st Battalion Alabama Artillery	August 23, 1864, Fort Morgan, Alabama	Steam Press No. 4 New Orleans, Louisiana transferred to Elmira October 8, 1864.	Died November 8, 1864 of Chronic Diarrhea, Grave No. 783. Headstone has W. B. Goldon.
Golds, Thomas D. Sergeant	16	April 18, 1861, Berryville, Virginia	Co. J, 2nd Virginia Infantry	May 12, 1864, Near Spotsylvania Court House, Virginia	Point Lookout, Maryland, transferred to Elmira Prison, NY, August 2, 1864	Exchanged February 20, 1865 at Boulware's or Cox Wharf on the James River, Virginia
Gollaspie, Jackson H. Private	Unk	March 15, 1862, Floyd Court House, Virginia	Co. B, 42nd Virginia Infantry	May 12, 1864, Spotsylvania Court House, Virginia	Point Lookout, Maryland, transferred to Elmira Prison, NY, August 2, 1864	Oath of Allegiance July 3, 1865
Gollaspie, Joseph Private	25	May 25, 1861, Floyd Court House, Virginia	Co. B, 42nd Virginia Infantry	May 12, 1864, Spotsylvania Court House, Virginia	Point Lookout, Maryland, transferred to Elmira Prison, NY, August 2, 1864	Oath of Allegiance July 30, 1865
Gollaspie, Willie Private	Unk	March 15, 1862, Floyd Court House, Virginia	Co. B, 42nd Virginia Infantry	May 12, 1864, Spotsylvania Court House, Virginia	Point Lookout, Maryland, transferred to Elmira Prison, NY, August 2, 1864	Oath of Allegiance June 27, 1865
Golliday, J. Private	Unk	Unknown	Signal Corps, Confederate States Army	August 11, 1864, Summit Point, Virginia	Old Capital Prison, Washington, DC transferred to Elmira Prison, NY, August 29, 1864	Oath of Allegiance July 7, 1865
Gollyhan, George Private	Unk	March 28, 1862, Fredericks-burg, Virginia	Captain Pollock's Company, Virginia Light Artillery	May 20, 1864, Stafford County, Virginia	Old Capital Prison, Washington, DC, transferred to Elmira July 23, 1864	Died April 14, 1865 of Chronic Diarrhea, Grave No. 2705
Gonde, Mathew Private	30	January 1, 1862, Georgetown, South Carolina	Co. A, 21st South Carolina Infantry	June 24, 1864, Near Petersburg, Virginia	Point Lookout, Maryland, transferred to Elmira Prison, NY, August 18, 1864	Exchanged March 2, 1865 at Boulware's Wharf on the James River, Virginia

Name & Rank	Age	Enlisted	Regiment and State	Where Captured	Prison	Remarks
Gonde, Stephen F. Private	Unk	January 1, 1862, Georgetown, South Carolina	Co. A, 21st South Carolina Infantry	June 24, 1864, Near Petersburg, Virginia	Point Lookout, Maryland, transferred to Elmira Prison, NY, August 18, 1864	Oath of Allegiance July 3, 1865
Gooch, Ferdinand Private	Unk	May 20, 1861, Palmyra, Virginia	Co. F, 44th Virginia Infantry	May 12, 1864, Spotsylvania Court House, Virginia	Point Lookout, Maryland, transferred to Elmira Prison, NY, August 2, 1864	Oath of Allegiance June 14, 1865
Gooch, William O. Private	Unk	May 20, 1861, Palmyra, Virginia	Co. F, 44th Virginia Infantry	May 12, 1864, Spotsylvania Court House, Virginia	Point Lookout, Maryland, transferred to Elmira Prison, NY, August 2, 1864	Exchanged March 14, 1865 at Boulware's Wharf on the James River, Virginia
Good, Allen W. Private	Unk	April 16, 1862, Rudes Hill, Virginia	Co. F, 2nd Virginia Infantry	May 12, 1864, Near Spotsylvania Court House, Virginia	Point Lookout, Maryland, transferred to Elmira Prison, NY, August 6, 1864	Exchanged February 13, 1865 at Boulware's wharf on the James River, Virginia
Good, George Thomas Private	29	March 2, 1863, Burton's Farm, Virginia	Co. C, 26th Virginia Infantry	June 16, 1864, Webb's Farm, Petersburg, Virginia. Gunshot Right Arm and Bayonet Wound Left Arm.	Old Capital Prison, Washington, DC transferred to Elmira Prison, NY, August 27, 1864	Died January 9, 1865, of Pneumonia, Grave No. 1218. Headstone has Thomas Goode.
Good, Sylvenus Private	24	May 1, 1862, Woodstock, Virginia	Co. K, 12th Virginia Cavalry	October 11, 1863, Culpeper, Virginia	Old Capital Prison, Washington, DC, transferred to Elmira July 23, 1864	Exchanged October 29, 1864 at Venus Point, Savannah River, GA.
Goode, A. C. Private	Unk	April 28, 1862, White Sulfur Springs, Virginia	Co. H, 22nd Virginia Infantry	June 3, 1864, Gaines Mill, Cold Harbor, Virginia	Point Lookout, Maryland, transferred to Elmira Prison, NY, July 17,1864	Exchanged at the James River, Virginia, March 10, 1865
Goode, Andrew Washington Private	23	April 23, 1861, Gloucester Court House, Virginia	Co. B, 26th Virginia Infantry	June 15, 1864, Near Petersburg, Virginia	Point Lookout, Maryland, transferred to Elmira Prison, NY, July 12, 1864	Died October 15, 1864 of Chronic Diarrhea, Grave No. 553

Name & Rank	Age	Enlisted	Regiment and State	Where Captured	Prison	Remarks
Goode, James T. Private	30	April 23, 1861, Gloucester Court House, Virginia	Co. B, 26th Virginia Infantry	June 15, 1864, Near Petersburg, Virginia	Point Lookout, Maryland, transferred to Elmira Prison, NY, July 12, 1864	Died September 20, 1864 of Typhoid Fever, Grave No. 509
Goode, Lemuel J. Private	Unk	July 12, 1861, Chesterfield, Virginia	Co. K, 6th Virginia Infantry	May 30, 1864, Mechanicsville, Virginia	Point Lookout, Maryland, transferred to Elmira Prison, NY, July 12, 1864	Exchanged February 25, 1864 on the James River, Virginia
Gooden, David James Private	18	February 3, 1862, Elizabethtown, NC, Bladen County, North Carolina	Co. I 36th Regiment North Carolina, 2nd Artillery	January 15, 1865, Fort Fisher, North Carolina	Elmira Prison, NY, February 1, 1865	Transferred for Exchange March 14, 1865 Boulware's Wharf, James River, VA. Died March 14, 1865.
Gooden, John D. Private	25	October 1, 1861, Knoxville, Tennessee	Co. B, 63rd Tennessee Infantry	May 16, 1864, Near Drury's Bluff, Virginia	Point Lookout, Maryland, transferred to Elmira Prison, NY, August 17, 1864	Exchanged February 25, 1865 at Boulware's or Cox Wharf on the James River, Virginia
Gooding, Arthur W. Private	Unk	Unknown	Co. A, 6th Virginia Cavalry	August 19, 1864, Waterford, Virginia	Old Capital Prison, Washington, DC transferred to Elmira Prison, NY, August 29, 1864	Oath of Allegiance May 29, 1865
Gooding, Eldred B. Sergeant	18	July 15, 1861, Whippy Swamp, South Carolina	Co. E, 11th South Carolina Infantry	January 15, 1865, Fort Fisher, North Carolina	February 1, 1865 Elmira Prison Camp, New York	Exchanged March 2, 1865 at Boulware's Wharf on the James River, Virginia
Goodman, Achilles H. Private	Unk	May 31, 1861, Yellow Branch, Virginia	Co. D, 42nd Virginia Infantry	May 12, 1864, Near Spotsylvania Court House, Virginia	Point Lookout, Maryland, transferred to Elmira Prison, NY, August 6, 1864	Oath of Allegiance June 14, 1865

Name & Rank	Age	Enlisted	Regiment and State	Where Captured	Prison	Remarks
Goodman, Christopher C. Sergeant	Unk	May 16, 1862, Fayetteville, Georgia	Co. G, 44th Georgia Infantry	May 10, 1864, Spotsylvania Court House, Virginia. Gunshot Wound Right Shoulder.	Old Capital Prison, Washington, DC transferred to Elmira Prison, NY, August 29, 1864	Died October 2, 1864 of Typhoid-Pneumonia, Grave No. 633
Goodman, David James Private	18	February 3, 1862, Elizabethtown, Bladen County, North Carolina	Co. J, 36th Regiment, 2nd North Carolina Artillery	January 15, 1865, Fort Fisher, North Carolina	February 1, 1865 Elmira Prison Camp, New York	Exchanged March 14, 1865 at Boulware's Wharf on the James River, Virginia
Goodman, Henry E. Private	41	July 18, 1863, Lenoir County, North Carolina	Co. G, 40th Regiment, 3rd North Carolina Artillery	January 15, 1865, Fort Fisher, North Carolina	January 30, 1865, Elmira Prison Camp, New York	Oath of Allegiance June 12, 1865
Goodman, Henry H. Private	32	April 16, 1862, Bold Brunswick Town, North Carolina	Co. G, 36th Regiment, 2nd North Carolina Artillery	January 15, 1865, Fort Fisher, North Carolina	February 1, 1865 Elmira Prison Camp, New York	Died February 21, 1865 of Variola (Smallpox), Grave No. 2237
Goodman, J. Private	Unk	Unknown	Co. G, 26th Georgia Infantry	May 20, 1864, Spotsylvania Court House, Virginia	Point Lookout, Maryland, transferred to Elmira Prison, NY, July 6, 1864	Oath of Allegiance June 21, 1865
Goodman, J. H. Private	Unk	Unknown	Co. J, 49th North Carolina Infantry	May 20, 1864, Aquia Creek, Spotsylvania Court House, Virginia	Point Lookout, Maryland, transferred to Elmira Prison, NY, July 6, 1864	Oath of Allegiance May 13, 1865
Goodman, J. J. Private	Unk	March 8, 1862, Lynchburg, Virginia	Co. D, 42nd Virginia Infantry	May 12, 1864, Near Spotsylvania Court House, Virginia	Point Lookout, Maryland, transferred to Elmira Prison, NY, August 6, 1864	Exchanged February 13, 1865 at Boulware's wharf on the James River, Virginia
Goodman, Jacob J. Private	30	September 12, 1861, Carthage, North Carolina	Co. C, 35th North Carolina Infantry	July 15, 1864, Petersburg, Virginia	Old Capital Prison, Washington, DC transferred to Elmira Prison, NY, August 27, 1864	Exchanged February 20, 1865 at Boulware's or Cox Wharf on the James River, Virginia

Name & Rank	Age	Enlisted	Regiment and State	Where Captured	Prison	Remarks
Goodman, John W. Private	Unk	August 16, 1863, Fredericks-burg, Virginia	Co. G, 3rd Virginia Cavalry	May 9, 1864, Spotsylvania Court House, Virginia	Point Lookout, Maryland, transferred to Elmira Prison, NY, August 17, 1864	Exchanged March 14, 1865 at Boulware's Wharf on the James River, Virginia
Goodman, Lycurgus L. Private	21	June 12, 1861, Weldon, North Carolina	Co. B, 5th North Carolina Infantry	May 12, 1864, Spotsylvania Court House, Virginia	Point Lookout, Maryland, transferred to Elmira Prison, NY, August 6, 1864	Oath of Allegiance June 21, 1865
Goodman, R. G. Private	Unk	May 31, 1861, Mason's Depot, Tennessee	Co. B, 1st Jackson's Tennessee Heavy Artillery	August 23, 1864, Fort Morgan, Alabama.	New Orleans, Louisiana transferred to Elmira Prison, NY, December 4, 1864.	Oath of Allegiance May 17, 1865
Goodman, Samuel C. Private	33	August 18, 1862, Statesville, North Carolina	Co. D, 7th North Carolina Infantry	May 6, 1864, Wilderness, Virginia	Point Lookout, Maryland, transferred to Elmira Prison, NY, August 14, 1864	Transferred for Exchange 10/11/64. Died 10/29/64 of Unknown Causes at Point Lookout, MD.
Goodpasture, William H. Private	30	January 5, 1863, Marion, Virginia	Co. F, 23rd Battalion Virginia Infantry	July 14, 1864, Near Washington, DC	Old Capital Prison, Washington, DC, transferred to Elmira July 23, 1864	Exchanged March 10, 1865 at Boulware's Wharf on the James River, Virginia
Goodson, George W. Private	Unk	Unknown	Co. H, 8th Louisiana Infantry	May 20, 1864, Spotsylvania Court House, Virginia	Point Lookout, Maryland, transferred to Elmira Prison, NY, July 6,1864	Died December 10, 1864 of Pneumonia, Grave No. 1048
Goodson, James Private	Unk	Unknown	Co. F, 3rd Alabama Infantry	May 20, 1864, Spotsylvania Court House, Virginia	Point Lookout, Maryland, transferred to Elmira Prison, NY, July 6,1864	Oath of Allegiance June 19, 1865
Goodson, James C. Private	Unk	October 17, 1863, Bryan County, Georgia	Co. K, 7th Georgia Cavalry	June 11, 1864, Trevilian Station, Louisa Court House, Virginia	Point Lookout, Maryland, transferred to Elmira Prison, NY, July 25, 1864	Died August 16, 1864 of Pneumonia, Grave No. 27

44

Name & Rank	Age	Enlisted	Regiment and State	Where Captured	Prison	Remarks
Goodson, Thomas Private	28	March 1, 1862, Swannanoa, North Carolina	Co. K, 11th North Carolina Infantry	July 14, 1863, Falling Waters, Maryland	Point Lookout, Maryland, transferred to Elmira Prison, NY, August 18, 1864	Transferred for Exchange 10/11/64. Died November 1, 1864 of Unknown Causes at Fort Monroe, VA
Goodson, William Private	Unk	February 19, 1864, Darlington District, South Carolina	Co. B, 21st South Carolina Infantry	June 17, 1864, Petersburg, Virginia	Point Lookout, Maryland, transferred to Elmira Prison, NY, July 30, 1864	Died September 26, 1864 of Typhoid Fever, Grave No. 449. Has GA not SC on Headstone.
Goodwin, Alexander Private	23	December 20, 1861, Camp Harlee, Cheraw, South Carolina	Co. B, 21st South Carolina Infantry	July 10, 1863, Morris Island, South Carolina	Point Lookout, Maryland, transferred to Elmira Prison, NY, August 18, 1864	Transferred For Exchange October 11, 1864 to Point Lookout Prison Camp, MD. Died October 15, 1864 of Chronic Diarrhea at Point Lookout Prison, MD.
Goodwin, David Private	Unk	May 30, 1861, Florence, South Carolina	Co. C, 8th South Carolina Infantry	July 27, 1864, Petersburg, Virginia	Point Lookout, Maryland, transferred to Elmira Prison, NY, August 12, 1864	Oath of Allegiance August 7, 1865
Goodwin, James H. Private	Unk	March 18, 1862, Salem, Virginia	Co. E, 42nd Virginia Infantry	May 12, 1864, Near Spotsylvania Court House, Virginia	Point Lookout, Maryland, transferred to Elmira Prison, NY, August 2, 1864	Oath of Allegiance June 21, 1865
Goodwin, James M. Private	17	June 20, 1863, Green City, Alabama	Co. J, 7th Alabama Cavalry	July 22, 1864, 15 Mile Station, Louisiana	New Orleans, LA, Transferred to Elmira Prison, NY, November 19, 1864	Exchanged February 13, 1865 at Boulware's wharf on the James River, Virginia

Name & Rank	Age	Enlisted	Regiment and State	Where Captured	Prison	Remarks
Goodwin, John A. Private	25	February 24, 1862, Wadesboro, North Carolina	Co. H, 43rd North Carolina Infantry	July 13, 1864, Near Washington, DC	Old Capital Prison, Washington, DC, transferred to Elmira July 23, 1864	Oath of Allegiance May 29, 1865
Goodwin, John M. Corporal	Unk	March 18, 1864, Salem, Virginia	Co. E, 42nd Virginia Infantry	May 12, 1864, Near Spotsylvania Court House, Virginia	Point Lookout, Maryland, transferred to Elmira Prison, NY, August 6, 1864	Exchanged March 2, 1865 at Akins Landing on the James River, Virginia
Goodwin, Joshua R. Private	Unk	September 21, 1862, Jefferson County, Alabama	Co. A, 21st Alabama Infantry	August 23, 1864, Fort Morgan, Alabama	Steam Press No. 4 New Orleans, Louisiana transferred to Elmira October 8, 1864.	Oath of Allegiance July 7, 1865
Goodwin, Samuel Private	Unk	May 10, 1862, Chesterfield, South Carolina	Co. D, 21st South Carolina Infantry	July 10, 1863, Morris Island, South Carolina	Point Lookout, Maryland, transferred to Elmira Prison, NY, August 18, 1864	Exchanged March 10, 1865 at Boulware's Wharf on the James River, Virginia
Goodwin, William L. Private	24	May 6, 1862, Mingo, North Carolina	Co. H, 51st North Carolina Infantry	May 31, 1864, Cold Harbor, Virginia	Point Lookout, Maryland, transferred to Elmira Prison, NY, July 17, 1864	Exchanged February 20, 1865 at Boulware's or Cox Wharf on the James River, Virginia
Goodwin, William P. Private	24	March 17, 1862, Memphis, Tennessee	Co. F, 12th Louisiana Infantry	September 19, 1864, Tensan Parish, Louisiana	Old Capital Prison, Washington, DC, transferred to Elmira Prison, NY, December 4, 1864	Exchanged February 20, 1865 at Boulware's or Cox Wharf on the James River, Virginia
Gope, J. D. Private	Unk	Unknown	Co. I, 51st North Carolina Infantry	June 1, 1864, Gaines Farm, Virginia	Point Lookout, Maryland, transferred to Elmira Prison, NY, July 17, 1864	Exchanged March 2, 1865 at Akins Landing on the James River, Virginia
Gordan, John W. Private	Unk	June 15, 1861, Buena Vista, Georgia	Co. K, 12th Georgia Infantry	May 10, 1864, Spotsylvania Court House, Virginia	Point Lookout, Maryland, transferred to Elmira Prison, NY, July 25, 1864	Oath of Allegiance June 21, 1865

Name & Rank	Age	Enlisted	Regiment and State	Where Captured	Prison	Remarks
Gordon, Charles P. Private	Unk	June 4, 1861, Camp Moore, Louisiana	Co. C, 6th Louisiana Infantry	May 5, 1864, Wilderness, Virginia	Point Lookout, Maryland, transferred to Elmira Prison, NY, August 17, 1864	Exchanged October 29, 1864 at Venus Point, Savannah River, GA.
Gordon, Frederick Corporal	22	May 26, 1861, Corinth, Mississippi	Co. A, 16th Mississippi Infantry	July 14, 1863, Falling Waters, Maryland	Point Lookout, Maryland, transferred to Elmira Prison, NY, August 18, 1864	Exchanged March 10, 1865 at Boulware's Wharf on the James River, Virginia
Gordon, James Private	Unk	April 23, 1861, Brownsburg, Virginia	Co. H, 25th Virginia Infantry	May 5, 1864, Wilderness, Virginia	Point Lookout, Maryland, transferred to Elmira Prison, NY, August 2, 1864	Exchanged March 10, 1865 at Boulware's Wharf on the James River, Virginia
Gordon, James M. Private	24	September 19, 1861, Kittrells, North Carolina	Co. J, 2nd North Carolina Cavalry	September 14, 1863, Near Culpepper, Virginia	Point Lookout, Maryland, transferred to Elmira Prison, NY, August 18, 1864	Died October 25, 1864 of Chronic Diarrhea, Grave No. 849
Gordon, John H. Private	Unk	Unknown	Co. G, 11th Virginia Cavalry	August 19, 1864, Montgomery County, Maryland	Old Capital Prison, Washington, DC transferred to Elmira Prison, NY, August 29, 1864	Oath of Allegiance May 19, 1865
Gordon, Richard Private	Unk	May 28, 1861, Lowry's Point, Virginia	Co. E, 55th Virginia Infantry	July 14, 1863, Falling Waters, Maryland	Point Lookout, Maryland, transferred to Elmira Prison, NY, August 18, 1864	Exchanged March 2, 1865 at Akins Landing on the James River, Virginia
Gordon, Samuel A. Private	Unk	April 18, 1861, Lexington, Virginia	Co. H, 27th Virginia Infantry	May 20, 1864, Spotsylvania Court House, Virginia	Point Lookout, Maryland, transferred to Elmira Prison, NY, July 6, 1864	Oath of Allegiance June 30, 1865

Name & Rank	Age	Enlisted	Regiment and State	Where Captured	Prison	Remarks
Gordon, William J. Private	22	September 11, 1862, Calhoun, Georgia	Co. B, 24th Georgia Infantry	August 16, 1864, Front Royal, Virginia	Old Capital Prison, Washington, DC transferred to Elmira Prison, NY, August 29, 1864	Died June 5, 1865 of Chronic Diarrhea at US Army Post Hospital, Elmira prison Camp, NY. No Grave Found at Woodlawn Cemetery, NY
Gore, R. H. Private	Unk	Unknown	Co. D, 12th Alabama Infantry	May 12, 1864, Spotsylvania Court House, Virginia	Point Lookout, Maryland, transferred to Elmira Prison, NY, August 17, 1864	Exchanged October 29, 1864 at Venus Point, Savannah River, GA.
Gore, Wesley P. Sergeant	18	June 29, 1861, Camp Howard, Brunswick County, North Carolina	Co. G, 20th North Carolina Infantry	May 12, 1864, Near Spotsylvania Court House, Virginia	Point Lookout Prison, Maryland. Transferred to Elmira Prison Camp New York August 14, 1864.	Exchanged March 2, 1865. Died March 24, 1865 of Scorbutis (Scurvy) at Jackson Hospital, Richmond, Virginia.
Gore, William Private	23	June 29, 1861, Camp Howard, Brunswick County, North Carolina	Co. G, 20th North Carolina Infantry	May 12, 1864, Near Spotsylvania Court House, Virginia	Point Lookout Prison, Maryland. Transferred to Elmira Prison Camp New York August 14, 1864.	Exchanged March 14, 1865 at Boulware's Wharf on the James River, Virginia
Gorman, John Private	Unk	August 26, 1861, Camden, Tennessee	Co. A, Jackson's 1st Regiment, Tennessee Heavy Artillery	August 23, 1864, Fort Morgan, Alabama	New Orleans, Louisiana transferred to Elmira Prison, NY, December 4, 1864.	Oath of Allegiance May 19, 1865
Gorman, Martin G. Private	44	July 22, 1861, Camp Moore, Louisiana	Co. C, 10th Louisiana Infantry	June 2, 1864, Brown's Farm, Cold Harbor, Virginia	Point Lookout, Maryland, transferred to Elmira Prison, NY, July 17, 1864	Exchanged February 13, 1865 at Boulware's wharf on the James River, Virginia

Name & Rank	Age	Enlisted	Regiment and State	Where Captured	Prison	Remarks
Goss, John W. Private	Unk	Unknown	Co. K, 23rd Virginia Cavalry	September 22, 1864, Fishers Hill, Virginia	Old Capital Prison, Washington, DC, transferred to Elmira December 17, 1864	Exchanged February 20, 1865 at Boulware's or Cox Wharf on the James River, Virginia
Gossage, Thomas J. Sergeant	Unk	August 9. 1861, Cumberland Gap, Tennessee	Co. D, 17th Tennessee Infantry	June 17, 1864, Petersburg, Virginia	Point Lookout, Maryland, transferred to Elmira Prison, NY, July 30, 1864	Exchanged February 13, 1865 at Boulware's wharf on the James River, Virginia
Gossett, W. A. Private	Unk	May 7, 1863, Laurens, South Carolina	Co. G, 27th South Carolina Infantry	June 24, 1864, Near Petersburg, Virginia	Point Lookout, Maryland, transferred to Elmira Prison, NY, August 18, 1864	Exchanged October 29, 1864 at Venus Point, Savannah River, GA.
Gossnell, George W. Private	Unk	June 9, 1864, Chesterfield, Virginia	Co. H, 22nd South Carolina Infantry	July 30, 1864, Petersburg, Virginia	Point Lookout, Maryland, transferred to Elmira Prison, NY, August 12, 1864	Died May 15, 1865 of Chronic Diarrhea, Grave No. 2806. Name Goshling on Headstone.
Gotcher, Z. P. Ord. Sergeant	Unk	August 15. 1861, Cumberland Gap, Tennessee	Co. D, 17th Tennessee Infantry	June 17, 1864, Petersburg, Virginia	Point Lookout, Maryland, transferred to Elmira Prison, NY, July 30, 1864	Exchanged February 25, 1865 at Boulware's or Cox Wharf on the James River, Virginia
Gott, A. S. Private	Unk	Unknown	Co. B, 50th Virginia Infantry	May 12, 1864, Spotsylvania Court House, Virginia	Point Lookout, Maryland, transferred to Elmira Prison, NY, August 2, 1864	Oath of Allegiance June 19, 1865
Gott, James E. Private	Unk	Unknown	Co. E, 50th Virginia Infantry	July 18, 1864, Snickers Gap, Virginia	Old Capital Prison, Washington, DC, transferred to Elmira Prison, NY, August 12, 1864	Oath of Allegiance June 19, 1865

Name & Rank	Age	Enlisted	Regiment and State	Where Captured	Prison	Remarks
Gott, R. Private	Unk	Unknown	Co. B, 50th Virginia Infantry	May 12, 1864, Spotsylvania Court House, Virginia	Point Lookout, Maryland, transferred to Elmira Prison, NY, August 2, 1864	Oath of Allegiance July 11, 1865
Goulding, John J. Private	Unk	May 9, 1861, New Orleans, Louisiana	Co. J, 2nd Louisiana Infantry	May 23, 1864, North Anna, Virginia	Point Lookout, Maryland, transferred to Elmira Prison, NY, July 25, 1864	Oath of Allegiance May 19, 1865
Gouldman, Asa J. Corporal	Unk	July 17, 1861, Dunnsville, Virginia	Co. D, 55th Virginia Infantry	May 5, 1864, Wilderness, Virginia	Point Lookout, Maryland, transferred to Elmira Prison, NY, August 14, 1864	Oath of Allegiance June 19, 1865
Gouldman, James T. Sergeant	Unk	July 24, 1861, Tappahannock, Virginia	Co. E, 55th Virginia Infantry	July 14, 1863, Falling Waters, Maryland	Point Lookout, Maryland, transferred to Elmira Prison, NY, August 18, 1864	Exchanged March 10, 1865 at Boulware's Wharf on the James River, Virginia
Gourley, James A. Private	Unk	March 1, 1862, Cherokee County, Georgia	Co. D, 14th Georgia Infantry	May 24, 1864, Hanover, Virginia	Point Lookout, Maryland, transferred to Elmira Prison, NY, July 12, 1864	Exchanged February 20, 1865 at Boulware's or Cox Wharf on the James River, Virginia
Gowan, Alexander Private	Unk	Unknown	Co. H, 50th Virginia Infantry	May 12, 1864, Spotsylvania Court House, Virginia	Point Lookout, Maryland, transferred to Elmira Prison, NY, August 2, 1864	Died September 21, 1864 of Hospital Gangrene, Grave No. 484. 5th Regiment on Headstone.
Gowan, Nelson Private	21	November 30, 1861, Asheboro, North Carolina	Co. F, 2nd Battalion North Carolina Infantry	May 12, 1864, Near Spotsylvania County Court House, Virginia	Point Lookout, Maryland, transferred to Elmira Prison, NY, August 14, 1864	Oath of Allegiance May 19, 1865
Gowan, Peter Private	20	February 24, 1862, Charleston, South Carolina	Co. A, 25th South Carolina Infantry	January 15, 1865, Fort Fisher, North Carolina	January 30, 1865, Elmira Prison Camp, New York	Oath of Allegiance July 21, 1865

Name & Rank	Age	Enlisted	Regiment and State	Where Captured	Prison	Remarks
Gowen, James T. Private	Unk	May 1, 1862, Wilmington, North Carolina	Co. G, 51st North Carolina Infantry	June 3, 1864, Gaines Mill, Cold Harbor, Virginia	Point Lookout, Maryland, transferred to Elmira Prison, NY, July 17, 1864	Oath of Allegiance June 21, 1865
Gower, D. S. Private	Unk	May 21, 1862, Richmond, Virginia	Co. B, 16th Georgia Infantry	August 16, 1864, Front Royal, Virginia	Old Capital Prison, Washington, DC transferred to Elmira Prison, NY, August 29, 1864	Oath of Allegiance June 16, 1865
Gower, Henry S. Private	Unk	October 13, 1863, Camp Holmes, Near Raleigh, North Carolina	Co. D, 36th Regiment, 2nd North Carolina Artillery	January 15, 1865, Fort Fisher, North Carolina	February 1, 1865 Elmira Prison Camp, New York	Died May 14, 1865 of Chronic Diarrhea, Grave No. 2800
Gowl, Peter S. Private	22	April 15, 1863, Harrisonburg, Virginia	Co. H, 12th Virginia Cavalry	September 14, 1863, Near Culpepper, Virginia	Point Lookout, Maryland, transferred to Elmira Prison, NY, August 18, 1864	Exchanged March 10, 1865 at Boulware's Wharf on the James River, Virginia
Goza, Robert D. Private	Unk	May 12, 1862, Savannah, Georgia	Co. D, 38th Georgia Infantry	August 10, 1864, Berryville, Virginia	Old Capital Prison, Washington, DC transferred to Elmira Prison, NY, August 29, 1864	Oath of Allegiance July 7, 1865
Grace, Andrew H. Sergeant	17	May 15, 1861, Hawkinsville, Georgia	Co. G, 8th Georgia Infantry	May 6, 1864, Wilderness, Virginia	Point Lookout, Maryland, transferred to Elmira Prison, NY, August 14, 1864	Oath of Allegiance June 19, 1865
Grace, Caleb H. Private	21	June 20, 1861, Abingdon, Virginia	Co. B, 48th Virginia Infantry	May 12, 1864, Spotsylvania Court House, Virginia	Point Lookout, Maryland, transferred to Elmira Prison, NY, August 2, 1864	Died February 17, 1865 of Pneumonia, Grave No. 2217
Grace, Frank M. Private	18	June 20, 1861, Abingdon, Virginia	Co. B, 48th Virginia Infantry	June 10, 1864, Spotsylvania Court House, Virginia	Point Lookout, Maryland, transferred to Elmira Prison, NY, July 25, 1864	Oath of Allegiance July 3, 1865

Name & Rank	Age	Enlisted	Regiment and State	Where Captured	Prison	Remarks
Gradeless, D. Private	Unk	April 5, 1862, Camp Manigault, Georgetown, South Carolina	Co. G, 21st South Carolina Infantry	June 24, 1864, Near Petersburg, Virginia	Point Lookout, Maryland, transferred to Elmira Prison, NY, August 18, 1864	Exchanged February 20, 1865 at Boulware's or Cox Wharf on the James River, Virginia
Grader, J. D. Private	Unk	Unknown	Co. J, 55th Virginia Infantry	May 6, 1864, Wilderness, Virginia	Point Lookout, Maryland, transferred to Elmira Prison, NY, August 14, 1864	Exchanged March 2, 1865 at Akins Landing on the James River, Virginia
Grady, James Private	Unk	April 22, 1861, Covington, Virginia	Captain Carpenter's Battery, Virginia Light Artillery	July 13, 1864, Near Washington, DC	Old Capital Prison, Washington, DC, transferred to Elmira July 23, 1864	Exchanged March 14, 1865 at Boulware's Wharf on the James River, Virginia
Grady, James H. Private	27	February 27, 1862, Rogers' Store, North Carolina	Co. I, 1st North Carolina Infantry	May 12, 1864, Spotsylvania Court House, Virginia	Point Lookout, Maryland, transferred to Elmira Prison, NY, August 6, 1864	Oath of Allegiance June 12, 1865
Grady, Lewis H. Private	22	July 13, 1863, Duplin County, North Carolina	Co. G, 40th Regiment, 3rd North Carolina Artillery	January 15, 1865, Fort Fisher, North Carolina	February 1, 1865 Elmira Prison Camp, New York	Exchanged March 2, 1865. Died March 15, 1865 of Pneumonia at Jackson Hospital, Richmond, Virginia.
Graham, Daniel Private	27	March 29, 1862, Cumberland County, North Carolina	Co. I, 51st North Carolina Infantry	June 1, 1864, Cold Harbor, Virginia	Point Lookout, Maryland, transferred to Elmira Prison, NY, July 17, 1864	Died July 24, 1864 from Fracture of Tibia and Foot Amputation, Grave No. 2848
Graham, David E. Private	Unk	March 1, 1863, Buckner's Neck, Virginia	Co. H, 25th Virginia Infantry	May 6, 1864, Wilderness, Virginia	Old Capital Prison, Washington, DC, transferred to Elmira Prison, NY, July 14, 1864	Died April 13, 1865 of Pneumonia, Grave No. 2685

Name & Rank	Age	Enlisted	Regiment and State	Where Captured	Prison	Remarks
Graham, Isaiah G. Private	Unk	July 11, 1861, Athens, Georgia	Co. C, 3rd Battalion Georgia Sharp Shooters	August 16, 1864, Front Royal, Virginia	Old Capital Prison, Washington, DC transferred to Elmira Prison, NY, August 29, 1864	Oath of Allegiance June 16, 1865
Graham Isreal Private	Unk	May 1, 1864, Hanover Junction, Virginia	Co. A, 1st Maryland Cavalry	May 27, 1864, Hanover Junction, Virginia	Point Lookout, Maryland, transferred to Elmira Prison, NY, July 11, 1864	Oath of Allegiance June 16, 1865
Graham, James Private	Unk	April 20, 1862, Marion Court House, South Carolina	Co. D, 25th South Carolina Infantry	January 15, 1865, Fort Fisher, North Carolina	January 30, 1865, Elmira Prison Camp, New York	Died February 4, 1865 of Remittent Fever, Grave No. 1887
Graham, R. M. Private	22	July 1, 1862, Zollicoffer, Tennessee	Co. F, 63rd Tennessee Infantry	June 17, 1864, Near Petersburg, Virginia	Point Lookout, Maryland, transferred to Elmira Prison, NY, July 23, 1864	Exchanged February 25, 1864 at Akins Landing on the James River, Virginia
Grahant, James M. Private	30	April 25, 1861, New Orleans, Louisiana	Co. J. 1st Louisiana Infantry	June 25, 1862, Williamsburg Road, Virginia	Old Capital Prison, Washington, DC, transferred to Elmira July 23, 1864	Exchanged October 29, 1864 at Venus Point, Savannah River, GA.
Grambling, Wilbur W. Private	19	February 20, 1862, Tallahassee, Florida	Co. K, 5th Florida Infantry	May 6, 1864, Wilderness, Virginia	Old Capital Prison, Washington, DC, transferred to Elmira July 23, 1864	Oath of Allegiance June 21, 1865
Gramling, Joel Private	35	March 26, 1862, Madison, Florida	Co. D, 5th Florida Infantry	May 6, 1864, Wilderness, Virginia. Gunshot Wound Left Shoulder.	Old Capital Prison, Washington, DC transferred to Elmira Prison, NY, August 27, 1864	Oath of Allegiance June 21, 1865
Gramling, M. L. Private	Unk	April 11, 1863, Coles Island, South Carolina	Co. F, 25th South Carolina Infantry	January 15, 1865, Fort Fisher, North Carolina	January 30, 1865, Elmira Prison Camp, New York	Oath of Allegiance July 7, 1865

Name & Rank	Age	Enlisted	Regiment and State	Where Captured	Prison	Remarks
Grandstaff, Hamilton P. Private	Unk	April 18, 1861, Harrisonburg, Virginia	Co. G, 10th Virginia Infantry	May 12, 1864, Spotsylvania Court House, Virginia	Point Lookout, Maryland, transferred to Elmira Prison, NY, August 2, 1864	Oath of Allegiance June 27, 1865
Granger, Joseph D. Private	23	February 28, 1862, Louisiana	Co. B, 10th Louisiana Infantry	May 12, 1864, Spotsylvania Court House, Virginia	Point Lookout, Maryland, transferred to Elmira Prison, NY, July 25, 1864	Died January 11, 1865 of Variola (Smallpox), Grave No. 1212
Granstaff, Noah J. Private	Unk	March 3, 1863, Edinburg, Virginia	Co. H, 7th Virginia Cavalry	September 14, 1863, Near Culpepper, Virginia	Point Lookout, Maryland, transferred to Elmira Prison, NY, August 18, 1864	Exchanged March 10, 1865 at Boulware's Wharf on the James River, Virginia
Grant, B. A. Private	Unk	January 20, 1862, Camp Hampton, South Carolina	Co. F, 4th South Carolina Cavalry	June 11, 1864, Trevilian Station, Louisa Court House, Virginia	Point Lookout, Maryland, transferred to Elmira Prison, NY, July 25, 1864	Oath of Allegiance June 14, 1865
Grant, Barnabas Private	Unk	January 12, 1862, Bennettsville, South Carolina	Co. E, 4th South Carolina Cavalry	June 11, 1864, Trevilian Station, Louisa Court House, Virginia	Point Lookout, Maryland, transferred to Elmira Prison, NY, July 23, 1864	Died January 31, 1865 of Chronic Diarrhea, Grave No. 1778
Grant, Benjamin Private	18	June 7, 1863, Richmond, Virginia	Co. E, 24th North Carolina Infantry	June 17, 1864, Petersburg, Virginia	Point Lookout, Maryland, transferred to Elmira Prison, NY, July 30, 1864	Oath of Allegiance June 27, 1865
Grant, E. F. Civilian	Unk	Unknown	Citizen of Surrey County, Virginia	July 1, 1864, Surrey County, Virginia	Point Lookout, Maryland, transferred to Elmira Prison, NY, July 25, 1864	Exchanged October 11, 1864. Nothing Further.
Grant, E. W. Private	Unk	Unknown	Co. J, 2nd Louisiana Cavalry	June 6, 1864, Morganza, Louisiana	Old Capital Prison, Washington, DC, transferred to Elmira Prison, NY, December 4, 1864	Exchanged February 25, 1865 at Boulware's or Cox Wharf on the James River, Virginia

Name & Rank	Age	Enlisted	Regiment and State	Where Captured	Prison	Remarks
Grant, John Private	Unk	September 6, 1863, Camp Prichard, South Carolina	Co. B, 4th South Carolina Cavalry	June 11, 1864, Trevilian Station, Louisa Court House, Virginia	Point Lookout, Maryland, transferred to Elmira Prison, NY, July 25, 1864	Exchanged March 2, 1865 at Akins Landing on the James River, Virginia
Grant, Peter Private	Unk	Unknown	Co. B, 3rd Louisiana Infantry	May 20, 1863, Milldale Hospital, Raymond, Mississippi	Point Lookout, Maryland, transferred to Elmira Prison, NY, August 18, 1864	Exchanged February 25, 1865 at Boulware's or Cox Wharf on the James River, Virginia
Grant, Solomon E. Private	Unk	April 16, 1864, Wilmington, North Carolina	Co. K, 10th Regiment, 1st North Carolina Artillery	January 15, 1865, Fort Fisher, North Carolina	January 30, 1865, Elmira Prison Camp, New York	Died March 6, 1865 of Diarrhea, Grave No. 2411
Grant, William R. Private	30	December 20, 1861, Cheraw, South Carolina	Co. D, 21st South Carolina Infantry	January 15, 1865, Fort Fisher, North Carolina	January 30, 1865, Elmira Prison Camp, New York	Exchanged March 2, 1865 at Boulware's Wharf on the James River, Virginia
Grantham, Alexander Private	25	May 9, 1861, Corinth, Mississippi	Co. I, 12th Mississippi Infantry	April 2, 1865, Petersburg, Virginia. Gunshot Wound Face.	Old Capital Prison, Washington, DC, transferred to Elmira Prison, NY, May 2, 1865.	Oath of Allegiance July 7, 1865
Grantham, John Q. Private	Unk	December 11, 1864, Fort Holmes, Brunswick County, North Carolina	Co. E, 40th Regiment, 3rd North Carolina Artillery	January 15, 1865, Fort Fisher, North Carolina	February 1, 1865, Elmira Prison Camp, New York	Exchanged March 14, 1865. Died April 5, 1865 of Typhoid Fever at Jackson Hospital, Richmond, Virginia
Grantham, Josiah L. Private	44	August 19, 1863, Fort Caswell, Brunswick County, North Carolina	Co. E, 40th Regiment, 3rd North Carolina Artillery	January 15, 1865, Fort Fisher, North Carolina	February 1, 1865, Elmira Prison Camp, New York	Died March 23, 1865 of Chronic Diarrhea, Grave No. 1514

Name & Rank	Age	Enlisted	Regiment and State	Where Captured	Prison	Remarks
Grantham, Robert W. Private	18	January 20, 1862, Darlington, South Carolina	Co. H, 21st South Carolina Infantry	January 15, 1865, Fort Fisher, North Carolina	January 30, 1865, Elmira Prison Camp, New York	Died March 5, 1865 of Pneumonia, Grave No. 2398. Headstone has 2nd South Carolina.
Grason, Kaja Mc Private	Unk	August 14, 1862, Statesville, North Carolina	Co. G, 18th North Carolina Infantry	May 12, 1864, Spotsylvania Court House, Virginia	Point Lookout, Maryland, transferred to Elmira Prison, NY, August 6, 1864	Oath of Allegiance June 30, 1865
Gravely, Jobeez E. Sergeant	Unk	June 22, 1861, Henry County, Virginia	Co. F, 42nd Virginia Infantry	May 12, 1864, Near Spotsylvania Court House, Virginia	Point Lookout, Maryland, transferred to Elmira Prison, NY, August 6, 1864	Exchanged March 2, 1865 at Akins Landing on the James River, Virginia
Graves, Jacob B. Private	35	August 13, 1862, Camp Hill, North Carolina	Co. G, 5th North Carolina Infantry	May 12, 1864, Spotsylvania Court House, Virginia	Point Lookout, Maryland, transferred to Elmira Prison, NY, August 6, 1864	Died December 2, 1864 of Hospital Gangrene, Grave No. 892
Graves, Jer. H. Corporal	Unk	March 10, 1862, Pittsylvania, Virginia	Co. G, 6th Virginia Cavalry	May 11, 1864, Yellow Tavern, Hanover County, Virginia	Point Lookout, Maryland, transferred to Elmira Prison, NY, August 17, 1864	Oath of Allegiance June 27, 1865
Graves, John F. Private	26	March 18, 1862, Mocksville, Davie County, North Carolina	Co. E, 42nd North Carolina Infantry	June 1, 1864, Gaines Farm, Virginia	Point Lookout, Maryland, transferred to Elmira Prison, NY, July 17, 1864	Exchanged March 2, 1865 at Akins Landing on the James River, Virginia
Graves, Marion Corporal	Unk	May 6, 1863, Coffee County, Alabama	Co. A, 61st Alabama Infantry	May 12, 1864, Spotsylvania Court House, Virginia	Point Lookout, Maryland, transferred to Elmira Prison, NY, July 30, 1864	Oath of Allegiance June 19, 1865
Graves, William Willer Private	41	July 1, 1862, North Garden, Virginia	Co. G, 46th Virginia Infantry	June 17, 1864, Petersburg, Virginia. Gunshot or Saber Wound, Left Side of Scalp.	Old Capital Prison, Washington, DC, transferred to Elmira December 17, 1864	Oath of Allegiance June 30, 1865

Name & Rank	Age	Enlisted	Regiment and State	Where Captured	Prison	Remarks
Gray, B. A. Private	Unk	June 7, 1864, Near Petersburg, Virginia	Co. H, 34th Virginia Infantry	June 15, 1864, Near Petersburg, Virginia	Point Lookout, Maryland, transferred to Elmira Prison, NY, July 12, 1864	Oath of Allegiance July 3, 1865
Gray, Benjamin Sergeant	Unk	May 24, 1861, Hillsboro, Alabama	Co. C, 9th Alabama Infantry	May 6, 1864, Wilderness, Virginia	Point Lookout, Maryland, transferred to Elmira Prison, NY, August 17, 1864	Oath of Allegiance June 14, 1865
Gray, Columbus T. Private	Unk	March 4, 1862, Clinton, Georgia	Co. F, 45th Georgia Infantry	May 6, 1864, Wilderness, Virginia	Point Lookout, Maryland, transferred to Elmira Prison, NY, August 14, 1864	Oath of Allegiance June 14, 1865
Gray, J. H. Civilian	Unk	Unknown	Citizen of Randolph County, North Carolina	April 21, 1864, Wilmington, North Carolina	Point Lookout, Maryland, transferred to Elmira Prison, NY, July 25, 1864	Died September 22, 1864 of Bronchitis and Chronic Diarrhea, Grave No. 489. Citizen of VA on Headstone.
Gray, James Alexander Private	19	July 16, 1864, Fort Fisher, North Carolina	Co. C, 36th Regiment, 2nd North Carolina Artillery	January 15, 1865, Fort Fisher, North Carolina	February 1, 1865, Elmira Prison Camp, New York	Exchanged March 2, 1865 at Boulware's Wharf on the James River, Virginia
Gray, James L. Private	32	March 27, 1862, Hicksford, Virginia	Co. F, 12th Virginia Infantry	October 27, 1864, Hatchers Run, Virginia. Gunshot Wound Left Foot.	Old Capital Prison, Washington, DC, transferred to Elmira Prison, NY, May 2, 1865.	Oath of Allegiance July 11, 1865
Gray, Jeremiah G. Private	Unk	September 5, 1861, Athens, Georgia	Co. D, Cobb's Legion Georgia	August 16, 1864, Front Royal, Virginia	Old Capital Prison, Washington, DC transferred to Elmira Prison, NY, August 29, 1864	Exchanged March 2, 1865 at Akins Landing on the James River, Virginia

Name & Rank	Age	Enlisted	Regiment and State	Where Captured	Prison	Remarks
Gray, Jesse L. Private	Unk	January 22, 1862, Fort Pillow, Tennessee	Co. B, 1st Jackson's Tennessee Heavy Artillery	August 23, 1864, Fort Morgan, Alabama.	New Orleans, Louisiana transferred to Elmira Prison, NY, December 4, 1864.	Exchanged February 25, 1865 at Boulware's or Cox Wharf on the James River, Virginia
Gray, John Private	Unk	Unknown	Co. K, 1st Virginia Cavalry	March 29, 1864, Shenandoah Valley, Bath, Virginia	Old Capital Prison, Washington, DC, transferred to Elmira July 23, 1864	Oath of Allegiance May 17, 1865
Gray, John T. Private	18	November 5, 1861, Camp Gaston, North Carolina	Co. E, 3rd North Carolina Cavalry	May 29, 1864, Nelson's Farm, Virginia	Point Lookout, Maryland, transferred to Elmira Prison, NY, July 11, 1864	Exchanged March 14, 1865 at Boulware's Wharf on the James River, Virginia
Gray, Oscar B. Private	Unk	April 3, 1862, Bryan County, Georgia	Co. H, 7th Georgia Cavalry	June 11, 1864, Trevilian Station, Louisa Court House, Virginia	Point Lookout, Maryland, transferred to Elmira Prison, NY, July 25, 1864	Died November 2, 1864 of Pneumonia, Grave No. 752
Gray, William Private	25	May 16, 1861, Columbia, North Carolina	Co. F, 32nd North Carolina Infantry	May 10, 1864, Near Mine Run, Spotsylvania, Virginia	Point Lookout, Maryland, transferred to Elmira Prison, NY, August 6, 1864	Oath of Allegiance June 27, 1865
Grayham, John H. Private	Unk	July 11, 1861, Athens, Georgia	Co. D, 3rd Battalion Georgia Sharp Shooters	August 16, 1864, Front Royal, Virginia	Old Capital Prison, Washington, DC transferred to Elmira Prison, NY, August 29, 1864	Oath of Allegiance June 16, 1865
Grayton, M. J. Private	Unk	Unknown	Co. C, 18th Georgia Infantry	June 1, 1864, Cold Harbor, Virginia	Point Lookout, Maryland, transferred to Elmira Prison, NY, July 17, 1864	Oath of Allegiance May 19, 1865
Greaves, John J. Private	25	May 16, 1861, Gloucester Point, Virginia	Co. A, 26th Virginia Infantry	June 15, 1864, Near Petersburg, Virginia	Point Lookout, Maryland, transferred to Elmira Prison, NY, July 17, 1864	Oath of Allegiance July 3, 1865

Name & Rank	Age	Enlisted	Regiment and State	Where Captured	Prison	Remarks
Greise, Armsted Private	Unk	Unknown	Captain Robinson's Home Guard, Florida	September 27, 1864, Marianna, Florida	New Orleans, Louisiana transferred to Elmira November 19, 1864.	Exchanged February 20, 1865 at Boulware's wharf on the James River, Virginia
Green, Ambrose G. Sergeant	18	June 10, 1861, Weldon, Halifax County, North Carolina	Co. K, 1st North Carolina Infantry	May 12, 1864, Spotsylvania Court House, Virginia	Point Lookout, Maryland, transferred to Elmira Prison, NY, August 6, 1864	Exchanged March 14, 1865 at Boulware's Wharf on the James River, Virginia
Green, Armistead D. Private	23	May 15, 1862, Camp Davis, North Carolina	Co. K, 43rd North Carolina Infantry	May 16, 1864, Near Drury's Bluff, Virginia	Point Lookout, Maryland, transferred to Elmira Prison, NY, August 18, 1864	Exchanged February 13, 1865 at Boulware's wharf on the James River, Virginia
Green, Council Private	22	May 3, 1861, Elizabethtown, North Carolina	Co. B, 18th North Carolina Infantry	May 12, 1864, Spotsylvania Court House, Virginia	Point Lookout, Maryland, transferred to Elmira Prison, NY, August 6, 1864	Oath of Allegiance May 29, 1865
Green, Elijah Private	24	May 27, 1861, Troy, Montgomery County, North Carolina	Co. C, 23rd North Carolina Infantry	May 12, 1864, Near Spotsylvania Court House, Virginia	Point Lookout Prison, Maryland. Transferred to Elmira Prison Camp New York August 14, 1864.	Died May 4, 1865 of Chronic Diarrhea, Grave No. 2760
Green, H. W. Private	Unk	September 3, 1862, Statesville, North Carolina	Co. E, 23rd North Carolina Infantry	May 12, 1864, Spotsylvania, Virginia	Old Capital Prison, Washington, DC, transferred to Elmira July 23, 1864	Died August 27, 1864 of Chronic Diarrhea, Grave No. 101
Green, Henry Private	27	May 3, 1861, Elizabethtown, North Carolina	Co. B, 18th North Carolina Infantry	May 12, 1864, Spotsylvania Court House, Virginia	Point Lookout, Maryland, transferred to Elmira Prison, NY, August 6, 1864	Exchanged February 13, 1865 at Boulware's wharf on the James River, Virginia

Name & Rank	Age	Enlisted	Regiment and State	Where Captured	Prison	Remarks
Green, Henry Private	Unk	September 17, 1862, Clifton, Virginia	Co. A, 9th Virginia Infantry	June 12, 1864, Cold Harbor, Virginia	Transferred From Point Lookout Prison, MD, July 12, 1864. Train Never Arrived at Elmira Prison Camp, NY.	Died July 15, 1864 in Train Wreck at Shohola, Pennsylvania.
Green, J. L. Private	42	August 28, 1863, Cleveland County, North Carolina	Co. H, 30th North Carolina Infantry	May 12, 1864, Near Spotsylvania Court House, Virginia	Point Lookout, Maryland, transferred to Elmira Prison, NY, August 14, 1864	Died October 4, 1864 of Chronic Diarrhea, Grave No. 600
Green, James A. Private	23	June 22, 1861, Richmond, Virginia	Co. K, 21st Virginia Infantry	May 20, 1864, Spotsylvania Court House, Virginia	Point Lookout, Maryland, transferred to Elmira Prison, NY, July 6, 1864	Oath of Allegiance June 11, 1865
Green, James A. W. Private	51	March 8, 1862, Richmond, Virginia	Co. H, 59th Virginia Infantry	May 8, 1864, Nottoway Bridge, Virginia	Point Lookout, Maryland, transferred to Elmira Prison, NY, August 17, 1864	Exchanged October 29, 1864 at Venus Point, Savannah River, GA.
Green, James Alex Private	Unk	April 24, 1862, Charleston, South Carolina	Co. B, 22nd South Carolina Infantry	July 30, 1864, Petersburg, Virginia	Point Lookout, Maryland, transferred to Elmira Prison, NY, August 12, 1864	Died May 21, 1865 of Chronic Diarrhea, Grave No. 2936
Green, James W. Corporal	Unk	April 19, 1862, Petersburg, Virginia	Capt. Pegram's Battery Virginia Light Artillery	July 30, 1864, Petersburg, Virginia	Point Lookout, Maryland, transferred to Elmira Prison, NY, August 12, 1864	Oath of Allegiance May 29, 1865
Green, John B. Private	Unk	January 6, 1863, Frederick County, Virginia	Co. H, 11th Virginia Cavalry	December 7, 1864, Cedar Creek, Shenandoah County, Virginia	Old Capital Prison, Washington, DC, transferred to Elmira Prison, NY, March 3, 1865.	Oath of Allegiance July 11, 1865
Green, John F. Private	Unk	Unknown	Co. D, 50th Virginia Infantry	May 12, 1864, Spotsylvania Court House, Virginia	Point Lookout, Maryland, transferred to Elmira Prison, NY, August 12, 1864	Oath of Allegiance June 30, 1865

Name & Rank	Age	Enlisted	Regiment and State	Where Captured	Prison	Remarks
Green, John H. Private	Unk	Unknown	Co. A, Ogden's Louisiana Cavalry	October 6, 1864, Clinton, Louisiana	New Orleans, Louisiana transferred to Elmira November 19, 1864.	Exchanged February 25, 1865 at Boulware's or Cox Wharf on the James River, Virginia
Green, Joshua G. Private	18	May 28, 1861, Meherrin, Virginia	Co. K, 21st Virginia Infantry	May 12, 1864, Spotsylvania Court House, Virginia	Point Lookout, Maryland, transferred to Elmira Prison, NY, August 2, 1864	Oath of Allegiance June 23, 1865
Green, Lewis Private	Unk	May 13, 1862, Savannah, Georgia	Co. E, 7th Georgia Cavalry	June 11, 1864, Trevilian Station, Louisa Court House, Virginia	Point Lookout, Maryland, transferred to Elmira Prison, NY, July 25, 1864	Exchanged February 20, 1865 at Boulware's or Cox Wharf on the James River, Virginia
Green, M. V. Private	Unk	September 3, 1862, Statesville, North Carolina	Co. C, 23rd North Carolina Infantry	May 12, 1864, Near Spotsylvania Court House, Virginia	Point Lookout, Maryland, transferred to Elmira Prison, NY, August 14, 1864	Exchanged October 29, 1864 at Venus Point, Savannah River, GA.
Green, Mitchell J. Private	Unk	September 9, 1861, Eden Station, Georgia	Co. D, 61st Georgia Infantry	May 12, 1864, Spotsylvania Court House, Virginia	Point Lookout, Maryland, transferred to Elmira Prison, NY, July 25, 1864	Oath of Allegiance June 21, 1865
Green, Nicholas T. Private	17	June 5, 1862, Oxford, North Carolina	Co. E, 23rd North Carolina Infantry	May 12, 1864, Near Spotsylvania Court House, Virginia	Point Lookout, Maryland, transferred to Elmira Prison, NY, August 14, 1864	Oath of Allegiance June 27, 1865
Green, R. A. Private	Unk	May 20, 1861, Jonesboro, Clayton County, Georgia	Co. E, 10th Georgia Infantry	July 29, 1864, Petersburg, Virginia	Point Lookout, Maryland, transferred to Elmira Prison, NY, August 12, 1864	Oath of Allegiance May 15, 1865
Green, Samuel Private	19	December 29, 1863, Fort Pender, North Carolina	Co. E, 36th Regiment, 2nd North Carolina Artillery	January 15, 1865, Fort Fisher, North Carolina	February 1, 1865, Elmira Prison Camp, New York	Oath of Allegiance July 3, 1865

Name & Rank	Age	Enlisted	Regiment and State	Where Captured	Prison	Remarks
Green, Thomas Sergeant	30	May 6, 1862, Shelby, North Carolina	Co. D, 55th Virginia Infantry	July 14, 1863, Falling Waters, Maryland	Point Lookout, Maryland, transferred to Elmira Prison, NY, August 18, 1864	Transferred For Exchange October 11, 1864 to Point Lookout Prison Camp, MD. Died November 13, 1864 at Port Royal, SC.
Green, William Private	26	July 15, 1862, Guilford County, North Carolina	Co. F, 1st North Carolina Infantry	May 12, 1864, Wilderness, Spotsylvania Court House, Virginia	Point Lookout, Maryland, transferred to Elmira Prison, NY, August 6, 1864	Oath of Allegiance June 16, 1865
Green, William Private	Unk	May 29, 1863, Mobile County, Alabama	Co. E, 61st Alabama Infantry	May 12, 1864, Spotsylvania Court House, Virginia	Point Lookout, Maryland, transferred to Elmira Prison, NY, July 30, 1864	Oath of Allegiance June 19, 1865
Green, Wyatt B. Private	Unk	August 24, 1861, Granada, Alabama	Co. A, 1st Alabama Artillery	August 23, 1864, Fort Morgan, Alabama	New Orleans, Louisiana transferred to Elmira Prison, NY, December 4, 1864.	Died March 2, 1865 of Bronchitis, Grave No. 2014
Green, Z. P. Private	61	February 11, 1863, Selma, Alabama's	Co. A, 1st Battalion Alabama Artillery	August 23, 1864, Fort Morgan, Alabama	New Orleans, Louisiana. Transferred to Elmira October 8, 1864	Died November 15, 1864 of Pleuro-Pneumonia, Grave No. 810
Green, Zachariah F. Private	27	December 17, 1861, Camp Trousdale, Tennessee	Co. H, 44th Tennessee Infantry	June 17, 1864, Petersburg, Virginia	Point Lookout, Maryland, transferred to Elmira Prison, NY, July 30, 1864	Oath of Allegiance March 10, 1865. Early Release per Lincoln's Proclamation, 12/8/1863.
Greenstreet, James F. Private	Unk	March 24, 1862, Fort Lowry, Virginia	Co. A, 55th Virginia Infantry	May 25, 1864, Spotsylvania Court House, Virginia	Point Lookout, Maryland, transferred to Elmira Prison, NY, July 11, 1864	Oath of Allegiance June 30, 1865

Name & Rank	Age	Enlisted	Regiment and State	Where Captured	Prison	Remarks
Greenway, William C. Private	25	July 1, 1862, Zollicoffer, Tennessee	Co. F, 63rd Tennessee Infantry	June 17, 1864, Petersburg, Virginia	Point Lookout, Maryland, transferred to Elmira Prison, NY, July 30, 1864	Exchanged February 25, 1865 at Boulware's or Cox Wharf on the James River, Virginia
Greenwood, Abel T. Private	Unk	February 11, 1864, Camp Near Orange, North Carolina	Co. B, 14th North Carolina Infantry	May 10, 1864, Spotsylvania Court House, Virginia	Point Lookout, Maryland, transferred to Elmira Prison, NY, July 23, 1864	Oath of Allegiance May 17, 1865
Greenwood, F. Sergeant	Unk	May 11, 1861, New Orleans, Louisiana	Co. C, 2nd Louisiana Infantry	May 12, 1864, Spotsylvania Court House, Virginia	Point Lookout, Maryland, transferred to Elmira Prison, NY, August 17, 1864	Exchanged February 25, 1865 at Boulware's or Cox Wharf on the James River, Virginia
Greenwood, Walter Private	Unk	July 17, 1861, Dunnsville, Virginia	Co. D, 55th Virginia Infantry	May 6, 1864, Wilderness, Virginia	Point Lookout, Maryland, transferred to Elmira Prison, NY, August 14, 1864	Oath of Allegiance June 16, 1865
Greer, E. W. Private	24	June 9, 1861, Camp Moore, Louisiana	Co. J, 15th Louisiana Infantry	August 17, 1864, Snickers Gap, Virginia	Old Capital Prison, Washington, DC transferred to Elmira Prison, NY, August 29, 1864	Oath of Allegiance May 19, 1865
Greer, Newton Private	17	September 14, 1862, Boone, North Carolina	Co. B, 37th North Carolina Infantry	May 24, 1864, Hanover Junction, Virginia	Point Lookout, Maryland, transferred to Elmira Prison, NY, July 12, 1864	Oath of Allegiance May 19, 1865
Greer, William Robert Private	Unk	January 4, 1863, Charleston, South Carolina	Co. B, 25th South Carolina Infantry	January 15, 1865, Fort Fisher, North Carolina	January 30, 1865, Elmira Prison Camp, New York	Oath of Allegiance June 23, 1865
Greever, Peter Private	Unk	July 17, 1861, Wyhteville, Virginia	Co. B, 50th Virginia Infantry	May 12, 1864, Spotsylvania Court House, Virginia	Point Lookout, Maryland, transferred to Elmira Prison, NY, August 2, 1864	Oath of Allegiance June 21, 1865

Name & Rank	Age	Enlisted	Regiment and State	Where Captured	Prison	Remarks
Gregg, Alex M. Sergeant	Unk	March 19, 1862, Pee Dee Bridge, South Carolina	Co. K, 21st South Carolina Infantry	January 15, 1865, Fort Fisher, North Carolina	January 30, 1865, Elmira Prison Camp, New York	Oath of Allegiance June 23, 1865
Gregg, E. W. Private	Unk	Unknown	Co. A, 21st Alabama Infantry	August 28, 1864, Fort Morgan, Louisiana	New Orleans, LA, Transferred to Elmira Prison, NY, November 19, 1864	Exchanged February 20, 1865 at Boulware's or Cox Wharf on the James River, Virginia
Gregg, John W. Private	Unk	May 20, 1862, Chesterfield, South Carolina	Co. B, 26th South Carolina Infantry	July 30, 1864, Petersburg, Virginia	Point Lookout, Maryland, transferred to Elmira Prison, NY, August 12, 1864	Exchanged October 29, 1864 at Venus Point, Savannah River, GA.
Gregg, Thomas C. Private	Unk	May 2, 1862, Camp Manigualt, South Carolina	Co. J, 21st South Carolina Infantry	January 15, 1865, Fort Fisher, North Carolina	January 30, 1865, Elmira Prison Camp, New York	Oath of Allegiance June 23, 1865
Gregg, W. W. Private	Unk	August 31, 1863, Marion, South Carolina	Co. J, 21st South Carolina Infantry	January 15, 1865, Fort Fisher, North Carolina	January 30, 1865, Elmira Prison Camp, New York	Exchanged February 20, 1865. Died February 20, 1865 of Unknown Causes, Brought from Flag Of Truce Boat Dead.
Gregory, Henry L. Private	Unk	June 22, 1861, Wytheville, Virginia	Co. B, 8th Virginia Cavalry	July 16, 1864, Loudoun County, Virginia	Old Capital Prison, Washington, DC, transferred to Elmira July 23, 1864	Oath of Allegiance July 3, 1865
Gregory, J. L. Sergeant	Unk	July 2, 1861, New Orleans, Louisiana	Co. K, 15th Louisiana Infantry	May 12, 1864, Spotsylvania Court House, Virginia	Point Lookout, Maryland, transferred to Elmira Prison, NY, July 25, 1864	Exchanged February 13, 1865 at Boulware's wharf on the James River, Virginia
Gregory, John Private	46	December 17, 1861, Unionville, South Carolina	Co. A, 18th South Carolina Infantry	July 30, 1864, Battle of the Crater, Petersburg, Virginia	Point Lookout, Maryland, transferred to Elmira Prison, NY, August 12, 1864	Died December 9, 1864 of Chronic Diarrhea, Grave No. 1164

Name & Rank	Age	Enlisted	Regiment and State	Where Captured	Prison	Remarks
Gregory, Silas E. Private	Unk	January 19, 1864, Orange County, Virginia	Co. K, 21st Virginia Infantry	May 12, 1864, Spotsylvania Court House, Virginia	Point Lookout, Maryland, transferred to Elmira Prison, NY, August 2, 1864	Transferred for Exchange 10/11/64. Died 11/8/64 at Sea.
Gregory, William A. Private	37	March 1, 1862, Person County, North Carolina	Co. J, 45th North Carolina Infantry	May 10, 1864, Spotsylvania Court House, Virginia	Point Lookout, Maryland, transferred to Elmira Prison, NY, August 6, 1864	Died September 17, 1864 of Hospital Gangrene, Grave No. 318. Regiment 51st on Headstone.
Gregory, William A. Private	19	February 28, 1862, Lumberton, North Carolina	Co. E, 51st North Carolina Infantry	May 10, 1864, Spotsylvania Court House, Virginia	Point Lookout, Maryland, transferred to Elmira Prison, NY, July 12, 1864	Oath of Allegiance July 13, 1865
Gregston, William A. Private	19	April 24, 1861, New Orleans, Louisiana	Co. F, Nelligan's 1st Louisiana Infantry	May 5, 1864, Wilderness, Virginia	Point Lookout, Maryland, transferred to Elmira Prison, NY, July 28,1864	Oath of Allegiance March 22, 1865
Gresham, William H. Private	Unk	May 6, 1862, Macon, Georgia	Co. J, 61st Georgia Infantry	May 12, 1864, Spotsylvania Court House, Virginia	Point Lookout, Maryland, transferred to Elmira Prison, NY, July 25, 1864	Oath of Allegiance June 21, 1865
Gressett, James P. Private	23	April 20, 1861, Belle Roi., Virginia	Co. A, 26th Virginia Infantry	June 15, 1864, Near Petersburg, Virginia	Point Lookout, Maryland, transferred to Elmira Prison, NY, July 17, 1864	Exchanged March 14, 1865 at Boulware's Wharf on the James River, Virginia
Grice, Franklin Private	Unk	April 3, 1862, Brownsville, South Carolina	Co. G, 27th South Carolina Infantry	June 24, 1864, Near Petersburg, Virginia	Point Lookout, Maryland, transferred to Elmira Prison, NY, August 18, 1864	Exchanged October 29, 1864 at Venus Point, Savannah River, GA.
Grice, Giles W. Private	Unk	October 23, 1861, Sampson County, North Carolina	Co. A, 36th Regiment, 2nd North Carolina Artillery	January 15, 1865, Fort Fisher, North Carolina	February 1, 1865, Elmira Prison Camp, New York	Died March 22, 1865 of Chronic Diarrhea, Grave No. 1517

Name & Rank	Age	Enlisted	Regiment and State	Where Captured	Prison	Remarks
Grice, John E. Private	23	August 12, 1861, Camp Butler, South Carolina	Co. B, 14th South Carolina Infantry	July 29, 1864, Petersburg, Virginia	Point Lookout, Maryland, transferred to Elmira Prison, NY, August 12, 1864	Transferred for Exchange 10/11/64. Died 11/6/64 of Chronic Diarrhea at Point Lookout, MD.
Grice, Nathan E. Private	Unk	August 4, 1863, Bryan County, Georgia	Co. K, 7th Georgia Cavalry	June 11, 1864, Trevilian Station, Louisa Court House, Virginia	Point Lookout, Maryland, transferred to Elmira Prison, NY, July 25, 1864	Died September 19, 1864 of Chronic Diarrhea, Grave No. 321
Grier, Thomas C. Private	34	December 20, 1861, Camp Harlee, Georgetown, South Carolina	Co. A, 21st South Carolina Infantry	January 15, 1865, Fort Fisher, North Carolina	January 30, 1865, Elmira Prison Camp, New York	Exchanged March 2, 1865 at Boulware's Wharf on the James River, Virginia
Grier, William S. Private	Unk	April 1, 1864, Charleston, South Carolina	Co. A, 21st South Carolina Infantry	January 15, 1865, Fort Fisher, North Carolina	January 30, 1865, Elmira Prison Camp, New York	Died March 12, 1865 of Chronic Diarrhea, Grave No. 1852
Griffen, David D. Private	Unk	March 16, 1862, Grove Hill, Alabama	Co. J, 5th Alabama Infantry	May 20, 1864, Spotsylvania Court House, Virginia	Point Lookout, Maryland, transferred to Elmira Prison, NY, July 6, 1864	Oath of Allegiance June 30, 1865
Griffen, John H. Private	Unk	June 13, 1861, Monroe, Georgia	Co. H, 9th Georgia Infantry	May 6, 1864, Wilderness, Virginia	Point Lookout, Maryland, transferred to Elmira Prison, NY, August 14, 1864	Died January 8, 1865 of Variola (Smallpox), Grave No. 1224.
Griffin, Absalom B. Private	Unk	April 11, 1863, Coles Island, South Carolina	Co. F, 25th South Carolina Infantry	January 15, 1865, Fort Fisher, North Carolina	January 30, 1865, Elmira Prison Camp, New York	Died May 6, 1865 of Chronic Diarrhea, Grave No. 2765
Griffin, Benjamin Private	23	July 24, 1861, Northampton County, North Carolina	Co. C, 32nd North Carolina Infantry	May 10, 1864, Near Mine Run, Spotsylvania, Virginia	Point Lookout, Maryland, transferred to Elmira Prison, NY, August 6, 1864	Died November 6, 1864 of Chronic Diarrhea, Grave No. 773. Name Griffith on Headstone.

Name & Rank	Age	Enlisted	Regiment and State	Where Captured	Prison	Remarks
Griffin, Charles P. Private	Unk	July 1, 1864, Anson County, North Carolina	Co. E, 33rd North Carolina Infantry	May 6, 1864, Wilderness, Virginia	Old Capital Prison, Washington, DC, transferred to Elmira July 23, 1864	Oath of Allegiance June 27, 1865
Griffin, Eli Private	Unk	February 27, 1863, Reidsville, Rockingham County, North Carolina	Co. E, 45th North Carolina Infantry	May 10, 1864, Spotsylvania Court House, Virginia	Point Lookout, Maryland, transferred to Elmira Prison, NY, August 6, 1864	Died February 5, 1865 of Variola (Smallpox), Grave No. 1909
Griffin, Henry J. F. Private	Unk	April 11, 1863, Coles Island, South Carolina	Co. F, 25th South Carolina Infantry	January 15, 1865, Fort Fisher, North Carolina	January 30, 1865, Elmira Prison Camp, New York	Died May 16, 1865 of Chronic Diarrhea, Grave No. 2963
Griffin, J. R. Private	25	February 25, 1862, Hardeeville, South Carolina	Co. J, 11th South Carolina Infantry	June 16, 1864, Petersburg, Virginia	Point Lookout, Maryland, transferred to Elmira Prison, NY, July 25, 1864	Exchanged February 13, 1865 at Boulware's wharf on the James River, Virginia
Griffin, Jackson J. Private	Unk	March 4, 1862, Perry, Georgia	Co. H, 45th Georgia Infantry	May 6, 1864, Wilderness, Virginia	Point Lookout, Maryland, transferred to Elmira Prison, NY, August 14, 1864	Died January 21, 1865 of Variola (Smallpox), Grave No. 1588. Headstone has 12th GA.
Griffin, James F. Private	19	March 20, 1862, Union County, North Carolina	Co. J, 53rd North Carolina Infantry	May 15, 1864, Spotsylvania Court House, Virginia	Point Lookout, Maryland, transferred to Elmira Prison, NY, July 6, 1864	Exchanged February 20, 1865 at Boulware's or Cox Wharf on the James River, Virginia
Griffin, James H. Private	23	February 1, 1862, Rich Square, North Carolina	Co. F, 1st North Carolina Infantry	May 12, 1864, Wilderness, Spotsylvania Court House, Virginia	Point Lookout, Maryland, transferred to Elmira Prison, NY, August 6, 1864	Oath of Allegiance May 29, 1865
Griffin, James L. Private	Unk	Unknown	Co. K, 19th Virginia Cavalry	July 15, 1864, Near Harper's Ferry, Loudoun County, Virginia	Old Capital Prison, Washington, DC, transferred to Elmira July 23, 1864	Died September 18, 1864 of Typhoid-Pneumonia, Grave No. 515

Name & Rank	Age	Enlisted	Regiment and State	Where Captured	Prison	Remarks
Griffin, Jesse Private	Unk	March 5, 1863, Richmond, Virginia	Co. F, 21st Virginia Infantry	May 20, 1864, Spotsylvania Court House, Virginia	Point Lookout, Maryland, transferred to Elmira Prison, NY, July 6, 1864	Exchanged October 29, 1864 at Venus Point, Savannah River, GA.
Griffin, John Private	Unk	February 27, 1863, Rockingham, North Carolina	Co. E, 45th North Carolina Infantry	May 10, 1864, Spotsylvania, Virginia	Old Capital Prison, Washington, DC, transferred to Elmira Prison, NY, July 25, 1864.	Died January 22, 1865 of Pneumonia, Grave No. 1602
Griffin, John D. Private	Unk	June 7, 1861, Macon, Georgia	Co. H, 12th Georgia Infantry	May 10, 1864, Spotsylvania Court House, Virginia	Point Lookout, Maryland, transferred to Elmira Prison, NY, July 25, 1864	Exchanged March 2, 1865 at Akins Landing on the James River, Virginia
Griffin, Louis F. Private	22	October 17, 1861, Manassas, Virginia	Co. G, 12th Mississippi Infantry	May 12, 1864, Spotsylvania, Virginia, Shell wound left leg, also wound near eye.	Old Capital Prison, Washington, DC, transferred to Elmira July 23, 1864	Exchanged October 29, 1864 at Venus Point, Savannah River, GA.
Griffin, Matthew Private	Unk	December 18, 1862, Macon, Georgia	Co. G, 51st Georgia Infantry	June 3, 1864, Gaines Farm Cold Harbor, Virginia	Point Lookout, Maryland, transferred to Elmira Prison, NY, July 17, 1864	Oath of Allegiance July 7, 1865
Griffin, Michael Private	Unk	June 22, 1862, Salt Sulfur Springs, Virginia	Co. F, 26th Battalion, Virginia Infantry	June 3, 1864, Gaines Farm, Cold Harbor, Virginia	Point Lookout, Maryland, transferred to Elmira Prison, NY, July 17, 1864	Oath of Allegiance June 19, 1865
Griffin, Robert D. Private	21	March 21, 1862, Colesville, North Carolina	Co. H, 22nd North Carolina Infantry	May 31, Mechanicsville, Virginia	Point Lookout, Maryland, transferred to Elmira Prison, NY, July 11, 1864	Oath of Allegiance June 14, 1865
Griffin, S. D. Private	Unk	April 11, 1863, Coles Island, South Carolina	Co. F, 25th South Carolina Infantry	January 15, 1865, Fort Fisher, North Carolina	January 30, 1865, Elmira Prison Camp, New York	Oath of Allegiance July 11, 1865
Griffin, Samuel N. Private	Unk	September 1, 1862, Columbia, South Carolina	Co. E, 6th South Carolina Cavalry	July 30, 1864, Lee's Mill, Petersburg, Virginia	Point Lookout, Maryland, transferred to Elmira Prison, NY, August 12, 1864	Exchanged March 14, 1865 at Boulware's Wharf on the James River, Virginia

Name & Rank	Age	Enlisted	Regiment and State	Where Captured	Prison	Remarks
Griffin, T. W. Private	Unk	March 4, 1862, Starkville, Lee County, Georgia	Co. E, 51st Georgia Infantry	June 3, 1864, Gaines Farm Cold Harbor, Virginia	Point Lookout, Maryland, transferred to Elmira Prison, NY, July 17,1864	Exchanged March 10, 1865 at Boulware's Wharf on the James River, Virginia
Griffin, W. J. Private	Unk	September 22, 1862, Waynesville, Georgia	Co. G, 7th Georgia Cavalry	June 11, 1864, Trevilian Station, Louisa Court House, Virginia	Point Lookout, Maryland, transferred to Elmira Prison, NY, July 25, 1864	Oath of Allegiance July 11, 1865
Griffith, Daniel Sergeant	Unk	September 23, 1861, Pocahontas, Arkansas	Co. B, 12th Battalion Arkansas Sharpshooters	May 17, 1863, Big Black River, Mississippi	Point Lookout, Maryland, transferred to Elmira Prison, NY, August 18, 1864	Exchanged February 13, 1865 at Boulware's or Cox Wharf on the James River, Virginia
Griffith, Richard Private	Unk	September 1, 1862, Leesburg, Virginia	Co. K, 1st Virginia Cavalry	June 27, 1864, Leesburg, Virginia	Old Capital Prison, Washington, DC, transferred to Elmira July 23, 1864	Oath of Allegiance May 29, 1865
Griffith, William A. C. Private	Unk	October 24, 1862, Randolph County, Alabama	Co. E, 61st Alabama Infantry	May 12, 1864, Spotsylvania Court House, Virginia	Point Lookout, Maryland, transferred to Elmira Prison, NY, July 30, 1864	Died October 12, 1864 of Chronic Diarrhea, Grave No. 566
Griffy, Barnett Private	38	April 5, 1862, Wilkes County, North Carolina	Co. K, 53rd North Carolina Infantry	July 13, 1864, Near Washington, DC	Old Capital Prison, Washington, DC, transferred to Elmira July 23, 1864	Exchanged February 20, 1865 at Boulware's or Cox Wharf on the James River, Virginia
Grigg, Richard Private	38	February 28, 1863, Cleveland County, North Carolina	Co. J, 38th North Carolina Infantry	July 14, 1863, Falling Waters, Maryland	Point Lookout, Maryland, transferred to Elmira Prison, NY, August 18, 1864	Exchanged March 10, 1865 at Boulware's Wharf on the James River, Virginia
Grigg, William N. Private	19	July 15, 1861, Valley Town, North Carolina	Co. D, 25th North Carolina Infantry	July 30, 1864, Petersburg, Virginia	Point Lookout, Maryland, transferred to Elmira Prison, NY, August 12, 1864	Exchanged March 2, 1865 at Akins Landing on the James River, Virginia

Name & Rank	Age	Enlisted	Regiment and State	Where Captured	Prison	Remarks
Griggs, Elisha Private	18	July 25, 1863, Fort Branch, North Carolina	Co. G, 40th Regiment, 3rd North Carolina Artillery	January 15, 1865, Fort Fisher, North Carolina	January 30, 1865, Elmira Prison Camp, New York	Oath of Allegiance June 12, 1865
Grim, T. Private	Unk	Unknown	Co. J, 23rd Virginia Cavalry	August 2, 1864, Fall Town, Loudoun County, Virginia	Old Capital Prison, Washington, DC, transferred to Elmira Prison, NY, August 12, 1864	Oath of Allegiance March 6, 1865
Grimes, William L. Corporal	26	May 1, 1862, South Mills, North Carolina	Co. D, 32nd North Carolina Infantry	May 10, 1864, Near Mine Run, Spotsylvania, Virginia	Point Lookout, Maryland, transferred to Elmira Prison, NY, August 6, 1864	Exchanged March 14, 1865 at Boulware's Wharf on the James River, Virginia
Grimsley, Bright Private	23	February 28, 1862, Lumberton, North Carolina	Co. H, 51st North Carolina Infantry	June 15, 1864, Petersburg, Virginia	Point Lookout, Maryland, transferred to Elmira Prison, NY, July 17, 1864	Oath of Allegiance July 3, 1865
Grimstead, David N. Private	18	May 7, 1863, King William County, Virginia	Co. C, 15th Virginia Cavalry	June 5, 1864, Shipyard, Currituck County, Virginia	Point Lookout Prison Camp, Maryland. Transferred to Elmira Prison Camp, New York August 17, 1864	Died October 19, 1864 of Pneumonia, Grave No. 540
Grinstead, William F. Private	Unk	March 4, 1862, Dublin, Laurens County, Georgia	Co. G, 49th Georgia Infantry	May 6, 1864, Wilderness, Virginia	Point Lookout, Maryland, transferred to Elmira Prison, NY, August 14, 1864	Died December 10, 1864 of Pneumonia, Grave No. 1152. Name Grimstead on Headstone.
Grinstead, William T. Private	Unk	June 8, 1861, Amelia County Court House, Virginia	Co. H, 44th Virginia Infantry	May 12, 1864, Spotsylvania Court House, Virginia	Point Lookout, Maryland, transferred to Elmira Prison, NY, August 2, 1864	Exchanged March 10, 1865 at Boulware's Wharf on the James River, Virginia

Name & Rank	Age	Enlisted	Regiment and State	Where Captured	Prison	Remarks
Grisham, James A. Private	25	July 1, 1861, Camp Carolina, North Carolina	Co. B, 12th North Carolina Infantry	May 12, 1864, Near Spotsylvania, Virginia	Point Lookout, Maryland, transferred to Elmira Prison, NY, August 14, 1864	Oath of Allegiance June 23, 1865
Grissard, John E. Engineer	Unk	Unknown	Unassigned	May 7, 1864, Homan's Mills, Virginia	Point Lookout, Maryland, transferred to Elmira Prison, NY, August 17, 1864	Died September 25, 1864 of Chronic Diarrhea and Erysipelas, Grave No. 357
Griswold, Albert C. Private	Unk	April 19, 1861, Norfolk, Virginia	Capt. Kevill's Battery, Richmond Howitzers, Virginia Artillery	July 7, 1864, Howlett's Farm, Virginia	Point Lookout, Maryland, transferred to Elmira Prison, NY, August 6, 1864	Exchanged February 20, 1865 at Boulware's or Cox Wharf on the James River, Virginia
Grogan, Charles T. Private	27	Unknown	Co. D, 5th North Carolina Cavalry	May 12, 1864, Spotsylvania Court House, Virginia	Point Lookout, Maryland, transferred to Elmira Prison, NY, July 25, 1864	Oath of Allegiance May 29, 1865
Grogan, James J. Private	Unk	October 9, 1862, Winchester, Virginia	Co. A, 2nd Battalion Maryland Infantry	July 29, 1864, Deserted to Union Lines, Petersburg, Virginia	Point Lookout, Maryland, transferred to Elmira Prison, NY, August 12, 1864	Oath of Allegiance January 6, 1865. Early Release per Lincoln's Proclamation, 12/8/1863.
Grogan, Jones P. Private	21	September 13, 1862, Kinston, North Carolina	Co. D, 5th North Carolina Infantry	May 12, 1864, Spotsylvania Court House, Virginia	Point Lookout, Maryland, transferred to Elmira Prison, NY, July 25, 1864	Oath of Allegiance May 29, 1865
Grogan, Joseph H. Private	Unk	March 17, 1862, Ridgeway, Virginia	Co. A, 42nd Virginia Infantry	July 16, 1864, Loudoun County, Virginia	Old Capital Prison, Washington, DC, transferred to Elmira July 23, 1864	Oath of Allegiance October 15, 1864
Grogg, Andrew H. Private	Unk	June 11, 1861, Hevener's Store, Virginia	Co. F, 25th Virginia Infantry	May 12, 1864, Spotsylvania Court House, Virginia	Point Lookout, Maryland, transferred to Elmira Prison, NY, August 12, 1864	Oath of Allegiance June 16, 1865

Name & Rank	Age	Enlisted	Regiment and State	Where Captured	Prison	Remarks
Grogg, Samuel Corporal	Unk	June 11, 1861, Hevener's Store, Virginia	Co. F, 25th Virginia Infantry	May 5, 1864, Wilderness, Virginia	Point Lookout, Maryland, transferred to Elmira Prison, NY, August 14, 1864	Oath of Allegiance June 19, 1865
Groom, Joseph T. Private	Unk	September 22, 1862, New Hope, Virginia	Co. C, 24th Virginia Cavalry	July 28, 1864, Petersburg, Virginia	Point Lookout, Maryland, transferred to Elmira Prison, NY, August 12, 1864	Exchanged March 10, 1864 at Boulware's Wharf on the James River, Virginia
Groome, Albert C. Private	Unk	February 8, 1862, Gloucester Point, Virginia	Co. B, 26th Virginia Infantry	June 15, 1864, Near Petersburg, Virginia	Point Lookout, Maryland, transferred to Elmira Prison, NY, July 12, 1864	Oath of Allegiance June 19, 1865
Grose, John Sergeant	21	October 16, 1861, Yadkinville, North Carolina	Co. B, 38th North Carolina Infantry	May 6, 1864, Wilderness, Virginia	Point Lookout, Maryland, transferred to Elmira Prison, NY, August 14, 1864	Oath of Allegiance May 29, 1865
Grose, John H. Private	19	October 16, 1861, Yadkinville, North Carolina	Co. B, 38th North Carolina Infantry	May 21, 1864, North Anna, Virginia	Point Lookout, Maryland, transferred to Elmira Prison, NY, July 23, 1864	Oath of Allegiance May 13, 1865
Grose, Nathan F. Private	18	February 15, 1863, Yadkinville, North Carolina	Co. B, 38th North Carolina Infantry	July 3, 1863, Gettysburg, Pennsylvania	Point Lookout, Maryland, transferred to Elmira Prison, NY, July 23, 1864	Oath of Allegiance May 29, 1865
Gross, Connor D. Private	19	March 1, 1862, Bear Creek, North Carolina	Co. E, 44th North Carolina Infantry	June 2, 1862, Cold Harbor, Virginia	Old Capital Prison, Washington, DC, transferred to Elmira December 17, 1864	Oath of Allegiance June 21, 1865
Gross, John Private	Unk	May 18, 1861, Lisbon, Virginia	Co. C, 42nd Virginia Infantry	May 12, 1864, Spotsylvania Court House, Virginia	Point Lookout, Maryland, transferred to Elmira Prison, NY, August 2, 1864	Oath of Allegiance June 21, 1865

Name & Rank	Age	Enlisted	Regiment and State	Where Captured	Prison	Remarks
Gross, John G. Private	Unk	January 6, 1862, Union Court House, South Carolina	Co. B, 15th South Carolina Infantry	July 27, 1864, Petersburg, Virginia	Point Lookout, Maryland, transferred to Elmira Prison, NY, August 12, 1864	Died December 7 1864 of Chronic Diarrhea, Grave No. 1186
Grouzard, John Private	Unk	July 16, 1861, Baton Rouge, Louisiana	Louisiana, Pointe Coupee Artillery	May 16, 1863, Champion Hill, Mississippi	Point Lookout, Maryland, transferred to Elmira Prison, NY, August 18, 1864	Exchanged February 25, 1865 at Boulware's wharf on the James River, Virginia
Grove, Jacob R. Private	Unk	April 18, 1861, Harrisonburg, Virginia	Co. B, 10th Virginia Infantry	May 12, 1864, Spotsylvania Court House, Virginia	Point Lookout, Maryland, transferred to Elmira Prison, New York, August 2, 1864	Died December 27, 1864 of Chronic Diarrhea, Grave No. 1458
Grove, Phillip Private	28	March 14, 1863, Camp Skinker, Virginia	Co. A, 10th Virginia Infantry	May 12, 1864, Spotsylvania Court House, Virginia	Point Lookout, Maryland, transferred to Elmira Prison, NY, August 2, 1864	Exchanged March 14, 1865 at Boulware's Wharf on the James River, Virginia
Groves, Jacob R. Private	Unk	April 18, 1861, Harrisburg, Virginia	Co. B, 10th Virginia Infantry	May 12, 1864, Spotsylvania, Virginia	Point Lookout Prison Camp, Maryland. Transferred to Elmira Prison, NY, August 2, 1864	Died December 27, 1864 of Chronic Diarrhea, Grave No. 1294
Grub, Absalom Private	Unk	October 15, 1862, Raleigh, North Carolina	Co. K, 42nd North Carolina Infantry	June 3, 1864, Gaines Mill, Cold Harbor, Virginia	Point Lookout, Maryland, transferred to Elmira Prison, NY, July 17, 1864	Exchanged 3/2/65. Died 4/5/65 of Debility at Jackson Hospital, Richmond, VA.
Grubb, James M. Private	24	October 1, 1862, Snickersville, Virginia	Co. C, 35th Battalion Virginia Cavalry	July 17, 1863, Snickers Gap, Virginia	Point Lookout, Maryland, transferred to Elmira Prison, NY, August 18, 1864	Exchanged March 2, 1865 at Akins Landing on the James River, Virginia

Name & Rank	Age	Enlisted	Regiment and State	Where Captured	Prison	Remarks
Grubb, John Sergeant	Unk	Unknown	Co. C, 19th Georgia Infantry	June 1, 1864, Gaines Mill, Cold Harbor, Virginia	Point Lookout, Maryland, transferred to Elmira Prison, NY, July 17, 1864	Exchanged October 29, 1864 at Venus Point, Savannah River, GA.
Grubbs, Charles W. Private	16	September 19, 1862, Near Martinsburg, Virginia	Co. I, 2nd Virginia Infantry	May 12, 1864, Near Spotsylvania Court House, Virginia	Point Lookout, Maryland, transferred to Elmira Prison, NY, August 6, 1864	Exchanged February 13, 1865 at Boulware's wharf on the James River, Virginia
Grubbs, Euell B. Private	Unk	July 15, 1861, Richmond, Virginia	Co. E, 44th Virginia Infantry	May 12, 1864, Spotsylvania Court House, Virginia	Point Lookout, Maryland, transferred to Elmira Prison, NY, August 2, 1864	Exchanged October 29, 1864 at Venus Point, Savannah River, GA.
Grubbs, James W. Private	Unk	November 1, 1863, Winston, North Carolina	Co. K, 52nd North Carolina Infantry	May 12, 1864, Spotsylvania Court House, Virginia	Point Lookout, Maryland, transferred to Elmira Prison, NY, July 30, 1864	Oath of Allegiance June 12, 1865
Grubbs, John Private	Unk	April 11, 1861, Buckhead, South Carolina	Co. B, 17th South Carolina Infantry	July 30, 1864, Near Petersburg, Virginia	Point Lookout, Maryland, transferred to Elmira Prison, NY, August 12, 1864	Oath of Allegiance July 7, 1865
Grubbs, John C. Private	Unk	April 20, 1864, Randolph County, North Carolina	Co. L, 22nd North Carolina Infantry	May 24, 1864, Hanover Junction, Virginia	Point Lookout, Maryland, transferred to Elmira Prison, NY, July 23, 1864	Exchanged October 29, 1864 at Venus Point, Savannah River, GA.
Grubbs, John W. Private	Unk	March 4, 1862, Jasper County, Georgia	Co. B, 44th Georgia Infantry	May 10, 1864, Spotsylvania, Virginia	Old Capital Prison, Washington, DC, transferred to Elmira July 23, 1864	Exchanged March 10, 1865 at Boulware's wharf on the James River, Virginia
Grubbs, P. Private	Unk	March 1, 1862, Winchester, Virginia	Co. C, 2nd Virginia Infantry	September 21, 1864, Warren County, Virginia	Old Capital Prison, Washington, DC, transferred to Elmira December 17, 1864	Oath of Allegiance June 21, 1865

Name & Rank	Age	Enlisted	Regiment and State	Where Captured	Prison	Remarks
Grubbs, R. D. Private	Unk	November 15, 1862, Richmond, Virginia	Co. E, 44th Virginia Infantry	May 12, 1864, Near Spotsylvania Court House, Virginia	Point Lookout Prison Camp, Maryland. Transferred to Elmira Prison, August 2, 1864	Died January 14, 1865 of Variola (Smallpox), Grave No. 1458
Guard, John E. Private	19	August 17, 1861, Powell's Point, Currituck County, North Carolina	Co. B, 8th North Carolina Infantry	June 1, 1864, Cold Harbor, Virginia	Point Lookout, Maryland, transferred to Elmira Prison, NY, July 17, 1864	Exchanged October 29, 1864 at Venus Point, Savannah River, GA.
Guatney, Magnes Private	26	May 15, 1862, Halifax County, North Carolina	Co. D, 24th North Carolina Infantry	June 17, 1864, Petersburg, Virginia	Point Lookout, Maryland, transferred to Elmira Prison, NY, July 30, 1864	Oath of Allegiance June 30, 1865
Gucenot, E. Civilian	Unk	Registered Enemy	Citizen of Louisiana	July 27, 1864, New Orleans, Louisiana	New Orleans, Louisiana transferred to Elmira November 19, 1864.	Died February 21, 1865 of Pneumonia, Grave No. 2297. Headstone has E. Grumon.
Guerrant, William F. Sergeant	Unk	June 6, 1861, New Canton, Virginia	Co. C, 44th Virginia Infantry	May 12, 1864, Spotsylvania Court House, Virginia	Point Lookout, Maryland, transferred to Elmira Prison, NY, August 2, 1864	Died September 12, 1864 of Chronic Diarrhea, Grave No. 189
Guerry, Mark Corporal	26	July 13, 1861, Jacksonville, Florida	Co. E, 2nd Florida Infantry	May 24, 1864, North Anna, Virginia	Point Lookout, Maryland, transferred to Elmira Prison, NY, July 25, 1864	Exchanged March 10, 1865 at Boulware's Wharf on the James River, Virginia
Guess, Henry W. Private	Unk	August 1, 1861, Decatur, Georgia	Co. D, 3rd Battalion Georgia Sharp Shooters	August 16, 1864, Front Royal, Virginia	Old Capital Prison, Washington, DC transferred to Elmira Prison, NY, August 29, 1864	Oath of Allegiance July 7, 1865
Guess, James W. P. Private	22	June 16, 1861, Washington County, Virginia	Co. J, 48th Virginia Infantry	May 12, 1864, Near Spotsylvania Court House, Virginia	Point Lookout, Maryland, transferred to Elmira Prison, NY, August 6, 1864	Exchanged February 20, 1865 at Boulware's or Cox Wharf on the James River, Virginia

Name & Rank	Age	Enlisted	Regiment and State	Where Captured	Prison	Remarks
Guess, John C. Private	22	March 14, 1864, Washington County, Virginia	Co. J, 48th Virginia Infantry	May 12, 1864, Near Spotsylvania Court House, Virginia	Point Lookout, Maryland, transferred to Elmira Prison, NY, August 6, 1864	Exchanged February 13, 1865 at Boulware's or Cox Wharf on the James River, Virginia
Guess, Nathan C. Private	Unk	June 16, 1861, Washington County, Virginia	Co. J, 48th Virginia Infantry	May 12, 1864, Near Spotsylvania Court House, Virginia	Point Lookout, Maryland, transferred to Elmira Prison, NY, August 6, 1864	Oath of Allegiance June 27, 1865
Guey, Tinsley Private	Unk	September 9, 1863, Macon, Georgia	Co. K, 12th Georgia Infantry	May 10, 1864, Spotsylvania Court House, Virginia	Point Lookout, Maryland, transferred to Elmira Prison, NY, July 25, 1864	Oath of Allegiance June 21, 1865
Guffey, John R. Private	Unk	January 4, 1864, Liberty Mills, Virginia	Co. H, 18th North Carolina Infantry	May 6, 1864, Wilderness, Virginia	Point Lookout, Maryland, transferred to Elmira Prison, NY, August 14, 1864	Transferred For Exchange October 11, 1864 to Point Lookout Prison Camp, MD. Nothing Further.
Guillman, J. M. Private	Unk	Unknown	Co. H, 8th North Carolina Infantry	June 1, 1864, Gaines Mill, Cold Harbor, Virginia	Point Lookout, Maryland, transferred to Elmira Prison, NY, July 17, 1864	Oath of Allegiance June 19, 1865
Guin, James B. Private	Unk	March 30, 1862, Camp Allegheny, Virginia	Co. F, 25th Virginia Infantry	May 6, 1864, Wilderness, Virginia	Old Capital Prison, Washington, DC, transferred to Elmira Prison, NY, July 14, 1864	Exchanged March 10, 1865 at Boulware's Wharf on the James River, Virginia
Guin, John V. Private	Unk	June 11, 1861, Hevener's Store, Virginia	Co. F, 25th Virginia Infantry	May 6, 1864, Wilderness, Virginia	Old Capital Prison, Washington, DC, transferred to Elmira Prison, NY, July 14, 1864	Exchanged February 13, 1864 on the James River, Virginia
Guin, Otho Private	24	June 11, 1861, Hevener's Store, Virginia	Co. F, 25th Virginia Infantry	May 6, 1864, Wilderness, Virginia	Old Capital Prison, Washington, DC, transferred to Elmira Prison, NY, July 14, 1864	Exchanged February 20, 1865 at Boulware's or Cox Wharf on the James River, Virginia

Name & Rank	Age	Enlisted	Regiment and State	Where Captured	Prison	Remarks
Guiton, Thomas W. Private	Unk	July 18, 1862, Cumberland County, North Carolina	Co. C, 3rd North Carolina Infantry	May 12, 1864, Near Spotsylvania Court House, Virginia	Point Lookout Prison, Maryland. Transferred to Elmira Prison Camp New York August 14, 1864.	Exchanged March 2, 1865 at Akins Landing on the James River, Virginia
Gum, William A. Private	Unk	April 18, 1861, Harrisonburg, Virginia	Co. H, 5th Virginia Infantry	May 12, 1864, Spotsylvania Court House, Virginia	Point Lookout, Maryland, transferred to Elmira Prison, NY, August 2, 1864	Oath of Allegiance June 27, 1865
Gunderson, Edward Private	25	March 21, 1862, New Orleans, Louisiana	Co. J, 6th Louisiana Infantry	May 5, 1864, Wilderness, Virginia	Point Lookout, Maryland, transferred to Elmira Prison, NY, August 17, 1864	Oath of Allegiance June 19, 1865
Gunnells, A. J. Private	Unk	1864 Virginia	Co. D, 3rd Battalion Georgia Sharp Shooters	August 16, 1864, Front Royal, Virginia	Old Capital Prison, Washington, DC transferred to Elmira Prison, NY, August 29, 1864	Exchanged October 29, 1864 at Venus Point, Savannah River, GA.
Gunnis, W. R. Sergeant	30	April 21, 1861, Memphis, Tennessee	Co. L, Jackson's 1st Regiment, Tennessee Heavy Artillery	August 23, 1864, Fort Morgan, Alabama	New Orleans, Louisiana transferred to Elmira Prison, NY, December 4, 1864.	Exchanged February 25, 1865 at Boulware's or Cox Wharf on the James River, Virginia
Gunter, J. R. Private	27	September 13, 1862, Chatham County, North Carolina	Co. E, 8th, North Carolina Infantry	June 1, 1864, Gaines Mill, Cold Harbor, Virginia	Point Lookout, Maryland, transferred to Elmira Prison, NY, July 17, 1864	Exchanged October 29, 1864 at Venus Point, Savannah River, GA.
Gunter, Napoleon B. Private	19	July 13, 1861, Camp Anderson, Tennessee	Co. G, 23rd Tennessee Infantry	June 17, 1864, Petersburg, Virginia	Point Lookout, Maryland, transferred to Elmira Prison, NY, July 30, 1864	Exchanged February 25, 1865 at Boulware's or Cox Wharf on the James River, Virginia
Gunter, Richard C. Private	18	July 20, 1863, Chatham County, North Carolina	Co. D, 35th North Carolina Infantry	June 17, 1864, Petersburg, Virginia	Point Lookout, Maryland, transferred to Elmira Prison, NY, July 30, 1864	Oath of Allegiance June 12, 1865

Name & Rank	Age	Enlisted	Regiment and State	Where Captured	Prison	Remarks
Gunter, Thomas D. Private	43	November 14, 1863, Ocala, Florida	Co. K, 9th Florida Infantry	August 14, 1864, Petersburg, Virginia	Old Capital Prison, Washington, DC transferred to Elmira Prison, NY, August 27, 1864	Died December 4, 1864, of Pneumonia, Grave No. 889
Gurgainus, James R. Private	Unk	October 20, 1864, Wilmington, North Carolina	Co. K, 10th Regiment, 1st North Carolina Artillery	January 15, 1865, Fort Fisher, North Carolina	January 30, 1865, Elmira Prison Camp, New York	Oath of Allegiance July 7, 1865
Gurganus, James R. Private	43	June 24, 1861, Williamston, North Carolina	Co. F, 1st North Carolina Infantry	May 12, 1864, Wilderness, Spotsylvania Court House, Virginia	Point Lookout, Maryland, transferred to Elmira Prison, NY, August 6, 1864	Died September 17, 1864 of Chronic Diarrhea, Grave No. 161. Name Garganous on Headstone.
Guthrie, George C. Sergeant	29	July 15, 1862, Raleigh, North Carolina	Co. E, 1st North Carolina Infantry	May 12, 1864, Spotsylvania Court House, Virginia	Point Lookout, Maryland, transferred to Elmira Prison, NY, August 6, 1864	Exchanged March 2, 1865 at Akins Landing on the James River, Virginia
Guthrie, Samuel W. Private	Unk	May 31, 1861, Atlanta, Georgia	Co. H, 7th Georgia Infantry	May 6, 1864, Wilderness, Virginia	Point Lookout, Maryland, transferred to Elmira Prison, NY, August 17, 1864	Exchanged October 29, 1864 at Venus Point, Savannah River, GA.
Guy, George W. Private	24	March 5, 1862, Franklin, North Carolina	Co. K, 1st North Carolina Cavalry	May 12, 1864, Spotsylvania Court House, Virginia	Point Lookout, Maryland, transferred to Elmira Prison, NY, August 12, 1864	Oath of Allegiance June 7, 1865
Guy, J. S. Sergeant	Unk	Unknown	Co. H, 5th Virginia Infantry	May 12, 1864 Spotsylvania Court House, Virginia	Point Lookout, Maryland, transferred to Elmira Prison, NY, August 2, 1864	Exchanged March 10, 1865 at Boulware's Wharf on the James River, Virginia
Guy, John J. Private	21	Unknown	Co. A, 51st North Carolina Infantry	June 1, 1864, Gaines Mill, Cold Harbor, Virginia	Point Lookout, Maryland, transferred to Elmira Prison, NY, July 17,1864	Oath of Allegiance June 21, 1865

Name & Rank	Age	Enlisted	Regiment and State	Where Captured	Prison	Remarks
Guy, William Private	24	April 30, 1862, Lillington, Harnett County, North Carolina	Co. C, 36th Regiment, 2nd North Carolina Artillery	January 15, 1865, Fort Fisher, North Carolina	February 1, 1865, Elmira Prison Camp, New York	Oath of Allegiance June 12, 1865
Guyer, William Private	Unk	May 13, 1862, Savannah, Georgia	Co. E, 7th Georgia Cavalry	June 11, 1864, Trevilian Station, Louisa Court House, Virginia	Point Lookout, Maryland, transferred to Elmira Prison, NY, July 25, 1864	Died January 3, 1865 of Pneumonia, Grave No. 1268
Guyton, J. S. Private	Unk	August 11, 1861, Richmond, Virginia	Co. E, 18th Georgia Infantry	June 1, 1864, Cold Harbor, Virginia	Point Lookout, Maryland, transferred to Elmira Prison, NY, July 17,1864	Exchanged March 14, 1865 at Boulware's Wharf on the James River, Virginia
Guyton, M. J. Private	Unk	March 28, 1863, Richmond, Virginia	Co. E, 18th Georgia Infantry	June 1, 1864, Cold Harbor, Virginia	Point Lookout, Maryland, transferred to Elmira Prison, NY, July 17,1864	Oath of Allegiance May 19, 1865
Gwin, R. H. Private	Unk	May 12, 1861, Gloucester Point, Virginia	Co. B, 26th Virginia Infantry	June 15, 1864, Petersburg, Virginia	Point Lookout, Maryland, transferred to Elmira Prison, NY, July 12, 1864	Died December 26, 1864 of Chronic Diarrhea, Grave No. 1286
Gwint, L. R. Private	Unk	Unknown	Co. B, 61st Alabama Infantry	May 20, 1864, Spotsylvania Court House, Virginia	Point Lookout, Maryland, transferred to Elmira Prison, NY, July 6, 1864	Exchanged March 2, 1865 at Akins Landing on the James River, Virginia
Gyles, F. A. Sergeant	21	February 24, 1862, Charleston, South Carolina	Co. A, 25th South Carolina Infantry	January 15, 1865, Fort Fisher, North Carolina	January 30, 1865, Elmira Prison Camp, New York	Exchanged March 14, 1865 at Boulware's Wharf on the James River, Virginia

Name & Rank	Age	Enlisted	Regiment and State	Where Captured	Prison	Remarks
Hacker, Newton Isaac Sergeant	Unk	September 20, 1862, Monroe County, Tennessee	Co. B, 62nd Tennessee Mounted Infantry	May 16, 1863, Big Black, Mississippi	Point Lookout, Maryland, transferred to Elmira Prison, NY, July 25, 1864	Oath of Allegiance May 19, 1865

Name & Rank	Age	Enlisted	Regiment and State	Where Captured	Prison	Remarks
Hackett, Christopher Sergeant	22	March 7, 1862, Greensboro, North Carolina	Co. B, 45th North Carolina Infantry	May 10, 1864, Spotsylvania Court House, Virginia	Point Lookout, Maryland, transferred to Elmira Prison, NY, July 25, 1864	Oath of Allegiance May 19, 1865
Hackett, William Private	23	July 22, 1861, Camp Moore, Louisiana	Co. A, 10th Louisiana Infantry	May 12, 1864, Spotsylvania Court House, Virginia	Point Lookout, Maryland, transferred to Elmira Prison, NY, July 25, 1864	Oath of Allegiance May 19, 1865
Hackler, Thomas K. Private	Unk	March 20, 1862, Elk Creek, Virginia	Co. F, 4th Virginia Infantry	May 12, 1864, Spotsylvania Court House, Virginia	Point Lookout, Maryland, transferred to Elmira Prison, NY, July 11,1864	Exchanged February 20, 1865 at Boulware's or Cox Wharf on the James River, Virginia
Hadaway, Edwin D. Private	Unk	August 25, 1862, Richmond, Virginia	Co. G, Cobb's Legion Georgia	August 16, 1864, Front Royal, Virginia	Old Capital Prison, Washington, DC transferred to Elmira Prison, NY, August 29, 1864	Oath of Allegiance July 11, 1865
Hadaway, J. P. M. Private	Unk	October 1, 1862, Calhoun, Georgia	Co. F, 24th Georgia Infantry	June 1, 1864, Cold Harbor, Virginia	Point Lookout, Maryland, transferred to Elmira Prison, NY, July 17,1864	Died November 11, 1864 of Pneumonia, Grave No. 795
Hadaway, W. K. Private	Unk	October 1, 1862, Calhoun, Georgia	Co. F, 24th Georgia Infantry	August 16, 1864, Front Royal, Virginia	Old Capital Prison, Washington, D. C., Transferred to Elmira August 28, 1864	Exchanged March 2, 1865 at Akins Landing on the James River, Virginia
Haddock, John Private	Unk	April 10, 1864, Camp Holmes, North Carolina	Co. C, 13th North Carolina Infantry	May 6, 1864, Wilderness, Virginia	Point Lookout, Maryland, transferred to Elmira Prison, NY, August 14, 1864	Died September 25, 1864 of Chronic Diarrhea, Grave No. 374
Haddock, Willard C. Private	Unk	May 8, 1862, Charleston, South Carolina	Co. A, 7th Georgia Cavalry	June 11, 1864, Trevilian Station, Louisa Court House, Virginia	Point Lookout, Maryland, transferred to Elmira Prison, NY, July 25, 1864	Oath of Allegiance June 19, 1865

Name & Rank	Age	Enlisted	Regiment and State	Where Captured	Prison	Remarks
Haddox, William S. Private	Unk	June 22, 1862, Martinsburg, Virginia	Co. D, 2nd Virginia Infantry	May 12, 1864, Near Spotsylvania Court House, Virginia	Point Lookout, Maryland, transferred to Elmira Prison, NY, August 6, 1864	Oath of Allegiance June 27, 1865
Haden, Daniel W. Private	Unk	March 21, 1862, Suffolk, Virginia	Co. J, 53rd Virginia Infantry	May 8, 1864, Near Petersburg, Virginia	Point Lookout, Maryland, transferred to Elmira Prison, NY, August 17, 1864	Oath of Allegiance June 19, 1865
Haden, George W. Private	Unk	March 4, 1864, Washington County, Virginia	Co. I, 48th Virginia Infantry	May 12, 1864, Near Spotsylvania Court House, Virginia	Point Lookout, Maryland, transferred to Elmira Prison, NY, August 6, 1864	Died November 11, 1864 of Typhoid Fever, Grave No. 796. Name Hayden on Headstone.
Haden, J. M. Private	Unk	February 5, 1864, Fluvanna, Virginia	Co. G, 5th Virginia Cavalry	June 11, 1864, Trevilian Station, Louisa Court House, Virginia	Point Lookout, Maryland, transferred to Elmira Prison, NY, July 25, 1864	Died October 11, 1864 of Chronic Diarrhea, Grave No. 576
Hadey, William Private	Unk	Unknown	Co. E, 3rd North Carolina Infantry	May 12, 1864, Spotsylvania Court House, Virginia	Point Lookout, Maryland, transferred to Elmira Prison, NY, August 14, 1864	Exchanged February 13, 1865 at Boulware's wharf on the James River, Virginia
Hager, Robert D. Private	19	March 17, 1862, Capt. Lowe's, North Carolina	Co. G, 52nd North Carolina Infantry	May 12, 1864, Spotsylvania Court House, Virginia	Point Lookout, Maryland, transferred to Elmira Prison, NY, August 12, 1864	Exchanged October 29, 1864 at Venus Point, Savannah River, GA.
Hagerty, Blassingame Private	17	April 27, 1861, Wetumpka, Alabama	Co. J, 3rd Alabama Infantry	May 8, 1864, Spotsylvania, Virginia	Point Lookout, Maryland, transferred to Elmira Prison, NY, August 12, 1864	Oath of Allegiance June 19, 1865
Haggard, J. W. Private	Unk	May 15, 1862, Camp Harris, Tennessee	Co. G, 17th Tennessee Infantry	June 17, 1864, Petersburg, Virginia	Point Lookout, Maryland, transferred to Elmira Prison, NY, July 30, 1864	Exchanged February 25, 1865 at Boulware's or Cox Wharf on the James River, Virginia

Name & Rank	Age	Enlisted	Regiment and State	Where Captured	Prison	Remarks
Haggard, Jesse M. Private	21	June 19, 1861, Camp Moore, New Orleans, Louisiana	Co. E, 8th Louisiana Infantry	April 9, 1865, Appomattox Court House, Virginia. Gunshot Wound Face, Left Eye.	Old Capital Prison, Washington, DC, transferred to Elmira Prison, NY, May 12, 1865.	Oath of Allegiance July 11, 1865
Haggard, John D. Private	30	July 18, 1864, St. Johns, Hertford County, North Carolina	Co. C, 3rd Battalion North Carolina Light Artillery	January 15, 1865, Fort Fisher, North Carolina	February 1, 1865, Elmira Prison Camp, New York	Oath of Allegiance May 29, 1865
Haggard, Samuel W. Private	Unk	November 1, 1862, Shelbyville, Tennessee	Co. G, 17th Tennessee Infantry	June 17, 1864, Petersburg, Virginia	Point Lookout, Maryland, transferred to Elmira Prison, NY, July 30, 1864	Exchanged February 25, 1865 at Boulware's or Cox Wharf on the James River, Virginia
Haggard, Squirs H. Private	Unk	August 23, 1861, Camp Trousdale, Tennessee	Co. D, 23rd Tennessee Infantry	June 17, 1864, Petersburg, Virginia	Point Lookout, Maryland, transferred to Elmira Prison, NY, July 30, 1864	Exchanged February 25, 1865 at Boulware's or Cox Wharf on the James River, Virginia
Hagler, John M. Private	26	August 20, 1862, Statesville, North Carolina	Co. B, 18th North Carolina Infantry	July 28, 1864, Malvern Hill, Virginia. Gunshot Right Shoulder and Lung.	Old Capital Prison, Washington, DC transferred to Elmira Prison, NY, August 27, 1864	Died November 28, 1864 of Pneumonia, Grave No. 900
Hagler, William C. Private	28	August 20, 1862, Statesville, North Carolina	Co. B, 18th North Carolina Infantry	May 12, 1864, Spotsylvania Court House, Virginia	Point Lookout, Maryland, transferred to Elmira Prison, NY, August 6, 1864	Died September 3, 1864 of Chronic Diarrhea, Grave No. 66
Hagood, Jesse M. Private	Unk	March 20, 1864, Fort Johnson, South Carolina	Co. F, 7th Battalion South Carolina Infantry	June 16, 1864, Petersburg, Virginia	Point Lookout, Maryland, transferred to Elmira Prison, NY, July 25, 1864	Died September 19, 1864 of Phthis Pulmonalis, Grave No. 500. Name Jesse M. Heygood on Headstone.

Name & Rank	Age	Enlisted	Regiment and State	Where Captured	Prison	Remarks
Hagy, David C. Sergeant	21	June 16, 1861, Washington County, Virginia	Co. J, 48th Virginia Infantry	May 12, 1864, Near Spotsylvania Court House, Virginia	Point Lookout, Maryland, transferred to Elmira Prison, NY, August 6, 1864	Exchanged October 29, 1864 at Venus Point, Savannah River, GA.
Hagy, William F. Private	Unk	February 19, 1863, Washington County, Virginia	Co. J, 48th Virginia Infantry	May 12, 1864, Near Spotsylvania Court House, Virginia	Point Lookout, Maryland, transferred to Elmira Prison, NY, August 6, 1864	Exchanged October 29, 1864 at Venus Point, Savannah River, GA.
Haigler, F. G. Private	Unk	May 22, 1862, Secessionville, James Island, South Carolina	Co. F, 25th South Carolina Infantry	January 15, 1865, Fort Fisher, North Carolina	January 30, 1865, Elmira Prison Camp, New York	Oath of Allegiance July 26, 1865
Hailey, Jackson Andrew Private	Unk	June 20, 1863, Sharpsburg, Virginia	Co. H, 5th Virginia Infantry	July 4, 1863, South Mountain, Virginia	Point Lookout, Maryland, transferred to Elmira Prison, NY, July 23, 1864	Died June 17, 1865 of Typhoid Fever, Grave No. 2878. Name H. Haley on Headstone.
Haines, Isaac B. Sergeant	Unk	May 18, 1861, Huntersville, Virginia	Co. I, 42nd Virginia Infantry	May 12, 1864, Spotsylvania Court House, Virginia	Point Lookout, Maryland, transferred to Elmira Prison, NY, August 12, 1864	Died October 13, 1864 of Pneumonia, Grave No. 569. Name Haynes on Headstone.
Haines, John T. Private	Unk	March 9, 1862, Fort Pillow, Tennessee	Co. B, 1st Jackson's Tennessee Heavy Artillery	August 23, 1864, Fort Morgan, Alabama.	New Orleans, Louisiana transferred to Elmira Prison, NY, December 4, 1864.	Died February 5, 1865 of Pthtisis Pneumonia, Grave No. 1898
Hains, Jonas N. Private	Unk	April 16, 1862, Rudes Hill, Virginia	Co. F, 2nd Virginia Infantry	May 12, 1864, Near Spotsylvania Court House, Virginia	Point Lookout, Maryland, transferred to Elmira Prison, NY, August 6, 1864	Exchanged February 20, 1865 at Boulware's or Cox Wharf on the James River, Virginia
Hair, Martin V. B. Private	27	October 13, 1862, Fayetteville, North Carolina	Co. F, 24th North Carolina Infantry	May 16, 1864, Near Drury's Bluff, Virginia	Point Lookout, Maryland, transferred to Elmira Prison, NY, August 18, 1864	Exchanged October 29, 1864 at Venus Point, Savannah River, GA.

Name & Rank	Age	Enlisted	Regiment and State	Where Captured	Prison	Remarks
Haire, George W. Private	26	October 3, 1861, Wadesboro, Anson County, North Carolina	Co. H, 43rd North Carolina Infantry	May 16, 1864, Near Drury's Bluff, Virginia	Point Lookout, Maryland, transferred to Elmira Prison, NY, August 17, 1864	Exchanged 3/2/65. Died 3/19/65 of Scorbutus (Scurvy) at Jackson Hospital, Richmond, VA.
Hairfield, Joseph W. Private	Unk	June 22, 1861, Henry County, Virginia	Co. F, 42nd Virginia Infantry	May 12, 1864, Near Spotsylvania Court House, Virginia	Point Lookout, Maryland, transferred to Elmira Prison, NY, August 6, 1864	Oath of Allegiance June 27, 1865
Haiston, Alexander M. H. Private	Unk	May 1, 1862, Fayetteville, Georgia	Co. C, 53rd Georgia Infantry	June 1, 1864, Gaines Mill, Cold Harbor, Virginia	Point Lookout, Maryland, transferred to Elmira Prison, NY, July 17, 1864	Exchanged March 14, 1865 at Boulware's Wharf on the James River, Virginia
Hale, Aaron K. Corporal	Unk	April 24, 1862, Camp Leon, Madison, Florida	Co. D, 5th Florida Infantry	May 12, 1864, Spotsylvania Court House, Virginia	Point Lookout, Maryland, transferred to Elmira Prison, NY, July 30, 1864	Died September 5, 1864 of Chronic Diarrhea, Grave No. 230
Hale, Benjamin Private	18	January 16, 1862, Weldon, Halifax County, North Carolina	Co. K, 1st North Carolina Infantry	May 12, 1864, Near Spotsylvania Court House, Virginia	Point Lookout Prison, Maryland. Transferred to Elmira Prison Camp New York August 6, 1864.	Oath of Allegiance June 30, 1865
Hale, Henry J. Private	Unk	December 11, 1861, Monticello, Florida	Co. A, 5th Florida Infantry	May 12, 1864, Spotsylvania Court House, Virginia	Point Lookout, Maryland, transferred to Elmira Prison, NY, August 12, 1864	Died September 20, 1864 of Chronic Diarrhea, Grave No. 495
Hale, Henry L. Private	Unk	February 28, 1864, Elk Creek, Virginia	Co. F, 4th Virginia Infantry	May 12, 1864, Spotsylvania Court House, Virginia	Point Lookout, Maryland, transferred to Elmira Prison, NY, August 2, 1864	Died September 2, 1864 of Typhoid Fever, Grave No. 80. Headstone has First Name Leander.

Name & Rank	Age	Enlisted	Regiment and State	Where Captured	Prison	Remarks
Hale, J. A. Private	Unk	Unknown	Co. D, 5th Virginia Infantry	May 20, 1864, Spotsylvania Court House, Virginia	Point Lookout, Maryland, transferred to Elmira Prison, NY, July 11, 1864	Exchanged February 20, 1865 at Boulware's or Cox Wharf on the James River, Virginia
Hale, Jacob L. Private	31	April 24, 1861, Elk Creek, Virginia	Co. F, 4th Virginia Infantry	May 12, 1864, Spotsylvania Court House, Virginia	Point Lookout, Maryland, transferred to Elmira Prison, NY, August 2, 1864	Oath of Allegiance June 27, 1865
Hale, James A. Private	Unk	October 24, 1861, Fort Lowrey, Virginia	Co. K, 9th Virginia Cavalry	April 19, 1864, on Potomac River Near Saint George's Island. Picked up by Gunboat.	Point Lookout, Maryland, transferred to Elmira Prison, NY, July 23, 1864	Oath of Allegiance May 13, 1865
Hale, John Private	Unk	March 20, 1862, Elk Creek, Virginia	Co. F, 4th Virginia Infantry	May 12, 1864, Spotsylvania Court House, Virginia	Point Lookout, Maryland, transferred to Elmira Prison, NY, August 2, 1864	Exchanged March 10, 1865 at Boulware's Wharf on the James River, Virginia
Hale, John T. Sergeant	34	June 12, 1861, New Orleans, Louisiana	Co. K, 14th Louisiana Infantry	May 12, 1864, Spotsylvania Court House, Virginia	Point Lookout, Maryland, transferred to Elmira Prison, NY, July 25, 1864	Exchanged February 13, 1865 at Boulware's Wharf on the James River, Virginia
Hale, Joshua B. Private	Unk	September 5, 1861, Camp Harmon, Virginia	Co. F, 4th Virginia Infantry	May 12, 1864, Spotsylvania Court House, Virginia	Point Lookout, Maryland, transferred to Elmira Prison, NY, August 2, 1864	Oath of Allegiance June 19, 1865
Hale, Rueben J. Private	Unk	March 9, 1861, Prattville, Alabama	Co. F, 1st Battalion Alabama Artillery	August 23, 1864, Fort Morgan, Alabama	Steam Press No. 4 New Orleans, Louisiana transferred to Elmira October 8, 1864.	Exchanged February 13, 1865 at Boulware's wharf on the James River, Virginia
Hale, Rufus H. Private	31	March 20, 1862, Elk Creek, Virginia	Co. F, 4th Virginia Infantry	May 12, 1864, Spotsylvania Court House, Virginia	Point Lookout, Maryland, transferred to Elmira Prison, NY, August 2, 1864	Exchanged February 13, 1865 at Boulware's Wharf on the James River, Virginia

Name & Rank	Age	Enlisted	Regiment and State	Where Captured	Prison	Remarks
Hale, William B. Sergeant	18	April 24, 1861, Elk Creek, Virginia	Co. F, 4th Virginia Infantry	May 12, 1864, Spotsylvania Court House, Virginia	Point Lookout, Maryland, transferred to Elmira Prison, NY, August 2, 1864	Exchanged March 10, 1865 at Boulware's Wharf on the James River, Virginia
Hale, William H. Private	Unk	September 4, 1862, Jefferson County, Alabama	Co. A, 21st Alabama Infantry	August 23, 1864, Fort Morgan, Alabama	Steam Press No. 4 New Orleans, Louisiana transferred to Elmira October 8, 1864.	Oath of Allegiance July 7, 1865
Hales, Samuel Private	53	March 2, 1862, Blockerville, Cumberland County, North Carolina	Co. D, 36th Regiment 2nd North Carolina Artillery	January 15, 1865, Fort Fisher, North Carolina	February 1, 1865, Elmira Prison Camp, New York	Exchanged March 2, 1865 at Boulware's Wharf on the James River, Virginia
Haley, D. L. Private	25	July 24, 1861, Camp McDonald, Cobb County, Georgia	Co. C, Phillips Legion Georgia	May 12, 1864, Spotsylvania Court House, Virginia	Point Lookout, Maryland, transferred to Elmira Prison, NY, August 12, 1864	Oath of Allegiance June 16, 1865
Haley, Harvey V. Corporal	Unk	January 1, 1862, Camp Harlee, Georgetown, South Carolina	Co. I, 25th South Carolina Infantry	January 15, 1865, Fort Fisher, North Carolina	January 30, 1865, Elmira Prison Camp, New York	Died March 12, 1865 of Diarrhea, Grave No. 1821
Haley, John B. Private	Unk	December 29, 1862, Virginia	Co. E, 1st Virginia Cavalry	June 21, 1864, Near White House, Virginia	Point Lookout, Maryland, transferred to Elmira Prison, NY, July 23, 1864	Oath of Allegiance May 17, 1865
Hall, Alexander A. Private	18	March 6, 1863, Hardeeville, South Carolina	Co. D, 11th South Carolina Infantry	January 15, 1865, Fort Fisher, North Carolina	February 1, 1865, Elmira Prison Camp, New York	Died April 2, 1865 of Rubeola (Measles), Grave No. 2581
Hall, Amos J. Private	31	December 2, 1862, Fort Fisher, North Carolina	Co. C, 36th Regiment 2nd North Carolina Artillery	January 15, 1865, Fort Fisher, North Carolina	February 1, 1865, Elmira Prison Camp, New York	Exchanged March 2, 1865 at Boulware's Wharf on the James River, Virginia

Name & Rank	Age	Enlisted	Regiment and State	Where Captured	Prison	Remarks
Hall, Andrew J. Private	Unk	June 17, 1861, Rocky Mount, Virginia	Co. K, 42nd Virginia Infantry	May 12, 1864, Spotsylvania Court House, Virginia	Point Lookout, Maryland, transferred to Elmira Prison, NY, August 2, 1864	Oath of Allegiance June 23, 1865
Hall, Charles Private	Unk	September 17, 1862, Coffee County, Alabama	Co. E, 1st Battalion Alabama Artillery	August 23, 1864, Fort Morgan, Louisiana	Steam Press No. 4, New Orleans, Louisiana transferred to Elmira October 8, 1864.	Died February 6, 1865 of Pneumonia, Grave No. 1892
Hall, Charles H. Private	Unk	October 1, 1861, Wareboro, Georgia	Co. K, 26th Georgia Infantry	May 6, 1864, Wilderness, Virginia	Point Lookout, Maryland, transferred to Elmira Prison, NY, August 14, 1864	Exchanged October 29, 1864 at Venus Point, Savannah River, GA.
Hall, Charles H. Private	20	June 10, 1861, Clinton, North Carolina	Co J, 20th North Carolina Infantry	May 12, 1864, Near Spotsylvania Court House, Virginia	Point Lookout, Maryland, transferred to Elmira Prison, NY, August 14, 1864	Exchanged March 2, 1865 at Akins Landing on the James River, Virginia
Hall, Charles H. Private	Unk	March 8, 1862, Lynchburg, Virginia	Co. D, 42nd Virginia Infantry	May 12, 1864, Near Spotsylvania Court House, Virginia	Point Lookout, Maryland, transferred to Elmira Prison, NY, August 6, 1864	Died December 30, 1864 of Pneumonia, Grave No. 1313
Hall, Daniel Private	25	January 13, 1862, Darlington District, South Carolina	Co. G, 21st South Carolina Infantry	January 15, 1865, Fort Fisher, North Carolina	January 30, 1865, Elmira Prison Camp, New York	Died February 25, 1865 of Pneumonia, Grave No. 2281
Hall, David T. Private	38	March 4, 1862, Ellisville, Bladen County, North Carolina	Co. C, 36th Regiment 2nd North Carolina Artillery	January 15, 1865, Fort Fisher, North Carolina	February 1, 1865, Elmira Prison Camp, New York	Oath of Allegiance July 7, 1865
Hall, Gaston W. Private	19	March 15, 1864, Fort Fisher, North Carolina	Co. H, 36th Regiment 2nd North Carolina Artillery	January 15, 1865, Fort Fisher, North Carolina	February 1, 1865, Elmira Prison Camp, New York	Died March 1, 1865 of Chronic Diarrhea, Grave No. 2109
Hall, George W. Private	24	April 26, 1861, Elizabethtown, North Carolina	Co. A, 18th North Carolina Infantry	May 12, 1864, Spotsylvania Court House, Virginia	Point Lookout, Maryland, transferred to Elmira Prison, NY, August 6, 1864	Oath of Allegiance June 30, 1865

Name & Rank	Age	Enlisted	Regiment and State	Where Captured	Prison	Remarks
Hall, Haynes L. Sergeant	21	March 31, 1862, Cumberland County, North Carolina	Co. J, 51st North Carolina Infantry	June 1, 1864, Cold Harbor, Virginia	Point Lookout, Maryland, transferred to Elmira Prison, NY, July 17,1864	Oath of Allegiance July 3, 1865
Hall, Henry Private	18	March 4, 1862, Clinton, North Carolina	Co. F, 20th North Carolina Infantry	July 10, 1864, Frederick Junction, Maryland	Old Capital Prison, Washington, DC, transferred to Elmira July 23, 1864	Oath of Allegiance May 15, 1865
Hall, Henry Private	21	February 24, 1862, Wadesboro, North Carolina	Co. H, 43rd North Carolina Infantry	July 16, 1864, Loudoun County, Virginia	Old Capital Prison, Washington, DC, transferred to Elmira July 23, 1864	Oath of Allegiance July 7, 1865
Hall, J. R. Private	Unk	Unknown	Co. B, 16th Virginia Infantry	May 24, 1864, North Anna, Virginia	Point Lookout, Maryland, transferred to Elmira Prison, NY, July 25, 1864	Oath of Allegiance April 18, 1865
Hall, Jacob S. Corporal	Unk	March 13, 1863, Frankford, Virginia	Co. E, 19th Virginia Cavalry	July 15, 1864, Loudoun County, Virginia	Old Capital Prison, Washington, DC, transferred to Elmira July 23, 1864	Oath of Allegiance July 3, 1865
Hall, James B. Private	Unk	May 15, 1862, Atlanta, Georgia	Co. D, 4th Georgia Infantry	July 12, 1864, Near Washington, DC. Gunshot Right Shoulder.	Old Capital Prison, Washington, DC transferred to Elmira Prison, NY, August 27, 1864	Oath of Allegiance July 7, 1865
Hall, James B. Private	Unk	August 26, 1863, Calhoun, Georgia	Co. G, 49th Georgia Infantry	May 6, 1864, Wilderness, Virginia	Point Lookout, Maryland, transferred to Elmira Prison, NY, August 14, 1864	Died February 16, 1865 of Variola (Smallpox), Grave No. 2201.
Hall, James E. Private	Unk	February 25, 1861, Selma, Alabama	Co. C, 1st Battalion Alabama Artillery	August 23, 1864, Fort Morgan, Alabama	New Orleans, Louisiana transferred to Elmira Prison, NY, December 4, 1864.	Died February 10, 1865 of Chronic Diarrhea, Grave No. 2091

Name & Rank	Age	Enlisted	Regiment and State	Where Captured	Prison	Remarks
Hall, James G. Private	Unk	March 8, 1862, Lynchburg, Virginia	Co. D, 42nd Virginia Infantry	May 12, 1864, Near Spotsylvania Court House, Virginia	Point Lookout, Maryland, transferred to Elmira Prison, NY, August 6, 1864	Died October 13, 1864 of Typhoid Fever, Grave No. 698
Hall, James H. Private	23	January 1, 1862, Georgetown, South Carolina	Co. K, 21st South Carolina Infantry	January 15, 1865, Fort Fisher, North Carolina	January 30, 1865, Elmira Prison Camp, New York	Died August 26, 1865 of Chronic Diarrhea, Grave No. 2857
Hall, Jesse Private	Unk	April 20, 1864 Camp Holmes, North Carolina	Co. H, 34th North Carolina Infantry	May 6, 1864, Wilderness, Virginia	Point Lookout, Maryland, transferred to Elmira Prison, NY, July 25, 1864. Ward No. 31	Died August 11, 1864 of Enteritis, Grave No. 137
Hall, Jesse Private	19	June 1, 1863, Fort Fisher, North Carolina	Co. J, 36th Regiment 2nd North Carolina Artillery	January 15, 1865, Fort Fisher, North Carolina	February 1, 1865, Elmira Prison Camp, New York	Died February 10, 1865 of Rubeola (Measles), Grave No. 2093
Hall, Jesse J. Sergeant	23	July 3, 1861, Atlanta, Georgia	Co. B, 11th Georgia Infantry	May 6, 1864, Wilderness, Virginia	Point Lookout, Maryland, transferred to Elmira Prison, NY, August 14, 1864	Oath of Allegiance June 23, 1865
Hall, Joel Private	Unk	May 31, 1861, Yellow Branch, Virginia	Co. D, 42nd Virginia Infantry	May 12, 1864, Near Spotsylvania Court House, Virginia	Point Lookout, Maryland, transferred to Elmira Prison, NY, August 2, 1864	Exchanged October 29, 1864 at Venus Point, Savannah River, GA.
Hall, John Sergeant	Unk	Unknown	Co. E, 3rd Battalion Georgia Sharp Shooters	August 16, 1864, Front Royal, Virginia	Old Capital Prison, Washington, DC transferred to Elmira Prison, NY, August 29, 1864	Oath of Allegiance May 29, 1865
Hall, John Private	Unk	October 1, 1863, Chatham County, North Carolina	Co. E, 26th North Carolina Infantry	May 12, 1864, Spotsylvania Court House, Virginia	Point Lookout, Maryland, transferred to Elmira Prison, NY, July 30, 1864	Exchanged February 20, 1865 at Boulware's or Cox Wharf on the James River, Virginia

Name & Rank	Age	Enlisted	Regiment and State	Where Captured	Prison	Remarks
Hall, John Private	Unk	Unknown	Co. A, 50th Virginia Infantry	May 12, 1864, Spotsylvania Court House, Virginia	Point Lookout, Maryland, transferred to Elmira Prison, NY, August 2, 1864	Died September 26, 1864 of Chronic Diarrhea, Grave No. 453
Hall, John A. W. Private	23	June 1, 1861, Lock's Creek, Fayetteville, North Carolina	Co. F, 24th North Carolina Infantry	June 17, 1864, Petersburg, Virginia	Point Lookout, Maryland, transferred to Elmira Prison, NY, July 30, 1864	Transferred for Exchange 10/11/64. Died 10/28/64 of Pneumonia at Point Lookout Prison Camp, MD.
Hall, John N. J. Private	17	April 18, 1861, Big Spring, Virginia	Co. B, 4th Virginia Infantry	July 10, 1864, Frederick Junction, Maryland	Old Capital Prison, Washington, DC, transferred to Elmira July 23, 1864	Oath of Allegiance May 19, 1865
Hall, John W. Corporal	Unk	July 13, 1861, Gloucester Point, Virginia	Co. B, 26th Virginia Infantry	June 15, 1864, Near Petersburg, Virginia	Point Lookout, Maryland, transferred to Elmira Prison, NY, July 12, 1864	Oath of Allegiance July 3, 1865
Hall, Lewis Private	17	August 7, 1864, St. Johns, Hertford County, North Carolina	Co. C, 3rd Battalion North Carolina Light Artillery	January 15, 1865, Fort Fisher, North Carolina	February 1, 1865, Elmira Prison Camp, New York	Died February 10, 1865 of Rubeola (Measles), Grave No. 2093
Hall, Lewis D. Private	Unk	September 20, 1863, Fort Fisher, North Carolina	Co. A, 36th Regiment 2nd North Carolina Artillery	January 15, 1865, Fort Fisher, North Carolina	February 1, 1865, Elmira Prison Camp, New York	Died March 19, 1865 of Variola (Smallpox), Grave No. 1960
Hall, Lorenzo Dow Private	45	Cumberland County, NC, 9/8/1863	3rd Co. B, 36th Regiment North Carolina, 2nd Artillery	January 15, 1865, Fort Fisher, North Carolina	January 30, 1865, Elmira Prison Camp, New York	Oath Of Allegiance July 7, 1865
Hall, Malcom Private	39	March 8, 1863, Fort Fisher, North Carolina	Co. C, 36th Regiment 2nd North Carolina Artillery	January 15, 1865, Fort Fisher, North Carolina	February 1, 1865, Elmira Prison Camp, New York	Oath of Allegiance July 11, 1865
Hall, Maurice Private	Unk	July 8, 1862, Fort Fisher, North Carolina	Co. C, 36th Regiment 2nd North Carolina Artillery	January 15, 1865, Fort Fisher, North Carolina	February 1, 1865, Elmira Prison Camp, New York	Oath of Allegiance June 12, 1865

Name & Rank	Age	Enlisted	Regiment and State	Where Captured	Prison	Remarks
Hall, P. J. Private	Unk	Unknown	Co. B, 16th Georgia Infantry	August 16, 1864, Front Royal, Virginia	Point Lookout, Maryland, transferred to Elmira Prison, NY, August 29, 1864	Transferred For Exchange October 11, 1864 to Point Lookout Prison, MD. Died October 24, 1864 of Unknown Causes.
Hall, Stephen W. Private	23	March 5, 1862, Harrison Creek, Cumberland County, North Carolina	Co. C, 36th Regiment 2nd North Carolina Artillery	January 15, 1865, Fort Fisher, North Carolina	February 1, 1865, Elmira Prison Camp, New York	Oath of Allegiance June 12, 1865
Hall, Thomas H. Private	Unk	August 20, 1864, Fort Fisher, North Carolina	Co. J, 36th Regiment 2nd North Carolina Artillery	January 15, 1865, Fort Fisher, North Carolina	February 1, 1865, Elmira Prison Camp, New York	Died February 16, 1865 of Pneumonia, Grave No. 2204
Hall, Thomas J. Private	19	March 11, 1862, Spring Garden, North Carolina	Co. D, 45th North Carolina Infantry	July 17,1864, Near Washington, DC	Old Capital Prison, Washington, DC, transferred to Elmira July 23, 1864	Exchanged March 14, 1865 at Boulware's Wharf on the James River, Virginia
Hall, W. A. Private	Unk	Unknown	Co, B, 22nd Alabama Infantry	June 3, 1864, Gaines Mill Cold Harbor, Virginia	Point Lookout, Maryland, transferred to Elmira Prison, NY, July 17,1864	Died March 9, 1865 of Pneumonia, Grave No. 1873
Hall, William Private	25	March 7, 1862, Duplin County, North Carolina	Co. B, 3rd North Carolina Infantry	May 12, 1864, Spotsylvania, Virginia	Point Lookout, Maryland, transferred to Elmira Prison, NY, August 14, 1864	Oath of Allegiance June 27, 1865
Hall, William Private	Unk	July 10, 1861, Wytheville, Virginia	Co. A, 50th Virginia Infantry	May 12, 1864, Spotsylvania Court House, Virginia	Point Lookout, Maryland, transferred to Elmira Prison, NY, August 2, 1864	Died March 16, 1865 of Pneumonia, Grave No. 1685
Hall, William B. Private	Unk	June 10, 1861, Morgan, Georgia	Co. D, 12th Georgia Infantry	May 10, 1864, Spotsylvania Court House, Virginia	Point Lookout, Maryland, transferred to Elmira Prison, NY, July 25, 1864	Oath of Allegiance June 16, 1865

Name & Rank	Age	Enlisted	Regiment and State	Where Captured	Prison	Remarks
Hall, William C. Corporal	24	September 10, 1861, Hillsboro, North Carolina	Co. K, 2nd North Carolina Cavalry	May 28, 1864, Hanover Junction, Virginia	Point Lookout, Maryland, transferred to Elmira Prison, NY, July 11, 1864	Died October 27, 1864 of Chronic Diarrhea, Grave No. 726
Hall, William C. Private	Unk	December 9, 1861, Camp Trousdale, Tennessee	Co. D, 44th Tennessee Infantry	June 17, 1864, Petersburg, Virginia	Point Lookout, Maryland, transferred to Elmira Prison, NY, July 30, 1864	Oath of Allegiance June 19, 1865
Hall, William C. Private	Unk	September 22, 1862, New Hope, Virginia	Co. C, 24th Virginia Cavalry	July 28, 1864, Petersburg, Virginia	Point Lookout, Maryland, transferred to Elmira Prison, NY, August 12, 1864	Transferred For Exchange October 11, 1864 to Point Lookout Prison Camp, MD. Nothing Further.
Hall, William D. Private	24	February 24, 1863, Clinton, Sampson County, North Carolina	Co. C, 36th Regiment 2nd North Carolina Artillery	January 15, 1865, Fort Fisher, North Carolina	February 1, 1865, Elmira Prison Camp, New York	Oath of Allegiance July 7, 1865
Hall, William H. Sergeant	Unk	May 31, 1861, Yellow Branch, Virginia	Co. D, 42nd Virginia Infantry	May 12, 1864, Near Spotsylvania Court House, Virginia	Point Lookout, Maryland, transferred to Elmira Prison, NY, August 6, 1864	Died March 4, 1865 of Diarrhea, Grave No. 1996. Headstone has 45th Virginia.
Hall, William H. Private	Unk	June 14, 1861, Richmond, Virginia	Co. D, 44th Virginia Infantry	May 12, 1864, Spotsylvania Court House, Virginia	Point Lookout, Maryland, transferred to Elmira Prison, NY, August 2, 1864	Oath of Allegiance July 16, 1865
Hall, William J. Private	34	May 8, 1862, Fort Fisher, North Carolina	Co. C, 36th Regiment 2nd North Carolina Artillery	January 15, 1865, Fort Fisher, North Carolina	February 1, 1865, Elmira Prison Camp, New York	Oath of Allegiance June 12, 1865
Hall, William M. Sergeant	Unk	May 31, 1861, Yellow Branch, Virginia	Co. D, 42nd Virginia Infantry	May 12, 1864, Near Spotsylvania Court House, Virginia	Point Lookout, Maryland, transferred to Elmira Prison, NY, August 6, 1864	Exchanged February 20, 1865 at Boulware's or Cox Wharf on the James River, Virginia

Name & Rank	Age	Enlisted	Regiment and State	Where Captured	Prison	Remarks
Hallman, John P. Corporal	Unk	July 19, 1861, Montgomery, Alabama	Co. G, 13th Alabama Infantry	May 12, 1864, Spotsylvania Court House, Virginia	Point Lookout, Maryland, transferred to Elmira Prison, NY, July 30, 1864	Oath of Allegiance June 23, 1865
Halsenback, Robert Private	Unk	July 20, 1862, Raleigh, North Carolina	Co. E, 35th North Carolina Infantry	June 17, 1864, Petersburg, Virginia	Point Lookout, Maryland, transferred to Elmira Prison, NY, July 30, 1864	Died August 9, 1864 of Typo Malaria Fever, Grave No. 139. Name Holsonbach on Headstone.
Halshouser, John R. Private	21	July 27, 1861, Salisbury, North Carolina	Co. K, 8th North Carolina Infantry	June 1, 1864, Gaines Farm Cold Harbor, Virginia	Point Lookout, Maryland, transferred to Elmira Prison, NY, July 17,1864	Oath of Allegiance July 3, 1865
Halstead, Hardin James Private	Unk	April 9, 1864, Halesford, Virginia	Co. E, 58th Virginia Infantry	May 20, 1864, Spotsylvania Court House, Virginia	Point Lookout, Maryland, transferred to Elmira Prison, NY, July 6,1864	Exchanged October 29, 1864 at Venus Point, Savannah River, GA.
Halterman, John W. Private	Unk	June 17, 1862, Huttonsville, Virginia	Co. A, 25th Virginia Infantry	May 12, 1864, Spotsylvania Court House, Virginia	Point Lookout, Maryland, transferred to Elmira Prison, NY, August 2, 1864	Oath of Allegiance June 27, 1865
Haltiwanger, James O. Private	16	March 8, 1862, Lake City, Florida	Co. B, 5th Florida Infantry	May 12, 1864, Spotsylvania Court House, Virginia	Point Lookout, Maryland, transferred to Elmira Prison, NY, August 12, 1864	Oath of Allegiance June 14, 1865
Halton, H. Corporal	Unk	Unknown	Co. D, 13th Alabama Infantry	May 12, 1864, Spotsylvania Court House, Virginia	Point Lookout, Maryland, transferred to Elmira Prison, NY, August 2, 1864	Oath of Allegiance May 15, 1865
Ham, J. B. Private	Unk	June 22, 1861, Camp McDonald, Georgia	Co. J, 18th Georgia Infantry	June 1, 1864, Cold Harbor, Virginia	Point Lookout, Maryland, transferred to Elmira Prison, NY, July 17,1864	Oath of Allegiance June 14, 1865

Name & Rank	Age	Enlisted	Regiment and State	Where Captured	Prison	Remarks
Ham, J. O. Private	Unk	Unknown	Co. K, 3rd North Carolina Infantry	May 28, 1864, Mocky Ferry, Virginia	Point Lookout, Maryland, transferred to Elmira Prison, NY, July 12, 1864	Exchanged October 11, 1864. Nothing Further.
Ham, William B. Sergeant	20	August 24, 1861, Kingsbury, North Carolina	Co. E, 8th North Carolina Infantry	June 1, 1864, Gaines Mill, Cold Harbor, Virginia	Transferred From Point Lookout Prison, MD, July 12, 1864. Train Never Arrived at Elmira Prison Camp, NY.	Died July 15, 1864 in Train Wreck at Shohola, Pennsylvania.
Ham, William H. Corporal	21	April 27, 1861, Snow Hill, North Carolina	Co. A, 3rd North Carolina Infantry	May 12, 1864, Near Spotsylvania Court House, Virginia	Point Lookout, Maryland, transferred to Elmira Prison, NY, August 14, 1864	Oath of Allegiance June 14, 1865
Hamby, John H. Private	22	March 14, 1862, Wilkesboro, North Carolina	Co. F, 52nd North Carolina Infantry	May 12, 1864, Spotsylvania Court House, Virginia	Point Lookout, Maryland, transferred to Elmira Prison, NY, August 12, 1864	Exchanged February 20, 1865 at Boulware's or Cox Wharf on the James River, Virginia.
Hamer, C. H. Private	38	October 20, 1863, Bennettsville, South Carolina	Co. F, 21st South Carolina Infantry	January 15, 1865, Fort Fisher, North Carolina	January 30, 1865, Elmira Prison Camp, New York	Died February 6, 1865 of Pneumonia, Grave No. 1919. Headstone has Hassler.
Hamer, James C. Private	42	May 1, 1864, Bennettsville, South Carolina	Co. F, 21st South Carolina Infantry	January 15, 1865, Fort Fisher, North Carolina	January 30, 1865, Elmira Prison Camp, New York	Died March 2, 1865 of Chronic Diarrhea, Grave No. 2022
Hames, Zealous Private	19	August 9, 1861, Mount Tabor, South Carolina	Co. H, 15th South Carolina Infantry	July 27, 1864, Petersburg, Virginia	Point Lookout, Maryland, transferred to Elmira Prison, NY, August 12, 1864	Transferred for Exchange 10/11/64. Died 11/11/64 of Chronic Diarrhea at US Army Hospital, Baltimore, MD.

Name & Rank	Age	Enlisted	Regiment and State	Where Captured	Prison	Remarks
Hamill, Thomas J. Sergeant	29	May 15, 1862, Halifax County, North Carolina	Co. F, 24th North Carolina Infantry	June 17, 1864, Petersburg, Virginia	Point Lookout, Maryland, transferred to Elmira Prison, NY, July 30, 1864	Oath of Allegiance June 21, 1865
Hamilton, David Private	Unk	September 14, 1862, Decatur, Georgia	Co. C, 24th Georgia Infantry	August 16, 1864, Front Royal, Virginia	Old Capital Prison, Washington, DC transferred to Elmira Prison, NY, August 29, 1864	Exchanged February 20, 1865 at Boulware's or Cox Wharf on the James River, Virginia
Hamilton, Henry C. Private	Unk	June 1, 1863, Columbus, Georgia	Co. K, 12th Georgia Infantry	May 10, 1864, Spotsylvania Court House, Virginia	Point Lookout, Maryland, transferred to Elmira Prison, NY, July 25, 1864	Died October 6, 1864 of Chronic Diarrhea, Grave No. 646
Hamilton, Jacob Private	Unk	July 21, 1862, Harrisonburg, Virginia	Co. G, 12th Virginia Cavalry	July 16, 1864, Frederick Junction, Maryland	Old Capital Prison, Washington, DC, transferred to Elmira July 23, 1864	Oath of Allegiance September 13, 1864. Early Release per Lincoln's Proclamation, 12/8/1863.
Hamilton, James W. Private	Unk	September 3, 1863, Orange County Court House, Virginia	Co. J, 5th Alabama Infantry	May 5, 1864, Wilderness, Virginia	Point Lookout, Maryland, transferred to Elmira Prison, NY, August 17, 1864	Transferred For Exchange October 11, 1864 to Point Lookout Prison Camp, MD. Died Unknown Date and Causes on Steamship *Northern Light*.
Hamilton, John Private	Unk	August 14, 1861, Mobile, Alabama	Co. F, 1st Battalion Alabama Artillery	August 23, 1864, Fort Morgan, Alabama	Steam Press No. 4 New Orleans, Louisiana transferred to Elmira October 8, 1864.	Oath of Allegiance May 15, 1865
Hamilton, Richard Private	26	June 24, 1861, Williamston, North Carolina	Co. F, 1st North Carolina Infantry	May 12, 1864, Wilderness, Spotsylvania Court House, Virginia	Point Lookout, Maryland, transferred to Elmira Prison, NY, August 6, 1864	Oath of Allegiance June 19, 1865

Name & Rank	Age	Enlisted	Regiment and State	Where Captured	Prison	Remarks
Hamilton, W. S. Private	44	September 16, 1863, Union County, North Carolina	Co. K, 30th North Carolina Infantry	May 20, 1864, Spotsylvania Court House, Virginia	Point Lookout, Maryland, transferred to Elmira Prison, NY, July 6, 1864	Exchanged October 29, 1864 at Venus Point, Savannah River, GA.
Hamilton, William H. Private	19	March 1, 1862, Friar's Point, Mississippi	Co. B, 33rd Mississippi Infantry	May 16, 1863, Champion Hill, Mississippi	Point Lookout, Maryland, transferred to Elmira Prison, NY, August 18, 1864	Transferred For Exchange 10/11/64 to Point Lookout Prison Camp, MD. Died 10/24/64 of Unknown Causes.
Hamilton, William W. Corporal	Unk	June 15, 1861, Buena Vista, Georgia	Co. K, 12th Georgia Infantry	May 10, 1864, Spotsylvania Court House, Virginia	Point Lookout, Maryland, transferred to Elmira Prison, NY, July 25, 1864	Died November 17, 1864 of Pneumonia, Grave No. 962
Hamington, J. L. Private	Unk	Unknown	Co. H, 13th North Carolina Cavalry	May 20, 1864, Spotsylvania Court House, Virginia	Point Lookout, Maryland, transferred to Elmira Prison, NY, July 6, 1864	Died February 7, 1865 of Smallpox. No Grave in Woodlawn Cemetery.
Hamlet, Nathanial M. Private Musician	20	January 1, 1862, Newbern, Craven County, North Carolina	Co. F, 36th Regiment 2nd North Carolina Artillery	January 15, 1865, Fort Fisher, North Carolina	February 1, 1865, Elmira Prison Camp, New York	Exchanged March 2, 1865 at Boulware's Wharf on the James River, Virginia
Hamlin, Thomas H. Private	15	Unknown	Capt. Cooper's Battery Virginia Light Artillery	July 15, 1864, Leasburg, Virginia	Old Capital Prison, Washington, DC, transferred to Elmira Prison, NY, August 12, 1864	Exchanged March 14, 1865 at Boulware's Wharf on the James River, Virginia
Hamme, F. Private	Unk	Unknown	Co. G, 13th North Carolina Infantry	May 20, 1864, Spotsylvania Court House, Virginia	Point Lookout, Maryland, transferred to Elmira Prison, NY, July 6, 1864	Oath of Allegiance June 30, 1865
Hammen, Charles E. Sergeant	Unk	April 18, 1861, McGaheys-ville, Virginia	Co. E, 10th Virginia Infantry	May 12, 1864, Spotsylvania Court House, Virginia	Point Lookout, Maryland, transferred to Elmira Prison, NY, August 2, 1864	Exchanged March 2, 1865 at Akins Landing on the James River, Virginia

Name & Rank	Age	Enlisted	Regiment and State	Where Captured	Prison	Remarks
Hammer, Leonard H. Private	Unk	May 14, 1861, Franklin, Virginia	Co. E, 25th Virginia Infantry	May 12, 1864, Spotsylvania Court House, Virginia	Point Lookout, Maryland, transferred to Elmira Prison, NY, August 12, 1864	Oath of Allegiance June 23, 1865
Hammer, William Harrison Private	Unk	May 14, 1861, Franklin, Virginia	Co. E, 25th Virginia Infantry	May 12, 1864, Spotsylvania Court House, Virginia	Point Lookout, Maryland, transferred to Elmira Prison, NY, August 12, 1864	Oath of Allegiance June 23, 1865
Hammer, William J. Sergeant	Unk	May 27, 1861, Buckhannon, Virginia	Co. B, 25th Virginia Infantry	May 12, 1864, Spotsylvania Court House, Virginia	Point Lookout, Maryland, transferred to Elmira Prison, NY, August 12, 1864	Oath of Allegiance June 16, 1865
Hammet, Julius S. Private	18	April 9, 1862, Charleston, South Carolina	Co. F, 18th South Carolina Infantry	July 30, 1864, Petersburg, Virginia	Point Lookout, Maryland, transferred to Elmira Prison, NY, August 12, 1864	Oath of Allegiance July 3, 1865
Hammom, Thomas Private	Unk	Unknown	Doyle's Home Guard Louisiana Cavalry	October 6, 1864, Clinton, Louisiana	New Orleans, Louisiana transferred to Elmira November 19, 1864.	Exchanged February 25, 1865 at Boulware's or Cox Wharf on the James River, Virginia
Hammond, John E. Private	22	April 15, 1863, Greenville, North Carolina	Co. E, 44th North Carolina Infantry	June 2, 1864, Gaines Farm Cold Harbor, Virginia	Point Lookout, Maryland, transferred to Elmira Prison, NY, July 17,1864	Died November 24, 1864 of Chronic Diarrhea, Grave No. 924
Hammond, John G. First Sergeant	Unk	May 14, 1862, Loachapoka, Alabama	Co. G, 47th Alabama Infantry	May 6, 1864, Wilderness, Virginia	Point Lookout, Maryland, transferred to Elmira Prison, NY, August 17, 1864	Exchanged October 29, 1864 at Venus Point, Savannah River, GA.
Hammond, Moses Private	27	May 3, 1862, Fort Caswell, Brunswick County, North Carolina	Co. E, 36th Regiment 2nd North Carolina Artillery	January 15, 1865, Fort Fisher, North Carolina	February 1, 1865, Elmira Prison Camp, New York	Oath of Allegiance June 23, 1865
Hammond, S. B. Private	Unk	March 13, 1863, Camp Pritchard, South Carolina	Co. H, 4th South Carolina Cavalry	May 30, 1864, Hall's Shop, Virginia	Point Lookout, Maryland, transferred to Elmira Prison, NY, July 12, 1864	Exchanged October 29, 1864 at Venus Point, Savannah River, GA.

Name & Rank	Age	Enlisted	Regiment and State	Where Captured	Prison	Remarks
Hammonds, William C. Private	30	April 23, 1861, Fair Bluff, North Carolina	Co. C, 20th North Carolina Infantry	May 20, 1864, Spotsylvania Court House, Virginia	Point Lookout, Maryland, transferred to Elmira Prison, NY, July 6, 1864	Oath of Allegiance June 3, 1865
Hammons, Jefferson P. Private	Unk	Unknown	Co. E, 50th Virginia Infantry	May 12, 1864, Spotsylvania Court House, Virginia	Point Lookout, Maryland, transferred to Elmira Prison, NY, August 2, 1864	Died December 12, 1864 of Pneumonia, Grave No. 1140. Name T. B. Hammonds on Headstone.
Hamner, James Private	Unk	February 13, 1864, Albemarle, North Carolina	Co. G, 5th Virginia Cavalry	May 11, 1864, Yellow Tavern, Hanover County, Virginia	Point Lookout, Maryland, transferred to Elmira Prison, NY, August 17, 1864	Oath of Allegiance June 14, 1865
Hampton, George H. Private	Unk	November 3, 1862, Camp Trousdale, Tennessee	Co. D, 17th Tennessee Infantry	June 17, 1864, Petersburg, Virginia	Point Lookout, Maryland, transferred to Elmira Prison, NY, July 30, 1864	Exchanged February 13, 1865 at Boulware's wharf on the James River, Virginia
Hampton, Henry G. Private	Unk	November 3, 1862, Camp Trousdale, Tennessee	Co. D, 17th Tennessee Infantry	June 17, 1864, Petersburg, Virginia	Point Lookout, Maryland, transferred to Elmira Prison, NY, July 30, 1864	Exchanged February 25, 1865 at Boulware's or Cox Wharf on the James River, Virginia
Hampton, J. M. Private	22	May 9, 1861, Rutherford County, North Carolina	Co. G, 16th North Carolina Infantry	May 6, 1864, Wilderness, Virginia	Point Lookout, Maryland, transferred to Elmira Prison, NY, August 14, 1864	Oath of Allegiance June 16, 1865
Hampton, R. F. Private	Unk	October 10, 1863, Charlottes-ville, Virginia	Co. A, 3rd Virginia Cavalry	August 16, 1864, Front Royal, Virginia	Point Lookout, Maryland, transferred to Elmira Prison, NY, August 29, 1864	Died October 13, 1864 of Chronic Diarrhea, Grave No. 697
Hamrick, Alfred W. Private	26	August 14, 1862, Statesville, North Carolina	Co. G, 18th North Carolina Infantry	May 12, 1864, Spotsylvania Court House, Virginia	Point Lookout, Maryland, transferred to Elmira Prison, NY, August 6, 1864	Exchanged February 20, 1865 at Boulware's or Cox Wharf on the James River, Virginia

Name & Rank	Age	Enlisted	Regiment and State	Where Captured	Prison	Remarks
Hamrick, Eli Private	24	May 7, 1862, Guiney Station, Virginia	Co. B, 34th North Carolina Infantry	May 6, 1864, Wilderness, Virginia	Point Lookout, Maryland, transferred to Elmira Prison, NY, August 14, 1864	Died November 16, 1864 of Remittent Fever, Grave No. 950. Name Harnick on Headstone.
Hamrick, William A. Private	Unk	April 29, 1862, Jefferson County, Florida	Co. G, 5th Florida Infantry	May 12, 1864, Spotsylvania Court House, Virginia	Point Lookout, Maryland, transferred to Elmira Prison, NY, July 30, 1864	Exchanged March 10, 1865 at Boulware's Wharf on the James River, Virginia
Hanchey, James W. Private	Unk	January 21, 1862, Kenansville, Duplin County, North Carolina	Co. B, 3rd North Carolina Infantry	May 12, 1864, Near Spotsylvania County Court House, Virginia	Point Lookout, Maryland, transferred to Elmira Prison, NY, August 14, 1864	Died March 20, 1865 of Variola (Smallpox), Grave No. 2142
Hancock, Caleb C. Private	24	December 19, 1861, Camp Gaston, North Carolina	Co. K, 3rd North Carolina Cavalry	May 29, 1864, Pamunkey, Virginia	Point Lookout, Maryland, transferred to Elmira Prison, NY, July 12, 1864	Oath of Allegiance June 28, 1865
Hancock, Henry Private	Unk	April 2, 1864, Tishomingo County, Mississippi	Co. D, 12th, Alabama Infantry	May 20, 1864, Spotsylvania Court House, Virginia	Point Lookout, Maryland, transferred to Elmira Prison, NY, July 6, 1864	Transferred for Exchange 10/11/64. Died 10/15/64 of Unknown Causes at US Army Hospital Baltimore, MD.
Hancock, James A. Private	Unk	Unknown	Co. E, 50th Virginia Infantry	May 6, 1864, Wilderness, Virginia	Point Lookout, Maryland, transferred to Elmira Prison, NY, August 14, 1864	Oath of Allegiance June 23, 1865
Hancock, Lowis D. Sergeant	Unk	Unknown	Co. E, 50th Virginia Infantry	May 5, 1864, Wilderness, Virginia	Point Lookout, Maryland, transferred to Elmira Prison, NY, August 14, 1864	Oath of Allegiance June 21, 1865
Hancock, William G. Private	Unk	March 15, 1862, Knoxville, Georgia	Co. C, 27th Georgia Infantry	June 1, 1864, Gaines Mill Cold Harbor, Virginia	Point Lookout, Maryland, transferred to Elmira Prison, NY, July 17,1864	Oath of Allegiance July 7, 1865

Name & Rank	Age	Enlisted	Regiment and State	Where Captured	Prison	Remarks
Hancock, William P. Private	Unk	Unknown	Co. E, 50th Virginia Infantry	May 6, 1864, Wilderness, Virginia	Point Lookout, Maryland, transferred to Elmira Prison, NY, August 14, 1864	Died November 11, 1864 of Chronic Diarrhea, Grave No. 792.
Hancock, Zumariah Private	Unk	July 18, 1863, Wilmington, North Carolina	Co. K, 10th Regiment, 1st North Carolina Artillery	January 15, 1865, Fort Fisher, North Carolina	January 30, 1865, Elmira Prison Camp, New York	Oath of Allegiance July 11, 1865
Hand, Joseph F. C. Private	Unk	June 4, 1861, Montevallo, Alabama	Co. C, 10th Alabama Infantry	May 6, 1864, Wilderness, Virginia	Point Lookout, Maryland, transferred to Elmira Prison, NY, August 17, 1864	Exchanged February 20, 1865 at Boulware's or Cox Wharf on the James River, Virginia
Handley, John A. Sergeant	21	March 4, 1862, Abbeville, Georgia	Co. E, 49th Georgia Infantry	May 6, 1864, Wilderness, Virginia	Point Lookout, Maryland, transferred to Elmira Prison, NY, August 14, 1864	Oath of Allegiance June 16, 1865
Handley, R. Perry Private	Unk	January 1, 1864, Richmond, Virginia	Co. H, 10th Virginia Cavalry	May 20, 1864, Spotsylvania Court House, Virginia	Point Lookout, Maryland, transferred to Elmira Prison, NY, July 6, 1864	Oath of Allegiance June 27, 1865
Hands, Columbus R. Private	22	August 25, 1862, Land Springs, Mississippi	Co. D, 13th, Mississippi Infantry	June 1, 1864, Cold Harbor, Virginia	Point Lookout, Maryland, transferred to Elmira Prison, NY, July 17,1864	Exchanged February 13, 1865 at Boulware's Wharf on the James River, Virginia
Hanes, W. H. Private	Unk	Unknown	Co. E, 16th Georgia Infantry	May 6, 1864, Wilderness, Virginia	Old Capital Prison, Washington, DC, transferred to Elmira Prison, NY, July 14, 1864	Oath of Allegiance May 29, 1865
Haney, D. W. Private	Unk	August 11, 1861, Gwinnett, Georgia	Co. H, 16th Georgia Infantry	June 1, 1864, Cold Harbor, Virginia	Point Lookout, Maryland, transferred to Elmira Prison, NY, July 17,1864	Oath of Allegiance July 7, 1865

Name & Rank	Age	Enlisted	Regiment and State	Where Captured	Prison	Remarks
Haney, James H. Private	Unk	October 10, 1864, Stanardsville, Virginia	Co. D, 34th, Virginia Infantry	June 15, 1864, Near Petersburg, Virginia	Point Lookout, Maryland, transferred to Elmira Prison, NY, July 17,1864	Oath of Allegiance June 16, 1865
Haney, Junis R. Private	Unk	April 18, 1861, Lexington, Virginia	Co. H, 27th Virginia Infantry	May 20, 1864, Spotsylvania Court House, Virginia	Point Lookout Prison. Transferred to Elmira Prison, New York, July 6, 1864.	Exchanged March 14, 1865 at Boulware's Wharf on the James River, Virginia
Haney, William E. Private	Unk	May 10, 1861, Lebanon, Virginia	Co. C, 4th Virginia Infantry	May 5, 1864, Wilderness, Virginia	Point Lookout, Maryland, transferred to Elmira Prison, NY, August 2, 1864	Died February 19, 1865 of Chronic Diarrhea, Grave No. 2358
Hanier, H. G. Private	Unk	Unknown	Co. F, 3rd North Carolina Infantry	May 12, 1864, Near Spotsylvania Court House, Virginia	Point Lookout, Maryland, transferred to Elmira Prison, NY, August 14, 1864	Oath of Allegiance June 23, 1865
Hanis, A. A. Private	Unk	Unknown	Co. C, 12th North Carolina Cavalry	May 20, 1864, Spotsylvania Court House, Virginia	Point Lookout, Maryland, transferred to Elmira Prison, NY, July 6, 1864	Oath of Allegiance June 27, 1865
Hankins, David M. Private	Unk	March 10, 1862, Pittsylvania, Virginia	Co. I, 21st, Virginia Infantry	May 20, 1864, Spotsylvania Court House, Virginia	Point Lookout, Maryland, transferred to Elmira Prison, NY, July 6,1864	Exchanged October 29, 1864 at Venus Point, Savannah River, GA.
Hankla, Benjamin L. Private	Unk	February 19, 1864, Dublin Depot, Virginia	Co. L, 26th Battalion, Virginia Infantry	June 3, 1864, Gaines Farm Cold Harbor, Virginia	Point Lookout, Maryland, transferred to Elmira Prison, NY, July 17,1864	Exchanged February 13, 1865 at Boulware's wharf on the James River, Virginia
Hanley, James Private	45	June 4, 1861, Camp Moore, Louisiana	Co. F, 6th Louisiana Infantry	May 5, 1864, Wilderness, Virginia	Point Lookout, Maryland, transferred to Elmira Prison, NY, August 17, 1864	Oath of Allegiance May 15, 1865

Name & Rank	Age	Enlisted	Regiment and State	Where Captured	Prison	Remarks
Hanly, D. S. Private	Unk	Unknown	Co. K, 50th Virginia Infantry	May 6, 1864, Wilderness, Virginia	Point Lookout, Maryland, transferred to Elmira Prison, NY, August 14, 1864	Oath of Allegiance June 16, 1865
Hanna, Q. T. Private	Unk	January 1, 1864, Lesciton, North Carolina	Co. K, 49th North Carolina Infantry	June 9, 1864, Chickahominy, Swamp, Virginia	Old Capital Prison, Washington, DC, transferred to Elmira July 23, 1864	Oath of Allegiance September 19, 1864
Hanna, William Private	Unk	June 14, 1861, Valdosta, Georgia	Co. J, 12th Georgia Infantry	May 10, 1864, Spotsylvania Court House, Virginia	Point Lookout, Maryland, transferred to Elmira Prison, NY, July 25, 1864	Exchanged March 2, 1865 at Akins Landing on the James River, Virginia
Hannon, Charles Sergeant	32	May 20, 1861, Mobile, Alabama	Co. J, 8th Alabama Infantry	May 6, 1864, Wilderness, Virginia	Point Lookout, Maryland, transferred to Elmira Prison, NY, August 17, 1864	Oath of Allegiance June 16, 1865
Hannon, Neill Sergeant	22	September 12, 1861, Carthage, North Carolina	Co. C, 35th North Carolina Infantry	June 17, 1864, Petersburg, Virginia	Point Lookout, Maryland, transferred to Elmira Prison, NY, July 30, 1864	Oath of Allegiance June 12, 1865
Hansard, Jepthy R. Private	Unk	March 4, 1862, Camp Bartow, Georgia	Co. H, 38th Georgia Infantry	May 20, 1864, Spotsylvania Court House, Virginia	Point Lookout, Maryland, transferred to Elmira Prison, NY, July 6,1864	Oath of Allegiance June 30, 1865
Hansard, Patrick H. Private	Unk	November 1, 1863, Orange County, Georgia	Co. H, 38th Georgia Infantry	July 8, 1864, Harper's Ferry, Virginia	Old Capital Prison, Washington, DC, transferred to Elmira July 23, 1864	Exchanged October 29, 1864 at Venus Point, Savannah River, GA.
Hansbrough, William L. Private	Unk	April 3, 1863, Culpepper Court House, Virginia	Co. C, 13th Virginia Infantry	May 20, 1864, Spotsylvania Court House, Virginia	Point Lookout, Maryland, transferred to Elmira Prison, NY, July 6,1864	Oath of Allegiance June 19, 1865

Name & Rank	Age	Enlisted	Regiment and State	Where Captured	Prison	Remarks
Hansford, Caroll M. Sergeant	Unk	October 31, 1863, Location Unknown	Co. L, 26th Battalion, Virginia Infantry	June 3, 1864, Gaines Farm Cold Harbor, Virginia	Point Lookout, Maryland, transferred to Elmira Prison, NY, July 17,1864	Exchanged February 25, 1865 at Boulware's or Cox Wharf on the James River, Virginia
Hansley, Jeremiah Private	18	May 13, 1861, Golden Place, Onslow County, North Carolina	Co. E, 3rd North Carolina Infantry	May 12, 1864, Spotsylvania Court House, Virginia	Point Lookout, Maryland, transferred to Elmira Prison, NY, August 14, 1864	Oath of Allegiance June 27, 1865
Hanson, Ambrose P. Private	Unk	July 26, 1861, Montgomery, Alabama	Co. E, 13th Alabama Infantry	May 12, 1864, Spotsylvania Court House, Virginia	Point Lookout, Maryland, transferred to Elmira Prison, NY, August 2, 1864	Oath of Allegiance June 19, 1865
Hanson, Robert S. Sergeant	21	July 3, 1861, Atlanta, Georgia	Co. A, 11th Georgia Infantry	May 6, 1864, Wilderness, Virginia	Old Capital Prison, Washington, DC, transferred to Elmira Prison, NY, July 14, 1864	Oath of Allegiance June 23, 1865
Hapner, John Private	17	March 14, 1862, Athens, Atlanta	Co. A, 9th Alabama Infantry	June 24, 1864, Near Petersburg, Virginia	Point Lookout, Maryland, transferred to Elmira Prison, NY, July 23, 1864	Oath of Allegiance May 19, 1865
Harbin, Harrison M. Private	21	March 20, 1862, Pickens District, South Carolina	Co. F, 1st South Carolina Infantry	May 12, 1864, Spotsylvania Court House, Virginia. Gunshot Wound Both Shoulders.	Old Capital Prison, Washington, DC transferred to Elmira Prison, NY, August 27, 1864	Exchanged February 20, 1865 at Boulware's or Cox Wharf on the James River, Virginia
Harbison, David C. Private	Unk	December 7, 1861, Camp Trousdale, Tennessee	Co. F, 44th Tennessee Infantry	May 16, 1864, Near Drury's Bluff, Virginia	Point Lookout, Maryland, transferred to Elmira Prison, NY, August 17, 1864	Exchanged February 13, 1865 at Boulware's wharf on the James River, Virginia
Harcum, Philip E. Private	Unk	March 2, 1862, White Stone, Virginia	Co. D, 55th Virginia Infantry	June 3, 1864, Old Church, Cold Harbor, Virginia	Point Lookout, Maryland, transferred to Elmira Prison, NY, July 17,1864	Died August 3, 1864 of Contusion of Abdomen, Grave No. 2

Name & Rank	Age	Enlisted	Regiment and State	Where Captured	Prison	Remarks
Hardaway, B. M. Private	Unk	Unknown	Co. A, Jackson's 1st Regiment, Tennessee Heavy Artillery	August 23, 1864, Fort Morgan, Alabama	New Orleans, Louisiana transferred to Elmira Prison, NY, December 4, 1864.	Exchanged February 25, 1865. Died March 28, 1865 of Typhoid Fever at U. S. Army Hospital, Baltimore, Maryland.
Hardaway, James H. Private	Unk	June 8, 1861, Amelia County Court House, Virginia	Co. H, 44th Virginia Infantry	May 12, 1864, Spotsylvania Court House, Virginia	Point Lookout, Maryland, transferred to Elmira Prison, NY, August 2, 1864	Exchanged February 13, 1865 at Boulware's wharf on the James River, Virginia
Hardbarger, Jacob Private	Unk	March 13, 1862, Salem, Virginia	Co. E, 42nd Virginia Infantry	July 18, 1864, Snickers Gap, Virginia	Old Capital Prison, Washington, DC, transferred to Elmira Prison, NY, August 12, 1864	Oath of Allegiance May 29, 1865
Hardee, John W. Private	31	September 21, 1861, Lowndes County, Georgia	Co. H, 26th Georgia Infantry	May 12, 1864, Spotsylvania Court House, Virginia. Gunshot Wound Left Hip and Arm.	Point Lookout Prison Camp, Maryland. Transferred to Elmira Prison, NY, July 25, 1864	Died February 25, 1865 of Chronic Diarrhea, Grave No. 2277
Hardeman, Zedekiah J. Private	Unk	May 14, 1862, Danielsville, Georgia	Co. A, 16th Georgia Infantry	August 16, 1864, Front Royal, Virginia	Point Lookout, Maryland, transferred to Elmira Prison, NY, August 29, 1864	Oath of Allegiance July 7, 1865
Harden, Angus Private	28	July 24, 1861, Lumberton, North Carolina	Co. D, 18th North Carolina Infantry	May 12, 1864, Spotsylvania Court House, Virginia	Point Lookout, Maryland, transferred to Elmira Prison, NY, August 6, 1864	Oath of Allegiance June 30, 1865
Hardgrove, Thomas M. Private	24	March 22, 1862, Winston, North Carolina	Co. K, 52nd North Carolina Infantry	May 6, 1864, Wilderness, Virginia	Point Lookout, Maryland, transferred to Elmira Prison, NY, August 12, 1864	Oath of Allegiance July 11, 1865

Name & Rank	Age	Enlisted	Regiment and State	Where Captured	Prison	Remarks
Hardin, Jacob Private	Unk	April 18, 1863, Macon, Georgia	Co. B, 64th Georgia Infantry	June 17, 1864, Petersburg, Virginia	Point Lookout, Maryland, transferred to Elmira Prison, NY, July 30, 1864	Died September 18, 1864 of Pneumonia, Grave No. 519
Harding, James Private	28	July 1, 1861, New Orleans, Louisiana	Co. H, 14th Louisiana Infantry	May 12, 1864, Wilderness, Virginia	Point Lookout, Maryland, transferred to Elmira Prison, NY, July 25, 1864	Exchanged February 13, 1865 at Boulware's wharf on the James River, Virginia
Harding, John W. Private	29	May 9, 1861, Manchester, Virginia	Co. J, 6th Virginia Infantry	May 12, 1864, Near Spotsylvania Court House, Virginia	Point Lookout, Maryland, transferred to Elmira Prison, NY, August 6, 1864	Oath of Allegiance June 14, 1865
Harding, William H. Private	21	June 4, 1861, Camp Moore, Louisiana	Co. K, 6th Louisiana Infantry	May 5, 1864, Wilderness, Virginia	Point Lookout, Maryland, transferred to Elmira Prison, NY, August 17, 1864	Exchanged February 25, 1865 at Boulware's or Cox Wharf on the James River, Virginia
Hardison, Jackson Corporal	22	January 28, 1862 Onslow County, North Carolina	Co. E, 3rd North Carolina Infantry	May 12, 1864, Near Spotsylvania Court House, Virginia	Point Lookout, Maryland, transferred to Elmira Prison, NY, August 14, 1864	Oath of Allegiance June 27, 1865
Hardison, James J. Private	Unk	March 1, 1862, Cumberland County, North Carolina	Co. I, 51st North Carolina Infantry	June 1, 1864, Cold Harbor, Virginia	Transferred From Point Lookout Prison, MD, July 12, 1864. Train Never Arrived at Elmira Prison Camp, NY.	Died July 15, 1864 in Train Wreck at Shohola, Pennsylvania.
Hardy, John H. Civilian	Unk	Chesterfield, Virginia	Citizen of Virginia	May 12, 1864, Manchester Station, Virginia	Point Lookout, Maryland, transferred to Elmira Prison, NY, July 23, 1864	Oath of Allegiance June 20, 1865
Hardy, Joseph H. Private	28	March 12, 1862, Ridgeway, Virginia	Co. F, 42nd Virginia Infantry	May 12, 1864, Near Spotsylvania Court House, Virginia	Point Lookout, Maryland, transferred to Elmira Prison, NY, August 6, 1864	Oath of Allegiance June 27, 1865

Name & Rank	Age	Enlisted	Regiment and State	Where Captured	Prison	Remarks
Hardy, Jules J. Private	18	June 19, 1861, Camp Moore, Louisiana	Co. C, 8th Louisiana Infantry	May 12, 1864, Spotsylvania Court House, Virginia	Point Lookout, Maryland, transferred to Elmira Prison, NY, August 17, 1864	Exchanged February 25, 1865 at Boulware's or Cox Wharf on the James River, Virginia
Hardy, Luther C. Private	Unk	June 7, 1861, Lunenburg Court House, Virginia	Co. G, 9th Virginia Cavalry	May 27, 1864, Guinea Station, Virginia	Point Lookout, Maryland, transferred to Elmira Prison, NY, July 12, 1864	Oath of Allegiance June 7, 1865
Hardy, T. J. Private	Unk	May 4, 1862, Georgia	Co. F, 3rd Battalion Georgia Sharp Shooters	August 16, 1864, Front Royal, Virginia	Old Capital Prison, Washington, DC transferred to Elmira Prison, NY, August 29, 1864	Oath of Allegiance June 16, 1865
Hardy, Thomas Private	Unk	July 2, 1862, Calhoun, Georgia	Co. K, 27th Georgia Infantry	June 1, 1864, Malvern Hill, Virginia	Point Lookout, Maryland, transferred to Elmira Prison, NY, July 17, 1864	Died March 21, 1865 of Pneumonia, Grave No. 1227
Hardy, William A. Private	Unk	August 10, 1861, Camp Butler, South Carolina	Co. B, 14th South Carolina Infantry	July 29, 1864, Petersburg, Virginia	Point Lookout, Maryland, transferred to Elmira Prison, NY, August 12, 1864	Oath of Allegiance May 19, 1865
Hardy, William H. Private	21	July 8, 1861, Griffin, Georgia	Co. K, 13th Georgia Infantry	May 10, 1864, Spotsylvania, Virginia	Old Capital Prison, Washington, DC, transferred to Elmira July 23, 1864	Exchanged March 10, 1865 at Boulware's Wharf on the James River, Virginia
Hare, Job Private	Unk	August 19, 1861, Gates County, North Carolina	Co. E, 33rd North Carolina Infantry	May 6, 1864, Wilderness, Virginia	Point Lookout, Maryland, transferred to Elmira Prison, NY, August 14, 1864	Oath of Allegiance June 30, 1865
Haren, Edward Jr. Private	Unk	Unknown	Ordinance Department Confederate States Army	September 19, 1864, Opposite Brunsburg, Louisiana	New Orleans, LA, Transferred to Elmira Prison, NY, November 19, 1864	Exchanged February 25, 1865 at Boulware's or Cox Wharf on the James River, Virginia

Name & Rank	Age	Enlisted	Regiment and State	Where Captured	Prison	Remarks
Hargett, John M. Private	Unk	October 25, 1863, Union County, North Carolina	Co. A, 48th North Carolina Infantry	May 12, 1864, Spotsylvania Court House, Virginia	Point Lookout Prison Camp, Maryland. Transferred to Elmira Prison, July 26, 1864	Died January 8, 1865 of Pneumonia, Grave No. 1227
Hargis, James W. Private	Unk	January 29, 1864, Bristol, Tennessee	Co. J, 14th Tennessee Infantry	May 6, 1864, Wilderness, Virginia	Point Lookout, Maryland, transferred to Elmira Prison, NY, July 23, 1864	Oath of Allegiance May 29, 1865
Hargiss, John W. Sergeant	Unk	December 9, 1861, Camp Trousdale, Tennessee	Co. K, 44th Tennessee Infantry	June 17, 1864, Petersburg, Virginia	Point Lookout, Maryland, transferred to Elmira Prison, NY, July 30, 1864	Oath of Allegiance May 19, 1865
Hargrove, David J. Sergeant	21	May 11, 1861, Bladen County, North Carolina	Co. H, 3rd North Carolina Infantry	May 12, 1864, Near Spotsylvania Court House, Virginia	Point Lookout, Maryland, transferred to Elmira Prison, NY, August 14, 1864	Oath of Allegiance June 30, 1865
Hargroves, Stephen B. Private	Unk	September 20, 1863, Decatur, Georgia	Co. E, 7th Georgia Cavalry	June 11, 1864, Trevilian Station, Louisa Court House, Virginia	Point Lookout, Maryland, transferred to Elmira Prison, NY, July 25, 1864	Oath of Allegiance June 14, 1865
Harley, James N. Private	27	June 24, 1861, Coosawhatchie, South Carolina	Co. E, 11th South Carolina Infantry	June 24, 1864, Near Petersburg, Virginia	Point Lookout, Maryland, transferred to Elmira Prison, NY, August 18, 1864	Oath of Allegiance July 3, 1865
Harley, John M. Private	21	June 16, 1861, Washington County, Virginia	Co. I, 48th Virginia Infantry	May 12, 1864, Spotsylvania, Virginia	Point Lookout Prison Camp, Maryland. Transferred to Elmira Prison, August 6, 1864	Died December 29, 1864 of Pneumonia, Grave No. 1299
Harley, Thomas J. Private	24	December 9, 1863, Ridgeville, South Carolina	Co. H, 6th South Carolina Cavalry	June 11, 1864, Trevilian Station, Louisa Court House, Virginia	Point Lookout, Maryland, transferred to Elmira Prison, NY, July 25, 1864	Exchanged March 14, 1865 at Boulware's Wharf on the James River, Virginia

Name & Rank	Age	Enlisted	Regiment and State	Where Captured	Prison	Remarks
Harlow, James W. Private	Unk	September 11, 1863, Fredericks-burg, Virginia	Co. J, 5th Virginia Cavalry	June 11, 1864, Trevilian Station, Louisa Court House, Virginia	Point Lookout, Maryland, transferred to Elmira Prison, NY, July 25, 1864	Oath of Allegiance June 19, 1865
Harlow, Ransom Private	22	July 10, 1861, Halifax County, North Carolina	Co. I, 5th North Carolina Infantry	May 12, 1864, Spotsylvania Court House, Virginia	Point Lookout, Maryland, transferred to Elmira Prison, NY, August 6, 1864	Oath of Allegiance June 27, 1865
Harlow, T. W. Private	Unk	May 20, 1861, Palmyra, Virginia	Co. F, 44th Virginia Infantry	May 12, 1864, Spotsylvania Court House, Virginia	Point Lookout, Maryland, transferred to Elmira Prison, NY, August 2, 1864	Oath of Allegiance June 14, 1865
Harlow, W. A. Private	Unk	February 10, 1863, Caroline County, Virginia	Co. F, 44th Virginia Infantry	May 12, 1864, Spotsylvania Court House, Virginia	Point Lookout, Maryland, transferred to Elmira Prison, NY, August 2, 1864	Oath of Allegiance June 14, 1865
Harman, Erastus F. Private	27	October 9, 1862, Tazewell County, Virginia	Co. I, 16th Virginia Cavalry	July 9, 1864, Frederick Junction, Maryland	Old Capital Prison, Washington, DC, transferred to Elmira July 23, 1864	Died January 13, 1865 of Chronic Diarrhea, Grave No. 1482
Harmon, B. F. Private	33	April 18, 1861, McGaheys-ville, Virginia	Co. H, 10th Virginia Infantry	May 20, 1864, Spotsylvania Court House, Virginia	Point Lookout, Maryland, transferred to Elmira Prison, NY, July 3, 1864	Exchanged February 13, 1865 at Boulware's wharf on the James River, Virginia
Harmon, Frederick L. Private	20	August 14, 1862, Statesville, North Carolina	Co. A, 18th North Carolina Infantry	May 12, 1864, Spotsylvania Court House, Virginia	Point Lookout, Maryland, transferred to Elmira Prison, NY, August 6, 1864	Exchanged February 13, 1865 at Boulware's wharf on the James River, Virginia
Harmon, H. W. Private	29	January 15, 1862, Martinsburg, Virginia	Co. G, 7th Virginia Cavalry	September 14, 1863, Near Culpepper, Virginia	Point Lookout, Maryland, transferred to Elmira Prison, NY, August 18, 1864	Exchanged October 29, 1864 at Venus Point, Savannah River, GA.

Name & Rank	Age	Enlisted	Regiment and State	Where Captured	Prison	Remarks
Harmon, Jacob H. Private	18	March 15, 1862, Gaston County, North Carolina	Co. K, 49th North Carolina Infantry	June 9, 1864, Chickahominy Swamp, Virginia	Old Capital Prison, Washington, DC, transferred to Elmira July 23, 1864	Oath of Allegiance September 19, 1864
Harmon, Rueben L. Private	21	April 26, 1861, White Plains, North Carolina	Co. D, 14th North Carolina Infantry	May 30, 1864, Mechanicsville, Virginia	Point Lookout, Maryland, transferred to Elmira Prison, NY, July 12, 1864	Exchanged October 29, 1864 at Venus Point, Savannah River, GA.
Harmon, Thomas Corporal	Unk	July 24, 1861, John Pasley's, Franklin County, Virginia	Co. E, 58th Virginia Infantry	May 20, 1864, Spotsylvania Court House, Virginia	Point Lookout, Maryland, transferred to Elmira Prison, NY, July 6, 1864	Exchanged February 20, 1865 at Boulware's or Cox Wharf on the James River, Virginia
Harmon, Thomas C. Corporal	18	September 1, 1861, Spartanburg, South Carolina	Co. J, 13th South Carolina Infantry	July 14, 1863, Falling Waters, Maryland	Point Lookout, Maryland, transferred to Elmira Prison, NY, August 18, 1864	Exchanged at Venus Point, Savannah River, GA, 10/29/1864.
Harn, William J. Private	Unk	July 6, 1863, Bryan County, Georgia	Co. H, 7th Georgia Cavalry	June 11, 1864, Trevilian Station, Louisa Court House, Virginia	Point Lookout, Maryland, transferred to Elmira Prison, NY, July 25, 1864	Died November 6, 1864 of Chronic Diarrhea, Grave No. 775
Harney, S. F. Private	Unk	Unknown	Engineering Department, Richmond, Virginia	April 10, 1865, Fairfax Station, Virginia	Old Capital Prison, Washington, DC, transferred to Elmira Prison, NY, May 2, 1865.	Oath of Allegiance July 7, 1865
Harold, Charles B. Private	Unk	May 18, 1861, Huntersville, Virginia	Co. I, 25th Virginia Infantry	May 12, 1864, Spotsylvania Court House, Virginia	Point Lookout, Maryland, transferred to Elmira Prison, NY, August 12, 1864	Exchanged October 29, 1864 at Venus Point, Savannah River, GA.
Harold, Elias Private	Unk	December 28, 1862, Camp Allegheny, Virginia	Co. H, 25th Virginia Infantry	May 5, 1864, Wilderness, Virginia	Point Lookout, Maryland, transferred to Elmira Prison, NY, August 2, 1864	Died September 11, 1864 of Pneumonia, Grave No. 261

Name & Rank	Age	Enlisted	Regiment and State	Where Captured	Prison	Remarks
Harp, William H. Private	18	June 11, 1861, Henderson, North Carolina	Co. G, 23rd North Carolina Infantry	May 12, 1864, Near Spotsylvania Court House, Virginia	Point Lookout Prison, Maryland. Transferred to Elmira Prison Camp New York August 14, 1864.	Died January 18, 1865 of Variola (Smallpox), Grave No.1430. Headstone has 20th North Carolina.
Harper, Henry T. P. Private	Unk	April 27, 1861, Richmond, Virginia	Co. H, 15th Virginia Infantry	June 3, 1864, Gaines Farm Cold Harbor, Virginia	Point Lookout, Maryland, transferred to Elmira Prison, NY, July 17,1864	Exchanged March 10, 1865 at Boulware's Wharf on the James River, Virginia
Harper, James N. Private	26	August 1, 1861, Troy, North Carolina	Co. E, 33rd North Carolina Infantry	May 12, 1864, Spotsylvania Court House, Virginia	Point Lookout, Maryland, transferred to Elmira Prison, NY, August 14, 1864	Oath of Allegiance June 19, 1865
Harper, Jesse P. Private	Unk	March 6, 1863, Macon, Georgia	Co. B 64th Georgia Infantry	August 16, 1864, New Market, Virginia	Old Capital Prison, Washington, DC transferred to Elmira Prison, NY, August 27, 1864	Oath of Allegiance May 29, 1865
Harper, Joseph W. S. Private	30	March 4, 1862, Bainbridge, Georgia	Co. F, 50th Georgia Infantry	June 1, 1864, Gaines Mill Cold Harbor, Virginia	Point Lookout, Maryland, transferred to Elmira Prison, NY, July 17,1864	Exchanged March 14, 1865 at Boulware's Wharf on the James River, Virginia
Harper, Montgomery G. Private	Unk	May 27, 1861, New Orleans, Louisiana	Co. E, 15th Louisiana Infantry	July 17,1864, Near Washington, DC	Old Capital Prison, Washington, DC, transferred to Elmira July 23, 1864	Oath of Allegiance May 15, 1865
Harralson, Basely Private	Unk	April 10, 1864, Camp Holmes, North Carolina	Co. A, 13th North Carolina Infantry	May 6, 1864, Wilderness, Virginia	Point Lookout, Maryland, transferred to Elmira Prison, NY, August 14, 1864	Died January 19, 1865 of Variola (Smallpox), Grave No. 1208. Name Barely on Headstone.

Name & Rank	Age	Enlisted	Regiment and State	Where Captured	Prison	Remarks
Harrell, Asa T. Private	Unk	Unknown	Co. B, 23rd North Carolina Infantry	July 12, 1864, Near Washington, DC	Old Capital Prison, Washington, DC. Transferred to Elmira Prison, New York August 17 1864	Died January 18, 1865 of Unknown Disease, Grave No. 1490
Harrell, Benjamin F. Private	Unk	March 8, 1862, Abbeville, Alabama	Co. B, 6th Alabama Infantry	May 8, 1864, Ely's Ford, Wilderness, Virginia	Point Lookout, Maryland, transferred to Elmira Prison, NY, August 17, 1864	Oath of Allegiance June 19, 1865
Harrell, Joseph H. Private	27	May 27, 1861, Wilmington, North Carolina	Co. D, 3rd North Carolina Infantry	May 12, 1864, Spotsylvania Court House, Virginia	Point Lookout, Maryland, transferred to Elmira Prison, NY, August 14, 1864	Oath of Allegiance June 19, 1865
Harrell, Nathan Private	Unk	May 19, 1863, Morris Island, South Carolina	Co. H, 21st South Carolina Infantry	July 10, 1863, Morris Island, South Carolina	Point Lookout, Maryland, transferred to Elmira Prison, NY, August 18, 1864	Transferred For Exchange October 11, 1864 to Point Lookout Prison Camp, MD.
Harrell, R. E. Private	Unk	Unknown	Co. E, 16th Georgia Infantry	May 6, 1864, Wilderness, Virginia	Old Capital Prison, Washington DC Transferred to Elmira Prison, NY, July 14, 1864	Died June 12, 1865 of Pneumonia, Grave No. 2883
Harrell, William A. Sergeant	37	July 5, 1861, Murfreesboro, North Carolina	Co. F, 1st North Carolina Infantry	May 12, 1864, Spotsylvania Court House, Virginia	Point Lookout, Maryland, transferred to Elmira Prison, NY, August 6, 1864	Oath of Allegiance May 29, 1865
Harrell, William H. Corporal	19	February 28, 1862, Lumberton, North Carolina	Co. E, 51st North Carolina Infantry	June 1, 1864, Cold Harbor, Virginia	Point Lookout, Maryland, transferred to Elmira Prison, NY, July 17,1864	Oath of Allegiance July 3, 1865
Harrelson, Isham West Private	30	April 16, 1862, Old Brunswick Town, North Carolina	Co. G, 36th Regiment 2nd North Carolina Artillery	January 15, 1865, Fort Fisher, North Carolina	February 1, 1865, Elmira Prison Camp, New York	Exchanged March 2, 1865 at Boulware's Wharf on the James River, Virginia

Name & Rank	Age	Enlisted	Regiment and State	Where Captured	Prison	Remarks
Harrington, Edward P. Private	18	February 14, 1862, Monroe County, North Carolina	Co. B, 43rd North Carolina Infantry	July 17,1864, Near Washington, DC	Old Capital Prison, Washington, DC, transferred to Elmira July 23, 1864	Oath of Allegiance May 17, 1865
Harrington, Lacy Private	25	September 17, 1861, Crockett, Texas	Co. J, 4th Texas Cavalry	July 31, 1864, Near Morganza, Louisiana	New Orleans, Louisiana transferred to Elmira November 19, 1864.	Oath of Allegiance June 14, 1865
Harris, Anderson K. Private	Unk	April 9, 1862, Wilmington, North Carolina	Co. A, 18th South Carolina Infantry	July 30, 1864, Battle of the Crater, Petersburg, Virginia	Point Lookout, Maryland, transferred to Elmira Prison, NY, August 12, 1864	Oath of Allegiance July 7, 1865
Harris, Britton Private	22	March 1, 1862, Troy, North Carolina	Co. F, 44th North Carolina Infantry	May 31, 1864, Gaines Farm, Cold Harbor, Virginia	Point Lookout, Maryland, transferred to Elmira Prison, NY, July 17,1864	Oath of Allegiance June 12, 1865
Harris, Columbus Private	Unk	Unknown	Co. D, 25th Tennessee Infantry	June 17, 1864, Petersburg, Virginia	Point Lookout, Maryland, transferred to Elmira Prison, NY, July 23, 1864	Exchanged March 2, 1865 at Akins Landing on the James River, Virginia
Harris, Darrell P. Private	Unk	August 8, 1862, Montgomery, Alabama	Co. F, 3rd Alabama Infantry	May 12, 1864, Spotsylvania Court House, Virginia	Point Lookout, Maryland, transferred to Elmira Prison, NY, August 12, 1864	Died June 21, 1865 of Pneumonia, Grave No. 2811
Harris, David Corporal	Unk	August 24, 1861, Lawrenceville, Georgia	Co. F, 24th Georgia Infantry	August 16, 1864, Front Royal, Virginia	Old Capital Prison, Washington, DC transferred to Elmira Prison, NY, August 29, 1864	Oath of Allegiance July 7, 1865
Harris, Edward Private	40	April 16, 1862, Old Brunswick Town, North Carolina	Co. G, 36th Regiment 2nd North Carolina Artillery	January 15, 1865, Fort Fisher, North Carolina	February 1, 1865, Elmira Prison Camp, New York	Died April 2, 1865 of Pneumonia, Grave No. 2585

Name & Rank	Age	Enlisted	Regiment and State	Where Captured	Prison	Remarks
Harris, Elisha K. Private	Unk	July 3, 1861, Lynchburg, Virginia	Co. G, 42nd Virginia Infantry	May 12, 1864, Near Spotsylvania, Virginia	Point Lookout, Maryland, transferred to Elmira Prison, NY, July 23, 1864	Died February 15, 1865 of Variola (Smallpox), Grave No. 2172
Harris, Franklin H. Private	18	January 20, 1862, Darlington District, South Carolina	Co. H, 21st South Carolina Infantry	January 15, 1865, Fort Fisher, North Carolina	January 30, 1865, Elmira Prison Camp, New York	Oath of Allegiance July 11, 1865
Harris, G. P. Private	Unk	Unable to Find Soldier's Records in Regimental Records	Fennog Battery State Unknown	October 6, 1864, Clinton, Louisiana	New Orleans, Louisiana transferred to Elmira November 19, 1864.	Exchanged February 25, 1865 at Boulware's or Cox Wharf on the James River, Virginia
Harris, G. Willis Private	27	March 1, 1862, Rogers Store, North Carolina	Co. J, 1st North Carolina Infantry	May 12, 1864, Near Spotsylvania Court House, Virginia	Point Lookout Prison, Maryland. Transferred to Elmira Prison Camp New York August 6, 1864.	Died June 24, 1865 of Chronic Diarrhea, Grave No. 2820
Harris, Guilford Private	25	August 12, 1861, Pitt County, North Carolina	Co. G, 8th North Carolina Infantry	May 31, 1864, Cold Harbor, Virginia	Point Lookout, Maryland, transferred to Elmira Prison, NY, July 11, 1864	Exchanged October 29, 1864 at Venus Point, Savannah River, GA.
Harris, Henry Private	34	May 14, 1862, Weldon, North Carolina	Co. K, 24th North Carolina Infantry	June 17, 1864, Petersburg, Virginia	Point Lookout, Maryland, transferred to Elmira Prison, NY, July 30, 1864	Oath of Allegiance July 3, 1865
Harris, Henry J, Private	Unk	June 15, 1861, Lynchburg, Virginia	Co. A, 42nd Virginia Infantry	May 12, 1864, Near Spotsylvania, Virginia	Point Lookout, Maryland, transferred to Elmira Prison, NY, July 23, 1864	Died September 13, 1864 of Pneumonia, Grave No. 263
Harris, Henry R. Private	Unk	September 16, 1861, Walton County, Georgia	Co. G, 35th Georgia Infantry	May 24, 1864, Hanover Junction, Virginia	Point Lookout, Maryland, transferred to Elmira Prison, NY, July 11, 1864	Exchanged March 2, 1865 at Akins Landing on the James River, Virginia

Name & Rank	Age	Enlisted	Regiment and State	Where Captured	Prison	Remarks
Harris, Henry T. Civilian	Unk	Culpepper County, Virginia	Citizen of Virginia	April 4, 1864, At Home in Culpepper County, Virginia	Point Lookout, Maryland, transferred to Elmira Prison, NY, ? 1864	Unknown
Harris, J. B. Private	Unk	Unknown	Co. I, 18th Georgia Infantry	June 1, Cold Harbor, Virginia	Point Lookout, Maryland, transferred to Elmira Prison, NY, July 17, 1864	Oath of Allegiance June 14, 1865
Harris, James Corporal	27	November 21, 1861, Spartanburg, South Carolina	Co. A, Holcombe Legion, South Carolina Infantry	May 7, 1864, Stony Creek, Virginia	Point Lookout, Maryland, transferred to Elmira Prison, NY, August 17, 1864	Exchanged October 29, 1864 at Venus Point, Savannah River, GA.
Harris, James A. Private	Unk	March 20, 1862, Buckingham County Court House, Virginia	Co. J, 21st Virginia Infantry	May 20, 1864, Spotsylvania Court House, Virginia	Point Lookout, Maryland, transferred to Elmira Prison, NY, July 6, 1864	Exchanged March 2, 1865 at Akins Landing on the James River, Virginia
Harris, James A. Private	Unk	May 27, 1861, Marion, Virginia	Co. B, 8th Virginia Cavalry	July 16, 1864, Loudoun County, Virginia	Old Capital Prison, Washington, DC, transferred to Elmira July 23, 1864	Died September 21, 1864 of Chronic Diarrhea, Grave No. 485
Harris, James F. Private	Unk	April 18, 1861, Marion, Virginia	Co. D, 4th Virginia Infantry	May 12, 1864 Spotsylvania Court House, Virginia	Point Lookout, Maryland, transferred to Elmira Prison, NY, August 2, 1864	Oath of Allegiance July 11, 1865
Harris, James R. Private	Unk	June 17, 1861, Conrad's Store, Virginia	Co. I, 10th Virginia Infantry	May 12, 1864, Spotsylvania Court House, Virginia	Point Lookout, Maryland, transferred to Elmira Prison, NY, August 2, 1864	Exchanged 10/29/64. Exchanged 11/15/64 at Venus Point, Savannah River, GA.
Harris, James W. Private	18	February 26, 1863, Rockingham County, North Carolina	Co. F, 45th North Carolina Infantry	March 25, 1865, Petersburg, Virginia. Gunshot Wound Left Hand.	Old Capital Prison, Washington DC Transferred to Elmira Prison, NY, May 12, 1865.	Oath of Allegiance July 3, 1865

Name & Rank	Age	Enlisted	Regiment and State	Where Captured	Prison	Remarks
Harris, John Private	Unk	Louisiana	Co. E, 10th Louisiana Infantry	July 13, 1864, Near Port Hudson, Louisiana	New Orleans, Louisiana transferred to Elmira November 19, 1864.	Oath of Allegiance May 17, 1865
Harris, John C. Private	35	March 17, 1862, Charlotte, North Carolina	Co. E, 17th South Carolina Infantry	March 25, 1865, Fort Stedman, Virginia. Contusion of Nose and Eye.	Old Capital Prison, Washington DC Transferred to Elmira Prison, NY, May 12, 1865.	Oath of Allegiance July 7, 1865
Harris, Joseph A. Corporal	18	August 11, 1861, Centerville, Virginia	Co. A, 13th Mississippi Infantry	May 5, 1864, Wilderness, Virginia	Point Lookout, Maryland, transferred to Elmira Prison, NY, August 14, 1864	Died October 10, 1864 of Chronic Diarrhea, Grave No. 684. Headstone has 15th Mississippi.
Harris, Joseph H. Private	Unk	May 24, 1861, Sussex Court Hose, Virginia	Co. A, 41st Virginia Infantry	May 24, 1864, North Anna, Virginia	Point Lookout, Maryland, transferred to Elmira Prison, NY, July 25, 1864	Died November 6, 1864 of Pneumonia, Grave No. 770
Harris, M. W. Private	Unk	July 10, 1861, Richmond, Virginia	Co. A, 38th Read's Battalion, Virginia Light Artillery	June 3, 1864, Gaines Farm, Cold Harbor, Virginia	Point Lookout, Maryland, transferred to Elmira Prison, NY, July 17, 1864	Oath of Allegiance June 16, 1865
Harris, Nathaniel P. Private	Unk	June 14, 1861, Valdosta, Georgia	Co. J, 12th Georgia Infantry	May 10, 1864, Spotsylvania Court House, Virginia	Point Lookout, Maryland, transferred to Elmira Prison, NY, July 25, 1864	Oath of Allegiance June 30, 1865
Harris, Noah Private	Unk	June 15, 1861, Lynchburg, Virginia	Co. A, 42nd Virginia Infantry	May 12, 1864, Spotsylvania Court House, Virginia	Point Lookout, Maryland, transferred to Elmira Prison, NY, August 2, 1864	Oath of Allegiance June 11, 1865
Harris, Richard P. Private	17	September 7, 1861, Camp Crabtree, Granville, North Carolina	Co. G, 30th North Carolina Infantry	May 12, 1864, Near Spotsylvania Court House, Virginia	Point Lookout, Maryland, transferred to Elmira Prison, NY, August 14, 1864	Oath of Allegiance June 19, 1865

Name & Rank	Age	Enlisted	Regiment and State	Where Captured	Prison	Remarks
Harris, Rueben, Private	26	February 27, 1862, Abbeville, Alabama	Co. B, 6th Alabama Infantry	July 14, 1864, Near Washington, D. C.	Old Capital Prison, Washington, DC, transferred to Elmira December 17, 1864	Exchanged February 13, 1865 at Boulware's Wharf on the James River, Virginia
Harris, Thomas, Private	Unk	Unknown	Co. J, 6th Virginia Cavalry	July 24, 1864, Culpepper County, Virginia	Old Capital Prison, Washington DC Transferred to Elmira Prison, NY, August 12, 1864	Exchanged October 29, 1864 at Venus Point, Savannah River, GA.
Harris, Thomas A., Private	Unk	June 15, 1861, Buena Vista, Georgia	Co. K, 12th Georgia Infantry	May 10, 1864, Spotsylvania Court House, Virginia	Point Lookout, Maryland, transferred to Elmira Prison, NY, July 25, 1864	Oath of Allegiance June 23, 1865
Harris, Thomas C., Private	Unk	March 8, 1862, Richmond, Mississippi	Co. C, 2nd Mississippi Infantry	July 14, 1863, Falling Waters, Maryland	Point Lookout, Maryland, transferred to Elmira Prison, NY, August 18, 1864	Exchanged March 10, 1865 at Boulware's Wharf on the James River, Virginia
Harris, Wiley, Private	32	August 24, 1861, Stewartsville, Bedford County, Virginia	Co. E, 58th Virginia Infantry	May 20, 1864, Spotsylvania Court House, Virginia	Point Lookout, Maryland, transferred to Elmira Prison, NY, July 6,1864	Oath of Allegiance June 30, 1865
Harris, William F., Private	22	April 19, 1861, Fishersville, Virginia	Co. H, 5th Virginia Infantry	May 12, 1864, Spotsylvania Court House, Virginia	Point Lookout, Maryland, transferred to Elmira Prison, NY, August 2, 1864	Exchanged March 10, 1865 at Boulware's Wharf on the James River, Virginia
Harris, Wilson W., Sergeant	25	Meet 16th 1861, Columbia, North Carolina	Co. A, 32nd North Carolina Infantry	May 10, 1864, Near Mine Run, Spotsylvania, Virginia	Point Lookout, Maryland, transferred to Elmira Prison, NY, August 6, 1864	Died January 29, 1865 of Variola (Smallpox), Grave No. 1795
Harrison, Andrew J., Sergeant Major	25	March 1, 1862, Roxboro, North Carolina	Field & Staff, 45th North Carolina Infantry	May 10, 1864, Spotsylvania Court House, Virginia	Point Lookout, Maryland, transferred to Elmira Prison, NY, August 6, 1864	Oath of Allegiance June 16, 1865

Name & Rank	Age	Enlisted	Regiment and State	Where Captured	Prison	Remarks
Harrison, B. S. Private	Unk	Unknown	Co. H, 8th Georgia Infantry	May 6, 1864, Wilderness, Virginia	Point Lookout, Maryland, transferred to Elmira Prison, NY, August 14, 1864	Died April 17, 1865 of Pneumonia, Grave No. 1353. Headstone has 49th GA.
Harrison, Benjamin Private	Unk	January 14, 1863, Hardeeville, South Carolina	Co. C, 11th South Carolina Infantry	June 18, 1864, Petersburg, Virginia	Point Lookout, Maryland, transferred to Elmira Prison, NY, July 30, 1864	Transferred For Exchange October 11, 1864 to Point Lookout Prison Camp, MD. Nothing Further.
Harrison, J. J. Private	30	January 1, 1863, Murfreesboro, Tennessee	Co. D, 25th Tennessee Infantry	May 16, 1864, Near Drury's Bluff, Virginia	Point Lookout, Maryland, transferred to Elmira Prison, NY, August 17, 1864	Exchanged October 29, 1864 at Venus Point, Savannah River, GA.
Harrison, John Alex Sergeant	28	May 1, 1861, Leasburg, North Carolina	Co. D, 13th North Carolina Infantry	May 10, 1864, Near Mine Run, Spotsylvania, Virginia	Point Lookout, Maryland, transferred to Elmira Prison, NY, August 6, 1864	Exchanged October 29, 1864 at Venus Point, Savannah River, GA.
Harrison, John S. Private	38	August 8, 1861, Oak Grove, Norfolk County, Virginia	Co. B, 61st Virginia Infantry	October 28, 1864, Weldon Railroad, Virginia. Gunshot Wound Left Side of Face.	Old Capital Prison, Washington, DC, transferred to Elmira December 17, 1864	Oath of Allegiance July 7, 1865
Harrison, John W. Sergeant	Unk	August 24, 1861, Habersham County, Georgia	Co. H, 24th Georgia Infantry	June 3, 1864, Gaines Mill Cold Harbor, Virginia	Point Lookout, Maryland, transferred to Elmira Prison, NY, July 17, 1864	Oath of Allegiance July 7, 1865
Harrison, Joseph J. Private	Unk	September 2, 1862, Butler County, Alabama	Co. A, 1st Alabama Artillery	August 23, 1864, Fort Morgan, Alabama	New Orleans, Louisiana transferred to Elmira Prison, NY, December 4, 1864.	Died January 17, 1865 of Pneumonia, Grave No. 1447
Harrison, Joseph M. Private	Unk	April 21, 1861, Norfolk County, Virginia	Co. F, 15th South Carolina Cavalry	June 15, 1864, Near Petersburg, Virginia	Point Lookout, Maryland, transferred to Elmira Prison, NY, July 25, 1864	Exchanged February 20, 1865 at Boulware's or Cox Wharf on the James River, Virginia

Name & Rank	Age	Enlisted	Regiment and State	Where Captured	Prison	Remarks
Harrison, Lee Private	Unk	Unknown	Co. H, 4th Virginia Cavalry	November 24, 1864, Front Royal, Virginia	November 11, 1864, Old Capital Prison, Washington, DC. February 4, 1865 Elmira, Prison Camp, NY	Exchanged March 14, 1865 at Boulware's Wharf on the James River, Virginia
Harrison, Lovick B. Sergeant	26	June 24, 1861, Williamston, North Carolina	Co. H, 1st North Carolina Infantry	May 12, 1864, Spotsylvania Court House, Virginia	Point Lookout, Maryland, transferred to Elmira Prison, NY, August 6, 1864	Died December 6, 1864 of Pleuro-Pneumonia, Grave No. 1026. Name Levich on Headstone.
Harrison, Silas E. Private	Unk	May 5, 1862, Marion, Alabama	Co. E, 41st Alabama Infantry	June 15, 1864, Petersburg, Virginia	Point Lookout, Maryland, transferred to Elmira Prison, NY, July 12, 1864	Exchanged March 14, 1865 at Boulware's Wharf on the James River, Virginia
Harrison, Thomas B. Private	Unk	March 4, 1862, Sandersville, Georgia	Co. C, 49th Georgia Infantry	May 6, 1864, Wilderness, Virginia	Point Lookout, Maryland, transferred to Elmira Prison, NY, August 14, 1864	Oath of Allegiance June 23, 1865
Harrison, Wiley Private	Unk	May 11, 1861, New Orleans, Louisiana	Co. K, 2nd Louisiana Infantry	May 12, 1864, Spotsylvania Court House, Virginia	Point Lookout, Maryland, transferred to Elmira Prison, NY, August 17, 1864	Exchanged February 25, 1865 at Boulware's or Cox Wharf on the James River, Virginia
Harrison, William H. Private	Unk	November 28, 1862, Bledsoe's Store, Virginia	Co. K, 44th Virginia Infantry	May 12, 1864, Spotsylvania Court House, Virginia	Point Lookout, Maryland, transferred to Elmira Prison, NY, August 2, 1864	Transferred for Exchange 10/11/64. Died 11/14/64 of Chronic Diarrhea. Buried at Hilton Head, SC.
Harrison, William H. B. Private	Unk	February 5, 1862, Norfolk, Virginia	Co. F, 46th Virginia Infantry	June 17, 1864, Petersburg, Virginia	Point Lookout, Maryland, transferred to Elmira Prison, NY, July 30, 1864	Oath of Allegiance May 29, 1865

Name & Rank	Age	Enlisted	Regiment and State	Where Captured	Prison	Remarks
Harriss, William L. Private	15	April 28, 1862, Camp Saunders, North Carolina	Co. B, 30th North Carolina Infantry	August 9, 1864, Bunker Hill, Virginia	Old Capital Prison, Washington, DC transferred to Elmira Prison, NY, August 29, 1864	Oath of Allegiance July 7, 1865
Harrow, J. W. Private	Unk	Unknown	Co. K, 26th Virginia Infantry	June 15, 1864, Near Petersburg, Virginia	Point Lookout, Maryland, transferred to Elmira Prison, NY, July 12, 1864	Exchanged March 10, 1865 at Boulware's Wharf on the James River, Virginia
Harruff, Andrew J. Private	30	July 17, 1861, Staunton, Virginia	Co. A, 52nd Virginia Infantry	May 30, 1864, Fair Oaks, Virginia	Point Lookout, Maryland, transferred to Elmira Prison, NY, July 8, 1864	Exchanged October 29, 1864 at Venus Point, Savannah River, GA.
Harsey, Wesley Private	21	November 1, 1861, Somerville, South Carolina	Co. G, 27th South Carolina Infantry	August 21, 1864, Weldon Railroad, Virginia. Gunshot Wound in Left Foot. Foot Amputated.	November 11, 1864, Old Capital Prison, Washington, DC. February 4, 1865 Elmira, Prison Camp, NY	Exchanged February 13, 1865 at Boulware's wharf on the James River, Virginia
Harshbarger, John Private	Unk	July 31, 1861, Staunton, Virginia	Co. F, 52nd Virginia, Infantry	May 30, 1864, Mechanicsville, Virginia	Point Lookout, Maryland, transferred to Elmira Prison, NY, July 9, 1864	Oath of Allegiance June 30, 1865
Hart, Harris Private	39	March 26, 1863, Chatham County, North Carolina	Co. G, 40th Regiment, 3rd North Carolina Artillery	January 15, 1865, Fort Fisher, North Carolina	January 30, 1865, Elmira Prison Camp, New York	Exchanged March 14, 1865 at Boulware's Wharf on the James River, Virginia
Hart, J. M. Private	Unk	December 20, 1863, Greenville, South Carolina	Co. H, 22nd South Carolina Infantry	July 30, 1864, Petersburg, Virginia	Point Lookout, Maryland, transferred to Elmira Prison, NY, August 12, 1864	Exchanged October 29, 1864 at Venus Point, Savannah River, GA.
Hart, Joseph W. Private	Unk	May 7, 1861, New Prospect, Virginia	Co. C, 26th North Carolina Infantry	June 17, 1864, Near Petersburg, Virginia	Point Lookout, Maryland, transferred to Elmira Prison, NY, July 30, 1864	Exchanged March 2, 1865 at Akins Landing on the James River, Virginia

Name & Rank	Age	Enlisted	Regiment and State	Where Captured	Prison	Remarks
Hart, Mathew Private	34	July 15, 1862, Raleigh, North Carolina	Co. D, 3rd North Carolina Infantry	May 12, 1864, Spotsylvania Court House, Virginia	Point Lookout, Maryland, transferred to Elmira Prison, NY, August 14, 1864	Oath of Allegiance June 27, 1865
Hart, Thomas Private	Unk	Unknown	Co. C, Ogden's Louisiana Cavalry	September 29, 1864, Natchez, Mississippi	New Orleans, Louisiana transferred to Elmira November 19, 1864.	Exchanged February 13, 1865 at Boulware's wharf on the James River, Virginia
Hart, Thomas J. Corporal	Unk	June 7, 1861, Richmond, Virginia	Co. C, 59th Virginia Infantry	June 18, 1864, Petersburg, Virginia	Point Lookout, Maryland, transferred to Elmira Prison, NY, July 30, 1864	Died November 1, 1864 of Pneumonia, Grave No. 750
Hart, William Private	23	June 4, 1861, Camp Moore, Louisiana	Co. J, 6th Louisiana Infantry	May 5, 1864, Wilderness, Virginia	Point Lookout, Maryland, transferred to Elmira Prison, NY, August 17, 1864	Exchanged February 13, 1865 at Boulware's wharf on the James River, Virginia
Harter, Charles H. Corporal	Unk	October 13, 1861, Mobile, Alabama	Co. A, 21st Alabama Infantry	August 23, 1864, Fort Morgan, Alabama	Steam Press No. 4 New Orleans, Louisiana transferred to Elmira October 8, 1864.	Oath of Allegiance May 17, 1865
Hartison, W. H. Private	Unk	Unknown	Co. H, 1st North Carolina Infantry	May 12, 1864, Wilderness, Spotsylvania Court House, Virginia	Point Lookout, Maryland, transferred to Elmira Prison, NY, August 6, 1864	Oath of Allegiance June 30, 1865
Hartless, Dabney Private	Unk	July 2, 1861, Bethel Am., Virginia	Co. F, 50th Virginia Infantry	May 12, 1864, Spotsylvania Court House, Virginia	Point Lookout, Maryland, transferred to Elmira Prison, NY, August 2, 1864	Transferred for Exchange 10/11/64. Died 10/29/64 of Pneumonia at Point Lookout, MD
Hartley, Bartlett Private	20	September 18, 1862, Boone, North Carolina	Co. E, 37th North Carolina Infantry	May 6, 1864, Wilderness, Virginia	Point Lookout, Maryland, transferred to Elmira Prison, NY, July 25, 1864	Died March 21, 1865 of Diarrhea, Grave No. 2488. Name Bartlett Hartell on Headstone.

Name & Rank	Age	Enlisted	Regiment and State	Where Captured	Prison	Remarks
Hartley, Hyram H. Private	23	July 13, 1862, Raleigh, North Carolina	Co. K, 15th North Carolina Infantry	May 12, 1864, Spotsylvania Court House, Virginia	Point Lookout, Maryland, transferred to Elmira Prison, NY, August 12, 1864	Exchanged February 13, 1865 at Boulware's wharf on the James River, Virginia
Hartman, Joseph W. Private	18	August 1, 1861, Danbury, North Carolina	Co. H, 53rd North Carolina Infantry	July 17, 1864, Near Washington, DC	Old Capital Prison, Washington, DC, transferred to Elmira July 23, 1864	Died September 14, 1864 of Chronic Diarrhea, Grave No. 268
Hartness, J. R. Private	Unk	April 18, 1864, Wilmington, North Carolina	Co. C, 17th South Carolina Infantry	July 30, 1864, Petersburg, Virginia	Point Lookout, Maryland, transferred to Elmira Prison, NY, August 12, 1864	Died March 20, 1865 of Diarrhea, Grave No. 1570
Hartsock, George H. Private	Unk	Unknown	Co. D, 22nd Virginia Cavalry	May 31, 1864, Hanover County Court House, Virginia	Point Lookout, Maryland, transferred to Elmira Prison, NY, July 25, 1864	Died January 18, 1865 of Chronic Diarrhea, Grave No. 1435.
Hartzog, Elias H. Private	Unk	March 26, 1863, Camp Whiting, South Carolina	Co. H, 17th South Carolina Infantry	July 30, 1864, Petersburg, Virginia	Point Lookout, Maryland, transferred to Elmira Prison, NY, August 12, 1864	Exchanged October 29, 1864 at Venus Point, Savannah River, GA.
Harvard, W. Private	Unk	Unknown	Co. J, 2nd Louisiana Cavalry	September 4, 1864, Near Port Pontchartrain, Louisiana	New Orleans, LA, Transferred to Elmira Prison, NY, November 19, 1864	Oath of Allegiance July 11, 1865
Harvel, Andrew J. Private	Unk	May 12, 1864, Place Unknown	Co. C, 12th Alabama Infantry	July 10, 1864, Harper's Ferry, Virginia	Old Capital Prison, Washington, DC, transferred to Elmira July 23, 1864	Died January 19, 1865 of Variola (Smallpox), Grave No. 1198. Headstone has Harville.
Harvel, Tristam Private	Unk	April 13, 1861, South Carolina	Co. G, 8th South Carolina Infantry	July 30, 1864, Petersburg, Virginia	Point Lookout, Maryland, transferred to Elmira Prison, NY, August 12, 1864	Exchanged October 29, 1864 at Venus Point, Savannah River, GA.

Name & Rank	Age	Enlisted	Regiment and State	Where Captured	Prison	Remarks
Harvell, William C. Private	Unk	Unknown	Ogden's Louisiana Cavalry	October 7, 1864, Near Greensburg, Louisiana	New Orleans, Louisiana transferred to Elmira November 19, 1864.	Exchanged March 10, 1865 at Boulware's Wharf on the James River, Virginia
Harveston, George W. Private	Unk	May 1, 1862, Augusta, Georgia	Co. F, 12th Battalion, Georgia Light Artillery	July 8, 1864, Harper's Ferry, Virginia	Old Capital Prison, Washington, DC, transferred to Elmira July 23, 1864	Died April 15, 1865 of Variola (Smallpox), Grave No. 2709
Harvey, Benjamin P. Corporal	Unk	March 10, 1862, Pittsylvania, Virginia	Co. G, 6th Virginia Cavalry	May 11, 1864, Yellow Tavern, Hanover County, Virginia	Point Lookout, Maryland, transferred to Elmira Prison, NY, August 17, 1864	Exchanged October 29, 1864 at Venus Point, Savannah River, GA.
Harvey, Moses J. Corporal	Unk	June 15, 1861, Buena Vista, Georgia	Co. H, 12th Georgia Infantry	May 12, 1864, Spotsylvania Court House, Virginia	Point Lookout, Maryland, transferred to Elmira Prison, NY, July 25, 1864	Exchanged October 29, 1864 at Venus Point, Savannah River, GA.
Harvey, Robert James Sergeant	49	January 23, 1862, Newbern, Craven County, North Carolina	Co. F, 36th Regiment 2nd North Carolina Artillery	January 15, 1865, Fort Fisher, North Carolina	February 1, 1865, Elmira Prison Camp, New York	Exchanged March 2, 1865 at Boulware's Wharf on the James River, Virginia
Harvey, Thomas E. Sergeant	23	May 18, 1861, Edenton, North Carolina	Co. A, 1st North Carolina Infantry	May 12, 1864, Spotsylvania Court House, Virginia	Point Lookout, Maryland, transferred to Elmira Prison, NY, August 6, 1864	Oath of Allegiance June 12, 1865
Harvey, Thomas M. Private	Unk	February 7, 1862, Camp Gist, South Carolina	Co. D, 2nd South Carolina Cavalry	September 22, 1863, Jack's Shop, Near Madison Court House, Virginia	Point Lookout, Maryland, transferred to Elmira Prison, NY, August 18, 1864	Exchanged March 10, 1865 at Boulware's Wharf on the James River, Virginia
Harvey, Zara Private	Unk	April 3, 1862, Bryan County, Georgia	Co. H, 7th Georgia Cavalry	June 11, 1864, Trevilian Station, Louisa Court House, Virginia	Point Lookout, Maryland, transferred to Elmira Prison, NY, July 25, 1864	Exchanged March 14, 1865 at Boulware's Wharf on the James River, Virginia

Name & Rank	Age	Enlisted	Regiment and State	Where Captured	Prison	Remarks
Harwell, C. C. Private	21	April 27, 1861, Newton, North Carolina	Co. DA, 12th North Carolina Infantry	August 12, 1864, Spotsylvania Court House, Virginia	Old Capital Prison, Washington, DC transferred to Elmira Prison, NY, August 29, 1864	Oath of Allegiance June 16, 1865
Harwood, Horatio W. Sergeant	26	April 20, 1861, Belle Roi., Virginia	Co. K, 26th Virginia Infantry	June 15, 1864, Near Petersburg, Virginia	Point Lookout, Maryland, transferred to Elmira Prison, NY, July 12, 1864	Exchanged October 29, 1864 at Venus Point, Savannah River, GA.
Haselden, Hugh G. Private	35	September 17, 1862, Georgetown, South Carolina	Co. F, 4th South Carolina Cavalry	May 28, 1864, Cold Harbor, Virginia. Gunshot Wound Neck	Old Capital Prison, Washington, DC transferred to Elmira Prison, NY, August 29, 1864	Died January 6, 1865 of Chronic Diarrhea, Grave No. 1243
Hashaw, Thomas Private	Unk	May 16, 1862, Alisona, Tennessee	Co. A, 17th Tennessee Infantry	June 17, 1864, Petersburg, Virginia	Point Lookout, Maryland, transferred to Elmira Prison, NY, July 30, 1864	Oath of Allegiance May 29, 1865
Haskins, Thomas William Private	Unk	March 4, 1862, Dublin, Georgia	Co. H, 14th Georgia Infantry	May 12, 1864, Spotsylvania Court House, Virginia	Point Lookout, Maryland, transferred to Elmira Prison, NY, July 30, 1864	Oath of Allegiance June 23, 1865
Haskins, William Private	Unk	October 11, 1864, Wayne County, North Carolina	Co. D, 40th Regiment, 3rd North Carolina Artillery	January 15, 1865, Fort Fisher, North Carolina	February 1, 1865, Elmira Prison Camp, New York	Died March 21, 1865 of Chronic Diarrhea, Grave No. 1529
Hassett, John Private	Unk	February 1, 1864, Dandrige, Tennessee	Co. J, 17th Tennessee Infantry	June 17, 1864, Petersburg, Virginia	Point Lookout, Maryland, transferred to Elmira Prison, NY, July 30, 1864	Died October 20, 1864 of Chronic Diarrhea, Grave No. 532
Hasstin, A. M. Private	Unk	April 28, 1862, Fayetteville, Georgia	Co. C, 53rd Georgia Infantry	June 1, 1864, Gaines Mill Cold Harbor, Virginia	Point Lookout, Maryland, transferred to Elmira Prison, NY, July 12, 1864	Exchanged March 14, 1865 at Boulware's Wharf on the James River, Virginia

Name & Rank	Age	Enlisted	Regiment and State	Where Captured	Prison	Remarks
Haste, Calvin A. Private	30	July 8, 1862, St. Johns, Hertford County, North Carolina	Co. C, 3rd Battalion North Carolina Light Artillery	January 15, 1865, Fort Fisher, North Carolina	February 1, 1865, Elmira Prison Camp, New York	Died February 14, 1865 of Peritonitis, Grave No. 2060
Hatch, J. S. Private	Unk	May 5, 1862, Zebulon, Georgia	Co. H, 53rd Georgia Infantry	June 1, 1864, Gaines Mill, Cold Harbor, Virginia	Transferred From Point Lookout Prison, MD, July 12, 1864. Train Never Arrived at Elmira Prison Camp, NY.	Died July 15, 1864 in Train Wreck at Shohola, Pennsylvania.
Hatcher, J. J. Private	Unk	Unknown	Co. A, 50th Virginia Infantry	May 12, 1864, Spotsylvania Court House, Virginia	Point Lookout, Maryland, transferred to Elmira Prison, NY, August 2, 1864	Died September 16, 1864 of Chronic Diarrhea, Grave No. 158
Hatcher, James M. Private	25	May 13, 1862, Bristol, Tennessee	Co. E, 63rd Tennessee Infantry	June 17, 1864, Petersburg, Virginia	Point Lookout, Maryland, transferred to Elmira Prison, NY, July 30, 1864	Died August 6, 1864 of Chronic Diarrhea, Grave No. 10. Name S. M. Hatcher on Headstone.
Hatcher, James W. Private	23	May 13, 1861, Liberty, Virginia	Co. C, 2nd Virginia Cavalry	May 12, 1864, Spotsylvania Court House, Virginia	Point Lookout, Maryland, transferred to Elmira Prison, NY, August 12, 1864	Exchanged March 14, 1865 at Boulware's Wharf on the James River, Virginia
Hatcher, John P. Private	Unk	June 11, 1861, Pickens County, Alabama	Co. H, 11th Alabama Infantry	July 2, 1864, Gettysburg, Pennsylvania	Fort Delaware, Delaware, transferred to Elmira Prison, NY, August 17, 1864	Died March 6, 1865 of Chronic Diarrhea, Grave No. 1959
Hatcher, Solomon O. Private	Unk	March 12, 1864, Henry County, Virginia	Co. F, 42nd Virginia Infantry	May 12, 1864, Near Spotsylvania Court House, Virginia	Point Lookout, Maryland, transferred to Elmira Prison, NY, July 23, 1864	Died September 24, 1864 of Chronic Diarrhea, Grave No. 458
Hatcher, William H. Private	Unk	December 31, 1863, Chesterfield, South Carolina	Co. D, 21st South Carolina Infantry	January 15, 1865, Fort Fisher, North Carolina	January 30, 1865, Elmira Prison Camp, New York	Died June 29, 1865 of Pneumonia, Grave No. 2826

Name & Rank	Age	Enlisted	Regiment and State	Where Captured	Prison	Remarks
Hatcher, William H. Private	27	May 22, 1861, Spoon Creek, Virginia	Co. H, 42nd Virginia Infantry	May 12, 1864, Spotsylvania Court House, Virginia	Point Lookout, Maryland, transferred to Elmira Prison, NY, July 30, 1864	Exchanged October 11, 1864. Nothing Further.
Hatfield, James W. Private	18	March 14, 1863, Charleston, South Carolina	Co. E, 7th Battalion South Carolina Infantry	August 21, 1864, Weldon Railroad, Near Petersburg, Virginia. Gunshot Scrotum and Testicle.	Old Capital Prison, Washington, DC transferred to Elmira Prison, NY, August 27, 1864	Died April 29, 1865 of Chronic Diarrhea, Grave No. 2730
Hatfield, William Private	Unk	July 30, 1861, Bowdon, Georgia	Co. B, Cobb's Legion Georgia	August 16, 1864, Front Royal, Virginia	Old Capital Prison, Washington, DC transferred to Elmira Prison, NY, August 29, 1864	Died November 14, 1864 of Chronic Diarrhea, Grave No. 812
Hathaway, James J. Private	18	May 1, 1862, Sparta, North Carolina	Co. F, 30th North Carolina Infantry	May 6, 1864, Wilderness, Virginia	Point Lookout, Maryland, transferred to Elmira Prison, NY, August 14, 1864	Oath of Allegiance June 27, 1865
Hathcock, Calvin Private	37	March 27, 1862, Salisbury, North Carolina	Co. C, 42nd North Carolina Infantry	June 3, 1864, Cold Harbor, Virginia	Point Lookout, Maryland, transferred to Elmira Prison, NY, July 17, 1864	Died November 3, 1864 of Chronic Diarrhea, Grave No. 759
Hathcock, Edney W. Private	17	September 7, 1861, Albemarle, North Carolina	Co. K, 28th North Carolina Infantry	May 12, 1864, Spotsylvania Court House, Virginia	Point Lookout, Maryland, transferred to Elmira Prison, NY, August 14, 1864	Exchanged February 13, 1865 at Boulware's wharf on the James River, Virginia
Hathcock, J. Z. A. Private	19	February 28, 1863, Stanly County, North Carolina	Co. H, 13th North Carolina Infantry	May 6, 1864, Wilderness, Virginia	Point Lookout, Maryland, transferred to Elmira Prison, NY, August 14, 1864	Oath of Allegiance June 27, 1865
Hatley, John M. Private	32	August 9, 1862, Mount Pleasant, North Carolina	Co. H, 8th North Carolina Infantry	June 1, 1864, Gaines Mill Cold Harbor, Virginia	Point Lookout, Maryland, transferred to Elmira Prison, NY, July 17, 1864	Died September 22, 1864 of Rubeola, Grave No. 938

Name & Rank	Age	Enlisted	Regiment and State	Where Captured	Prison	Remarks
Hatley, Simeon Private	33	August 8, 1862, Camp Hill, Stanly County, North Carolina	Co. F, 5th North Carolina Infantry	May 20, 1864, Spotsylvania Court House, Virginia	Point Lookout, Maryland, transferred to Elmira Prison, NY, July 6,1864	Oath of Allegiance June 11, 1865
Hatley, William W. Private	34	August 18, 1862, Mount Pleasant, North Carolina	Co. H, 8th North Carolina Infantry	June 1, 1864, Gaines Mill Cold Harbor, Virginia	Point Lookout, Maryland, transferred to Elmira Prison, NY, July 17, 1864	Died May 16, 1865 of Chronic Diarrhea, Grave No. 2958
Hatton, William L. Sergeant	Unk	Unknown	Co. A, 5th Battalion Home Guards, Louisiana	September 27, 1864, Marianna, Florida	New Orleans, Louisiana transferred to Elmira November 19, 1864.	Died December 24, 1864 of Chronic Diarrhea, Grave No. 1101
Havcoff, T. J. Private	Unk	April 20, 1861, Belle Roi., Virginia	Co. A, 26th Virginia Infantry	June 15, 1864, Near Petersburg, Virginia	Point Lookout, Maryland, transferred to Elmira Prison, NY, July 12, 1864	Oath of Allegiance July 3, 1865
Havely, C. B. Corporal	22	April 14, 1862, Knoxville, Tennessee	Co. A, 63rd Tennessee Infantry	May 16, 1864, Near Drury's Bluff, Virginia	Point Lookout, Maryland, transferred to Elmira Prison, NY, August 17, 1864	Exchanged March 10, 1865 at Boulware's Wharf on the James River, Virginia
Hawes, L. A. Private	27	February 21, 1864, Wetumpka, Alabama	Co. F, 1st Battalion Alabama Artillery	August 23, 1864, Fort Morgan, Alabama	Steam Press No. 4 New Orleans, Louisiana transferred to Elmira October 8, 1864.	Died November 10, 1864 of Pneumonia, Grave No. 831. Headstone has Hawse.
Hawkes, William J. Private	Unk	August 1, 1864, Richmond, Virginia	Co. E, 3rd Virginia Cavalry	August 16, 1864, Front Royal, Virginia	Point Lookout, Maryland, transferred to Elmira Prison, NY, August 29, 1864	Exchanged March 14, 1865 at Boulware's Wharf on the James River, Virginia
Hawkins, A. J. Private	Unk	Unknown	Co. G, 53rd North Carolina Infantry	May 20, 1864, Spotsylvania Court House, Virginia	Point Lookout, Maryland, transferred to Elmira Prison, NY, July 23, 1864	Exchanged October 11, 1864. Nothing Further.

Name & Rank	Age	Enlisted	Regiment and State	Where Captured	Prison	Remarks
Hawkins, A. L. Sergeant	21	July 30, 1861, Livingston, Tennessee	Co. J, 25th Tennessee Infantry	May 16, 1864, Near Drury's Bluff, Virginia	Point Lookout, Maryland, transferred to Elmira Prison, NY, August 17, 1864	Exchanged February 25, 1865 at Boulware's or Cox Wharf on the James River, Virginia
Hawkins, J. T. Private	Unk	Unknown	Co. B, Hood's Battalion Virginia Reserve Infantry	June 15, 1864, Near Petersburg, Virginia	Point Lookout, Maryland, transferred to Elmira Prison, NY, July 12, 1864	Exchanged October 29, 1864 at Venus Point, Savannah River, GA.
Hawkins, John C. Private	Unk	March 1, 1864, Bat Tracy, Tennessee	Co. A, Jackson's 1st Regiment, Tennessee Heavy Artillery	August 23, 1864, Fort Morgan, Alabama	New Orleans, Louisiana transferred to Elmira Prison, NY, December 4, 1864.	Exchanged March 14, 1865 at Boulware's Wharf on the James River, Virginia
Hawkins, John P. Sailor	Unk	Unknown	Confederate States Navy	January 15, 1865, Fort Fisher, North Carolina	February 1, 1865, Elmira Prison Camp, New York	Oath of Allegiance May 17, 1865
Hawkins, Major B. Private	19	October 9, 1861, Enfield, Halifax County, North Carolina	Co. F, 36th Regiment 2nd North Carolina Artillery	January 15, 1865, Fort Fisher, North Carolina	February 1, 1865, Elmira Prison Camp, New York	Died February 13, 1865 of Pneumonia, Grave No. 2046
Hawkins, Michael L. Private	22	April 28, 1861, New Orleans, Louisiana	Co. D, 1st Louisiana Infantry	May 20, 1864, Near Spotsylvania, Virginia	Point Lookout, Maryland, transferred to Elmira Prison, NY, July 23, 1864	Died March 16, 1865 of Variola (Smallpox), Grave No. 1684, Name on Headstone: William L.
Hawkins, Peter Private	Unk	December 28, 1861, Camp Hampton, Columbia, South Carolina	Co. C, 7th Battalion, South Carolina Infantry	September 14, 1863, Near Culpepper, Virginia	Point Lookout, Maryland, transferred to Elmira Prison, NY, August 18, 1864	Exchanged March 10, 1865 at Boulware's Wharf on the James River, Virginia
Hawkins, S. M. Sergeant	Unk	Unknown	Co. H, 22nd South Carolina Infantry	July 30, 1864, Petersburg, Virginia	Point Lookout, Maryland, transferred to Elmira Prison, NY, August 12, 1864	Exchanged March 2, 1865 at Akins Landing on the James River, Virginia

Name & Rank	Age	Enlisted	Regiment and State	Where Captured	Prison	Remarks
Hawkins, Samuel S. Private	35	September 24, 1861, Wilkesboro, North Carolina	Co. F, 37th North Carolina Infantry	May 12, 1864, Spotsylvania Court House, Virginia. Wound Right Arm.	Old Capital Prison, Washington DC Transferred to Elmira Prison, NY, August 12, 1864	Transferred For Exchange October 11, 1864 to Point Lookout Prison Camp, MD. Nothing Further
Hawkins, Thomas Private	Unk	July 8, 1862, Hillsboro, North Carolina	Co. F, 33rd North Carolina Infantry	May 6, 1864, Wilderness, Virginia	Old Capital Prison, Washington DC Transferred to Elmira Prison, NY, July 14, 1864	Transferred 10/11/64. Died 10/26/64 of Chronic Diarrhea at Point Lookout, MD
Hawkins, W. B. Private	Unk	February 23, 1864, Notasulga, Alabama	Co. F, 1st Battalion Alabama Artillery	August 23, 1864, Fort Morgan, Alabama	Steam Press No. 4 New Orleans, Louisiana transferred to Elmira October 8, 1864.	Oath of Allegiance July 11, 1865
Hawkins, William H. Private	Unk	March 6, 1861, Selma, Alabama	Co. C, 1st Battalion Alabama Artillery	August 23, 1864, Fort Morgan, Alabama	New Orleans, Louisiana transferred to Elmira Prison, NY, December 4, 1864.	Oath of Allegiance May 19, 1865
Hawley, William H. Private	Unk	April 29, 1862, White Sulfur Springs, Virginia	Co. C, 26th Battalion Virginia Infantry	June 3, 1864, Gaines Mill Cold Harbor, Virginia	Point Lookout, Maryland, transferred to Elmira Prison, NY, July 17,1864	Exchanged March 2, 1865 at Akins Landing on the James River, Virginia
Hawn, Joseph Corporal	26	August 14, 1862, Statesville, North Carolina	Co. A, 18th North Carolina Infantry	May 6, 1864, Wilderness, Virginia	Point Lookout, Maryland, transferred to Elmira Prison, NY, August 14, 1864	Oath of Allegiance June 23, 1865
Hawood, B. Private	Unk	Unknown	Co. H, 30th Virginia Infantry	May 26, 1864, Port Royal, Virginia	Point Lookout, Maryland, transferred to Elmira Prison, NY, July 12, 1864	Exchanged October 11, 1864. Nothing Further.
Hawpe, James W. Private	Unk	November 27, 1863, Greenville, Virginia	Co. I, 52nd Virginia, Infantry	May 30, 1864, Mechanicsville, Virginia	Point Lookout, Maryland, transferred to Elmira Prison, NY, July 9, 1864	Oath of Allegiance June 30, 1865

Name & Rank	Age	Enlisted	Regiment and State	Where Captured	Prison	Remarks
Haws, Rodolphus Private	Unk	February 5, 1861, Montgomery, Alabama	Co. A, 1st Alabama Artillery	August 23, 1864, Fort Morgan, Alabama	New Orleans, Louisiana transferred to Elmira Prison, NY, December 4, 1864.	Oath of Allegiance May 17, 1865
Hawthorne, Andrew C. Private	18	Unknown	Co. F, 26th North Carolina Infantry	May 12, 1864, Spotsylvania Court House, Virginia	Point Lookout, Maryland, transferred to Elmira Prison, NY, July 30, 1864	Oath of Allegiance May 2, 1865
Hawthorne, Robert Private	Unk	Unknown	2nd Battery Maryland Artillery	July 10, 1864, Rockville, Maryland	Old Capital Prison, Washington, DC, transferred to Elmira July 23, 1864	Oath of Allegiance May 17, 1865
Hawthorne, Thomas W. Corporal	Unk	February 12, 1863, Camp Canonselet, Virginia	Co. M, 12th Louisiana Infantry	May 16, 1863, Baker's Creek, Champion Hill, Mississippi	Point Lookout, Maryland, transferred to Elmira Prison, NY, August 18, 1864	Exchanged February 25, 1865 at Boulware's wharf on the James River, Virginia
Hay, William W. Corporal	19	September 5, 1861, Dawson, Georgia	Co. K, 31st Georgia Infantry	January 27, 1865, Fort Stevens, DC. Gunshot Fracture Left Thigh.	November 11, 1864, Old Capital Prison, Washington, DC. February 4, 1865 Elmira, Prison Camp, NY	Exchanged February 13, 1865 at Boulware's wharf on the James River, Virginia
Hayes, B. R. Private	Unk	Unknown	Co. J, 1st South Carolina	June 9, 1864, Gaines Mill Cold Harbor, Virginia	Point Lookout, Maryland, transferred to Elmira Prison, NY, July 30, 1864	Oath of Allegiance July 3, 1865
Hayes, Burrell H. Private	Unk	September 24, 1862, Martinsburg, Virginia	Co. H, 4th Virginia Infantry	May 12, 1864, Spotsylvania Court House, Virginia	Point Lookout, Maryland, transferred to Elmira Prison, NY, August 2, 1864	Exchanged October 29, 1864 at Venus Point, Savannah River, GA.
Hayes, John Private	Unk	Unknown	Co. F, 24th North Carolina Infantry	June 17, 1864, Petersburg, Virginia	Point Lookout, Maryland, transferred to Elmira Prison, NY, July 30, 1864	Oath of Allegiance June 11, 1865

Name & Rank	Age	Enlisted	Regiment and State	Where Captured	Prison	Remarks
Hayes, N. T. Private	Unk	Unknown	Co. K, 11th Georgia Infantry	June 1, 1864, Cold Harbor, Virginia	Point Lookout, Maryland, transferred to Elmira Prison, NY, July 17,1864	Oath of Allegiance July 7, 1865
Hayes, Richard H. S. Private	Unk	November 25, 1863, Eastville, Alabama	Co. E, 13th Alabama Infantry	May 24, 1864, North Anna, Virginia	Point Lookout, Maryland, transferred to Elmira Prison, NY, July 25, 1864	Oath of Allegiance May 14, 1865
Hayes, Tobias R. Private	Unk	October 13, 1861, Mobile, Alabama	Co. A, 21st Alabama Infantry	August 23, 1864, Fort Morgan, Alabama	Steam Press No. 4 New Orleans, Louisiana transferred to Elmira October 8, 1864.	Oath of Allegiance July 7, 1865
Hayes, Wilson Enos Private	Unk	November 20, 1863, Green Ponch, South Carolina	Co. F, 4th South Carolina Cavalry	May 30, 1864, Cold Harbor, Virginia	Point Lookout, Maryland, transferred to Elmira Prison, NY, July 12, 1864	Oath of Allegiance June 19, 1865
Haymans, Stoughton Sergeant	Unk	April 3, 1862, Bryan County, Georgia	Co. H, 7th Georgia Cavalry	June 11, 1864, Trevilian Station, Louisa Court House, Virginia	Point Lookout, Maryland, transferred to Elmira Prison, NY, July 25, 1864	Transferred for Exchange 10/11/64. Died 10/30/64 of Unknown Disease at Fort Monroe, VA.
Haynes, G. W. Private	Unk	March 8, 1862, Fort Pillow, Tennessee	Co. B, 1st Jackson's Tennessee Heavy Artillery	August 23, 1864, Fort Morgan, Alabama.	New Orleans, Louisiana transferred to Elmira Prison, NY, December 4, 1864.	Exchanged February 25, 1865 at Boulware's or Cox Wharf on the James River, Virginia
Haynes, H. H. Sergeant	Unk	Unknown	Co. B, 2nd Georgia Infantry	July 4, 1864, Rockville, Maryland	Old Capital Prison, Washington, DC, transferred to Elmira July 23, 1864	Oath of Allegiance June 16, 1865
Haynes, Henry H. Private	Unk	March 4, 1862, Augusta, Georgia	Co. A, 45th Georgia Infantry	June 23, 1864, Near Petersburg, Virginia	Point Lookout Prison Camp, Maryland. Transferred to Elmira Prison, July 17, 1864	Died December 13, 1864 of Chronic Diarrhea, Grave No. 1141

Name & Rank	Age	Enlisted	Regiment and State	Where Captured	Prison	Remarks
Haynes, James W. Corporal	Unk	July 12, 1862, Hartwell, Georgia	Co. B, 24th Georgia Infantry	August 16, 1864, Front Royal, Virginia	Old Capital Prison, Washington, DC transferred to Elmira Prison, NY, August 29, 1864	Oath of Allegiance June 16, 1865
Haynes, Nathanial Asbury Private	Unk	December 28, 1861, Camp Hampton, South Carolina	Co. F, Holcombe Legion, South Carolina	May 8, 1864, Jarrett's Depot, Virginia	Point Lookout, Maryland, transferred to Elmira Prison, NY, August 17, 1864	Exchanged March 2, 1865 at Akins Landing on the James River, Virginia
Haynes, R. H. Sergeant	26	April 14, 1862, Union Springs, Alabama	Co. L, 3rd Alabama Infantry	May 12, 1864, Spotsylvania, Virginia. Gunshot Wound Chest	Old Capital Prison, Washington, DC, transferred to Elmira July 23, 1864	Exchanged March 10, 1865 at Boulware's Wharf on the James River, Virginia
Haynes, Robert P. Sergeant	Unk	May 1, 1862, White Sulfur Springs, Virginia	Co. H, 26th Battalion Virginia Infantry	June 3, 1864, Gaines Mill, Cold Harbor, Virginia	Transferred From Point Lookout Prison, MD, July 12, 1864. Train Never Arrived at Elmira Prison Camp, NY.	Died July 15, 1864 in Train Wreck at Shohola, Pennsylvania.
Haynes, William A. Private	17	December 10, 1863, Haig, South Carolina	Co. B, 26th Virginia Infantry	June 15, 1864, Petersburg, Virginia	Point Lookout, Maryland, transferred to Elmira Prison, NY, July 12, 1864	Oath of Allegiance July 3, 1865
Haynes, William L. Private	24	October 16, 1861, Yadkinville, North Carolina	Co. B, 38th North Carolina Infantry	May 6, 1864, Wilderness, Virginia	Point Lookout, Maryland, transferred to Elmira Prison, NY, August 14, 1864	Exchanged February 20, 1865 at Boulware's or Cox Wharf on the James River, Virginia
Hayney, Junius R. Private	Unk	April 18, 1861, Lexington, Virginia	Co. H, 27th Virginia Infantry	May 20, 1864, Spotsylvania Court House, Virginia	Point Lookout, Maryland, transferred to Elmira Prison, NY, July 6, 1864	Exchanged March 14, 1865 at Boulware's Wharf on the James River, Virginia

Name & Rank	Age	Enlisted	Regiment and State	Where Captured	Prison	Remarks
Haynie, James B. Private	28	August 20, 1862, Raleigh, North Carolina	Co. K, 43rd North Carolina Infantry	May 10, 1864, Spotsylvania Court House, Virginia	Point Lookout, Maryland, transferred to Elmira Prison, NY, August 14, 1864	Died December 8, 1864 of Chronic Diarrhea, Grave No. 1168
Hays, Barrett C. Sergeant	Unk	August 24, 1861, Habersham County, Georgia	Co. K, 24th Georgia Infantry	August 16, 1864, Front Royal, Virginia	Old Capital Prison, Washington, DC transferred to Elmira Prison, NY, August 29, 1864	Oath of Allegiance July 7, 1865
Hays, Bennet J. Corporal	28	March 10, 1862, Lumberton, North Carolina	Co. F, 51st North Carolina Infantry	June 15, 1864, Bottoms Church, Near Petersburg, Near Bermuda Hundred, Virginia	Point Lookout, Maryland, transferred to Elmira Prison, NY, July 12,1864	Exchanged October 29, 1864 at Venus Point, Savannah River, GA.
Hays, Charles F. Private	Unk	April 20, 1862, Marion Court House, South Carolina	Co. D, 25th South Carolina Infantry	January 15, 1865, Fort Fisher, North Carolina	January 30, 1865, Elmira Prison Camp, New York	Died March 23, 1865 of Pneumonia, Grave No. 1515. Headstone has C. F. Hayes.
Hays, James N. Private	Unk	June 16, 1863, James Island, South Carolina	Co. D, 25th South Carolina Infantry	January 15, 1865, Fort Fisher, North Carolina	January 30, 1865, Elmira Prison Camp, New York	Oath of Allegiance June 23, 1865
Hays, Wilson Enos Private	Unk	November 20, 1863, Green Pond, South Carolina	Co. F, 4th South Carolina Cavalry	May 30, 1864, Cold Harbor, Virginia	Point Lookout Prison, Maryland, transferred to Elmira Prison, New York, July 12, 1864	Oath of Allegiance June 19, 1865
Haywood, F. P. Private	Unk	Unknown	Co. A, Captain Godwin's Home Guard Florida	September 27, 1864, Marianna, Florida	New Orleans, Louisiana transferred to Elmira November 19, 1864.	Oath of Allegiance December 12, 1864 Due to Debility. Early Release Granted by Commissary General of Prisoners.

Name & Rank	Age	Enlisted	Regiment and State	Where Captured	Prison	Remarks
Haywood, William M. Sergeant	22	May 18, 1861, Seven Mile Ford, Virginia	Co. D, 48th Virginia Infantry	May 5, 1864, Wilderness, Virginia. Gunshot Wound Left Ankle	Old Capital Prison, Washington, DC, transferred to Elmira July 23, 1864	Oath of Allegiance May 17, 1865
Hazelwood, John W. Private	Unk	April 7, 1864, Camp Gauley, Virginia	Co. D, 22nd Virginia Infantry	June 3, 1864, Gaines Farm Cold Harbor, Virginia	Point Lookout, Maryland, transferred to Elmira Prison, NY, July 17,1864	Died October 7, 1864 of Chronic Diarrhea Grave No. 588
Head, Joseph Private	Unk	August 19, 1862, Calhoun, Georgia	Co. E, 44th Georgia Infantry	May 20, 1864, Spotsylvania Court House, Virginia	Point Lookout, Maryland, transferred to Elmira Prison, NY, July 6, 1864	Exchanged March 10, 1865 at Boulware's Wharf on the James River, Virginia
Head, Thomas M. Private	Unk	July 9, 1861, Jackson, Georgia	Co. J, 14th Georgia Infantry	May 12, 1864, Spotsylvania Court House, Virginia	Point Lookout, Maryland, transferred to Elmira Prison, NY, July 30, 1864	Oath of Allegiance May 29, 1865
Head, William E. Private	17	April 9, 1864, Auburn, Alabama	Co. A, 1st Alabama Artillery	August 23, 1864, Fort Morgan, Alabama.	New Orleans, Louisiana transferred to Elmira Prison, NY, December 4, 1864.	Died February 17, 1865 of Pneumonia, Grave No. 2231
Heady, Charles Private	30	October 23, 1861, New Hanover, North Carolina	Co. D, 36th Regiment 2nd North Carolina Artillery	January 15, 1865, Fort Fisher, North Carolina	February 1, 1865, Elmira Prison Camp, New York	Died May 27, 1865 of Rheumatism, Grave No. 2914
Heald, S. L. Private	Unk	September 4, 1863, Palmyra, Georgia	Co. A, 20th Battalion Georgia Cavalry	June 11, 1864, Trevilian Station, Louisa Court House, Virginia	Point Lookout, Maryland, transferred to Elmira Prison, NY, July 25, 1864	Died February 11, 1865 of Variola (Smallpox), Grave No. 2079
Healer, J. B. Private	Unk	Unknown	Co. F, 17th South Carolina Infantry	July 30, 1864, Near Petersburg, Virginia	Point Lookout, Maryland, transferred to Elmira Prison, NY, August 12, 1864	Died September 1, 1864 of Chronic Diarrhea, Grave No. 77. Name Beheler on Headstone.

Name & Rank	Age	Enlisted	Regiment and State	Where Captured	Prison	Remarks
Healey, John T. Private	23	June 19, 1861, Camp Moore, Louisiana	Co. F, 8th Louisiana Infantry	May 12, 1864, Spotsylvania Court House, Virginia	Point Lookout, Maryland, transferred to Elmira Prison, NY, August 17, 1864	Exchanged February 25, 1865 at Boulware's or Cox Wharf on the James River, Virginia
Heard, James W. C. Private	19	Unknown	Co. E, 19th Georgia Infantry	August 19, 1864, Petersburg, Virginia. Gunshot Wound Left Foot.	Old Capital Prison, Washington, DC, transferred to Elmira December 17, 1864	Died March 10, 1865 of Pneumonia, Grave No. 1860
Hearn, E. M. Sergeant	Unk	November 1, 1862, Lebanon, Tennessee	Co. A, Jackson's 1st Regiment, Tennessee Heavy Artillery	August 23, 1864, Fort Morgan, Alabama	New Orleans, Louisiana transferred to Elmira Prison, NY, December 4, 1864.	Exchanged February 25, 1865 at Boulware's or Cox Wharf on the James River, Virginia
Hearon, Edward L. Private	Unk	March 16, 1862, Grove Hill, Alabama	Co. J, 5th Alabama Infantry	May 5, 1864, Wilderness, Virginia	Point Lookout, Maryland, transferred to Elmira Prison, NY, August 17, 1864	Died December 11, 1864 of Pneumonia, Grave No. 1041
Heart, John Private	Unk	March 17, 1862, New Orleans, Louisiana	Co. B, 6th Louisiana Infantry	May 5, 1864, Wilderness, Virginia	Point Lookout, Maryland, transferred to Elmira Prison, NY, August 17, 1864	Oath of Allegiance May 17, 1865
Heath, George Private	18	March 15, 1862, Union Parish, Louisiana	Co. A, 6th Louisiana Infantry	May 5, 1864, Wilderness, Virginia	Point Lookout, Maryland, transferred to Elmira Prison, NY, August 17, 1864	Oath of Allegiance June 27, 1865
Heath, James P. Private	26	April 23, 1861, Snow Hill, North Carolina	Co. A, 3rd North Carolina Infantry	May 12, 1864, Spotsylvania Court House, Virginia	Point Lookout, Maryland, transferred to Elmira Prison, NY, August 14, 1864	Exchanged March 10, 1865 at Boulware's Wharf on the James River, Virginia
Heath, John T. Private	28	May 24, 1861, Trenton, North Carolina	Co. G, 2nd North Carolina Infantry	November 7, 1863, Kelly's Ford, Rappahannock Virginia	Point Lookout, Maryland, transferred to Elmira Prison, NY, August 18, 1864	Exchanged March 10, 1865 at Boulware's Wharf on the James River, Virginia

Name & Rank	Age	Enlisted	Regiment and State	Where Captured	Prison	Remarks
Heath, Josiah J. F. Corporal	19	July 6, 1861, Wilmington, North Carolina	Co. I, 18th North Carolina Infantry	May 12, 1864, Spotsylvania Court House, Virginia	Point Lookout, Maryland, transferred to Elmira Prison, NY, August 6, 1864	Transferred for Exchange 10/11/64. Died 11/3/64 of Unknown Causes at Fort Monroe, VA.
Heath, Robert Sailor	Unk	Unknown	Confederate States Navy	January 15, 1865, Fort Fisher, North Carolina	February 1, 1865, Elmira Prison Camp, New York	Oath of Allegiance July 18, 1865
Heath, William M. Private	Unk	May 2, 1862, Macon, Georgia	Co. J, 61st Georgia Infantry	May 20, 1864, Spotsylvania Court House, Virginia	Point Lookout, Maryland, transferred to Elmira Prison, NY, July 6, 1864	Exchanged March 2, 1865 at Akins Landing on the James River, Virginia
Heatherington W. H. Private	Unk	May 25, 1862, Camp Moore, Louisiana	Co. A, 4th Louisiana Cavalry	October 6, 1864, Clinton, Louisiana	New Orleans, Louisiana transferred to Elmira November 19, 1864.	Exchanged February 25, 1865 at Boulware's or Cox Wharf on the James River, Virginia
Heaton, Joseph Pennal Private	Unk	September 3, 1861, Camp Butler, South Carolina	Co. I, 14th South Carolina Infantry	July 29, 1864, Petersburg, Virginia	Point Lookout, Maryland, transferred to Elmira Prison, NY, August 12, 1864	Exchanged February 13, 1865 at Boulware's Wharf on the James River, Virginia
Heavner, Fredrick Private	28	March 15, 1862, Lincolnton, North Carolina	Co. I, 23rd North Carolina Infantry	July 14, 1864, Near Washington, DC	Old Capital Prison, Washington, DC, transferred to Elmira July 23, 1864	Exchanged February 13, 1865 at Boulware's wharf on the James River, Virginia
Hebert, Jean A. Private	Unk	Unknown	Co. C, 4th Louisiana Cavalry	September 11, 1864, Near Plaquemine, Louisiana	New Orleans, LA, Transferred to Elmira Prison, NY, November 19, 1864	Exchanged March 10, 1865 at Boulware's Wharf on the James River, Virginia
Heck, W. S. Private	Unk	May 1, 1863, Fetterman, Virginia	Co. A, 25th Virginia Infantry	May 12, 1864, Spotsylvania Court House, Virginia	Point Lookout, Maryland, transferred to Elmira Prison, NY, August 2, 1864	Exchanged March 2, 1865 at Akins Landing on the James River, Virginia

Name & Rank	Age	Enlisted	Regiment and State	Where Captured	Prison	Remarks
Heckel, Andrew J. Private	Unk	September 1, 1862, James Island, South Carolina	Co. F, 25th South Carolina Infantry	January 15, 1865, Fort Fisher, North Carolina	January 30, 1865, Elmira Prison Camp, New York	Died February 9, 1865 of Typhoid Fever, Grave No. 1951
Heckler, W. T. Private	Unk	April 1, 1864, Kinston, North Carolina	Co. C, 38th Read's Battalion, Virginia Light Artillery	June 3, 1864, Gaines Farm Cold Harbor, Virginia	Point Lookout, Maryland, transferred to Elmira Prison, NY, July 17, 1864	Oath of Allegiance June 27, 1865
Hedgepath, John S. Private	17	Unknown	Co. F, 36th Regiment 2nd North Carolina Artillery	January 15, 1865, Fort Fisher, North Carolina	February 1, 1865, Elmira Prison Camp, New York	Died February 10, 1865 of Pneumonia, Grave No. 1945
Hedrick, Levi Private	37	March 31, 1863, Newton, North Carolina	Co. F, 32nd North Carolina Infantry	May 10, 1864, Wilderness, Virginia	Point Lookout, Maryland, transferred to Elmira Prison, NY, August 6, 1864	Died January 14, 1865 of Chronic Diarrhea, Grave No. 1470. Name Hendrick on Headstone.
Hedrick, Richard S. Sergeant	23	May 18, 1861, Edenton, North Carolina	Co. A, 1st North Carolina Infantry	May 12, 1864, Spotsylvania Court House, Virginia	Point Lookout, Maryland, transferred to Elmira Prison, NY, August 6, 1864	Oath of Allegiance June 12, 1865
Hedrick, William P. Private	18	April 5, 1862, Camp Shenandoah, Virginia	Co. E, 25th Virginia Infantry	May 12, 1864, Spotsylvania Court House, Virginia	Point Lookout, Maryland, transferred to Elmira Prison, NY, August 12, 1864	Oath of Allegiance June 27, 1865
Hefflefinger, Henry A. Private	Unk	June 22, 1861, Wytheville, Virginia	Co. K, 50th Virginia Infantry	July 18, 1864, Snickers Gap, Virginia	Old Capital Prison, Washington DC Transferred to Elmira Prison, NY, August 12, 1864	Oath of Allegiance June 23, 1865
Hefner, Burrell C. Private	18	April 13, 1863, Camp Holmes, North Carolina	Co. F, 32nd North Carolina Infantry	May 10, 1864, Wilderness, Virginia	Point Lookout, Maryland, transferred to Elmira Prison, NY, August 6, 1864	Oath of Allegiance June 27, 1865

Name & Rank	Age	Enlisted	Regiment and State	Where Captured	Prison	Remarks
Hefner, Elcanah R. Corporal	Unk	October 31, 1861, Newton, North Carolina	Co. E, 38th North Carolina Infantry	May 6, 1864, Wilderness, Virginia	Point Lookout, Maryland, transferred to Elmira Prison, NY, August 14, 1864	Transferred for Exchange 10/11/64. Died 10/14/64 of Unknown Causes at US Army Hospital, Baltimore, MD.
Hefner, James P. Private	Unk	May 18, 1861, Sutton, Virginia	Co. C, 25th Virginia Infantry	May 6, 1864, Wilderness, Virginia	Old Capital Prison, Washington DC Transferred to Elmira Prison, NY, July 14, 1864	Oath of Allegiance June 27, 1865
Hefner, James W. Private	Unk	June 13, 1861, Conrad's, Virginia	Co. G, 25th Virginia Infantry	May 6, 1864, Wilderness, Virginia	Old Capital Prison, Washington DC Transferred to Elmira Prison, NY, July 14, 1864	Oath of Allegiance June 23, 1865
Hefner, Levi Private	21	August 13, 1861, Newton, North Carolina	Co. C, 28th North Carolina Infantry	May 12, 1864, Spotsylvania Court House, Virginia	Point Lookout, Maryland, transferred to Elmira Prison, NY, August 14, 1864	Oath of Allegiance July 7, 1865
Hefner, Samuel C. Private	Unk	May 18, 1861, Sutton, Virginia	Co. C, 25th Virginia Infantry	May 6, 1864, Wilderness, Virginia	Old Capital Prison, Washington DC Transferred to Elmira Prison, NY, July 14, 1864	Oath of Allegiance June 27, 1865
Hefner, Samuel N. Private	Unk	May 21, 1864, Hendersonville, North Carolina	Co. D, 6th North Carolina Cavalry	June 22, 1864, Jackson's Mills, Near Kinston, North Carolina	Point Lookout, Maryland, transferred to Elmira Prison, NY, July 25, 1864	Died February 17, 1865 of Chronic Diarrhea, Grave No. 2214
Heidt, George Private	Unk	November 1, 1863, Georgetown, South Carolina	Co. E, 7th Georgia Cavalry	June 11, 1864, Trevilian Station, Louisa Court House, Virginia	Point Lookout, Maryland, transferred to Elmira Prison, NY, July 25, 1864	Oath of Allegiance July 17, 1865

Name & Rank	Age	Enlisted	Regiment and State	Where Captured	Prison	Remarks
Heiflebower, Edward L. Private	Unk	April 25, 1862, Hainesville, Virginia	Co. J, 12th Virginia Cavalry	April 12, 1865, Fairfax Station, Virginia	Old Capital Prison, Washington DC Transferred to Elmira Prison, NY, May 2, 1865.	Oath of Allegiance July 19, 1865
Heileg, Julius Corporal	18	June 8, 1861, Salisbury, North Carolina	Co. K, 5th North Carolina Infantry	May 9, 1864, Spotsylvania, Virginia. Gunshot Wound Right Arm and Ear	Old Capital Prison, Washington, DC, transferred to Elmira July 23, 1864	Exchanged October 29, 1864 at Venus Point, Savannah River, GA.
Heim, Michael Private	20	June 19, 1861, Camp Moore, Louisiana	Co. K, 8th Louisiana Infantry	May 12, 1864, Spotsylvania Court House, Virginia	Point Lookout, Maryland, transferred to Elmira Prison, NY, August 17, 1864	Exchanged March 10, 1865 at Boulware's Wharf on the James River, Virginia
Helbert, George W. Private	44	August 13, 1863, Zollicoffer, Tennessee	Co. F, 63rd Tennessee Infantry	June 17, 1864, Petersburg, Virginia	Point Lookout, Maryland, transferred to Elmira Prison, NY, July 30, 1864	Died September 3, 1864 of Chronic Diarrhea, Grave No. 224
Helfer, Pleasant E. Private	Unk	October 20, 1863, Wilmington, North Carolina	Co. K, 42nd North Carolina Infantry	June 3, 1864, Cold Harbor, Virginia	Point Lookout, Maryland, transferred to Elmira Prison, NY, July 17,1864	Died December 2, 1864 of Pneumonia, Grave No. 893
Helmick, George A. Private	Unk	May 18, 1861, Huntersville, Virginia	Co. I, 25th Virginia Infantry	May 12, 1864, Spotsylvania Court House, Virginia	Point Lookout, Maryland, transferred to Elmira Prison, NY, August 12, 1864	Oath of Allegiance May 29, 1865
Helms, Albert Private	Unk	February 15, 1862, Union County, North Carolina	Co. C, 42nd North Carolina Infantry	June 3, 1864, Cold Harbor, Virginia	Point Lookout, Maryland, transferred to Elmira Prison, NY, July 17,1864	Exchanged March 10, 1865 at Boulware's Wharf on the James River, Virginia
Helms, C. N. Private	Unk	January ?, 1862, Montgomery, Alabama	Co. F, 3rd Alabama Infantry	May 5, 1864, Wilderness, Virginia	Point Lookout, Maryland, transferred to Elmira Prison, NY, August 17, 1864	Died November 26, 1864 of Typhoid-Pneumonia, Grave No. 979

Name & Rank	Age	Enlisted	Regiment and State	Where Captured	Prison	Remarks
Helms, John Private	Unk	February 15, 1862, Union County, North Carolina	Co. C, 42nd North Carolina Infantry	June 3, 1864, Cold Harbor, Virginia	Point Lookout, Maryland, transferred to Elmira Prison, NY, July 17,1864	Oath of Allegiance June 30, 1865
Helms, M. H. Private	18	October 20, 1861, Richmond, Virginia	Co. C, 1st North Carolina Cavalry	September 22, 1863, Near Madison Court House, Virginia	Point Lookout, Maryland, transferred to Elmira Prison, NY, August 18, 1864	Transferred For Exchange 10/11/64 to Point Lookout Prison, MD. Died 10/20/64 of Chronic Diarrhea at US Army Hospital, Baltimore, MD.
Helms, Matthew Private	Unk	February 22, 1863, Salem, Virginia	Co. B, 14th Virginia Cavalry	July 16, 1864, Loudoun County, Virginia	Old Capital Prison, Washington, DC, transferred to Elmira July 23, 1864	Died January 18, 1865 of Pneumonia, Grave No. 1434
Helms, Tobias Private	23	May 5, 1862, Union County, North Carolina	Co. J, 53rd North Carolina Infantry	May 12, 1864, Spotsylvania, Virginia, Gunshot Wound Upper or Thigh	Old Capital Prison, Washington, DC, transferred to Elmira July 23, 1864	Exchanged February 13, 1865 at Boulware's wharf on the James River, Virginia
Helsebeck, Gaston J. Private	Unk	July 2, 1862, Pfafftown, North Carolina	Co. C, 33rd North Carolina Infantry	July 28, 1864, Deep Bottom, Virginia. Gunshot Wound Right Lower Leg, Amputated.	Old Capital Prison, Washington, DC, transferred to Elmira December 17, 1864	Exchanged February 13, 1865 at Boulware's Wharf on the James River, Virginia
Helton, Hollis Private	30	March 17, 1862, Smerna or Griffins, North Carolina	Co. E, 48th North Carolina Infantry	May 24, 1864, Hanover Junction, Virginia	Point Lookout, Maryland, transferred to Elmira Prison, NY, July 12, 1864	Died September 14, 1864 of Pneumonia, Grave No. 284
Hembree, William J. Sergeant	18	August 15, 1861, Carroll County, Georgia	Co. F, Cobb's Legion Georgia	August 16, 1864, Front Royal, Virginia	Old Capital Prison, Washington, DC transferred to Elmira Prison, NY, August 29, 1864	Oath of Allegiance July 11, 1865

Name & Rank	Age	Enlisted	Regiment and State	Where Captured	Prison	Remarks
Hemphill, John L. Private	Unk	March 19, 1862, Abbeville District, South Carolina	Co. G, 1st South Carolina Infantry	July 14, 1863, Falling Waters, Maryland	Point Lookout, Maryland, transferred to Elmira Prison, NY, August 18, 1864	Exchanged February 25, 1865 at Boulware's or Cox Wharf on the James River, Virginia
Hempstead, James A. Private	20	May 13, 1862, Richmond, Virginia	Co. R, 10th Virginia Cavalry	July 14, 1863, Falling Waters, Maryland	Point Lookout, Maryland, transferred to Elmira Prison, NY, August 18, 1864	Exchanged March 10, 1865 at Boulware's Wharf on the James River, Virginia
Henderson, Alfred D. Private	Unk	June 1, 1864, Randolph, Georgia	Co. J, 48th Georgia Infantry	August 16, 1864, New Market, Virginia	Old Capital Prison, Washington, DC transferred to Elmira Prison, NY, August 27, 1864	Oath of Allegiance May 19, 1865
Henderson, Andrew Private	Unk	October 8, 1863, Sullivan's Island, South Carolina	Co. H, 22nd South Carolina Infantry	July 30, 1864, Near Petersburg, Virginia	Point Lookout, Maryland, transferred to Elmira Prison, NY, August 12, 1864	Died December 26, 1864 of Variola (Smallpox), Grave No. 1292
Henderson, B. F. Private	Unk	Unknown	Co. J, 3rd Texas Cavalry	August 25, 1864, Clinton, Louisiana	New Orleans, LA, Transferred to Elmira Prison, NY, November 19, 1864	Exchanged March 10, 1865 at Boulware's Wharf on the James River, Virginia
Henderson, David W. Private	18	June 11, 1861, Cobb County, Georgia	Co. C, Phillips Legion, Georgia	June 2, 1864, Gaines Farm Cold Harbor, Virginia	Point Lookout, Maryland, transferred to Elmira Prison, NY, July 17,1864	Oath of Allegiance June 23, 1865
Henderson, H. S. Private	25	January 1, 1863, Mississippi	Co. J, 1st Missouri Cavalry	May 17, 1863, Big Black Bridge, Champion Hill, Mississippi	Point Lookout, Maryland, transferred to Elmira Prison, NY, August 18, 1864	Exchanged February 13, 1865 at Boulware's wharf on the James River, Virginia

Name & Rank	Age	Enlisted	Regiment and State	Where Captured	Prison	Remarks
Henderson, Henry Private	Unk	October 12, 1863, Columbia, South Carolina	Co. L, 1st South Carolina Infantry	July 29, 1864, Petersburg, Virginia	Point Lookout, Maryland, transferred to Elmira Prison, NY, August 12, 1864	Exchanged February 13, 1865 at Boulware's wharf on the James River, Virginia
Henderson, Hiram F. Private	26	June 15, 1861, Washington, Virginia	Co. F, 48th Virginia Infantry	May 12, 1864, Spotsylvania Court House, Virginia	Point Lookout, Maryland, transferred to Elmira Prison, NY, August 2, 1864	Oath of Allegiance June 27, 1865
Henderson, James Private	Unk	April 1, 1862, Abingdon, Virginia	Co. F, 48th Virginia Infantry	May 12, 1864, Spotsylvania Court House, Virginia	Point Lookout, Maryland, transferred to Elmira Prison, NY, August 2, 1864	Oath of Allegiance June 14, 1865
Henderson, James H. Private	26	April 15, 1861, Shreveport, Louisiana	Co. A, 1st Louisiana Infantry	July 10, 1864, Near Frederick, Maryland	Old Capital Prison, Washington, DC, transferred to Elmira July 23, 1864	Exchanged February 25, 1865 at Boulware's or Cox Wharf on the James River, Virginia
Henderson, John A. Sergeant	26	February 26, 1862, Camp Leon, Madison, Florida	Co. D, 5th Florida Infantry	May 12, 1864, Spotsylvania Court House, Virginia	Point Lookout, Maryland, transferred to Elmira Prison, NY, July 30, 1864	Oath of Allegiance June 23, 1865
Henderson, John A. Private	Unk	April 1, 1862, Abingdon, Virginia	Co. F, 48th Virginia Infantry	May 12, 1864, Spotsylvania Court House, Virginia	Point Lookout, Maryland, transferred to Elmira Prison, NY, August 12, 1864	Exchanged February 20, 1865 at Boulware's or Cox Wharf on the James River, Virginia
Henderson, John Wood Private	32	August 15, 1862, Iredell County, North Carolina	Co. I, 37th North Carolina Infantry	July 29, 1864, Petersburg, Virginia	Point Lookout, Maryland, transferred to Elmira Prison, NY, August 12, 1864	Oath of Allegiance June 27, 1865
Henderson, Levi O. Private	26	May 14, 1862, Camp McCarthy, Near Orange Spring, Putnam County, Florida	Co. B, 9th Florida Infantry	July 29, 1864, Deserted to Union Lines, Petersburg, Virginia	Point Lookout, Maryland, transferred to Elmira Prison, NY, August 12, 1864	Oath of Allegiance January 30, 1865. Early Release per Lincoln's Proclamation, 12/8/1863.

Name & Rank	Age	Enlisted	Regiment and State	Where Captured	Prison	Remarks
Henderson, William A. Private	26	April 19, 1862, Jonesboro, Tennessee	Co. D, 63rd Tennessee Infantry	June 17, 1864, Petersburg, Virginia	Point Lookout, Maryland, transferred to Elmira Prison, NY, July 30, 1864	Exchanged October 29, 1864 at Venus Point, Savannah River, GA.
Henderson, William N. Private	28	July 16, 1862, Raleigh, North Carolina	Co. D, 14th North Carolina Infantry	May 20, 1864, Spotsylvania Court House, Virginia	Point Lookout, Maryland, transferred to Elmira Prison, NY, July 30, 1864	Exchanged October 29, 1864 at Venus Point, Savannah River, GA.
Henderson, Z. W. Private	26	July 5, 1862, Camp Randolph, Georgia	Co. K, 10th Georgia Infantry	May 6, 1864, Wilderness, Virginia	Point Lookout, Maryland, transferred to Elmira Prison, NY, August 14, 1864	Oath of Allegiance June 16, 1865
Hendon, H. T. Sergeant	Unk	July 8, 1861, Griffin, Georgia	Co. B, 13th Georgia Infantry	July 14, 1864, Near Washington, DC	Old Capital Prison, Washington, DC, transferred to Elmira July 23, 1864	Exchanged March 10, 1865 at Boulware's Wharf on the James River, Virginia
Hendrick, John E. Private	33	May 14, 1861, Cumberland Court House, Virginia	Co. G, 3rd Virginia Cavalry	May 9, 1864, Spotsylvania Court House, Virginia	Point Lookout, Maryland, transferred to Elmira Prison, NY, August 17, 1864	Died February 28, 1865 of Chronic Diarrhea, Grave No. 2118
Hendrick, W. J. Private	Unk	May 22, 1862, Augusta, Georgia	Co. F, 38th Georgia Infantry	June 1, 1864, Cold Harbor, Virginia	Point Lookout, Maryland, transferred to Elmira Prison, NY, July 17, 1864	Transferred for Exchange 10/11/64. Died November 10, 1864 at Sea.
Hendricks, George Civilian	Unk	Randolph County, Virginia	Citizen of Virginia	April 21, 1864, Wilmington, North Carolina	Old Capital Prison, Washington, DC, transferred to Elmira July 23, 1864	Died October 28, 1864 of Chronic Diarrhea, Grave No. 724
Hendricks, Lemuel S. Private	29	July 13, 1861, Jacksonville, Florida	Co. E, 2nd Florida Infantry	May 12, 1864, Spotsylvania Court House, Virginia	Point Lookout, Maryland, transferred to Elmira Prison, NY, August 12, 1864	Died January 13, 1865 of Chronic Diarrhea, Grave No. 1481

Name & Rank	Age	Enlisted	Regiment and State	Where Captured	Prison	Remarks
Hendricks, T. M. Private	Unk	February 17, 1863, Charleston, South Carolina	Co. B, 27th South Carolina Infantry	June 24, 1864, Near Petersburg, Virginia	Point Lookout, Maryland, transferred to Elmira Prison, NY, August 18, 1864	Died November 13, 1864 of Pneumonia, Grave No. 817
Hendricks, William W. Private	Unk	September 8, 1863, Columbia, South Carolina	Co. C, 22nd South Carolina Infantry	July 30, 1864, Petersburg, Virginia	Point Lookout, Maryland, transferred to Elmira Prison, NY, August 12, 1864	Transferred for Exchange 10/11/64. Died 10/26/64 of Chronic Diarrhea at Point Lookout, MD.
Hendrix, Daniel J. Corporal	Unk	March 25, 1862, Columbia, South Carolina	Co. C, 1st South Carolina Infantry	July 29, 1864, Petersburg, Virginia	Point Lookout, Maryland, transferred to Elmira Prison, NY, August 12, 1864	Oath of Allegiance June 3, 1865
Hendrix, Eli A. Sergeant	25	July 20, 1861, Fayetteville, North Carolina	Co. E, 8th North Carolina Infantry	May 31, 1864, Cold Harbor, Virginia	Point Lookout, Maryland, transferred to Elmira Prison, NY, July 12, 1864	Exchanged October 29, 1864 at Venus Point, Savannah River, GA.
Hendrix, Henry B. Private	Unk	January 10, 1862, Columbia, South Carolina	Co. C, 22nd South Carolina Infantry	July 30, 1864, Petersburg, Virginia	Point Lookout, Maryland, transferred to Elmira Prison, NY, August 12, 1864	Died March 29, 1865 of Chronic Diarrhea, Grave No. 2487. Name N. B. Hendricks on Headstone.
Hendrix, John Z. Private	28	May 1, 1862, Camp Leon, Madison, Florida	Co. D, 5th Florida Infantry	May 12, 1864, Spotsylvania Court House, Virginia	Point Lookout, Maryland, transferred to Elmira Prison, NY, July 30, 1864	Oath of Allegiance June 16, 1865
Hendrixon, Thomas W. Private	Unk	March 1, 1862, Vernon, Louisiana	Co. M, 12th Louisiana Infantry	May 16, 1863, Baker's Creek, Champion Hill, Mississippi	Point Lookout, Maryland, transferred to Elmira Prison, NY, August 18, 1864	Exchanged March 10, 1865. Died June 3, 1865 of Unknown Causes at Jackson Hospital, Richmond, VA

Name & Rank	Age	Enlisted	Regiment and State	Where Captured	Prison	Remarks
Henkle, Isaac D. Corporal	Unk	May 14, 1861, Franklin, Virginia	Co. E, 25th Virginia Infantry	May 5, 1864, Wilderness, Virginia	Point Lookout, Maryland, transferred to Elmira Prison, NY, August 14, 1864	Oath of Allegiance June 21, 1865
Henly, Edward Private	Unk	May 16, 1861, Radfordsville, Perry County, Alabama	Co. K, 8th Alabama Infantry	July 4, 1864, Gettysburg, Pennsylvania. Gunshot Wound Right Wrist.	Point Lookout, Maryland, transferred to Elmira Prison, NY, August 17, 1864	Oath of Allegiance June 19, 1865
Henly, Lewis D. Sergeant	21	April 20, 1861, Pickensville, Alabama	Co. H, 5th Alabama Infantry	March 25, 1865, Petersburg, Virginia. Gunshot Wound Left Thigh.	Old Capital Prison, Washington DC Transferred to Elmira Prison, NY, May 2, 1865.	Oath of Allegiance July 7, 1865
Hennesee, Patrick R. A. Private	22	July 25, 1861, Tullahoma, Tennessee	Co. E, 25th Tennessee Infantry	May 16, 1864, Near Drury's Bluff, Virginia	Point Lookout, Maryland, transferred to Elmira Prison, NY, August 17, 1864	Exchanged February 25, 1865 at Boulware's or Cox Wharf on the James River, Virginia
Hennesee, William A. Private	18	July 25, 1861, Tullahoma, Tennessee	Co. E, 25th Tennessee Infantry	May 16, 1864, Near Drury's Bluff, Virginia	Point Lookout, Maryland, transferred to Elmira Prison, NY, August 17, 1864	Exchanged February 25, 1865 at Boulware's or Cox Wharf on the James River, Virginia
Henning, James D. Corporal	28	February 28, 1862, Camp Pickens, Standardsville, Virginia	Co. D, 34th, Virginia Infantry	June 15, 1864, Near Petersburg, Virginia	Point Lookout, Maryland, transferred to Elmira Prison, NY, July 12, 1864	Exchanged March 10, 1865 at Boulware's Wharf on the James River, Virginia
Henning, Lorenzo D. Private	Unk	May 1, 1862, White Sulfur Springs, Virginia	Co. F, 22nd Virginia Infantry	June 3, 1864, Gaines Farm Cold Harbor, Virginia	Point Lookout, Maryland, transferred to Elmira Prison, NY, July 17, 1864	Died January 24, 1865 of Variola (Smallpox) Grave No. 1624
Hennissey, John Private	Unk	June 12, 1861, New Orleans, Louisiana	Co. K, 14th Louisiana Infantry	May 12, 1864, Spotsylvania Court House, Virginia	Point Lookout, Maryland, transferred to Elmira Prison, NY, July 25, 1864	Exchanged February 25, 1865 at Boulware's or Cox Wharf on the James River, Virginia

Name & Rank	Age	Enlisted	Regiment and State	Where Captured	Prison	Remarks
Henrick, William Sergeant	Unk	June 11, 1861, New Orleans, Louisiana	Co. J, 15th Louisiana Infantry	July 17,1864, Near Washington, DC	Old Capital Prison, Washington, DC, transferred to Elmira Prison, NY, July 23, 1864	Exchanged February 25, 1865 at Boulware's Wharf on the James River, Virginia
Henry, Edward J. Private	Unk	June 12, 1861, LaFayette, Walker County, Georgia	Co. G, 9th Georgia Infantry	May 6, 1864, Wilderness, Virginia	Old Capital Prison, Washington, DC, transferred to Elmira Prison, NY, July 14, 1864	Transferred For Exchange October 11, 1864 to Point Lookout Prison Camp, MD. Nothing Further.
Henry, Hiram Private	25	May 10, 1861, Camp Moore, Louisiana	Co. C, 5th Louisiana Infantry	May 5, 1864, Wilderness, Virginia	Point Lookout, Maryland, transferred to Elmira Prison, NY, August 17, 1864	Oath of Allegiance May 5, 1865
Henry, Joseph O. Private	Unk	Unknown	Co. J, 2nd Louisiana Cavalry	September 20, 1864, Near Morganza, Louisiana	Fort Columbus, NY Harbor, transferred to Elmira Prison, NY, December 4, 1864.	Orders for Elmira Prison, NY. Transferred to US Army Hospital Fort Columbus, NY Harbor. No Further Information Available.
Hensill, R. Private	Unk	October 6, 1862, Striders Mill, Virginia	Co. F, 1st Virginia Cavalry	August 22, 1864, Sharpsburg, Maryland	Old Capital Prison, Washington, DC transferred to Elmira Prison, NY, August 29, 1864	Exchanged March 14, 1865 at Boulware's Wharf on the James River, Virginia
Hensill, William J. Private	Unk	June 28, 1863, Shepherds-town, Virginia	Co. F, 1st Virginia Cavalry	August 22, 1864, Sharpsburg, Maryland	Old Capital Prison, Washington, DC transferred to Elmira Prison, NY, August 29, 1864	Exchanged October 29, 1864 at Venus Point, Savannah River, GA.
Henslee, Thomas N. Private	Unk	January 1, 1862, Tullahoma, Tennessee	Co. B, 17th Tennessee Infantry	June 17, 1864, Petersburg, Virginia	Point Lookout, Maryland, transferred to Elmira Prison, NY, July 30, 1864	Oath of Allegiance May 25, 1865

Name & Rank	Age	Enlisted	Regiment and State	Where Captured	Prison	Remarks
Hensley, Hiram L. Private	24	May 1, 1861, Burnsville, North Carolina	Co. C, 16th North Carolina Infantry	May 23, 1864, North Anna River, Virginia. Gunshot Wound Head and Scalp.	Old Capital Prison, Washington, DC, transferred to Elmira Prison, NY, August 12, 1864	Exchanged March 10, 1865 at Boulware's Wharf on the James River, Virginia
Hensley, James D. Corporal	Unk	April 20, 1861, Lexington, Virginia	Co. H, 4th Virginia Infantry	May 12, 1864, Spotsylvania Court House, Virginia	Point Lookout, Maryland, transferred to Elmira Prison, NY, August 2, 1864	Exchanged October 29, 1864 at Venus Point, Savannah River, GA.
Hensley, James H. Private	24	August 4, 1861, Milboro, Scott County, Virginia	Co. H, 48th Virginia Infantry	May 12, 1864, Near Spotsylvania Court House, Virginia	Point Lookout, Maryland, transferred to Elmira Prison, NY, August 6, 1864	Exchanged October 29, 1864 at Venus Point, Savannah River, GA.
Hensley, John H. Private	Unk	June 17, 1861, Rocky Mount, Virginia	Co. K, 42nd Virginia Infantry	May 12, 1864, Spotsylvania Court House, Virginia	Point Lookout, Maryland, transferred to Elmira Prison, NY, August 2, 1864	Oath of Allegiance June 27, 1865
Hensley, Robert A. Private	Unk	May 1, 1864, Pisgah Church, Virginia	Co. H, 42nd Virginia Infantry	May 12, 1864, Near Spotsylvania Court House, Virginia	Point Lookout, Maryland, transferred to Elmira Prison, NY, August 6, 1864	Transferred For Exchange October 11, 1864 to Point Lookout Prison Camp, MD. Nothing Further.
Hensley, Samuel Private	Unk	December 7, 1861, Camp Trousdale, Tennessee	Co. E, 44th Tennessee Infantry	June 17, 1864, Petersburg, Virginia	Point Lookout, Maryland, transferred to Elmira Prison, NY, July 30, 1864	Exchanged October 11, 1864. Nothing Further.
Henson, A. Newton Private	Unk	February 22, 1863, Camp Jenkins, North Carolina	Co. I, 17th South Carolina Infantry	July 30, 1864, Petersburg, Virginia	Point Lookout, Maryland, transferred to Elmira Prison, NY, August 12, 1864	Exchanged October 29, 1864 at Venus Point, Savannah River, GA.
Henson, George W. Private	Unk	March 10, 1862, Winchester, Virginia	Co. A, 2nd Virginia Infantry	May 12, 1864, Near Spotsylvania Court House, Virginia	Point Lookout, Maryland, transferred to Elmira Prison, NY, August 6, 1864	Oath of Allegiance May 15, 1865

Name & Rank	Age	Enlisted	Regiment and State	Where Captured	Prison	Remarks
Henson, James T. Private	Unk	May 6, 1862, Fair Play, Alabama	Co. K, 44th Alabama Infantry	July 29, 1864, Petersburg, Virginia	Point Lookout, Maryland, transferred to Elmira Prison, NY, August 12, 1864	Oath of Allegiance June 14, 1865
Hentz, F. W. Private	Unk	Unknown	Co. A, Captain Norwood's Home Guard Florida	September 27, 1864, Marianna, Florida	New Orleans, Louisiana transferred to Elmira November 19, 1864.	Exchanged March 2, 1865 at Akins Landing on the James River, Virginia
Herbert, John R. Private	Unk	Unknown	Co. F, 13th, Virginia Infantry	May 20, 1864, Spotsylvania Court House, Virginia	Point Lookout, Maryland, transferred to Elmira Prison, NY, July 12, 1864	Exchanged March 10, 1865 at Boulware's Wharf on the James River, Virginia
Hereford, Josiah Sergeant	Unk	June 22, 1861, Henry County, Virginia	Co. F, 42nd Virginia Infantry	May 12, 1864, Near Spotsylvania Court House, Virginia	Point Lookout, Maryland, transferred to Elmira Prison, NY, August 6, 1864	Oath of Allegiance June 23, 1865
Herman, Abel Private	Unk	August 13, 1861, Newton, North Carolina	Co. C, 28th North Carolina Infantry	July 14, 1863, Falling Waters, Maryland	Point Lookout, Maryland, transferred to Elmira Prison, NY, August 18, 1864	Died September 12, 1864 of Chronic Diarrhea, Grave No. 186. Headstone has Harmon.
Herman, Rufus D. Private	17	August 13, 1861, Newton, North Carolina	Co. C, 28th North Carolina Infantry	July 29, 1864, Petersburg, Virginia	Point Lookout, Maryland, transferred to Elmira Prison, NY, August 12, 1864	Oath of Allegiance July 3, 1865
Herndon, H. G. Corporal	Unk	August 28, 1861, Waterboro, South Carolina	Co. J, 11th South Carolina Infantry	June 24, 1864, Petersburg, Virginia	Point Lookout, Maryland, transferred to Elmira Prison, NY, August 18, 1864	Exchanged March 14, 1865 at Boulware's Wharf on the James River, Virginia
Herndon, James Private	21	July 15, 1862, Durham's Department, North Carolina	Co. F, 1st North Carolina Infantry	May 12, 1864, Wilderness, Spotsylvania Court House, Virginia	Point Lookout, Maryland, transferred to Elmira Prison, NY, August 6, 1864	Exchanged October 29, 1864 at Venus Point, Savannah River, GA.

Name & Rank	Age	Enlisted	Regiment and State	Where Captured	Prison	Remarks
Herndon, John Private	Unk	April 21, 1861, Memphis, Tennessee	Co. A, Jackson's 1st Regiment, Tennessee Heavy Artillery	August 23, 1864, Fort Morgan, Alabama	New Orleans, Louisiana transferred to Elmira Prison, NY, December 4, 1864.	Oath of Allegiance May 19, 1865
Herr, Henry Private	27	June 12, 1861, New Orleans, Louisiana	Co. K, 14th Louisiana Infantry	May 12, 1864, Spotsylvania Court House, Virginia	Point Lookout, Maryland, transferred to Elmira Prison, NY, July 25, 1864	Exchanged February 13, 1865 at Boulware's wharf on the James River, Virginia
Herrell, J. G. Citizen	Unk	Unknown	North Carolina Citizen	January 15, 1865, Fort Fisher, North Carolina	January 31, 1865, Elmira Prison Camp, New York	Died of Variola (Smallpox), Grave Not Found At Woodlawn Cemetery.
Herring, Benjamin Private	38	September 25, 1864, Fort Holmes, Brunswick County, North Carolina	Co. G, 40th Regiment, 3rd North Carolina Artillery	January 15, 1865, Fort Fisher, North Carolina	February 1, 1865, Elmira Prison Camp, New York	Died May 22, 1865 of Chronic Diarrhea, Grave No. 2932
Herring, Benjamin F. Corporal	15	October 14, 1861, Red Banks, Robeson County, North Carolina	Co. G, 40th Regiment, 3rd North Carolina Artillery	January 15, 1865, Fort Fisher, North Carolina	February 1, 1865, Elmira Prison Camp, New York	Oath of Allegiance May 17, 1865
Herring, Henderson Private	37	March 13, 1863, Camp Gregg, North Carolina	Co. E, 13th North Carolina Infantry	June 5, 1864, Cold Harbor, Virginia	Point Lookout, Maryland, transferred to Elmira Prison, NY, July 25, 1864	Oath of Allegiance September 19, 1864. Early Release per Lincoln's Proclamation, 12/8/1863.
Herring, James Private	16	July 14, 1863, Wayne County, North Carolina	Co. G, 40th Regiment, 3rd North Carolina Artillery	January 15, 1865, Fort Fisher, North Carolina	January 30, 1865 Elmira Prison Camp, New York	Died April 21, 1865 of Chronic Diarrhea, Grave No. 1386
Herring, John W. Sergeant	25	May 11, 1861, New Orleans, Louisiana	Co. K, 2nd Louisiana Infantry	May 12, 1864, Spotsylvania Court House, Virginia	Point Lookout, Maryland, transferred to Elmira Prison, NY, August 17, 1864	Exchanged October 29, 1864 at Venus Point, Savannah River, GA.

Name & Rank	Age	Enlisted	Regiment and State	Where Captured	Prison	Remarks
Herring, Oliver Private	Unk	March 10, 1864, Camp Holmes, North Carolina	Co. F, 51st North Carolina Infantry	May 16, 1864, Near Drury's Bluff, Virginia	Point Lookout, Maryland, transferred to Elmira Prison, NY, August 18, 1864	Died October 3, 1864 of Chronic Diarrhea, Grave No. 622
Herring, Stephen A. Private	Unk	July 15, 1862, Duplin County, North Carolina	Co. E, 61st North Carolina Infantry	August 27, 1863, Battery Wagner, Morris Island, South Carolina	Point Lookout, Maryland, transferred to Elmira Prison, NY, August 18, 1864	Exchanged October 29, 1864 at Venus Point, Savannah River, GA.
Herring, T. J. Private	Unk	August 15, 1862, Dale County, Alabama	Co. H, 15th Alabama Infantry	May 12, 1864, Spotsylvania Court House, Virginia	Point Lookout, Maryland, transferred to Elmira Prison, NY, July 30, 1864	Died June 4, 1865 of Chronic Diarrhea, Grave No. 2895
Herrings, Joseph B. Private	18	May 9, 1861, Clinton, North Carolina	Co. D, 20th North Carolina Infantry	May 12, 1864, Near Spotsylvania Court House, Virginia	Point Lookout Prison, Maryland. Transferred to Elmira Prison Camp New York August 14, 1864.	Oath of Allegiance June 23, 1865
Herrington, Elias M. Second Lieutenant	Unk	July 30, 1861, Salem, Virginia	Co. K, 8th Virginia Infantry	January 15, 1865, Farquier County, Virginia	November 11, 1864, Old Capital Prison, Washington, DC. February 4, 1865 Elmira, Prison Camp, NY	Oath of Allegiance July 7, 1865
Herron, Michael Private	26	June 7, 1861, Camp Moore, Louisiana	Co. C, 7th Louisiana Infantry	May 11, 1864, Near Spotsylvania Court House, Virginia	Point Lookout, Maryland, transferred to Elmira Prison, NY, August 17, 1864	Exchanged February 13, 1865 at Boulware's wharf on the James River, Virginia
Hershberger, John S. Private	Unk	June 2, 1861, Luray, Virginia	Co. K, 10th Virginia Infantry	May 12, 1864, Near Spotsylvania Court House, Virginia	Point Lookout, Maryland, transferred to Elmira Prison, NY, August 2, 1864	Exchanged February 20, 1865 at Boulware's or Cox Wharf on the James River, Virginia

Name & Rank	Age	Enlisted	Regiment and State	Where Captured	Prison	Remarks
Herst, J. G. Private	Unk	August 24, 1861, Lawrenceville, Georgia	Co. F, 24th Georgia Infantry	August 16, 1864, Front Royal, Virginia	Old Capital Prison, Washington, DC transferred to Elmira Prison, NY, August 29, 1864	Exchanged February 20, 1865 at Boulware's or Cox Wharf on the James River, Virginia
Hess, Thomas Private	Unk	Unknown	Co. E, 50th Virginia Infantry	May 12, 1864, Spotsylvania Court House, Virginia	Point Lookout, Maryland, transferred to Elmira Prison, NY, August 2, 1864	Oath of Allegiance July 3, 1865
Hesser, Andrew M. Private	28	July 24, 1861, Union, Virginia	Co. A, 6th Cavalry, Virginia	July 19, 1864, Petersburg, Virginia	Old Capital Prison, Washington, D. C., transferred to Elmira July 23, 1864	Exchanged March 10, 1865 at Boulware's Wharf on the James River, Virginia
Hesser, Colvert C. Private	Unk	June 27, 1863, Snickersville, Virginia	Co. A, 6th Cavalry, Virginia	June 1, 1864, Cold Harbor, Virginia	Point Lookout, Maryland, transferred to Elmira Prison, NY, July 17, 1864	Oath of Allegiance May 31, 1865
Hessey, Edward H. Private	35	June 9, 1861, Camp Jackson, Virginia	Co. B, 2nd Virginia Infantry	May 12, 1864, Near Spotsylvania Court House, Virginia	Point Lookout, Maryland, transferred to Elmira Prison, NY, August 6, 1864	Exchanged October 29, 1864 at Venus Point, Savannah River, GA.
Hester, David D. Private	18	January 1, 1864, Elizabethtown, Bladen County, North Carolina	Co. K, 40th Regiment, 3rd North Carolina Artillery	January 15, 1865, Fort Fisher, North Carolina	February 1, 1865, Elmira Prison Camp, New York	Died February 6, 1865 of Pneumonia-Typhoid Fever, Grave No. 1910
Hester, Jasper Private	18	June 8, 1864, Fort Holmes, Brunswick County, North Carolina	Co. K, 40th Regiment, 3rd North Carolina Artillery	January 15, 1865, Fort Fisher, North Carolina	February 1, 1865, Elmira Prison Camp, New York	Died February 28, 1865 of Typhoid Fever, Grave No. 2133
Hester, Stephen Private	21	October 2, 1862, Raleigh, North Carolina	Co. K, 28th North Carolina Infantry	May 12, 1864, Spotsylvania Court House, Virginia	Point Lookout, Maryland, transferred to Elmira Prison, NY, August 14, 1864	Died September 20, 1864 of Pneumonia, Grave No. 350

Name & Rank	Age	Enlisted	Regiment and State	Where Captured	Prison	Remarks
Hester, William B. Private	18	January 1, 1864, Elizabethtown, Bladen County, North Carolina	Co. K, 40th Regiment, 3rd North Carolina Artillery	January 15, 1865, Fort Fisher, North Carolina	February 1, 1865, Elmira Prison Camp, New York	Exchanged March 2, 1865 at Boulware's Wharf on the James River, Virginia
Hester, William J. Private	19	January 1, 1864, Elizabethtown, Bladen County, North Carolina	Co. K, 40th Regiment, 3rd North Carolina Artillery	January 15, 1865, Fort Fisher, North Carolina	February 1, 1865, Elmira Prison Camp, New York	Died March 29, 1865 of Pneumonia, Grave No. 2589
Hestle, W. J. Private	Unk	January 29, 1864, Wilcox, Alabama	Co. F, 1st Battalion Alabama Artillery	August 23, 1864, Fort Morgan, Alabama	Steam Press No. 4 New Orleans, Louisiana transferred to Elmira October 8, 1864.	Oath of Allegiance June 21, 1865
Hewett, Abel K. Private	21	May 25, 1861, Camp Howard, Brunswick County, North Carolina	Co. G, 3rd North Carolina Infantry	May 12, 1864, Near Spotsylvania Court House, Virginia	Point Lookout, Maryland, transferred to Elmira Prison, NY, August 14, 1864	Oath of Allegiance June 27, 1865
Hewett, Doherty W. Private	17	October 26, 1863, Fort Campbell, Brunswick County, North Carolina	Co. G, 36th Regiment 2nd North Carolina Artillery	January 15, 1865, Fort Fisher, North Carolina	February 1, 1865, Elmira Prison Camp, New York	Died March 26, 1865 of Pneumonia, Grave No. 1680
Hewett, Richard Private	Unk	May 28, 1861, Warrenton, Virginia	Co. C, 49th Virginia Infantry	September 19, 1864, Farquier County, Virginia	Old Capital Prison, Washington, DC transferred to Elmira Prison, NY, August 27, 1864	Oath of Allegiance July 11, 1865
Hewitt, Allen Private	Unk	April 25, 1864, Decatur, Georgia	Co. E, 12th Georgia Infantry	July 17,1864, Near Washington, DC	Old Capital Prison, Washington, DC, transferred to Elmira July 23, 1864	Exchanged 2/20/64. Died 3/12/65 of Intermittent Fever at Jackson Hospital Richmond, VA.
Hewitt, Ephram Private	19	May 4, 1864, Brunswick County, North Carolina	Co. G, 36th Regiment 2nd North Carolina Artillery	January 15, 1865, Fort Fisher, North Carolina	February 1, 1865, Elmira Prison Camp, New York	Exchanged March 2, 1865 at Boulware's Wharf on the James River, Virginia

Name & Rank	Age	Enlisted	Regiment and State	Where Captured	Prison	Remarks
Hewitt, Isaiah Private	26	September 4, 1863, Fort Campbell, Brunswick County, North Carolina	Co. G, 36th Regiment 2nd North Carolina Artillery	January 15, 1865, Fort Fisher, North Carolina	February 1, 1865, Elmira Prison Camp, New York	Exchanged February 20, 1865 at Boulware's or Cox Wharf on the James River, Virginia
Hewitt, J. R. Private	Unk	Unknown	Co. B, 36th Regiment 2nd North Carolina Artillery	January 15, 1865, Fort Fisher, North Carolina	February 1, 1865, Elmira Prison Camp, New York	Transferred to USA General Hospital July 13, 1865. No Additional Information.
Hewitt, John J. Private	Unk	June 21, 1861, Valdosta, Georgia	Co. J, 12th Georgia Infantry	May 10, 1864, Spotsylvania Court House, Virginia	Point Lookout, Maryland, transferred to Elmira Prison, NY, July 25, 1864	Oath of Allegiance June 30, 1865
Hewitt, Theodore F. Private	17	January 28, 1862, Onslow County, North Carolina	Co. G, 3rd North Carolina Infantry	May 12, 1864, Near Spotsylvania Court House, Virginia	Point Lookout Prison, Maryland. Transferred to Elmira Prison Camp New York August 14, 1864.	Exchanged October 29, 1864 at Venus Point, Savannah River, GA.
Hibbits, Ira K. Sergeant	Unk	December 30, 1861, Nashville, Tennessee	Co. J, 44th Tennessee Infantry	May 16, 1864, Near Drury's Bluff, Virginia	Point Lookout, Maryland, transferred to Elmira Prison, NY, August 17, 1864	Oath of Allegiance May 15, 1865
Hibble, M. C. Private	Unk	June 2, 1861, Gloucester Court House, Virginia	Co. C, 24th Virginia Cavalry	July 28, 1864, Petersburg, Virginia	Point Lookout, Maryland, transferred to Elmira Prison, NY, August 12, 1864	Died January 27, 1865 of Chronic Diarrhea, Grave No. 1647
Hickey, William Private	27	July 3, 1861, Atlanta, Georgia	Co. B, 11th Georgia Infantry	May 6, 1864, Wilderness, Virginia	Old Capital Prison, Washington, DC, transferred to Elmira Prison, NY, July 14, 1864	Oath of Allegiance July 11, 1865
Hickman, Eli Private	Unk	January 25, 1864, Raleigh, North Carolina	Co. G, 26th North Carolina Infantry	May 12, 1864, Spotsylvania Court House, Virginia	Point Lookout, Maryland, transferred to Elmira Prison, NY, July 30, 1864	Died January 27, 1865 of Variola (smallpox), Grave No. 1640

Name & Rank	Age	Enlisted	Regiment and State	Where Captured	Prison	Remarks
Hickman, Harrison Private	Unk	October 9, 1863, Lewisburg, Virginia	Co. A, 26th Virginia Infantry	June 3, 1864, Gaines Farm Cold Harbor, Virginia	Point Lookout, Maryland, transferred to Elmira Prison, NY, July 17,1864	Died May 14, 1864 of Chronic Diarrhea Grave No. 2803
Hickman, J. Private	Unk	Unknown	Co. A, 25th Virginia Infantry	May 12, 1864, Spotsylvania Court House, Virginia	Point Lookout, Maryland, transferred to Elmira Prison, NY, August 2, 1864	Transferred for Exchange October 11, 1864. Nothing Further.
Hickman, Robert Private	33	September 2, 1861, Smithville, Brunswick County, North Carolina	Co. C, 30th North Carolina Infantry	May 12, 1864, Near Spotsylvania Court House, Virginia	Point Lookout, Maryland, transferred to Elmira Prison, NY, August 14, 1864	Died December 6, 1864 of Pneumonia, Grave No. 1022
Hickman, Samuel H. Corporal	18	May 25, 1861, Camp Howard, Brunswick County, North Carolina	Co. G, 3rd North Carolina Infantry	May 12, 1864, Near Spotsylvania Court House, Virginia	Point Lookout, Maryland, transferred to Elmira Prison, NY, August 14, 1864	Oath of Allegiance August 7, 1865
Hickman, Stewart Corporal	24	April 16, 1862, Old Brunswick Town, North Carolina	Co. G, 36th Regiment 2nd North Carolina Artillery	January 15, 1865, Fort Fisher, North Carolina	February 1, 1865, Elmira Prison Camp, New York	Oath of Allegiance August 7, 1865
Hickman, William B. Private	17	Unknown	Co. E, 36th Regiment 2nd North Carolina Artillery	January 15, 1865, Fort Fisher, North Carolina	February 1, 1865, Elmira Prison Camp, New York	Died February 28, 1865 of Chronic Diarrhea, Grave No. 2117
Hickok, James W. Private	31	April 17, 1861, Christians-burg, Virginia	Co. G, 4th Virginia Infantry	May 12, 1864, Spotsylvania Court House, Virginia	Point Lookout, Maryland, transferred to Elmira Prison, NY, August 2, 1864	Exchanged February 20, 1865 at Boulware's or Cox Wharf on the James River, Virginia
Hicks, A. W. Private	Unk	Unknown	Co. H, 8th North Carolina Infantry	May 6, 1864, Wilderness, Virginia	Point Lookout, Maryland, transferred to Elmira Prison, NY, August 14, 1864	Oath of Allegiance June 23, 1865
Hicks, George T. Private	18	June 25, 1863, Fort Johnson, North Carolina	Co. G, 40th Regiment, 3rd North Carolina Artillery	January 15, 1865, Fort Fisher, North Carolina	January 30, 1865, Elmira Prison Camp, New York	Died March 31, 1865 of Pneumonia, Grave No. 2599

Name & Rank	Age	Enlisted	Regiment and State	Where Captured	Prison	Remarks
Hicks, Henry C. Sergeant	20	August 6, 1861, Crabtree, Raleigh, North Carolina	Co. D, 31st North Carolina Infantry	June 1, 1864, Gaines Farm Cold Harbor, Virginia	Point Lookout, Maryland, transferred to Elmira Prison, NY, July 17,1864	Exchanged March 2, 1865 at Akins Landing on the James River, Virginia
Hicks, Hiram M. Private	Unk	March 4, 1864, Fayetteville, Georgia	Co. G, 44th Georgia Infantry	June 10, 1864, Spotsylvania Court House, Virginia	Point Lookout, Maryland, transferred to Elmira Prison, NY, July 25, 1864	Oath of Allegiance July 11, 1865
Hicks, J. D. Private	Unk	August 16, 1863, Camp Jackson, Georgia	Co. D, 20th Georgia Cavalry	May 28, 1864, Hall's Shop, Virginia	Point Lookout, Maryland, transferred to Elmira Prison, NY, July 12, 1864	Died September 12, 1864 of Chronic Diarrhea, Grave No. 179
Hicks, James Private	Unk	Unknown	Co. G, 20th North Carolina Infantry	August 22, 1864, Charlestown, Virginia	Old Capital Prison, Washington, DC transferred to Elmira Prison, NY, August 29, 1864	Oath of Allegiance May 29, 1865
Hicks, James F. Private	Unk	July 24, 1861, Hartwell, Georgia	Co. B, 3rd Battalion Georgia Sharp Shooters	August 16, 1864, Front Royal, Virginia	Old Capital Prison, Washington, DC transferred to Elmira Prison, NY, August 29, 1864	Oath of Allegiance June 21, 1865
Hicks, James H. Private	19	June 10, 1861, Wilmington, North Carolina	Co. F, 3rd North Carolina Infantry	May 12, 1864, Spotsylvania Court House, Virginia	Point Lookout, Maryland, transferred to Elmira Prison, NY, August 14, 1864	Oath of Allegiance May 19, 1865
Hicks, John C. Private	Unk	March 13, 1862, Hamer, Banks County, Georgia	Co. A, 24th Georgia Infantry	August 16, 1864, Front Royal, Virginia	Old Capitol Prison, Washington, D. C., transferred to Elmira October 28, 1864	Died October 19, 1864 of Chronic Diarrhea, Grave No. 530
Hicks, Marion H. Sergeant	35	December 7, 1861, Camp Trousdale, Tennessee	Co. B, 44th Tennessee Infantry	June 17, 1864, Petersburg, Virginia	Point Lookout, Maryland, transferred to Elmira Prison, NY, July 30, 1864	Oath of Allegiance May 2, 1865

Name & Rank	Age	Enlisted	Regiment and State	Where Captured	Prison	Remarks
Hicks, Peyton Private	Unk	May 12, 1862, Camp McIntosh, North Carolina	Co. D, 1st North Carolina Infantry	May 30, 1864, Cold Harbor, Virginia	Point Lookout, Maryland, transferred to Elmira Prison, NY, July 12, 1864	Died September 30, 1864 of Typhoid-Pneumonia, Grave No. 405
Hicks, R. D. Private	Unk	July 2, 1861, Bethel, Virginia	Co. C, 50th Virginia Infantry	May 12, 1864, Spotsylvania Court House, Virginia	Point Lookout, Maryland, transferred to Elmira Prison, NY, July 30, 1864	Oath of Allegiance June 23, 1865
Hicks, Thornton Private	Unk	July 25, 1863, Danbury, North Carolina	Co. F, 21st North Carolina Infantry	August 21, 1864, Charlestown, Virginia	Old Capital Prison, Washington, DC transferred to Elmira Prison, NY, August 29, 1864	Died February 13, 1865 of Chronic Diarrhea, Grave No. 2048
Hickson, John Civilian	Unk	Unknown	Citizen of Loudoun County, Virginia	January 13, 1864, Loudoun County, Virginia	Point Lookout, Maryland, transferred to Elmira Prison, NY, July 25, 1864	Oath of Allegiance November 30, 1864. Early Release Per Lincoln's Proclamation, 12/8/1863.
Hickson, William L. Private	Unk	April 30, 1862, McClellans-ville, South Carolina	Co. H, 26th South Carolina Infantry	July 30, 1864, Petersburg, Virginia	Point Lookout, Maryland, transferred to Elmira Prison, NY, August 12, 1864	Died October 6, 1864 of Typhoid-Pneumonia, Grave No. 584
Higdon, J. T. Private	Unk	January 2, 1864, Butler County, Alabama	Co. A, 1st Alabama Artillery	August 23, 1864, Fort Morgan, Alabama	New Orleans, Louisiana transferred to Elmira Prison, NY, December 4, 1864.	Died January 11, 1865 of Pneumonia, Grave No. 1483
Higginbotham Lewis W. Private	30	August 13, 1862, Lake City, Florida	Co. D, 2nd Battalion Florida Infantry	June 27, 1864, Near Petersburg, Florida	Point Lookout, Maryland, transferred to Elmira Prison, NY, July 25, 1864	Exchanged March 2, 1865 at Akins Landing on the James River, Virginia
Higgins, Benjamin F. Private	19	July 1, 1861, Jacksonville, Onslow County, North Carolina	Co. G, 3rd North Carolina Infantry	May 12, 1864, Near Spotsylvania Court House, Virginia	Point Lookout Prison, Maryland. Transferred to Elmira Prison Camp, New York, August 14, 1864.	Exchanged March 2, 1865 at Akins Landing on the James River, Virginia

Name & Rank	Age	Enlisted	Regiment and State	Where Captured	Prison	Remarks
Higgins, George Y. Corporal	Unk	July 1, 1861, Selma, Alabama	Jeff Davis Alabama Artillery	May 5, 1864, Wilderness, Virginia	Point Lookout, Maryland, transferred to Elmira Prison Camp, NY, August 17, 1864	Oath of Allegiance May 16, 1865
Higgins, John Y. Sergeant	Unk	June 13, 1861, Lebanon, DeKalb County, Alabama	Co. E, 12th Alabama Infantry	July 17, 1864, Near Washington, DC	Old Capital Prison, Washington, DC, transferred to Elmira Prison, NY, July 23, 1864	Oath of Allegiance May 29, 1865
Higgins, Thomas Sergeant	Unk	May 9, 1861, New Orleans, Louisiana	Co. B, 2nd Louisiana Infantry	May 20, 1864, Spotsylvania Court House, Virginia	Point Lookout, Maryland, transferred to Elmira Prison, NY, July 3, 1864	Exchanged February 13, 1865 at Boulware's wharf on the James River, Virginia
Higgins, William Private	Unk	July 18, 1863, Secessionville, South Carolina	Co. J, 11th South Carolina Infantry	June 18, 1864, Petersburg, Virginia	Point Lookout, Maryland, transferred to Elmira Prison, NY, July 30, 1864	Exchanged October 29, 1864 at Venus Point, Savannah River, GA.
Higgs, Henry Private	28	March 24, 1862, Luray, Virginia	Co. K, 10th Virginia Infantry	May 12, 1864, Spotsylvania Court House, Virginia	Point Lookout, Maryland, transferred to Elmira Prison, NY, August 2, 1864	Oath of Allegiance June 27, 1865
Higgs, William Corporal	Unk	May 19, 1861, New Orleans, Louisiana	Co. A, 59th Virginia Infantry	June 17, 1864, Petersburg, Virginia	Point Lookout, Maryland, transferred to Elmira Prison, NY, July 30, 1864	Died November 16, 1864 of Chronic Diarrhea, Grave No. 957
High, E. D. Private	Unk	August 10, 1861, Albany, Georgia	Co. D, Cobb's Legion, Georgia	May 31, 1864, Hanover Court House, Cold Harbor, Virginia	Point Lookout, Maryland, transferred to Elmira Prison, NY, July 17, 1864	Exchanged October 29, 1864 at Venus Point, Savannah River, GA.
Hight, John H. Private	28	March 9, 1862, Greenville, Virginia	Co. E, 5th Virginia Infantry	September 22, 1864, Fishers Hill, Virginia	Old Capital Prison, Washington, DC, transferred to Elmira Prison, NY, December 17, 1864	Exchanged March 10, 1865 at Boulware's Wharf on the James River, Virginia

Name & Rank	Age	Enlisted	Regiment and State	Where Captured	Prison	Remarks
Hightower, Charnel Private	Unk	July 11, 1861, Wrightsville, Johnson County, Georgia	Co. E, 14th Georgia Infantry	May 6, 1864, Wilderness, Virginia	Old Capital Prison, Washington, DC, transferred to Elmira Prison, NY, July 14, 1864	Oath of Allegiance May 11, 1865
Higman, Abram R. Private	Unk	February 11, 1863, Bastross, Louisiana	Co. F, 12th Louisiana Infantry	May 16, 1863, Baker's Creek, Champion Hill, Mississippi	Point Lookout, Maryland, transferred to Elmira Prison, NY, August 18, 1864	Exchanged October 29, 1864 at Venus Point, Savannah River, GA.
Hildreth, Thomas Private	43	August 20, 1863, Fort Branch, Martin County, North Carolina	Co. G, 40th Regiment, 3rd North Carolina Artillery	January 15, 1865, Fort Fisher, North Carolina	January 30, 1865, Elmira Prison Camp, New York	Died March 2, 1865 of Pneumonia, Grave No. 2007
Hiles, Thompson Private	Unk	May 16, 1861, Alisona, Tennessee	Co. A, 17th Tennessee Infantry	June 17, 1864, Petersburg, Virginia	Point Lookout, Maryland, transferred to Elmira Prison, NY, July 30, 1864	Exchanged February 25, 1865 at Boulware's or Cox Wharf on the James River, Virginia
Hill, Abraham R. Private	Unk	April 24, 1862, Swift Run Gap, Virginia	Co. E, 2nd, Virginia Infantry	May 20, 1864, Spotsylvania Court House, Virginia	Point Lookout, Maryland, transferred to Elmira Prison, NY, July 6, 1864	Oath of Allegiance June 30, 1865
Hill, Benjamin F. Private	Unk	December 30, 1861, Nashville, Tennessee	Co. J, 44th Tennessee Infantry	May 16, 1864, Near Drury's Bluff, Virginia	Point Lookout, Maryland, transferred to Elmira Prison, NY, August 17, 1864	Oath of Allegiance May 15, 1865
Hill, Benjamin F. P. Private	Unk	October 28, 1863, Augusta, Georgia	Co. A, 16th Georgia Infantry	August 16, 1864, Front Royal, Virginia	Point Lookout, Maryland, transferred to Elmira Prison, NY, August 29, 1864	Oath of Allegiance July 11, 1865
Hill, Duncan Private	23	September 25, 1861, Camp Branch, Roxboro, North Carolina	Co. E, 35th North Carolina Infantry	June 17, 1864, Petersburg, Virginia	Point Lookout, Maryland, transferred to Elmira Prison, NY, July 30, 1864	Oath of Allegiance July 3, 1865

Name & Rank	Age	Enlisted	Regiment and State	Where Captured	Prison	Remarks
Hill, Elias Private	Unk	May 13, 1862, Darlington, South Carolina	Co. B, 21st South Carolina Infantry	January 15, 1865, Fort Fisher, North Carolina	January 30, 1865, Elmira Prison Camp, New York	Died May 2, 1865 of Chronic Diarrhea, Grave No. 2744
Hill, H. H. Private	Unk	March 4, 1862, LaFayette, Georgia	Co. G, 11th Georgia Infantry	May 6, 1864, Wilderness, Virginia	Old Capital Prison, Washington, DC, transferred to Elmira Prison, NY, July 14, 1864	Oath of Allegiance June 23, 1865
Hill, Henry W. Private	17	March 28, 1861, Rome, Georgia	Co. K, 21st Georgia Infantry	May 12, 1864, Spotsylvania Court House, Virginia	Old Capital Prison, Washington, DC, transferred to Elmira Prison, NY, August 12, 1864	Oath of Allegiance June 14, 1865
Hill, James private	Unk	July 30, 1861, Bowdon, Georgia	Co. B, Cobb's Legion Georgia	August 16, 1864, Front Royal, Virginia	Old Capital Prison, Washington, DC transferred to Elmira Prison, NY, August 29, 1864	Died March 25, 1865 of Pneumonia, Grave No. 2464
Hill, James J. Private	Unk	May 1, 1863, Jackson, South Carolina	Co. I, 18th South Carolina Infantry	July 30, 1864, Petersburg, Virginia	Point Lookout, Maryland, transferred to Elmira Prison, NY, August 12, 1864	Died October 14, 1864 of Erysipelas, Grave No. 704
Hill, John Sergeant	Unk	July 3, 1861, Lynchburg, Virginia	Co. G, 42nd Virginia Infantry	May 12, 1864, Spotsylvania Court House, Virginia	Point Lookout, Maryland, transferred to Elmira Prison, NY, August 6, 1864	Died October 19, 1864 of Chronic Diarrhea, Grave No. 538
Hill, John F. Sergeant	Unk	May 16, 1861, Alisona, Tennessee	Co. A, 17th Tennessee Infantry	June 17, 1864, Petersburg, Virginia	Point Lookout, Maryland, transferred to Elmira Prison, NY, July 30, 1864	Exchanged February 25, 1865 at Boulware's or Cox Wharf on the James River, Virginia
Hill, John W. Private	19	June 3, 1861, Wise County Court House, Virginia	Co. H, 50th Virginia Infantry	May 6, 1864, Wilderness, Virginia	Point Lookout, Maryland, transferred to Elmira Prison, NY, August 14, 1864	Died December 15, 1864 of Pneumonia, Grave No. 1060

Name & Rank	Age	Enlisted	Regiment and State	Where Captured	Prison	Remarks
Hill, Laban L. Private	Unk	October 1, 1862, Snickersville, Virginia	Co. A, 6th Virginia Cavalry	July 17, 1864, Petersburg, Virginia	Old Capital Prison, Washington, DC, transferred to Elmira July 23, 1864	Exchanged March 10, 1865 at Boulware's Wharf on the James River, Virginia
Hill, Merritt R. Sergeant	23	September 19, 1861, Dalton, Georgia	Co. F, 60th Georgia Infantry	May 12, 1864, Spotsylvania, Virginia	Point Lookout, Maryland, transferred to Elmira Prison, NY, August 17, 1864	Died January 12, 1865 of Chronic Diarrhea, Grave No. 1195
Hill, Owen C. Sergeant	21	July 1, 1861, Jacksonville, Onslow County, North Carolina	Co. G, 3rd North Carolina Infantry	May 12, 1864, Near Spotsylvania Court House, Virginia	Point Lookout Prison, Maryland. Transferred to Elmira Prison Camp New York August 14, 1864.	Exchanged February 20, 1865 at Boulware's or Cox Wharf on the James River, Virginia
Hill, Pinkney Private	32	May 14, 1862, Lenoir County, North Carolina	Co. E, 61st North Carolina Infantry	August 27, 1863, Battery Wagner, Morris Island, South Carolina	Point Lookout, Maryland, transferred to Elmira Prison, NY, August 18, 1864	Exchanged March 10, 1865 at Boulware's Wharf on the James River, Virginia
Hill, Richard C. Private	Unk	July 15, 1862, Lenoir County, North Carolina	Co. E, 61st North Carolina Infantry	August 27, 1863, Battery Wagner, Morris Island, South Carolina	Point Lookout, Maryland, transferred to Elmira Prison, NY, August 18, 1864	Exchanged March 10, 1865 at Boulware's Wharf on the James River, Virginia
Hill, Robert F. Private	Unk	July 9, 1861, Dublin, Georgia	Co. H, 14th Georgia Infantry	May 12, 1864, Spotsylvania Court House, Virginia	Point Lookout, Maryland, transferred to Elmira Prison, NY, July 30, 1864	Oath of Allegiance June 12, 1865
Hill, Thomas W. Private	Unk	Unknown	Co. H, 26th North Carolina Infantry	Unknown	Unknown	Died April 18, 1865 of Unknown Disease, Grave No. 1491
Hill, W. E. Corporal	Unk	June 17, 1862, Savannah, Georgia	Co. B, 7th Georgia Cavalry	June 11, 1864, Trevilian Station, Louisa Court House, Virginia	Point Lookout, Maryland, transferred to Elmira Prison, NY, July 25, 1864	Exchanged October 29, 1864 at Venus Point, Savannah River, GA.

Name & Rank	Age	Enlisted	Regiment and State	Where Captured	Prison	Remarks
Hill, Walter Private	Unk	May 8, 1862, Augusta, Georgia	Co. A, 7th Georgia Cavalry	June 11, 1864, Trevilian Station, Louisa Court House, Virginia	Point Lookout, Maryland, transferred to Elmira Prison, NY, July 25, 1864	Died December 8, 1864 of Typhoid-Pneumonia, Grave No. 1179
Hill, Webb H. Private	21	October 9, 1861, Enfield, Wayne County, North Carolina	Co. F, 36th Regiment 2nd North Carolina Artillery	January 15, 1865, Fort Fisher, North Carolina	February 1, 1865, Elmira Prison Camp, New York	Oath of Allegiance May 29, 1865
Hill, William E. Sergeant	Unk	August 13, 1861, Center Hill, Georgia	Co. B, 16th Georgia Infantry	June 1, 1864, Cold Harbor, Virginia	Point Lookout, Maryland, transferred to Elmira Prison, NY, July 17,1864	Oath of Allegiance June 7, 1865
Hill, William H. Private	Unk	October 11, 1861, Savannah, Georgia	Co. G, 60th Georgia Infantry	May 6, 1864, Wilderness, Virginia	Old Capital Prison, Washington, DC, transferred to Elmira Prison, NY, July 14, 1864	Died November 14, 1864 of Pneumonia, Grave No. 814
Hill, William J. Private	Unk	February 22, 1862, Conyers, South Carolina	Co. A, 3rd Battalion, Georgia Sharp Shooters	July 29, 1864, Near Petersburg, Virginia	Point Lookout, Maryland, transferred to Elmira Prison, NY, August 12, 1864	Oath of Allegiance June 14, 1865
Hillery, William H. Private	Unk	September 1, 1863, Camp Miller, Virginia	Co. D, 20th Virginia Cavalry	August 4, 1864, Sharpsburg, Maryland	Old Capital Prison, Washington, DC, transferred to Elmira Prison, NY, August 12, 1864	Oath of Allegiance July 11, 1865
Hilliard, John C. Private	48	June 4, 1861, Camp Moore, Louisiana	Co. D, 6th Louisiana Infantry	May 5, 1864, Wilderness, Virginia	Point Lookout, Maryland, transferred to Elmira Prison, NY, August 17, 1864	Exchanged February 20, 1865. Died March 4, 1865 of Erysipelas at CSA Hospital No. 9, Richmond, VA.
Hilliard, Thomas H. Private	27	June 1, 1862, Richmond, Virginia	Co. E, 12th North Carolina Infantry	May 12, 1864, Near Spotsylvania, Virginia	Point Lookout, Maryland, transferred to Elmira Prison, NY, August 14, 1864	Oath of Allegiance June 23, 1865

Name & Rank	Age	Enlisted	Regiment and State	Where Captured	Prison	Remarks
Hilliard, William J. Private	Unk	April 28, 1862, New Hanover County, North Carolina	Co. E, 51st North Carolina Infantry	May 16, 1864, Near Drury's Bluff, Virginia	Point Lookout, Maryland, transferred to Elmira Prison, NY, August 18, 1864	Exchanged at Venus Point, Savannah River, GA, 10/29/1864.
Hillingham, James H. Sergeant	Unk	Unknown	Co. J, 2nd Virginia Infantry	May 12, 1864, Near Spotsylvania Court House, Virginia	Point Lookout, Maryland, transferred to Elmira Prison, NY, August 6, 1864	Oath of Allegiance June 27, 1865
Hillman, Henry W. Private	28	April 15, 1862, Buena Vista, Georgia	Co. K, 12th Georgia Infantry	May 10, 1864, Spotsylvania Court House, Virginia	Point Lookout, Maryland, transferred to Elmira Prison, NY, July 25, 1864	Oath of Allegiance June 20, 1865
Hilly, T. R. Private	21	July 13, 1861, Hartwell, Georgia	Co. C, 16th Georgia Infantry	June 1, 1864, Gaines Farm Cold Harbor, Virginia	Point Lookout, Maryland, transferred to Elmira Prison, NY, July 17,1864	Oath of Allegiance July 3, 1865
Hillyard, John W. Corporal	18	May 7, 1861, New Prospect, Virginia	Co. C, 26th North Carolina Infantry	May 12, 1864, Spotsylvania Court House, Virginia	Point Lookout, Maryland, transferred to Elmira Prison, NY, July 30, 1864	Transferred for Exchange 10/11/64. Died 10/26/64 at Point Lookout Prison Camp, MD.
Hilton, James M. Private	30	July 15, 1861, Guilford County, North Carolina	Co. A, 1st North Carolina Infantry	May 12, 1864, Spotsylvania Court House, Virginia	Point Lookout, Maryland, transferred to Elmira Prison, NY, August 6, 1864	Oath of Allegiance May 19, 1865
Hilton, Jonathan W. Sergeant	27	June 26, 1861, Scott County, Virginia	Co. H, 42nd Virginia Infantry	May 12, 1864, Near Spotsylvania Court House, Virginia	Point Lookout, Maryland, transferred to Elmira Prison, NY, August 6, 1864	Exchanged October 29, 1864 at Venus Point, Savannah River, GA.
Hilton, W. Private	Unk	Unknown	Co. C, 18th Georgia Infantry	June 1, 1864, Cold Harbor, Virginia	Point Lookout, Maryland, transferred to Elmira Prison, NY, July 17,1864	Exchanged October 29, 1864 at Venus Point, Savannah River, GA.

Name & Rank	Age	Enlisted	Regiment and State	Where Captured	Prison	Remarks
Hilton, W. A. Private	Unk	March 13, 1862, Hamer, Banks County Georgia	Co. A, 24th Georgia Infantry	June 1, 1864, Cold Harbor, Virginia	Point Lookout, Maryland, transferred to Elmira Prison, NY, July 17,1864	Exchanged February 20, 1865 at Boulware's or Cox Wharf on the James River, Virginia
Hilton, William L. Corporal	Unk	March 19, 1862, Scott County, Virginia	Co. H, 48th Virginia Infantry	May 12, 1864, Near Spotsylvania Court House, Virginia	Point Lookout, Maryland, transferred to Elmira Prison, NY, August 6, 1864	Exchanged October 29, 1864 at Venus Point, Savannah River, GA.
Hilton, William T. Private	23	June 26, 1861, Scott County, Virginia	Co. H, 48th Virginia Infantry	May 12, 1864, Near Spotsylvania Court House, Virginia	Point Lookout, Maryland, transferred to Elmira Prison, NY, August 6, 1864	Exchanged October 29, 1864 at Venus Point, Savannah River, GA.
Himes, James Private	Unk	May 16, 1861, Alisona, Tennessee	Co. A, 17th Tennessee Infantry	June 17, 1864, Petersburg, Virginia	Point Lookout, Maryland, transferred to Elmira Prison, NY, July 30, 1864	Oath of Allegiance May 29, 1865
Hine, Edward A. Private	29	March 18, 1862, Winston, North Carolina	Co. K, 52nd North Carolina Infantry	May 12, 1864, Spotsylvania Court House, Virginia	Point Lookout, Maryland, transferred to Elmira Prison, NY, July 30, 1864	Oath of Allegiance June 12, 1865
Hinely, Israel Private	Unk	April 29, 1862, Camp Leon, Madison, Florida	Co. D, 5th Florida Infantry	May 12, 1864, Spotsylvania Court House, Virginia	Point Lookout, Maryland, transferred to Elmira Prison, NY, July 30, 1864	Oath of Allegiance July 11, 1865
Hines, Edward Private	19	May 31, 1861, Middle Sound, New Hanover County, North Carolina	Co. E, 1st North Carolina Infantry	May 12, 1864, Spotsylvania Court House, Virginia	Point Lookout, Maryland, transferred to Elmira Prison, NY, August 6, 1864	Oath of Allegiance June 14, 1865
Hines, Henry C. Private	25	August 6, 1861, Lenoir County, North Carolina	Co. A, 40th Regiment, 3rd North Carolina Artillery	January 15, 1865, Fort Fisher, North Carolina	February 1, 1865, Elmira Prison Camp, New York	Died March 26, 1865 of Pneumonia, Grave No. 2465

Name & Rank	Age	Enlisted	Regiment and State	Where Captured	Prison	Remarks
Hines, J. M. Private	Unk	February 22, 1862, Linden, Texas	Co. J, 32nd Texas Cavalry	September 19, 1864, Tensan Parish, Louisiana	New Orleans, LA, Transferred to Elmira Prison, NY, November 19, 1864	Died April 13, 1865 of Variola (Smallpox), Grave No. 2702. Headstone has G. W. Hines 34th Texas Cavalry
Hines, James W. Sergeant	Unk	May 14, 1862, Camp Leon, Florida	Co. K, 5th Florida Infantry	May 12, 1864, Spotsylvania Court House, Virginia	Point Lookout, Maryland, transferred to Elmira Prison, NY, August 12, 1864	Exchanged March 14, 1865 at Boulware's Wharf on the James River, Virginia
Hines, John Private	Unk	October 15, 1862, Charleston, South Carolina	Co. C, 27th South Carolina Infantry	June 24, 1864, Near Petersburg, Virginia	Point Lookout, Maryland, transferred to Elmira Prison, NY, July 23, 1864	Oath of Allegiance May 17, 1865
Hines, John H. Private	23	May 10, 1861, Morganton, North Carolina	Co. E, 16th North Carolina Infantry	May 6, 1864, Wilderness, Virginia	Point Lookout, Maryland, transferred to Elmira Prison, NY, August 14, 1864	Died January 26, 1865 of Pneumonia, Grave No. 1633
Hines, Neill W. Private	20	August 22, 1862, Wilkes County, North Carolina	Co. D, 18th North Carolina Infantry	May 12, 1864, Spotsylvania Court House, Virginia	Point Lookout, Maryland, transferred to Elmira Prison, NY, August 6, 1864	Died March 18, 1865 of Diarrhea, Grave No. 1725
Hines, Robert B. Private	Unk	Unknown	Co. F, 5th Texas Cavalry	August 5, 1864, Cross Bayou, Louisiana	New Orleans, LA, Transferred to Elmira Prison, NY, November 19, 1864	Oath of Allegiance June 16, 1865
Hines, Thomas Private	Unk	November 10, 1862, Smithville, North Carolina	Co. K, 66th North Carolina Infantry	June 17, 1864, Petersburg, Virginia	Point Lookout, Maryland, transferred to Elmira Prison, NY, July 25, 1864	Died September 23, 1864 of Chronic Diarrhea, Grave No. 462
Hines, William Private	Unk	September 1, 1862, Dale County, Alabama	Co. A, 6th Alabama Infantry	May 12, 1864, Spotsylvania Court House, Virginia	Point Lookout, Maryland, transferred to Elmira Prison, NY, August 17, 1864	Oath of Allegiance June 14, 1865

Name & Rank	Age	Enlisted	Regiment and State	Where Captured	Prison	Remarks
Hinkle, William Private	Unk	March 19, 1863, Frankford, Virginia	Co. B, 19th Virginia Cavalry	July 16, 1864, Loudoun County, Virginia	Old Capital Prison, Washington, DC, transferred to Elmira July 23, 1864	Died November 21, 1864 of Chronic Diarrhea, Grave No. 937
Hinnant, George S. Private	19	August 28, 1861, Alston, South Carolina	Co. F, 12th South Carolina Infantry	May 9, 1864, Spotsylvania Court House, Virginia. Gunshot Wound Right Hand. Amputation of Arm.	Old Capital Prison, Washington, DC, transferred to Elmira Prison, NY, March 3, 1865.	Oath of Allegiance June 30, 1865
Hinnon, T. Private	Unk	Unknown	Co. C, 1st North Carolina Infantry	June 10, 1864, Spotsylvania, Virginia	Point Lookout, Maryland, transferred to Elmira Prison, NY, July 25, 1864	Oath of Allegiance June 14, 1865
Hinseman, Levi Private	34	October 15, 1862, Camp, North Carolina	Co. A, 52nd North Carolina Infantry	May 12, 1864, Spotsylvania Court House, Virginia	Point Lookout, Maryland, transferred to Elmira Prison, NY, July 30, 1864	Oath of Allegiance June 12, 1865
Hinsey, Henry Private	Unk	April 23, 1862, Camp Leon, Florida	Co. A, 5th Florida Infantry	May 12, 1864, Spotsylvania Court House, Virginia	Point Lookout, Maryland, transferred to Elmira Prison, NY, August 12, 1864	Exchanged March 2, 1865 at Akins Landing on the James River, Virginia
Hinsey, John R. Private	18	August 1, 1862, Monticello, Florida	Co. A, 5th Florida Infantry	May 12, 1864, Spotsylvania Court House, Virginia	Point Lookout, Maryland, transferred to Elmira Prison, NY, August 12, 1864	Oath of Allegiance June 14, 1865
Hinson, Charles R. Private	28	February 24, 1864, Wadesboro, North Carolina	Co H, 43rd North Carolina Infantry	May 16, 1864, Near Drury's Bluff, Virginia	Point Lookout, Maryland, transferred to Elmira Prison, NY, August 18, 1864	Oath of Allegiance June 12, 1865
Hinson, Eli Private	17	December 8, 1863, Fort Pender, Brunswick County, North Carolina	Co. E, 36th Regiment 2nd North Carolina Artillery	January 15, 1865, Fort Fisher, North Carolina	February 1, 1865, Elmira Prison Camp, New York	Oath of Allegiance July 19, 1865

Name & Rank	Age	Enlisted	Regiment and State	Where Captured	Prison	Remarks
Hinson, Elias A. Corporal	21	March 4, 1862, Wilmington, North Carolina	Co. E, 36th Regiment 2nd North Carolina Artillery	January 15, 1865, Fort Fisher, North Carolina	February 1, 1865, Elmira Prison Camp, New York	Died March 13, 1865 of Pneumonia, Grave No. 2431
Hinson, George W. Private	20	March 24, 1862, Salisbury, North Carolina	Co. C, 42nd North Carolina Infantry	June 3, 1864, Cold Harbor, Virginia	Point Lookout, Maryland, transferred to Elmira Prison, NY, July 17,1864	Oath of Allegiance June 21, 1865
Hinson, Jimpsey Private	Unk	April 28, 1864, New Hanover, North Carolina	Co. E, 36th Regiment 2nd North Carolina Artillery	January 15, 1865, Fort Fisher, North Carolina	February 1, 1865, Elmira Prison Camp, New York	Died March 7, 1865 of Chronic Diarrhea, Grave No. 2401. Headstone has Jacob Hinson.
Hinson, John Private	24	December 20, 1861, Georgetown, South Carolina	Co. A, 21st South Carolina Infantry	January 15, 1865, Fort Fisher, North Carolina	January 30, 1865, Elmira Prison Camp, New York	Died May 19, 1865 of Pneumonia, Grave No. 2947
Hinson, John Private	18	February 1, 1862, Salisbury, North Carolina	Co. C, 42nd North Carolina Infantry	June 3, 1864, Cold Harbor, Virginia	Point Lookout, Maryland, transferred to Elmira Prison, NY, July 17,1864	Oath of Allegiance June 21, 1865
Hinson, Joshua Private	24	May 10, 1862, Lenoir County, North Carolina	Co. E, 61st North Carolina Infantry	August 27, 1863, Battery Wagner, Morris Island, South Carolina	Point Lookout, Maryland, transferred to Elmira Prison, NY, August 18, 1864	Oath of Allegiance July 11, 1865
Hinson, Joshua P. Private	18	July 29, 1863, Fort Anderson, Brunswick County, North Carolina	Co. E, 36th Regiment 2nd North Carolina Artillery	January 15, 1865, Fort Fisher, North Carolina	February 1, 1865, Elmira Prison Camp, New York	Died April 7, 1865 of Chronic Diarrhea, Grave No. 2636. Headstone has J. B. Henson.
Hinson, Richard Private	Unk	December 5, 1863, Goldsboro, North Carolina	Co. F, 10th Regiment, 1st North Carolina Artillery	January 15, 1865, Fort Fisher, North Carolina	January 30, 1865, Elmira Prison Camp, New York	Oath of Allegiance May 29, 1865

Name & Rank	Age	Enlisted	Regiment and State	Where Captured	Prison	Remarks
Hinson, Rowan M. Sergeant	18	March 13, 1862, Salisbury, North Carolina	Co. C, 42nd North Carolina Infantry	June 3, 1864, Cold Harbor, Virginia	Point Lookout, Maryland, transferred to Elmira Prison, NY, July 17, 1864	Died September 22, 1864 of Typhoid Fever, Grave No. 481
Hinson, William H. Private	36	March 26, 1863, Chatham County, North Carolina	Co. G, 40th Regiment, 3rd North Carolina Artillery	January 15, 1865, Fort Fisher, North Carolina	January 30, 1865, Elmira Prison Camp, New York	Oath of Allegiance June 12, 1865
Hinton, Bernard A. Private	21	October 19, 1861, Elizabethtown, Bladen County, North Carolina	Co. J, 36th Regiment 2nd North Carolina Artillery	January 15, 1865, Fort Fisher, North Carolina	February 1, 1865, Elmira Prison Camp, New York	Exchanged March 2, 1865 at Boulware's Wharf on the James River, Virginia
Hinton, George W. Private	23	May 15, 1861, Johnston County, North Carolina	Co. C, 24th North Carolina Infantry	June 17, 1864, Petersburg, Virginia	Point Lookout, Maryland, transferred to Elmira Prison, NY, July 30, 1864	Died September 17, 1864 of Chronic Diarrhea, Grave No. 212
Hinton, Malachi Private	Unk	September 20, 1863, Clayton, North Carolina	Co. C, 24th North Carolina Infantry	June 17, 1864, Petersburg, Virginia	Point Lookout, Maryland, transferred to Elmira Prison, NY, July 30, 1864	Exchanged October 29, 1864 at Venus Point, Savannah River, GA.
Hiott, Joseph Private	Unk	November 1, 1862, Walterboro, South Carolina	Co. J, 11th South Carolina Infantry	June 16, 1864, Petersburg, Virginia	Point Lookout, Maryland, transferred to Elmira Prison, NY, July 25, 1864	Exchanged October 29, 1864 at Venus Point, Savannah River, GA.
Hiott, Lawrence P. Private	Unk	February 25, 1862, Hardeeville, South Carolina	Co. J, 11th South Carolina Infantry	June 16, 1864, Petersburg, Virginia	Point Lookout, Maryland, transferred to Elmira Prison, NY, July 25, 1864	Died October 26, 1864 of Chronic Diarrhea, Grave No. 850
Hipes, John W. Private	Unk	April 29, 1862, White Sulfur Springs, Virginia	Co. C, 26th Battalion Georgia Infantry	June 3, 1864, Gaines Mill Cold Harbor, Virginia	Point Lookout, Maryland, transferred to Elmira Prison, NY, July 17, 1864	Died August 22, 1864 of Chronic Diarrhea, Grave No. 32
Hipp, James F. Private	26	August 15, 1862, Iredell County, North Carolina	Co. I, 37th North Carolina Infantry	July 29, 1864, Petersburg, Virginia	Point Lookout, Maryland, transferred to Elmira Prison, NY, August 12, 1864	Oath of Allegiance July 3, 1865

Name & Rank	Age	Enlisted	Regiment and State	Where Captured	Prison	Remarks
Hirschler, Isaac Private	22	July 7, 1862, Wilmington, North Carolina	Co. D, 1st Battalion North Carolina Heavy Artillery	January 15, 1865, Fort Fisher, North Carolina	February 1, 1865, Elmira Prison Camp, New York	Oath of Allegiance May 13, 1865
Hiser, Noah Private	20	April 6, 1862, Camp Shenandoah, Virginia	Co. K, 25th Virginia Infantry	May 5, 1864, Wilderness, Virginia	Point Lookout, Maryland, transferred to Elmira Prison, NY, July 23, 1864	Oath of Allegiance May 15, 1865
Hitchcock, Samuel Private	20	Unknown	Co. J, 2nd North Carolina Infantry	July 9, 1864, Frederick, Maryland	Old Capital Prison, Washington, DC transferred to Elmira Prison, NY, August 27, 1864	Oath of Allegiance July 7, 1865
Hite, Cornelius Randolph Private	19	March 20, 1863, Fauquier County, Virginia	Co. H, 4th Virginia Cavalry	February 6, 1864, Fauquier County, Virginia	Old Capital Prison, Washington, DC, transferred to Elmira Prison, NY, August 12, 1864	Oath of Allegiance June 19, 1865
Hitlenbrandt, Daniel Private	Unk	October 20, 1863, Morganton, North Carolina	Co. B, 54th North Carolina Infantry	July 16, 1864, Loudoun County, Virginia	Old Capital Prison, Washington, DC, transferred to Elmira July 23, 1864	Died February 20, 1865 of Diarrhea, Grave No. 2333
Hix, James P. Corporal	Unk	August 1, 1861, Cumberland Gap, Tennessee	Co. A, 17th Tennessee Infantry	June 17, 1864, Petersburg, Virginia	Point Lookout, Maryland, transferred to Elmira Prison, NY, July 30, 1864	Died November 11, 1864 of Chronic Diarrhea, Grave No. 791
Hix, Jeremiah G. Private	Unk	March 10, 1862, Decatur, Georgia	Co. C, Cobb's Legion Georgia	August 16, 1864, Front Royal, Virginia	Old Capital Prison, Washington, DC transferred to Elmira Prison, NY, August 29, 1864	Oath of Allegiance July 11, 1865
Hix, John Private	Unk	April 10, 1862, Brushy Ridge, Virginia	Co. A, 22nd Virginia Infantry	June 3, 1864, Gaines Farm Cold Harbor, Virginia	Point Lookout, Maryland, transferred to Elmira Prison, NY, July 17,1864	Died September 2, 1864 of Chronic Diarrhea Grave No. 63

Name & Rank	Age	Enlisted	Regiment and State	Where Captured	Prison	Remarks
Hix, William G. Private	Unk	April 1, 1861, Lacy's Store, Virginia	Co. B, 44th Virginia Infantry	May 12, 1864, Spotsylvania Court House, Virginia	Point Lookout, Maryland, transferred to Elmira Prison, NY, August 2, 1864	Exchanged October 29, 1864 at Venus Point, Savannah River, GA.
Hixon, William A. Private	Unk	October 17, 1862, Paris, Virginia	Co. A, 6th Virginia Cavalry	December 9, 1863, Loudoun County, Virginia	Point Lookout, Maryland, transferred to Elmira Prison, NY, August 17, 1864	Transferred For Exchange October 11, 1864 to Point Lookout Prison Camp, MD. Died October 27, 1864 of Chronic Diarrhea.
Hoard, J. R. Corporal	23	October 8, 1861, Hamilton, Martin County, North Carolina	Co. F, 31st North Carolina Infantry	May 31, 1864, Gaines Mill Cold Harbor, Virginia	Point Lookout, Maryland, transferred to Elmira Prison, NY, July 17,1864	Exchanged March 14, 1865 at Boulware's Wharf on the James River, Virginia
Hoard, James Private	26	June 25, 1861, Plymouth, North Carolina	Co. H, 1st North Carolina Infantry	May 12, 1864, Spotsylvania, Virginia	Point Lookout, Maryland, transferred to Elmira Prison, NY, August 6, 1864	Died March 28, 1861 of Pneumonia. No Grave Found in Woodlawn National Cemetery.
Hoard, Wylie J. Corporal	17	October 8, 1861, Hamilton, Martin County, North Carolina	Co. F, 31st North Carolina Infantry	May 31, 1864, Gaines Mill Cold Harbor, Virginia	Point Lookout, Maryland, transferred to Elmira Prison, NY, July 17,1864	Oath of Allegiance July 11, 1865
Hobbs, George A. Corporal	Unk	March 31, 1862, Williamston, North Carolina	Co. K, 10th Regiment, 1st North Carolina Artillery	January 15, 1865, Fort Fisher, North Carolina	January 30, 1865, Elmira Prison Camp, New York	Died March 21, 1865 of Phthisis, Grave No. 1546
Hobbs, Joseph E. Private	33	May 13, 1861, Golden Place, Onslow County, North Carolina	Co. E, 3rd North Carolina Infantry	May 12, 1864, Spotsylvania Court House, Virginia	Point Lookout, Maryland, transferred to Elmira Prison, NY, August 14, 1864	Oath of Allegiance June 30, 1865

Name & Rank	Age	Enlisted	Regiment and State	Where Captured	Prison	Remarks
Hobbs, Thomas A. J. Corporal	23	May 2, 1862, Goldsboro, North Carolina	Co. E, 3rd North Carolina Infantry	May 12, 1864, Near Spotsylvania Court House, Virginia	Point Lookout, Maryland, transferred to Elmira Prison, NY, August 14, 1864	Oath of Allegiance June 27, 1865
Hobson, Thomas R. Sergeant	19	May 13, 1861, Lynchburg, Virginia	Co. H, 11th Mississippi Infantry	June 3, 1864, Near Old Church, Cold Harbor, Virginia	Point Lookout, Maryland, transferred to Elmira Prison, NY, July 12, 1864	Oath of Allegiance June 27, 1865
Hockaday, Bennett Private	26	February 26, 1862, Fayetteville, Cumberland County, North Carolina	Co. A, 36th Regiment 2nd North Carolina Artillery	January 15, 1865, Fort Fisher, North Carolina	February 1, 1865, Elmira Prison Camp, New York	Died March 5, 1865 of Variola (Smallpox), Grave No. 1966
Hocott, B. C. Private	15	April 9, 1864, Bristol, Tennessee	Co. B, 3rd Battalion South Carolina Infantry	May 23, 1864, North Anna, Virginia	Point Lookout, Maryland, transferred to Elmira Prison, NY, July 23, 1864	Escaped December 13, 1864
Hocut, Caswell Private	Unk	September 20, 1863, Clayton, North Carolina	Co. C, 24th North Carolina Infantry	June 17, 1864, Petersburg, Virginia	Point Lookout, Maryland, transferred to Elmira Prison, NY, July 30, 1864	Exchanged 11/15/1864 at Venus Point, October River, GA
Hodge, Elihue S. Private	17	January 1, 1862, Camp Harlee, Georgetown, South Carolina	Co. I, 25th South Carolina Infantry	January 15, 1865, Fort Fisher, North Carolina	January 30, 1865, Elmira Prison Camp, New York	Exchanged February 20, 1865. Died March 4, 1865 at Richmond Wayside Hospital #9, VA.
Hodge, George W. Private	Unk	November 22, 1864, Union Mills, Virginia	Co. C, 6th Alabama Infantry	May 5, 1864, Ely's Ford, Wilderness, Virginia	Point Lookout Prison Camp, Maryland. Transferred to Elmira Prison Camp, NY, August 17, 1864	Died April 6, 1865 of Variola (Smallpox), Grave No. 2659
Hodge, James B. Private	22	January 1, 1862, Camp Harlee, Georgetown, South Carolina	Co. I, 25th South Carolina Infantry	January 15, 1865, Fort Fisher, North Carolina	January 30, 1865, Elmira Prison Camp, New York	Died April 10, 1865 of Chronic Diarrhea, Grave No. 2606

Name & Rank	Age	Enlisted	Regiment and State	Where Captured	Prison	Remarks
Hodge, John P. Private	18	July 15, 1861, Whippy Swamp, South Carolina	Co. D, 11th South Carolina Infantry	January 15, 1865, Fort Fisher, North Carolina	February 1, 1865, Elmira Prison Camp, New York	Oath of Allegiance August 7, 1865
Hodge, Lewis Sergeant	22	July 15, 1861, Whippy Swamp, South Carolina	Co. D, 11th South Carolina Infantry	January 15, 1865, Fort Fisher, North Carolina	February 1, 1865, Elmira Prison Camp, New York	Oath of Allegiance July 13, 1865
Hodge, Samuel N. Private	21	January 1, 1862, Camp Harlee, Georgetown, South Carolina	Co. I, 25th South Carolina Infantry	January 15, 1865, Fort Fisher, North Carolina	January 30, 1865, Elmira Prison Camp, New York	Died February 11, 1865 of Chronic Diarrhea, Grave No. 2175. Headstone has S. B. Hodges.
Hodge, William H. Private	21	December 28, 1861, Georgetown, South Carolina	Co. K, 21st South Carolina Infantry	January 15, 1865, Fort Fisher, North Carolina	January 30, 1865, Elmira Prison Camp, New York	Died March 7, 1865 of Diarrhea, Grave No. 2392
Hodgen, D. M. Private	31	March 10, 1862, Montevallo, Alabama	Co. C, 10th Alabama Infantry	May 7, 1864, Wilderness, Virginia	Point Lookout, Maryland, transferred to Elmira Prison, NY, August 17, 1864	Oath of Allegiance May 29, 1865
Hodgerson, Lewis J. Private	36	March 8, 1861, Montgomery, Alabama	Co. A, 1st Alabama Artillery	August 23, 1864, Fort Morgan, Alabama	New Orleans, Louisiana transferred to Elmira Prison, NY, December 4, 1864.	Died January 17, 1865 of Pneumonia, Grave No. 1437
Hodges, F. T. Private	Unk	May 8, 1862, Camp Capers, South Carolina	Co. F, Holcombe Legion, South Carolina	May 8, 1864, Jarrett's Depot, Virginia	Point Lookout, Maryland, transferred to Elmira Prison, NY, August 17, 1864	Oath of Allegiance June 21, 1865
Hodges, Jacob Landsman	Unk	Unknown	Confederate States Navy	May 5, 1864, Albemarle Sound on Steamer CSS Bombshell	Point Lookout, Maryland, transferred to Elmira Prison, NY, August 17, 1864	Oath of Allegiance June 16, 1865
Hodges, James H. Private	Unk	May 14, 1862, Sandersville, Georgia	Co. E, 12th Battalion Georgia Light Artillery	March 25, 1865, Petersburg, Virginia. Gunshot Wound Temple and Scalp.	Old Capital Prison, Washington, DC, transferred to Elmira Prison, NY, May 2, 1865.	Oath of Allegiance July 7, 1865

Name & Rank	Age	Enlisted	Regiment and State	Where Captured	Prison	Remarks
Hodges, John H. Private	23	April 18, 1861, Blacksburg, Virginia	Co. E, 4th Virginia Infantry	May 12, 1864, Near Spotsylvania Court House, Virginia	Point Lookout, Maryland, transferred to Elmira Prison, NY, August 2, 1864	Exchanged March 2, 1865 at Boulware's Wharf on the James River, Virginia
Hodges, John H. Private	44	September 1, 1863, Robison County, North Carolina	Co. B, 36th Regiment 2nd North Carolina Artillery	January 15, 1865, Fort Fisher, North Carolina	February 1, 1865, Elmira Prison Camp, New York	Exchanged 3/14/65. Died 3/27/65 of Chronic Diarrhea at CSA Way Hospital, Greensboro, North Carolina
Hodges, John W. Private	Unk	July 10, 1861, Winchester, Virginia	Co. F, 5th, Virginia Infantry	May 20, 1864, Spotsylvania Court House, Virginia	Point Lookout, Maryland, transferred to Elmira Prison, NY, July 6, 1864	Oath of Allegiance June 16, 1865
Hodges, Richard A. Private	23	December 17, 1861, Camp Trousdale, Tennessee	Co. H, 44th Tennessee Infantry	June 17, 1864, Petersburg, Virginia	Point Lookout, Maryland, transferred to Elmira Prison, NY, July 23, 1864	Oath of Allegiance May 10, 1865
Hodges, S. B. Sergeant	Unk	July 20, 1861, Sandy Springs, South Carolina	Co. F, Holcombe Legion, South Carolina	May 8, 1864, Jarrett's Depot, Virginia	Point Lookout, Maryland, transferred to Elmira Prison, NY, August 17, 1864	Oath of Allegiance June 14, 1865
Hodges, T. J. Private	Unk	October 3, 1863, Bryan County, Georgia	Co. H, 7th Georgia Cavalry	June 11, 1864, Trevilian Station, Louisa Court House, Virginia	Point Lookout, Maryland, transferred to Elmira Prison, NY, July 25, 1864	Died November 18, 1864 of Chronic Diarrhea, Grave No. 965
Hodges, Thomas R. Private	Unk	October 9, 1862, Franklin County, Virginia	Co. F, 25th North Carolina Infantry	June 17, 1864, Petersburg, Virginia	Point Lookout, Maryland, transferred to Elmira Prison, NY, July 30, 1864	Died October 3, 1864 of Scorbutus (Scurvy) Grave No. 615
Hodges, William Private	44	December 1, 1863, Camp Duke, South Carolina	Co. C, 46th Virginia Infantry	June 17, 1864, Petersburg, Virginia	Point Lookout, Maryland, transferred to Elmira Prison, NY, July 30, 1864	Died September 11, 1864 of Chronic Diarrhea, Grave No. 260

Name & Rank	Age	Enlisted	Regiment and State	Where Captured	Prison	Remarks
Hodgins, William B. Private	47	July 20, 1861, Camp Pickens, Anderson District, South Carolina	Co. C, 1st South Carolina Infantry	July 14, 1863, Falling Waters, Maryland	Point Lookout, Maryland, transferred to Elmira Prison, NY, August 18, 1864	Died September 20, 1864 of Chronic Diarrhea, Grave No. 325
Hodnett, George A. Private	Unk	June 22, 1861, Richmond, Virginia	Co. C, 46th Virginia Infantry	June 16, 1864, Petersburg, Virginia	Point Lookout, Maryland, transferred to Elmira Prison, NY, August 18, 1864	Exchanged March 10, 1865 at Boulware's Wharf on the James River, Virginia
Hoerick, Adam J. Private	Unk	December 22, 1862, Guinness Station, Virginia	Co. D, 2nd Virginia Infantry	May 12, 1864, Near Spotsylvania Court House, Virginia	Point Lookout, Maryland, transferred to Elmira Prison, NY, August 6, 1864	Oath of Allegiance June 21, 1865
Hoey, S. A. Private	Unk	June 16, 1863, Raleigh, North Carolina	Co. F, 3rd North Carolina Cavalry	May 27, 1864, Hanover Town, Virginia	Point Lookout, Maryland, transferred to Elmira Prison, NY, July 12, 1864	Exchanged February 20, 1865 at Boulware's or Cox Wharf on the James River, Virginia
Hofauger, George W. Private	18	April 15, 1862, Richmond, Virginia	Co. D, 5th Virginia Cavalry	June 8, 1864, Bottoms Bridge, Virginia	Point Lookout, Maryland, transferred to Elmira Prison, NY, July 25, 1864	Oath of Allegiance May 29, 1865
Hoffman, D. Private	Unk	April 18, 1864, Greenbrier, Virginia	Co. H, 22nd Virginia Infantry	June 3, 1864, Gaines Farm Cold Harbor, Virginia	Point Lookout, Maryland, transferred to Elmira Prison, NY, July 17, 1864	Oath of Allegiance July 3, 1865
Hoffman, Jacob Private	Unk	September 27, 1862, Richmond, Virginia	Co. G, 42nd Virginia Cavalry	December 13, 1863, Charles City Court House, Virginia	Point Lookout, Maryland, transferred to Elmira Prison, NY, July 23, 1864	Oath of Allegiance May 15, 1865
Hoffman, Robert N. Private	21	April 18, 1861, Halltown, Virginia	Co. B, 2nd Virginia Infantry	May 12, 1864, Spotsylvania Court House, Virginia	Point Lookout, Maryland, transferred to Elmira Prison, NY, August 2, 1864	Exchanged March 2, 1865 at Akins Landing on the James River, Virginia

Name & Rank	Age	Enlisted	Regiment and State	Where Captured	Prison	Remarks
Hoffman, Waldemar Private	Unk	Unknown	Getting's Battalion Texas Infantry	July 22, 1864, Near Brownsville, Texas	New Orleans, LA, Transferred to Elmira Prison, NY, November 19, 1864	Died December 28, 1864 of Pneumonia, Grave No. 1304
Hoffmaster, John W. Private	Unk	September 25, 1861, Charlestown, Virginia	Co. B, 12th Virginia Cavalry	March 4, 1865, Jefferson County, Virginia	Old Capital Prison, Washington, DC, transferred to Elmira Prison, NY, May 12, 1865.	Oath of Allegiance July 11, 1865
Hogan, A. N. Private	Unk	May 31, 1861, Yellow Branch, Virginia	Co. I, 42nd Virginia Infantry	May 12, 1864, Spotsylvania Court House, Virginia	Point Lookout, Maryland, transferred to Elmira Prison, NY, August 12, 1864	Transferred to US Army Hospital, Elmira, New York, July 13, 1865. Nothing Further.
Hogan, P. L. Private	Unk	March 12, 1864, Columbia, South Carolina	Co. E, 3rd Battalion South Carolina Infantry	July 29, 1864, Petersburg, Virginia	Point Lookout, Maryland, transferred to Elmira Prison, NY, August 12, 1864	Oath of Allegiance May 17, 1865
Hogg, James M. Private	21	April 20, 1861, Belle Roi., Virginia	Co. G, 26th Virginia Infantry	June 15, 1864, Near Petersburg, Virginia	Point Lookout, Maryland, transferred to Elmira Prison, NY, July 17,1864	Oath of Allegiance June 27, 1865
Hogg, Levi B. Private	24	March 2, 1862, Newbern, North Carolina	Co. E, 7th North Carolina Infantry	May 6, 1864, Wilderness, Virginia	Point Lookout, Maryland, transferred to Elmira Prison, NY, August 14, 1864	Oath of Allegiance June 19, 1865
Hogg, Marcellus L. Private	20	May 16, 1861, Gloucester Point, Virginia	Co. G, 26th Virginia Infantry	June 15, 1864, Near Petersburg, Virginia	Point Lookout, Maryland, transferred to Elmira Prison, NY, July 17,1864	Oath of Allegiance June 27, 1865
Hogsett, William R. Private	Unk	May 18, 1861, Huntersville, Virginia	Co. I, 25th Virginia Infantry	May 12, 1864, Spotsylvania Court House, Virginia	Point Lookout, Maryland, transferred to Elmira Prison, NY, August 12, 1864	Exchanged February 20, 1865 at Boulware's or Cox Wharf on the James River, Virginia

Name & Rank	Age	Enlisted	Regiment and State	Where Captured	Prison	Remarks
Hogston, John Corporal	Unk	July 30, 1861, Marion, Virginia	Co. D, 4th Virginia Infantry	May 20, 1864, Spotsylvania Court House, Virginia	Point Lookout, Maryland, transferred to Elmira Prison, NY, July 6, 1864	Oath of Allegiance June 19, 1865
Holcomb, Andrew J. Private	20	May 28, 1861, Corinth, Mississippi	Co. K, 17th Mississippi Infantry	May 8, 1864, Spotsylvania Court House, Virginia	Point Lookout, Maryland, transferred to Elmira Prison, NY, July 23, 1864	Oath of Allegiance May 19, 1865
Holcomb, Joseph A. Corporal	Unk	March 30, 1863, Monroe County, Virginia	Co. A, 26th Virginia Infantry	May 31, 1864, Chickahominy, Cold Harbor, Virginia	Point Lookout, Maryland, transferred to Elmira Prison, NY, July 11, 1864	Oath of Allegiance June 27, 1865
Holcomb, Newton J. Private	Unk	August 24, 1861, Habersham County, Georgia	Co. H, 24th Georgia Infantry	August 16, 1864, Front Royal, Virginia	Old Capital Prison, Washington, DC transferred to Elmira Prison, NY, August 29, 1864	Oath of Allegiance June 14, 1865
Holcomb, William M. Private	Unk	August 24, 1861, White County, Georgia	Co. C, 24th Georgia Infantry	August 16, 1864, Front Royal, Virginia	Old Capital Prison, Washington, DC transferred to Elmira Prison, NY, August 29, 1864	Died March 17, 1865 of Variola (Smallpox), Grave No. 1711
Holcombe, Sherwood Private	Unk	April 18, 1863, Macon, Georgia	Co. B, 64th Georgia Infantry	June 17, 1864, Petersburg, Virginia	Point Lookout, Maryland, transferred to Elmira Prison, NY, July 30, 1864	Died March 20, 1865 of General Debility, Grave No. 1568
Holden, Nathan E. Private	20	September 4, 1863, Fort Caswell, Brunswick County, North Carolina	Co. G, 36th Regiment 2nd North Carolina Artillery	January 15, 1865, Fort Fisher, North Carolina	February 1, 1865, Elmira Prison Camp, New York	Died February 28, 1865 of Chronic Diarrhea, Grave No. 2130
Holden, Richard A. Private	17	February 28, 1864, Fort Fisher, North Carolina	Co. G, 36th Regiment 2nd North Carolina Artillery	January 15, 1865, Fort Fisher, North Carolina	February 1, 1865, Elmira Prison Camp, New York	Oath of Allegiance July 3, 1865

Name & Rank	Age	Enlisted	Regiment and State	Where Captured	Prison	Remarks
Holden, Richard W. Private	42	August 24, 1863, Fort Caswell, Brunswick County, North Carolina	Co. G, 36th Regiment 2nd North Carolina Artillery	January 15, 1865, Fort Fisher, North Carolina. Gunshot Wound Right Breast.	February 1, 1865, Elmira Prison Camp, New York.	Exchanged February 20, 1865. Died March 12, 1865 of Variola at Howard Grove Hospital, Richmond, VA.
Holden, Willis Private	34	May 15, 1862, Camp McIntosh, Goldsboro, North Carolina	Co. J, 1st North Carolina Infantry	May 12, 1864, Near Spotsylvania Court House, Virginia	Point Lookout Prison, Maryland. Transferred to Elmira Prison Camp New York August 6, 1864.	Exchanged February 13, 1865 at Boulware's wharf on the James River, Virginia
Holder, Charles Private	Unk	August 1, 1862, Drury's Bluff, Virginia	Co. H, 49th, Virginia Infantry	May 20, 1864, Spotsylvania Court House, Virginia	Point Lookout, Maryland, transferred to Elmira Prison, NY, July 6, 1864	Exchanged March 14, 1865 at Boulware's Wharf on the James River, Virginia
Holder, Jacob Private	Unk	December 25, 1862, Mocksville, North Carolina	Co. M, 7th Confederate Cavalry	May 6, 1864, Buck Island, Virginia	Point Lookout, Maryland, transferred to Elmira Prison, NY, August 17, 1864	Transferred For Exchange 10/11/64 to Point Lookout Prison Camp, MD. Died 11/5/64 of Unknown Causes at Fort Monroe, VA.
Holder, Nathan B. Private	Unk	Unknown	Co. C, 7th Texas Cavalry	November 20, 1863, Camp Price, Louisiana	New Orleans, LA, Transferred to Elmira Prison, NY, November 19, 1864	Died March 1, 1865 of Chronic Diarrhea, Grave No. 2107. Headstone has N. B. Holden.
Holder, Sampson Private	40	March 6, 1862, Newton Grove, North Carolina	Co H, 20th North Carolina Infantry	May 12, 1864, Near Spotsylvania Court House, Virginia	Point Lookout, Maryland, transferred to Elmira Prison, NY, August 14, 1864	Oath of Allegiance June 30, 1865

Name & Rank	Age	Enlisted	Regiment and State	Where Captured	Prison	Remarks
Holder, Stark H. Private	Unk	March 4, 1862, Calhoun County, Georgia	Co. E, 51st Georgia Infantry	June 3, 1864, Gaines Farm Cold Harbor, Virginia	Point Lookout Prison, Maryland Transferred July 17, 1864 to Elmira, NY	Died July 21, 1865 of Unknown Causes, Grave No. 2865. Name S. H. Holden on Headstone.
Holder, William Private	Unk	March 12, 1862, Asheboro, North Carolina	Co. F, 2nd Battalion North Carolina Infantry	July 10, 1864, Frederick Junction, Maryland	Old Capital Prison, Washington, DC, transferred to Elmira July 23, 1864	Died October 4, 1864 of Chronic Diarrhea, Grave No. 609
Holderfield, J. T. Private	23	July 28, 1861, Cedar Fork, North Carolina	Co. G, 7th North Carolina Infantry	May 6, 1864, Wilderness, Virginia	Point Lookout, Maryland, transferred to Elmira Prison, NY, August 14, 1864	Exchanged February 13, 1865 at Boulware's wharf on the James River, Virginia
Holdman, David M. Private	Unk	March 15, 1862, Lawrenceville, Georgia	Co. F, 24th Georgia Infantry	June 1, 1864, Cold Harbor, Virginia	Point Lookout, Maryland, transferred to Elmira Prison, NY, July 17, 1864	Exchanged October 29, 1864 at Venus Point, Savannah River, GA.
Holiday, John D. Private	Unk	March 15, 1864, Orange Court House, North Carolina	Co. J, 1st North Carolina Infantry	May 12, 1864, Near Spotsylvania Court House, Virginia	Point Lookout Prison, Maryland. Transferred to Elmira Prison Camp New York August 6, 1864.	Died September 16, 1864 of Typhoid Fever, Grave No. 166
Holland, Alfred Berry Corporal	18	December 4, 1861, Mountain Spring, Anderson District, South Carolina	Co. D, 18th South Carolina Infantry	July 30, 1864, Petersburg, Virginia	Point Lookout, Maryland, transferred to Elmira Prison, NY, August 12, 1864	Oath of Allegiance May 29, 1865
Holland, James W. Sergeant	22	April 20, 1861, Camp Moore, New Orleans, Louisiana	Co. J, 15th Louisiana Infantry	May 12, 1864, Spotsylvania Court House, Virginia	Point Lookout, Maryland, transferred to Elmira Prison, NY, July 25, 1864	Exchanged October 29, 1864 at Venus Point, Savannah River, GA.

Name & Rank	Age	Enlisted	Regiment and State	Where Captured	Prison	Remarks
Holland, Matthew Private	37	October 9, 1863, Clinton, Sampson County, North Carolina	Co. C, 36th Regiment 2nd North Carolina Artillery	January 15, 1865, Fort Fisher, North Carolina	February 1, 1865 Elmira Prison Camp, New York	Died April 7, 1865 of Chronic Diarrhea, Grave No. 2657
Holland, Phineas A. Private	18	August 22, 1861, Cleveland County, North Carolina	Co. H, 28th North Carolina Infantry	May 24, 1864, Spotsylvania Court House, Virginia	Point Lookout, Maryland, transferred to Elmira Prison, NY, July 11, 1864	Exchanged March 10, 1865 at Boulware's Wharf on the James River, Virginia
Holland, Richard H. Private	26	February 19, 1862, Entrenched Camp, Virginia	Co. E, 6th Virginia Infantry	July 30, 1864, Petersburg, Virginia. Gunshot Wound Left Forearm.	November 11, 1864, Old Capital Prison, Washington, DC. February 4, 1865 Elmira, Prison Camp, NY	Exchanged March 14, 1865 at Boulware's Wharf on the James River, Virginia
Holland, Thomas P. Private	28	April 20, 1861, Griffin, Georgia	Co. D, 2nd Battalion Georgia Infantry	June 24, 1864, Near Petersburg, Virginia	Point Lookout, Maryland, transferred to Elmira Prison, NY, July 23, 1864	Oath of Allegiance March 6, 1865
Holland, William M. Private	35	December 9, 1861, Camp Trousdale, Tennessee	Co. D, 44th Tennessee Infantry	June 17, 1864, Petersburg, Virginia	Point Lookout, Maryland, transferred to Elmira Prison, NY, July 30, 1864	Oath of Allegiance May 12, 1865
Hollandsworth, Harrison Private	Unk	July 3, 1861, Lynchburg, Virginia	Co. G, 42nd Virginia Infantry	May 12, 1864, Near Spotsylvania Court House, Virginia	Point Lookout, Maryland, transferred to Elmira Prison, NY, August 6, 1864	Died January 23, 1865 of Pneumonia, Grave No. 1608. Name Hollingsworth on Headstone.
Hollar, Jacob Private	29	August 14, 1862, Statesville, North Carolina	Co. A, 18th North Carolina Infantry	May 12, 1864, Spotsylvania Court House, Virginia	Point Lookout, Maryland, transferred to Elmira Prison, NY, August 6, 1864	Oath of Allegiance June 30, 1865
Hollen, Peter Sergeant	Unk	July 29, 1861, Fairfax Station, Virginia	Co. D, 10th Virginia Infantry	May 12, 1864, Spotsylvania Court House, Virginia	Point Lookout, Maryland, transferred to Elmira Prison, NY, August 2, 1864	Exchanged March 14, 1865 at Boulware's Wharf on the James River, Virginia

Name & Rank	Age	Enlisted	Regiment and State	Where Captured	Prison	Remarks
Holley, James Private	Unk	July 13, 1861, Jacksonville, Florida	Co. K, 2nd Florida Infantry	May 12, 1864, Spotsylvania Court House, Virginia	Point Lookout, Maryland, transferred to Elmira Prison, NY, August 12, 1864	Exchanged February 13, 1865 at Boulware's Wharf on the James River, Virginia
Holley, James Private	Unk	Unknown	Co. B, 48th Virginia Infantry	May 12, 1864, Spotsylvania Court House, Virginia	Point Lookout, Maryland, transferred to Elmira Prison, NY, August 2, 1864	Exchanged February 20, 1865 at Boulware's or Cox Wharf on the James River, Virginia
Holley, Silus Private	Unk	May 1, 1862, Cumberland County, North Carolina	Co. J, 51st North Carolina Infantry	May 16, 1864, Near Drury's Bluff, Virginia	Point Lookout, Maryland, transferred to Elmira Prison, NY, August 18, 1864	Exchanged at Venus Point, Savannah River, GA, 10/29/1864.
Holliday, John R. Sergeant	Unk	July 2, 1861, New Orleans, Louisiana	Co. J, 15th Louisiana Infantry	May 12, 1864, Spotsylvania Court House, Virginia	Point Lookout, Maryland, transferred to Elmira Prison, NY, July 25, 1864	Exchanged February 13, 1865 at Boulware's wharf on the James River, Virginia
Holliman, S. B. Private	Unk	August 6, 1863, Decatur, Georgia	Co. C, 20th Battalion Georgia Cavalry	June 2, 1864, Cold Harbor, Virginia	Point Lookout, Maryland, transferred to Elmira Prison, NY, July 17,1864	Died September 27, 1864 of Chronic Diarrhea, Grave No. 382
Holliman, William M. Private	Unk	September 29, 1863, Macon, Georgia	Co. E, 12th Georgia Infantry	May 10, 1864, Spotsylvania Court House, Virginia	Point Lookout, Maryland, transferred to Elmira Prison, NY, July 25, 1864	Died August 27, 1864 of Chronic Diarrhea, Grave No. 106
Hollingsworth D. T. Private	21	May 20, 1861, Louisburg, North Carolina	Co. K, 32nd North Carolina Infantry	May 10, 1864, Near Mine Run, Virginia	Point Lookout, Maryland, transferred to Elmira Prison, NY, August 6, 1864	Died February 23, 1865 of Pleuritis, Grave No. 2266
Hollingsworth Edward C. Private	Unk	March 27, 1861, Selma, Alabama	Co. C, 1st Battalion Alabama Artillery	August 23, 1864, Fort Morgan, Alabama	New Orleans, Louisiana transferred to Elmira Prison, NY, December 4, 1864.	Oath of Allegiance June 21, 1865

Name & Rank	Age	Enlisted	Regiment and State	Where Captured	Prison	Remarks
Hollis, Harrison B. Sergeant	17	July 23, 1861, Staunton, Virginia	Co. H, 52nd Virginia, Infantry	May 30, 1864, Mechanicsville, Virginia	Point Lookout, Maryland, transferred to Elmira Prison, NY, July 9, 1864	Exchanged October 29, 1864 at Venus Point, Savannah River, GA.
Hollis, James Civilian	Unk	Unknown	North Carolina Citizen	January 15, 1865, Fort Fisher, North Carolina	February 1, 1865 Elmira Prison Camp, New York	Died February 16, 1865 of Rubeola (Measles), Grave No. 2178
Holloway, Y. E. Private	Unk	March 10, 1862, Cahaba, Alabama	Co. F, 5th, Alabama Infantry	May 20, 1864, Spotsylvania Court House, Virginia	Point Lookout, Maryland, transferred to Elmira Prison, NY, July 6, 1864	Exchanged October 29, 1864 at Venus Point, Savannah River, GA.
Holman, J. D. B. Private	27	July 7, 1861, Mocksville, North Carolina	Co. H, 5th North Carolina Infantry	May 11, 1864, Beaver Dam Station, Virginia	Point Lookout, Maryland, transferred to Elmira Prison, NY, August 17, 1864	Died January 3, 1865 of Chronic Diarrhea, Grave No. 1265
Holman, John Private	Unk	Unknown	Co. F, 11th Florida Infantry	July 29, 1864, Petersburg, Virginia	Point Lookout, Maryland, transferred to Elmira Prison, NY, August 12, 1864	Exchanged March 14, 1865 at Boulware's Wharf on the James River, Virginia
Holmes, George W. Private	Unk	August 24, 1861, Habersham County, Georgia	Co. H, 24th Georgia Infantry	June 3, 1864, Gaines Mill Cold Harbor, Virginia	Point Lookout, Maryland, transferred to Elmira Prison, NY, July 17, 1864	Exchanged February 20, 1865 at Boulware's or Cox Wharf on the James River, Virginia
Holmes, Harrison Civilian	Unk	Unknown	Citizen of Prince William County, Virginia	December 16, 1863, Prince William County, Virginia	Point Lookout, Maryland, transferred to Elmira Prison, NY, July 25, 1864	Died October 8, 1864 of Chronic Diarrhea, Grave No. 661
Holmes, J. H. Private	Unk	December 7, 1863, Decatur, Georgia	Co. C, 18th Georgia Infantry	June 1, 1864, Cold Harbor, Virginia	Point Lookout, Maryland, transferred to Elmira Prison, NY, July 17, 1864	Exchanged October 29, 1864 at Venus Point, Savannah River, GA.

Name & Rank	Age	Enlisted	Regiment and State	Where Captured	Prison	Remarks
Holmes, John W. Sergeant	23	May 3, 1861, Jerusalem, Virginia	Co. D, 3rd Virginia Infantry	May 6, 1864, Wakefield, Virginia	Point Lookout, Maryland, transferred to Elmira Prison, NY, August 17, 1864	Oath of Allegiance June 23, 1865
Holmes, Samuel D. Private	Unk	July 17, 1861, Decatur, Georgia	Co. E, 7th Georgia Infantry	August 1, 1864, Turkey Bend, Virginia	Point Lookout, Maryland, transferred to Elmira Prison, NY, August 18, 1864	Oath of Allegiance June 16, 1865
Holmes, William Private	17	Unknown	Co. A, Battalion Washington Louisiana Artillery	May 1, 1864, Petersburg, Virginia	New Orleans, Louisiana transferred to Elmira November 19, 1864.	Exchanged February 13, 1865 at Boulware's wharf on the James River, Virginia
Holmes, William E. Corporal	27	May 7, 1862, Charleston, South Carolina	Co. A, 25th South Carolina Infantry	January 15, 1865, Fort Fisher, North Carolina	January 30, 1865, Elmira Prison Camp, New York	Oath of Allegiance June 19, 1865
Holobaugh, George M. Private	19	July 21, 1861, Salisbury, North Carolina	Co. K, 8th North Carolina	May 31, 1864, Cold Harbor, Virginia	Point Lookout, Maryland, transferred to Elmira Prison, NY, July 17,1864	Exchanged March 2, 1865 at Akins Landing on the James River, Virginia
Holsinger, Noah Private	Unk	April 10, 1863, Lacy Springs, Virginia	Co. H, 12th Virginia Cavalry	September 14, 1863, Near Culpepper, Virginia	Point Lookout, Maryland, transferred to Elmira Prison, NY, August 18, 1864	Exchanged March 10, 1865 at Boulware's Wharf on the James River, Virginia
Holstein, D. O. Private	Unk	Unknown	Co. A, Harrison's 3rd Louisiana Cavalry	September 30, 1864, Cecily Island, Louisiana	New Orleans, Louisiana transferred to Elmira November 19, 1864.	Exchanged February 25, 1865 at Boulware's or Cox Wharf on the James River, Virginia
Holstein, Joseph A. Private	Unk	April 21, 1863, James Island, South Carolina	Co. G, 25th South Carolina Infantry	January 15, 1865, Fort Fisher, North Carolina	January 30, 1865, Elmira Prison Camp, New York	Died March 7, 1865, Diarrhea, Grave No. 2381
Holstine, Van B. Private	21	June 22, 1861, Charleston, Virginia	Co. J, 22nd, Virginia Infantry	May 30, 1864, Hanover Junction, Virginia	Point Lookout, Maryland, transferred to Elmira Prison, NY, July 12, 1864	Exchanged October 29, 1864 at Venus Point, Savannah River, GA.

Name & Rank	Age	Enlisted	Regiment and State	Where Captured	Prison	Remarks
Holt, Alpheus Private	Unk	Unknown	Co. B, Hood's Battalion Virginia Reserve Infantry	June 15, 1864, Near Petersburg, Virginia	Point Lookout, Maryland, transferred to Elmira Prison, NY, July 30, 1864	Oath of Allegiance July 3, 1865
Holt, Daniel C. Private	Unk	March 6, 1864, Camp Holmes, North Carolina	Co. E, 13th North Carolina Infantry	May 6, 1864, Wilderness, Virginia	Point Lookout, Maryland, transferred to Elmira Prison, NY, August 14, 1864	Died February 14, 1865 of Variola (Smallpox), Grave No. 2164. Headstone has 12th LA.
Holt, David Private	Unk	April 18, 1864, Gordonville, Virginia	Co. C, 53rd Georgia Infantry	June 1, 1864, Gaines Mill Cold Harbor, Virginia	Point Lookout, Maryland, transferred to Elmira Prison, NY, July 17, 1864	Exchanged October 29, 1864 at Venus Point, Savannah River, GA.
Holt, E. F. Private	21	May 1, 1861, Raleigh, North Carolina	Co. H, 1st North Carolina Infantry	May 12, 1864, Spotsylvania Court House, Virginia	Point Lookout, Maryland, transferred to Elmira Prison, NY, August 6, 1864	Oath of Allegiance June 30, 1865
Holt, James P. Private	39	September 20, 1861, Camp of Instruction Near Raleigh, Chatham County, North Carolina	Co. B, 35th North Carolina Infantry	June 17, 1864, Near Petersburg, Virginia	Point Lookout, Maryland, transferred to Elmira Prison, NY, July 30, 1864	Exchanged October 29, 1864 at Venus Point, Savannah River, GA.
Holt, Martin N. Private	36	August 25, 1864, Coosa County, Alabama	Co. C, 12th Alabama Infantry	April 25, 1865, Fort Steadman, Virginia	Old Capital Prison, Washington, DC. Transferred to Elmira Prison Camp, NY, May 12, 1865.	Died July 17, 1865 of Unknown Disease, Grave No. 2870
Holt, Thomas Private	Unk	May 1, 1862, Fayetteville, Georgia	Co. C, 53rd Georgia Infantry	June 1, 1864, Gaines Mill Cold Harbor, Virginia	Point Lookout, Maryland, transferred to Elmira Prison, NY, July 17,1864	Oath of Allegiance June 14, 1865
Holton, Charles H. Private	16	February 1, 1864, Charlotte, North Carolina	Co. K, 45th North Carolina Infantry	July 17,1864, Near Washington, DC	Old Capital Prison, Washington, DC, transferred to Elmira July 23, 1864	Exchanged March 14, 1865 at Boulware's Wharf on the James River, Virginia

Name & Rank	Age	Enlisted	Regiment and State	Where Captured	Prison	Remarks
Holtree, Richard J. Sergeant	Unk	Unknown	Co. B, 1st Battalion Louisiana Cavalry	October 14, 1864, Harrisonburg, Louisiana	Old Capital Prison, Washington, DC, transferred to Elmira Prison, NY, December 4, 1864	Died February 19, 1865 of Pneumonia, Grave No. 2324. Headstone has Horttree.
Holtzclaw, Henry Private	Unk	November 7, 1861, Camp Wayne, Georgia	Co. G, 61st Georgia Infantry	May 12, 1864, Spotsylvania Court House, Virginia	Point Lookout, Maryland, transferred to Elmira Prison, NY, July 25, 1864	Exchanged February 20, 1865 at Boulware's or Cox Wharf on the James River, Virginia
Homblock, Charles Private	30	April 1, 1862, New Orleans, Louisiana	Co. K, 14th Louisiana Infantry	May 12, 1864, Spotsylvania Court House, Virginia	Point Lookout, Maryland, transferred to Elmira Prison, NY, July 23, 1864	Oath of Allegiance May 29, 1865
Homburger, J. Private	Unk	March 7, 1864, Monroe County, Louisiana	Co. A, Harrison's 3rd Louisiana Cavalry	September 30, 1864, Tensan Parish, Louisiana	New Orleans, Louisiana transferred to Elmira November 19, 1864.	Exchanged February 25, 1865 at Boulware's or Cox Wharf on the James River, Virginia
Honeycutt, Hillary H. Private	42	July 23, 1863, Wilmington, North Carolina	Co. G, 40th Regiment, 3rd North Carolina Artillery	January 15, 1865, Fort Fisher, North Carolina	February 1, 1865 Elmira Prison Camp, New York	Exchanged March 2, 1865 at Boulware's Wharf on the James River, Virginia
Honeycutt, J. F. Private	18	May 5, 1861, Statesville, Iredell County, North Carolina	Co. A, 4th North Carolina Infantry	August 10, 1864, Summit Point, Virginia	Old Capital Prison, Washington, DC transferred to Elmira Prison, NY, August 27, 1864	Oath of Allegiance May 17, 1865
Honeycutt, M. N. Private	22	July 2, 1862, Salisbury, North Carolina	Co. B, 57th North Carolina Infantry	August 6, 1864, Hallstown, Maryland	Old Capital Prison, Washington, DC transferred to Elmira Prison, NY, August 27, 1864	Oath of Allegiance May 29, 1865

Name & Rank	Age	Enlisted	Regiment and State	Where Captured	Prison	Remarks
Honeycutt, Miles C. Private	23	September 1, 1861, Sampson County, North Carolina	Co. A, 30th North Carolina Infantry	September 22, 1864, Fishers Hill, Virginia	November 11, 1864, Old Capital Prison, Washington, DC. February 4, 1865 Elmira, Prison Camp, NY	Oath of Allegiance May 29, 1865
Honts, Alexander H. Private	Unk	January 11, 1864, Camp Instruction, Virginia	Co. L, 26th Battalion Virginia Infantry	June 3, 1864, Gaines Farm Cold Harbor, Virginia	Point Lookout, Maryland, transferred to Elmira Prison, NY, July 17,1864	Oath of Allegiance July 7, 1865
Hood, Dutton Corporal	Unk	July 1, 1861, Scott Creek, Scott County, Virginia	Co. A, 48th Virginia Infantry	May 12, 1864 Spotsylvania Court House, Virginia	Point Lookout, Maryland, transferred to Elmira Prison, NY, August 2, 1864	Oath of Allegiance June 23, 1865
Hood, H. T. Private	Unk	April 17, 1862, Columbus, Georgia	Co. A, 31st Georgia Infantry	May 20, 1864, Spotsylvania Court House, Virginia	Point Lookout, Maryland, transferred to Elmira Prison, NY, July 6, 1864	Exchanged February 20, 1865 at Boulware's or Cox Wharf on the James River, Virginia
Hood, James Private	Unk	Unknown	Co. G, 21st South Carolina Infantry	Unknown	Unknown	Died March 28, 1865 of Unknown Disease, Grave No. 2509
Hood, James A. Private	Unk	May 6, 1862, Pike County, Georgia	Co. D, 12th Georgia Infantry	May 10, 1864, Spotsylvania Court House, Virginia	Point Lookout, Maryland, transferred to Elmira Prison, NY, July 25, 1864	Oath of Allegiance June 27, 1865
Hood, John M. Sergeant	Unk	July 27, 1861, Newberry, South Carolina	Co. B, McCreary's 1st South Carolina Infantry	May 24, 1864, Hanover Junction, Virginia	Point Lookout, Maryland, transferred to Elmira Prison, NY, July 12,1864	Exchanged March 10, 1865 at Boulware's Wharf on the James River, Virginia
Hood, Robert Private	18	November 15, 1861, Elizabeth City, North Carolina	Co. J, 5th North Carolina Infantry	May 6, 1864, Wilderness, Virginia	Point Lookout, Maryland, transferred to Elmira Prison, NY, August 14, 1864	Oath of Allegiance June 23, 1865

Name & Rank	Age	Enlisted	Regiment and State	Where Captured	Prison	Remarks
Hood, Robert B. Sergeant	26	July 16, 1862, Camp Holmes, Raleigh, North Carolina	Co. E, 24th North Carolina Infantry	June 17, 1864, Petersburg, Virginia	Point Lookout, Maryland, transferred to Elmira Prison, NY, July 30, 1864	Died October 26, 1864 of Chronic Diarrhea, Grave No. 854. Name Robin Bold Hood on Headstone.
Hood, W. H. Private	Unk	Unknown	Co. A, Powers Cavalry, Mississippi	September 10, 1864, Near Matches, Louisiana	New Orleans, LA, Transferred to Elmira Prison, NY, November 19, 1864	Exchanged February 25, 1865 at Boulware's or Cox Wharf on the James River, Virginia
Hook, Samuel P. Private	Unk	April 11, 1862, Coles Island, South Carolina	Co. G, 25th South Carolina Infantry	January 15, 1865, Fort Fisher, North Carolina	January 30, 1865, Elmira Prison Camp, New York	Died March 8, 1865 of Pneumonia, Grave No. 2374. Headstone has L. P. Hooks.
Hooker, Clarkson Private	15	November 1, 1862, Asheboro, North Carolina	Co. F, 2nd Battalion North Carolina Infantry	July 10, 1864, Frederick Junction, Maryland	Old Capital Prison, Washington, DC, transferred to Elmira July 23, 1864	Oath of Allegiance May 29, 1865
Hooks, Andrew Private	28	February 24, 1862, Wadesboro, North Carolina	Co. H, 43rd North Carolina Infantry	May 16, 1864, Near Drury's Bluff, Virginia	Point Lookout, Maryland, transferred to Elmira Prison, NY, August 17, 1864	Transferred For Exchange October 11, 1864 to Point Lookout Prison Camp, MD. Died of Unknown Causes October 21, 1864.
Hooks, Daniel Private	Unk	March 4, 1862, Starkville, Lee County, Georgia	Co. B, 51st Georgia Infantry	June 3, 1864, Gaines Farm Cold Harbor, Virginia	Point Lookout, Maryland, transferred to Elmira Prison, NY, July 17,1864	Died September 19, 1864 of Typhoid Fever Grave No. 511
Hooks, William L. Private	Unk	June 22, 1861, Camp McDonald, Georgia	Co. J, 18th Georgia Infantry	June 1, 1864, Cold Harbor, Virginia	Point Lookout, Maryland, transferred to Elmira Prison, NY, July 17,1864	Oath of Allegiance July 7, 1865

Name & Rank	Age	Enlisted	Regiment and State	Where Captured	Prison	Remarks
Hooper, Anderson W. C. Private	Unk	May 20, 1862, Richmond, Virginia	Co. D, 24th Georgia Infantry	June 1, 1864, Cold Harbor, Virginia	Point Lookout, Maryland, transferred to Elmira Prison, NY, July 17,1864	Exchanged October 29, 1864 at Venus Point, Savannah River, GA.
Hooper, James A. Private	22	July 3, 1861, Atlanta, Georgia	Co. C, 11th Georgia Infantry	May 6, 1864, Wilderness, Virginia	Point Lookout, Maryland, transferred to Elmira Prison, NY, August 14, 1864	Oath of Allegiance June 20, 1865
Hooper, James S. Private	Unk	September 8, 1862, Clayton, Georgia	Co. C, 24th Georgia Infantry	August 16, 1864, Front Royal, Virginia	Old Capital Prison, Washington, DC transferred to Elmira Prison, NY, August 29, 1864	Exchanged February 20, 1865 at Boulware's or Cox Wharf on the James River, Virginia
Hooper, W. A. Private	Unk	Unknown	Co. D, 24th Georgia Infantry	June 1, 1864, Cold Harbor, Virginia	Point Lookout, Maryland, transferred to Elmira Prison, NY, July 15,1864	No Additional Information.
Hooter, John W. Private	Unk	Unknown	Co. A, Woods Regiment Confederate Cavalry	August 31, 1864, Grand Gulf, Mississippi	Fort Columbus, NY Harbor, transferred to Elmira Prison, NY, December 4, 1864.	Died December 17, 1864 of Pneumonia, Grave No. 1283
Hoover, David M. Corporal	25	January 2, 1862, Camp Lee, South Carolina	Co. G, 17th South Carolina Infantry	April 25, 1865, Fort Steadman, Virginia. Gunshot Wound Right Hip.	Old Capital Prison, Washington, DC, transferred to Elmira Prison, NY, May 12, 1865.	Oath of Allegiance July 7, 1865
Hoover, George W. Private	Unk	May 27, 1861, Buckhannon, Virginia	Co. B, 25th Virginia Infantry	May 12, 1864, Spotsylvania Court House, Virginia	Point Lookout, Maryland, transferred to Elmira Prison, NY, August 12, 1864	Oath of Allegiance June 16, 1865
Hope, Lawson H Private	Unk	July 9, 1861, Cumming, Georgia	Co. E, 14th Georgia Infantry	May 12, 1864, Spotsylvania Court House, Virginia	Point Lookout, Maryland, transferred to Elmira Prison, NY, August 12, 1864	Oath of Allegiance June 23, 1865

Name & Rank	Age	Enlisted	Regiment and State	Where Captured	Prison	Remarks
Hope, Thomas S. Private	22	March 15, 1862, Lincolnton, North Carolina	Co. B, 23rd North Carolina Infantry	July 15, 1864, Sharpsburg, Maryland. Deserted to Union Lines.	Old Capital Prison, Washington, DC, transferred to Elmira Prison, NY, August 12, 1864	Oath of Allegiance December 23, 1864. Early Release per Lincoln's Proclamation, 12/8/1863.
Hopkins, D. A. Private	22	October 14, 1861, High House, Wake County, North Carolina	Co. H, 31st North Carolina Infantry	June 1, 1864, Gaines Mill Cold Harbor, Virginia	Point Lookout, Maryland, transferred to Elmira Prison, NY, July 17, 1864	Exchanged March 10, 1865 at Boulware's Wharf on the James River, Virginia
Hopkins, David L. Sergeant	25	February 27, 1862, Reidsville, North Carolina	Co. E, 45th North Carolina Infantry	April 25, 1865, Fort Steadman, Virginia. Gunshot Wound Left Hip.	Old Capital Prison, Washington, DC, transferred to Elmira Prison, NY, May 12, 1865.	Oath of Allegiance June 23, 1865
Hopkins, George W. Corporal	18	May 18, 1861, Seven Mile Ford, Virginia	Co. D, 48th Virginia Infantry	May 12, 1864, Spotsylvania Court House, Virginia	Point Lookout, Maryland, transferred to Elmira Prison, NY, August 2, 1864	Died April 24, 1865 of Chronic Diarrhea, Grave No. 1408
Hopkins, Luke H. Private	28	June 24, 1861, Williamston, North Carolina	Co. H, 1st North Carolina Infantry	May 12, 1864, Spotsylvania Court House, Virginia	Point Lookout, Maryland, transferred to Elmira Prison, NY, August 6, 1864	Died February 20, 1865 of variola (Smallpox), Grave No. 2314
Hopkins, Noah B. Corporal	18	May 18, 1861, Seven Mile Ford, Virginia	Co. D, 48th Virginia Infantry	May 12, 1864, Spotsylvania Court House, Virginia	Point Lookout, Maryland, transferred to Elmira Prison, NY, August 2, 1864	Oath of Allegiance, May 29, 1865
Hopkins, William P. Private	18	July 1, 1862, Raleigh, North Carolina	Co. K, 1st North Carolina Infantry	May 12, 1864, Spotsylvania Court House, Virginia	Point Lookout, Maryland, transferred to Elmira Prison, NY, August 6, 1864	Died October 5, 1864 of Chronic Diarrhea, Grave No. 601
Horn, Henry W. Private	Unk	October 11, 1861, Savannah, Georgia	Co. G, 60th Georgia Infantry	May 23, 1864, North Anna, Virginia	Point Lookout, Maryland, transferred to Elmira Prison, NY, July 11, 1864	Exchanged March 2, 1865 on Boulware's Wharf the James River, Virginia

Name & Rank	Age	Enlisted	Regiment and State	Where Captured	Prison	Remarks
Horn, Lewis H. Private	19	August 17, 1862, Raleigh, North Carolina	Co. J, 18th North Carolina Infantry	May 6, 1864, Wilderness, Virginia	Point Lookout, Maryland, transferred to Elmira Prison, NY, August 14, 1864	Exchanged October 29, 1864 at Venus Point, Savannah River, GA.
Horn, Little Berry Private	33	March 5, 1862, Wilmington, North Carolina	Co. E, 36th Regiment 2nd North Carolina Artillery	January 15, 1865, Fort Fisher, North Carolina	February 1, 1865 Elmira Prison Camp, New York	Exchanged February 20, 1865 at Boulware's or Cox Wharf on the James River, Virginia
Horn, W. W. Private	38	May 11, 1862, Gourdins Department, Williamsburg District, South Carolina	Co. I, 25th South Carolina Infantry	January 15, 1865, Fort Fisher, North Carolina	January 30, 1865, Elmira Prison Camp, New York	Oath of Allegiance July 11, 1865
Horn, William W. Private	17	April 12, 1864, Shelby, North Carolina	Co. E, 12th North Carolina Infantry	May 12, 1864, Near Spotsylvania, Virginia	Point Lookout, Maryland, transferred to Elmira Prison, NY, August 14, 1864	Exchanged October 29, 1864 at Venus Point, Savannah River, GA.
Hornady, Lewis D. Private	31	April 28, 1862, Jonesboro, North Carolina	Co. H, 30th North Carolina Infantry	May 12, 1864, Near Spotsylvania Court House, Virginia	Point Lookout, Maryland, transferred to Elmira Prison, NY, August 14, 1864	Oath of Allegiance June 27, 1865
Horne, Daniel W. Private	31	May 7, 1862, Fort Fisher, North Carolina	Co. C, 36th Regiment 2nd North Carolina Artillery	January 15, 1865, Fort Fisher, North Carolina	February 1, 1865 Elmira Prison Camp, New York	Died March 26, 1865 of Variola (Smallpox), Grave No. 2470
Horne, Pleasant Private	41	September 13, 1863, Camp Holmes, North Carolina	Co. H, 30th North Carolina Infantry	May 12, 1864, Near Spotsylvania Court House, Virginia	Point Lookout, Maryland, transferred to Elmira Prison, NY, August 14, 1864	Died October 25, 1864 of Scorbutus (Scurvy), Grave No. 378
Horne, William B. Private	Unk	July 18, 1862, Cumberland County, North Carolina	Co. C, 3rd North Carolina Infantry	May 12, 1864, Near Spotsylvania Court House, Virginia	Point Lookout Prison, Maryland. Transferred to Elmira Prison Camp New York August 14, 1864.	Oath of Allegiance June 30, 1865

Name & Rank	Age	Enlisted	Regiment and State	Where Captured	Prison	Remarks
Horne, William J. Private	18	July 26, 1863, Fort Fisher, North Carolina	Co. C, 36th Regiment 2nd North Carolina Artillery	January 15, 1865, Fort Fisher, North Carolina	February 1, 1865 Elmira Prison Camp, New York	Died March 7, 1865 of Chronic Diarrhea, Grave No. 2399
Horner, David H. Private	Unk	March 17, 1862, Charlotte, North Carolina	Co. E, 17th South Carolina Infantry	March 25, 1865, Fort Stedman, Virginia. Contusion of Nose and Eye.	Old Capital Prison, Washington, DC, transferred to Elmira Prison, NY, May 12, 1865.	Oath of Allegiance July 7, 1865
Horrogan, Daniel Private	26	June 4, 1861, Camp Moore, Louisiana	Co. J, 6th Louisiana Infantry	May 5, 1864, Wilderness, Virginia	Point Lookout, Maryland, transferred to Elmira Prison, NY, August 17, 1864	Exchanged February 25, 1865 at Boulware's or Cox Wharf on the James River, Virginia
Horton, George P. Private	Unk	June 29, 1864, Fort Holmes, North Carolina	Co. G, 40th Regiment, 3rd North Carolina Artillery	January 15, 1865, Fort Fisher, North Carolina	January 30, 1865, Elmira Prison Camp, New York	Oath of Allegiance June 12, 1865
Horton, J. H. Private	30	September 6, 1862, Fort Morgan, Alabama	Co. C, 1st Battalion Alabama Artillery	August 23, 1864, Fort Morgan, Alabama	New Orleans, Louisiana transferred to Elmira Prison, NY, December 4, 1864.	Orders for Elmira, NY. Died in Transit January 31, 1865 of Variola at US Army Hospital Fort Columbus, NY Harbor.
Horton, Lewis Private	Unk	March 1, 1864, Savannah, Georgia	Co. K, Holcombe Legion, South Carolina Infantry	May 7, 1864, Stony Creek, Virginia	Point Lookout, Maryland, transferred to Elmira Prison, NY, August 17, 1864	Transferred for Exchange February 20, 1865. Died March 2, 1865 of Chronic Diarrhea at US Army Hospital, Baltimore, MD.
Horton, Nimrod R. Private	18	November 21, 1861, Spartanburg, South Carolina	Co. A, Holcombe Legion, South Carolina Infantry	May 7, 1864, Stony Creek, Virginia	Point Lookout, Maryland, transferred to Elmira Prison, NY, August 17, 1864	Exchanged February 13, 1865 at Boulware's wharf on the James River, Virginia

Name & Rank	Age	Enlisted	Regiment and State	Where Captured	Prison	Remarks
Horton, Solomon D. Private	Unk	March 13, 1862, Charleston, South Carolina	Co. E, 11th South Carolina Infantry	June 24, 1864, Near Petersburg, Virginia	Point Lookout, Maryland, transferred to Elmira Prison, NY, August 18, 1864	Oath of Allegiance June 16, 1865
Horton, Thomas F. Private	19	May 5, 1862, Jonesboro, Tennessee	Co. D, 63rd Tennessee Infantry	June 17, 1864, Petersburg, Virginia	Point Lookout, Maryland, transferred to Elmira Prison, NY, July 30, 1864	Exchanged February 25, 1865 at Boulware's or Cox Wharf on the James River, Virginia
Hoskins, George O. Private	22	July 15, 1862, Guilford County, North Carolina	Co. F, 1st North Carolina Infantry	May 12, 1864, Wilderness, Spotsylvania Court House, Virginia	Point Lookout, Maryland, transferred to Elmira Prison, NY, August 6, 1864	Oath of Allegiance May 17, 1865
Hotsfield, J. W. Private	Unk	Unknown	Co. A, Captain Norwood's Home Guard Florida	September 27, 1864, Marianna, Florida	New Orleans, Louisiana. Had Received Orders to Be Transferred to Elmira Prison, NY, November 19, 1864 Stayed on Because of Illness.	Died February 16, 1865 of Chronic Diarrhea at Fort Columbus, New York Harbor.
Hottle, David H. Sergeant	Unk	March 14, 1862, Woodstock, Virginia	Co. K, 7th Virginia Cavalry	September 22, 1863, Near Madison Court House, Virginia	Point Lookout, Maryland, transferred to Elmira Prison, NY, August 18, 1864	Oath of Allegiance May 13, 1865
Houching, G. L. Private	Unk	February 13, 1864, Albemarle, North Carolina	Co. G, 5th Virginia Cavalry	May 11, 1864, Yellow Tavern, Hanover County, Virginia	Point Lookout, Maryland, transferred to Elmira Prison, NY, August 17, 1864	Oath of Allegiance June 14, 1865
Hough, Nathanial G. Private	Unk	March 13, 1864, Longs, North Carolina	Co. F, 48th North Carolina Infantry	May 10, 1864, Near Mine Run, Spotsylvania, Virginia	Point Lookout, Maryland, transferred to Elmira Prison, NY, August 6, 1864	Died July 13, 1865 of Chronic Diarrhea, Grave No. 2876. Name Daniel on Headstone.

Name & Rank	Age	Enlisted	Regiment and State	Where Captured	Prison	Remarks
Houghton, William H. Private	Unk	May 1, 1861, Lewis County, Virginia	Co. B, 41st Battalion Virginia Cavalry	July 16, 1864, Harper's Ferry, Virginia. Gunshot Wound of Hand.	Old Capital Prison, Washington, DC, transferred to Elmira Prison, NY, August 12, 1864	Exchanged March 2, 1865 at Akins Landing on the James River, Virginia
Houltz, James Private	Unk	June 7, 1861, Staunton, Virginia	Co. D, 25th Virginia Infantry	May 12, 1864, Spotsylvania Court House, Virginia	Point Lookout, Maryland, transferred to Elmira Prison, NY, August 2, 1864	Exchanged March 2, 1865 on the James River, Virginia
House, A. C. Corporal	Unk	May 12, 1862, Goodwater, Alabama	Co. A, 59th Alabama Infantry	June 17, 1864, Petersburg, Virginia	Point Lookout, Maryland, transferred to Elmira Prison, NY, July 30, 1864	Oath of Allegiance June 19, 1865
House, E. W. Private	Unk	March 24, 1862, Pickensville, Alabama	Co. C, 5th Alabama Infantry	May 5, 1864, Wilderness, Virginia	Point Lookout, Maryland, transferred to Elmira Prison, NY, August 17, 1864	Exchanged March 2, 1865 at Akins Landing on the James River, Virginia
House, James M. Private	Unk	August 24, 1861, White County, Georgia	Co. C, 24th Georgia Infantry	August 16, 1864, Front Royal, Virginia	Old Capital Prison, Washington, DC transferred to Elmira Prison, NY, August 29, 1864	Died February 26, 1865 of Variola (Smallpox), Grave No. 2137
House, John H. Private	18	September 15, 1863, Brunswick County, North Carolina	Co. F, 36th Regiment 2nd North Carolina Artillery	January 15, 1865, Fort Fisher, North Carolina	February 1, 1865 Elmira Prison Camp, New York	Oath of Allegiance July 7, 1865
House, John W. Private	Unk	April 22, 1864, Concord, North Carolina	Co. H, 8th North Carolina Infantry	June 1, 1864, Gaines Mill Cold Harbor, Virginia	Point Lookout, Maryland, transferred to Elmira Prison, NY, July 17,1864	Died September 26, 1864 of Rubeola, Grave No. 457
House, Samuel Sergeant	25	April 21, 1861, Memphis, Tennessee	Co. A, 1st Tennessee Heavy Artillery	August 23, 1864, Fort Morgan, Alabama	Fort Columbus, New York Harbor. Transferred February 4, 1865 Elmira, Prison Camp, NY	Exchanged March 10, 1865 at Boulware's Wharf on the James River, Virginia

Name & Rank	Age	Enlisted	Regiment and State	Where Captured	Prison	Remarks
Houser, Theodore Private	26	April 28, 1861, New Orleans, Louisiana	Co. D, 1st Louisiana Infantry	May 8, 1864, Wilderness Cold Harbor, Virginia	Point Lookout, Maryland, transferred to Elmira Prison, NY, July 23, 1864	Oath of Allegiance May 15, 1865
Housley, J. M. Private	23	November 6, 1861, Cleveland, Tennessee	Co. H, 63rd Tennessee Infantry	June 17, 1864, Petersburg, Virginia	Point Lookout, Maryland, transferred to Elmira Prison, NY, July 30, 1864	Exchanged February 25, 1865 at Boulware's or Cox Wharf on the James River, Virginia
Houston, John J. Private	Unk	September 3, 1862, Sumter City, Alabama	Co. D, Jeff Davis Legion Mississippi Cavalry	June 11, 1864, Trevilian Station, Louisa Court House, Virginia	Point Lookout, Maryland, transferred to Elmira Prison, NY, July 25, 1864	Transported to Venus Point, Savannah River, GA, 11/15/1864
Houston, Persis D. Private	Unk	May 15, 1862, Camp Harris, Tennessee	Co. C, 17th Tennessee Infantry	June 17, 1864, Petersburg, Virginia	Point Lookout, Maryland, transferred to Elmira Prison, NY, July 30, 1864	Oath of Allegiance April 3, 1865
Houts, James P. Sergeant	Unk	June 4, 1861, Salem, Virginia	Co. E, 42nd Virginia Infantry	May 12, 1864, Near Spotsylvania Court House, Virginia	Point Lookout, Maryland, transferred to Elmira Prison, NY, August 6, 1864	Exchanged March 14, 1865 at Boulware's Wharf on the James River, Virginia
Hovis, Jacob D. Private	Unk	August 12, 1862, Statesville, North Carolina	Co. H, 37th North Carolina Infantry	July 29, 1864, Petersburg, Virginia	Point Lookout, Maryland, transferred to Elmira Prison, NY, August 12, 1864	Oath of Allegiance June 12, 1865
Hovis, Moses Private	19	March 25, 1862, Lincoln County, North Carolina	Co. H, 52nd North Carolina Infantry	May 12, 1864, Spotsylvania Court House, Virginia	Point Lookout, Maryland, transferred to Elmira Prison, NY, August 12, 1864	Oath of Allegiance June 12, 1865
Howard, G. W. James Private	Unk	Unknown	Co. I, 18th South Carolina Infantry	July 30, 1864, Petersburg, Virginia	Point Lookout, Maryland, transferred to Elmira Prison, NY, August 12, 1864	Died January 19, 1865 of Variola (Smallpox), Grave No. 1199

Name & Rank	Age	Enlisted	Regiment and State	Where Captured	Prison	Remarks
Howard, George W. Private	28	December 20, 1862, Edgecombe County, North Carolina	Co. K, 3rd North Carolina Cavalry	May 27, 1864, Pamunkey, Virginia	Point Lookout, Maryland, transferred to Elmira Prison, NY, July 26, 1864	Oath of Allegiance July 26, 1865
Howard, Fleet. H. Private	21	September 11, 1861, Sampson County, North Carolina	Co. A, 13th North Carolina Infantry	May 12, 1864, Spotsylvania Court House, Virginia	Point Lookout, Maryland, transferred to Elmira Prison, NY, August 14, 1864	Exchanged October 29, 1864 at Venus Point, Savannah River, GA.
Howard, Harrison H. Private	20	April 26, 1861, Mocksville, North Carolina	Co. F, 13th North Carolina Infantry	May 6, 1864, Wilderness, Virginia	Point Lookout Prison Camp, Maryland. Transferred to Elmira Prison, NY, August 14, 1864	Died February 13, 1865 of Variola (Smallpox), Grave No. 2032
Howard, Henry O. Color Sergeant	20	April 29, 1861, Yanceyville, North Carolina	Co. A, 13th North Carolina Infantry	May 6, 1864, Wilderness, Virginia	Point Lookout, Maryland, transferred to Elmira Prison, NY, August 14, 1864	Oath of Allegiance June 16, 1865
Howard, Isaac Private	Unk	February 20, 1863, Albany, Georgia	Co. D, 64th Georgia Infantry	August 18, 1864, New Market, Virginia	Point Lookout, Maryland, transferred to Elmira Prison, NY, August 29, 1864	Exchanged February 13, 1865 at Boulware's Wharf on the James River, Virginia
Howard, James H. Private	Unk	Unknown	Co. B, Mosby's Regiment Virginia Cavalry	January 15, 1865, Farquier County, Virginia	November 11, 1864, Old Capital Prison, Washington, DC. February 4, 1865 Elmira, Prison Camp, NY	Exchanged March 14, 1865 at Boulware's Wharf on the James River, Virginia
Howard, James M. Private	Unk	June 13, Lebanon, DeKalb County, Alabama	Co. E, 12th, Alabama Infantry	May 20, 1864, Spotsylvania Court House, Virginia	Point Lookout, Maryland, transferred to Elmira Prison, NY, July 6, 1864	Oath of Allegiance June 30, 1865

Name & Rank	Age	Enlisted	Regiment and State	Where Captured	Prison	Remarks
Howard, John Private	Unk	June 4, 1861, Camp Moore, New Orleans, Louisiana	Co. C, 6th Louisiana Infantry	May 5, 1864, Wilderness, Virginia	Point Lookout, Maryland, transferred to Elmira Prison, NY, August 18, 1864	Transferred February 15, 1865 to The US Army Baltimore, MD. Oath of Allegiance June 10, 1865
Howard, John E. Private	Unk	September 1, 1862, Richmond, Virginia	Co. C, 1st Maryland Cavalry	July 16, 1864, Loudoun County, Virginia	Old Capital Prison, Washington, DC, transferred to Elmira July 23, 1864	Exchanged October 29, 1864 at Venus Point, Savannah River, GA.
Howard, John J. Private	Unk	February 22, 1862, Blockers, Alabama	Co. C, 1st Battalion Alabama Artillery	August 23, 1864, Fort Morgan, Alabama	Steam Press No. 4 New Orleans, Louisiana transferred to Elmira October 8, 1864.	Died November 22, 1864 of Chronic Diarrhea, Grave No. 926
Howard, John L. Private	Unk	April 28, 1862, Camp Pillow, South Carolina	Co. I, 17th South Carolina Infantry	July 30, 1864, Near Petersburg, Virginia	Point Lookout, Maryland, transferred to Elmira Prison, NY, August 12, 1864	Died March 16, 1865 of Diarrhea, Grave No. 1705
Howard, John L. Private	26	February 1, 1864, New Market, Virginia	Co. A, 35th Battalion Virginia Cavalry	July 21, 1864, Captured Near North Fork, Loudoun County, Virginia	Old Capital Prison, Washington, DC, transferred to Elmira Prison, NY, August 12, 1864	Exchanged March 10, 1865 at Boulware's Wharf on the James River, Virginia
Howard, John W. Corporal	Unk	Unknown	Co. K, 22nd North Carolina Infantry	May 24, 1864, North Anna, Virginia	Point Lookout, Maryland, transferred to Elmira Prison, NY, July 23, 1864	Died October 24, 1864 of Chronic Diarrhea, Grave No. 847
Howard, Joseph A. Private	35	January 1, 1862, Georgetown, South Carolina	Co. A, 21st South Carolina Infantry	June 24, 1864, Near Petersburg, Virginia	Point Lookout, Maryland, transferred to Elmira Prison, NY, August 18, 1864	Died September 28, 1864 of Chronic Diarrhea, Grave No. 394
Howard, Levi Private	20	April 27, 1861, Newton, North Carolina	Co. F, 32nd North Carolina Infantry	May 10, 1864, Wilderness, Virginia	Point Lookout, Maryland, transferred to Elmira Prison, NY, August 6, 1864	Oath of Allegiance June 30, 1865

Name & Rank	Age	Enlisted	Regiment and State	Where Captured	Prison	Remarks
Howard, W. S. Private	Unk	March 16, 1862, Autauga, Alabama	Co. B, 59th Alabama Infantry	June 17, 1864, Petersburg, Virginia	Point Lookout, Maryland, transferred to Elmira Prison, NY, July 30, 1864	Oath of Allegiance June 19, 1865
Howard, William Private	24	April 14, 1862, Lenoir County, North Carolina	Co. E, 61st North Carolina Infantry	July 27, 1863, Morris Island, South Carolina	Point Lookout Prison Camp, Maryland. Transferred to Elmira Prison Camp July 25, 1864	Died October 12, 1864 of Chronic Diarrhea, Grave. 696
Howard, William Private	18	September 1, 1864, Duplin County, North Carolina	Co. D, 1st Battalion North Carolina Heavy Artillery	January 15, 1865, Fort Fisher, North Carolina	February 1, 1865 Elmira Prison Camp, New York	Died May 1, 1865 of Chronic Diarrhea, Grave No. 2736
Howard, William Key Private	Unk	March 19, 1863, Culpepper, Virginia	Co. E, 4th Virginia Cavalry	August 16, 1864, Front Royal, Virginia	Point Lookout, Maryland, transferred to Elmira Prison, NY, August 29, 1864	Exchanged February 13, 1865 at Boulware's Wharf on the James River, Virginia
Howe, David R. T. Corporal	Unk	July 19, 1861, Montgomery, Alabama	Co. I, 13th Alabama Infantry	May 12, 1864, Spotsylvania Court House, Virginia	Point Lookout, Maryland, transferred to Elmira Prison, NY, August 12, 1864	Died May 1, 1865 of Chronic Diarrhea, Grave No. 2742
Howe, J. T. Private	Unk	April 13, 1863, Wilmington, North Carolina	Co. G, 18th South Carolina Infantry	July 30, 1864, Petersburg, Virginia	Point Lookout, Maryland, transferred to Elmira Prison, NY, August 12, 1864	Died September 24, 1864 of Typhoid Fever, Grave No. 459
Howe, Nathanial S. Private	Unk	January 22, 1862, Columbia, South Carolina	Co. B, 22nd South Carolina Infantry	June 17, 1864, Petersburg, Virginia	Point Lookout, Maryland, transferred to Elmira Prison, NY, July 30, 1864	Died November 23, 1864 of Chronic Diarrhea, Grave No. 930
Howell, Abner Private	24	June 10, 1861, Weldon, North Carolina	Co. K, 1st North Carolina Infantry	Unknown	Point Lookout Prison Camp, Maryland. Transferred to Elmira Prison, August 6, 1864	Died December 30, 1864 of Unknown Disease, Grave No. 1320

Name & Rank	Age	Enlisted	Regiment and State	Where Captured	Prison	Remarks
Howell, Curtis D. Private	Unk	September 20, 1862, Goldsboro, North Carolina	Co. F, 10th Regiment, 1st North Carolina Artillery	January 15, 1865, Fort Fisher, North Carolina	January 30, 1865, Elmira Prison Camp, New York	Oath of Allegiance May 29, 1865
Howell, Daniel Corporal	Unk	March 4, 1862, Camilla, Georgia	Co. C, 51st Georgia Infantry	June 2, 1864, Gaines Farm Cold Harbor, Virginia	Point Lookout Prison, Maryland Transferred July 17,1864 to Elmira, NY	Oath of Allegiance July 11, 1865
Howell, Ezekiel H. Private	22	April 22, 1864, Shelby, North Carolina	Co. E, 12th North Carolina Infantry	May 12, 1864, Near Spotsylvania, Virginia	Point Lookout, Maryland, transferred to Elmira Prison, NY, August 14, 1864	Oath of Allegiance June 23, 1865
Howell, Isaac T. Private	Unk	May 14, 1863, Atlanta, Georgia	Co. B 64th Georgia Infantry	August 16, 1864, New Market, Virginia	Old Capital Prison, Washington, DC transferred to Elmira Prison, NY, August 27, 1864	Oath of Allegiance May 17, 1865
Howell, J. B. Private	Unk	May 28, 1863, Morris Island, South Carolina	Co. H, 21st South Carolina Infantry	July 10, 1863, Morris Island, South Carolina	Point Lookout, Maryland, transferred to Elmira Prison, NY, August 18, 1864	Exchanged October 29, 1864 at Venus Point, Savannah River, GA.
Howell, J. L. Private	Unk	Unknown	Co. D, 12th Alabama Infantry	May 12, 1864, Spotsylvania Court House, Virginia	Point Lookout, Maryland, transferred to Elmira Prison, NY, August 12, 1864	Oath of Allegiance June 14, 1865
Howell, James C. Private	39	May 29, 1861, Stevensville, Virginia	Co. K, 34th Virginia Infantry	June 15, 1864, Near Petersburg, Virginia	Point Lookout Prison, Maryland Transferred July 12,1864 to Elmira, NY	Exchanged March 14, 1865 on the James River, Virginia
Howell, John H. Private	19	August 28, 1861, Lancasterville, South Carolina	Co. J, 12th South Carolina Infantry	July 14, 1863, Falling Waters, Maryland	Point Lookout, Maryland, transferred to Elmira Prison, NY, August 18, 1864	Exchanged at Venus Point, Savannah River, GA, 10/29/1864

Name & Rank	Age	Enlisted	Regiment and State	Where Captured	Prison	Remarks
Howell, Julius A. Private	28	April 28, 1862, Albemarle, North Carolina	Co. J, 52nd North Carolina Infantry	July 14, 1863, Falling Waters, Maryland	Point Lookout, Maryland, transferred to Elmira Prison, NY, August 18, 1864	Exchanged at Venus Point, Savannah River, GA, 10/29/1864
Howell, Kader Private	18	July 12, 1861, Halifax County, North Carolina	Co. C, 5th North Carolina Infantry	May 12, 1864, Spotsylvania Court House, Virginia	Point Lookout, Maryland, transferred to Elmira Prison, NY, August 6, 1864	Oath of Allegiance May 29, 1865
Howell, L. D. Private	Unk	March 8, 1863, Goldsboro, North Carolina	Co. F, 10th Regiment, 1st North Carolina Artillery	January 15, 1865, Fort Fisher, North Carolina	January 30, 1865, Elmira Prison Camp, New York	Died May 22, 1865 of Chronic Diarrhea, Grave No. 2933
Howell, Leonard R. Private	Unk	September 4, 1862, Highland, Virginia	Co. A, 62nd Virginia Mounted Infantry	July 14, 1864, Hagerstown, Maryland	Old Capital Prison, Washington, DC, transferred to Elmira July 23, 1864	Oath of Allegiance July 7, 1865
Howell, Levi D. Private	43	March 8, 1864, Goldsboro, North Carolina	Co. F, 10th Regiment, 1st North Carolina Artillery	January 15, 1865, Fort Fisher, North Carolina	January 30, 1865 Elmira Prison Camp, New York	Died May 22, 1865 of Chronic Diarrhea, Grave No. 2933
Howell, M. Private	Unk	Unknown	Co. H, 3rd Alabama Infantry	July 17,1864, Near Washington, DC	Old Capital Prison, Washington, DC, transferred to Elmira Prison, NY, July 23, 1864	Exchanged March 14, 1865 at Boulware's Wharf on the James River, Virginia
Howell, Ralph Private	22	March 3, 1862, Wilmington, New Hanover County, North Carolina	Co. D, 36th Regiment North Carolina, 2nd Artillery	January 15, 1865, Fort Fisher, North Carolina	February 1, 1865 Elmira Prison Camp, New York	Oath Of Allegiance July 7, 1865
Howell, Richard M. Private	27	June 28, 1861, Beaufort, North Carolina	Co. F, 10th Regiment, 1st North Carolina Artillery	January 15, 1865, Fort Fisher, North Carolina	January 30, 1865, Elmira Prison Camp, New York	Exchanged February 20, 1865 at Boulware's or Cox Wharf on the James River, Virginia

Name & Rank	Age	Enlisted	Regiment and State	Where Captured	Prison	Remarks
Howell, Thomas Private	Unk	May 14, 1863, Atlanta, Georgia	Co. B 64th Georgia Infantry	August 16, 1864, New Market, Virginia	Old Capital Prison, Washington, DC transferred to Elmira Prison, NY, August 27, 1864	Died April 18, 1865, of Pneumonia, Grave No. 1360
Howser, Charles T. J. Sergeant	16	August 4, 1861, Lincolnton, North Carolina	Co. D, 1st North Carolina Infantry	May 12, 1864, Spotsylvania Court House, Virginia	Point Lookout, Maryland, transferred to Elmira Prison, NY, August 6, 1864	Oath of Allegiance June 21, 1865
Howser, Joseph H. Private	Unk	March 21, 1862, Scott County, Virginia	Co. H, 48th Virginia Infantry	May 12, 1864, Near Spotsylvania Court House, Virginia	Point Lookout, Maryland, transferred to Elmira Prison, NY, August 6, 1864	Exchanged March 2, 1865 at Akins Landing on the James River, Virginia
Hoyle, Phillip A. Private	Unk	October 2, 1863, Camp Vance, North Carolina	Co. F, 23rd North Carolina Infantry	May 12, 1864, Near Spotsylvania Court House, Virginia	Point Lookout, Maryland, transferred to Elmira Prison, NY, August 18, 1864	Oath of Allegiance June 30, 1865
Hoyle, William H. Corporal	Unk	August 20, 1861, Tallahassee, Florida	Co. M, 2nd Florida Infantry	May 12, 1864, Spotsylvania Court House, Virginia	Point Lookout, Maryland, transferred to Elmira Prison, NY, August 12, 1864	Died February 18, 1865 of Chronic Diarrhea, Grave No. 2223
Hubbard, D. C. Sergeant	24	April 7, 1862, Petersburg, Virginia	Co. K, 5th Virginia Cavalry	May 11, 1864, Yellow Tavern, Virginia	Point Lookout, Maryland, transferred to Elmira Prison, NY, July 12,1864	Oath of Allegiance May 15, 1865
Hubbard, J. B. Private	Unk	Unknown	Co. H, 25th South Carolina Infantry	January 15, 1865, Fort Fisher, North Carolina	January 30, 1865, Elmira Prison Camp, New York	Transferred to Post Hospital July 13, 1865. No Additional Information.
Hubbard, James W. Private	Unk	March 25, 1862, Patrick County, Virginia	Co. D, 12th Virginia Infantry	May 12, 1864, Spotsylvania Court House, Virginia	Point Lookout, Maryland, transferred to Elmira Prison, NY, August 12, 1864	Exchanged February 20, 1865 at Boulware's or Cox Wharf on the James River, Virginia

Name & Rank	Age	Enlisted	Regiment and State	Where Captured	Prison	Remarks
Hubbard, Richard F. Private	Unk	April 24, 1862, Granada, Mississippi	Co. K, 33rd Mississippi Infantry	May 16, 1863, Champion Hill, Mississippi	Point Lookout, Maryland, transferred to Elmira Prison, NY, August 18, 1864	Exchanged March 10, 1865 at Boulware's wharf on the James River, Virginia
Hubbard, Thomas Private	Unk	March 3, 1864, Thunderbolt, Georgia	Co. G, 7th Georgia Cavalry	June 11, 1864, Trevilian Station, Louisa Court House, Virginia	Point Lookout, Maryland, transferred to Elmira Prison, NY, July 25, 1864	Oath of Allegiance July 11, 1865
Hubble, Juston C. Sergeant	Unk	Unknown	Co. E, 50th Virginia Infantry	May 12, 1864, Spotsylvania Court House, Virginia	Point Lookout, Maryland, transferred to Elmira Prison, NY, August 2, 1864	Transferred for Exchange 10/11/64. Died 11/1/64 of Unknown Causes at Fort Monroe, VA.
Hudgens, Charles Private	Unk	July 16, 1863, Winchester, Virginia	Co. C, 1st Maryland Cavalry	July 13, 1864, Rockville, Maryland	Old Capital Prison, Washington, DC, transferred to Elmira July 23, 1864	Oath of Allegiance May 15, 1865
Hudgins, Albert F. Private	22	July 23, 1861, Matthews Court House, Virginia	Co. F, 5th Virginia Cavalry	May 11, 1864, Yellow Tavern, Hanover County, Virginia	Point Lookout, Maryland, transferred to Elmira Prison, NY, August 17, 1864	Oath of Allegiance June 19, 1865
Hudgins, Rueben B. Sergeant	Unk	June 6, 1861, New Canton, Virginia	Co. C, 44th Virginia Infantry	May 12, 1864, Spotsylvania Court House, Virginia	Point Lookout, Maryland, transferred to Elmira Prison, NY, August 2, 1864	Exchanged October 29, 1864 at Venus Point, Savannah River, GA.
Hudgins, Thomas H. Private	28	May 5, 1861, Roxboro, North Carolina	Co. A, 24th North Carolina Infantry	June 17, 1864, Petersburg, Virginia	Point Lookout, Maryland, transferred to Elmira Prison, NY, July 30, 1864	Exchanged March 14, 1865 at Boulware's Wharf on the James River, Virginia
Hudgins, Thomas J. Sergeant	Unk	June 6, 1861, New Canton, Virginia	Co. C, 44th Virginia Infantry	May 12, 1864, Spotsylvania Court House, Virginia	Point Lookout, Maryland, transferred to Elmira Prison, NY, August 2, 1864	Exchanged October 29, 1864 at Venus Point, Savannah River, GA.

Name & Rank	Age	Enlisted	Regiment and State	Where Captured	Prison	Remarks
Hudgins, W. H. Private	Unk	May 15, 1862, New Kent, Virginia	Co. D, 26th Virginia Infantry	May 8, 1864, Nottoway Bridge, Virginia	Point Lookout, Maryland, transferred to Elmira Prison, NY, August 17, 1864	Died March 9, 1865 of Chronic Diarrhea, Grave No. 1875. Name Hodgins on Headstone.
Hudler, David Private	23	August 15, 1862, Statesville, North Carolina	Co. B, 37th North Carolina Infantry	May 12, 1864, Spotsylvania Court House, Virginia	Point Lookout, Maryland, transferred to Elmira Prison, NY, August 12, 1864	Oath of Allegiance June 23, 1865
Hudson, Benjamin G. Private	32	March 22, 1862, Porter's Precinct, Virginia	Co. B, 15th Virginia Cavalry	June 10, 1864, Chickahominy, Cold Harbor, Virginia	Point Lookout, Maryland, transferred to Elmira Prison, NY, July 30, 1864	Died September 16, 1864 of Chronic Diarrhea, Grave No. 310
Hudson, Ephraim Green Sergeant	25	July 20, 1861, Camp Pickens, Sandy Springs, Anderson District, South Carolina	Co. C, Orr's Regiment 1st South Carolina infantry	July 28, 1864, Malvern Hill, Virginia. Gunshot Wound Right Thigh.	Old Capital Prison, Washington, DC, transferred to Elmira December 17, 1864	Died February 26, 1865 of Variola (Smallpox), Grave No. 2286
Hudson, Irvin Private	26	May 9, 1862, Wadesboro, North Carolina	Co. I, 43rd North Carolina Infantry	July 17, 1864, Near Washington, DC	Old Capital Prison, Washington, DC, transferred to Elmira July 23, 1864	Oath of Allegiance June 3, 1865
Hudson, J. Thomas Private	Unk	July 31, 1861, Hickory Flat, Alabama	Co. F, 14th Alabama Infantry	May 24, 1864, North Anna River, Hanover Junction, Virginia	Point Lookout, Maryland, transferred to Elmira Prison, NY, July 12, 1864	Oath of Allegiance June 19, 1865
Hudson, James Private	20	June 12, 1861, Halifax County, North Carolina	Co. K, 1st North Carolina Infantry	May 12, 1864, Near Spotsylvania Court House, Virginia	Point Lookout Prison, Maryland. Transferred to Elmira Prison Camp New York August 6, 1864.	Oath of Allegiance June 30, 1865
Hudson, John M. Private	26	September 5, 1861, Dawson, Georgia	Co. H, 31st Georgia Infantry	May 20, 1864, Spotsylvania Court House, Virginia	Point Lookout, Maryland, transferred to Elmira Prison, NY, July 6, 1864	Oath of Allegiance June 30, 1865

Name & Rank	Age	Enlisted	Regiment and State	Where Captured	Prison	Remarks
Hudson, Joshua B. Private	Unk	September 21, 1861, Conyers, Georgia	Co. B, 35th Georgia Infantry	May 6, 1864, Wilderness, Virginia	Point Lookout, Maryland, transferred to Elmira Prison, NY, August 14, 1864	Died February 19, 1865 of Variola (Smallpox), Grave No. 2331. Headstone has 25th GA.
Hudson, Thomas Private	Unk	September 8, 1863, Fort Johnson, South Carolina	Co. K, 21st South Carolina Infantry	January 15, 1865, Fort Fisher, North Carolina	January 30, 1865, Elmira Prison Camp, New York	Oath of Allegiance June 30, 1865
Hudson, William Private	34	July 15, 1862, Raleigh, North Carolina	Co. C, 5th North Carolina Infantry	May 12, 1864, Spotsylvania Court House, Virginia	Point Lookout, Maryland, transferred to Elmira Prison, NY, August 6, 1864	Died December 10, 1864 of Pneumonia, Grave No. 1045
Hudson, William A. Corporal	22	October 31, 1861, Pickens District, South Carolina	Co. B, 2nd South Carolina Infantry	June 3, 1864, Mechanicsville, Virginia	Point Lookout, Maryland, transferred to Elmira Prison, NY, July 17,1864	Died September 9, 1864 of Pneumonia, Grave No. 202
Hudson, William D. Sergeant	Unk	July 15, 1861, Elberton, Georgia	Co. C, 15th Georgia Infantry	July 3, 1863, Gettysburg, Pennsylvania	Point Lookout, Maryland, transferred to Elmira Prison, NY, August 18, 1864	Exchanged February 25, 1865 at Boulware's or Cox Wharf on the James River, Virginia
Huestess, George W. Private	37	September 1, 1863, Bennettsville, South Carolina	Co. F, 21st South Carolina Infantry	August 21, 1864, Weldon Railroad, Virginia	Old Capital Prison, Washington, DC, transferred to Elmira December 17, 1864	Died March 29, 1865 of Diarrhea, Grave No. 2515. Headstone has G. W. Husless.
Huff, Edward H. Private	28	April 22, 1861, Washington, Virginia	Co. B, 6th Virginia Cavalry	May 12, 1864, Spotsylvania Court House, Virginia	Point Lookout, Maryland, transferred to Elmira Prison, NY, August 12, 1864	Oath of Allegiance June 27, 1865
Huff, Eli B. Private	20	June 12, 1861, Miledgeville, Georgia	Co. F, 9th Georgia Infantry	May 24, 1864, Hanover Junction, Virginia	Point Lookout, Maryland, transferred to Elmira Prison, NY, July 11, 1864	Exchanged March 14, 1865 at Boulware's Wharf on the James River, Virginia

Name & Rank	Age	Enlisted	Regiment and State	Where Captured	Prison	Remarks
Huff, George P. Private	26	September 10, 1862, Newport, Cooke County, Tennessee	Co. J, 62nd Tennessee Mounted Infantry	May 16, 1863, Big Black, Mississippi	Point Lookout, Maryland, transferred to Elmira Prison, NY, July 25, 1864	Died August 16, 1864 of Chronic Diarrhea, Grave No. 124
Huff, H. J. Private	Unk	August 27, 1862, Milledgeville, Georgia	Co. F, 9th Georgia Infantry	May 6, 1864, Wilderness, Virginia	Old Capital Prison, Washington, DC, transferred to Elmira Prison, NY, July 14, 1864	Oath of Allegiance June 23, 1865
Huffer, Samuel Private	Unk	July 16, 1861, Staunton, Virginia	Co. D, 52nd Virginia, Infantry	May 30, 1864, Mechanicsville, Virginia	Point Lookout, Maryland, transferred to Elmira Prison, NY, July 9, 1864	Oath of Allegiance June 30, 1865
Huffman, Andrew Private	Unk	April 11, 1862, Coles Island, South Carolina	Co. F, 25th South Carolina Infantry	January 15, 1865, Fort Fisher, North Carolina	January 30, 1865, Elmira Prison Camp, New York	Died April 6, 1865 of Chronic Diarrhea, Grave No. 2641
Huffman, Andrew J. Private	Unk	July 22, 1861, Davis' Barracks, Virginia	Co. G, 49th Virginia Infantry	April 14, 1864, Rappahannock County, Virginia	Old Capital Prison, Washington, DC, transferred to Elmira July 23, 1864	Oath of Allegiance June 30, 1865
Huffman, D. J. Private	Unk	April 11, 1862, Coles Island, South Carolina	Co. F, 25th South Carolina Infantry	January 15, 1865, Fort Fisher, North Carolina	January 30, 1865, Elmira Prison Camp, New York	Oath of Allegiance July 11, 1865
Huffman, Daniel W. Private	18	August 13, 1861, Newton, North Carolina	Co. C, 33rd North Carolina Infantry	May 12, 1864, Spotsylvania Court House, Virginia	Point Lookout, Maryland, transferred to Elmira Prison, NY, August 14, 1864	Oath of Allegiance June 19, 1865
Huffman, James Private	Unk	June 17, 1861, Conrad's Store, Virginia	Co. I, 10th Virginia Infantry	May 12, 1864, Spotsylvania Court House, Virginia	Point Lookout, Maryland, transferred to Elmira Prison, NY, August 2, 1864	Oath of Allegiance June 27, 1865
Huffman, James D. Private	Unk	June 15, 1861, Macon, Georgia	Co. D, 12th Georgia Infantry	May 10, 1864, Spotsylvania Court House, Virginia	Point Lookout, Maryland, transferred to Elmira Prison, NY, July 25, 1864	Oath of Allegiance June 16, 1865

Name & Rank	Age	Enlisted	Regiment and State	Where Captured	Prison	Remarks
Huffman, M. P. Private	Unk	September 7, 1862, Murfreesboro, Tennessee	Co. B, 17th Tennessee Infantry	June 17, 1864, Petersburg, Virginia	Point Lookout, Maryland, transferred to Elmira Prison, NY, July 30, 1864	Exchanged February 25, 1865 at Boulware's or Cox Wharf on the James River, Virginia
Huffman, Milton Private	18	April 14, 1864, Camp Wyatt, Hanover County, North Carolina	Co. D, 36th Regiment 2nd North Carolina Artillery	January 15, 1865, Fort Fisher, North Carolina	February 1, 1865 Elmira Prison Camp, New York	Oath of Allegiance March 14, 1865
Hufford, John Private	Unk	April 7, 1862, Virginia	Co. J, 50th Virginia Infantry	May 6, 1864, Wilderness, Virginia	Point Lookout, Maryland, transferred to Elmira Prison, NY, August 14, 1864	Died April 10, 1865 of Chronic Diarrhea, Grave No. 2664
Huffstetler, Henry C. Private	20	March 15, 1862, Gaston County, North Carolina	Co. K, 49th North Carolina Infantry	June 9, 1864, Chickahominy Swamp, Cold Harbor, Virginia	Old Capital Prison, Washington, DC, transferred to Elmira July 23, 1864	Oath of Allegiance September 19, 1864
Huggins, Christopher C. Sergeant	24	February 21, 1862, Marion District, South Carolina	Co. L, 21st South Carolina Infantry	January 15, 1865, Fort Fisher, North Carolina	January 30, 1865, Elmira Prison Camp, New York	Oath of Allegiance June 23, 1865
Huggins, W. J. Private	Unk	February 29, 1864, Marion, South Carolina	Co. J, 21st South Carolina Infantry	June 24, 1864, Petersburg, Virginia	Point Lookout, Maryland, transferred to Elmira Prison, NY, August 18, 1864	Died September 27, 1864 of Chronic Diarrhea, Grave No. 385
Hughes, Alfred Private	Unk	January 25, 1864, Bristol, Tennessee	Co. J, 14th Tennessee Infantry	May 23, 1864, Mudd Tavern, Spotsylvania, Virginia	Point Lookout, Maryland, transferred to Elmira Prison, NY, July 25, 1864	Oath of Allegiance May 19, 1865
Hughes, Daniel H. Private	Unk	March 12, 1862, Randolph County, North Carolina	Co. L, 22nd North Carolina Infantry	May 30, 1864, Hanover Junction, Virginia	Point Lookout, Maryland, transferred to Elmira Prison, NY, July 11, 1864	Died March 17, 1864 of Diarrhea, Grave No. 1713
Hughes, David Private	Unk	June 1, 1861, Hillsville, Carroll County, Virginia	Co. D, 29th Virginia Infantry	March 30, 1864, Cherry Grove, Virginia	Point Lookout, Maryland, transferred to Elmira Prison, NY, July 26, 1864	Oath of Allegiance 11/1/1864. Early Release per Lincoln's Proclamation, 12/8/1863.

Name & Rank	Age	Enlisted	Regiment and State	Where Captured	Prison	Remarks
Hughes, Edward Private	45	September 25, 1863, Campbell, Virginia	Co. J, 2nd Virginia Cavalry	May 12, 1864, Near Spotsylvania Court House, Virginia	Point Lookout, Maryland, transferred to Elmira Prison, NY, July 23, 1864	Oath of Allegiance May 29, 1865
Hughes, Ephraim P. Private	Unk	January 6, 1862, Union Court House, South Carolina	Co. B, 15th South Carolina Infantry	July 27, 1864, Petersburg, Virginia	Point Lookout, Maryland, transferred to Elmira Prison, NY, August 12, 1864	Oath of Allegiance July 3, 1865
Hughes, Jesse G. Private	Unk	September 8, 1862, Frederick, Maryland	Co. K, 44th Virginia Infantry	May 12, 1864, Spotsylvania Court House, Virginia	Point Lookout, Maryland, transferred to Elmira Prison, NY, August 2, 1864	Exchanged March 10, 1865 at Boulware's Wharf on the James River, Virginia
Hughes, John J. Private	Unk	June 11, 1861, Georgia	Co. F, 3rd Battalion Georgia Sharp Shooters	August 16, 1864, Front Royal, Virginia	Old Capital Prison, Washington, DC transferred to Elmira Prison, NY, August 29, 1864	Exchanged October 29, 1864 at Venus Point, Savannah River, GA.
Hughes, Michael Corporal	Unk	April 25, 1861, New Orleans, Louisiana	Co. E, 1st Louisiana Infantry	May 12, 1864, Spotsylvania Court House, Virginia	Point Lookout, Maryland, transferred to Elmira Prison, NY, August 14, 1864	Exchanged February 13, 1865 at Boulware's wharf on the James River, Virginia
Hughes, Milcajah K. Private	Unk	November 4, 1863, Richmond, Virginia	Co. G, 6th Virginia Cavalry	May 11, 1864, Yellow Tavern, Hanover County, Virginia	Point Lookout, Maryland, transferred to Elmira Prison, NY, August 17, 1864	Died October 19, 1864 of Chronic Diarrhea, Grave No. 539
Hughes, Miles Private	Unk	Unknown	Co. L, 32nd North Carolina Infantry	May 20, 1864, Spotsylvania Court House, Virginia	Point Lookout, Maryland, transferred to Elmira Prison, NY, July 6, 1864	Died December 25, 1864 of Pneumonia, Grave No. 1110
Hughes, Milton T. Private	Unk	May 18, 1864, Raleigh, North Carolina	Co. F, 2nd North Carolina Infantry	July 8, 1864, Harper's Ferry, Virginia	Old Capital Prison, Washington, DC, transferred to Elmira July 23, 1864	Exchanged February 20, 1865 at Boulware's or Cox Wharf on the James River, Virginia

Name & Rank	Age	Enlisted	Regiment and State	Where Captured	Prison	Remarks
Hughes, R. F. Private	Unk	Unknown	Co. J, 32nd North Carolina Infantry	May 20, 1864, Spotsylvania Court House, Virginia	Point Lookout, Maryland, transferred to Elmira Prison, NY, July 6, 1864	Exchanged February 25, 1865 at Boulware's or Cox Wharf on the James River, Virginia
Hughes, Simon J. Private	19	November 5, 1864, Columbia, South Carolina	Co. C, 22nd South Carolina Infantry	March 29, 1865, Hatchers Run, Virginia. Gunshot Wound Left Side of Chest.	Old Capital Prison, Washington, DC, transferred to Elmira Prison, NY, May 12, 1865.	Oath of Allegiance July 7, 1865
Hughes, T. S. Private	Unk	January 15, 1864, Charleston, South Carolina	Co. F, 17th South Carolina Infantry	July 30, 1864, Petersburg, Virginia	Point Lookout, Maryland, transferred to Elmira Prison, NY, August 12, 1864	Oath of Allegiance July 3, 1865
Hughes, W. Private	Unk	Unknown	Co. E, 5th Alabama Infantry	August 10, 1864, Summit Point, Virginia	Old Capital Prison, Washington, DC transferred to Elmira Prison, NY, August 29, 1864	Exchanged March 2, 1865 at Akins Landing on the James River, Virginia
Hughes, William J. Corporal	Unk	June 11, 1861, Bledsoe's, Fluvanna County, Virginia	Co. K, 44th Virginia Infantry	May 12, 1864, Spotsylvania Court House, Virginia	Point Lookout, Maryland, transferred to Elmira Prison, NY, August 2, 1864	Exchanged March 10, 1865 at Boulware's Wharf on the James River, Virginia
Hughes, William K. Private	Unk	April 4, 1863, Abingdon, Virginia	Co. I, 26th Battalion, Virginia Infantry	June 3, 1864, Gaines Farm Cold Harbor, Virginia	Point Lookout, Maryland, transferred to Elmira Prison, NY, July 17, 1864	Exchanged February 13, 1865 on the James River, Virginia
Hughes, William W. Sergeant	Unk	January 10, 1862, Columbia, South Carolina	Co. C, 22nd South Carolina Infantry	July 30, 1864, Petersburg, Virginia	Point Lookout, Maryland, transferred to Elmira Prison, NY, August 12, 1864	Oath of Allegiance July 3, 1865
Hughey, G. P. Private	Unk	April 14, 1864, Oatland Island, South Carolina	Co. F, Holcombe Legion, South Carolina	May 8, 1864, Jarrett's Depot, Virginia	Point Lookout, Maryland, transferred to Elmira Prison, NY, August 17, 1864	Oath of Allegiance July 7, 1865

Name & Rank	Age	Enlisted	Regiment and State	Where Captured	Prison	Remarks
Hughlet, James H. Private	24	January 27, 1862, Covington, Tennessee	Co. A, Jackson's 1st Regiment, Tennessee Heavy Artillery	August 23, 1864, Fort Morgan, Alabama	New Orleans, Louisiana transferred to Elmira Prison, NY, December 4, 1864.	Exchanged February 13, 1865 at Boulware's wharf on the James River, Virginia
Hughs, Alexander Private	Unk	November 2, 1861, Jekyll Island, Georgia	Co. E, 61st Georgia Infantry	May 12, 1864, Spotsylvania Court House, Virginia	Point Lookout, Maryland, transferred to Elmira Prison, NY, July 25, 1864	Oath of Allegiance June 30, 1865
Huit, Ambrose M. Private	37	March 31, 1863, Newton, North Carolina	Co. F, 32nd North Carolina Infantry	May 10, 1864, Wilderness, Virginia	Point Lookout, Maryland, transferred to Elmira Prison, NY, August 6, 1864	Died February 28, 1865 of Diarrhea, Grave No. 2143
Hulfish, James P. Private	Unk	September 27, 1862, Stryder's Mill, Virginia	Co. A, 4th Virginia Cavalry	August 16, 1864, Front Royal, Virginia	Point Lookout, Maryland, transferred to Elmira Prison, NY, August 29, 1864	Oath of Allegiance June 21, 1865
Hull, Alexander S. Private	21	December 25, 1861, Springfield, Missouri	Co. K, 1st Missouri Cavalry	May 17, 1863, Big Black Bridge, Champion Hill, Mississippi	Point Lookout, Maryland, transferred to Elmira Prison, NY, August 18, 1864	Exchanged February 13, 1865 at Boulware's wharf on the James River, Virginia
Hull, John N. Corporal	Unk	July 31, 1861, Marion, Virginia	Co. D, 4th Virginia Infantry	May 12, 1864 Spotsylvania Court House, Virginia	Point Lookout, Maryland, transferred to Elmira Prison, NY, August 2, 1864	Exchanged March 10, 1865 at Boulware's Wharf on the James River, Virginia
Hull, Samuel Private	23	June 24, 1861, Coosawhatchie, South Carolina	Co. E, 11th South Carolina Infantry	June 24, 1864, Near Petersburg, Virginia	Point Lookout, Maryland, transferred to Elmira Prison, NY, August 18, 1864	Died March 18, 1865 of Chronic Diarrhea, Grave No. 1723
Hulme, John W. Private	27	December 21, 1861, Nashville, Tennessee	Co. J, 44th Tennessee Infantry	June 17, 1864, Petersburg, Virginia	Point Lookout, Maryland, transferred to Elmira Prison, NY, July 30, 1864	Oath of Allegiance April 22, 1865. Early Release per Lincoln's Proclamation, 12/8/1863.

Name & Rank	Age	Enlisted	Regiment and State	Where Captured	Prison	Remarks
Hultsman, Benjamin N. Private	19	June 20, 1861, Rockport, Arkansas	Co. F, 3rd Arkansas Infantry	May 12, 1864, Spotsylvania Court House, Virginia	Point Lookout, Maryland, transferred to Elmira Prison, NY, July 30, 1864	Exchanged February 13, 1865 at Boulware's wharf on the James River, Virginia
Humble, Oliver Private	Unk	June 20, 1862, Charlottes-ville, Virginia	Co. C, 6th Louisiana Infantry	May 5, 1864, Wilderness, Virginia	Point Lookout, Maryland, transferred to Elmira Prison, NY, August 17, 1864	Exchanged February 13, 1865 at Boulware's wharf on the James River, Virginia
Hume, R. E. Civilian	Unk	Unknown	Citizen of Culpeper County, Virginia	January 12, 1864, Culpeper County, Virginia	Point Lookout, Maryland, transferred to Elmira Prison, NY, July 25, 1864	Oath of Allegiance June 20, 1865
Hummer, Braden E. Private	Unk	May 1, 1862, Swift River Gap, Virginia	Co. A, 35th Battalion Virginia Cavalry	August 16, 1863, Loudoun County, Virginia	Point Lookout, Maryland, transferred to Elmira Prison, NY, August 18, 1864	Exchanged March 10, 1865 at Boulware's Wharf on the James River, Virginia
Humphrey, James W. Private	Unk	December 3, 1862, Golden Place, North Carolina	Co. H, 3rd North Carolina Cavalry	June 23, 1864, Petersburg, Virginia	Point Lookout, Maryland, transferred to Elmira Prison, NY, July 23, 1864	Died April 3, 1865 of Variola (Smallpox), Grave No. 2661
Humphrey, Martin Private	19	May 6, 1861, Jacksonville, North Carolina	Co. B, 24th North Carolina Infantry	June 17, 1864, Petersburg, Virginia	Point Lookout, Maryland, transferred to Elmira Prison, NY, July 30, 1864	Died September 26, 1864 of Chronic Diarrhea, Grave No. 380
Humphreys, Elliott Private	37	February 28, 1863, Rockingham, North Carolina	Co. C, 13th North Carolina Infantry	May 6, 1864, Wilderness, Virginia	Point Lookout, Maryland, transferred to Elmira Prison, NY, August 14, 1864	Died January 18, 1865 of Pleuro-Pneumonia, Grave No. 779
Humphreys, George Corporal	Unk	July 8, 1861, Camp Trousdale, Tennessee	Co. B, 17th Tennessee Infantry	June 17, 1864, Petersburg, Virginia	Point Lookout, Maryland, transferred to Elmira Prison, NY, July 30, 1864	Exchanged February 25, 1865 at Boulware's or Cox Wharf on the James River, Virginia

Name & Rank	Age	Enlisted	Regiment and State	Where Captured	Prison	Remarks
Humphreys, John Private	19	June 16, 1861, Washington County, Virginia	Co. J, 48th Virginia Infantry	May 12, 1864, Near Spotsylvania Court House, Virginia	Point Lookout, Maryland, transferred to Elmira Prison, NY, August 6, 1864	Exchanged February 20, 1865 at Boulware's or Cox Wharf on the James River, Virginia
Humphreys, Robert R. Private	Unk	June 8, 1862, Camp Heth, Virginia	Co. F, 26th Battalion, Virginia Infantry	June 3, 1864, Gaines Farm Cold Harbor, Virginia	Point Lookout, Maryland, transferred to Elmira Prison, NY, July 17, 1864	Oath of Allegiance July 3, 1865
Humphries, James Rolen Private	Unk	January 10, 1863, Place Unknown	Co. E, 50th Virginia Infantry	May 12, 1864, Spotsylvania Court House, Virginia	Point Lookout, Maryland, transferred to Elmira Prison, NY, August 18, 1864	Exchanged March 10, 1865 at Boulware's Wharf on the James River, Virginia
Humphries, W. L. Private	Unk	March 26, 1863, Newberry, South Carolina	Co. E, 27th South Carolina Infantry	June 24, 1864, Near Petersburg, Virginia	Point Lookout, Maryland, transferred to Elmira Prison, NY, August 18, 1864	Died October 1, 1864 of Unknown Causes, Grave No. 404
Hundley, James T. C. Private	20	May 29, 1861, Stevensville, Virginia	Co. K, 34th Virginia Infantry	June 15, 1864, Near Petersburg, Virginia	Point Lookout, Maryland, transferred to Elmira Prison, NY, July 12, 1864	Oath of Allegiance June 19, 1865
Hundley, Wiley D. Private	Unk	June 29, 1861, Pittsylvania, Virginia	Co. J, 21st Virginia Infantry	May 12, 1864, Near Spotsylvania Court House, Virginia	Point Lookout, Maryland, transferred to Elmira Prison, NY, August 6, 1864	Exchanged February 20, 1865 at Boulware's or Cox Wharf on the James River, Virginia
Hungerpiler, Jacob J. Private	Unk	April 11, 1862, Coles Island, South Carolina	Co. G, 27th South Carolina Infantry	June 24, 1864, Near Petersburg, Virginia	Point Lookout, Maryland, transferred to Elmira Prison, NY, August 18, 1864	Died February 13, 1865 of Peritonitis, Grave No. 2068. Headstone has Hungerfeler.
Hunley, John H. Private	27	June 1, 1861, Stokes County, North Carolina	Co. H, 22nd North Carolina Infantry	May 6, 1864, Wilderness, Virginia	Point Lookout, Maryland, transferred to Elmira Prison, NY, August 14, 1864	Exchanged February 13, 1865 at Boulware's wharf on the James River, Virginia

Name & Rank	Age	Enlisted	Regiment and State	Where Captured	Prison	Remarks
Hunnicutt, Archibald\n\nPrivate	26	May 23, 1861, Raleigh, North Carolina	Co. F, 32nd North Carolina Infantry	May 12, 1864, Spotsylvania Court House, Virginia	Point Lookout, Maryland, transferred to Elmira Prison, NY, August 6, 1864	Oath of Allegiance May 13, 1865
Hunnicutt, John T.\n\nCorporal	20	July 20, 1861, Camp Pickens, Anderson District, South Carolina	Co. C, 1st South Carolina Infantry	July 14, 1863, Falling Waters, Maryland	Point Lookout, Maryland, transferred to Elmira Prison, NY, August 18, 1864	Died September 24, 1864 of Chronic Diarrhea, Grave No. 471. Headstone has Honeycutt.
Hunseiker, G. D.\n\nPrivate	23	July 15, 1862, Raleigh, North Carolina	Co. E, 3rd North Carolina Infantry	May 20, 1864, Spotsylvania Court House, Virginia	Point Lookout, Maryland, transferred to Elmira Prison, NY, July 3, 1864	Exchanged March 2, 1865 at Akins Landing on the James River, Virginia
Hunsucker, Nelson W.\n\nSergeant	Unk	April 27, 1861, Newton, North Carolina	Co. F, 32nd North Carolina Infantry	May 10, 1864, Wilderness, Virginia	Point Lookout, Maryland, transferred to Elmira Prison, NY, August 6, 1864	Oath of Allegiance June 23, 1865
Hunt, James F.\n\nPrivate	Unk	April 1, 1864, Danielsville, Georgia	Co. A, 16th Georgia Infantry	August 16, 1864, Front Royal, Virginia	Point Lookout, Maryland, transferred to Elmira Prison, NY, August 29, 1864	Oath of Allegiance June 21, 1865
Hunt, James W. H.\n\nPrivate	Unk	March 10, 1862, Camp Bartow, Georgia	Co. J, 38th Georgia Infantry	May 20, 1864, Spotsylvania Court House, Virginia	Point Lookout, Maryland, transferred to Elmira Prison, NY, July 6, 1864	Exchanged March 10, 1865 at Boulware's Wharf on the James River, Virginia
Hunt, John E.\n\nPrivate	Unk	May 13, 1862, Charleston, South Carolina	Co. A, 21st South Carolina Infantry	June 24, 1864, Near Petersburg, Virginia	Point Lookout, Maryland, transferred to Elmira Prison, NY, August 18, 1864	Exchanged March 2, 1865 at Akins Landing on the James River, Virginia
Hunt, Lewis H.\n\nPrivate	Unk	February 1, 1864, Upperville, Virginia	Co. A, 6th Virginia Cavalry	June 1, 1864, Cold Harbor, Virginia	Point Lookout, Maryland, transferred to Elmira Prison, NY, July 17, 1864	Oath of Allegiance May 29, 1865

Name & Rank	Age	Enlisted	Regiment and State	Where Captured	Prison	Remarks
Hunt, Richard Private	28	June 18, 1861, East Bend, North Carolina	Co. F, 28th North Carolina Infantry	May 6, 1864, Wilderness, Virginia	Point Lookout, Maryland, transferred to Elmira Prison, NY, August 14, 1864	Oath of Allegiance May 19, 1865
Hunt, S. J. W. Private	Unk	March 10, 1862, Camp Bartow, Georgia	Co. J, 38th Georgia Infantry	May 20, 1864, Spotsylvania Court House, Virginia	Point Lookout, Maryland, transferred to Elmira Prison, NY, July 6, 1864	Exchanged March 10, 1865 at Boulware's Wharf on the James River, Virginia
Hunt, William H. Private	Unk	June 18, 1861, Danielsville, Georgia	Co. A, 16th Georgia Infantry	August 16, 1864, Front Royal, Virginia	Point Lookout, Maryland, transferred to Elmira Prison, NY, August 29, 1864	Died February 23, 1865 of Variola (Smallpox), Grave No. 2262. Headstone has 61st Georgia.
Hunter, H. C. Private	Unk	January 20, 1862, Darlington District, South Carolina	Co. G, 21st South Carolina Infantry	July 10, 1863, Morris Island, South Carolina	Point Lookout, Maryland, transferred to Elmira Prison, NY, August 18, 1864	Exchanged October 29, 1864 at Venus Point, Savannah River, GA.
Hunter, Henry Lee Private	27	March 1, 1864, Taylorsville, North Carolina	Co. K, 23rd North Carolina Infantry	August 11, 1864, Winchester, Virginia	Old Capital Prison, Washington, DC transferred to Elmira Prison, NY, August 27, 1864	Oath of Allegiance May 13, 1865
Hunter, James L. Private	Unk	May 27, 1862, Salt Sulfur Springs, Virginia	Co. F, 26th Battalion, Virginia Infantry	June 3, 1864, Gaines Farm Cold Harbor, Virginia	Point Lookout, Maryland, transferred to Elmira Prison, NY, July 17, 1864	Oath of Allegiance July 3, 1865
Hunter, Martin Private	28	March 3, 1862, Wilmington, North Carolina	Co. E, 30th North Carolina Infantry	May 12, 1864, Near Spotsylvania Court House, Virginia	Point Lookout, Maryland, transferred to Elmira Prison, NY, August 14, 1864	Oath of Allegiance June 23, 1865
Hunter, Stephen Private	18	February 8, 1863, Livingston, Tennessee	Co. D, 25th Tennessee Infantry	May 16, 1864, Near Drury's Bluff, Virginia	Point Lookout, Maryland, transferred to Elmira Prison, NY, August 17, 1864	Died September 14, 1864 of Chronic Diarrhea, Grave No. 278

Name & Rank	Age	Enlisted	Regiment and State	Where Captured	Prison	Remarks
Hunter, Thomas C. Private	Unk	April 20, 1861, London Bridge, Lynnhaven Beach, Virginia	Co. K, 15th Virginia Cavalry	September 14, 1863, Near Culpepper, Virginia	Point Lookout, Maryland, transferred to Elmira Prison, NY, August 18, 1864	Exchanged March 10, 1865 at Boulware's Wharf on the James River, Virginia
Hunter, Virgil A. P. Sergeant	Unk	July 19, 1861, Montgomery, Alabama	Co. D, 13th Alabama Infantry	May 12, 1864, Spotsylvania Court House, Virginia	Point Lookout, Maryland, transferred to Elmira Prison, NY, August 2, 1864	Oath of Allegiance May 15, 1865
Hunter, W. F. Private	Unk	January 16, 1862, Chesterfield, South Carolina	Co. B, 26th South Carolina Infantry	July 30, 1864, Petersburg, Virginia	Point Lookout, Maryland, transferred to Elmira Prison, NY, August 12, 1864	Exchanged October 29, 1864 at Venus Point, Savannah River, GA.
Hunter, William H. Sergeant	22	August 1, 1861, Livingston, Tennessee	Co. D, 25th Tennessee Infantry	May 16, 1864, Near Drury's Bluff, Virginia	Point Lookout, Maryland, transferred to Elmira Prison, NY, August 17, 1864	Exchanged February 13, 1865 at Boulware's wharf on the James River, Virginia
Hunter, William N. Private	Unk	April 29, 1862, White Sulfur Springs, Virginia	Co. F, 26th Battalion, Virginia Infantry	June 3, 1864, Gaines Farm Cold Harbor, Virginia	Point Lookout, Maryland, transferred to Elmira Prison, NY, July 17, 1864	Oath of Allegiance July 3, 1865
Hunter, William W. N. Sergeant	19	October 16, 1861, Lenoir County, North Carolina	Co. G, 40th Regiment, 3rd North Carolina Artillery	January 15, 1865, Fort Fisher, North Carolina	January 30, 1865 Elmira Prison Camp New York	Oath of Allegiance June 12, 1865
Huntley, Elijah D. Corporal	30	July 20, 1863, Fort Branch, Martin County, North Carolina	Co. G, 40th Regiment, 3rd North Carolina Artillery	January 15, 1865, Fort Fisher, North Carolina	January 30, 1865 Elmira Prison Camp New York	Exchanged March 14, 1865 at Boulware's Wharf on the James River, Virginia
Hurley, Cornelius Private	26	May 27, 1861, New Orleans, Louisiana	Co. B, 15th Louisiana Infantry	May 12, 1864, Spotsylvania Court House, Virginia	Point Lookout, Maryland, transferred to Elmira Prison, NY, July 25, 1864	Oath of Allegiance May 19, 1865

Name & Rank	Age	Enlisted	Regiment and State	Where Captured	Prison	Remarks
Hurley, John Private	33	January 1, 1862, Richmond, Virginia	Co. E, 59th Virginia Infantry	June 17, 1864, Petersburg, Virginia	Point Lookout, Maryland, transferred to Elmira Prison, NY, July 30, 1864	Exchanged October 29, 1864 at Venus Point, Savannah River, GA.
Hurlocker, Moses Private	25	July 20, 1861, Fayetteville, North Carolina	Co. E, 8th North Carolina Infantry	May 31, 1864, Cold Harbor, Virginia	Point Lookout, Maryland, transferred to Elmira Prison, NY, July 12, 1864	Oath of Allegiance June 12, 1865
Hurly, Daniel Private	Unk	April 2, 1862, New Orleans, Louisiana	Co. G, Miles Legion Louisiana	September 19, 1864, Atchafalaya, Louisiana	New Orleans, LA, Transferred to Elmira Prison, NY, November 19, 1864	Died December 15, 1864 of Pneumonia, Grave No. 1119. Headstone has Hurley.
Hurly, John No. 2 Corporal	Unk	May 23, 1861, Guntersville, Marshall County, Alabama	Co. B, 9th Alabama Infantry	August 16, 1864, New Market, Virginia	Old Capital Prison, Washington, DC transferred to Elmira Prison, NY, August 27, 1864	Oath of Allegiance May 15, 1865
Hurst, Thomas J. Private	23	May 6, 1861, Mobile, Alabama	Co. E, 8th Alabama Infantry	May 24, 1864, North Anna, Virginia	Point Lookout, Maryland, transferred to Elmira Prison, NY, July 23, 1864	Oath of Allegiance May 19, 1865
Hurt, George H. Private	21	May 29, 1861, Stevensville, Georgia	Co. K, 34th Virginia Infantry	June 15, 1864, Near Petersburg, Virginia	Point Lookout, Maryland, transferred to Elmira Prison, NY, July 12, 1864	Oath of Allegiance July 7, 1865
Hurt, Kindred Private	Unk	January 6, 1864, Charleston, South Carolina	Co. C, 1st South Carolina Infantry	July 29, 1864, Petersburg, Virginia	Point Lookout, Maryland, transferred to Elmira Prison, NY, August 12, 1864	Died December 6, 1864 of Chronic Diarrhea, Grave No. 1189

Name & Rank	Age	Enlisted	Regiment and State	Where Captured	Prison	Remarks
Hurt, Thomas W. Sergeant	Unk	July 21, 1862, Washington County, Virginia	Co. I, 26th Battalion, Virginia Infantry	June 3, 1864, Gaines Mill Cold Harbor, Virginia	Point Lookout, Maryland, transferred to Elmira Prison, NY, July 17, 1864	Died July 22, 1864 of Chronic Diarrhea, Grave No. 2849. Headstone has 20th VA.
Hurt, William W. Private	Unk	March 1, 1862, Gloucester Point, Virginia	Co. D, 26th Virginia Infantry	June 15, 1864, Petersburg, Virginia	Point Lookout, Maryland, transferred to Elmira Prison, NY, July 30, 1864	Died March 14, 1865 Chronic Diarrhea. Grave No. 2422. Name William A. Hunt on Headstone.
Hurter, John Christopher Private	Unk	April 23, 1861, Mobile, Alabama	Co. E, 3rd Alabama Infantry	May 12, 1864, Spotsylvania Court House, Virginia	Point Lookout, Maryland, transferred to Elmira Prison, NY, August 12, 1864	Oath of Allegiance June 16, 1865
Huse, A. C. Private	Unk	Unknown	Co. E, 50th Virginia Infantry	May 12, 1864, Spotsylvania Court House, Virginia	Point Lookout, Maryland, transferred to Elmira Prison, NY, August 2, 1864	Oath of Allegiance June 19, 1865
Huse, D. W. Corporal	Unk	Unknown	Co. E, 50th Virginia Infantry	May 12, 1864, Spotsylvania Court House, Virginia	Point Lookout, Maryland, transferred to Elmira Prison, NY, August 2, 1864	Exchanged March 14, 1865 at Boulware's Wharf on the James River, Virginia
Hustmayer, William J. Sergeant	Unk	May 9, 1861, New Orleans, Louisiana	Co. B, 2nd Louisiana Infantry	May 12, 1864, Spotsylvania Court House, Virginia	Point Lookout, Maryland, transferred to Elmira Prison, NY, August 17, 1864	Exchanged October 29, 1864 at Venus Point, Savannah River, GA.
Hutches, James Private	Unk	Unknown	Co. G, 2nd Louisiana Cavalry	October 27, 1864, Bayou Grosstete, Point Coupee Parish, Louisiana	New Orleans, Louisiana transferred to Elmira November 19, 1864.	Exchanged February 25, 1865 at Boulware's or Cox Wharf on the James River, Virginia

Name & Rank	Age	Enlisted	Regiment and State	Where Captured	Prison	Remarks
Hutchinson, David W. Private	40	March 15, 1862, Gaston County, North Carolina	Co. K, 49th North Carolina Infantry	June 9, 1864, Chickahominy Swamp, Cold Harbor, Virginia	Old Capital Prison, Washington, DC, transferred to Elmira July 23, 1864	Oath of Allegiance September 19, 1864
Hutchinson, Henry Private	Unk	July 27, 1863, Abbeville, South Carolina	Co. C, 6th South Carolina Cavalry	June 11, 1864, Trevilian Station, Louisa Court House, Virginia	Point Lookout, Maryland, transferred to Elmira Prison, NY, July 25, 1864	Oath of Allegiance June 16, 1865
Hutchinson, John S. Corporal	20	April 18, 1861, Edingburg, Virginia	Co. F, 10th, Virginia Infantry	May 20, 1864, Spotsylvania Court House, Virginia	Point Lookout, Maryland, transferred to Elmira Prison, NY, July 6, 1864	Exchanged February 20, 1865 at Boulware's or Cox Wharf on the James River, Virginia
Hutchison, A. J. Private	45	September 22, 1863, Cabarrus County, North Carolina	Co. A, 30th North Carolina Infantry	May 12, 1864, Near Spotsylvania Court House, Virginia	Point Lookout, Maryland, transferred to Elmira Prison, NY, August 14, 1864	Died February 28, 1865 of Variola (Smallpox), Grave No. 2124
Hutchison, Aaron Private	25	September 20, 1861, Homer, Texas	Co. D, 7th Texas Cavalry	July 22, 1864, Concordia, Louisiana	New Orleans, LA, Transferred to Elmira Prison, NY, November 19, 1864	Oath of Allegiance June 16, 1865
Hutchison, G. Private	Unk	February 4, 1862, Fort Pillow, Tennessee	Co. B, 1st Jackson's Tennessee Heavy Artillery	August 23, 1864, Fort Morgan, Alabama.	New Orleans, Louisiana transferred to Elmira Prison, NY, December 4, 1864.	Exchanged February 13, 1865 at Boulware's wharf on the James River, Virginia
Hutchison, James A. Private	Unk	December 21, 1862, Chaffin's Farm, Virginia	Co. K, 46th Virginia Infantry	June 17, 1864, Petersburg, Virginia	Point Lookout, Maryland, transferred to Elmira Prison, NY, July 30, 1864	Oath of Allegiance June 21, 1865
Hutchison, James P. Sergeant	45	July 2, 1862, Camp Moore, Louisiana	Co. F, Wingfield's 3rd Louisiana Cavalry	September 16, 1864, Greenville Springs, Near East Baton Rouge, Louisiana	New Orleans, Louisiana transferred to Elmira November 19, 1864.	Exchanged February 25, 1865 at Boulware's or Cox Wharf on the James River, Virginia

Name & Rank	Age	Enlisted	Regiment and State	Where Captured	Prison	Remarks
Hutchison, Larry N. Private	22	September 1, 1863, Marion, South Carolina	Co. B, 21st South Carolina Infantry	August 21, 1864, Petersburg, Virginia. Gunshot Wound Right Forearm, Arm Amputated.	Old Capital Prison, Washington, DC, transferred to Elmira December 17, 1864	Exchanged February 13, 1865 at Boulware's Wharf on the James River, Virginia
Hux, Benjamin G. Private	18	June 8, 1863, Fort Caswell, Brunswick County, North Carolina	Co. F, 36th Regiment 2nd North Carolina Artillery	January 15, 1865, Fort Fisher, North Carolina	February 1, 1865 Elmira Prison Camp, New York	Oath of Allegiance July 26, 1865
Hux, Eldridge Private	23	June 12, 1861, Halifax County, North Carolina	Co. K, 1st North Carolina Infantry	May 12, 1864, Near Spotsylvania Court House, Virginia	Point Lookout Prison, Maryland. Transferred to Elmira Prison Camp New York August 6, 1864.	Died March 3, 1865 of Diarrhea, Grave No. 1990. Headstone has Eldred Hucks.
Hux, Gardner H. Private	15	October 25, 1864, Halifax County, North Carolina	Co. F, 36th Regiment 2nd North Carolina Artillery	January 15, 1865, Fort Fisher, North Carolina	February 1, 1865 Elmira Prison Camp, New York	Oath of Allegiance June 23, 1865
Hyce, James Private	Unk	Unknown	Co. F, 14th Louisiana Cavalry	September 24, 1864, Near Port Hudson, Louisiana	New Orleans, Louisiana transferred to Elmira November 19, 1864.	Exchanged February 13, 1865 at Boulware's Wharf on the James River, Virginia

Name & Rank	Age	Enlisted	Regiment and State	Where Captured	Prison	Remarks
Ide, Joseph E. Private	44	August 1, 1861, Salisbury, North Carolina	Co. K, 8th North Carolina Infantry	May 30, 1864, Cold Harbor, Virginia	Point Lookout, Maryland, transferred to Elmira Prison, NY, July 12, 1864	Exchanged February 25, 1865 at Boulware's or Cox Wharf on the James River, Virginia
Idol, David Harrison Drum Major	32	November 1, 1862, Teague Town, North Carolina	Co. G, 2nd Battalion North Carolina Infantry	July 26, 1864, Fort Stevens, Virginia	Old Capital Prison, Washington, DC, transferred to Elmira Prison, NY, July 23, 1864	Oath of Allegiance May 15, 1865

Name & Rank	Age	Enlisted	Regiment and State	Where Captured	Prison	Remarks
Ikner, Ward Private	Unk	February 2, 1863, Camp Whiting, Wilmington, North Carolina	Co. G, 51st North Carolina Infantry	June 3, 1864, Gains Mill, Cold Harbor, Virginia	Point Lookout Prison Camp, Maryland. Transferred to Elmira Prison Camp July 17, 1864	Died November 18, 1864 of Remittent Fever, Grave No. 970
Iler, A. J. Sergeant	Unk	May 15, 1863, Bryan County, Georgia	Co. H, 7th Georgia Cavalry	June 11, 1864, Trevilian Station, Louisa Court House, Virginia	Point Lookout, Maryland, transferred to Elmira Prison, NY, July 25, 1864	Oath of Allegiance July 7, 1865
Imbler, Stephen Private	Unk	August 8, 1862, Petersburg, Virginia	Co. H, 48th North Carolina Infantry	June 4, 1864, Gaines Farm Cold Harbor, Virginia	Point Lookout, Maryland, transferred to Elmira Prison, NY, July 17,1864	Exchanged March 14, 1865 at Boulware's Wharf on the James River, Virginia
Impock, W. H. Private	Unk	Unknown	Co. B, 5th North Carolina Infantry	May 12, 1864, Spotsylvania Court House, Virginia	Point Lookout, Maryland, transferred to Elmira Prison, NY, August 6, 1864	Oath of Allegiance June 30, 1865
Inabnet, Andrew J. Private	Unk	April 11, 1862, Coles Island, South Carolina	Co. G, 25th South Carolina Infantry	January 15, 1865, Fort Fisher, North Carolina	January 30, 1865, Elmira Prison Camp, New York	Oath of Allegiance June 23, 1865
Inabnet, Charles G. Private	Unk	April 11, 1862, Coles Island, South Carolina	Co. G, 25th South Carolina Infantry	January 15, 1865, Fort Fisher, North Carolina	January 30, 1865, Elmira Prison Camp, New York	Oath of Allegiance July 7, 1865
Ingle, Anthony H. Corporal	21	June 16, 1861, Washington County, Virginia	Co. J, 48th Virginia Infantry	May 12, 1864, Near Spotsylvania Court House, Virginia	Point Lookout, Maryland, transferred to Elmira Prison, NY, August 6, 1864	Oath of Allegiance June 19, 1865
Ingle, John C. Private	33	July 15, 1862, Raleigh, North Carolina	Co. E, 1st North Carolina Infantry	May 12, 1864, Spotsylvania Court House, Virginia	Point Lookout, Maryland, transferred to Elmira Prison, NY, August 6, 1864	Oath of Allegiance June 19, 1865

Name & Rank	Age	Enlisted	Regiment and State	Where Captured	Prison	Remarks
Ingles, Elisha McC. Sergeant	20	April 17, 1861, Christiansburg, Virginia	Co. G, 4th Virginia Infantry	May 12, 1864, Spotsylvania Court House, Virginia	Point Lookout, Maryland, transferred to Elmira Prison, NY, August 2, 1864	Oath of Allegiance June 21, 1865
Ingold, Edward Private	35	July 15, 1862, Raleigh, North Carolina	Co. E, 1st North Carolina Infantry	May 12, 1864, Spotsylvania Court House, Virginia	Point Lookout, Maryland, transferred to Elmira Prison, NY, August 6, 1864	Oath of Allegiance May 19, 1865
Ingram, David B. Private	Unk	December 19, 1862, Macon, Georgia	Co. D, 12th Georgia Infantry	May 10, 1864, Spotsylvania Court House, Virginia	Point Lookout, Maryland, transferred to Elmira Prison, NY, July 30, 1864	Died January 10, 1865 of Phthisis Pulmonalis, Grave No. 1496
Ingram, H. F. Private	Unk	April 21, 1861, Memphis, Tennessee	Co. A, Jackson's 1st Regiment, Tennessee Heavy Artillery	August 23, 1864, Fort Morgan, Alabama	New Orleans, Louisiana transferred to Elmira Prison, NY, December 4, 1864.	Exchanged February 25, 1865 at Boulware's or Cox Wharf on the James River, Virginia
Ingram, Hughes M. Private	48	February 24, 1862, Wadesboro, North Carolina	Co. H, 43rd North Carolina Infantry	May 30, 1864, Cold Harbor, Virginia	Old Capital Prison, Washington, DC, transferred to Elmira, NY, March 3, 1865.	Oath of Allegiance June 12, 1865
Ingram, James L. Private	Unk	May 8, 1862, Morgan, Georgia	Co. D, 12th Georgia Infantry	May 10, 1864, Spotsylvania Court House, Virginia	Point Lookout, Maryland, transferred to Elmira Prison, NY, July 30, 1864	Oath of Allegiance June 14, 1865
Inman, William P. Private	25	April 17, 1861, Wytheville, Virginia	Co. A, 4th Virginia Infantry	May 10, 1864, Spotsylvania Court House, Virginia	Point Lookout, Maryland, transferred to Elmira Prison, NY, July 25, 1864	Died February 6, 1865 of Pneumonia, Grave No. 1913

Name & Rank	Age	Enlisted	Regiment and State	Where Captured	Prison	Remarks
Irby, F. S. Private	23	February 27, 1862, Vernon, Louisiana	Co. A, 9th Louisiana Infantry	May 12, 1864, Spotsylvania Court House, Virginia	Point Lookout, Maryland, transferred to Elmira Prison, NY, August 17, 1864	Died September 27, 1864 of Congestion of the Brain, Grave No. 390. Headstone has P. S. Irby.
Irby, William Private	18	February 2, 1863, Fort Caswell, North Carolina	Co. F, 36th Regiment 2nd North Carolina Artillery	January 15, 1865, Fort Fisher, North Carolina	February 1, 1865 Elmira Prison Camp, New York	Oath of Allegiance June 12, 1865
Irick, Elliott H. Private	31	May 1, 1862, Secessionville, James Island, South Carolina	Co. G, 25th South Carolina Infantry	January 15, 1865, Fort Fisher, North Carolina	January 30, 1865, Elmira Prison Camp, New York	Exchanged February 20, 1865 at Boulware's or Cox Wharf on the James River, Virginia
Irick, Laban A. Corporal	Unk	April 11, 1862, Coles Island, South Carolina	Co. G, 25th South Carolina Infantry	January 15, 1865, Fort Fisher, North Carolina	January 30, 1865, Elmira Prison Camp, New York	Oath of Allegiance July 11, 1865
Irvin, E. A. Private	Unk	February 25, 1864, Jefferson, Georgia	Co. C, 18th Georgia Infantry	June 1, 1864, Cold Harbor, Virginia	Point Lookout, Maryland, transferred to Elmira Prison, NY, July 17, 1864	Oath of Allegiance June 21, 1865
Irvin, Maslin B. Private	Unk	October 15, 1862, Greenbrier, Virginia	Co. C, 14th Virginia Cavalry	July 14, 1864, Near Washington, DC	Old Capital Prison, Washington, DC, transferred to Elmira Prison, NY, July 25, 1864.	Exchanged February 13, 1865 at Boulware's wharf on the James River, Virginia
Irving, Averet S. Sergeant	Unk	June 11, 1861, Bledsoe's Store, Virginia	Co. I, 44th Virginia Infantry	May 12, 1864, Spotsylvania Court House, Virginia	Point Lookout, Maryland, transferred to Elmira Prison, NY, August 2, 1864	Exchanged October 29, 1864 at Venus Point, Savannah River, GA.
Irving, David Private	27	June 19, 1861, Camp Moore, New Orleans, Louisiana	Co. H, 8th Louisiana Infantry	November 7, 1863, Rappahannock Station, Virginia	Old Capital Prison, Washington, DC transferred to Elmira, NY, August 29, 1864	Exchanged October 29, 1864 at Venus Point, Savannah River, GA.

Name & Rank	Age	Enlisted	Regiment and State	Where Captured	Prison	Remarks
Irving, W. Private	Unk	Unknown	Co. J, 3rd Louisiana Cavalry	September 14, 1864, Tunica, Louisiana	New Orleans, Louisiana transferred to Elmira November 19, 1864.	Exchanged February 13, 1865 at Boulware's Wharf on the James River, Virginia
Irwin, William J. Private	Unk	April 1, 1864, Columbia, South Carolina	Co. B, Hampton Legion, South Carolina	July 27, 1864, Petersburg, Virginia	Point Lookout, Maryland, transferred to Elmira Prison, NY, August 12, 1864	Died August 28, 1864 of Chronic Diarrhea, Grave No. 49
Isbell, Thomas E. Private	Unk	July 11, 1861, Lynchburg, Virginia	Co. I, 42nd Virginia Infantry	May 12, 1864, Spotsylvania Court House, Virginia	Point Lookout, Maryland, transferred to Elmira Prison, NY, August 12, 1864	Exchanged February 20, 1865 at Boulware's or Cox Wharf on the James River, Virginia
Isley, Alfred Private	Unk	June 27, 1864, Alamance County, North Carolina	Co. A, 53rd North Carolina Infantry	July 17, 1864, Near Washington, DC,	Old Capital Prison, Washington, DC, transferred to Elmira July 23, 1864	Oath of Allegiance May 17, 1865
Isley, Austin Private	35	July 15, 1862, Raleigh, North Carolina	Co. E, 1st North Carolina Infantry	May 12, 1864, Spotsylvania Court House, Virginia	Point Lookout, Maryland, transferred to Elmira Prison, NY, August 6, 1864	Transferred for Exchange 2/13/65. Due to Illness Sent to US Army Hospital, Baltimore, MD. Oath of Allegiance June 10, 1865.
Isley, George Private	22	July 15, 1862, Raleigh, North Carolina	Co. E, 1st North Carolina Infantry	May 12, 1864, Spotsylvania Court House, Virginia	Point Lookout, Maryland, transferred to Elmira Prison, NY, August 6, 1864	Oath of Allegiance June 19, 1865
Isley, Lewis C. Sergeant	18	July 5, 1861, Halifax County, North Carolina	Co. I, 8th North Carolina Infantry	June 1, 1864, Cold Harbor, Virginia	Point Lookout, Maryland, transferred to Elmira Prison, NY, July 17, 1864	Exchanged March 2, 1865 at Akins Landing on the James River, Virginia

Name & Rank	Age	Enlisted	Regiment and State	Where Captured	Prison	Remarks
Isley, Presley W. Private	30	February 27, 1862, Reidsville, Rockingham County, North Carolina	Co. J, 45th North Carolina Infantry	May 10, 1864, Spotsylvania Court House, Virginia	Point Lookout, Maryland, transferred to Elmira Prison, NY, August 6, 1864	Exchanged October 29, 1864 at Venus Point, Savannah River, GA.
Isom, James Private	Unk	Unknown	Co. B, 1st Jackson's Tennessee Heavy Artillery	August 23, 1864, Fort Morgan, Alabama.	New Orleans, Louisiana transferred to Elmira Prison, NY, December 4, 1864.	Exchanged February 13, 1865 at Boulware's wharf on the James River, Virginia
Israel, John Private	Unk	June 2, 1863, Wilmington, North Carolina	Co. E, 51st North Carolina Infantry	June 1, 1864, Cold Harbor, Virginia	Point Lookout, Maryland, transferred to Elmira Prison, NY, July 17,1864	Died September 6, 1864 of Dropsy from Hepatic Disease, Grave No. 242
Israel, Joseph Private	Unk	June 1, 1863, Coffee County, Alabama	Co. C, 61st Alabama Infantry	Unknown	Point Lookout Prison Camp, Maryland. Transferred to Elmira Prison, NY, Date Unknown	Died March 22, 1865 of Unknown Disease, Grave No. 1541
Ives, John P. Private	28	June 3, 1861, New Berne, North Carolina	Co. J, 2nd North Carolina Infantry	May 19, 1864, Spotsylvania Court House, Virginia. Gunshot Wound Left Leg.	Old Capital Prison, Washington, DC, transferred to Elmira Prison, NY, August 12, 1864	Exchanged October 29, 1864 at Venus Point, Savannah River, GA.
Ivester, William Private	Unk	July 24, 1861, Clarksville, Georgia	Co. E, 16th Georgia Infantry	June 1, 1864, Cold Harbor, Virginia	Point Lookout, Maryland, transferred to Elmira Prison, NY, July 17,1864	Oath of Allegiance July 11, 1865
Ivey, Alfred S. Private	23	May 18, 1861, Lumberton, North Carolina	Co. D, 18th North Carolina Infantry	May 12, 1864, Spotsylvania Court House, Virginia	Point Lookout, Maryland, transferred to Elmira Prison, NY, August 6, 1864	Oath of Allegiance June 27, 1865

Name & Rank	Age	Enlisted	Regiment and State	Where Captured	Prison	Remarks
Ivey, John A. Private	46	December 21, 1861, Fort Fisher, North Carolina	Co. J, 36th Regiment 2nd North Carolina Artillery	January 15, 1865, Fort Fisher, North Carolina	February 1, 1865, Elmira Prison Camp, New York	Exchanged March 2, 1865 at Boulware's Wharf on the James River, Virginia
Ivey, O. R. Private	Unk	Unknown	Co. D, 49th North Carolina Infantry	June 2, 1864, Bermuda Hundred, Virginia	Point Lookout, Maryland, transferred to Elmira Prison, NY, July 12,1864	Exchanged March 10, 1865 at Boulware's Wharf on the James River, Virginia
Izler, Adolphus M. Private	Unk	April 11, 1862, Coles Island, South Carolina	Co. G, 25th South Carolina Infantry	January 15, 1865, Fort Fisher, North Carolina	January 30, 1865, Elmira Prison Camp, New York	Exchanged March 14, 1865 at Boulware's Wharf on the James River, Virginia
Izler, Benjamin P. Sergeant	Unk	April 11, 1862, Coles Island, South Carolina	Co. G, 25th South Carolina Infantry	January 15, 1865, Fort Fisher, North Carolina	January 30, 1865, Elmira Prison Camp, New York	Oath of Allegiance June 14, 1865

Name & Rank	Age	Enlisted	Regiment and State	Where Captured	Prison	Remarks
Jack, William Z. B. Corporal	Unk	April 9, 1862, Shenandoah Mt., Virginia	Co. H, 52nd, Virginia Infantry	May 30, 1864 Mechanicsville, Virginia	Point Lookout, Maryland, transferred to Elmira Prison, NY, July 8, 1864	Oath of Allegiance May 19, 1865
Jackard, H. L. Private	Unk	Unknown	Co. A, 8th Virginia Cavalry	May 30, 1864, Bottoms Bridge, Virginia	Point Lookout, Maryland, transferred to Elmira Prison, NY, July 25, 1864	Oath of Allegiance May 13, 1865
Jacks, Isaac M. Private	Unk	September 1, 1862, Coosa, Alabama	Co. K, 59th Alabama Infantry	June 17, 1864, Petersburg, Virginia	Point Lookout, Maryland, transferred to Elmira Prison, NY, July 30, 1864	Oath of Allegiance May 19, 1865

Name & Rank	Age	Enlisted	Regiment and State	Where Captured	Prison	Remarks
Jacks, William H. H. Private	Unk	February 24, 1862, Jefferson, North Carolina	Co. A, 1st North Carolina Cavalry	September 22, 1863, Near Madison Court House, Virginia	Point Lookout, Maryland, transferred to Elmira Prison, NY, August 18, 1864	Transferred For Exchange October 11, 1864 to Point Lookout Prison Camp, MD. Died November 4, 1864 of Unknown Causes at Fort Monroe, Virginia
Jackson, Alfred Webb Private	37	October 25, 1863, Fort Fisher, North Carolina	Co. E, 36th Regiment 2nd North Carolina Artillery	January 15, 1865, Fort Fisher, North Carolina	February 1, 1865 Elmira Prison Camp, New York	Exchanged March 2, 1865. Died March 24, 1865 of Chronic Diarrhea at Way Station Hospital No. 1, Weldon, North Carolina.
Jackson, Allen M. Private	42	May 6, 1863, Fort Fisher, North Carolina	Co. E, 36th Regiment 2nd North Carolina Artillery	January 15, 1865, Fort Fisher, North Carolina	February 1, 1865 Elmira Prison Camp, New York	Oath of Allegiance July 3, 1865
Jackson, Andrew Private	46	September 7, 1862, Kinston, North Carolina	Co. J, 2nd North Carolina Cavalry	June 3, 1864, Gaines Mill Cold Harbor, Virginia	Point Lookout, Maryland, transferred to Elmira Prison, NY, July 17, 1864	Exchanged March 14, 1865 at Boulware's Wharf on the James River, Virginia
Jackson, Andrew D. Private	Unk	Unknown	Co. B, 68th North Carolina Infantry	June 8, 1864, Shiloh, Camden County, North Carolina	Point Lookout, Maryland, transferred to Elmira Prison, NY, July 12, 1864	Died December 4, 1864 of Chronic Diarrhea, Grave No. 884. Name Henry A. on Headstone.
Jackson, Andrew J. Private	Unk	March 29, 1862, Lewisburg, Virginia	Co. D, 26th Battalion Virginia Infantry	June 3, 1864, Gaines Farm Cold Harbor, Virginia	Point Lookout, Maryland, transferred to Elmira Prison, NY, July 17, 1864	Oath of Allegiance August 7, 1865
Jackson, Blackman Private	37	February 18, 1863, Sampson County, North Carolina	Co. A, 36th Regiment, 2nd North Carolina Artillery	January 15, 1865, Fort Fisher, North Carolina	February 1, 1865 Elmira Prison Camp, New York	Exchanged March 14, 1865 at Boulware's Wharf on the James River, Virginia

Name & Rank	Age	Enlisted	Regiment and State	Where Captured	Prison	Remarks
Jackson, Calvin Corporal	Unk	August 24, 1861, Clarksville, Habersham County, Georgia	Co. A, 24th Georgia Infantry	August 16, 1864, Front Royal, Virginia	Old Capital Prison, Washington, DC transferred to Elmira Prison, NY, August 29, 1864	Oath of Allegiance June 21, 1865
Jackson, Charles Private	Unk	October 10, 1862, Bennettesville, South Carolina	Co. E, 4th South Carolina Cavalry	May 30, 1864 Hanover Junction, Virginia	Point Lookout, Maryland, transferred to Elmira Prison, NY, July 11, 1864	Exchanged October 29, 1864 at Venus Point, Savannah River, GA.
Jackson, Curtis A. Private	Unk	August 24, 1861, White County, Georgia	Co. C, 24th Georgia Infantry	June 1, 1864, Cold Harbor, Virginia	Point Lookout, Maryland, transferred to Elmira Prison, NY, July 12, 1864	Died January 2, 1865 of Hospital Gangrene, Grave No. 1505
Jackson, Elisha Private	Unk	March 1, 1862, Richmond, Virginia	Co. E, 17th Virginia Infantry	July 21, 1863, Manassas Gap, Virginia	Point Lookout, Maryland, transferred to Elmira Prison, NY, August 18, 1864	Exchanged March 10, 1865 at Boulware's Wharf on the James River, Virginia
Jackson, George A. Private	Unk	August 6, 1863, Greensboro, Georgia	Co. F, 7th Georgia Cavalry	June 11, 1864, Trevilian Station, Louisa Court House, Virginia	Point Lookout, Maryland, transferred to Elmira Prison, NY, July 25, 1864	Oath of Allegiance June 21, 1865
Jackson, George G. Corporal	21	July 15, 1861, Selma, Alabama	Jeff Davis Alabama Artillery	May 5, 1864, Wilderness, Virginia	Point Lookout, Maryland, transferred to Elmira Prison, NY, August 17, 1864	Escaped October 7, 1864 by Tunneling Under Fence.
Jackson, Isaac Private	Unk	May 25, 1862, Floyd Court House, Virginia	Co. B, 42nd Virginia Infantry	May 12, 1864, Spotsylvania Court House, Virginia	Point Lookout, Maryland, transferred to Elmira Prison, NY, August 2, 1864	Died January 25, 1865 of Chronic Diarrhea, Grave No. 1620
Jackson, J. Private	Unk	Unknown	Co. B, 64th Georgia Infantry	July 29, 1864, Deserted to Union Lines, Petersburg, Virginia	Point Lookout, Maryland, transferred to Elmira Prison, NY, August 12, 1864	Oath of Allegiance November 30, 1864. Early Release per Lincoln's Proclamation, 12/8/1863.

Name & Rank	Age	Enlisted	Regiment and State	Where Captured	Prison	Remarks
Jackson, J. C. Private	Unk	June 18, 1864, Columbia, South Carolina	Co. G, 18th South Carolina Infantry	July 30, 1864, Petersburg, Virginia	Point Lookout, Maryland, transferred to Elmira Prison, NY, August 12, 1864	Exchanged October 29, 1864 at Venus Point, Savannah River, GA.
Jackson, J. W. Private	Unk	May 6. 1862, Cumberland County, North Carolina	Co. I, 51st North Carolina Infantry	June 1, 1864, Cold Harbor, Virginia	Point Lookout, Maryland, transferred to Elmira Prison, NY, July 12, 1864	Exchanged October 29, 1864 at Venus Point, Savannah River, GA.
Jackson, James Private	Unk	April 1, 1864, Richmond, Virginia	Co. B, 3rd Battalion Georgia Sharp shooters	August 16, 1864, Front Royal, Virginia	Old Capital Prison, Washington, DC transferred to Elmira Prison, NY, August 29, 1864	Oath of Allegiance June 21, 1865
Jackson, James M. Private	30	February 27, 1862, Reidsville, Rockingham County, North Carolina	Co. G, 45th North Carolina Infantry	May 10, 1864, Spotsylvania Court House, Virginia	Point Lookout, Maryland, transferred to Elmira Prison, NY, August 6, 1864	Oath of Allegiance June 14, 1865
Jackson, John Private	18	July 19, 1861, Halifax County, North Carolina	Co. K, 1st North Carolina Infantry	May 12, 1864, Spotsylvania Court House, Virginia	Point Lookout Prison Camp, Maryland. Transferred to Elmira Prison, NY, August 6, 1864	Died February 27, 1865 of Chronic Diarrhea, Grave No. 2152
Jackson, John Private	Unk	May 13, 1862, New Hanover County, North Carolina	Co. I, 51st North Carolina Infantry	June 1, 1864, Cold Harbor, Virginia	Point Lookout, Maryland, transferred to Elmira Prison, NY, July 17,1864	Exchanged October 29, 1864 at Venus Point, Savannah River, GA.
Jackson, John M. Private	Unk	July 19, 1861, Monroe, Georgia	Co. F, 16th Georgia Infantry	June 1, 1864, Cold Harbor, Virginia	Point Lookout, Maryland, transferred to Elmira Prison, NY, July 12, 1864	Oath of Allegiance July 7, 1865
Jackson, John M. Private	35	January 1, 1862, Camp Hampton, Columbia, South Carolina	Co. F, 18th South Carolina Infantry	July 30, 1864, Petersburg, Virginia	Fort Columbus, N Y Harbor, transferred to Elmira Prison, NY, December 4, 1864.	Exchanged February 20, 1865 at Boulware's or Cox Wharf on the James River, Virginia

Name & Rank	Age	Enlisted	Regiment and State	Where Captured	Prison	Remarks
Jackson, John W. Private	Unk	June 2, 1861, Jackson, Tennessee	Co. L, 3rd Kentucky Infantry	May 16, 1863, Champion Hill, Mississippi	Point Lookout, Maryland, transferred to Elmira Prison, NY, July 25, 1864	Died October 6, 1864 of Chronic Diarrhea, Grave No. 583
Jackson, Joseph C. Private	29	January 23, 1862, Windsor, North Carolina	Co. C, 11th North Carolina Infantry	July 14, 1863, Falling Waters, Maryland	Point Lookout, Maryland, transferred to Elmira Prison, NY, August 18, 1864	Died November 12, 1864 of Hospital Gangrene, Grave No. 819
Jackson, Joseph C. Private	Unk	January 12, 1862, Bennettsville, South Carolina	Co. E, 4th South Carolina Cavalry	June 11, 1864, Trevilian Station, Louisa Court House, Virginia	Point Lookout, Maryland, transferred to Elmira Prison, NY, July 11, 1864. Ward No. 26	Died August 12, 1864 of Chronic Diarrhea, Grave No. 133
Jackson, Kelly W. Private	25	October 22, 1861, Clinton, North Carolina	Co. D, 38th North Carolina Infantry	May 10, 1864, Near Spotsylvania County Court House, Virginia	Point Lookout, Maryland, transferred to Elmira Prison, NY, August 14, 1864	Exchanged March 2, 1865 at Boulware's Wharf on the James River, Virginia
Jackson, Lewis Private	18	April 5, 1862, Hall's Store, North Carolina	Co. K, 51st North Carolina Infantry	June 15, 1864, Bottoms Church, Near Petersburg, Near Bermuda Hundred, Virginia	Point Lookout, Maryland, transferred to Elmira Prison, NY, July 12, 1864	Oath of Allegiance July 3, 1865
Jackson, Martin V. Private	Unk	August 5, 1862, Chattahoochee, Florida	Co. A, 11th Florida Infantry	July 29, 1864, Petersburg, Virginia	Point Lookout, Maryland, transferred to Elmira Prison, NY, August 12, 1864	Oath of Allegiance May 29, 1865
Jackson, Micajah C. Private	Unk	November 21, 1863, Raleigh, North Carolina	Co. B, 52nd North Carolina Infantry	May 12, 1864, Spotsylvania Court House, Virginia	Point Lookout, Maryland, transferred to Elmira Prison, NY, July 23, 1864	Oath of Allegiance May 13, 1865
Jackson, Nathan H. Private	38	February 18, 1863, Sampson County, North Carolina	Co. A, 36th Regiment, 2nd North Carolina Artillery	January 15, 1865, Fort Fisher, North Carolina	February 1, 1865 Elmira Prison Camp, New York	Died February 11, 1865 of Pneumonia, Grave No. 2094

Name & Rank	Age	Enlisted	Regiment and State	Where Captured	Prison	Remarks
Jackson, Noah R. Private	21	September 21, 1861, Cartage, North Carolina	Co. C, 35th North Carolina Infantry	June 17, 1864, Petersburg, Virginia	Point Lookout, Maryland, transferred to Elmira Prison, NY, July 25, 1864	Oath of Allegiance May 19, 1865
Jackson, R. Private	Unk	Unknown	Co. E, 2nd Virginia Artillery	May 12, 1864, Spotsylvania Court House, Virginia	Point Lookout, Maryland, transferred to Elmira Prison, NY, August 12, 1864	Died May 19, 1865 of Variola (Smallpox), Grave No. 2944
Jackson, Randall L. Private	Unk	August 24, 1861, White County, Georgia	Co. C, 24th Georgia Infantry	August 16, 1864, Front Royal, Virginia	Old Capital Prison, Washington, DC transferred to Elmira Prison, NY, August 29, 1864	Exchanged February 13, 1865 at Boulware's wharf on the James River, Virginia
Jackson, Robert C. Private	18	Unknown	Co. H, 11th Virginia Cavalry	December 6, 1864, Stone Bridge, Virginia	November 11, 1864, Old Capital Prison, Washington, DC. February 4, 1865 Elmira, Prison Camp, NY	Exchanged March 14, 1865 at Boulware's Wharf on the James River, Virginia
Jackson, W. P. Private	Unk	Unknown	Co. D, Gober's Battalion Louisiana Cavalry	October 3, 1864, Dutch Store, Ascension Parish, Louisiana	New Orleans, Louisiana transferred to Elmira November 19, 1864.	Exchanged February 25, 1865 at Boulware's or Cox Wharf on the James River, Virginia
Jackson, William Private	22	August 12, 1861, Pitt County, North Carolina	Co. G, 8th North Carolina Infantry	June 1, 1864, Cold Harbor, Virginia	Point Lookout, Maryland, transferred to Elmira Prison, NY, July 17, 1864	Exchanged March 2, 1865 at Akins Landing on the James River, Virginia
Jackson, William G. Private	Unk	June 9, 1861, Jones County, Georgia	Co. B, 12th Georgia Infantry	May 10, 1864, Spotsylvania Court House, Virginia	Point Lookout, Maryland, transferred to Elmira Prison, NY, July 25, 1864	Oath of Allegiance June 14, 1865
Jackson, William H. Private	20	June 2, 1861, Little Plymouth, Virginia	Co. G, 26th Virginia Infantry	June 15, 1864, Near Petersburg, Virginia	Point Lookout, Maryland, transferred to Elmira Prison, NY, July 12, 1864	Oath of Allegiance July 12, 1865

Name & Rank	Age	Enlisted	Regiment and State	Where Captured	Prison	Remarks
Jackson, William M. Private	Unk	May 1, 1862, Fayetteville, Georgia	Co. C, 53rd Georgia Infantry	June 1, 1864, Gaines Mill, Cold Harbor, Virginia	Transferred From Point Lookout Prison, MD, July 12, 1864. Train Never Arrived at Elmira Prison Camp, NY.	Died July 15, 1864 in Train Wreck at Shohola, Pennsylvania.
Jacobs, Andrew J. Private	Unk	March 23, 1862, Georgetown, South Carolina	Co. A, 21st South Carolina Infantry	June 24, 1864, Near Petersburg, Virginia	Point Lookout, Maryland, transferred to Elmira Prison, NY, August 18, 1864	Died November 1, 1864 of Pneumonia, Grave No. 756
Jacobs, Henry Private	Unk	Unknown	Co. B, 1st Virginia Cavalry	July 15, 1864, Rockville, Maryland	Old Capital Prison, Washington, DC, transferred to Elmira Prison, NY, July 25, 1864.	Oath of Allegiance May 29, 1865
Jacobs, Jason Private	32	February 11, 1862, St. Johns, North Carolina	Co. F, 1st North Carolina Infantry	May 12, 1864, Spotsylvania Court House, Virginia	Point Lookout, Maryland, transferred to Elmira Prison, NY, August 6, 1864	Died May 16, 1865 of Chronic Diarrhea, Grave No. 2957
Jacobs, Lewis A. Corporal	Unk	October 13, 1862, Richmond, Virginia	Co. E, 25th Battalion Virginia Infantry	July 12, 1864, Cox's Farm, Virginia	Point Lookout, Maryland, transferred to Elmira Prison, NY, August 6, 1864	Oath of Allegiance July 3, 1865
Jacobs, Robert Private	Unk	May 20, 1862, Camp Harris, Tennessee	Co. D, 17th Tennessee Infantry	June 17, 1864, Petersburg, Virginia	Point Lookout, Maryland, transferred to Elmira Prison, NY, July 30, 1864	Exchanged February 25, 1865 at Boulware's or Cox Wharf on the James River, Virginia
Jacobs, Snowden Private	24	December 25, 1861, Bennettsville, South Carolina	Co. F, 21st South Carolina Infantry	January 15, 1865, Fort Fisher, North Carolina	January 30, 1865 Elmira Prison Camp, New York	Oath of Allegiance July 7, 1865
Jamerson, Joseph D. Private	Unk	April 26, 1862, Talbotton, Georgia	Co. F, 4th Georgia Infantry	May 20, 1864, Spotsylvania Court House, Virginia	Point Lookout, Maryland, transferred to Elmira Prison, NY, July 6, 1864	Exchanged February 25, 1865 at Boulware's or Cox Wharf on the James River, Virginia

Name & Rank	Age	Enlisted	Regiment and State	Where Captured	Prison	Remarks
James, Abel Corporal	Unk	June 9, 1861, Jones County, Georgia	Co. B, 12th Georgia Infantry	May 10, 1864, Spotsylvania Court House, Virginia	Point Lookout, Maryland, transferred to Elmira Prison, NY, July 25, 1864	Oath of Allegiance June 27, 1865
James, Andrew F. Corporal	21	August 31, 1861, Spartanburg Court House, South Carolina	Co. B, 13th South Carolina Infantry	May 12, 1864, Spotsylvania Court House, Virginia. Wounded in Back and Left Side of Neck by a Shell.	Point Lookout, Maryland, transferred to Elmira Prison, NY, August 29, 1864	Transferred For Exchange October 11, 1864 to Point Lookout Prison Camp, MD. Died October 22, 1864 of Unknown Causes.
James, B. F. Corporal	Unk	January 10, 1862, Camp Hampton, Columbia, South Carolina	Co. I, 18th South Carolina Infantry	July 30, 1864, Petersburg, Virginia	Point Lookout, Maryland, transferred to Elmira Prison, NY, August 12, 1864	Oath of Allegiance July 19, 1865
James, Edwin Private	Unk	June 7, 1861, Camp Moore, Louisiana	Co. G, 7th Louisiana Infantry	May 11, 1864, Spotsylvania Court House, Virginia	Point Lookout, Maryland, transferred to Elmira Prison, NY, July 3, 1864	Escaped the night of July 8, 1864 by Scaling a Fence. Never Recaptured.
James, Henry L. Private		February 10, 1864, Kinston, North Carolina	Co. G, 43rd North Carolina Infantry	May 30, 1864 Mechanicsville, Virginia	Point Lookout, Maryland, transferred to Elmira Prison, NY, July 11, 1864	Died September 21, 1864 of Remittent Fever, Grave No. 338
James, James C. Private	24	October 1, 1861, Nashville, Tennessee	Co. A, 1st Tennessee Heavy Artillery	August 23, 1864, Fort Morgan, Alabama	Fort Columbus, New York Harbor. Transferred February 4, 1865 Elmira, Prison Camp, NY	Died March 16, 1865 of Diarrhea, Grave No. 1694
James, James V. Corporal	16	December 20, 1861, Brittons Neck, South Carolina	Co. J, 21st South Carolina Infantry	June 24, 1864, Near Petersburg, Virginia	Point Lookout, Maryland, transferred to Elmira Prison, NY, August 18, 1864	Exchanged March 14, 1865 at Boulware's Wharf on the James River, Virginia
James, Joel P. Private	27	December 5, 1861, Sac River, St. Clair County, Missouri	Co. K, 1st Missouri Cavalry	May 17, 1863, Big Black Bridge, Champion Hill, Mississippi	Point Lookout, Maryland, transferred to Elmira Prison, NY, August 18, 1864	Exchanged October 29, 1864 at Venus Point, Savannah River, GA.

Name & Rank	Age	Enlisted	Regiment and State	Where Captured	Prison	Remarks
James, John B. Private	26	May 25, 1861, Morrisville, Virginia	Co. J, 11th Virginia Infantry	September 14, 1863, Kelly's Ford, Virginia	Point Lookout, Maryland, transferred to Elmira Prison, NY, August 18, 1864	Died February 10, 1865 of Variola (Smallpox), Grave No. 2080
James, John F. Corporal	22	December 4, 1861, Pickens Court House, South Carolina	Co. F, 1st South Carolina Cavalry	September 14, 1863, Captured on Pickett Duty Near Culpepper, Virginia	Point Lookout, Maryland, transferred to Elmira Prison, NY, August 18, 1864	Exchanged October 29, 1864 at Venus Point, Savannah River, GA.
James, Lewis Private	17	July 19, 1862 Graham, North Carolina	Co. I, 8th North Carolina Infantry	May 31, 1864, Cold Harbor, Virginia	Point Lookout, Maryland, transferred to Elmira Prison, NY, July 11, 1864	Exchanged March 2, 1865 at Akins Landing on the James River, Virginia
James, Lycurgus Private	21	May 16, 1862, Corinth, Mississippi	Co. K, 1st Missouri Cavalry	May 17, 1863, Big Black Bridge, Champion Hill, Mississippi	Point Lookout, Maryland, transferred to Elmira Prison, NY, August 18, 1864	Exchanged October 29, 1864 at Venus Point, Savannah River, GA.
James, Marshall E. Private	28	December 4, 1861, Randolph County, North Carolina	Co. F, 2nd Battalion North Carolina Infantry	May 10, 1864, Near Spotsylvania Court House, Virginia	Point Lookout, Maryland, transferred to Elmira Prison, NY, August 14, 1864	Died November 22, 1864 of Pneumonia, Grave No. 935
James, Meridith Clay Private	Unk	Unknown	Co. A, Mosby's Regiment Virginia Cavalry	July 18, 1864, Point Rocks, Maryland	Old Capital Prison, Washington, DC, transferred to Elmira, NY, August 12, 1864	Oath of Allegiance November 3, 1864. Early Release per Lincoln's Proclamation, 12/8/1863.
James, Rueben H. Private	Unk	April 15, 1864, Union County, North Carolina	Co. I, 53rd North Carolina Infantry	May 6, 1864, Wilderness, Virginia	Old Capital Prison, Washington, DC, transferred to Elmira July 23, 1864	Exchanged October 29, 1864 at Venus Point, Savannah River, GA.
James, T. J. Corporal	Unk	May 28, 1861, Matthews County Court House, Virginia	Co. D, 26th North Carolina Infantry	June 17, 1864, Near Petersburg, Virginia	Point Lookout, Maryland, transferred to Elmira Prison, NY, July 30, 1864	Exchanged October 29, 1864 at Venus Point, Savannah River, GA.

Name & Rank	Age	Enlisted	Regiment and State	Where Captured	Prison	Remarks
James, Thomas B. Private	Unk	May 28, 1861, Matthews County Court House, Virginia	Co. F, 26th North Carolina Infantry	June 17, 1864, Near Petersburg, Virginia	Point Lookout, Maryland, transferred to Elmira Prison, NY, July 30, 1864	Oath of Allegiance July 3, 1865
James, Thomas J. Private	Unk	June 2, 1863, Caroline County, Virginia	Co. B, 12th Georgia Infantry	May 10, 1864, Spotsylvania Court House, Virginia	Point Lookout, Maryland, transferred to Elmira Prison, NY, July 25, 1864	Oath of Allegiance June 16, 1865
James, William J. Private	Unk	June 9, 1861, Jones County, Georgia	Co. B, 12th Georgia Infantry	May 10, 1864, Spotsylvania Court House, Virginia	Point Lookout, Maryland, transferred to Elmira Prison, NY, July 25, 1864	Died October 1, 1864 of Typhoid-Pneumonia, Grave No. 413
Jamison, A. R. Private	Unk	February 20, 1863, Charleston, South Carolina	Co. G, 5th South Carolina Cavalry	May 28, 1864, Hall's Shop, Virginia	Point Lookout, Maryland, transferred to Elmira Prison, NY, July 12, 1864	Exchanged October 29, 1864 at Venus Point, Savannah River, GA.
Jamison, John F. Sergeant	21	December 31, 1861, Columbia, South Carolina	Co. G, 18th South Carolina Infantry	July 30, 1864, Petersburg, Virginia	Point Lookout, Maryland, transferred to Elmira Prison, NY, August 12, 1864	Oath of Allegiance July 3, 1865
Jamison, William T. Private	18	July 9, 1861, Staunton, Virginia	Co. A, 52nd Virginia Infantry	May 30, 1864 Mechanicsville, Virginia	Point Lookout, Maryland, transferred to Elmira Prison, NY, July 9, 1864	Oath of Allegiance June 19, 1865
January, George W. Private	22	August 29, 1862, Camp Little, Mississippi	Co. F, 3rd Battalion Missouri Cavalry	May 17, 1863, Big Black Bridge, Champion Hill, Mississippi	Point Lookout, Maryland, transferred to Elmira Prison, NY, August 18, 1864	Exchanged October 29, 1864 at Venus Point, Savannah River, GA.
Jarman, Jobe Private	16	February 6, 1864, Hamilton, North Carolina	Co. A, 35th North Carolina Infantry	June 17, 1864, Petersburg, Virginia	Point Lookout, Maryland, transferred to Elmira Prison, NY, July 30, 1864	Oath of Allegiance May 19, 1865
Jarratt, P. T. Private	Unk	March 13, 1862, Henry County, Virginia	Co. G, 42nd Virginia Infantry	May 12, 1864, Near Spotsylvania Court House, Virginia	Point Lookout, Maryland, transferred to Elmira Prison, NY, August 6, 1864	Died September 27, 1864 of Rubeola (Measles), Grave No. 444

Name & Rank	Age	Enlisted	Regiment and State	Where Captured	Prison	Remarks
Jarratt, Patrick F. Private	Unk	March 13, 1862, Henry County, Virginia	Co. G, 42nd Virginia Infantry	May 12, 1864, Near Spotsylvania Court House, Virginia	Point Lookout, Maryland, transferred to Elmira Prison, NY, August 6, 1864	Exchanged October 29, 1864 at Venus Point, Savannah River, GA.
Jarrell, Richard H. Private	21	June 24, 1861, Coosawhatchie, South Carolina	Co. E, 11th South Carolina Infantry	June 24, 1864, Near Petersburg, Virginia	Point Lookout, Maryland, transferred to Elmira Prison, NY, August 18, 1864	Exchanged October 29, 1864 at Venus Point, Savannah River, GA.
Jarrell, Zimri Private	Unk	June 5, 1861, Asheboro, North Carolina	Co. J, 22nd North Carolina Infantry	May 5, 1864, Wilderness, Virginia	Point Lookout, Maryland, transferred to Elmira Prison, NY, August 14, 1864	Oath of Allegiance June 30, 1865
Jarvis, Alexander V. Corporal	22	August 1, 1861, Currituck County, North Carolina	Co. B, 8th North Carolina Infantry	May 30, 1864, Cold Harbor, Virginia	Point Lookout, Maryland, transferred to Elmira Prison, NY, July 11, 1864	Oath of Allegiance June 30, 1865
Jarvis, James Private	20	March 4, 1862, Salisbury, North Carolina	Co. D, 42nd North Carolina Infantry	June 2, 1864, Cold Harbor, Virginia	Point Lookout, Maryland, transferred to Elmira Prison, NY, July 17,1864	Exchanged October 29, 1864 at Venus Point, Savannah River, GA.
Jarvis, James O. M. Private	Unk	November 22, 1862, Knoxville, Tennessee	Co. H, 47th Alabama Infantry	May 23, 1864, North Anna, Hanover Junction, Virginia	Point Lookout, Maryland, transferred to Elmira Prison, NY, August 17, 1864	Exchanged October 29, 1864 at Venus Point, Savannah River, GA.
Jarvis, William Private	24	March 4, 1862, Salisbury, North Carolina	Co. D, 42nd North Carolina Infantry	June 2, 1864, Cold Harbor, Virginia	Point Lookout, Maryland, transferred to Elmira Prison, NY, July 11, 1864	Oath of Allegiance June 21, 1865
Jarvis, William H. Private	Unk	August 1, 1861, Staunton, Virginia	Co. H, 25th Virginia Infantry	May 12, 1864, Spotsylvania Court House, Virginia	Point Lookout, Maryland, transferred to Elmira Prison, NY, August 12, 1864	Exchanged October 29, 1864 at Venus Point, Savannah River, GA.
Jasper, David N. Sergeant	Unk	June 7, 1861, New Market, Virginia	Co. H, 49th, Virginia Infantry	May 30, 1864, Gaines Mill Cold Harbor, Virginia	Point Lookout, Maryland, transferred to Elmira Prison, NY, July 11,1864	Oath of Allegiance June 14, 1865

Name & Rank	Age	Enlisted	Regiment and State	Where Captured	Prison	Remarks
Jasper, Henry N. Sergeant	25	May 20, 1861, Louisburg, North Carolina	Co. K, 32nd North Carolina Infantry	May 10, 1864, Near Mine Run Spotsylvania, Virginia	Point Lookout, Maryland, transferred to Elmira Prison, NY, August 6, 1864	Exchanged March 10, 1865 at Boulware's Wharf on the James River, Virginia
Jefferds, Joseph B. Private	Unk	February 27, 1862, Pee Dee Bridge, South Carolina	Co. K, 21st South Carolina Infantry	January 15, 1865, Fort Fisher, North Carolina	January 30, 1865 Elmira Prison Camp, New York	Oath of Allegiance July 3, 1865
Jefferson, John Private	Unk	May 29, 1864, Petersburg, Virginia	Co. B, 3rd Archer's Battalion, Virginia Reserves Infantry	June 9, 1864, Petersburg, Virginia	Point Lookout, Maryland, transferred to Elmira Prison, NY, July 12,1864	Exchanged October 29, 1864 at Venus Point, Savannah River, GA.
Jeffreys, Archibald Private	Unk	May 22, 1864, Fort Morgan, Alabama	Co. E, 1st Battalion Alabama Artillery	August 23, 1864, Fort Morgan, Alabama	Steam Press No. 4 New Orleans, Louisiana transferred to Elmira Prison, NY, October 8, 1864.	Exchanged February 20, 1865 at Boulware's or Cox Wharf on the James River, Virginia
Jeffreys, Newton A. Private	21	March 27, 1862, Greensboro, North Carolina	Co. C, 45th North Carolina Infantry	May 10, 1864, Spotsylvania Court House, Virginia	Point Lookout, Maryland, transferred to Elmira Prison, NY, August 6, 1864	Oath of Allegiance June 12, 1865
Jeffrie, George W. Private	20	February 15, 1862, Dandridge, Jefferson County, Tennessee	Co. C, 39th Tennessee Infantry	August 10, 1864, Rockville, Maryland	Old Capital Prison, Washington, DC transferred to Elmira Prison, NY, August 29, 1864	Died March 27, 1865 of Pneumonia, Grave No. 2497. Headstone has Jeffers also 31st Arty.
Jeffries, John Corporal	21	September 25, 1861, Camp Branch, Roxboro, North Carolina	Co. E, 35th North Carolina Infantry	June 17, 1864, Petersburg, Virginia	Point Lookout, Maryland, transferred to Elmira Prison, NY, July 30, 1864	Died March 10, 1865 of Diarrhea, Grave No. 1880
Jeffords, Joseph B. Private	26	February 20, 1862, Pee Dee, South Carolina	Co. K, 21st South Carolina Volunteers	January 15, 1865, Fort Fisher, North Carolina	January 30, 1865 Elmira Prison Camp, New York	Oath Of Allegiance July 3, 1865

Name & Rank	Age	Enlisted	Regiment and State	Where Captured	Prison	Remarks
Jelks, Cincinnatus Private	21	May 29, 1861, Goldsboro, North Carolina	Co. H, 2nd North Carolina Infantry	July 12, 1864, Near Washington, DC,	Old Capital Prison, Washington, DC, transferred to Elmira July 23, 1864	Oath of Allegiance May 29, 1865
Jenkins, Christy J. Private	Unk	March 17, 1862 Dallas, Gaston County, North Carolina	Co. M, 16th North Carolina Infantry	May 12, 1864, Spotsylvania Court House, Virginia	Point Lookout, Maryland, transferred to Elmira Prison, NY, August 12, 1864	Exchanged March 2, 1865 at Akins Landing on the James River, Virginia
Jenkins, Daniel R. Private	Unk	Unknown	Co. I, 6th North Carolina Infantry	May 30, 1864 Mechanicsville, Virginia	Point Lookout, Maryland, transferred to Elmira Prison, NY, July 12, 1864	Oath of Allegiance May 13, 1865
Jenkins, Edward Private	Unk	September 20, 1862, Snickersville, Virginia	Co. A, 6th Virginia Cavalry	February 1, 1865, Clark County, Virginia	Old Capital Prison, Washington, DC, transferred to Elmira, NY, March 3, 1865.	Oath of Allegiance June 30, 1865
Jenkins, Elbert H. Private	Unk	April 14, 1864, Bristol, Tennessee	Co. J, 14th Tennessee Infantry	May 6, 1864, Wilderness, Virginia	Point Lookout, Maryland, transferred to Elmira Prison, NY, July 23, 1864	Died November 11, 1864 of Chronic Diarrhea, Grave No. 1551
Jenkins, James G. Corporal	Unk	March 11, 1864, Warrenton, Virginia	Co. A, 35th Virginia Cavalry	April 21, 1865, Prospect Hill, Virginia	Old Capital Prison, Washington, DC, transferred to Elmira, NY, May 12, 1865.	Oath of Allegiance July 7, 1865
Jenkins, John H. Sergeant	Unk	July 29, 1861, Lineville, Talladega County, Alabama	Co. J, 14th Alabama Infantry	May 24, 1864, North Anna River, Hanover Junction, Virginia	Point Lookout, Maryland, transferred to Elmira Prison, NY, July 11, 1864	Exchanged March 10, 1865 at Boulware's Wharf on the James River, Virginia
Jenkins, John R. Private	21	April 18, 1861, Winchester, Virginia	Co. F, 2nd Virginia Infantry	May 12, 1864, Near Spotsylvania Court House, Virginia	Point Lookout, Maryland, transferred to Elmira Prison, NY, August 2, 1864	Oath of Allegiance June 27, 1865

Name & Rank	Age	Enlisted	Regiment and State	Where Captured	Prison	Remarks
Jenkins, Littleton B. Corporal	Unk	July 9, 1861, Dublin, Georgia	Co. H, 14th Georgia Infantry	May 12, 1864, Spotsylvania Court House, Virginia	Point Lookout, Maryland, transferred to Elmira Prison, NY, July 30, 1864	Oath of Allegiance July 19, 1865
Jenkins, Meridith T. Private	Unk	June 1, 1862, Camp Mangum, North Carolina	Co. K, 54th North Carolina Infantry	November 7, 1864, Rappahanock Ford, Virginia	Point Lookout, Maryland, transferred to Elmira Prison, NY, July 23, 1864	Died March 13, 1865 of Chronic Diarrhea, Grave No. 2429. Name Henry Jenkins Appears on Headstone.
Jenkins, R. O. Private	Unk	December 31, 1861, Columbia, South Carolina	Co. G, 18th South Carolina Infantry	July 30, 1864, Petersburg, Virginia	Point Lookout, Maryland, transferred to Elmira Prison, NY, August 12, 1864	Died April 21, 1865 of Pneumonia, Grave No. 1388
Jenkins, Robert A. Private	Unk	February 15, 1864, Orange County, Virginia	Co. D, 15th, Virginia Cavalry	May 28, 1864, Gaines Mill Cold Harbor, Virginia	Point Lookout, Maryland, transferred to Elmira Prison, NY, July 12,1864	Exchanged October 29, 1864 at Venus Point, Savannah River, GA.
Jenkins, Samuel Private	41	August 19, 1863, Fort Branch, Martin County, North Carolina	Co. F, 40th Regiment, 3rd North Carolina Artillery	January 15, 1865, Fort Fisher, North Carolina	January 30, 1865 Elmira Prison Camp, New York	Oath of Allegiance June 23, 1865
Jenkins, William H. Sergeant	29	April 20, 1861, E. H. Rowe's Store, Virginia	Co. F, 26th North Carolina Infantry	June 17, 1864, Near Petersburg, Virginia	Point Lookout, Maryland, transferred to Elmira Prison, NY, July 30, 1864	Oath of Allegiance July 15, 1865
Jenkins, William R. Private	20	February 21, 1862, Concord, North Carolina	Co. A, 33rd North Carolina Infantry	May 6, 1864, Wilderness, Virginia	Point Lookout, Maryland, transferred to Elmira Prison, NY, August 14, 1864	Oath of Allegiance May 17, 1865
Jenkins, Wilson S. Private	22	August 1, 1861, Waynesboro, Georgia	Co. E, Cobb's Legion Georgia	August 16, 1864, Front Royal, Virginia	Old Capital Prison, Washington, DC transferred to Elmira Prison, NY, August 29, 1864	Oath of Allegiance June 21, 1865

Name & Rank	Age	Enlisted	Regiment and State	Where Captured	Prison	Remarks
Jennings, Churchwell M. Private	Unk	April 5, 1862, Wytheville, Virginia	Co. C, 29th, Virginia Infantry	June 1, 1864, Gaines Mill Cold Harbor, Virginia	Point Lookout, Maryland, transferred to Elmira Prison, NY, July 12, 1864	Died May 3, 1865 of Debility, Grave No. 2909
Jennings, Joseph Private	Unk	December 15, 1863, Mount Pleasant, South Carolina	Co. G, 27th South Carolina Infantry	June 24, 1864, Near Petersburg, Virginia	Point Lookout, Maryland, transferred to Elmira Prison, NY, August 17, 1864	Exchanged October 29, 1864 at Venus Point, Savannah River, GA.
Jernell, Hamilton J. Private	19	April 18, 1861, Blacksburg, Virginia	Co. E, 4th Virginia Infantry	May 12, 1864, Near Spotsylvania Court House, Virginia	Point Lookout, Maryland, transferred to Elmira Prison, NY, August 2, 1864	Oath of Allegiance August 7, 1865
Jernigan, Cader R. Private	24	May 10, 1861, Newton Grove, North Carolina	Co. H, 20th North Carolina Infantry	May 20, 1864, Spotsylvania Court House, Virginia	Point Lookout, Maryland, transferred to Elmira Prison, NY, July 6, 1864	Oath of Allegiance June 16, 1865
Jernigan, Delancey A. Private	20	March 7, 1862, Wilmington, North Carolina	Co. H, 51st North Carolina Infantry	June 1, 1864, Cold Harbor, Virginia	Point Lookout, Maryland, transferred to Elmira Prison, NY, July 12, 1864	Died October 6, 1864 of Chronic Diarrhea, Grave No. 596
Jernigan, George W. Private	19	January 8, 1862, Fort Johnson, North Carolina	Co. E, 28th North Carolina Infantry	May 20, 1864, Spotsylvania Court House, Virginia	Point Lookout, Maryland, transferred to Elmira Prison, NY, July 3, 1864	Died February 12, 1865 of Variola (Smallpox), Grave No. 2072
Jernigan, Lewis M. Private	28	May 10, 1861, Newton Grove, North Carolina	Co. H, 20th North Carolina Infantry	May 20, 1864, Spotsylvania Court House, Virginia	Point Lookout, Maryland, transferred to Elmira Prison, NY, July 6, 1864	Died December 28, 1864 of Pneumonia, Grave No. 1297
Jernigan, William H. Sergeant	26	April 1, 1862, Windsor, North Carolina	Co. G, 32nd North Carolina Infantry	May 10, 1864, Wilderness, Virginia	Point Lookout, Maryland, transferred to Elmira Prison, NY, August 6, 1864	Exchanged March 10, 1865 at Boulware's Wharf on the James River, Virginia

Name & Rank	Age	Enlisted	Regiment and State	Where Captured	Prison	Remarks
Jesse, Elisha B. Corporal	23	December 31, 1861, Springfield, Missouri	Co. H, 1st Missouri Cavalry	May 17, 1863, Big Black Bridge, Champion Hill, Mississippi	Point Lookout, Maryland, transferred to Elmira Prison, NY, August 18, 1864	Exchanged February 13, 1865 at Boulware's wharf on the James River, Virginia
Jessop, Thomas Private	26	July 15, 1862, Guilford County, North Carolina	Co. A, 1st North Carolina Infantry	May 12, 1864, Wilderness, Spotsylvania Court House, Virginia	Point Lookout, Maryland, transferred to Elmira Prison, NY, August 6, 1864	Oath of Allegiance May 17, 1865
Jessup, William F. Private	Unk	May 6, 1862, Macon, Georgia	Co. J, 61st Georgia Infantry	May 12, 1864, Spotsylvania Court House, Virginia	Point Lookout, Maryland, transferred to Elmira Prison, NY, July 25, 1864	Died July 9, 1865 of Pneumonia, Grave No. 2843
Jeter, Joseph F. Private	Unk	March 11, 1862, Richmond, Virginia	Co. G, 22nd Battalion Virginia, Infantry	May 11, 1864, Hanover Court House, Virginia	Point Lookout, Maryland, transferred to Elmira Prison, NY, July 11, 1864	Oath of Allegiance May29, 1865
Jett, Abvarada D. Private	Unk	February 24, 1862, Camp Clifton, Fredericksburg, Virginia	Co. A, 47th Virginia Infantry	May 5, 1864, Wilderness, Virginia	Point Lookout, Maryland, transferred to Elmira Prison, NY, July 23, 1864	Oath of Allegiance May 15, 1865
Jewell, James W. Private	Unk	March 17, 1862, Luray, Virginia	Co. K, 10th Virginia Infantry	May 12, 1864, Spotsylvania Court House, Virginia	Point Lookout, Maryland, transferred to Elmira Prison, NY, August 2, 1864	Oath of Allegiance June 27, 1865
Jewell, M. S. Private	Unk	Unknown	Co. E, 16th Georgia Infantry	May 6, 1864, Wilderness, Virginia	Old Capital Prison, Washington, DC, transferred to Elmira, NY, July 14, 1864	Exchanged March 10, 1865 at Boulware's Wharf on the James River, Virginia
Jimmerson, Samuel W. Private	Unk	March 14, 1864, Camp Vance, North Carolina	Co. G, 37th North Carolina Infantry	July 29, 1864, Near Darby Town, Petersburg Virginia	Point Lookout, Maryland, transferred to Elmira Prison, NY, August 12, 1864	Oath of Allegiance July 3, 1865

Name & Rank	Age	Enlisted	Regiment and State	Where Captured	Prison	Remarks
Job, Jesse R. Private	Unk	March 1, 1864, Orange County Court House, North Carolina	Co. H, 1st North Carolina Infantry	May 12, 1864, Wilderness, Spotsylvania Court House, Virginia	Point Lookout, Maryland, transferred to Elmira Prison, NY, August 6, 1864	Died January 13, 1865 of Pneumonia, Grave No. 1471
Job, Jonathan F. Private	21	July 8, 1862, Greensboro, North Carolina	Co. H, 1st North Carolina Infantry	May 12, 1864, Wilderness, Spotsylvania Court House, Virginia	Point Lookout, Maryland, transferred to Elmira Prison, NY, August 6, 1864	Died April 8, 1865 of Chronic Diarrhea, Grave No. 2632.
John, Levi Private	Unk	May 12, 1863, Troy, Alabama	Co. G, 59th Alabama Infantry	May 18, 1864, Near Drury's Bluff, Virginia	Point Lookout, Maryland, transferred to Elmira Prison, NY, July 25, 1864	Oath of Allegiance May 19, 1865
John, Shadrick Private	Unk	Unknown	Co. A, Captain Jones' Home Guard Florida	September 27, 1864, Marianna, Florida	New Orleans, Louisiana transferred to Elmira November 19, 1864.	Oath of Allegiance May 29, 1865
Johnnett, William Henry Corporal	Unk	June 19, 1861, Camp Moore, Louisiana	Co. B, 8th Louisiana Infantry	May 12, 1864, Spotsylvania Court House, Virginia	Point Lookout, Maryland, transferred to Elmira Prison, NY, August 17, 1864	Exchanged March 2, 1865 at Akins Landing on the James River, Virginia
Johns, B. F. Private	Unk	Unknown	Co. E, 16th Georgia Infantry	May 6, 1864, Wilderness, Virginia	Old Capital Prison, Washington, DC, transferred to Elmira, NY, July 14, 1864	Exchanged February 20, 1865 at Boulware's or Cox Wharf on the James River, Virginia
Johns, Decatur M. Private	Unk	June 11, 1861, Hevener's Store, Virginia	Co. F, 25th Virginia Infantry	May 12, 1864, Spotsylvania Court House, Virginia	Point Lookout, Maryland, transferred to Elmira Prison, NY, August 12, 1864	Died September 9, 1864 of Chronic Diarrhea, Grave No. 201
Johns, Enoch Private	Unk	Unknown	Co. A, Captain Jones' Home Guard Florida	September 27, 1864, Marianna, Florida	New Orleans, Louisiana transferred to Elmira November 19, 1864.	Died December 27, 1864 of Variola (Smallpox), Grave No. 1290

Name & Rank	Age	Enlisted	Regiment and State	Where Captured	Prison	Remarks
Johns, R. Private	Unk	Unknown	Co. B, 2nd North Carolina Infantry	May 20, 1864, Spotsylvania Court House, Virginia	Point Lookout, Maryland, transferred to Elmira Prison, NY, August 12, 1864	Oath of Allegiance June 16, 1865
Johnsey, Nelson M. Private	Unk	Unknown	Co. B, 60th Georgia Infantry	May 20, 1864, Spotsylvania Court House, Virginia	Point Lookout, Maryland, transferred to Elmira Prison, NY, August 12, 1864	Oath of Allegiance May 17, 1865
Johnson, A. B. Private	Unk	Unknown	Co. E, 16th Georgia Infantry	May 6, 1864, Wilderness, Virginia	Old Capital Prison, Washington, DC, transferred to Elmira, NY, July 14, 1864	Transferred for Exchange 10/11/64. Died 11/8/64 of Unknown Causes at Fort Monroe, VA.
Johnson, A. D. Corporal	19	May 2, 1862, Guineas, Virginia	Co. J, 5th Virginia Cavalry	May 11, 1864, Yellow Tavern, Hanover County, Virginia	Point Lookout, Maryland, transferred to Elmira Prison, NY, August 17, 1864	Died March 30, 1865 of Diarrhea, Grave No. 2535
Johnson, A. I. Private	Unk	September 16, 1861, Montgomery, Alabama	Co. B, 59th Alabama Infantry	June 18, 1864, Petersburg, Virginia	Point Lookout, Maryland, transferred to Elmira Prison, NY, July 25, 1864	Oath of Allegiance May 19, 1865
Johnson, A. L. Private	31	September 23, 1862, Camp Holmes, North Carolina	Co. C, 30th North Carolina Infantry	May 12, 1864, Near Spotsylvania Court House, Virginia	Point Lookout, Maryland, transferred to Elmira Prison, NY, August 14, 1864	Oath of Allegiance June 23, 1865
Johnson, A. R. Sergeant	22	May 18, 1861, Rome, Georgia	Co. A, 8th Georgia Infantry	May 6, 1864, Wilderness, Virginia	Point Lookout, Maryland, transferred to Elmira Prison, NY, August 14, 1864	Exchanged March 10, 1865 at Boulware's Wharf on the James River, Virginia
Johnson, Adam G. Corporal	Unk	August 14, 1861, Livingston, Alabama	Co. H, 5th Alabama Infantry	May 5, 1864, Wilderness, Virginia	Point Lookout, Maryland, transferred to Elmira Prison, NY, August 17, 1864	Died April 13, 1865, of Pneumonia, Grave No. 2703

Name & Rank	Age	Enlisted	Regiment and State	Where Captured	Prison	Remarks
Johnson, Alfayette P. Private	20	July 4, 1861, Talladega, Alabama	Co. B, 5th Alabama Infantry	April 2, 1865, Petersburg, Virginia	Old Capital Prison, Washington, DC, transferred to Elmira Prison, NY, May 2, 1865.	Oath of Allegiance July 11, 1865
Johnson, Amos Private	28	June 26, 1862, Wilson, North Carolina	Co. H, 7th Confederate Cavalry	May 7, 1864, Lyttleton, Virginia	Point Lookout, Maryland, transferred to Elmira Prison, NY, August 17, 1864	Transferred For Exchange October 11, 1864 to Point Lookout Prison Camp, MD. Died November 3, 1864 of Unknown Causes, at Fort Monroe, VA
Johnson, Amos Private	28	January 25, 1862, Robeson County, North Carolina	Co. C, 36th Regiment, 2nd North Carolina Artillery	January 15, 1865, Fort Fisher, North Carolina	February 1, 1865 Elmira Prison Camp, New York	Died April 16, 1865 of Chronic Diarrhea, Grave No. 2721
Johnson, Amos J. Sergeant	20	June 17, 1861, Kenansville, Duplin County, North Carolina	Co. B, 3rd North Carolina Infantry	May 12, 1864, Near Spotsylvania Court House, Virginia	Point Lookout, Maryland, transferred to Elmira Prison, NY, August 14, 1864	Oath of Allegiance June 27, 1865
Johnson, Anderson Sergeant	Unk	January 10, 1862, Columbia, South Carolina	Co. C, 22nd South Carolina Infantry	July 30, 1864, Petersburg, Virginia	Point Lookout, Maryland, transferred to Elmira Prison, NY, August 12, 1864	Died October 21, 1864 of Pneumonia, Grave No. 523
Johnson, Andrew Private	Unk	August 25, 1863, Knoxville, Tennessee	Co. B, 1st Tennessee Infantry	May 6, 1864, Wilderness, Virginia	Point Lookout, Maryland, transferred to Elmira Prison, NY, July 23, 1864	Oath of Allegiance May 15, 1865
Johnson, Benjamin D. Sergeant	Unk	June 6, 1861, South Quay, Virginia	Co. K, 41st Virginia Infantry	July 30, 1864, Petersburg, Virginia	Point Lookout, Maryland, transferred to Elmira Prison, NY, August 12, 1864	Exchanged February 20, 1865 at Boulware's or Cox Wharf on the James River, Virginia

Name & Rank	Age	Enlisted	Regiment and State	Where Captured	Prison	Remarks
Johnson, C. C. Private	Unk	August 28, 1863, Dublin, Virginia	Co. I, 26th Battalion, Virginia Infantry	June 3, 1864, Gaines Farm Cold Harbor, Virginia	Point Lookout, Maryland, transferred to Elmira Prison, NY, July 17, 1864	Oath of Allegiance July 3, 1865
Johnson, Charles A. Private	Unk	June 20, 1863, Greene County, Alabama	Co. B, 7th Alabama Cavalry	July 22, 1863, Mobile Point, Louisiana	New Orleans, LA, Transferred to Elmira Prison, NY, November 19, 1864	Oath of Allegiance May 17, 1865
Johnson, Creed F. Private	18	July 15, 1861, Henderson County, North Carolina	Co. H, 25th North Carolina Infantry	July 30, 1864, Petersburg, Virginia	Point Lookout, Maryland, transferred to Elmira Prison, NY, August 12, 1864	Oath of Allegiance May 29, 1865
Johnson, Edwin Sergeant	21	March 17, 1862, Wilson, North Carolina	Co. G, 5th North Carolina Infantry	May 12, 1864, Spotsylvania Court House, Virginia	Point Lookout, Maryland, transferred to Elmira Prison, NY, August 6, 1864	Died September 13, 1864 of Pneumonia, Grave No. 184. Name Edward on Headstone.
Johnson, F. J. Private	34	March 22, 1862, Porter's Precinct, Virginia	Co. B, 15th Virginia Cavalry	September 14, 1863, Near Culpepper, Virginia	Point Lookout, Maryland, transferred to Elmira Prison, NY, August 18, 1864	Exchanged March 10, 1865 at Boulware's Wharf on the James River, Virginia
Johnson, Franklin D. Private	42	Unknown	Co. B, 1st Tennessee Heavy Artillery	August 23, 1864, Fort Morgan, Alabama	Fort Columbus, New York Harbor. Transferred February 4, 1865 Elmira, Prison Camp, NY	Exchanged March 10, 1865 at Boulware's Wharf on the James River, Virginia
Johnson, Franklin R. Private	Unk	May 9, 1861, New Orleans, Louisiana	Co. H, 2nd Louisiana Infantry	May 12, 1864, Spotsylvania Court House, Virginia	Point Lookout, Maryland, transferred to Elmira Prison, NY, August 17, 1864	Exchanged February 25, 1865 at Boulware's or Cox Wharf on the James River, Virginia
Johnson, George Private	Unk	July 15, 1862, Hendersonville, North Carolina	Co. D, 6th North Carolina Cavalry	June 22, 1864, Jackson's Mills, Near Kinston, North Carolina	Point Lookout, Maryland, transferred to Elmira Prison, NY, July 25, 1864	Oath of Allegiance July 3, 1865

Name & Rank	Age	Enlisted	Regiment and State	Where Captured	Prison	Remarks
Johnson, George D. Private	24	July 15, 1862, Raleigh, North Carolina	Co. C, 5th North Carolina Infantry	July 14, 1864, Near Washington, DC	Old Capital Prison, Washington DC. Transferred to Elmira Prison Camp New York July 25, 1864.	Oath of Allegiance July 11, 1865
Johnson, George W. Private	18	July 1, 1863, Knoxville, Tennessee	Co. B, 63rd Tennessee Infantry	May 16, 1864, Near Drury's Bluff, Virginia	Point Lookout, Maryland, transferred to Elmira Prison, NY, August 17, 1864	Exchanged February 25, 1865 at Boulware's or Cox Wharf on the James River, Virginia
Johnson, George W. Sergeant Major	Unk	May 14, 1861, Franklin, Virginia	Co. E, 25th Virginia Infantry	May 12, 1864, Spotsylvania Court House, Virginia	Point Lookout, Maryland, transferred to Elmira Prison, NY, August 12, 1864	Exchanged March 14, 1865 at Boulware's Wharf on the James River, Virginia
Johnson, H. G. Private	Unk	Unknown	Co. C, 12th North Carolina Infantry	May 20, 1864, Spotsylvania Court House, Virginia	Point Lookout, Maryland, transferred to Elmira Prison, NY, July 6, 1864	Transferred for Exchange October 11, 1864. No Further Information.
Johnson, Haywood Private	33	July 16, 1862, Raleigh, North Carolina	Co. D, 5th North Carolina Infantry	May 12, 1864, Spotsylvania Court House, Virginia	Point Lookout, Maryland, transferred to Elmira Prison, NY, August 6, 1864	Oath of Allegiance May 29, 1865
Johnson, Henry Private	Unk	March 7, 1862, Halifax County, North Carolina	Co. A, 24th North Carolina Infantry	June 9, 1864, Near Bottoms Bridge, Chickahominy Swamp, Cold Harbor, Virginia	Old Capital Prison, Washington, DC, transferred to Elmira July 23, 1864	Oath of Allegiance May 17, 1865
Johnson, Henry A. Private	Unk	March 16, 1864, Augusta, Alabama	Co. B, 59th Alabama Infantry	June 16, 1864, Near Petersburg, Virginia	Point Lookout, Maryland, transferred to Elmira Prison, NY, July 30, 1864	Died December 9, 1864 of Pneumonia, Grave No. 1034

Name & Rank	Age	Enlisted	Regiment and State	Where Captured	Prison	Remarks
Johnson, Henry P. Private	Unk	Unknown	Co. F, 1st Maryland Cavalry	July 8, 1864, Boonesboro, Maryland	Old Capital Prison, Washington DC. Transferred to Elmira Prison Camp, New York, July 25, 1864.	Oath of Allegiance November 4, 1864 by Orders of Commissary General of Prisoners.
Johnson, Hesikish H. Private	Unk	Unknown	Co. A, 50th Virginia Infantry	May 12, 1864, Spotsylvania Court House, Virginia	Point Lookout, Maryland, transferred to Elmira Prison, NY, August 2, 1864	Died March 13, 1865 of Chronic Diarrhea, Grave No. 1824
Johnson, Isaac Private	Unk	August 1, 1861, Waynesboro, Georgia	Co. E, Cobb's Legion Georgia	August 16, 1864, Front Royal, Virginia	Old Capital Prison, Washington, DC transferred to Elmira Prison, NY, August 29, 1864	Exchanged March 14, 1865 at Boulware's Wharf on the James River, Virginia
Johnson, J. Private	Unk	Unknown	Co. H, 50th Virginia Infantry	May 12, 1864, Spotsylvania Court House, Virginia	Point Lookout, Maryland, transferred to Elmira Prison, NY, August 2, 1864	Oath of Allegiance July 3, 1865
Johnson, J. R. Private	Unk	May 9, 1861, New Orleans, Louisiana	Co. H, 2nd Louisiana Infantry	May 12, 1864, Spotsylvania Court House, Virginia	Point Lookout, Maryland, transferred to Elmira Prison, NY, August 17, 1864	Exchanged February 13, 1865 at Boulware's wharf on the James River, Virginia
Johnson, J. W. Private	Unk	November 9, 1863, Talladega, Alabama	Jeff Davis Alabama Artillery	May 5, 1864, Wilderness, Virginia	Point Lookout, Maryland, transferred to Elmira Prison, NY, August 17, 1864	Died February 13, 1865 of General Debility, Grave No. 2045. Headstone has Carter's battery, VA.
Johnson, J. W. Corporal	Unk	January 11, 1863, Henry County, Virginia	Co. F, 21st Virginia Infantry	May 12, 1864, Spotsylvania Court House, Virginia	Point Lookout, Maryland, transferred to Elmira Prison, NY, August 2, 1864	Oath of Allegiance June 23, 1865

Name & Rank	Age	Enlisted	Regiment and State	Where Captured	Prison	Remarks
Johnson, Jackson Private	Unk	March 4, 1862, Pike County, Georgia	Co. B, 44th Georgia Infantry	July 12, 1864, Near Washington, DC,	Old Capital Prison, Washington, DC, transferred to Elmira July 23, 1864	Exchanged March 7, 1865 at Akins Landing on the James River, Virginia
Johnson, Jacob C. Private	Unk	June 10, 1861, Morgan, Georgia	Co. D, 12th Georgia Infantry	May 10, 1864, Spotsylvania Court House, Virginia	Point Lookout, Maryland, transferred to Elmira Prison, NY, July 30, 1864	Oath of Allegiance June 14, 1865
Johnson, James Private	Unk	May 27, 1861, Atlanta, Georgia	Co. E, 6th Georgia infantry	August 19, 1864, Petersburg, Virginia. Gunshot Fracture of Humerus Left Arm. Arm Amputated.	Old Capital Prison, Washington, DC, transferred to Elmira December 17, 1864	Exchanged March 10, 1865 at Boulware's Wharf on the James River, Virginia
Johnson, James Private	18	May 16, 1863, Fort Fisher, North Carolina	Co. C, 36th Regiment, 2nd North Carolina Artillery	January 15, 1865, Fort Fisher, North Carolina	February 1, 1865 Elmira Prison Camp, New York	Exchanged February 20, 1865 at Boulware's or Cox Wharf on the James River, Virginia
Johnson, James Private	Unk	May 12, 1863, Place Unknown	Co. B, 50th Virginia Infantry	May 12, 1864, Spotsylvania, Virginia	Point Lookout, Maryland, transferred to Elmira Prison, NY, July 23, 1864	Oath of Allegiance May 19, 1865
Johnson, James A. Private	20	May 1, 1861, Leasburg, North Carolina	Co. D, 13th North Carolina Infantry	May 24, 1864, Butler's Mills, Virginia	Point Lookout, Maryland, transferred to Elmira Prison, NY, July 25, 1864	Oath of Allegiance June 30, 1865
Johnson, James H. Private	23	May 1, 1862, Knoxville, Tennessee	Co. B, 63rd Tennessee Infantry	May 16, 1864, Near Drury's Bluff, Virginia	Point Lookout, Maryland, transferred to Elmira Prison, NY, August 17, 1864	Exchanged February 25, 1865 at Boulware's or Cox Wharf on the James River, Virginia
Johnson, James Henry Private	Unk	July 21, 1861, Goldsboro, North Carolina	Co. F, 10th Regiment, 1st North Carolina Artillery	January 15, 1865, Fort Fisher, North Carolina	January 30, 1865, Elmira Prison Camp, New York	Oath of Allegiance July 11, 1865

Name & Rank	Age	Enlisted	Regiment and State	Where Captured	Prison	Remarks
Johnson, Jeffrey Private	Unk	May 12, 1863, Place Unknown	Co. B, 50th Virginia Infantry	May 12, 1864, Spotsylvania, Virginia	Point Lookout, Maryland, transferred to Elmira Prison, NY, July 23, 1864	Died May 21, 1865 Chronic Diarrhea, Grave No. 2938
Johnson, John Private	45	July 9, 1861, Goldsboro, North Carolina	Co. F, 10th Regiment, 1st North Carolina Artillery	January 15, 1865, Fort Fisher, North Carolina	January 30, 1865, Elmira Prison Camp, New York	Oath of Allegiance July 26, 1865
Johnson, John Private	30	February 21, 1862, Charleston, South Carolina	Co. E, 25th South Carolina Infantry	January 15, 1865, Fort Fisher, North Carolina	January 30, 1865, Elmira Prison Camp, New York	Oath of Allegiance May 13, 1865
Johnson, John Private	Unk	June 12, 1861, Centre Cross, Virginia	Co. H, 55th Virginia Infantry	May 6, 1864, Wilderness, Virginia	Point Lookout, Maryland, transferred to Elmira Prison, NY, August 14, 1864	Exchanged March 2, 1865 at Akins Landing on the James River, Virginia
Johnson, John A. Private	28	March 15, 1862, Roswell, Georgia	Co. E, Cobb's Legion Georgia	May 12, 1864, Spotsylvania Court House, Virginia	Point Lookout, Maryland, transferred to Elmira Prison, NY, August 12, 1864	Exchanged February 20, 1865 at Boulware's or Cox Wharf on the James River, Virginia
Johnson, John A. Private	18	January 6, 1863, Fort Fisher, North Carolina	Co. C, 36th Regiment, 2nd North Carolina Artillery	January 15, 1865, Fort Fisher, North Carolina	February 1, 1865 Elmira Prison Camp, New York	Died February 23, 1865 of Dysentery, Grave No. 2257
Johnson, John D. Private	Unk	May 1, 1862, Savannah, Georgia	Co. C, 26th Georgia Infantry	May 20, 1864, Spotsylvania Court House, Virginia	Point Lookout, Maryland, transferred to Elmira Prison, NY, July 6, 1864	Oath of Allegiance June 16, 1865
Johnson, John D. Private	24	September 15, 1862, Camp Mangum, Raleigh, North Carolina	Co. B, 31st North Carolina Infantry	June 1, 1864, Cold Harbor, Virginia	Transferred From Point Lookout Prison, MD, July 12, 1864. Train Never Arrived at Elmira Prison Camp, NY.	Died from Injuries July 18, 1864 Suffered in Train Wreck, Shohola, Pennsylvania.

Name & Rank	Age	Enlisted	Regiment and State	Where Captured	Prison	Remarks
Johnson, John F. Private	Unk	April 20, 1862, Marion Court House, South Carolina	Co. D, 25th South Carolina Infantry	January 15, 1865, Fort Fisher, North Carolina	January 30, 1865, Elmira Prison Camp, New York	Exchanged February 20, 1865 at Boulware's or Cox Wharf on the James River, Virginia
Johnson, John J. Private	38	January 1, 1862, Camp Harllee, Georgetown, South Carolina	Co. J, 25th South Carolina Infantry	January 15, 1865, Fort Fisher, North Carolina	January 30, 1865 Elmira Prison Camp, New York	Died February 16, 1865 of Remittent Fever, Grave No. 2210
Johnson, John J. Private	Unk	May 30, 1862, Columbia, South Carolina	Co. C, 22nd South Carolina Infantry	July 30, 1864, Petersburg, Virginia	Point Lookout, Maryland, transferred to Elmira Prison, NY, August 12, 1864	Exchanged October 29, 1864 at Venus Point, Savannah River, GA.
Johnson, John R. Private	Unk	Unknown	Co. J, 19th Texas Cavalry	September 19, 1864, Tensan Parish, Louisiana	New Orleans, LA, Transferred to Elmira Prison, NY, November 19, 1864	Oath of Allegiance May 17, 1865
Johnson, John W. Private	Unk	May 21, 1863, Camp of Instruction, Virginia	Co. I, 26th Battalion, Virginia Infantry	June 3, 1864, Gaines Mill Cold Harbor, Virginia	Point Lookout, Maryland, transferred to Elmira Prison, NY, July 17, 1864	Transferred for Exchange October 11, 1864. Died in Steamship *Northern Light.*
Johnson, John W. Corporal	Unk	April 1, 1862, Abingdon, Virginia	Co. F, 48th Virginia Infantry	May 12, 1864, Spotsylvania Court House, Virginia	Point Lookout, Maryland, transferred to Elmira Prison, NY, August 2, 1864	Exchanged October 29, 1864 at Venus Point, Savannah River, GA.
Johnson, Joseph L. Private	18	April 15, 1862, Murfreesboro, North Carolina	Co. C, 24th North Carolina Infantry	June 17, 1864, Petersburg, Virginia	Point Lookout, Maryland, transferred to Elmira Prison, NY, July 30, 1864	Oath of Allegiance June 16, 1865
Johnson, Lafayette Marion Private	Unk	November 1, 1863, Raleigh, North Carolina	Co. H, 45th North Carolina Infantry	July 12, 1864, Near Washington, DC,	Old Capital Prison, Washington, DC, transferred to Elmira July 23, 1864	Oath of Allegiance May 29, 1865

Name & Rank	Age	Enlisted	Regiment and State	Where Captured	Prison	Remarks
Johnson, Larry Private	23	July 8, 1861, At Home, North Carolina	Co. F, 10th Regiment, 1st North Carolina Artillery	January 15, 1865, Fort Fisher, North Carolina	January 30, 1865, Elmira Prison Camp, New York	Died February 26, 1865 of Pneumonia, Grave No. 2158
Johnson, Levi Private	Unk	Unknown	Co. B, 50th Virginia Infantry	May 12, 1864, Spotsylvania, Virginia	Point Lookout, Maryland, transferred to Elmira Prison, NY, July 23, 1864	Oath of Allegiance May 19, 1865
Johnson, M. P. Private	Unk	August 1, 1863, James Island, South Carolina	Co. I, 25th South Carolina Infantry	January 15, 1865, Fort Fisher, North Carolina	January 30, 1865, Elmira Prison Camp, New York	Died March 23, 1865 of Variola (Smallpox), Grave No. 2443
Johnson, Marion Private	31	September 23, 1862, Camp Holmes, North Carolina	Co. H, 30th North Carolina Infantry	May 12, 1864, Near Spotsylvania Court House, Virginia	Point Lookout, Maryland, transferred to Elmira Prison, NY, August 14, 1864	Exchanged October 29, 1864 at Venus Point, Savannah River, GA.
Johnson, Matt T. Private	Unk	August 28, 1863, Smithville, North Carolina	Co. F, 10th Regiment, 1st North Carolina Artillery	January 15, 1865, Fort Fisher, North Carolina	January 30, 1865, Elmira Prison Camp, New York	Oath of Allegiance July 11, 1865
Johnson, Napoleon B. Private	36	January 14, 1863, Richmond, Virginia	Co. H, 46th Virginia Infantry	June 15, 1864, Petersburg, Virginia. Gunshot Wound Left Knee. Left Leg Amputated Below Knee.	Point Lookout, Maryland, transferred to Elmira Prison, NY, August 29, 1864	Oath of Allegiance June 21, 1865
Johnson, Owen L. Private	24	September 7, 1861, Unknown Place	Captain Carters Co., Virginia Light Artillery	May 10, 1864, Spotsylvania, Virginia. Gunshot Wounds Right Shoulder, Right Hip, Severe, and Scalp.	Old Capital Prison, Washington, DC, transferred to Elmira December 4, 1864	Exchanged February 25, 1865 at Boulware's or Cox Wharf on the James River, Virginia
Johnson, Philip Private	Unk	May 28, 1863, Atlanta, Georgia	Co. H, 64th Georgia Infantry	August 11, 1864, New Market, Virginia	Point Lookout, Maryland, transferred to Elmira Prison, NY, August 29, 1864	Transferred For Exchange October 11, 1864 to Point Lookout Prison Camp, MD. Died October 18, 1864 of Unknown Causes.

Name & Rank	Age	Enlisted	Regiment and State	Where Captured	Prison	Remarks
Johnson, Richard M. Private	Unk	May 12, 1862, Fayetteville, Cumberland County, North Carolina	Co. C, 36th Regiment, 2nd North Carolina Artillery	January 15, 1865, Fort Fisher, North Carolina	February 1, 1865 Elmira Prison Camp, New York	Died February 20, 1865 of Pneumonia, Grave No. 2332
Johnson, Robert Private	Unk	September 1, 1862, Grahamville, South Carolina	Co. J, 27th South Carolina Infantry	June 24, 1864, Near Petersburg, Virginia	Point Lookout, Maryland, transferred to Elmira Prison, NY, August 18, 1864	Oath of Allegiance June 16, 1865
Johnson, Robert F. Private	Unk	June 12, 1861, Milledgeville, Georgia	Co. F, 9th Georgia Infantry	May 6, 1864, Wilderness, Virginia	Point Lookout, Maryland, transferred to Elmira Prison, NY, August 14, 1864	Died January 19, 1865 of Pneumonia, Grave No. 1204
Johnson, Rueben Private	Unk	March 16, 1861, Autauga, Alabama	Co. E, 1st Battalion Alabama Artillery	August 23, 1864, Fort Morgan, Alabama	Steam Press No. 4 New Orleans, Louisiana transferred to Elmira Prison, NY, October 8, 1864.	Oath of Allegiance July 7, 1865
Johnson, Rufus Private	Unk	July 18, 1862, Cumberland County, North Carolina	Co. C, 3rd North Carolina Infantry	May 12, 1864, Near Spotsylvania Court House, Virginia	Point Lookout Prison, Maryland. Transferred to Elmira Prison Camp New York August 14, 1864.	Oath of Allegiance June 16, 1865
Johnson, S. L. Private	Unk	Unknown	11th Battalion Louisiana Infantry	September 16, 1864, Greenville Springs, Near East Baton Rouge, Louisiana	New Orleans, Louisiana transferred to Elmira November 19, 1864.	Died December 14, 1860 Ford of Typhoid-Pneumonia, Grave No. 1125. Headstone has J. L. Johnson and Powers' Regiment.
Johnson, Samuel L. Private	24	August 19, 1861, Camp Pulaski, Louisiana	Co. J, 15th Louisiana Infantry	May 12, 1864, Spotsylvania Court House, Virginia	Point Lookout, Maryland, transferred to Elmira Prison, NY, July 25, 1864	Exchanged February 13, 1865 at Boulware's wharf on the James River, Virginia

Name & Rank	Age	Enlisted	Regiment and State	Where Captured	Prison	Remarks
Johnson, Solomon D. Private	Unk	June 11, 1861, Drayton, Georgia	Co. J, 12th Georgia Infantry	May 10, 1864, Spotsylvania Court House, Virginia	Point Lookout, Maryland, transferred to Elmira Prison, NY, July 25, 1864	Oath of Allegiance June 21, 1865
Johnson, Stephen H. Corporal	24	June 1, 1861, Lock's Creek, Fayetteville, North Carolina	Co. F, 24th North Carolina Infantry	June 17, 1864, Petersburg, Virginia	Point Lookout, Maryland, transferred to Elmira Prison, NY, July 30, 1864	Oath of Allegiance June 16, 1865
Johnson, T. B. K. Private	Unk	September 4, 1863, Georgetown, Georgia	Co. B, 7th Georgia Cavalry	June 11, 1864, Trevilian Station, Louisa Court House, Virginia	Point Lookout, Maryland, transferred to Elmira Prison, NY, July 25, 1864	Exchanged October 29, 1864 at Venus Point, Savannah River, GA.
Johnson, Thomas Private	Unk	June 5, 1862, Corinth, Mississippi	Co. M, 1st Texas Infantry	May 24, 1864, Near Spotsylvania Court House, Virginia	Point Lookout, Maryland, transferred to Elmira Prison, NY, July 23, 1864	Exchanged March 14, 1865 at Boulware's Wharf on the James River, Virginia
Johnson, Thomas D. Private	Unk	Unknown	Co. K, 44th Virginia Infantry	May 12, 1864, Spotsylvania Court House, Virginia	Point Lookout, Maryland, transferred to Elmira Prison, NY, August 2, 1864	Oath of Allegiance June 27, 1865
Johnson, Thomas G. Private	Unk	July 1, 1862, Hurtford, County, North Carolina	Co. C, 33rd North Carolina Infantry	May 13, 1864, Spotsylvania Court House, Virginia	Point Lookout, Maryland, transferred to Elmira Prison, NY, August 14, 1864	Oath of Allegiance June 16, 1865
Johnson, Thomas L. R. Private	Unk	September 19, 1861, Dalton, Georgia	Co. B, 60th Georgia Infantry	May 20, 1864, Spotsylvania Court House, Virginia	Point Lookout, Maryland, transferred to Elmira Prison, NY, July 6, 1864	Exchanged October 29, 1864 at Venus Point, Savannah River, GA.
Johnson, W. H. Private	Unk	June 10, 1864, Chaffin's Farm, Virginia	Co. B, 59th Alabama Infantry	June 17, 1864, Petersburg, Virginia	Point Lookout, Maryland, transferred to Elmira Prison, NY, July 25, 1864	Exchanged March 2, 1865 at Akins Landing on the James River, Virginia

Name & Rank	Age	Enlisted	Regiment and State	Where Captured	Prison	Remarks
Johnson, W. Newton Corporal	Unk	January 10, 1862, Columbia, South Carolina	Co. C, 22nd South Carolina Infantry	July 30, 1864, Petersburg, Virginia	Point Lookout, Maryland, transferred to Elmira Prison, NY, August 12, 1864	Exchanged 3/14/65. Died 4/28/65 of Bronchitis at Confederate States Army Hospital, No. 11, Charlotte, NC.
Johnson, Wellington Private	23	June 3, 1861, Lacey Springs, Virginia	Co. H, 10th, Virginia Cavalry	May 14, 1864, Spotsylvania Court House, Virginia	Point Lookout, Maryland, transferred to Elmira Prison, NY, July 6, 1864	Exchanged March 10, 1865 at Boulware's Wharf on the James River, Virginia
Johnson, William Private	Unk	Unknown	Co. J, 9th Alabama Infantry	May 6, 1864, Wilderness, Virginia	Point Lookout, Maryland, transferred to Elmira Prison, NY, August 17, 1864	Oath of Allegiance June 14, 1865
Johnson, William Private	Unk	February 18, 1864, Greenville, Tennessee	Co. B, 1st Tennessee Infantry	May 22, 1864, Bull's Church, Wilderness, Virginia	Point Lookout, Maryland, transferred to Elmira Prison, NY, July 23, 1864	Oath of Allegiance January 24, 1865 Early Release per Lincoln's Proclamation, 12/8/1863.
Johnson, William B. Sergeant	18	May 15, 1862, Clayton, Johnston County, North Carolina	Co. C, 24th North Carolina Infantry	June 17, 1864, Petersburg, Virginia	Point Lookout, Maryland, transferred to Elmira Prison, NY, July 30, 1864	Oath of Allegiance June 16, 1865
Johnson, William C. Private	22	May 30, 1861, Garysburg, North Carolina	Co. C, 5th North Carolina Infantry	May 12, 1864, Spotsylvania Court House, Virginia	Point Lookout, Maryland, transferred to Elmira Prison, NY, August 6, 1864	Oath of Allegiance June 12, 1865
Johnson, William F. Private	27	October 28, 1861, Wilmington, North Carolina	Co. E, 36th Regiment 2nd North Carolina Artillery	January 15, 1865, Fort Fisher, North Carolina	February 1, 1865 Elmira Prison Camp, New York	Exchanged March 2, 1865. Died March 9, 1865 of Chronic Diarrhea at Moore Hospital, Richmond, Virginia
Johnson, William H. Private	21	July 3, 1861, Atlanta, Georgia	Co. B, 11th Georgia Infantry	May 6, 1864, Wilderness, Virginia	Old Capital Prison, Washington, DC, transferred to Elmira, NY, July 14, 1864	Died February 16, 1865 of Chronic Rheumatism, Grave No. 2196

Name & Rank	Age	Enlisted	Regiment and State	Where Captured	Prison	Remarks
Johnson, William H. Sergeant	22	April 20, 1861, Sampson County, North Carolina	Co. A, 30th North Carolina Infantry	May 12, 1864, Near Spotsylvania Court House, Virginia	Point Lookout, Maryland, transferred to Elmira Prison, NY, August 14, 1864	Oath of Allegiance June 19, 1865
Johnson, William M. H. Private	25	March 18, 1862, Winston, North Carolina	Co. K, 52nd North Carolina Infantry	May 12, 1864, Spotsylvania Court House, Virginia	Point Lookout, Maryland, transferred to Elmira Prison, NY, July 30, 1864	Died January 18, 1865 of Pneumonia, Grave No. 1436
Johnson, William R. Private	Unk	July 1, 1862, Newberry, South Carolina	Co. B, 3rd South Carolina Infantry	May 25, 1864, Hanover, Virginia	Point Lookout, Maryland, transferred to Elmira Prison, NY, July 11, 1864	Oath of Allegiance June 19, 1865
Johnson, William S. Private	Unk	August 29, 1864, Camp Randolph, Georgia	Co. B, 44th Georgia Infantry	July 12, 1864, Near Washington, DC. Bayonet Wound of Right Thigh.	Old Capital Prison, Washington DC. Transferred to Elmira Prison Camp New York July 25, 1864.	Exchanged February 20, 1865 at Boulware's or Cox Wharf on the James River, Virginia
Johnston, Andrew W. Private	30	July 26, 1861, R. Chapel, North Carolina	Co. F, 1st North Carolina Infantry	May 12, 1864, Wilderness, Spotsylvania Court House, Virginia	Point Lookout, Maryland, transferred to Elmira Prison, NY, August 6, 1864	Exchanged March 14, 1865 at Boulware's Wharf on the James River, Virginia
Johnston, Henry Tobias Private	18	August 14, 1861, Mount Pleasant, North Carolina	Co. E, 8th North Carolina Infantry	May 31, 1864, Cold Harbor, Virginia	Point Lookout, Maryland, transferred to Elmira Prison, NY, July 11, 1864	Oath of Allegiance July 3, 1865
Johnston, Jessup L. Sergeant	Unk	July 9, 1861, Cumming, Georgia	Co. E, 14th Georgia Infantry	June 2, 1864, Old Church Cold Harbor, Virginia	Point Lookout, Maryland, transferred to Elmira Prison, NY, July 12,1864	Exchanged March 10 at Boulware's or Cox Wharf on the James River, Virginia
Johnston, John Private	22	June 4, 1861, Camp Moore, Louisiana	Co. F, 6th Louisiana Infantry	May 5, 1864, Wilderness, Virginia	Point Lookout, Maryland, transferred to Elmira Prison, NY, August 17, 1864	Oath of Allegiance May 17, 1865

Name & Rank	Age	Enlisted	Regiment and State	Where Captured	Prison	Remarks
Johnston, John B. Private	31	May 24, 1861, Gadsen, Alabama	Co. A, 1st Alabama Artillery	August 23, 1864, Fort Morgan, Alabama	New Orleans, Louisiana transferred to Elmira Prison, NY, December 4, 1864.	Orders for Elmira, New York. Died in Transit January 11, 1865 of Variola at US Army Hospital Fort Columbus, New York Harbor
Johnston, Joseph R. Private	Unk	May 4, 1864, Petersburg, Virginia	Co. A, 3rd Archer's Battalion, Virginia Reserves Infantry	June 9, 1864, Petersburg, Virginia	Point Lookout, Maryland, transferred to Elmira Prison, NY, July 12,1864	Exchanged October 29, 1864 at Venus Point, Savannah River, GA.
Johnston, Josiah S. Private	40	March 19, 1862, South Washington, North Carolina	Co. K, 3rd North Carolina Infantry	May 12, 1864, Near Spotsylvania Court House, Virginia	Point Lookout Prison, Maryland. Transferred to Elmira Prison Camp New York August 14, 1864.	Oath of Allegiance June 16, 1865
Johnston, Maxwell Private	40	March 10, 1863, Newton, North Carolina	Co. F, 23rd North Carolina Infantry	May 20, 1864, Spotsylvania Court House, Virginia	Point Lookout, Maryland, transferred to Elmira Prison, NY, July 6, 1864	Exchanged October 29, 1864 at Venus Point, Savannah River, GA.
Johnston, Michael Private	Unk	March 1, 1863, Knoxville, Tennessee	Co. A, 3rd Tennessee, Lillard's Mounted Infantry	May 17, 1863, Big Black, Mississippi	Point Lookout, Maryland, transferred to Elmira Prison, NY, August 18, 1864	Exchanged October 29, 1864 at Venus Point, Savannah River, GA.
Johnston, Nathanial G. Sergeant	Unk	April 22, 1862, Roanoke, Alabama	Co. I, 13th Alabama Infantry	May 12, 1864, Spotsylvania Court House, Virginia	Point Lookout, Maryland, transferred to Elmira Prison, NY, August 12, 1864	Oath of Allegiance June 19, 1865
Johnston, Philip R. Private	Unk	March 12, 1862, 6 Mile, Centerville, Alabama	Co. F, 44th Alabama Infantry	May 6, 1864, wilderness, Virginia	Point Lookout, Maryland, transferred to Elmira Prison, NY, August 17, 1864	Exchanged October 29, 1864 at Venus Point, Savannah River, GA.
Johnston, W. W. Private	Unk	June 7, 1864, Fort Morgan, Alabama	Co. A, 1st Alabama Artillery	August 23, 1864, Fort Morgan, Alabama.	New Orleans, Louisiana transferred to Elmira Prison, NY, December 4, 1864.	Oath of Allegiance July 26, 1865

Name & Rank	Age	Enlisted	Regiment and State	Where Captured	Prison	Remarks
Johnston, William M. Private	Unk	April 21, 1862, Staunton, Virginia	Co. J, 4th Virginia Infantry	May 12, 1864, Near Spotsylvania Court House, Virginia	Point Lookout, Maryland, transferred to Elmira Prison, NY, August 6, 1864	Exchanged March 2, 1865 at Akins Landing on the James River, Virginia
Johnston, William S. Private	Unk	August 29, 1862, Camp Randolph, Georgia	Co. B, 44th Georgia Infantry	May 12, 1864, Spotsylvania, Virginia, Bayonet Wound Right Thigh	Old Capital Prison, Washington, DC, transferred to Elmira July 23, 1864	Exchanged February 20, 1865 at Boulware's or Cox Wharf on the James River, Virginia
Joiner, Bristow Cook	Unk	Unknown	CSS Steamer Arrow, Confederate States Navy	July 28, 1864, Bennett's Creek, North Carolina	Point Lookout, Maryland, transferred to Elmira Prison, NY, August 18, 1864	Died March 4, 1865 of Variola (Smallpox), Grave No. 1968. Headstone has Joince.
Joiner, William H. Private	Unk	August 12, 1862, Staunton, Virginia	Co. H, 34th Virginia Infantry	June 15, 1864, Near Petersburg, Virginia	Point Lookout, Maryland, transferred to Elmira Prison, NY, July 12, 1864	Oath of Allegiance July 7, 1865
Jolley, Daniel J. Private	Unk	July 1, 1863, Wilmington, North Carolina	Co. G, 51st North Carolina Infantry	June 3, 1864, Gaines Mill Cold Harbor, Virginia	Point Lookout, Maryland, transferred to Elmira Prison, NY, July 12, 1864	Oath of Allegiance July 3, 1865
Jolley, James R. Private	Unk	February 21, 1863, Fredericksburg, Virginia	Co. F, 60th Georgia Infantry	June 3, 1864, Cold Harbor, Virginia	Point Lookout, Maryland, transferred to Elmira Prison, NY, July 17, 1864	Died October 7, 1864 of Typhoid Fever, Grave No. 593
Jolley, William Private	23	February 26, 1862, Chapel Hill, North Carolina	Co. G, 11th North Carolina Infantry	July 14, 1863, Falling Waters, Maryland	Point Lookout, Maryland, transferred to Elmira Prison, NY, August 18, 1864	Transferred for Exchange 10/11/1864. Died November 14, 1864 of Unknown Causes at Port Royal, SC.
Jolly, James Private	23	June 15, 1861, Camp Wyatt, Wilmington, North Carolina	Co. H, 18th North Carolina Infantry	July 29, 1864, Petersburg, Virginia	Point Lookout, Maryland, transferred to Elmira Prison, NY, August 12, 1864	Oath of Allegiance July 3, 1865

Name & Rank	Age	Enlisted	Regiment and State	Where Captured	Prison	Remarks
Jolly, William Sergeant	32	July 15, 1862, Raleigh, North Carolina	Co. D, 3rd North Carolina Infantry	May 12, 1864, Near Spotsylvania, Virginia	Point Lookout, Maryland, transferred to Elmira Prison, NY, August 14, 1864	Oath of Allegiance June 27, 1865
Jonas, Andrew Corporal	18	March 17, 1862, Lincolnton, North Carolina	Co. D, 1st North Carolina Infantry	May 12, 1864, Spotsylvania Court House, Virginia	Point Lookout, Maryland, transferred to Elmira Prison, NY, August 6, 1864	Oath of Allegiance June 19, 1865
Jonas, Daniel Private	40	March 24, 1862, Lincolnton, Lincoln County, North Carolina	Co. D, 1st North Carolina Infantry	May 12, 1864, Spotsylvania Court House, Virginia	Point Lookout Prison Camp, Maryland. Transferred to Elmira Prison, August 6, 1864	Died January 17, 1865 of Pneumonia, Grave No. 1442
Jones, A. S. Private	Unk	Unknown	Co. H, 6th North Carolina Infantry	June 6, 1864, Near Chickahominy Swamp, Cold Harbor, Virginia	Point Lookout, Maryland, transferred to Elmira Prison, NY, July 25, 1864	Exchanged March 2, 1865 at Akins Landing on the James River, Virginia
Jones, Alexander F. Private	19	June 1, 1861, Richmond County, North Carolina	Co. F, 18th North Carolina Infantry	May 6, 1864, Wilderness, Virginia	Point Lookout, Maryland, transferred to Elmira Prison, NY, August 6, 1864	Died March 29, 1865 of Diarrhea, Grave No. 2522
Jones, Alfred C. Private	18	September 20, 1861, Catawba Station, North Carolina	Co. F, 32nd North Carolina Infantry	May 10, 1864, Wilderness, Virginia	Point Lookout, Maryland, transferred to Elmira Prison, NY, August 6, 1864	Oath of Allegiance Date Unknown
Jones, Alsey J. Private	38	April 9, 1863, Raleigh, North Carolina	Co. K, 56th North Carolina Infantry	March 25, 1865, Petersburg, Virginia. Gunshot Wound Right Jaw, Severe.	Old Capital Prison, Washington, DC. Transferred to Elmira Prison Camp, NY, May 2, 1865.	Died July 11, 1865 Chronic Diarrhea, Grave No. 2846
Jones, Alson G. Corporal	19	March 20, 1862, Danbury, Stokes County, North Carolina	Co. H, 53rd North Carolina Infantry	July 12, 1864, Near Washington, DC	Old Capital Prison, Washington DC. Transferred to Elmira Prison Camp, NY July 25, 1864.	Oath of Allegiance June 21, 1865

Name & Rank	Age	Enlisted	Regiment and State	Where Captured	Prison	Remarks
Jones, Atlas H. Private	21	January 21, 1862, Rolesville, North Carolina	Co. I, 1st North Carolina Infantry	May 12, 1864, Near Spotsylvania Court House, Virginia	Point Lookout Prison Camp, Maryland. Transferred to Elmira Prison, August 6, 1864	Died January 22, 1865 of Chronic Diarrhea, Grave No. 1598
Jones, B. B. Corporal	Unk	May 13, 1862, Savannah, Georgia	Co. E, 7th Georgia Cavalry	June 11, 1864, Louisa Court House, Trevilian Station, Virginia	Point Lookout, Maryland, transferred to Elmira Prison, NY, July 30, 1864	Died January 17, 1865 of Chronic Diarrhea, Grave No. 1440
Jones, Bartemus P. Ordinance Sergeant	33	September 30, 1861, Beaufort County, North Carolina	Co. B, 40th Regiment, 3rd North Carolina Artillery	January 15, 1865, Fort Fisher, North Carolina	February 1, 1865 Elmira Prison Camp, New York	Died April 1, 1865 of Variola (Smallpox), Grave No. 2583
Jones, Benjamin A. Corporal	Unk	May 20, 1861, Palmyra, Virginia	Co. F, 44th Virginia Infantry	May 12, 1864, Spotsylvania Court House, Virginia	Point Lookout, Maryland, transferred to Elmira Prison, NY, August 2, 1864	Exchanged March 10, 1865 at Boulware's Wharf on the James River, Virginia
Jones, Britton Private	Unk	August 21, 1864, Washington County, North Carolina	Co. D, 40th Regiment North Carolina 3rd Artillery	January 15, 1865, Fort Fisher, North Carolina	February 1, 1865 Elmira Prison Camp, New York	Oath of Allegiance July 7, 1865
Jones, Burrell F. Private	18	May 10, 1861, Columbus, Georgia	Co. A, 10th Georgia Infantry	May 6, 1864, Wilderness, Virginia, Gunshot Wound Left Thigh	Old Capital Prison, Washington, DC, transferred to Elmira, NY, July 23, 1864	Oath of Allegiance May 19, 1865
Jones, Cadwallader, A. Private	Unk	Unknown	Co. I, 6th North Carolina Infantry	May 30, 1864 Mechanicsville, Virginia	Point Lookout, Maryland, transferred to Elmira Prison, NY, July 12, 1864	Died April 27, 1865 of Chronic Diarrhea, Grave No. 2724
Jones, Charles H. Private	Unk	September 10, 1861, Richmond, Virginia	Co. D, 3rd Battalion Georgia Sharp Shooters	August 16, 1864, Front Royal, Virginia	Old Capital Prison, Washington, DC transferred to Elmira Prison, NY, August 29, 1864	Oath of Allegiance May 19, 1865
Jones, D. H. Sergeant	20	July 2, 1862, Charleston, South Carolina	Co. A, 25th South Carolina Infantry	January 15, 1865, Fort Fisher, North Carolina	January 30, 1865, Elmira Prison Camp, New York	Oath of Allegiance June 19, 1865

Name & Rank	Age	Enlisted	Regiment and State	Where Captured	Prison	Remarks
Jones, Daniel M. Private	Unk	February 2, 1863, Georgetown, South Carolina	Co. H, 7th Battalion South Carolina infantry	May 16, 1864, Near Drury's Bluff, Virginia	Point Lookout, Maryland, transferred to Elmira Prison, NY, August 17, 1864	Died October 10, 1864 of Chronic Diarrhea, Grave No. 666
Jones, Daniel S. Private	Unk	June 17, 1863, Wilmington, North Carolina	Co. K, 10th Regiment, 1st North Carolina Artillery	January 15, 1865, Fort Fisher, North Carolina	January 30, 1865, Elmira Prison Camp, New York	Oath of Allegiance June 23, 1865
Jones, David Private	20	March 27, 1863, Mooresfield, Virginia	Co. F, 7th Virginia Cavalry	September 14, 1863, Near Culpepper, Virginia	Point Lookout, Maryland, transferred to Elmira Prison, NY, August 18, 1864	Exchanged March 10, 1865 at Boulware's Wharf on the James River, Virginia
Jones, David Private	Unk	March 15, 1862, Ridgeway, Virginia	Co. A, 42nd Virginia Infantry	May 12, 1864, Spotsylvania Court House, Virginia	Point Lookout, Maryland, transferred to Elmira Prison, NY, August 2, 1864	Died December 23, 1864 of Pneumonia, Grave No. 1096
Jones, David D. Private	Unk	March 1, 1862, Lillington, Cumberland County, North Carolina	Co. I, 51st North Carolina Infantry	June 1, 1864, Cold Harbor, Virginia	Point Lookout, Maryland, transferred to Elmira Prison, NY, July 12, 1864	Exchanged February 13, 1865 at Boulware's wharf on the James River, Virginia
Jones, David J. Private	Unk	April 25, 1862, Whiteville, North Carolina	Co. E, 51st North Carolina Infantry	June 1, 1864, Gaines Mill Cold Harbor, Virginia	Point Lookout, Maryland, transferred to Elmira Prison, NY, July 9, 1864	Exchanged March 14, 1865 at Boulware's Wharf on the James River, Virginia
Jones, David W. Private	Unk	Unknown	Co. H, 12th North Carolina Infantry	May 20, 1864, Spotsylvania Court House, Virginia	Point Lookout, Maryland, transferred to Elmira Prison, NY, July 6, 1864	Died December 2, 1864, Pneumonia, Grave No. 1009. Has 5th VA on Headstone.
Jones, Franklin A. Private	Unk	August 17, 1864, Wayne County, North Carolina	Co. D, 40th Regiment, 3rd North Carolina Artillery	January 15, 1865, Fort Fisher, North Carolina	February 1, 1865 Elmira Prison Camp, New York	Oath of Allegiance May 29, 1865
Jones, George W. Private	Unk	March 10, 1862, Hanover County, Virginia	Captain Woolfolk's Battery, Virginia Light Artillery	May 25, 1864, Hanover Junction, Virginia	Point Lookout, Maryland, transferred to Elmira Prison, NY, July 25, 1864	Died September 7, 1864 of Chronic Diarrhea, Grave No. 248

Name & Rank	Age	Enlisted	Regiment and State	Where Captured	Prison	Remarks
Jones, George W. Private	Unk	January 9, 1864, Montgomery, Alabama	Co. E, 1st Battalion Alabama Artillery	August 23, 1864, Fort Morgan, Alabama	Steam Press No. 4 New Orleans, Louisiana transferred to Elmira Prison, NY, October 8, 1864.	Exchanged February 13, 1865 at Boulware's wharf on the James River, Virginia
Jones, George W. Private	30	March 7, 1864, Camp, Virginia	Co. E, 4th Virginia Infantry	May 12, 1864, Spotsylvania Court House, Virginia	Point Lookout, Maryland, transferred to Elmira Prison, NY, July 25, 1864	Oath of Allegiance May 14, 1865
Jones, H. Private	Unk	Unknown	Co. C, 1st North Carolina Infantry	Unknown	Unknown	Died July 15, 1865 of Unknown Disease, Grave No. 2875
Jones, H. H. Private	Unk	March 3, 1862, Berlin, Arkansas	Co. B, 3rd Arkansas Infantry	May 5, 1864, Wilderness, Virginia	Point Lookout, Maryland, transferred to Elmira Prison, NY, July 30, 1864	Exchanged October 29, 1864 at Venus Point, Savannah River, GA.
Jones, H. J. Private	Unk	Unknown	Co. L, 21st South Carolina Infantry	January 15, 1865, Fort Fisher, North Carolina	January 30, 1865 Elmira Prison Camp, New York	Exchanged March 14, 1865 at Boulware's Wharf on the James River, Virginia
Jones, H. K. Private	Unk	March 10, 1864, Rogers Store, North Carolina	Co. J, 1st North Carolina Infantry	May 12, 1864, Near Spotsylvania Court House, Virginia	Point Lookout Prison, Maryland. Transferred to Elmira Prison Camp New York August 6, 1864.	Transferred for Exchanged 10/29/64 at Venus Point, Savannah River, GA.
Jones, H. N. Private	Unk	April 27, 1864, Columbia, South Carolina	Co. H, 17th South Carolina Infantry	July 30, 1864, Petersburg, Virginia	Point Lookout, Maryland, transferred to Elmira Prison, NY, August 12, 1864	Exchanged October 29, 1864 at Venus Point, Savannah River, GA.
Jones, Hardy Private	Unk	February 1, 1864, Cumberland County, North Carolina	Co. F, 24th North Carolina Infantry	June 17, 1864, Near Petersburg, Virginia	Point Lookout, Maryland, transferred to Elmira Prison, NY, July 30, 1864	Transferred for Exchanged 10/29/64 at Venus Point, Savannah River, GA.

Name & Rank	Age	Enlisted	Regiment and State	Where Captured	Prison	Remarks
Jones, Henry L. Private	Unk	July 9, 1861, Forsyth, Georgia	Co. A, 14th Georgia Infantry	May 6, 1864, Wilderness, Virginia	Point Lookout, Maryland, transferred to Elmira Prison, NY, August 14, 1864	Exchanged March 14, 1865 at Boulware's Wharf on the James River, Virginia
Jones, J. A. Private	46	January 21, 1864, Marion, South Carolina	Co. L, 21st South Carolina Infantry	January 15, 1865, Fort Fisher, North Carolina	January 30, 1865 Elmira Prison Camp, New York	Died February 26, 1865 of Chronic Diarrhea, Grave No. 2122
Jones, J. Charles Corporal	Unk	April 15, 1861, Livingston, Alabama	Co. G, 5th Alabama Infantry	May 5, 1864, Wilderness, Virginia	Point Lookout, Maryland, transferred to Elmira Prison, NY, August 17, 1864	Oath of Allegiance May 29, 1865
Jones, J. G. Private	Unk	November 23, 1863, Georgetown, Georgia	Co. E, 7th Georgia Cavalry	June 11, 1864, Louisa Court House, Trevilian Station, Virginia	Point Lookout, Maryland, transferred to Elmira Prison, NY, July 30, 1864	Oath of Allegiance June 14, 1865
Jones, James Private	20	July 1, 1863, Charlestown, Virginia	Co. A, 12th Virginia Cavalry	May 12, 1864, Jefferson County, Virginia	Old Capital Prison, Washington DC. Transferred to Elmira Prison Camp, NY July 25, 1864.	Exchanged March 14, 1865 at Boulware's Wharf on the James River, Virginia
Jones, James A. Corporal	Unk	February 28, 1862, Young's Crossroads, North Carolina	Co. J, 23rd North Carolina Infantry	May 12, 1864, Near Spotsylvania Court House, Virginia	Point Lookout Prison, Maryland. Transferred to Elmira Prison Camp New York August 14, 1864.	Oath of Allegiance June 16, 1865
Jones, James E. Private	18	March 23, 1864, Edgecombe County, North Carolina	Co. D, 40th Regiment, 3rd North Carolina Artillery	January 15, 1865, Fort Fisher, North Carolina	February 1, 1865 Elmira Prison Camp, New York	Oath of Allegiance June 21, 1865
Jones, James M. Sergeant	27	March 9, 1861, Selma, Alabama	Co. E, 1st Battalion Alabama Artillery	August 23, 1864, Fort Morgan, Alabama	Steam Press No. 4 New Orleans, Louisiana transferred to Elmira Prison, NY, October 8, 1864.	Died November 29, 1864 of Chronic Diarrhea, Grave No. 985

Name & Rank	Age	Enlisted	Regiment and State	Where Captured	Prison	Remarks
Jones, James M. Private	33	May 28, 1861, Davis Mills, Virginia	Co. F, 2nd Virginia Cavalry	May 12, 1864, Spotsylvania Court House, Virginia	Point Lookout, Maryland, transferred to Elmira Prison, NY, August 12, 1864	Oath of Allegiance June 21, 1865
Jones, James M. Corporal	20	June 28, 1862, Huttonsville, Virginia	Co. A, 25th Virginia Infantry	May 5, 1864, Wilderness, Virginia	Point Lookout, Maryland, transferred to Elmira Prison, NY, July 23, 1864	Oath of Allegiance May 29, 1865
Jones, James R. Private	22	August 3, 1861, Fayetteville, North Carolina	Co. E, 8th North Carolina Infantry	May 31, 1864, Cold Harbor, Virginia	Point Lookout, Maryland, transferred to Elmira Prison, NY, July 12, 1864	Oath of Allegiance March 22, 1865
Jones, James S. Private	Unk	March 8, 1861, Autauga, Alabama	Co. E, 1st Battalion Alabama Artillery	August 23, 1864, Fort Morgan, Alabama	Steam Press No. 4, New Orleans, Louisiana transferred to Elmira Prison, NY, October 8, 1864.	Oath of Allegiance May 17, 1865
Jones, Jeremiah Corporal	22	May 18, 1861, Edenton, North Carolina	Co. A, 1st North Carolina Infantry	May 12, 1864, Wilderness (Spotsylvania), Virginia	Point Lookout, Maryland, transferred to Elmira Prison, NY, August 6, 1864	Exchanged March 14, 1864 at Boulware's Wharf on the James River, Virginia
Jones, John A. Private	Unk	January 27, 1863, Camp of Instruction, Virginia	Co. F, 26th Battalion, Virginia Infantry	June 3, 1864, Gaines Mill Cold Harbor, Virginia	Point Lookout, Maryland, transferred to Elmira Prison, NY, July 17, 1864	Oath of Allegiance July 3, 1865
Jones, John B. Private	Unk	September 6, 1862, Covington, Alabama	Co. C, 1st Battalion Alabama Artillery	August 23, 1864, Fort Morgan, Alabama	New Orleans, Louisiana transferred to Elmira Prison, NY, December 4, 1864.	Died February 20, 1865 of Pneumonia, Grave No. 2317
Jones, John B. Private	43	January 28, 1862, Jacksonville, Onslow County, North Carolina	Co. G, 3rd North Carolina Infantry	May 12, 1864, Near Spotsylvania Court House, Virginia	Point Lookout Prison, Maryland. Transferred to Elmira Prison Camp New York August 14, 1864.	Exchanged February 20, 1865 at Boulware's or Cox Wharf on the James River, Virginia

Name & Rank	Age	Enlisted	Regiment and State	Where Captured	Prison	Remarks
Jones, John B. Sergeant	Unk	June 4, 1861, Fork of Wilson, Virginia	Co. D, 50th Virginia Infantry	May 12, 1864, Spotsylvania Court House, Virginia	Point Lookout, Maryland, transferred to Elmira Prison, NY, August 2, 1864	Died May 10, 1865 of Pneumonia, Grave No. 2793
Jones, John L. Private	Unk	August 1, 1863, Montgomery County, Alabama	Co. B, 61st Alabama Infantry	May 12, 1864, Spotsylvania Court House, Virginia	Point Lookout, Maryland, transferred to Elmira Prison, NY, July 30, 1864	Died September 1, 1864 of Scorbutus (Scurvy), Grave No. 76
Jones, John P. Private	21	May 6, 1861, Jacksonville, North Carolina	Co. B, 24th North Carolina Infantry	June 17, 1864, Petersburg, Virginia	Point Lookout, Maryland, transferred to Elmira Prison, NY, July 30, 1864	Exchanged March 2, 1865 at Akins Landing on the James River, Virginia
Jones, John R. Private	23	Unknown	Co. F, 7th Virginia Cavalry	December 2, 1864, Hampshire County, Virginia	Old Capital Prison, Washington, DC, transferred to Elmira, NY, December 17, 1864	Exchanged March 14, 1865 at Boulware's Wharf on the James River, Virginia
Jones, John V. Corporal	37	July 15, 1862, Fayetteville, North Carolina	Co. H, 33rd North Carolina Infantry	July 29, 1864, Petersburg, Virginia	Point Lookout, Maryland, transferred to Elmira Prison, NY, August 12, 1864	Exchanged October 29, 1864 at Venus Point, Savannah River, GA.
Jones, John W. Corporal	19	May 4, 1861, Stokes County, North Carolina	Co. A, 2nd Battalion North Carolina Infantry	May 12, 1864, Near Spotsylvania County Court House, Virginia	Point Lookout, Maryland, transferred to Elmira Prison, NY, August 14, 1864	Oath of Allegiance July 3, 1865
Jones, John W. Private	Unk	April 18, 1861, Jefferson Court House, Virginia	Co. A, 2nd Virginia Infantry	May 12, 1864, Near Spotsylvania Court House, Virginia	Point Lookout, Maryland, transferred to Elmira Prison, NY, August 6, 1864	Exchanged March 2, 1865 at Akins Landing on the James River, Virginia
Jones, Joseph P. Private	19	January 9, 1864, Montgomery, Alabama	Co. E, 1st Battalion Alabama Artillery	August 23, 1864, Fort Morgan, Alabama	Steam Press No. 4, New Orleans, Louisiana transferred to Elmira Prison, NY, October 8, 1864.	Oath of Allegiance May 17, 1865

Name & Rank	Age	Enlisted	Regiment and State	Where Captured	Prison	Remarks
Jones, Joseph T. Private	25	May 20, 1861, Louisburg, North Carolina	Co. K, 32nd North Carolina Infantry	March 25, 1865, Fort Stedman, Virginia. Gunshot Wound Right Arm Above the Elbow.	Old Capital Prison, Washington, DC, transferred to Elmira Prison, NY, May 2, 1865.	Oath of Allegiance June 30, 1865
Jones, L. R. Civilian	Unk	Unknown	Citizen of Louisiana	September 19, 1864, St. Joseph, Louisiana	New Orleans, LA, Transferred to Elmira Prison, NY, November 19, 1864	Oath of Allegiance June 20, 1865
Jones, Lawrence B. Private	Unk	February 21, 1863, Richmond, Virginia	Co. E, 25th Battalion Virginia Infantry	July 12, 1864, Cox's Farm, Virginia	Point Lookout, Maryland, transferred to Elmira Prison, NY, August 6, 1864	Oath of Allegiance February 2, 1865 Early Release per Lincoln's Proclamation, 12/8/1863.
Jones, Leroy Z. Corporal	Unk	July 5, 1861, Buffalo Gap, Virginia	Co. D, 44th Virginia Infantry	May 12, 1864, Spotsylvania Court House, Virginia	Point Lookout, Maryland, transferred to Elmira Prison, NY, August 2,1864	Exchanged October 29, 1864 at Venus Point, Savannah River, GA.
Jones, Love Private	26	March 5, 1863, Cumberland County, North Carolina	Co. J, 16th North Carolina Infantry	June 2, 1864, Old Church, Cold Harbor, Virginia	Point Lookout, Maryland, transferred to Elmira Prison, NY, July 17,1864	Exchanged October 29, 1864 at Venus Point, Savannah River, GA.
Jones, Maryus Corporal	Unk	January 8, 1863, Saluda, Virginia	Co. D, 24th Virginia Cavalry	July 28, 1864, Petersburg, Virginia	Point Lookout, Maryland, transferred to Elmira Prison, NY, August 12, 1864	Exchanged October 29, 1864 at Venus Point, Savannah River, GA.
Jones, P. D. Private	Unk	Unknown	Co. D, 40th Regiment, 3rd North Carolina Artillery	January 15, 1865, Fort Fisher, North Carolina	February 1, 1865 Elmira Prison Camp, New York	Oath of Allegiance July 7, 1865
Jones, R. A. Private	Unk	June 28, 1862, Huttonsville, Virginia	Co. A, 25th Virginia Infantry	May 12, 1864, Spotsylvania Court House, Virginia	Point Lookout, Maryland, transferred to Elmira Prison, NY, August 2, 1864	Oath of Allegiance June 16, 1865

Name & Rank	Age	Enlisted	Regiment and State	Where Captured	Prison	Remarks
Jones, Richard A. Private	25	October 1, 1862, Raleigh, North Carolina	Co. I, 32nd North Carolina Infantry	May 10, 1864, Wilderness, Virginia	Point Lookout, Maryland, transferred to Elmira Prison, NY, August 6, 1864	Oath of Allegiance May 29, 1865
Jones, Richard M. Private	Unk	April 17, 1861, Christiansburg, Virginia	Co. G, 4th Virginia Infantry	May 5, 1864, Wilderness, Virginia	Point Lookout, Maryland, transferred to Elmira Prison, NY, August 2, 1864	Oath of Allegiance June 19, 1865
Jones, Robert M. Corporal	24	May 1, 1861, Leasburg, North Carolina	Co. D, 13th North Carolina Infantry	May 24, 1864, Butler's Mills, Virginia	Point Lookout, Maryland, transferred to Elmira Prison, NY, July 11, 1864	Oath of Allegiance June 19, 1865
Jones, Robert T. Private	27	April 12, 1862, Hendersonville, North Carolina	Co. A, 56th North Carolina Infantry	April 2, 1865, Five Forks, Virginia. Gunshot Wound Left Shoulder.	Old Capital Prison, Washington, DC, transferred to Elmira Prison, NY, May 2, 1865.	Oath of Allegiance July 7, 1865
Jones, Rueben Private	20	September 3, 1861, Richmond, Virginia	Co. K, 13th Georgia Infantry	May 6, 1864, Wilderness, Virginia	Old Capital Prison, Washington, DC, transferred to Elmira, NY, July 14, 1864	Oath of Allegiance June 19, 1865
Jones, Silas V. Private	20	May 29, 1861, Stevensville, Virginia	Co. K, 34th Virginia Infantry	June 15, 1864, Near Petersburg, Virginia	Point Lookout, Maryland, transferred to Elmira Prison, NY, July 12, 1864	Point Lookout, Maryland, transferred to Elmira Prison, NY, July 23, 1864
Jones, Stephen Private	Unk	Unknown	Co. B, 50th Virginia Infantry	May 12, 1864, Spotsylvania Court House, Virginia	Point Lookout, Maryland, transferred to Elmira Prison, NY, August 2, 1864	Oath of Allegiance June 19, 1865
Jones, Theodore F. Sergeant	Unk	August 2, 1861, Bowling Green, Virginia	Co. G, 47th Virginia Infantry	May 6, 1864, Wilderness, Virginia	Point Lookout, Maryland, transferred to Elmira Prison, NY, August 14, 1864	Oath of Allegiance June 14, 1865

Name & Rank	Age	Enlisted	Regiment and State	Where Captured	Prison	Remarks
Jones, Thomas A. Private	32	August 1, 1862, Richmond, Virginia	Co. H, 14th Virginia Cavalry	May 11, 1864, Yellow Tavern, Hanover County, Virginia	Point Lookout, Maryland, transferred to Elmira Prison, NY, August 17, 1864	Died November 6, 1864 of Chronic Diarrhea, Grave No. 763. Headstone has Benjamin Guthrie.
Jones, Thomas B. Private	28	July 17, 1862, Randolph County, North Carolina	Co. H, 3rd North Carolina Infantry	May 12, 1864, Near Spotsylvania, Virginia	Point Lookout, Maryland, transferred to Elmira Prison, NY, August 14, 1864	Exchanged October 29, 1864 at Venus Point, Savannah River, GA.
Jones, Thomas C. Private	Unk	June 11, 1861, Hevener's Store, Virginia	Co. F, 25th Virginia Infantry	May 5, 1864, Wilderness, Virginia	Point Lookout, Maryland, transferred to Elmira Prison, NY, August 17, 1864	Oath of Allegiance June 23, 1865
Jones, Thomas H. Sergeant	42	March 1, 1862, Aor Creek, Virginia	Co. K, 47th Virginia Infantry	May 6, 1864, Wilderness, Virginia	Point Lookout, Maryland, transferred to Elmira Prison, NY, July 23, 1864	Oath of Allegiance May 19, 1865
Jones, Thomas J. Private	19	March 24, 1862, Davis' X-Roads, North Carolina	Co. K, 12th North Carolina Infantry	May 12, 1864, Near Spotsylvania, Virginia	Point Lookout, Maryland, transferred to Elmira Prison, NY, August 14, 1864	Exchanged 10/29/65. Died 1/1/65 of Chronic Diarrhea at 2nd Division Hospital, Savannah, GA
Jones, Thomas L. Sergeant	22	May 16, 1861, Columbia, North Carolina	Co. A, 32nd North Carolina Infantry	May 10, 1864, Spotsylvania Court House, Virginia	Point Lookout, Maryland, transferred to Elmira Prison, NY, August 6, 1864	Exchanged March 10, 1865 at Boulware's Wharf on the James River, Virginia
Jones, W. H. Private	19	July 15, 1862, Raleigh, North Carolina	Co. G, 1st North Carolina Infantry	May 12, 1864, Wilderness, Spotsylvania Court House, Virginia	Point Lookout, Maryland, transferred to Elmira Prison, NY, August 6, 1864	Died March 28, 1865 of Diarrhea, Grave No. 2499
Jones, W. H. Private	Unk	April 26, 1864, Richmond, Virginia	Co. A, 3rd Virginia Cavalry	August 16, 1864, Front Royal, Virginia	Old Capital Prison, Washington, DC transferred to Elmira Prison, NY, August 29, 1864	Exchanged February 13, 1865 at Boulware's wharf on the James River, Virginia

Name & Rank	Age	Enlisted	Regiment and State	Where Captured	Prison	Remarks
Jones, W. L. Private	Unk	May 3, 1862, Griffin, Georgia	Co. H, 13th Georgia Infantry	May 20, 1864, Spotsylvania Court House, Virginia	Point Lookout, Maryland, transferred to Elmira Prison, NY, July 6, 1864	Point Lookout, Maryland, transferred to Elmira Prison, NY, July 23, 1864
Jones, W. T. Private	Unk	July 1, 1863, Carrollton, Alabama	Co. A, 7th Alabama Cavalry	July 22, 1864, Swans Place, Tensan Parish, Louisiana	New Orleans, LA, Transferred to Elmira Prison, NY, November 19, 1864	Died March 10, 1865 of Variola (Smallpox), Grave No. 1853
Jones, Walter G. Private	22	July 23, 1861, Mathews Court House, Virginia	Co. K, 5th, Virginia Cavalry	May 31, 1864 Cold Harbor, Virginia	Point Lookout, Maryland, transferred to Elmira Prison, NY, July 11, 1864	Exchanged March 14, 1865 at Boulware's Wharf on the James River, Virginia
Jones, Wesley A. Private	19	February 21, 1862, Rogers Store, North Carolina	Co. J, 1st North Carolina Infantry	May 12, 1864, Near Spotsylvania Court House, Virginia	Point Lookout Prison, Maryland. Transferred to Elmira Prison Camp New York August 6, 1864.	Died November 17, 1864 of Chronic Diarrhea, Grave No. 961. Headstone has A. W. Jones.
Jones, Whitmel Private	Unk	August 22, 1861, Edenton, North Carolina	Co. A, 1st North Carolina Infantry	May 12, 1864, Wilderness, Spotsylvania Court House, Virginia	Point Lookout, Maryland, transferred to Elmira Prison, NY, August 6, 1864	Oath of Allegiance June 19, 1865
Jones, Wiley A. Private	30	March 8, 1862, Salisbury, North Carolina	Co. C, 42nd North Carolina Infantry	June 1, 1864, Gaines Farm Cold Harbor, Virginia	Point Lookout, Maryland, transferred to Elmira Prison, NY, July 12, 1864	Oath of Allegiance June 14, 1865
Jones, William Private	23	May 11, 1862, Boone, North Carolina	Co. D, 1st North Carolina Cavalry	May 27, 1864, Hanover Junction, Virginia	Point Lookout, Maryland, transferred to Elmira Prison, NY, July 6, 1864	Exchanged October 29, 1864 at Venus Point, Savannah River, GA.
Jones, William Private	46	March 3, 1862, Magnolia, North Carolina	Co. C, 51st North Carolina Infantry	June 15, 1864, Petersburg, Virginia	Point Lookout, Maryland, transferred to Elmira Prison, NY, July 9, 1864	Died October 28, 1864 of Typhoid-Pneumonia, Grave No. 717

Name & Rank	Age	Enlisted	Regiment and State	Where Captured	Prison	Remarks
Jones, William Private	21	April 26, 1861, Townesville, North Carolina	Co. P, 12th North Carolina Infantry	May 20, 1864, Spotsylvania Court House, Virginia	Point Lookout, Maryland, transferred to Elmira Prison, NY, July 6, 1864	Exchanged October 29, 1864 at Venus Point, Savannah River, GA.
Jones, William Private	19	May 21, 1861, Graham, North Carolina	Co. H, 15th North Carolina Infantry	May 6, 1864, Wilderness, Virginia	Point Lookout, Maryland, transferred to Elmira Prison, NY, August 14, 1864	Exchanged February 20, 1865 at Boulware's or Cox Wharf on the James River, Virginia
Jones, William Private	Unk	October 23, 1863, Columbia, South Carolina	Co. B, 23rd South Carolina Infantry	June 17, 1864, Near Petersburg, Virginia	Point Lookout, Maryland, transferred to Elmira Prison, NY, July 30, 1864	Transferred for Exchange 10/11/64. Died 10/28/64 of Chronic Diarrhea at Point Lookout Prison Camp, MD.
Jones, William Apcatesby Private	Unk	Unknown	Co. H, 26th Battalion Virginia Infantry	June 3, 1864, Gaines Farm, Cold Harbor, Virginia	Transferred From Point Lookout Prison, MD, July 12, 1864. Train Never Arrived at Elmira Prison Camp, NY.	Died July 15, 1864 in Train Wreck at Shohola, Pennsylvania.
Jones, William A. Private	Unk	April 1, 1863, Warm Springs, Virginia	Co. J, 20th Virginia Cavalry	August 11, 1864, Berryville, Virginia	Point Lookout, Maryland, transferred to Elmira Prison, NY, August 29, 1864	Exchanged February 25, 1865 at Boulware's or Cox Wharf on the James River, Virginia
Jones, William A. Private	Unk	April 1, 1862, Gordonville, Virginia	Co. J, 53rd Virginia Infantry	May 10, 1864, Near Petersburg, Virginia	Point Lookout, Maryland, transferred to Elmira Prison, NY, August 17, 1864	Died March 27, 1865 of Diarrhea, Grave No. 2505
Jones, William C. Private	19	January 28, 1862, Jacksonville, Onslow County, North Carolina	Co. G, 3rd North Carolina Infantry	May 12, 1864, Near Spotsylvania Court House, Virginia	Point Lookout Prison, Maryland. Transferred to Elmira Prison Camp New York August 14, 1864.	Oath of Allegiance June 12, 1865

Name & Rank	Age	Enlisted	Regiment and State	Where Captured	Prison	Remarks
Jones, William D. Private	36	September 15, 1861, Allegheny County, North Carolina	Co. K, 37th North Carolina Infantry	May 12, 1864, Spotsylvania Court House, Virginia	Point Lookout, Maryland, transferred to Elmira Prison, NY, August 12, 1864	Exchanged October 29, 1864 at Venus Point, Savannah River, GA.
Jones, William J. Sergeant	23	March 14, 1862, Jasper, Florida	Co. B, 5th Florida Infantry	May 12, 1864, Spotsylvania Court House, Virginia	Point Lookout, Maryland, transferred to Elmira Prison, NY, July 30, 1864	Oath of Allegiance June 19, 1865
Jones, William J. Sergeant	Unk	April 28, 1861, New Orleans, Louisiana	Co. A, 1st Louisiana Infantry	May 5, 1864, Wilderness, Virginia	Point Lookout, Maryland, transferred to Elmira Prison, NY, August 17, 1864	Exchanged February 25, 1865 at Boulware's or Cox Wharf on the James River, Virginia
Jones, William M. Corporal	Unk	July 4, 1861, Selma, Alabama	Co. F, 1st Battalion Alabama Artillery	August 23, 1864, Fort Morgan, Alabama	Steam Press No. 4 New Orleans, Louisiana transferred to Elmira Prison, NY, October 8, 1864.	Oath of Allegiance May 17, 1865
Jones, William M. Private	19	February 12, 1862, Raleigh, North Carolina	Co. I, 3rd North Carolina Cavalry	May 24, 1864 Hanover Junction, Virginia	Point Lookout, Maryland, transferred to Elmira Prison, NY, July 8, 1864	Exchanged October 29, 1864 at Venus Point, Savannah River, GA.
Jones, William P. Private	Unk	September 18, 1861, Camp Potomac, Virginia	Co. E, 9th Virginia Cavalry	September 14, 1863, Near Culpepper, Virginia	Point Lookout, Maryland, transferred to Elmira Prison, NY, August 18, 1864	Exchanged March 10, 1865 at Boulware's Wharf on the James River, Virginia
Jones, William T. Private	18	May 30, 1861, Weldon, North Carolina	Co. H, 5th North Carolina Infantry	May 12, 1864, Spotsylvania Court House, Virginia	Point Lookout, Maryland, transferred to Elmira Prison, NY, August 6, 1864	Died November 23, 1864 of Chronic Diarrhea, Grave No. 920
Joor, John P. Private	Unk	Unknown	Co. J, 3rd Louisiana Cavalry	October 10, 1864, Bayou Sara, Louisiana	New Orleans, Louisiana transferred to Elmira November 19, 1864.	Oath of Allegiance April 3, 1865

Name & Rank	Age	Enlisted	Regiment and State	Where Captured	Prison	Remarks
Jordan, A. C. Corporal	Unk	August 24, 1861, Palmer, Georgia	Co. A, 24th Georgia Infantry	August 16, 1864, Front Royal, Virginia	Old Capital Prison, Washington, DC transferred to Elmira Prison, NY, August 29, 1864	Died February 13, 1865 of Variola (Smallpox), Grave No. 2073
Jordan, Abram Private	Unk	September 22, 1862, Waynesville, Georgia	Co. G, 7th Georgia Cavalry	June 11, 1864, Trevilian Station, Louisa Court House, Virginia	Point Lookout, Maryland, transferred to Elmira Prison, NY, July 25, 1864	Died October 23, 1864 of Chronic Diarrhea, Grave No. 865
Jordan, Elijah P. Private	21	May 18, 1862, Loachapoka, Tallapoosa County, Alabama	Co. I, 47th Alabama Infantry	May 6, 1864, Wilderness, Virginia	Point Lookout, Maryland, transferred to Elmira Prison, NY, August 17, 1864	Exchanged February 20, 1865. Died April 26, 1865 of Chronic Diarrhea at US Army Hospital, Baltimore, MD.
Jordan, George F. Private	18	April 14, 1863, Wilmington, North Carolina	Co. B, 4th North Carolina Infantry	May 30, 1864, Old Church Cold Harbor, Virginia	Point Lookout, Maryland, transferred to Elmira Prison, NY, July 12, 1864	Oath of Allegiance June 30, 1865
Jordan, Grey J. Private	32	February 16, 1862, Carterett County, North Carolina	Co. F, 7th North Carolina Infantry	July 14, 1863, Falling Waters, Maryland	Point Lookout, Maryland, transferred to Elmira Prison, NY, August 18, 1864	Exchanged March 10, 1865 at Boulware's Wharf on the James River, Virginia
Jordan, J. T. Private	Unk	Unknown	Co. B, 1st Jackson's Tennessee Heavy Artillery	August 23, 1864, Fort Morgan, Alabama.	New Orleans, Louisiana transferred to Elmira Prison, NY, December 4, 1864.	Exchanged February 25, 1865 at Boulware's or Cox Wharf on the James River, Virginia
Jordan, Jacob Private	Unk	Unknown	Co. A, 50th Virginia Infantry	May 12, 1864, Spotsylvania Court House, Virginia	Point Lookout, Maryland, transferred to Elmira Prison, NY, August 2, 1864	Exchanged March 2, 1865 at Akins Landing on the James River, Virginia
Jordan, James M. Private	Unk	September 28, 1862, Camp Randolph, Georgia	Co. A, 27th Georgia Infantry	June 16, 1864, Petersburg, Virginia	Point Lookout, Maryland, transferred to Elmira Prison, NY, July 25, 1864	Died January 26, 1865 of Chronic Diarrhea, Grave No. 1628

Name & Rank	Age	Enlisted	Regiment and State	Where Captured	Prison	Remarks
Jordan, John A. Private	26	April 15, 1861, Pittsboro, North Carolina	Co. I, 32nd North Carolina Infantry	May 10, 1864, Wilderness, Virginia	Point Lookout, Maryland, transferred to Elmira Prison, NY, August 6, 1864	Died March 7, 1865 of Diarrhea, Grave No. 2404
Jordan, John J. 1st Sergeant	Unk	June 10, 1861, Richmond, Virginia	Co. F, 44th Virginia Infantry	May 12, 1864, Spotsylvania Court House, Virginia	Point Lookout, Maryland, transferred to Elmira Prison, NY, August 2, 1864	Died December 4, 1864 of Chronic Diarrhea, Grave No. 890.
Jordan, John W. Corporal	18	June 15, 1862, Columbia, South Carolina	Co. G, 6th South Carolina Cavalry	June 11, 1864, Trevilian Station, Louisa Court House, Virginia	Point Lookout, Maryland, transferred to Elmira Prison, NY, July 25, 1864	Died August 19, 1864 of Chronic Diarrhea. Grave No. 486
Jordan, John W. Corporal	Unk	Unknown	Co. B, Hood's Battalion Virginia Reserves	June 15, 1864, Jordan's Farm, Near Petersburg, Virginia	Point Lookout, Maryland, transferred to Elmira Prison, NY, July 25, 1864	Oath of Allegiance May 17, 1865
Jordan, Joseph E. Sergeant	24	May 20, 1861, Black Walnut, Virginia	Co. C, 3rd Virginia Cavalry	August 16, 1864, Front Royal, Virginia	Point Lookout, Maryland, transferred to Elmira Prison, NY, August 29, 1864	Exchanged March 14, 1865 at Boulware's Wharf on the James River, Virginia
Jordan, Kenion Private	23	July 29, 1861, Beaufort, North Carolina	Co. F, 10th Regiment, 1st North Carolina Artillery	January 15, 1865, Fort Fisher, North Carolina	January 30, 1865, Elmira Prison Camp, New York	Died March 10, 1865 of Pneumonia, Grave No. 1864. Headstone has Kenyon Jordan.
Jordan, Lewis G. Private	22	August 13, 1861, Forestville, Wake County, North Carolina	Co. J, 1st North Carolina Infantry	May 12, 1864, Near Spotsylvania Court House, Virginia	Point Lookout Prison, Maryland. Transferred to Elmira Prison Camp New York August 6, 1864.	Oath of Allegiance June 19, 1865

Name & Rank	Age	Enlisted	Regiment and State	Where Captured	Prison	Remarks
Jordan, Newton Sergeant	Unk	August 24, 1861, Banks County, Georgia	Co. A, 24th Georgia Infantry	August 16, 1864, Front Royal, Virginia	Old Capital Prison, Washington, DC transferred to Elmira Prison, NY, August 29, 1864	Transferred For Exchange October 11, 1864 to Point Lookout Prison Camp, MD. Died Aboard Steamship "Northern Light" of Unknown Causes and Date.
Jordan, Thomas W. Private	Unk	April 13, 1864, Homer, Georgia	Co. A, 24th Georgia Infantry	August 16, 1864, Front Royal, Virginia	Old Capital Prison, Washington, DC transferred to Elmira Prison, NY, August 29, 1864	Died February 15, 1865 of Variola (Smallpox), Grave No. 2174
Jordan, W. K. Private	Unk	March 30, 1862, Camp Mannigault, South Carolina	Co. J, 21st South Carolina Infantry	June 24, 1864, Near Petersburg, Virginia	Point Lookout, Maryland, transferred to Elmira Prison, NY, August 18, 1864	Died September 16, 1864 of Chronic Diarrhea, Grave No. 168
Jordan, William H. Private	22	May 18, 1862, Loachapoka, Tallapoosa County, Alabama	Co. I, 47th Alabama Infantry	May 6, 1864, Wilderness, Virginia	Point Lookout, Maryland, transferred to Elmira Prison, NY, August 17, 1864	Oath of Allegiance June 14, 1865
Jordan, William H. Private	Unk	April 15, 1862, Buena Vista, Georgia	Co. K, 12th Georgia Infantry	May 10, 1864, Spotsylvania Court House, Virginia	Point Lookout, Maryland, transferred to Elmira Prison, NY, July 25, 1864	Died May 16, 1865 of Chronic Diarrhea, Grave No. 2960
Jordan, William R. Private	24	March 27, 1862, Clinton, North Carolina	Co. K, 51st North Carolina Infantry	June 15, 1864, Petersburg, Virginia	Point Lookout, Maryland, transferred to Elmira Prison, NY, July 12, 1864	Oath of Allegiance July 3, 1865
Jordan, Wilson Private	58	March 26, 1862, Newland, Avery County, North Carolina	Co. C, 3rd Battalion, North Carolina Light Artillery	January 15, 1865, Fort Fisher, North Carolina	February 1, 1865, Elmira Prison Camp, New York	Exchanged March 14, 1865 at Boulware's Wharf on the James River, Virginia

Name & Rank	Age	Enlisted	Regiment and State	Where Captured	Prison	Remarks
Jordan, Wyatt G. Private	28	May 1, 1863, Raleigh, North Carolina	Co. J, 32nd North Carolina Infantry	May 10, 1864, Wilderness, Virginia	Point Lookout, Maryland, transferred to Elmira Prison, NY, July 23, 1864	Oath of Allegiance May 29, 1865
Joseph, William M. Private	Unk	May 10, 1862, Augusta, Georgia	Co. D, 12th Battalion Georgia Light Artillery	July 12, 1864, Near Washington, DC,	Old Capital Prison, Washington, DC, transferred to Elmira, NY, July 23, 1864	Oath of Allegiance April 6, 1865
Josey, Moses C. Private	20	May 29, 1861, Charlotte, North Carolina	Co. G, 6th North Carolina Infantry	July 8, 1864, Harpers Ferry, Virginia	Old Capital Prison, Washington DC. Transferred to Elmira Prison Camp, NY July 25, 1864.	Oath of Allegiance May 29, 1865
Joyce, James K. P. Private	17	March 11, 1862, Spring Garden, North Carolina	Co. J, 45th North Carolina Infantry	May 20, 1864, Spotsylvania Court House, Virginia	Point Lookout, Maryland, transferred to Elmira Prison, NY, July 6, 1864	Exchanged October 29, 1864 at Venus Point, Savannah River, GA.
Joyner, Archer Private	Unk	March 1, 1862, Suffolk, Virginia	Co. C, 13th Virginia Cavalry	June 1, 1864, Ashland, Cold Harbor, Virginia	Transferred From Point Lookout Prison, MD, July 12, 1864. Train Never Arrived at Elmira Prison Camp, NY.	Died July 15, 1864 in Train Wreck at Shohola, Pennsylvania.
Joyner, Elijah J. Private	33	July 15, 1862, Nash County, North Carolina	Co. D, 1st North Carolina Infantry	May 12, 1864, Spotsylvania Court House, Virginia	Point Lookout, Maryland, transferred to Elmira Prison, NY, August 6, 1864	Exchanged October 29, 1864 at Venus Point, Savannah River, GA.
Joyner, George W. Sergeant	Unk	January 9, 1862, Columbia, South Carolina	Co. E, 22nd South Carolina Infantry	July 30, 1864, Petersburg, Virginia	Point Lookout, Maryland, transferred to Elmira Prison, NY, August 12, 1864	Exchanged February 13, 1865 at Boulware's Wharf on the James River, Virginia

Name & Rank	Age	Enlisted	Regiment and State	Where Captured	Prison	Remarks
Joyner, J. R. Private	Unk	Unknown	Co. K, 12th North Carolina Infantry	May 12, 1864, Spotsylvania, Virginia	Point Lookout Prison Camp, Maryland. Transferred to Elmira Prison Camp, NY, August 6, 1864	Died May 7, 1865 of Chronic Diarrhea, Grave No. 2767. Headstone has Joiner.
Joyner, James H. Private	34	May 16, 1862, Fort St. Philip, Brunswick County, North Carolina	Co. G, 36th Regiment 2nd North Carolina Artillery	January 15, 1865, Fort Fisher, North Carolina	February 1, 1865 Elmira Prison Camp, New York	Exchanged February 20, 1865. Died March 20, 1865 of Unknown Disease at Pettigrew Hospital, Raleigh, NC
Joyner, John T. Private	Unk	December 19, 1862, Pitt County, North Carolina	Co. I, 3rd North Carolina Cavalry	May 16, 1864, Half-Way House, Near Drewrys Bluff, Virginia	Point Lookout, Maryland, transferred to Elmira Prison, NY, July 12, 1864	Died April 3, 1865 of Chronic Valvular Disease of Heart, Grave No. 2547. Last Name Joyner on Headstone.
Joyner, Samuel Sergeant	43	March 1, 1862, Whiteville, Columbus County, North Carolina	Co. E, 36th Regiment 2nd North Carolina Artillery	January 15, 1865, Fort Fisher, North Carolina	February 1, 1865 Elmira Prison Camp, New York	Died February 28, 1865 of Gangrene of Feet, Grave No. 2148
Joyner, Willis B. Private	40	Unknown	Co. K, 12th North Carolina Infantry	March 25, 1865, Petersburg, Virginia. Gunshot Wound of Scalp.	Old Capital Prison, Washington, DC, transferred to Elmira Prison, NY, May 2, 1865.	Oath of Allegiance June 30, 1865
Judge, John J. Sergeant	20	October 9, 1861, Enfield, Halifax County, North Carolina	Co. F, 36th Regiment, 2nd North Carolina Artillery	January 15, 1865, Fort Fisher, North Carolina	February 1, 1865 Elmira Prison Camp, New York	Exchanged March 14, 1865 at Boulware's Wharf on the James River, Virginia
Judkins, Joseph G. Private	Unk	Unknown	Co. B, Hood's Battalion, Virginia Reserve Infantry	June 15, 1864, Petersburg, Virginia	Point Lookout, Maryland, transferred to Elmira Prison, NY, July 30, 1864	Died October 11, 1864 of Chronic Diarrhea, Grave No. 693

Name & Rank	Age	Enlisted	Regiment and State	Where Captured	Prison	Remarks
Judy, Martin Private	Unk	April 15, 1862, Valley Mills, Virginia	Co. E, 25th Virginia Infantry	May 12, 1864, Spotsylvania Court House, Virginia	Point Lookout, Maryland, transferred to Elmira Prison, NY, August 12, 1864	Exchanged March 14, 1865 at Boulware's Wharf on the James River, Virginia
Judy, Ruben F. Private	Unk	June 1, 1861, Luray County, Virginia	Co. H, 33rd Virginia Infantry	July 8, 1864, Harpers Ferry, Virginia	Old Capital Prison, Washington DC. Transferred to Elmira Prison Camp, NY, July 25, 1864.	Oath of Allegiance June 21, 1865
Juit, Michael Private	Unk	Unknown	Co. B, 23rd Virginia Infantry	July 15, 1864, Leesburg, Virginia	Old Capital Prison, Washington, DC, transferred to Elmira, NY, August 12, 1864	Oath of Allegiance May 17, 1865
June, S. N. Private	17	April 12, 1862, Battery Island, South Carolina	Co. C, 25th South Carolina Infantry	January 15, 1865, Fort Fisher, North Carolina	January 30, 1865, Elmira Prison Camp, New York	Oath of Allegiance July 19, 1865
Juneau, J. J. Sergeant	Unk	May 9, 1861, Camp Walker, New Orleans, Louisiana	Co. E, 2nd Louisiana Infantry	May 12, 1864, Spotsylvania Court House, Virginia	Point Lookout, Maryland, transferred to Elmira Prison, NY, August 17, 1864	Exchanged February 25, 1865 at Boulware's or Cox Wharf on the James River, Virginia
Justice, Benjamin Private Musician	25	April 4, 1863, North Carolina	Co. E, 36th Regiment 2nd North Carolina Artillery	January 15, 1865, Fort Fisher, North Carolina	February 1, 1865 Elmira Prison Camp, New York	Oath of Allegiance May 15, 1865
Justice, Sparral Private	Unk	May 25, 1861, Floyd Court House, Virginia	Co. B, 42nd Virginia Infantry	May 12, 1864, Spotsylvania Court House, Virginia	Point Lookout, Maryland, transferred to Elmira Prison, NY, August 2, 1864	Died January 19, 1865 of Variola (Smallpox), Grave No. 1209
Justier, Abent W. Private	Unk	October 22, 1862, Murfreesboro, Tennessee	Co. H, 23rd Tennessee Infantry	June 17, 1864, Petersburg, Virginia	Point Lookout, Maryland, transferred to Elmira Prison, NY, July 30, 1864	Exchanged February 13, 1865 at Boulware's wharf on the James River, Virginia

Name & Rank	Age	Enlisted	Regiment and State	Where Captured	Prison	Remarks
Justus, J. B. Private	Unk	Unknown	Co. A, Captain Norwood's Home Guard Florida	September 27, 1864, Marianna, Florida	New Orleans, Louisiana transferred to Elmira November 19, 1864.	Exchanged February 20, 1865 at Boulware's wharf on the James River, Virginia

Name & Rank	Age	Enlisted	Regiment and State	Where Captured	Prison	Remarks
Kackley, Joseph Private	23	March 6, 1862, Berryville, Virginia	Co. F, 7th Virginia Cavalry	September 14, 1863, Near Culpepper, Virginia	Point Lookout, Maryland, transferred to Elmira Prison, NY, August 18, 1864	Exchanged March 10, 1865 at Boulware's Wharf on the James River, Virginia
Kale, Noah J. Private	26	October 1, 1862, Catawba Station, North Carolina	Co. F, 32nd North Carolina Infantry	May 10, 1864, Wilderness, Virginia	Point Lookout, Maryland, transferred to Elmira Prison, NY, August 6, 1864	Oath of Allegiance June 19, 1865
Kale, William R. Private	Unk	Unknown	Co. B, 2nd North Carolina Infantry	June 1, 1864, Norfolk County, Virginia	Point Lookout, Maryland, transferred to Elmira Prison, NY, July 25, 1864	Oath of Allegiance May 29, 1865
Kalliher, Dennis Private	30	May 28, 1861, Lynchburg, Virginia	Captain Hardwick's Company Lee's Battery, Virginia Light Artillery	July 12, 1864, Near Washington, DC	Old Capital Prison, Washington DC. Transferred to Elmira Prison Camp New York July 25, 1864.	Died December 24, 1864 of Pneumonia, Grave No. 1106
Kanady, Robert J. Private	Unk	September 17, 1861, Eastville, Alabama	Co. E, 13th Alabama Infantry	May 12, 1864, Spotsylvania Court House, Virginia	Point Lookout, Maryland, transferred to Elmira Prison, NY, August 2, 1864	Transferred for Exchange 10/11/64. Died 10/26/64 of Chronic Diarrhea at Point Lookout, MD.
Kanode, Blackford C. Private	Unk	October 8, 1862, Bunker Hill, Virginia	Co. A, 2nd Virginia Infantry	May 12, 1864, Near Spotsylvania Court House, Virginia	Point Lookout, Maryland, transferred to Elmira Prison, NY, August 6, 1864	Oath of Allegiance May 17, 1865

Name & Rank	Age	Enlisted	Regiment and State	Where Captured	Prison	Remarks
Karn, John Civilian	Unk	Louisiana	Citizen of Louisiana	August 26, 1864, Clinton, Louisiana	New Orleans, LA, Transferred to Elmira Prison, NY, November 19, 1864	Oath of Allegiance June 20, 1865
Karnes, Samuel S. Private	Unk	May 18, 1861, Lisbon, Virginia	Co. C, 42nd Virginia Infantry	May 12, 1864, Spotsylvania Court House, Virginia	Point Lookout, Maryland, transferred to Elmira Prison, NY, August 2, 1864	Oath of Allegiance June 19, 1865
Karney, John Private	30	June 10, 1862, Union City, Mississippi	Co. E, 12th Mississippi Infantry	August 21, 1864, Weldon Railroad, Virginia. Gunshot Wound Left Side Chest, Severe.	Old Capital Prison, Washington, DC, transferred to Elmira Prison, NY, December 17, 1864	Exchanged February 25, 1865 at Boulware's or Cox Wharf on the James River, Virginia
Karney, Martin V. Corporal	22	March 29, 1862, Des Arc, Arkansas	Co. F, 1st Missouri Cavalry	May 17, 1863, Big Black River, Mississippi	Point Lookout, Maryland, transferred to Elmira Prison, NY, August 18, 1864	Died December 18, 1864 of Chronic Diarrhea, Grave No. 1279. Headstone has Matthew V.
Karrer, Gutlope F. Private	Unk	March 26, 1862, Walhalla, South Carolina	Co. C, 1st South Carolina Infantry	July 14, 1863, Falling Waters, Maryland	Point Lookout, Maryland, transferred to Elmira Prison, NY, August 18, 1864	Exchanged March 10, 1865 at Boulware's Wharf on the James River, Virginia
Kascoe, J. F. Private	17	December 20, 1861, Chesterfield District, South Carolina	Co. E, 21st South Carolina Infantry	June 24, 1864, Petersburg, Virginia	Point Lookout, Maryland, transferred to Elmira Prison, NY, August 18, 1864	Exchanged March 14, 1865 at Boulware's Wharf on the James River, Virginia
Kasson, Leverett Private	Unk	June 19, 1861, New Orleans, Louisiana	Co. J, 18th Louisiana Infantry	October 9, 1864, Vermillion, Louisiana	New Orleans, Louisiana transferred to Elmira November 19, 1864.	Oath of Allegiance April 3, 1865
Kating, George P. Private	Unk	Unknown	Co. H, 1st Maryland Cavalry	December 3, 1864, Luray Valley, Loudoun County, Virginia	Old Capital Prison, Washington, DC, transferred to Elmira Prison, NY, December 17, 1864	Exchanged March 10, 1865 at Boulware's Wharf on the James River, Virginia

Name & Rank	Age	Enlisted	Regiment and State	Where Captured	Prison	Remarks
Kaufman, Stephen Private	Unk	May 20, 1861, Camp Martin, Lynchburg, Virginia	Co. J, 14th Louisiana Infantry	July 12, 1864, Near Washington, DC	Old Capital Prison, Washington, DC, transferred to Elmira Prison, NY, July 23, 1864	Oath of Allegiance May 15, 1865
Keachey, George W. Private	Unk	March 14, 1861, Skipperville, Alabama	Co. F, 1st Battalion Alabama Artillery	August 23, 1864, Fort Morgan, Alabama	Steam Press No. 4 New Orleans, Louisiana transferred to Elmira Prison, NY, October 8, 1864.	Exchanged March 14, 1865 at Boulware's Wharf on the James River, Virginia
Kean, Patrick H. Corporal	23	July 22, 1861, Camp Moore, Louisiana	Co. G, 10th Louisiana Infantry	May 12, 1864, Spotsylvania Court House, Virginia	Point Lookout, Maryland, transferred to Elmira Prison, NY, July 25, 1864	Exchanged February 25, 1865 at Boulware's or Cox Wharf on the James River, Virginia
Keane, Edward Private	18	October 5, 1861, Mobile, Alabama	Co. A, 21st Alabama Infantry	August 23, 1864, Fort Morgan, Alabama	Steam Press No. 4 New Orleans, Louisiana transferred to Elmira Prison, NY, October 8, 1864.	Died January 5, 1865 of Chronic Diarrhea, Grave No. 1238
Keane, William L. Private	Unk	March 20, 1862, Camp Gist, South Carolina	Co. B, 5th South Carolina Cavalry	June 6, 1864, Near Wilson's Landing, Bermuda Hundred, Virginia	Point Lookout, Maryland, transferred to Elmira Prison, NY, July 12, 1864	Exchanged October 29, 1864 at Venus Point, Savannah River, GA.
Kearney, John Private	Unk	January 20, 1863, Camp Gregg, Virginia	Co. D, 22nd Battalion Virginia Infantry	May 6, 1864, Wilderness, Virginia	Point Lookout, Maryland, transferred to Elmira Prison, NY, August 14, 1864	Oath of Allegiance May 15, 1865
Kearny, Henry Private	Unk	March 11, 1861, New Orleans, Louisiana	Co. A, 2nd Louisiana Infantry	December 3, 1863, Morton's Ford, Virginia	Old Capital Prison, Washington, DC, transferred to Elmira prison Camp, NY, July 12, 1864.	No Additional Information.
Keatley, James Private	21	June 6, 1862, Centerville, Virginia	Co. H, 26th Battalion, Virginia Infantry	June 3, 1864, Gaines Mill Cold Harbor, Virginia	Point Lookout, Maryland, transferred to Elmira Prison, NY, July 17, 1864	Exchanged October 29, 1864 at Venus Point, Savannah River, GA.

Name & Rank	Age	Enlisted	Regiment and State	Where Captured	Prison	Remarks
Keaton, Madison Private	Unk	May 31, 1861, Lynchburg, Virginia	Co. J, 24th Virginia Infantry	May 18, 1864, Spring Hill, Virginia	Point Lookout, Maryland, transferred to Elmira Prison, NY, July 23, 1864	Died December 20, 1864 of Chronic Diarrhea, Grave No. 1079
Kee, Ransom R. Corporal	Unk	April 28, 1862, Camp Pillow, South Carolina	Co. I, 17th South Carolina Infantry	July 30, 1864, Petersburg, Virginia	Point Lookout, Maryland, transferred to Elmira Prison, NY, August 12, 1864	Died May 28, 1865 of Pneumonia, Grave No. 2912. Name Key on Headstone.
Keefe, John Private	Unk	Unknown	Co. G, 48th Mississippi Infantry	July 30, 1864, Petersburg, Virginia	Point Lookout, Maryland, transferred to Elmira Prison, NY, August 12, 1864	Oath of Allegiance May 29, 1865
Keefe, John William Private	Unk	November 1, 1862, Winchester, Virginia	Co. D, 2nd Virginia Infantry	May 12, 1864, Near Spotsylvania Court House, Virginia	Point Lookout, Maryland, transferred to Elmira Prison, NY, August 6, 1864	Oath of Allegiance February 20, 1865. Early Release per Lincoln's Proclamation, 12/8/1863.
Keel, C. Wise S. Private	Unk	August 10, 1861, Barnwell District, South Carolina	Co. A, 1st South Carolina Infantry	July 29, 1864, Petersburg, Virginia	Point Lookout, Maryland, transferred to Elmira Prison, NY, August 12, 1864	Oath of Allegiance July 3, 1865
Keeler, Isaac N. Private	Unk	December 17, 1861, Harrisonburg, Virginia	Co. B, 10th Virginia Infantry	May 12, 1864, Spotsylvania Court House, Virginia	Point Lookout, Maryland, transferred to Elmira Prison, NY, August 2, 1864	Oath of Allegiance April 3, 1865. Early Release per Lincoln's Proclamation, 12/8/1863.
Keen, Alexander Private	Unk	May 13, 1862, Isabella, Georgia	Co. F, 59th Georgia Infantry	May 6, 1864, Wilderness, Virginia	Old Capital Prison, Washington, DC, transferred to Elmira Prison, NY, July 14, 1864	Oath of Allegiance June 19, 1865

Name & Rank	Age	Enlisted	Regiment and State	Where Captured	Prison	Remarks
Keen, Moses H. Private	38	March 8, 1862, Lake City, Florida	Co. B, 5th Florida Infantry	May 12, 1864, Spotsylvania, Virginia	Point Lookout Prison Camp, Maryland. Transferred to Elmira Prison Camp, New York July 6, 1864	Died August 19, 1864 of Chronic Diarrhea, Grave No. 117
Keener, Abraham L. Private	Unk	August 24, 1861, Clayton, Georgia	Co. A, 24th Georgia Infantry	August 16, 1864, Front Royal, Virginia	Old Capital Prison, Washington, DC transferred to Elmira Prison, NY, August 29, 1864	Oath of Allegiance, June 21, 1865
Keener, Albert Private	Unk	May 1, 1863, Fetterman, Virginia	Co. A, 25th Virginia Infantry	May 12, 1864, Spotsylvania Court House, Virginia	Point Lookout, Maryland, transferred to Elmira Prison, NY, August 2, 1864	Oath of Allegiance June 16, 1865
Keener, E. E. Private	Unk	June 21, 1863, Fetterman, Virginia	Co. A, 25th Virginia Infantry	May 12, 1864, Spotsylvania Court House, Virginia	Point Lookout, Maryland, transferred to Elmira Prison, NY, August 2, 1864	Oath of Allegiance June 16, 1865
Keener, J. M. Private	Unk	September 8, 1862, Clayton, Georgia	Co. A, 24th Georgia Infantry	August 16, 1864, Front Royal, Virginia	Old Capital Prison, Washington, DC transferred to Elmira Prison, NY, August 29, 1864	Oath of Allegiance, June 21, 1865
Keener, John Private	Unk	June 21, 1863, Fetterman, Virginia	Co. A, 25th Virginia Infantry	May 12, 1864, Spotsylvania Court House, Virginia	Point Lookout, Maryland, transferred to Elmira Prison, NY, August 12, 1864	Oath of Allegiance July 11, 1865
Keener, Marcus Private	24	September 6, 1862, Statesville, North Carolina	Co. D, 23rd North Carolina Infantry	May 12, 1864, Near Spotsylvania Court House, Virginia	Point Lookout Prison, Maryland. Transferred to Elmira Prison Camp New York August 14, 1864.	Exchanged October 29, 1864 at Venus Point, Savannah River, GA.

Name & Rank	Age	Enlisted	Regiment and State	Where Captured	Prison	Remarks
Kees, John Private	31	October 10, 1862, Camp Homes, Wilkes, County, North Carolina	Co. K, 53rd North Carolina Infantry	July 12, 1864, Near Washington, DC	Old Capital Prison, Washington DC. Transferred to Elmira Prison Camp, NY, July 25, 1864.	Oath of Allegiance May 19, 1865
Keesee, George A. F. Private	Unk	August 24, 1861, Hamer, Banks County, Georgia	Co. A, 24th Georgia Infantry	June 1, 1864, Cold Harbor, Virginia	Point Lookout, Maryland, transferred to Elmira Prison, NY, July 12, 1864	Oath of Allegiance May 29, 1865
Keeth, Griffin Private	Unk	May 6, 1862, Savannah, Georgia	Co. J, 60th Georgia Infantry	September 22, 1864, Fishers Hill, Virginia	November 11, 1864, Old Capital Prison, Washington, DC. February 4, 1865 Elmira, Prison Camp, NY	Oath of Allegiance June 14, 1865
Keeth, John N. Private	Unk	October 13, 1861, Mobile, Alabama	Co. A, 21st Alabama Infantry	August 23, 1864, Fort Morgan, Alabama	Steam Press No. 4 New Orleans, Louisiana transferred to Elmira Prison, NY, October 8, 1864.	Oath of Allegiance June 21, 1865
Keever, James Private	25	August 31, 1861, Lincolnton, North Carolina	Co. E, 34th North Carolina Infantry	May 6, 1864, Wilderness, Virginia	Point Lookout, Maryland, transferred to Elmira Prison, NY, August 14, 1864	Oath of Allegiance June 30, 1865
Keever, John L. Private	23	September 1, 1861, Camp Pickens, Manassas, Virginia	Co. A, 8th Louisiana Infantry	May 12, 1864, Spotsylvania Court House, Virginia	Point Lookout, Maryland, transferred to Elmira Prison, NY, August 2,1864	Oath of Allegiance May 13, 1865
Kehey, M. L. Private	Unk	March 8, 1862, Westville, Alabama	Co. E, 15th Alabama Infantry	May 6, 1864, Wilderness, Virginia	Point Lookout, Maryland, transferred to Elmira Prison, NY, August 17, 1864	Exchanged March 14, 1865 at Boulware's Wharf on the James River, Virginia
Keiley, Anthony M. Private	Unk	May 4, 1864, Petersburg, Virginia	Co. B, 3rd Archer's Battalion, Virginia Reserves Infantry	June 9, 1864, Petersburg, Virginia	Point Lookout, Maryland, transferred to Elmira Prison, NY, July 12, 1864	Exchanged October 29, 1864 at Venus Point, Savannah River, GA.

Name & Rank	Age	Enlisted	Regiment and State	Where Captured	Prison	Remarks
Keiningham, J. C. Private	Unk	January 15, 1863, Richmond, Virginia	Co. D, 1st Virginia Infantry	May 16, 1864, Near Drury's Bluff, Virginia	Point Lookout, Maryland, transferred to Elmira Prison, NY, August 17, 1864	Exchanged March 14, 1865 at Boulware's Wharf on the James River, Virginia
Keister, David Private	38	March 1, 1863, Salem, Virginia	Co. L, 4th Virginia Infantry	May 12, 1864, Near Spotsylvania Court House, Virginia	Point Lookout, Maryland, transferred to Elmira Prison, NY, August 6, 1864	Exchanged March 14, 1865 at Boulware's Wharf on the James River, Virginia
Keith, Duncan Private	Unk	April 24, 1863, Wilmington, North Carolina	Co. F, 10th Regiment, 1st North Carolina Artillery	January 15, 1865, Fort Fisher, North Carolina	January 30, 1865, Elmira Prison Camp, New York	Oath of Allegiance June 12, 1865
Keith, Thomas E. Private	20	July 19, 1861, Montgomery, Alabama	Co. D, 13th Alabama Infantry	May 5, 1864, Spotsylvania Court House, Virginia	Point Lookout, Maryland, transferred to Elmira Prison, NY, July 30, 1864	Exchanged March 10, 1865. Records also Indicate Prisoner Died in Transit from Point Lookout July 30, 1864 of Acute Dysentery.
Kellam, James T. Corporal	27	April 1, 1862, Windsor, North Carolina	Co. G, 32nd North Carolina Infantry	May 10, 1864, Wilderness, Virginia	Point Lookout, Maryland, transferred to Elmira Prison, NY, August 6, 1864	Oath of Allegiance April 1, 1865. Early Release per Lincoln's Proclamation, 12/8/1863.
Kellam, John A. Private	Unk	August 24, 1862, Richmond, Virginia	Co. F, 46th Virginia Infantry	June 17, 1864, Near Petersburg, Virginia	Point Lookout, Maryland, transferred to Elmira Prison, NY, July 30, 1864	Died December 1, 1864 of Pneumonia, Grave No. 894
Kellam, Nathaniel S. Private	22	May 23, 1861, Greensboro, North Carolina	Co. E, 22nd North Carolina Infantry	May 6, 1864, Wilderness, Virginia	Point Lookout, Maryland, transferred to Elmira Prison, NY, August 14, 1864	Exchanged February 13, 1865 at Boulware's wharf on the James River, Virginia
Keller, F. Thomas Private	Unk	July 4, 1862, Salisbury, North Carolina	Co. A, 57 North Carolina Infantry	July 12, 1864, Near Washington, DC	Old Capital Prison, Washington DC. Transferred to Elmira Prison Camp, NY, July 25, 1864.	Exchanged March 2, 1865 at Akins Landing on the James River, Virginia

Name & Rank	Age	Enlisted	Regiment and State	Where Captured	Prison	Remarks
Keller, J. A. Private	Unk	May 8, 1864, Columbia, South Carolina	Co. B, 7th Georgia Cavalry	June 11, 1864, Trevilian Station, Louisa Court House, Virginia	Point Lookout, Maryland, transferred to Elmira Prison, NY, July 12, 1864	Exchanged October 29, 1864 at Venus Point, Savannah River, GA.
Keller, James F. Private	Unk	December 14, 1863, Talladega, Alabama	Co. D, 13th Alabama Infantry	May 12, 1864, Spotsylvania Court House, Virginia	Point Lookout, Maryland, transferred to Elmira Prison, NY, July 30, 1864	Exchanged October 29, 1864 at Venus Point, Savannah River, GA.
Keller, Noah Private	38	November 1, 1861, Camp Argyle, Carolina City, North Carolina	Co. A, 7th North Carolina Infantry	May 6, 1864, Wilderness, Virginia	Point Lookout, Maryland, transferred to Elmira Prison, NY, August 14, 1864	Died February 12, 1865 of Variola (Smallpox), Grave No. 2075
Kelley, Alexander Private	40	March 15, 1864, Macon, Georgia	Co. A, 14th Georgia Infantry	May 6, 1864, Wilderness, Virginia	Point Lookout, Maryland, transferred to Elmira Prison, NY, August 14, 1864	Exchanged 2/13/65. Died 4/9/65 of Chronic Diarrhea at US Army Hospital Baltimore, MD.
Kelley, Enoch Sergeant	Unk	May 31, 1862, Philippi, Virginia	Co. A, 25th Virginia Infantry	May 12, 1864, Spotsylvania Court House, Virginia	Point Lookout, Maryland, transferred to Elmira Prison, NY, August 2, 1864	Died October 25, 1864 of Chronic Diarrhea, Grave No. 710
Kelley, James Private	Unk	Unknown	Co. A, 21st Virginia Cavalry	July 14, 1864, Ellicott's Mills, Virginia	Old Capital Prison, Washington DC. Transferred to Elmira Prison Camp, NY, July 25, 1864.	Oath of Allegiance May 29, 1865
Kelley, James M. Private	Unk	August 13, 1861, Camp Moore, Louisiana	Co. K, 12th Louisiana Infantry	May 16, 1863, Baker's Creek, Champion Hill, Mississippi	Point Lookout, Maryland, transferred to Elmira Prison, NY, August 18, 1864	Exchanged February 25, 1865 at Boulware's wharf on the James River, Virginia
Kelley, John C. Private	Unk	May 1, 1862, Anderson, South Carolina	Co. H, 25th South Carolina Infantry	January 15, 1865, Fort Fisher, North Carolina	January 30, 1865, Elmira Prison Camp, New York	Died February 28, 1865 of Variola (Smallpox), Grave No. 2112

Name & Rank	Age	Enlisted	Regiment and State	Where Captured	Prison	Remarks
Kelley, John H. Corporal	24	July 1, 1861, Pittsylvania, Virginia	Co. H, 21st Virginia Infantry	May 12, 1864, Spotsylvania, Virginia. Gunshot Wound Right Leg and Arm.	Old Capital Prison, Washington, DC, transferred to Elmira Prison, NY, December 17, 1864	Exchanged February 25, 1865 at Boulware's or Cox Wharf on the James River, Virginia
Kelley, Joseph H. Private	Unk	April 18, 1861, Harrisonburg, Virginia	Co. B, 10th Virginia Infantry	May 12, 1864, Spotsylvania Court House, Virginia	Point Lookout, Maryland, transferred to Elmira Prison, NY, August 2, 1864	Oath of Allegiance June 16, 1865
Kelley, Thomas D. Private	Unk	August 24, 1861, Habersham County, Georgia	Co. A, 24th Georgia Infantry	August 16, 1864, Front Royal, Virginia	Old Capital Prison, Washington, DC transferred to Elmira Prison, NY, August 29, 1864	Died January 5, 1865 of Variola (Smallpox), Grave No. 1258. Headstone has Keeler.
Kelley, William D. Private	Unk	September 4, 1862, Highland, Louisiana	Co. D, 62nd Mounted Virginia Infantry	July 16, 1864, Near Harpers Ferry, Loudoun County, Virginia	Old Capital Prison, Washington DC. Transferred to Elmira Prison Camp, NY, July 25, 1864.	Exchanged March 14, 1865 at Boulware's Wharf on the James River, Virginia
Kellum, Reddin Private	19	May 6, 1861, Jacksonville, North Carolina	Co. B, 24th North Carolina Infantry	June 17, 1864, Petersburg, Virginia	Point Lookout, Maryland, transferred to Elmira Prison, NY, July 30, 1864	Died November 24, 1864 of Chronic Diarrhea, Grave No. 921
Kelly, George Frank Private	Unk	May 13, 1861, Aldie, Virginia	Co. D, 8th Virginia Infantry	October 5, 1863, Aldie, Loudoun County, Virginia.	Point Lookout, Maryland, transferred to Elmira Prison, NY, July 23, 1864	Oath of Allegiance May 13, 1865
Kelly, Henry Private	Unk	Unknown	Co. G, 21st South Carolina Infantry	January 15, 1865, Fort Fisher, North Carolina	January 30, 1965 Elmira Prison Camp, New York	Oath of Allegiance June 14, 1865
Kelly, J. M. Private	24	May 28, 1862, Charleston, South Carolina	Co. A, 25th South Carolina Infantry	January 15, 1865, Fort Fisher, North Carolina	January 30, 1865, Elmira Prison Camp, New York	Died February 13, 1865 of Pneumonia, Grave No. 2067

Name & Rank	Age	Enlisted	Regiment and State	Where Captured	Prison	Remarks
Kelly, James A. Sergeant	18	December 23, 1861, Darlington District, South Carolina	Co. B, 21st South Carolina Infantry	January 15, 1865, Fort Fisher, North Carolina	January 30, 1965 Elmira Prison Camp, New York	Died February 6, 1865 of Pneumonia, Grave No. 1912. Headstone has Kelley.
Kelly, James B. Private	Unk	February 18, 1864, Montgomery, Alabama	Co. A, 1st Battalion Alabama Artillery	August 23, 1864, Fort Morgan, Alabama	New Orleans, Louisiana transferred to Elmira Prison, NY, December 4, 1864.	Oath of Allegiance July 7, 1865
Kelly, James L. B. Private	21	January 10, 1862, Camp Hampton, Columbia, South Carolina	Co. J, 18th South Carolina Infantry	June 16, 1864, Petersburg, Virginia	Point Lookout, Maryland, transferred to Elmira Prison, NY, July 25, 1864	Oath of Allegiance May 15, 1865
Kelly, John Private	Unk	April 28, 1861, New Orleans, Louisiana	Co. D, 1st Louisiana Infantry	May 5, 1864, Wilderness, Virginia	Point Lookout, Maryland, transferred to Elmira Prison, NY, August 17, 1864	Exchanged February 25, 1865 at Boulware's or Cox Wharf on the James River, Virginia
Kelly, John B. Private	Unk	May 11, 1861, Gadsen, Alabama	Co. A, 1st Alabama Artillery	August 23, 1864, Fort Morgan, Alabama	New Orleans, Louisiana transferred to Elmira Prison, NY, December 4, 1864.	Oath of Allegiance May 29, 1865
Kelly, Patrick Private	19	June 4, 1861, Camp Moore, Louisiana	Co. H, 6th Louisiana Infantry	November 9, 1863, Rappahannock Station, Virginia	Point Lookout, Maryland, transferred to Elmira Prison, NY, July 12, 1864	Exchanged October 29, 1864 at Venus Point, Savannah River, GA.
Kelly, Simon Private	Unk	March 15, 1864, Darlington District, South Carolina	Co. G, 21st South Carolina Infantry	January 15, 1865, Fort Fisher, North Carolina	January 30, 1965 Elmira Prison Camp, New York	Died February 16, 1865 of Pneumonia, Grave No. 2202
Kelly, Thomas Private	Unk	January 20, 1862, Darlington District, South Carolina	Co. G, 21st South Carolina Infantry	January 15, 1865, Fort Fisher, North Carolina	January 30, 1965 Elmira Prison Camp, New York	Oath of Allegiance July 3, 1865

Name & Rank	Age	Enlisted	Regiment and State	Where Captured	Prison	Remarks
Kelly, William Private	23	May 1, 1861, Norfolk, Virginia	Co. D, 6th Virginia Infantry	July 5, 1864, Petersburg, Virginia	Old Capital Prison, Washington DC. Transferred to Elmira Prison Camp, NY, July 25, 1864.	Oath of Allegiance May 19, 1865
Kelly, William P. Sergeant	Unk	October 1, 1861, Macon, Georgia	Co. J, 61st Georgia Infantry	May 12, 1864, Spotsylvania, Virginia	Point Lookout, Maryland, transferred to Elmira Prison, NY, July 23, 1864	Oath of Allegiance May 13, 1865
Kelly, William P. Private	16	April 15, 1862, Camp McIntosh, Goldsboro, North Carolina	Co. C, 1st North Carolina Infantry	May 12, 1864, Near Spotsylvania Court House, Virginia	Point Lookout Prison, Maryland. Transferred to Elmira Prison Camp New York August 6, 1864.	Exchanged March 14, 1865 at Boulware's Wharf on the James River, Virginia
Kelton, Joseph Seaman	Unk	Unknown	Confederate States Navy	July 1, 1864, Deserted on James River, Virginia	Point Lookout, Maryland, transferred to Elmira Prison, NY, July 25, 1864	Oath of Allegiance November 3, 1864. Early Release per Lincoln's Proclamation, 12/8/1863.
Kemp, Edward H. Private	Unk	January 15, 1864, Selma, Alabama	Co. E, 1st Battalion Alabama Artillery	August 23, 1864, Fort Morgan, Alabama	Steam Press No. 4, New Orleans, Louisiana transferred to Elmira Prison, NY, October 8, 1864.	Died March 17, 1865 of Diarrhea, Grave No. 1697
Kemp, Francis M. Private	23	May 10, 1861, Jackson County, Florida	Co. F, 2nd Florida Infantry	May 12, 1864, Spotsylvania Court House, Virginia	Point Lookout, Maryland, transferred to Elmira Prison, NY, August 12, 1864	Exchanged February 20, 1865 at Boulware's or Cox Wharf on the James River, Virginia
Kemp, Joseph R. Corporal	18	May 10, 1861, Bladen County, North Carolina	Co. B, 3rd North Carolina Infantry	May 12, 1864, Near Spotsylvania Court House, Virginia	Point Lookout, Maryland, transferred to Elmira Prison, NY, August 14, 1864	Died February 15, 1865 of Variola (Smallpox), Grave No. 2177. Name J. A. Kamp on Headstone.

Name & Rank	Age	Enlisted	Regiment and State	Where Captured	Prison	Remarks
Kemp, Lewis M. Private	25	April 20, 1861, Belle Roi, Gloucester, Virginia	Co. A, 26th Virginia Infantry	June 15, 1864, Near Petersburg, Virginia	Point Lookout, Maryland, transferred to Elmira Prison, NY, July 12, 1864	Exchanged March 2, 1865 at Akins Landing on the James River, Virginia
Kemp, M. P. Private	Unk	November 21, 1861, Mobile, Alabama	Co. F, 1st Battalion Alabama Artillery	August 23, 1864, Fort Morgan, Alabama	Steam Press No. 4 New Orleans, Louisiana transferred to Elmira Prison, NY, October 8, 1864.	Oath of Allegiance June 21, 1865
Kemp, William M. Private	Unk	April 28, 1862, Marietta, Georgia	Co. M, Phillips Legion, Georgia	July 29, 1864, Petersburg, Virginia	Point Lookout, Maryland, transferred to Elmira Prison, NY, August 12, 1864	Died February 26, 1865 of Pneumonia, Grave No. 2163
Kemp, Wyatt H. Private	Unk	May 30, 1862, Charleston, South Carolina	Co. C, 22nd South Carolina Infantry	July 30, 1864, Petersburg, Virginia	Point Lookout, Maryland, transferred to Elmira Prison, NY, August 12, 1864	Died September 8, 1864 of Acute Diarrhea, Grave No. 211
Kemp, Wyndham Peter Private	21	April 20, 1861, Belle Roi., Virginia	Co. A, 26th Virginia Infantry	June 15, 1864, Near Petersburg, Virginia	Point Lookout, Maryland, transferred to Elmira Prison, NY, July 12, 1864	Exchanged October 29, 1864 at Venus Point, Savannah River, GA.
Kendall, Larkin L. Private	Unk	April 24, 1862, Elksville, Wilkes County, North Carolina	Co. K, 42nd North Carolina Infantry	June 3, 1864, Gaines Farm Cold Harbor, Virginia	Point Lookout, Maryland, transferred to Elmira Prison, NY, July 12, 1864	Oath of Allegiance May 19, 1865
Kendall, Samuel M. Private	Unk	September 23, 1863, Kinston, North Carolina	Co. K, 42nd North Carolina Infantry	June 3, 1864, Gaines Farm Cold Harbor, Virginia	Point Lookout, Maryland, transferred to Elmira Prison, NY, July 12, 1864	Died December 13, 1864 of Pneumonia, Grave No. 1131
Kendrick, William P. Private	Unk	February 18, 1864, Henry County, Virginia	Co. H, 42nd Virginia Infantry	May 12, 1864, Near Spotsylvania Court House, Virginia	Point Lookout, Maryland, transferred to Elmira Prison, NY, August 6, 1864	Died February 1, 1865 of Chronic Diarrhea, Grave No. 1770

Name & Rank	Age	Enlisted	Regiment and State	Where Captured	Prison	Remarks
Kenedy, Thomas J. Private	Unk	February 20, 1862, Atlanta, Georgia	Co. F, 8th Georgia Infantry	May 6, 1864, Wilderness, Virginia	Point Lookout, Maryland, transferred to Elmira Prison, NY, August 14, 1864	Died March 2, 1865 of Pneumonia, Grave No. 2021
Kenneday, Emanuel Private	25	March 10, 1862, Greensboro, North Carolina	Co. B, 45th North Carolina Infantry	May 24, 1864, Hanover Junction, Virginia	Point Lookout, Maryland, transferred to Elmira Prison, NY, July 23, 1864	Oath of Allegiance May 29, 1865
Kennedy, A. J. Private	Unk	February 12, 1863, Abingdon, Virginia	Co. D, 26th Battalion Virginia Infantry	June 3, 1864, Gaines Farm Cold Harbor, Virginia	Point Lookout, Maryland, transferred to Elmira Prison, NY, July 12, 1864	Died March 6, 1865 of Phthisis, Grave No. 2394
Kennedy, James Private	Unk	July 22, 1861, Camp Moore, Louisiana	Co. K, 10th Louisiana Infantry	May 12, 1864, Spotsylvania Court House, Virginia	Point Lookout, Maryland, transferred to Elmira Prison, NY, July 25, 1864	Oath of Allegiance May 14, 1865
Kennedy, John Private	Unk	Unknown	Co. A, 21st Alabama Infantry	August 23, 1864, Fort Morgan, Alabama	Steam Press No. 4 New Orleans, Louisiana transferred to Elmira Prison, NY, October 8, 1864.	Oath of Allegiance June 30, 1865
Kennedy, John Private	33	June 7, 1861, Camp Moore, Tangipahoa Parish, Louisiana	Co. F, 7th Louisiana Infantry	July 8, 1864, Harper's Ferry, Virginia	Old Capital Prison, Washington, DC, transferred to Elmira Prison, NY, August 12, 1864	Exchanged February 25, 1865 at Boulware's or Cox Wharf on the James River, Virginia
Kennedy, John Private	Unk	Unknown	Co. B, 24th North Carolina Infantry	June 17, 1864, Petersburg, Virginia	Point Lookout, Maryland, transferred to Elmira Prison, NY, July 30, 1864	Exchanged February 20, 1865 at Boulware's or Cox Wharf on the James River, Virginia
Kennedy, Levi B. Private	Unk	April 15, 1864, Camp Holmes, North Carolina	Co. F, 10th Regiment, 1st North Carolina Artillery	January 15, 1865, Fort Fisher, North Carolina	January 30, 1865, Elmira Prison Camp, New York	Died February 6, 1865 of Chronic Diarrhea, Grave No. 1893

Name & Rank	Age	Enlisted	Regiment and State	Where Captured	Prison	Remarks
Kennedy, Lorenzo P. Private	Unk	July 24, 1861, Clarksville, Georgia	Co. E, 16th Georgia Infantry	June 1, 1864, Cold Harbor, Virginia	Point Lookout, Maryland, transferred to Elmira Prison, NY, July 12, 1864	Died February 2, 1865 of Phthisis Pulmonalis, Grave No. 1774
Kennedy, Philip Private	Unk	April 30, 1861, New Orleans, Louisiana	Co. H, 5th Louisiana Infantry	May 5, 1864, Wilderness, Virginia	Point Lookout, Maryland, transferred to Elmira Prison, NY, August 17, 1864	Oath of Allegiance May 13, 1865
Kennedy, William Private	22	May 16, 1861, Columbia, North Carolina	Co. F, 32nd North Carolina Infantry	May 10, 1864, Near Spotsylvania Court House, Virginia	Point Lookout, Maryland, transferred to Elmira Prison, NY, August 6, 1864	Died April 12, 1865 of Chronic Diarrhea, Grave No. 2689
Kennedy, William J. Private	39	March 15, 1863, Fort Fisher, North Carolina	Co. C, 36th Regiment North Carolina Artillery	January 15, 1865, Fort Fisher, North Carolina	February 1, 1865, Elmira Prison Camp, New York	Oath of Allegiance June 12, 1865
Kennemore, Jacob Private	Unk	Unknown	Co. D, 18th South Carolina Infantry	July 30, 1864, Petersburg, Virginia	Point Lookout, Maryland, transferred to Elmira Prison, NY, August 12, 1864	Exchanged October 29, 1864 at Venus Point, Savannah River, GA.
Kennemore, Moses Private	Unk	February 12, 1863, Camp Pickens, South Carolina	Co. D, 18th South Carolina Infantry	July 30, 1864, Petersburg, Virginia	Point Lookout, Maryland, transferred to Elmira Prison, NY, August 12, 1864	Died September 29, 1864 of Chronic Diarrhea, Grave No. 434. Name Kinemore on Headstone.
Kennerly, J. C. Private	Unk	Unknown	6th Field Battery Louisiana Light Artillery	October 3, 1864, Atchafalaya, Louisiana	New Orleans, Louisiana transferred to Elmira November 19, 1864.	Exchanged February 13, 1865 at Boulware's Wharf on the James River, Virginia
Kennett, James M. Private	Unk	May 25, 1862, Floyd Court House, Virginia	Co. B, 42nd Virginia Infantry	May 12, 1864, Spotsylvania Court House, Virginia	Point Lookout, Maryland, transferred to Elmira Prison, NY, August 2, 1864	Exchanged March 14, 1865 at Boulware's Wharf on the James River, Virginia

Name & Rank	Age	Enlisted	Regiment and State	Where Captured	Prison	Remarks
Kenny, Edward Sergeant	Unk	July 20, 1861, Richmond, Virginia	Co. F, 59th Virginia Infantry	June 17, 1864, Petersburg, Virginia	Point Lookout, Maryland, transferred to Elmira Prison, NY, July 30, 1864	Oath of Allegiance May 29, 1865
Kenny, George W. Private	Unk	June 2, 1861, Corinth, Alabama	Co. G, 6th Alabama Infantry	May 5, 1864, Wilderness, Virginia	Point Lookout, Maryland, transferred to Elmira Prison, NY, August 17, 1864	Oath of Allegiance June 19, 1865
Kent, Charles E. Private	Unk	Unknown	Co. F, 50th Virginia Infantry	May 12, 1864, Spotsylvania Court House, Virginia	Point Lookout, Maryland, transferred to Elmira Prison, NY, August 2, 1864	Exchanged October 29, 1864 at Venus Point, Savannah River, GA.
Kent, George W. Private	20	March 1, 1862, Union, Virginia	Co. H, 1st Virginia Cavalry	July 18, 1863, Snickers Gap, Virginia	Point Lookout, Maryland, transferred to Elmira Prison, NY, August 18, 1864	Exchanged February 20, 1865 at Boulware's or Cox Wharf on the James River, Virginia
Kent, Newton C. Private	Unk	August 14, 1861, Graysport, Mississippi	Co. D, 48th Mississippi Infantry	July 10, 1864, Petersburg, Virginia	Prison, Washington DC. Transferred to Elmira Prison Camp New York July 25, 1864.	Oath of Allegiance June 16, 1865
Kent, Randolph Private	Unk	November 16, 1862, Greenville, Alabama	Co. H, 59th Alabama Infantry	May 16, 1864, Drury's Bluff, Virginia	Point Lookout, Maryland, transferred to Elmira Prison, NY, July 25, 1864	Exchanged March 14, 1865 at Boulware's Wharf on the James River, Virginia
Kent, Richard Private	Unk	Unknown	Co. B, Robertson's Squadron Texas Cavalry	August 5, 1864, Near Cross Bayou, Louisiana	New Orleans, LA, Transferred to Elmira Prison, NY, November 19, 1864	Died February 4, 1865 of Variola (Smallpox), Grave No. 1739
Kephart, Jasper C. Private	Unk	March 28, 1864, Brownsburg, Virginia	Co. A, 35th Battalion Virginia Cavalry	July 29, 1864, Leesburg, Virginia	Old Capital Prison, Washington, DC, transferred to Elmira Prison, NY, August 12, 1864	Oath of Allegiance June 14, 1865

Name & Rank	Age	Enlisted	Regiment and State	Where Captured	Prison	Remarks
Keplingher, J. F. Private	Unk	August 1, 1864, Shepherd, Virginia	Co. F, 1st Virginia Cavalry	August 22, 1864, Sharpsburg, Virginia	Old Capital Prison, Washington, DC transferred to Elmira Prison, NY, August 29, 1864	Oath of Allegiance, June 21, 1865
Keply, Jacob N. Private	30	July 5, 1862, Salisbury, North Carolina	Co. K, 57 North Carolina Infantry	July 10, 1864, Harpers Ferry, Virginia	Old Capital Prison, Washington DC. Transferred to Elmira Prison Camp, NY, July 25, 1864.	Transferred for Exchanged 10/29/64 at Venus Point, Savannah River, GA.
Kerfoot, Jackson A. Private	27	April 25, 1861, Harper's Ferry, Virginia	Co. C, 2nd Virginia Infantry	May 12, 1864, Near Spotsylvania Court House, Virginia	Point Lookout, Maryland, transferred to Elmira Prison, NY, August 6, 1864	Oath of Allegiance June 16, 1865
Kerley, Elisha Private	29	October 18, 1863, Camp Holmes, North Carolina	Co. F, 32nd North Carolina Infantry	May 10, 1864, Wilderness, Virginia	Point Lookout, Maryland, transferred to Elmira Prison, NY, August 6, 1864	Transferred for Exchange 10/11/64. Died 10/22/64 of Unknown Disease at Point Lookout, MD
Kernaghan, William G. Private	Unk	August 16, 1861, Hamburg, Edgefield District, South Carolina	Co. A, 1st South Carolina Infantry	May 24, 1864, North Anna, Virginia	Point Lookout, Maryland, transferred to Elmira Prison, NY, August 17, 1864	Exchanged February 13, 1865 at Boulware's Wharf on the James River, Virginia
Kernegay, James H. Private	23	October 1, 1863, Raleigh, North Carolina	Co. B, 52nd North Carolina Infantry	July 14, 1863, Falling Waters, Maryland	Point Lookout, Maryland, transferred to Elmira Prison, NY, August 18, 1864	Exchanged March 10, 1865 at Boulware's Wharf on the James River, Virginia
Kernick, Benjamin F. Private	26	July 1, 1861, Markham, Virginia	Co. A, 38th Battalion Virginia Light Artillery	September 1, 1863, Mathias Point, Front Royal, Virginia	Point Lookout, Maryland, transferred to Elmira Prison, NY, August 18, 1864	Exchanged March 10, 1865 at Boulware's Wharf on the James River, Virginia
Kerr, Columbus Private	21	June 7, 1861, Statesville, North Carolina	Co. C, 4th North Carolina Infantry	May 30, 1864 Mechanics-ville, Virginia	Point Lookout, Maryland, transferred to Elmira Prison, NY, July 11, 1864	Oath of Allegiance May 19, 1865

Name & Rank	Age	Enlisted	Regiment and State	Where Captured	Prison	Remarks
Kerr, John C. Private	Unk	Unknown	Co. H, 26th North Carolina Infantry	July 14, 1864, Near Washington, DC	Old Capital Prison, Washington DC. Transferred to Elmira Prison Camp, NY, July 25, 1864.	Exchanged March 2, 1865 at Akins Landing on the James River, Virginia
Kerr, Milton Private	45	March 1, 1862, Piney Woods, North Carolina	Co. A, 51st North Carolina Infantry	June 1, 1864, Gaines Mill Cold Harbor, Virginia	Point Lookout, Maryland, transferred to Elmira Prison, NY, July 12, 1864	Died February 13, 1865 of Chronic Diarrhea, Grave No. 2036
Kerr, William D. Sergeant	23	May 2, 1862, Camp Morgan, North Carolina	Co. A, 51st North Carolina Infantry	June 1, 1864, Gaines Mill, Virginia	Point Lookout, Maryland, transferred to Elmira Prison, NY, July 12, 1864	Exchanged 3/2/65. Died 3/17/65 of Debility at Jackson Hospital, Richmond, VA.
Kerr, William J. Private	Unk	January 14, 1862, Camp Hampton, South Carolina	Co. D, 17th South Carolina Infantry	July 30, 1864, Petersburg, Virginia	Point Lookout, Maryland, transferred to Elmira Prison, NY, August 12, 1864	Oath of Allegiance June 19, 1865
Kersey, Stephen Private	40	March 6, 1862, Greensboro, North Carolina	Co. B, 45th North Carolina Infantry	June 11, 1864, Orange County, Virginia	Old Capital Prison, Washington DC. Transferred to Elmira Prison Camp, NY, July 25, 1864.	Exchanged March 14, 1865 at Boulware's Wharf on the James River, Virginia
Kesler, W. A. Private	19	July 22, 1861, Salisbury, North Carolina	Co. K, 8th North Carolina Infantry	June 1, 1864, Gaines Farm Cold Harbor, Virginia	Point Lookout, Maryland, transferred to Elmira Prison, NY, July 12, 1864	Oath of Allegiance September 11, 1865
Kesner, John Private	Unk	Unknown	Co. K, 48th Virginia Infantry	May 12, 1864, Spotsylvania Court House, Virginia	Point Lookout, Maryland, transferred to Elmira Prison, NY, August 2, 1864	Died February 14, 1865 of Chronic Diarrhea, Grave No. 2054, Name Kuesner 40th VA on Headstone.

Name & Rank	Age	Enlisted	Regiment and State	Where Captured	Prison	Remarks
Ketcham, James P. Sergeant	28	July 1, 1861, Jacksonville, Onslow County, North Carolina	Co. G, 3rd North Carolina Infantry	May 12, 1864, Near Spotsylvania Court House, Virginia	Point Lookout Prison, Maryland. Transferred to Elmira Prison Camp New York August 14, 1864.	Exchanged October 29, 1864 at Venus Point, Savannah River, GA.
Ketchey, David A. Private	27	September 6, 1862, Camp Hill, North Carolina	Co. C, 18th North Carolina Infantry	May 12, 1864, Spotsylvania Court House, Virginia	Point Lookout, Maryland, transferred to Elmira Prison, NY, August 6, 1864	Oath of Allegiance June 27, 1865
Ketchie, M. M. Private	Unk	February 15, 1864, Concord, North Carolina	Co. H, 8th North Carolina Infantry	May 31, 1864, Old Church Cold Harbor, Virginia	Point Lookout, Maryland, transferred to Elmira Prison, NY, July 12, 1864	Oath of Allegiance June 12, 1865
Ketham, James P. Sergeant	28	July 1, 1861, Jacksonville, Onslow County, North Carolina	Co. G, 3rd North Carolina Infantry	May 12, 1864, Near Spotsylvania Court House, Virginia	Point Lookout, Maryland, transferred to Elmira Prison, NY, August 14, 1864	Exchanged October 29, 1864 at Venus Point, Savannah River, GA.
Ketner, John P. Private	26	March 19, 1862, Concorde, North Carolina	Co. A, 52nd North Carolina Infantry	May 12, 1864, Spotsylvania Court House, Virginia	Point Lookout, Maryland, transferred to Elmira Prison, NY, July 30, 1864	Died September 20, 1864 of Chronic Diarrhea and Scurvy, Grave No. 327
Kevan, Alexander Thomas Corporal	Unk	April 20, 1861, Belle Roi., Virginia	Co. G, 26th Virginia Infantry	June 15, 1864, Near Petersburg, Virginia	Point Lookout, Maryland, transferred to Elmira Prison, NY, July 12, 1864	Oath of Allegiance June 14, 1865
Kevan, John R. Private	18	April 20, 1861, Belle Roi., Virginia	Co. G, 26th Virginia Infantry	June 15, 1864, Near Petersburg, Virginia	Point Lookout, Maryland, transferred to Elmira Prison, NY, July 12, 1864	Oath of Allegiance June 14, 1865
Key, David Private	28	August 16, 1861, Camp Butler, South Carolina	Co. K, 14th South Carolina Infantry	July 29, 1864, Petersburg, Virginia	Point Lookout, Maryland, transferred to Elmira Prison, NY, August 12, 1864	Died April 1, 1865 of Pneumonia, Grave No. 2596

Name & Rank	Age	Enlisted	Regiment and State	Where Captured	Prison	Remarks
Key, John W. Private	20	August 28, 1861, Memphis, Tennessee	Co. B, Woods Regiment, C. S. A.	May 16, 1862, Champion Hill, Mississippi	Point Lookout, Maryland, transferred to Elmira Prison, NY, August 18, 1864	Exchanged March 10, 1865 at Boulware's wharf on the James River, Virginia
Key, Peter S. Private		August 12, 1862, Staunton, Virginia	Co. H, 34th Virginia Infantry	June 15, 1864, Near Petersburg, Virginia	Point Lookout, Maryland, transferred to Elmira Prison, NY, July 12, 1864	Died October 19, 1864 of Chronic Diarrhea, Grave No. 528
Keys, Isaac Private	Unk	September 30, 1863, Lewisburg, Virginia	Co. A, 26th Battalion, Virginia Infantry	May 31, 1864, Chickahominy, Cold Harbor, Virginia	Point Lookout, Maryland, transferred to Elmira Prison, NY, July 11, 1864	Died September 28, 1864 of Anasarca or Edema, Grave No. 430
Keys, James Private	Unk	February 16, 1863, Monroe, Virginia	Co. A, 26th Battalion, Virginia Infantry	June 3, 1864, Gaines Mill Cold Harbor, Virginia	Point Lookout, Maryland, transferred to Elmira Prison, NY, July 17, 1864	Exchanged October 29, 1864 at Venus Point, Savannah River, GA.
Keyser, Marshall D. Private	Unk	April 9, 1862, Shenandoah, Virginia	Co. K, 52nd Virginia Infantry	May 22, 1864, Hanover Junction, Virginia	Point Lookout, Maryland, transferred to Elmira Prison, NY, July 25, 1864	Exchanged October 29, 1864 at Venus Point, Savannah River, GA.
Kibler, Hiram C. Private	Unk	March 12, 1862, Luray, Virginia	Co. K, 10th Virginia Infantry	May 12, 1864, Spotsylvania Court House, Virginia	Point Lookout, Maryland, transferred to Elmira Prison, NY, August 2, 1864	Oath of Allegiance June 27, 1865
Kibler, Rueben A. Private	Unk	June 2, 1862, Luray, Virginia	Co. K, 10th Virginia Infantry	May 12, 1864, Spotsylvania Court House, Virginia	Point Lookout, Maryland, transferred to Elmira Prison, NY, August 2, 1864	Oath of Allegiance June 27, 1865
Kicklighter, James Private	Unk	October 9, 1863, Bryan County, Georgia	Co. H, 7th Georgia Cavalry	June 11, 1864, Trevilian Station, Louisa Court House, Virginia	Point Lookout, Maryland, transferred to Elmira Prison, NY, July 25, 1864	Exchanged February 13, 1865 at Boulware's wharf on the James River, Virginia

Name & Rank	Age	Enlisted	Regiment and State	Where Captured	Prison	Remarks
Kidd, Demarquis L. Private	Unk	Unknown	Co. C, 48th Virginia Infantry	May 5, 1864, Wilderness, Virginia	Point Lookout, Maryland, transferred to Elmira Prison, NY, August 12, 1864	Oath of Allegiance July 11, 1865
Kidd, F. C. Private	37	June 1, 1862, Sausalito, Tennessee	Co. A, Jackson's 1st Regiment, Tennessee Heavy Artillery	August 23, 1864, Fort Morgan, Alabama	New Orleans, Louisiana transferred to Elmira Prison, NY, December 4, 1864.	Exchanged February 25, 1865 at Boulware's or Cox Wharf on the James River, Virginia
Kidd, Fields A. Private	Unk	June 11, 1861, Bledsoe's, Fluvanna County, Virginia	Co. K, 44th Virginia Infantry	September 13, 1864, Fluvanna County, Virginia	Point Lookout Prison Camp, Maryland. Transferred to Elmira Prison Camp, New York August 2, 1864	Died September 13, 1864 of Chronic Diarrhea, Grave No. 271
Kidd, James M. Private	Unk	April 23, 1862, Fairburn, Campbell County, Georgia	Co. C, 35th Georgia Infantry	May 5, 1864, Wilderness, Virginia	Point Lookout, Maryland, transferred to Elmira Prison, NY, August 17, 1864	Died April 20, 1865 of Chronic Diarrhea, Grave No. 1381
Kidd, Lorenzo D. Private	23	May 1, 1861, Massey's Mill, Nelson County, Virginia	Co. G, 19th Virginia Infantry	March 31, 1865, Petersburg, Virginia. Gunshot Wound Right Leg.	Old Capital Prison, Washington, DC, transferred to Elmira Prison, NY, May 2, 1865.	Oath of Allegiance July 7, 1865
Kidd, Samuel G. Private	Unk	June 11, 1861, Bledsoe's Store, Virginia	Co. K, 44th Virginia Infantry	May 12, 1864, Spotsylvania Court House, Virginia	Point Lookout, Maryland, transferred to Elmira Prison, NY, August 2, 1864	Exchanged October 29, 1864 at Venus Point, Savannah River, GA.
Kidd, W. L. Private	Unk	August 19, 1861, Bethel, Tennessee	Co. A, Jackson's 1st Regiment, Tennessee Heavy Artillery	August 23, 1864, Fort Morgan, Alabama	New Orleans, Louisiana transferred to Elmira Prison, NY, December 4, 1864.	Exchanged March 10, 1865 at Boulware's Wharf on the James River, Virginia
Kidd, William Private	Unk	April 15, 1862, Buena Vista, Georgia	Co. K, 12th Georgia Infantry	May 10, 1864, Spotsylvania Court House, Virginia	Point Lookout, Maryland, transferred to Elmira Prison, NY, July 25, 1864	Oath of Allegiance June 19, 1865

Name & Rank	Age	Enlisted	Regiment and State	Where Captured	Prison	Remarks
Kies, Jacob Private	Unk	Unknown	Co. B, 1st Jackson's Tennessee Heavy Artillery	August 23, 1864, Fort Morgan, Alabama.	New Orleans, Louisiana transferred to Elmira Prison, NY, December 4, 1864.	Exchanged February 25, 1865 at Boulware's or Cox Wharf on the James River, Virginia
Kiker, William M. Private	22	May 15, 1862, Camp Davis, North Carolina	Co. K, 43rd North Carolina Infantry	May 25, 1864, Hanover Junction, Virginia	Point Lookout, Maryland, transferred to Elmira Prison, NY, July 11, 1864	Exchanged March 14, 1865 at Boulware's Wharf on the James River, Virginia
Kilby, William Private	34	October 20, 1863, Camp Holmes, Wilkesboro, North Carolina	Co. F, 37th North Carolina Infantry	July 29, 1864, Near Darby Town, Petersburg Virginia	Point Lookout, Maryland, transferred to Elmira Prison, NY, August 12, 1864	Died May 3, 1865 of General Debility, Grave No. 2749
Kilby, William A. Landsman	Unk	Unknown	Confederate States Navy	May 5, 1864, Albemarle Sound on Steamer CSS Bombshell	Point Lookout, Maryland, transferred to Elmira Prison, NY, August 17, 1864	Oath of Allegiance June 16, 1865
Kilcrease, Abram Private	Unk	October 10, 1863, Jacksonboro, South Carolina	Co. B, 6th South Carolina Cavalry	June 11, 1864, Trevilian Station, Louisa Court House, Virginia	Point Lookout, Maryland, transferred to Elmira Prison, NY, July 25, 1864	Exchanged February 13, 1865 at Boulware's wharf on the James River, Virginia
Kile, John R. Sergeant	Unk	May 18, 1861, Franklin, Virginia	Co. K, 25th Virginia Infantry	May 12, 1864, Spotsylvania Court House, Virginia	Point Lookout, Maryland, transferred to Elmira Prison, NY, August 12, 1864	Exchanged February 20, 1865 at Boulware's or Cox Wharf on the James River, Virginia
Kilgore, Berry A. Private	Unk	August 24, 1861, Lawrenceville, Georgia	Co. F, 24th Georgia Infantry	June 1, 1864, Cold Harbor, Virginia	Point Lookout, Maryland, transferred to Elmira Prison, NY, July 12, 1864	Oath of Allegiance July 7, 1865
Kilgore, James Private	Unk	July 19, 1861, Camp Bartow, Monroe, Georgia	Co. C, 9th Georgia Infantry	May 12, 1864, Spotsylvania Court House, Virginia	Point Lookout, Maryland, transferred to Elmira Prison, NY, August 14, 1864	Died September 14, 1864 of Chronic Diarrhea, Grave No. 287

Name & Rank	Age	Enlisted	Regiment and State	Where Captured	Prison	Remarks
Killebrew, J. J. Private	Unk	May 8, 1862, Buena Vista, Georgia	Co. G, 59th Georgia Infantry	May 6, 1864, Wilderness, Virginia	Old Capital Prison, Washington, DC, transferred to Elmira Prison, NY, July 14, 1864	Transferred for Exchange 10/11/64. Died 10/26/64 of Chronic Diarrhea at Point Lookout, ND.
Killen, Daniel Private	26	July 2, 1861, New Orleans, Louisiana	Co. H, 14th Louisiana Infantry	May 5, 1864, Wilderness, Virginia	Point Lookout, Maryland, transferred to Elmira Prison, NY, July 25, 1864	Exchanged October 29, 1864 at Venus Point, Savannah River, GA.
Killet, E. Private	Unk	Unknown	Co. B, 8th North Carolina Infantry	June 1, 1864, Cold Harbor, Virginia	Point Lookout, Maryland, transferred to Elmira Prison, NY, July 12, 1864	Oath of Allegiance July 3, 1865
Killgro, Leroy Private	Unk	January 4, 1862, Savannah, Georgia	Co. A, 31st Georgia Infantry	May 20, 1864, Spotsylvania Court House, Virginia	Point Lookout, Maryland, transferred to Elmira Prison, NY, July 3, 1864	Exchanged March 10, 1865 at Boulware's Wharf on the James River, Virginia
Killingsworth, James G. Sergeant	Unk	March 4, 1862, Fort Gaines, Georgia	Co. I, 51st Georgia Infantry	June 3, 1864, Gaines Farm Cold Harbor, Virginia	Point Lookout, Maryland, transferred to Elmira Prison, NY, July 12, 1864	Died March 20, 1865 of Variola (Smallpox), Grave No. 1552
Kilmer, Harrison D. Private	Unk	April 10, 1862, Shepherds, Virginia	Co. D, 12th Virginia Cavalry	April 3, 1865, Burkley County, Virginia	Old Capital Prison, Washington, DC, transferred to Elmira Prison, NY, May 12, 1865.	Oath of Allegiance June 27, 1865
Kimball, James John Private	Unk	August 13, 1861, Camp Moore, Louisiana	Co. C, 12th Louisiana Infantry	May 17, 1863, Big Black River, Mississippi	Point Lookout, Maryland, transferred to Elmira Prison, NY, August 18, 1864	Exchanged October 29, 1864 at Venus Point, Savannah River, GA.
Kimball, W. H. Private	Unk	Unknown	Captain Robinson's Home Guard, Florida	September 27, 1864, Marianna, Florida	New Orleans, Louisiana transferred to Elmira November 19, 1864.	Oath of Allegiance May 29, 1865

Name & Rank	Age	Enlisted	Regiment and State	Where Captured	Prison	Remarks
Kimbrew, William W. Sergeant	Unk	June 9, 1861, Bibb County, Georgia	Co. H, 12th Georgia Infantry	July 12, 1864, Near Washington, DC	Old Capital Prison, Washington DC. Transferred to Elmira Prison Camp, NY, July 25, 1864.	Exchanged March 10, 1865 at Boulware's Wharf on the James River, Virginia
Kimbro, William Private	Unk	August 24, 1861, Lawrenceville, Georgia	Co. A, 24th Georgia Infantry	August 16, 1864, Front Royal, Virginia	Old Capital Prison, Washington, DC transferred to Elmira Prison, NY, August 29, 1864	Died September 29, 1864 of Chronic Diarrhea, Grave No. 427
Kimes, William Private	39	June 14, 1861, Jefferson Court House, Virginia	Co. A, 2nd Virginia Infantry	May 12, 1864, Near Spotsylvania Court House, Virginia	Point Lookout, Maryland, transferred to Elmira Prison, NY, August 6, 1864	Exchanged February 20, 1865 at Boulware's or Cox Wharf on the James River, Virginia
Kimmel, John W. Private	Unk	August 23, 1861, Charlestown, Virginia	Co. C, 12th Virginia Cavalry	May 12, 1864, Spotsylvania Court House, Virginia	Point Lookout, Maryland, transferred to Elmira Prison, NY, August 14, 1864	Oath of Allegiance June 21, 1865
Kincannon, F. P. Private	24	October 4, 1862, Cleveland, Tennessee	Co. H, 63rd Tennessee Infantry	June 17, 1864, Petersburg, Virginia	Point Lookout, Maryland, transferred to Elmira Prison, NY, July 30, 1864	Exchanged October 29, 1864. Died November 12, 1864 and buried at Port Royal, SC.
Kinder, H. Private	Unk	July 2, 1861, Wytheville, Virginia	Co. B, 50th Virginia Infantry	May 12, 1864, Spotsylvania Court House, Virginia	Point Lookout, Maryland, transferred to Elmira Prison, NY, August 2, 1864	Transferred For Exchange October 11, 1864 to Point Lookout Prison Camp, MD. Nothing Further.
King, A. H. Sergeant	Unk	Unknown	Co. B, 1st Maryland Cavalry	October 27, 1864, Fauquier County, Virginia	Old Capital Prison, Washington, DC, transferred to Elmira Prison, NY, December 17, 1864	Oath of Allegiance June 19, 1865

Name & Rank	Age	Enlisted	Regiment and State	Where Captured	Prison	Remarks
King, Aisgall Private	25	July 15, 1862, Raleigh, North Carolina	Co. J, 3rd North Carolina Infantry	May 12, 1864, Near Spotsylvania Court House, Virginia	Point Lookout Prison, Maryland. Transferred to Elmira Prison Camp New York August 14, 1864.	Died March 29, 1865 of Variola (Smallpox), Grave No. 2510
King, Alfred Private	Unk	September 19, 1862, Raleigh, North Carolina	Co. D, 8th North Carolina Infantry	June 1, 1864, Gaines Farm Cold Harbor, Virginia	Point Lookout, Maryland, transferred to Elmira Prison, NY, July 17, 1864	Died October 21, 1864 of Chronic Diarrhea, Grave No. 876
King, Allen F. Private	22	April 1, 1864, Wake County, North Carolina	Co. E, 30th North Carolina Infantry	May 20, 1864, Spotsylvania, Virginia	Point Lookout, Maryland, transferred to Elmira Prison, NY, July 6,1864	Exchanged October 29, 1864 at Venus Point, Savannah River, GA.
King, Anguish McD Private	Unk	May 7, 1862, Macon, Georgia	Co. J, 61st Georgia Infantry	May 12, 1864, Spotsylvania Court House, Virginia	Point Lookout, Maryland, transferred to Elmira Prison, NY, July 25, 1864	Exchanged February 20, 1865 at Boulware's or Cox Wharf on the James River, Virginia
King, Barnabas S. Private	Unk	March 30, 1863, Wilmington, North Carolina	Co. F, 10th Regiment, 1st North Carolina Artillery	January 15, 1865, Fort Fisher, North Carolina	January 30, 1865, Elmira Prison Camp, New York	Died February 24, 1865 of Chronic Diarrhea, Grave No. 2252
King, C. B. Private	Unk	December 25, 1863, Mobile, Alabama	Co. A, 1st Alabama Artillery	August 23, 1864, Fort Morgan, Alabama	New Orleans, Louisiana transferred to Elmira Prison, NY, December 4, 1864.	Died January 30, 1865 of Pneumonia, Grave No. 1791
King, Caswell Private	39	April 1, 1864, Wake County, North Carolina	Co. D, 30th North Carolina Infantry	May 12, 1864, Near Spotsylvania Court House, Virginia	Point Lookout, Maryland, transferred to Elmira Prison, NY, August 14, 1864	Died March 6, 1865 of Diarrhea, Grave No. 2402
King, Chapman Private	20	April 2, 1862, Virginia	Co. J, 50th Virginia Infantry	May 6, 1864, Wilderness, Virginia	Point Lookout, Maryland, transferred to Elmira Prison, NY, August 14, 1864	Died April 18, 1865 of Chronic Diarrhea, Grave No. 1347

Name & Rank	Age	Enlisted	Regiment and State	Where Captured	Prison	Remarks
King, Chester B. Private	Unk	Unknown	Co. H, 50th Virginia Infantry	May 12, 1864, Spotsylvania Court House, Virginia	Point Lookout, Maryland, transferred to Elmira Prison, NY, August 2, 1864	Oath of Allegiance June 16, 1865
King, Cornelius Private	25	June 7, 1861, Camp Moore, New Orleans, Louisiana	Co. C, 7th Louisiana Infantry	May 11, 1864, Spotsylvania Court House, Virginia	Point Lookout, Maryland, transferred to Elmira Prison, NY, August 17, 1864	Oath of Allegiance May 19, 1865
King, E. P. Private	Unk	Unknown	Co. H, 13th Louisiana Infantry	May 20, 1864, Spotsylvania Court House, Virginia	Point Lookout, Maryland, transferred to Elmira Prison, NY, July 6, 1864	Died May 7, 1865 Of Chronic Diarrhea, Grave No. 2769. Has 13th GA on Headstone.
King, Edward H. Private	18	May 8, 1862, Goldsboro, North Carolina	Co. E, 3rd North Carolina Infantry	May 12, 1864, Spotsylvania Court House, Virginia	Point Lookout, Maryland, transferred to Elmira Prison, NY, August 14, 1864	Exchanged October 29, 1864 at Venus Point, Savannah River, GA.
King, George B. Private	18	May 6, 1862, Elizabethtown, Bladen County, North Carolina	Co. K, 40th Regiment, North Carolina Artillery	January 15, 1865, Fort Fisher, North Carolina	February 1, 1865, Elmira Prison Camp, New York	Oath of Allegiance June 21, 1865
King, George B. Corporal	Unk	May 27, 1861, Buckhannon, Virginia	Co. B, 25th Virginia Infantry	May 12, 1864, Spotsylvania Court House, Virginia	Point Lookout, Maryland, transferred to Elmira Prison, NY, August 12, 1864	Oath of Allegiance June 30, 1865
King, H. C. Private	Unk	Unknown	Co. A, Captain Jones' Home Guard Florida	September 27, 1864, Marianna, Florida	New Orleans, Louisiana transferred to Elmira November 19, 1864.	Exchanged February 13, 1865 at Boulware's Wharf on the James River, Virginia
King, Harvey M. Private	Unk	July 22, 1863, Wytheville, Virginia	Co. B, 29th Virginia Infantry	May 13, 1864, Near Fort Darling, Virginia	Point Lookout, Maryland, transferred to Elmira Prison, NY, July 25, 1864	Died January 15, 1865 of Chronic Diarrhea, Grave No. 1449

Name & Rank	Age	Enlisted	Regiment and State	Where Captured	Prison	Remarks
King, Hiram Private	Unk	September 7, 1862, Coffee County, Alabama	Co. D, 1st Battalion Alabama Artillery	August 23, 1864, Fort Morgan, Alabama	Steam Press No. 4, New Orleans, Louisiana transferred to Elmira Prison, NY, October 8, 1864.	Died December 5, 1864 of Pleuro-Pneumonia, Grave No. 1031
King, Hubbard Private	17	May 3, 1862, Goldsboro, North Carolina	Co. G, 45th North Carolina Infantry	May 10, 1864, Spotsylvania, Virginia. Gunshot Wound Left Thigh.	Old Capital Prison, Washington, DC. Transferred to Elmira Prison Camp, NY, July 25, 1864.	Died March 26, 1865 of Diarrhea, Grave No. 2473
King, I. P. Z. Sergeant	Unk	February 15, 1863, Darlington District, South Carolina	Co. B, 21st South Carolina Infantry	January 15, 1865, Fort Fisher, North Carolina	January 30, 1965 Elmira Prison Camp, New York	Oath of Allegiance July 11, 1865
King, Jacob Sergeant	25	May 3, 1862, Macon, Georgia	Captain Slayton's Battery Macon Light Artillery, Georgia Artillery	June 17, 1864, Near Petersburg, Virginia	Point Lookout, Maryland, transferred to Elmira Prison, NY, July 30, 1864	Oath of Allegiance May 17, 1865
King, James Private	31	August 2, 1862, Fort St. Philips, Brunswick County, North Carolina	Co. G, 36th Regiment North Carolina Artillery	January 15, 1865, Fort Fisher, North Carolina	February 1, 1865, Elmira Prison Camp, New York	Died March 2, 1865 of Variola (smallpox), Grave No. 2115
King, James A. Private	Unk	August 1, 1861, Richmond, Virginia	2nd Battalion Maryland Artillery	May 11, 1864, Yellow Tavern, Hanover County, Virginia	Point Lookout, Maryland, transferred to Elmira Prison, NY, August 17, 1864	Oath of Allegiance June 14, 1865
King, James A. Private	Unk	March 15, 1862, Floyd Court House, Virginia	Co. B, 42nd Virginia Infantry	May 12, 1864, Spotsylvania Court House, Virginia	Point Lookout, Maryland, transferred to Elmira Prison, NY, August 2, 1864	Oath of Allegiance May 29, 1865
King, James A. J. Private	Unk	May 6, 1863, Coffee County, Alabama	Co. G, 61st Alabama Infantry	May 20, 1864, Spotsylvania Court House, Virginia	Point Lookout, Maryland, transferred to Elmira Prison, NY, July 6, 1864	Oath of Allegiance August 7, 1865

Name & Rank	Age	Enlisted	Regiment and State	Where Captured	Prison	Remarks
King, James M. Private	Unk	July 13, 1861, Camp McDonald, Georgia	Co. F, 18th Georgia Infantry	June 1, 1864, Cold Harbor, Virginia	Point Lookout, Maryland, transferred to Elmira Prison, NY, July 17, 1864	Oath of Allegiance July 7, 1865
King, James S. Civilian	Unk	Unknown	Citizen of Prince William County, Virginia	November 26, 1863, Prince William County, Virginia	Point Lookout, Maryland, transferred to Elmira Prison, NY, July 25, 1864	Exchanged March 10, 1865 at Boulware's Wharf on the James River, Virginia
King, James T. Private	Unk	June 25, 1861, Wytheville, Virginia	Co. I, 50th Virginia Infantry	May 12, 1864, Spotsylvania Court House, Virginia	Point Lookout, Maryland, transferred to Elmira Prison, NY, August 2, 1864	Oath of Allegiance June 27, 1865
King, James W. Private	Unk	July 10, 1861, Danielsville, Georgia	Co. A, 16th Georgia Infantry	August 16, 1864, Front Royal, Virginia	Old Capital Prison, Washington, DC transferred to Elmira Prison, NY, August 29, 1864	Exchanged March 2, 1865 at Akins Landing on the James River, Virginia
King, Jared M. Private	25	July 25, 1861, Tullahoma, Tennessee	Co. E, 25th Tennessee Infantry	June 17, 1864, Near Petersburg, Virginia	Point Lookout, Maryland, transferred to Elmira Prison, NY, July 30, 1864	Exchanged February 20, 1865 at Boulware's or Cox Wharf on the James River, Virginia
King, John J. Private	34	March 3, 1862 Fort Marks, Florida	Co. G, 5th Florida Infantry	May 12, 1864, Spotsylvania Court House, Virginia	Point Lookout, Maryland, transferred to Elmira Prison, NY, July 30, 1864	Oath of Allegiance June 19, 1865
King, John L. Civilian	Unk	Unknown	Citizen of Prince William County, Virginia	November 26, 1863, Prince William Court House, Virginia	Point Lookout, Maryland, transferred to Elmira Prison, NY, July 17,1864	No Additional Information.
King, John R. Private	21	June 15, 1861, Wilmington, North Carolina	Co. E, 3rd North Carolina Infantry	May 12, 1864, Near Spotsylvania, Virginia	Point Lookout, Maryland, transferred to Elmira Prison, NY, August 14, 1864	Oath of Allegiance June 27, 1865

Name & Rank	Age	Enlisted	Regiment and State	Where Captured	Prison	Remarks
King, John Rufus Private	Unk	May 14, 1863, Warm Springs, Virginia	Co. B, 25th Virginia Infantry	May 12, 1864, Spotsylvania Court House, Virginia	Point Lookout, Maryland, transferred to Elmira Prison, NY, July 30, 1864	Oath of Allegiance June 14, 1865
King, John W. Private	Unk	April 23, 1862, Campbell County, Georgia	Co. C, 35th Georgia Infantry	May 24, 1864, North Anna, Virginia	Point Lookout, Maryland, transferred to Elmira Prison, NY, July 25, 1864	Oath of Allegiance May 29, 1865
King, Josiah Private	Unk	March 2, 1864, Anderson, South Carolina	Co. F, 1st South Carolina Infantry	May 24, 1864, Jericho Ford, Hanover Junction, Virginia	Point Lookout, Maryland, transferred to Elmira Prison, NY, July 23, 1864	Died September 12, 1864 of Chronic Diarrhea, Grave No. 174
King, P. Civilian	Unk	Louisiana	Citizen of Louisiana	May 6, 1864, Bayou Lafourche, Louisiana	New Orleans, Louisiana transferred to Elmira November 19, 1864.	Died March 16, 1865 of Chronic Diarrhea, Grave No. 1695
King, Philip Private	39	April 20, 1861, San Antonio, Texas	Co. A, Edgar's Co. 1st Texas Field Artillery	March 21, 1864, Natchitoches, Louisiana	New Orleans, LA, Transferred to Elmira Prison, NY, November 19, 1864	Oath of Allegiance May 19, 1865
King, Richard Private	23	July 16, 1861, Forestville, Wake County, North Carolina	Co I, 1st North Carolina Infantry	May 12, 1864, Spotsylvania Court House, Virginia	Point Lookout, Maryland, transferred to Elmira Prison, NY, August 6,1864	Oath of Allegiance June 27, 1865
King, Robert Private	Unk	Unknown	Co. K, 50th Virginia Infantry	May 12, 1864, Spotsylvania Court House, Virginia	Point Lookout, Maryland, transferred to Elmira Prison, NY, August 2, 1864	Exchanged February 13, 1865 at Boulware's wharf on the James River, Virginia
King, Rufus Private	Unk	Unknown	Co. J, 7th Alabama Cavalry	July 22, 1864, 15 Mile Station at Camp Gonzalez on the Pensacola Railroad, Louisiana	New Orleans, LA, Transferred to Elmira Prison, NY, November 19, 1864	Exchanged February 20, 1865 at Boulware's or Cox Wharf on the James River, Virginia

Name & Rank	Age	Enlisted	Regiment and State	Where Captured	Prison	Remarks
King, Rufus Private	47	July 3, 1861, Brundidge, Alabama	Co. F, 15th Alabama Infantry	May 6, 1864, Wilderness, Virginia	Point Lookout, Maryland, transferred to Elmira Prison, NY, August 17, 1864	Died February 1, 1865 of Pneumonia, Grave No. 1773
King, Russell Private	Unk	Unknown	Co. J, 50th Virginia Infantry	July 18, 1864, Snickers Gap, Virginia	Old Capital Prison, Washington, DC, transferred to Elmira Prison, NY, August 12, 1864	Exchanged 3/14/65. Died 3/25/65 of Chronic Diarrhea at Chimborazo Hospital No. 2, Richmond, VA.
King, T. P. Private	18	December 23, 1861, Georgetown, South Carolina	Co. B, 21st South Carolina Infantry	January 15, 1865, Fort Fisher, North Carolina	January 30, 1965 Elmira Prison Camp, New York	Oath of Allegiance July 11, 1865
King, Thomas A. Private	17	March 13, 1861, Clarksville, Georgia	Co. K, 24th Georgia Infantry	June 1, 1864, Cold Harbor, Virginia	Point Lookout, Maryland, transferred to Elmira Prison, NY, July 12, 1864	Oath of Allegiance July 7, 1865
King, Thomas E. Private	25	May 13, 1861, Golden Hill, Onslow County, North Carolina	Co. E, 3rd North Carolina Infantry	May 12, 1864, Near Spotsylvania Court House, Virginia	Point Lookout, Maryland, transferred to Elmira Prison, NY, July 23, 1864	Oath of Allegiance May 17, 1865
King, Thomas H. Private	Unk	Unknown	Co. H, 50th Virginia Infantry	May 12, 1864, Spotsylvania Court House, Virginia	Point Lookout, Maryland, transferred to Elmira Prison, NY, August 2, 1864	Oath of Allegiance July 7, 1865
King, Wesley Private	Unk	Unknown	Co. H, 21st South Carolina Infantry	January 15, 1865, Fort Fisher, North Carolina	January 30, 1965 Elmira Prison Camp, New York	Died June 23, 1865 of Chronic Diarrhea, Grave No. 2818
King, William Private	25	June 10, 1861, Halifax County, North Carolina	Co. K, 1st North Carolina Infantry	May 12, 1864, Spotsylvania Court House, Virginia	Point Lookout, Maryland, transferred to Elmira Prison, NY, August 6,1864	Oath of Allegiance June 27, 1865
King, William Private	Unk	April 28, 1862, Camp Narrows, Virginia	Co. K, 50th Virginia Infantry	May 12, 1864, Spotsylvania Court House, Virginia	Point Lookout, Maryland, transferred to Elmira Prison, NY, August 2, 1864	Died March 12, 1865 of Pneumonia, Grave No. 2427

Name & Rank	Age	Enlisted	Regiment and State	Where Captured	Prison	Remarks
King, William S. Sergeant	35	June 3, 1861, New Orleans, Louisiana	Co. B, 14th Louisiana Infantry	May 5, 1864, Wilderness, Virginia	Point Lookout, Maryland, transferred to Elmira Prison, NY, July 25, 1864	Exchanged February 25, 1865 at Boulware's or Cox Wharf on the James River, Virginia
King, William S. Private	Unk	April 25, 1862, Macon, Georgia	Co. J, 61st Georgia Infantry	May 12, 1864, Spotsylvania Court House, Virginia	Point Lookout, Maryland, transferred to Elmira Prison, NY, July 25, 1864	Oath of Allegiance June 23, 1865
King, William T. Private	Unk	Unknown	Co. A, Captain Parson's Home Guard Florida	September 27, 1864, Marianna, Florida	New Orleans, Louisiana transferred to Elmira November 19, 1864.	Died January 13, 1865 of Chronic Bronchitis, Grave No. 1468
Kingman, John W. Private	Unk	February 15, 1864, Charleston, South Carolina	Co. A, 25th South Carolina Infantry	January 15, 1865, Fort Fisher, North Carolina	January 30, 1865, Elmira Prison Camp, New York	Exchanged March 14, 1865 at Boulware's Wharf on the James River, Virginia
Kingry, John W. Private	Unk	June 17, 1861, Rocky Mount, Virginia	Co. K, 42nd Virginia Infantry	May 12, 1864, Spotsylvania Court House, Virginia	Point Lookout, Maryland, transferred to Elmira Prison, NY, August 2, 1864	Exchanged October 29, 1864 at Venus Point, Savannah River, GA.
Kingsolver, Anthony F. Private	19	June 16, 1861, Washington County, Virginia	Co. I, 48th Virginia Infantry	May 12, 1864, Near Spotsylvania Court House, Virginia	Point Lookout, Maryland, transferred to Elmira Prison, NY, August 6, 1864	Died January 14, 1865 of Variola (Smallpox) Grave No. 1459
Kinlaw, Anderson W. Private	Unk	November 20, 1864, Fort Holmes, Brunswick County, North Carolina	Co. K, 40th Regiment, 3rd North Carolina Artillery	January 15, 1865, Fort Fisher, North Carolina	February 1, 1865, Elmira Prison Camp, New York	Exchanged February 20, 1865 at Boulware's or Cox Wharf on the James River, Virginia
Kinlaw, Benjamin Corporal	Unk	May 6, 1862, Elizabethtown, Bladen County, North Carolina	Co. K, 40th Regiment, North Carolina Artillery	January 15, 1865, Fort Fisher, North Carolina	February 1, 1865, Elmira Prison Camp, New York	Died April 16, 1865 of Chronic Diarrhea, Grave No. 2720

Name & Rank	Age	Enlisted	Regiment and State	Where Captured	Prison	Remarks
Kinlaw, Neill Private	43	August 18, 1863, Lumberton, Robison County, North Carolina	Co. K, 40th Regiment, North Carolina Artillery	January 15, 1865, Fort Fisher, North Carolina	February 1, 1865, Elmira Prison Camp, New York	Died February 20, 1865 of Diarrhea, Grave No. 2334
Kinnery, David W. Private	17	March 1, 1864, Wilmington, North Carolina	Co. C, 42nd North Carolina Infantry	June 3, 1864, Cold Harbor, Virginia	Point Lookout, Maryland, transferred to Elmira Prison, NY, July 12, 1864	Exchanged October 29, 1864 at Venus Point, Savannah River, GA.
Kinney, A. D. Private	Unk	Unknown	Co. D, 11th North Carolina Infantry	May 30, 1864 Mechanics-ville, Virginia	Point Lookout, Maryland, transferred to Elmira Prison, NY, July 11, 1864	Oath of Allegiance June 30, 1865
Kinney, Clingman Private	17	July 19, 1861, Graham, North Carolina	Co. I, 8th North Carolina Infantry	June 1, 1864, Cold Harbor, Virginia	Point Lookout, Maryland, transferred to Elmira Prison, NY, July 12, 1864	Died October 21, 1864 of Chronic Diarrhea, Grave No. 875
Kinney, William Private	Unk	October 31, 1863, Charles City Court House, Virginia	Co. H, 24th Virginia Infantry	December 13, 1863, Charles City Court House, Virginia	Point Lookout, Maryland, transferred to Elmira Prison, NY, July 23, 1864	Oath of Allegiance May 15, 1865
Kinnple, Edward B. Private	Unk	June 10, 1861, Mt. Meridian, Virginia	Co. B, 10th Virginia Infantry	May 12, 1864, Spotsylvania Court House, Virginia	Point Lookout, Maryland, transferred to Elmira Prison, NY, August 2, 1864	Oath of Allegiance June 14, 1865
Kinny, John J. Private	23	May 22, 1861, New Orleans, Louisiana	Co. E, 7th Louisiana Infantry	May 11, 1864, Near Spotsylvania Court House, Virginia	Point Lookout, Maryland, transferred to Elmira Prison, NY, August 17, 1864	Oath of Allegiance May 29, 1865
Kinny, John L. Private	Unk	July 25, 1862, Near Richmond, Virginia	Co. A, 49th Georgia Infantry	May 12, 1864, Spotsylvania Court House, Virginia	Point Lookout, Maryland, transferred to Elmira Prison, NY, August 12, 1864	Exchanged October 29, 1864 at Venus Point, Savannah River, GA.
Kinny, William M. Private	30	September 10, 1862, Raleigh, North Carolina	Co. I, 8th North Carolina Infantry	May 31, 1864, Cold Harbor, Virginia	Point Lookout, Maryland, transferred to Elmira Prison, NY, July 11, 1864	Oath of Allegiance May 19, 1865

Name & Rank	Age	Enlisted	Regiment and State	Where Captured	Prison	Remarks
Kinsey, Allan Private	Unk	December 9, 1861, Camp Hampton, South Carolina	Co. H, 17th South Carolina Infantry	July 30, 1864, Petersburg, Virginia	Point Lookout, Maryland, transferred to Elmira Prison, NY, August 12, 1864	Exchanged October 29, 1864 at Venus Point, Savannah River, GA.
Kinsey, John W. Private	Unk	October 25, 1863, Greenville, Alabama	Co. E, 1st Battalion Alabama Artillery	August 23, 1864, Fort Morgan, Alabama	Steam Press No. 4, New Orleans, Louisiana transferred to Elmira Prison, NY, October 8, 1864.	Oath of Allegiance July 11, 1865
Kinzer, Jacob S. Private	23	April 18, 1861, Blacksburg, Virginia	Co. E, 4th Virginia Infantry	May 12, 1864, Near Spotsylvania Court House, Virginia	Point Lookout, Maryland, transferred to Elmira Prison, NY, August 2, 1864	Exchanged March 14, 1865 at Boulware's Wharf on the James River, Virginia
Kirby, Dixon Private	Unk	The 29th 1861, Camp Holmes, Near Raleigh, North Carolina	Co. K, 10th Regiment, 1st North Carolina Artillery	January 15, 1865, Fort Fisher, North Carolina	January 30, 1865 Elmira Prison Camp, New York	Died April 13, 1865 of Variola (Smallpox), Grave No. 2700
Kirby, J. R. Private	Unk	Scottsville, Virginia	Co. K, 26th Virginia Infantry	May 12, 1864, Spotsylvania, Virginia	Point Lookout, Maryland, transferred to Elmira Prison, NY, July 12, 1864	Oath of Allegiance June 27, 1865
Kirby, James H. Private	Unk	July 30, 1863, Lewisburg, Virginia	Co. A, 26th Virginia Infantry	May 31, 1864, Cold Harbor, Virginia	Point Lookout, Maryland, transferred to Elmira Prison, NY, July 12, 1864	Died September 12, 1864 of Pneumonia, Grave No. 181
Kirby, James W. Private	18	March 1, 1862, Baton Rouge, Louisiana	Co. B, 7th Louisiana Infantry	May 12, 1864, Spotsylvania Court House, Virginia	Point Lookout, Maryland, transferred to Elmira Prison, NY, August 17, 1864	Died October 10, 1864 of Chronic Diarrhea, Grave No. 665
Kirby, William H. Private	26	April 22, 1861, Wadesboro, North Carolina	Co. H, 14th North Carolina Infantry	May 22, 1864, Hanover Junction, Virginia	Point Lookout, Maryland, transferred to Elmira Prison, NY, July 11, 1864. Ward No. 26	Died August 7, 1864, Pneumonia, Grave No. 13

Name & Rank	Age	Enlisted	Regiment and State	Where Captured	Prison	Remarks
Kirk, James B. Private	Unk	December 9, 1861, Camp Trousdale, Tennessee	Co. A, 44th Tennessee Infantry	June 17, 1864, Petersburg, Virginia	Point Lookout, Maryland, transferred to Elmira Prison, NY, July 30, 1864	Oath of Allegiance May 2, 1865
Kirk, John G. Private	Unk	February 18, 1864, Greenville, Tennessee	Co. B, 1st Tennessee Infantry	May 6, 1864, Wilderness, Virginia	Point Lookout, Maryland, transferred to Elmira Prison, NY, July 23, 1864	Oath of Allegiance April 1, 1865
Kirk, Joseph P. Private	Unk	June 3, 1862, Richmond, Virginia	Co. J, 59th Virginia Infantry	May 8, 1864, Nottoway Bridge, Virginia	Point Lookout, Maryland, transferred to Elmira Prison, NY, August 17, 1864	Died September 15, 1864 of Chronic Diarrhea, Grave No. 299
Kirkland, J. M. Private	Unk	October 15, 1863, Johns Island, South Carolina	Co. F, 6th South Carolina Cavalry	July 30, 1864, Lee's Mill, Petersburg, Virginia	Point Lookout, Maryland, transferred to Elmira Prison, NY, August 12, 1864	Oath of Allegiance June 14, 1865
Kirkland, J. William Private	Unk	Unknown	Co. B, Paine's Battalion Louisiana Cavalry	September 12, 1864, Morganza, Louisiana	New Orleans, LA, Transferred to Elmira Prison, NY, November 19, 1864	Died December 8, 1864, of Chronic Diarrhea, Grave No. 1171
Kirkman, Elisha W. Private	28	October 1, 1862, Drury's Bluff, Virginia	Co. B, 45th North Carolina Infantry	May 20, 1864, Spotsylvania Court House, Virginia	Point Lookout, Maryland, transferred to Elmira Prison, NY, July 3, 1864	Exchanged October 29, 1864 at Venus Point, Savannah River, GA.
Kirkman, J. H. Civilian	Unk	Unknown	Citizen of Guilford County, North Carolina	April 21, 1864, Wilmington, North Carolina	Point Lookout, Maryland, transferred to Elmira Prison, NY, July 25, 1864	Oath of Allegiance June 12, 1865
Kirkner, Charles H. Private	Unk	May 27, 1861, Lynchburg, Virginia	Co. E, 24th Virginia Infantry	May 13, 1864, Near Fort Darling, Virginia	Point Lookout, Maryland, transferred to Elmira Prison, NY, August 17, 1864	Oath of Allegiance June 16, 1865

Name & Rank	Age	Enlisted	Regiment and State	Where Captured	Prison	Remarks
Kirkpatrick, Andrew J. Private	Unk	December 21, 1861, Nashville, Tennessee	Co. J, 44th Tennessee Infantry	June 17, 1864, Petersburg, Virginia	Point Lookout, Maryland, transferred to Elmira Prison, NY, July 30, 1864	Oath of Allegiance February 27, 1865. Early Release per Lincoln's Proclamation, 12/8/1863.
Kirkpatrick, Charles M. Private	25	June 6, 1861, Bath County Court House, Virginia	Co. H, 25th Virginia Infantry	May 6, 1864, Wilderness, Virginia	Old Capital Prison, Washington, DC, transferred to Elmira Prison, NY, July 14, 1864	Oath of Allegiance June 27, 1865
Kirkpatrick, James F. Private	Unk	June 17, 1861, Warrenton, Virginia	Co. C, 49th Virginia Infantry	February 15, 1865, Loudoun County, Virginia	Old Capital Prison, Washington, DC, transferred to Elmira Prison, NY, March 27, 1865.	Oath of Allegiance July 11, 1865
Kirkpatrick, Walker S. Private	Unk	August 1, 1861, Covington, Newton County, Georgia	Co. A, Cobb's Legion Georgia	August 16, 1864, Front Royal, Virginia	Old Capital Prison, Washington, DC transferred to Elmira Prison, NY, August 29, 1864	Oath of Allegiance July 7, 1865
Kirkpatrick, William H. Sergeant	Unk	September 5, 1861, Athens, Georgia	Co. D, Cobb's Legion Georgia	August 16, 1864, Front Royal, Virginia	Old Capital Prison, Washington, DC transferred to Elmira Prison, NY, August 29, 1864	Transferred For Exchange October 11, 1864 to Point Lookout Prison Camp, MD. Died November 1, 1864 of Chronic Diarrhea.
Kirks, Samuel R. Private	Unk	March 17, 1862, Henry County, Virginia	Co. F, 42nd Virginia Infantry	May 12, 1864, Near Spotsylvania Court House, Virginia	Point Lookout, Maryland, transferred to Elmira Prison, NY, August 6, 1864	Oath of Allegiance June 27, 1865
Kisor, George M. Private	Unk	August 8, 1862, Camp Hill, Stanly County, North Carolina	Co. F, 5th North Carolina Infantry	May 12, 1864, Spotsylvania Court House, Virginia	Point Lookout, Maryland, transferred to Elmira Prison, NY, August 6, 1864	Died March 27, 1865 of Pneumonia, Grave No. 2524. Name Kiser on Headstone.

Name & Rank	Age	Enlisted	Regiment and State	Where Captured	Prison	Remarks
Kistler, Roderick M. Private	27	August 20, 1862, Statesville, North Carolina	Co. J, 7th North Carolina Infantry	May 6, 1864, Wilderness, Virginia	Point Lookout, Maryland, transferred to Elmira Prison, NY, August 14, 1864	Exchanged February 20, 1865 at Boulware's or Cox Wharf on the James River, Virginia
Kitchen, Thomas W. Private	Unk	Unknown	Co. B, Hood's Battalion, Virginia Reserves	June 15, 1864, Petersburg, Virginia	Point Lookout, Maryland, transferred to Elmira Prison, NY, July 30, 1864	Died April 12, 1865 of Chronic Diarrhea, Grave No. 2694
Kite, Andrew J. Private	Unk	June 1, 1861, Luray County, Virginia	Co. H, 33rd Virginia Infantry	July 8, 1864, Harpers Ferry, Virginia	Old Capital Prison, Washington DC. Transferred to Elmira Prison Camp New York, July 25, 1864.	Exchanged February 20, 1865. Died March 7, 1865 of Chronic Diarrhea at Chimborazo Hospital #2, Richmond, VA.
Kite, Siram N. Private	Unk	June 2, 1862, Luray, Virginia	Co. K, 10th Virginia Infantry	May 12, 1864, Spotsylvania Court House, Virginia	Point Lookout, Maryland, transferred to Elmira Prison, NY, August 2, 1864	Oath of Allegiance June 19, 1865
Kittrell, John S. Private	18	August 6, 1861, Pitt County, North Carolina	Co. G, 8th North Carolina Infantry	June 1, 1864, Cold Harbor, Virginia	Point Lookout, Maryland, transferred to Elmira Prison, NY, July 12, 1864	Oath of Allegiance July 3, 1865
Kivett, Talton Private	21	June 10, 1861, Cedar Falls, North Carolina	Co. E, 22nd North Carolina Infantry	May 6, 1864, Wilderness, Virginia	Point Lookout, Maryland, transferred to Elmira Prison, NY, August 14, 1864	Died March 16, 1865 of Variola (Smallpox), Grave No. 1709. F. Kirett, 22nd SC on Headstone.
Klepper, Henry Private	Unk	April 14, 1864, Bristol, Tennessee	Co. A, 14th Tennessee Infantry	May 6, 1864, Wilderness, Virginia	Point Lookout, Maryland, transferred to Elmira Prison, NY, July 23, 1864	Died November 11, 1864 of Chronic Diarrhea, Grave No. 786. Name Clepper Appears on Headstone.

Name & Rank	Age	Enlisted	Regiment and State	Where Captured	Prison	Remarks
Kline, Edward D. Private	26	July 15, 1862, Forsyth County, North Carolina	Co. G, 33rd North Carolina Infantry	May 12, 1864, Spotsylvania Court House, Virginia	Point Lookout, Maryland, transferred to Elmira Prison, NY, August 14, 1864	Oath of Allegiance June 21, 1865
Kline, Snowden B. Private	Unk	July 20, 1863, Fishers Hill, Virginia	Co. F, 18th Virginia Cavalry	August 10, 1864, Summit Point, Virginia	Old Capital Prison, Washington, DC transferred to Elmira Prison, NY, August 29, 1864	Oath of Allegiance May 29, 1865
Kling, Bernard Private	Unk	May 5, 1862, Camp Moore, Louisiana	Co. E, 28th Louisiana Infantry	October 12, 1864, Near Hampton's Ferry, Louisiana	New Orleans, Louisiana transferred to Elmira November 19, 1864.	Exchanged February 13, 1865 at Boulware's wharf on the James River, Virginia
Kling, Cyrille Private	Unk	April 3, 1862, Ascension Parish, Louisiana	Co. E, 28th Louisiana Infantry	October 12, 1864, Near Hampton's Ferry, Louisiana	New Orleans, Louisiana transferred to Elmira November 19, 1864.	Exchanged February 25, 1865. Died March 8, 1865 of Chronic Diarrhea at General Hospital No. 9, Richmond VA.
Klopfer, John Sergeant	Unk	June 4, 1861, Camp Moore, New Orleans, Louisiana	Co. G, 6th Louisiana Infantry	May 5, 1864, Wilderness, Virginia	Point Lookout, Maryland, transferred to Elmira Prison, NY, July 25, 1864	Oath of Allegiance November 4, 1864. Early Release per Lincoln's Proclamation, 12/8/1863.
Klutts, Julius A. Private	Unk	February 26, 1864, Salisbury, North Carolina	Co. C, 57th North Carolina Infantry	July 8, 1864, Harpers Ferry, Virginia	Old Capital Prison, Washington DC. Transferred to Elmira Prison Camp, New York, July 25, 1864.	Oath of Allegiance May 29, 1865
Knauff, Henry J. Private	25	July 21, 1863, Columbia, South Carolina	Co. G, 6th South Carolina Cavalry	June 11, 1864, Trevilian Station, Louisa Court House, Virginia	Point Lookout, Maryland, transferred to Elmira Prison, NY, July 25, 1864	Oath of Allegiance June 16, 1865

Name & Rank	Age	Enlisted	Regiment and State	Where Captured	Prison	Remarks
Knight, A. N. 1st Sergeant	Unk	September 22, 1862, Waynesville, Georgia	Co. G, 7th Georgia Cavalry	June 11, 1864, Trevilian Station, Louisa Court House, Virginia	Point Lookout, Maryland, transferred to Elmira Prison, NY, July 25, 1864	Died September 15, 1864 of Chronic Diarrhea, Grave No. 290
Knight, J. A. Private	Unk	May 11, 1861, New Orleans, Louisiana	Co. K, 2nd Louisiana Infantry	May 5, 1864, Wilderness, Virginia	Point Lookout, Maryland, transferred to Elmira Prison, NY, August 17, 1864	Exchanged February 13, 1865 at Boulware's wharf on the James River, Virginia
Knight, J. F. Private	Unk	May 20, 1862, Darlington District, South Carolina	Co. G, 21st South Carolina Infantry	June 17, 1864, Petersburg, Virginia	Point Lookout, Maryland, transferred to Elmira Prison, NY, July 30, 1864	Oath of Allegiance July 3, 1865
Knight, James P. Private	Unk	March 6, 1862, Etowah, Georgia	Co. D, 18th Georgia Infantry	June 1, 1864, Cold Harbor, Virginia	Point Lookout, Maryland, transferred to Elmira Prison, NY, July 17, 1864	Oath of Allegiance June 21, 1865
Knight, John Private	26	August 3, 1864, St. Johns, Hertford County North Carolina	Co. C, 3rd Battalion, North Carolina Light Artillery	January 15, 1865, Fort Fisher, North Carolina	February 1, 1865, Elmira Prison Camp, New York	Died April 15, 1865 of Typhoid Fever, Grave No. 2714
Knight, John F. Private	Unk	Unknown	Co, C, 64th Georgia Infantry	August 16, 1864, New Market, Virginia	Old Capital Prison, Washington, DC transferred to Elmira Prison, NY, August 29, 1864	Died January 24, 1865 of Variola (Smallpox), Grave No. 1621
Knight, John H. Private	Unk	April 4, 1864, Bristol, Tennessee	Co. D, 7th Tennessee Infantry	May 22, 1864, South Anna River, Near Hanover Junction, Virginia	Point Lookout, Maryland, transferred to Elmira Prison, NY, July 25, 1864	Oath of Allegiance May 17, 1865
Knight, Joseph Private	Unk	October 30, 1862, Clark, Virginia	Co. F, 6th Virginia Cavalry	August 14, 1864, White Post., Virginia	Old Capital Prison, Washington, DC transferred to Elmira Prison, NY, August 29, 1864	Oath of Allegiance June 21, 1865

Name & Rank	Age	Enlisted	Regiment and State	Where Captured	Prison	Remarks
Knight, Joseph A. Private	Unk	July 22, 1861, Camp McDonald, Georgia	Co. D, 18th Georgia Infantry	June 1, 1864, Cold Harbor, Virginia	Point Lookout, Maryland, transferred to Elmira Prison, NY, July 17, 1864	Died February 22, 1865 of Variola (Smallpox), Grave No. 2250
Knight, Joseph M. Private	21	May 20, 1862, Camp Harris, Tennessee	Co. D, 17th Tennessee Infantry	June 17, 1864, Petersburg, Virginia	Point Lookout, Maryland, transferred to Elmira Prison, NY, July 30, 1864	Oath of Allegiance April 26, 1865
Knight, Mark A. Private	Unk	May 28, 1861, Lexington, Virginia	Co. F, 15th Georgia Infantry	September 1, 1863, United States Ford, Virginia	Point Lookout, Maryland, transferred to Elmira Prison, NY, August 18, 1864	Exchanged February 25, 1865 at Boulware's or Cox Wharf on the James River, Virginia
Knight, Thomas F. Private	Unk	Unknown	Co. H, 33rd Virginia Infantry	July 8, 1864, Harpers Ferry, Virginia	Old Capital Prison, Washington DC. Transferred to Elmira Prison Camp, New York, July 25, 1864.	Oath of Allegiance May 29, 1865
Knight, William M. Private	Unk	May 6, 1861, Grove Hill, Alabama	Co. J, 5th Alabama Infantry	May 5, 1864, Wilderness, Virginia	Point Lookout, Maryland, transferred to Elmira Prison, NY, August 17, 1864	Died November 16, 1864 of Chronic Diarrhea, Grave No. 955
Knipe, J. A. Private	Unk	Unknown	Co. E, 32nd North Carolina Infantry	May 10, 1864, Wilderness, Virginia	Point Lookout, Maryland, transferred to Elmira Prison, NY, August 6, 1864	Exchanged February 25, 1865 at Boulware's Wharf on the James River, Virginia
Knode, George W. Private	Unk	Unknown	Co. C, 2nd Virginia Infantry	May 27, 1864, Hall's Shop, Virginia	Point Lookout, Maryland, transferred to Elmira Prison, NY, July 12, 1864	Died September 12, 1864 of Chronic Diarrhea, Grave No. 192
Knott, John Henry Private	22	April 26, 1861, Townsville, North Carolina	Co. B, 12th North Carolina Infantry	May 12, 1864, Near Spotsylvania, Virginia	Point Lookout, Maryland, transferred to Elmira Prison, NY, August 14, 1864	Died May 26, 1865 of Erysipelas, Grave No. 2919

Name & Rank	Age	Enlisted	Regiment and State	Where Captured	Prison	Remarks
Knox, Gardner Private	27	June 24, 1863, Raleigh, North Carolina	Co. C, 2nd North Carolina Infantry	May 20, 1864, Near Spotsylvania Court House, Virginia	Point Lookout Prison Camp, Maryland. Transferred to Elmira Prison, July 6, 1864	Died February 28, 1865 of Diarrhea, Grave No. 2150
Knox, James S. Private	25	May 9, 1863, Charlotte, North Carolina	Co. B, 53rd North Carolina Infantry	July 12, 1864, Near Washington D. C. Gunshot Wound Right Thigh.	Old Capital Prison, Washington, DC, transferred to Elmira Prison, NY, December 17, 1864	Exchanged March 10, 1865 at Boulware's Wharf on the James River, Virginia
Koeppen, Henry C. Private	22	April 10, 1862, Greenville, Alabama	Co. B, 1st Battalion Alabama Artillery	August 8, 1864, Fort Gaines, Alabama	Steam Press No. 4 New Orleans, Louisiana transferred to Elmira Prison, NY, October 8, 1864.	Oath of Allegiance May 17, 1865
Koger, Pinkney Private	Unk	March 13, 1862, Henry County, Virginia	Co. G, 42nd Virginia Infantry	May 12, 1864, Near Spotsylvania Court House, Virginia	Point Lookout, Maryland, transferred to Elmira Prison, NY, August 6, 1864	Oath of Allegiance June 30, 1865
Koiner, Hiram C. Private	19	July 15, 1861, Waynesboro, Virginia	Co. B, 52nd Virginia Infantry	May 30, 1864 Mechanics-ville, Virginia	Point Lookout, Maryland, transferred to Elmira Prison, NY, July 9, 1864	Oath of Allegiance May 29, 1865
Koiner, Livingston R. Private	Unk	April 16, 1862, Elk Run, Rudes Hill, Virginia	Co. D, 2nd Virginia Infantry	May 12, 1864, Near Spotsylvania Court House, Virginia	Point Lookout, Maryland, transferred to Elmira Prison, NY, August 6, 1864	Exchanged March 2, 1865. Died April 10, 1865 of Typhoid Fever at Jackson Hospital, Richmond, VA.
Kolwyck, A. D. Private	Unk	December 7, 1861, Decatur County, Tennessee	Co. A, Jackson's 1st Regiment, Tennessee Heavy Artillery	August 23, 1864, Fort Morgan, Alabama	New Orleans, Louisiana transferred to Elmira Prison, NY, December 4, 1864.	Died December 17, 1864 of Variola (Smallpox). Grave No. 1735. Headstone has A. D. Kolwick.

Name & Rank	Age	Enlisted	Regiment and State	Where Captured	Prison	Remarks
Koonce, Richard H. Private	20	June 30, 1861, Trenton, North Carolina	Co. G, 2nd North Carolina Infantry	May 30, 1864 Mechanics-ville, Virginia	Point Lookout, Maryland, transferred to Elmira Prison, NY, July 11, 1864	Oath of Allegiance June 30, 1865
Koontz, K. Z. Private	21	August 8, 1863, Petersburg, Virginia	Co. H, 48th North Carolina Infantry	June 3, 1864, Gaines Farm Cold Harbor, Virginia	Point Lookout, Maryland, transferred to Elmira Prison, NY, July 12, 1864	Oath of Allegiance July 3, 1865
Koontz, Peter W. Private	Unk	April 23, 1862, Elk Run, Virginia	Co. B, 10th Virginia Infantry	May 12, 1864, Spotsylvania Court House, Virginia	Point Lookout, Maryland, transferred to Elmira Prison, NY, August 2, 1864	Exchanged March 10, 1865 at Boulware's Wharf on the James River, Virginia
Kornbacker, J. J. Private	Unk	September 14, 1862, Point Coupee, Mississippi	Co. H, 1st Mississippi Light Artillery	August 25, 1864, Clinton, Louisiana	New Orleans, LA, Transferred to Elmira Prison, NY, November 19, 1864	Exchanged February 13, 1865 at Boulware's wharf on the James River, Virginia
Kornegay, Dickson W. Private	16	October 16, 1861, Wayne County, North Carolina	Co. F, 40th Regiment, 3rd North Carolina Artillery	January 15, 1865, Fort Fisher, North Carolina	January 30, 1865 Elmira Prison Camp, New York	Exchanged February 20, 1865 at Boulware's or Cox Wharf on the James River, Virginia
Kornegay, Joseph E. Private	16	April 13, 1864, Fort Holmes, Brunswick County, North Carolina	Co. G, 40th Regiment, North Carolina Artillery	January 15, 1865, Fort Fisher, North Carolina	February 1, 1865, Elmira Prison Camp, New York	Exchanged March 2, 1865 at Boulware's Wharf on the James River, Virginia
Kornegay, Wesley Corporal	17	October 16, 1861, Duplin County, North Carolina	Co. F, 40th Regiment, 3rd North Carolina Artillery	January 15, 1865, Fort Fisher, North Carolina	January 30, 1865 Elmira Prison Camp, New York	Died April 27, 1865 of Chronic Diarrhea, Grave No. 2725. Headstone has Wesley Kernezay.
Kroll, Felix Sergeant	Unk	Unknown	Co. C, 6th Louisiana Infantry	July 8, 1864, Harpers Ferry, Virginia	Old Capital Prison, Washington DC. Transferred to Elmira Prison Camp, NY July 25, 1864.	Exchanged March 2, 1865 at Akins Landing on the James River, Virginia

Name & Rank	Age	Enlisted	Regiment and State	Where Captured	Prison	Remarks
Krystian, Merry G. Private	Unk	July 14, 1861, Maxeys, Georgia	Co. K, 8th Georgia Infantry	July 8, 1863, Fairfield, Virginia	Point Lookout Prison Camp, Maryland. Transferred to Elmira Prison, Date Unknown	Died March 13, 1865 of Chronic Diarrhea, Grave No. 1826
Kupferi-schmidt, Otto Private	Unk	Unknown	Co. A, Mosby's Regiment Virginia Cavalry	June 1, 1864, Falls Church Cold Harbor, Virginia	Old Capital Prison, Washington, DC, transferred to Elmira Prison, NY, August 12, 1864	Oath of Allegiance July 3, 1865
Kuschke, Herman Private	47	June 4, 1861, Camp Moore, Louisiana	Co. G, 6th Louisiana Infantry	May 5, 1864, Wilderness, Virginia	Point Lookout, Maryland, transferred to Elmira Prison, NY, July 23, 1864	Oath of Allegiance May 15, 1865
Kyle, Pleasant H. Private	22	June 22, 1861, Union City, Tennessee	Co. A, 13th Mississippi Infantry	April 6, 1865, Sailor's Creek, Virginia. Gunshot Wound Right Leg.	Old Capital Prison, Washington, DC, transferred to Elmira Prison, NY, May 12, 1865.	Oath of Allegiance July 11, 1865
Kyles, James Private	Unk	April 27, 1863, Swannanoa, North Carolina	Co. H, 11th North Carolina Infantry	July 14, 1863, Falling Waters, Maryland	Point Lookout, Maryland, transferred to Elmira Prison, NY, August 18, 1864	Died November 20, 1864 of Chronic Diarrhea, Grave No. 947
Kymrey, Manlove Sergeant	30	March 25, 1862, Albemarle, North Carolina	Co. J, 52nd North Carolina Infantry	July 14, 1863, Falling Waters, Maryland	Point Lookout, Maryland, transferred to Elmira Prison, NY, August 18, 1864	Exchanged February 13, 1865 at Boulware's wharf on the James River, Virginia

Name & Rank	Age	Enlisted	Regiment and State	Where Captured	Prison	Remarks
Labell, William H. Private	Unk	Unknown	Co. B, 7th Virginia Cavalry	July 24, 1864, Canons on James River, Virginia	Point Lookout, Maryland, transferred to Elmira Prison, NY, August 12, 1864	Oath of Allegiance May 29, 1865

Name & Rank	Age	Enlisted	Regiment and State	Where Captured	Prison	Remarks
Lablanc, Dosite Private	Unk	Unknown	Co. C, 4th Louisiana Cavalry	September 11, 1864, Near Plaquemine, Louisiana	New Orleans, LA, Transferred to Elmira Prison, NY, November 19, 1864	Died January 20, 1865 of Pneumonia, Grave No. 1201. Headstone has Dosite Loblane.
Laborde, Seweard Private	Unk	May 19, 1861, Camp Walker, New Orleans, Louisiana	Co. E, 2nd Louisiana Infantry	May 12, 1864, Spotsylvania Court House, Virginia	Point Lookout, Maryland, transferred to Elmira Prison, NY, August 17, 1864	Oath of Allegiance June 30, 1865
Lack, Joseph L. Private	25	May 14, 1862, Grenada, Mississippi	Co. C, 42nd Mississippi Infantry	May 24, 1864, Cold Harbor, Virginia	Point Lookout, Maryland, transferred to Elmira Prison, NY, July 11, 1864	Oath of Allegiance May 19, 1865
Lacock, H. Private	Unk	August 24, 1863, Point Coupee Parish, Louisiana	Co. J, 2nd Louisiana Cavalry	September 29, 1864, Point Coupee Parish, Louisiana	New Orleans, Louisiana transferred to Elmira November 19, 1864.	Exchanged February 13, 1865 at Boulware's Wharf on the James River, Virginia
Lacomb, Austin Private	Unk	June 4, 1861, Camp Moore, Louisiana	Co. C, 6th Louisiana Infantry	May 5, 1864, Wilderness, Virginia	Point Lookout, Maryland, transferred to Elmira Prison, NY, August 17, 1864	Exchanged February 25, 1865 at Boulware's or Cox Wharf on the James River, Virginia
LaCoste, G. Civilian	Unk	Registered Enemy	Citizen of Louisiana	July 27, 1864, New Orleans, Louisiana	New Orleans, Louisiana transferred to Elmira November 19, 1864.	Oath of Allegiance June 20, 1865
Ladd F. M. Private	Unk	Unknown	Co. F, Holcombe Legion, South Carolina Infantry	Unknown	Unknown	Died March 14, 1865 of Unknown Disease, Grave No. 2189
Ladd, John B. Private	17	January 25, 1864, Richmond, Virginia	Co. E, 25th Battalion Virginia Infantry	July 12, 1864, Cox's Farm, Virginia	Point Lookout, Maryland, transferred to Elmira Prison, NY, August 6, 1864	Oath of Allegiance June 21, 1865

Name & Rank	Age	Enlisted	Regiment and State	Where Captured	Prison	Remarks
Ladd, John W. Private	Unk	October 19, 1861, Richmond, Virginia	Co. G, 59th Virginia Infantry	May 8, 1864, Nottoway Bridge, Virginia	Point Lookout, Maryland, transferred to Elmira Prison, NY, August 17, 1864	Died January 3, 1865 of Chronic Diarrhea, Grave No. 1260. Headstone has G. W. Ladd, 55th VA.
Ladd, T. M. Private	Unk	Unknown	Conscript	Unknown	Point Lookout, Maryland, transferred to Elmira Prison, NY, July 17,1864	Died February 14, 1865 of Chronic Diarrhea, No Grave at Woodlawn Cemetery.
Lael, Calvin Private	Unk	February 14, 1864, Near Hanover Junction, Virginia	Co. D, 12th North Carolina Infantry	May 9, 1864, Spotsylvania Court House, Virginia	Old Capital Prison, Washington DC. Transferred to Elmira Prison Camp, NY, July 25, 1864.	Oath of Allegiance June 27, 1865
Lael, Cicero Private	19	March 15, 1862, Newton, North Carolina	Co. C, 28th North Carolina Infantry	July 29, 1864, Petersburg, Virginia	Point Lookout, Maryland, transferred to Elmira Prison, NY, August 12, 1864	Died January 4, 1865 of Pneumonia, Grave No. 1262. Lail 25th NC on Headstone.
Laffler, Jacob M. Private	Unk	Unknown	Co. H, 11th North Carolina Infantry	May 30, 1864 Mechanics-ville, Virginia	Point Lookout, Maryland, transferred to Elmira Prison, NY, July 11, 1864	Exchanged March 14, 1865 at Boulware's Wharf on the James River, Virginia
Laffoon, Moses Private	19	August 27, 1862, Raleigh, North Carolina	Co. C, 61st North Carolina Infantry	June 16, 1864, Petersburg, Virginia	Point Lookout, Maryland, transferred to Elmira Prison, NY, July 25, 1864	Exchanged October 29, 1864 at Venus Point, Savannah River, GA.
Laffoon, William G. Private	21	August 10, 1861, Dobson, North Carolina	Co. B, 2nd Battalion North Carolina Infantry	May 10, 1864, Near Spotsylvania County Court House, Virginia	Point Lookout, Maryland, transferred to Elmira Prison, NY, August 14, 1864	Died November 2, 1864 of Chronic Diarrhea, Grave No. 758. Name Laffloon on Headstone.
Lafitte, Joseph V. Corporal	Unk	May 6, 1861, Grove Hill, Alabama	Co. J, 5th Alabama Infantry	May 5, 1864, Wilderness, Virginia	Point Lookout, Maryland, transferred to Elmira Prison, NY, August 17, 1864	Oath of Allegiance June 10, 1865

Name & Rank	Age	Enlisted	Regiment and State	Where Captured	Prison	Remarks
Lake, Peter Private	25	February 15, 1862, New Orleans, Louisiana	Co. D, 5th Louisiana Infantry	May 24, 1864, North Anna, Virginia	Point Lookout, Maryland, transferred to Elmira Prison, NY, July 25, 1864	Oath of Allegiance March 22, 1865
Lake, Richard C. Private	Unk	August 20, 1862, Mill Point, Virginia	Co. G, 25th Virginia Infantry	May 6, 1864, Wilderness, Virginia	Old Capital Prison, Washington, DC, transferred to Elmira Prison, NY, July 14, 1864	Exchanged February 20, 1865 at Boulware's or Cox Wharf on the James River, Virginia
Lalonde, Georges Private	25	July 22, 1861, Camp Moore, Louisiana	Co. K, 10th Louisiana Infantry	May 5, 1864, Wilderness, Virginia	Point Lookout, Maryland, transferred to Elmira Prison, NY, July 25, 1864	Oath of Allegiance May 21, 1865
Lamarr, Francis M. Corporal	23	July 2, 1861, Nickelsville, Scott County, Virginia	Co. B, 48th Virginia Infantry	May 12, 1864, Spotsylvania Court House, Virginia	Point Lookout, Maryland, transferred to Elmira Prison, NY, August 12, 1864	Died January 25, 1865 of Chronic Diarrhea, Grave No. 1625
Lamb, Alpheus L. Private	21	June 5, 1861, Asheboro, North Carolina	Co. J, 22nd North Carolina Infantry	May 24, 1864, Hanover Junction, Virginia	Point Lookout, Maryland, transferred to Elmira Prison, NY, July 11, 1864	Oath of Allegiance May 17, 1865
Lamb, Burgess Private	18	June 5, 1861, Asheboro, North Carolina	Co. I, 22nd North Carolina Infantry	May 24, 1864, Hanover, Virginia	Point Lookout, Maryland, transferred to Elmira Prison, NY, July 12,1864	Oath of Allegiance July 26, 1865
Lamb, James Private	Unk	January 10, 1864, Fort Holmes, North Carolina	Co. F, 10th Regiment, 1st North Carolina Artillery	January 15, 1865, Fort Fisher, North Carolina	January 30, 1865, Elmira Prison Camp, New York	Died April 19, 1865 of Chronic Diarrhea, Grave No. 2335.
Lamb, John Private	Unk	February 11, 1863, Charleston, South Carolina	Co. G, 27th South Carolina Infantry	June 18, 1864, Near Petersburg, Virginia	Point Lookout, Maryland, transferred to Elmira Prison, NY, July 30, 1864	Transferred for Exchange 10/11/64. Died 11/1/64 of Chronic Diarrhea at Fort Monroe, VA.

Name & Rank	Age	Enlisted	Regiment and State	Where Captured	Prison	Remarks
Lamb, Lewis Z. Private	Unk	April 18, 1861, Conrad's Store, Virginia	Co. I, 10th Virginia Infantry	May 12, 1864, Spotsylvania Court House, Virginia	Point Lookout, Maryland, transferred to Elmira Prison, NY, August 2, 1864	Oath of Allegiance June 27, 1865
Lamb, Thomas Private	28	Unknown	Co. J, 17th North Carolina Infantry	July 14, 1863, Falling Waters, Maryland	Point Lookout, Maryland, transferred to Elmira Prison, NY, August 18, 1864	Oath of Allegiance June 12, 1865
Lamb, Thomas L. Private	Unk	March 30, 1862, Charleston, South Carolina	Co. I, 22nd South Carolina Infantry	July 30, 1864, Petersburg, Virginia	Point Lookout, Maryland, transferred to Elmira Prison, NY, August 12, 1864	Exchanged March 14, 1865 at Boulware's Wharf on the James River, Virginia
Lamb, William Private	Unk	February 4, 1863, Camp Randolph, Virginia	Co. D, 34th, Virginia Infantry	June 15, 1864, Near Petersburg, Virginia	Point Lookout, Maryland, transferred to Elmira Prison, NY, July 12, 1864	Oath of Allegiance July 3, 1865
Lamberson, Eli Private	21	March 20, 1862, Elizabethtown, Bladen County, North Carolina	Co. H, 36th Regiment 2nd North Carolina Artillery	January 15, 1865, Fort Fisher, North Carolina	February 1, 1865 Elmira Prison Camp, New York	Died March 7, 1865 of Diarrhea, Grave No. 2382
Lambert, Green Private	Unk	February 20, 1864, Decatur, Georgia	Co. B, 27th Georgia Infantry	June 1, 1864, Gaines Mill Cold Harbor, Virginia	Point Lookout, Maryland, transferred to Elmira Prison, NY, July 12, 1864	Died December 28, 1864 of Pneumonia, Grave No. 1306
Lambert, James L. Private	Unk	Unknown	Co. E, 50th Virginia Infantry	May 12, 1864, Spotsylvania Court House, Virginia	Point Lookout, Maryland, transferred to Elmira Prison, NY, August 2, 1864	Exchanged October 29, 1864 at Venus Point, Savannah River, GA.
Lambert, John J. Private	19	May 28, 1861, Cartersville, North Carolina	Co. E, 26th North Carolina Infantry	May 12, 1864, Spotsylvania Court House, Virginia	Point Lookout, Maryland, transferred to Elmira Prison, NY, July 30, 1864	Oath of Allegiance June 23, 1865
Lambert, John M. Private	21	February 8, 1862, Randolph County, North Carolina	Co. E, 44th North Carolina Infantry	June 2, 1864, Talapatomoy Creek, Gaines Farm Cold Harbor, Virginia	Point Lookout, Maryland, transferred to Elmira Prison, NY, July 12, 1864	Oath of Allegiance July 3, 1865

Name & Rank	Age	Enlisted	Regiment and State	Where Captured	Prison	Remarks
Lambert, Mark Martin Private	Unk	July 11, 1863, Ritchie County, Virginia	Co. A, 46th Virginia Cavalry	July 16, 1864, Near Harpers Ferry, Loudoun County, Virginia	Old Capital Prison, Washington DC. Transferred to Elmira Prison Camp, NY, July 25, 1864.	Exchanged March 14, 1865 at Boulware's Wharf on the James River, Virginia
Lambert, Samuel D. Private	Unk	July 15, 1862, Raleigh, North Carolina	Co. C, 5th North Carolina Infantry	June 10, 1864, Spotsylvania Court House, Virginia	Point Lookout, Maryland, transferred to Elmira Prison, NY, July 25, 1864	Transferred For Exchange October 11, 1864 to Point Lookout Prison Camp, MD. Nothing Further.
Lambeth, Samuel Private	41	February 27, 1862, Reidsville, Rockingham County, North Carolina	Co. E, 45th North Carolina Infantry	May 10, 1864, Spotsylvania Court House, Virginia	Point Lookout, Maryland, transferred to Elmira Prison, NY, August 6, 1864	Died March 4, 1865 of Diarrhea, Grave No. 1987
Lamkin, John C. Sergeant	Unk	June 4, 1861, Warsaw, Virginia	Co. E, 48th Virginia Infantry	June 2, 1864, Near Talapatomoy Creek, Old Church, Cold Harbor, Virginia	Point Lookout, Maryland, transferred to Elmira Prison, NY, July 6, 1864	Exchanged March 14, 1865 at Boulware's Wharf on the James River, Virginia
Lamkin, Samuel R. Private	18	April 20, 1861, Holmesville, Mississippi	Co. E, 16th Mississippi Infantry	August 21, 1864, Weldon Railroad, Near Petersburg, VA. Gunshot Wound Left Arm, Severe. Amputation of Left Arm.	Old Capital Prison, Washington, DC transferred to Elmira Prison, NY, August 27, 1864	Exchanged February 20, 1865 at Boulware's or Cox Wharf on the James River, Virginia
Lamkin, T. C. Private	Unk	August 4, 1863, Columbia County, Georgia	Co. C, 20th Battalion Georgia Cavalry	June 1, 1864, Gaines Farm, Cold Harbor, Virginia	Transferred From Point Lookout Prison, MD, July 12, 1864. Train Never Arrived at Elmira Prison Camp, NY.	Died July 15, 1864 in Train Wreck at Shohola, Pennsylvania.
Lampe, Isaac M. Private	26	April 18, 1861, Marion, Virginia	Co. D, 4th Virginia Infantry	May 12, 1864, Spotsylvania Court House, Virginia. Gunshot Boned Right of Spine.	Old Capital Prison, Washington, DC transferred to Elmira Prison, NY, August 29, 1864	Oath of Allegiance, May 12, 1865

Name & Rank	Age	Enlisted	Regiment and State	Where Captured	Prison	Remarks
Lanagan, Thomas Corporal	34	June 5, 1861, Memphis, Tennessee	Co. A, Jackson's 1st Regiment, Tennessee Heavy Artillery	August 23, 1864, Fort Morgan, Alabama	New Orleans, Louisiana transferred to Elmira Prison, NY, December 4, 1864.	Exchanged February 25, 1865 at Boulware's or Cox Wharf on the James River, Virginia
Lancaster, Crofford C. Private	27	July 29, 1861, Whiteville, North Carolina	Co. C, 18th North Carolina Infantry	May 12, 1864, Spotsylvania Court House, Virginia	Point Lookout, Maryland, transferred to Elmira Prison, NY, August 6, 1864	Exchanged October 29, 1864 at Venus Point, Savannah River, GA.
Lance, Michael Private	Unk	February 11, 1862, Hiawassee, Georgia	Co. C, 24th Georgia Infantry	June 1, 1864, Cold Harbor, Virginia	Point Lookout, Maryland, transferred to Elmira Prison, NY, July 12, 1864	Oath of Allegiance June 14, 1865
Lancer, Francis M. Private	Unk	March 8, 1862, Camp Leon, Madison, Florida	Co. D, 5th Florida Infantry	May 12, 1864, Spotsylvania Court House, Virginia	Point Lookout, Maryland, transferred to Elmira Prison, NY, July 30, 1864	Died December 9, 1864 of Pneumonia, Grave No. 1172. Name Lanier on Headstone.
Land, John H. Private	Unk	February 12, 1864, Campbell, Virginia	Co. E, 5th Virginia Cavalry	May 11, 1864, Yellow Tavern, Hanover County, Virginia	Point Lookout, Maryland, transferred to Elmira Prison, NY, August 17, 1864	Exchanged October 29, 1864 at Venus Point, Savannah River, GA.
Land, Joseph H. Sergeant	Unk	June 15, 1861, Lynchburg, Virginia	Co. A, 42nd Virginia Infantry	May 12, 1864, Spotsylvania Court House, Virginia	Point Lookout, Maryland, transferred to Elmira Prison, NY, August 2, 1864	Oath of Allegiance June 19, 1865
Land, William M. Private	Unk	July 20, 1862, Columbia, South Carolina	Co. M, 1st Palmetto Sharpshooters South Carolina	June 1, 1864, Old Church Cold Harbor, Virginia	Point Lookout, Maryland, transferred to Elmira Prison, NY, July 12, 1864	Oath of Allegiance June 14, 1865
Landers, John G. Private	35	August 13, 1862, Calhoun, Georgia	Co. E, 44th Georgia Infantry	May 10, 1864, Spotsylvania Court House, Virginia	Old Capital Prison, Washington DC. Transferred to Elmira Prison Camp, NY, July 25, 1864.	Oath of Allegiance June 16, 1865

Name & Rank	Age	Enlisted	Regiment and State	Where Captured	Prison	Remarks
Landing, J. T. Private	Unk	May 13, 1862, Savannah, Georgia	Co. E, 7th Georgia Cavalry	June 11, 1864, Louisa Court House, Trevilian Station, Virginia	Point Lookout, Maryland, transferred to Elmira Prison, NY, July 30, 1864	Exchanged February 20, 1865. Died March 28, 1865 of Diarrhea at Hospital #10, Salisbury, NC.
Landing, Joseph F. Private	22	July 6, 1861, Halifax County, North Carolina	Co. H, 5th North Carolina Infantry	August 16, 1864, Gates County, North Carolina and	Point Lookout, Maryland, transferred to Elmira Prison, NY, August 18, 1864	Oath of Allegiance May 29, 1865
Landreth, Samuel Private	33	August 15, 1862, Statesville, North Carolina	Co. B, 37th North Carolina Infantry	May 12, 1864, Spotsylvania Court House, Virginia	Point Lookout, Maryland, transferred to Elmira Prison, NY, August 12, 1864	Oath of Allegiance June 27, 1865
Landrum, John J. Sergeant	Unk	July 11, 1861, Lynchburg, Virginia	Co. I, 42nd Virginia Infantry	May 12, 1864, Spotsylvania Court House, Virginia	Point Lookout, Maryland, transferred to Elmira Prison, NY, August 2, 1864	Exchanged March 10, 1865 at Boulware's Wharf on the James River, Virginia
Landrum, Josephus A. Private	Unk	February 8, 1862, Gloucester Point, Virginia	Co. G, 26th Virginia Infantry	June 15, 1864, Petersburg, Virginia	Point Lookout, Maryland, transferred to Elmira Prison, NY, July 30, 1864	Exchanged March 14, 1865 at Boulware's Wharf on the James River, Virginia
Landrum, Samuel P. Private	Unk	July 11, 1862, Lynchburg, Virginia	Co. I, 42nd Virginia Infantry	May 12, 1864, Near Spotsylvania Court House, Virginia	Point Lookout, Maryland, transferred to Elmira Prison, NY, August 6, 1864	Oath of Allegiance June 27, 1865
Landvoight, Edwin Private	Unk	Unknown	Co. A, Jackson's 1st Regiment, Tennessee Heavy Artillery	August 23, 1864, Fort Morgan, Alabama	New Orleans, Louisiana transferred to Elmira Prison, NY, December 4, 1864.	Exchanged March 10, 1865 at Boulware's Wharf on the James River, Virginia
Lane, Andrew J. Private	28	May 1, 1862, South Mills, North Carolina	Co. D, 32nd North Carolina Infantry	May 10, 1864, Near Spotsylvania Court House, Virginia	Point Lookout, Maryland, transferred to Elmira Prison, NY, August 6, 1864	Died February 25, 1865 of Chronic Diarrhea, Grave No. 2293

Name & Rank	Age	Enlisted	Regiment and State	Where Captured	Prison	Remarks
Lane, C. T. Corporal	26	July 3, 1861, Atlanta, Georgia	Co. K, 11th Georgia Infantry	May 6, 1864, Wilderness, Virginia	Point Lookout, Maryland, transferred to Elmira Prison, NY, August 14, 1864	Oath of Allegiance June 30, 1865
Lane, Charles W. Private	Unk	May 20, 1861, Nashville, Tennessee	Co. I, 7th Tennessee Infantry	June 2, 1864, Near Old Church Cold Harbor, Virginia	Point Lookout, Maryland, transferred to Elmira Prison, NY, July 12, 1864	Exchanged February 25, 1865 at Boulware's or Cox Wharf on the James River, Virginia
Lane, Henry Private	25	May 18, 1861, Edenton, North Carolina	Co. A, 1st North Carolina Infantry	May 12, 1864, Wilderness, Spotsylvania Court House, Virginia	Point Lookout, Maryland, transferred to Elmira Prison, NY, August 6, 1864	Died February 12, 1865 of Variola (Smallpox), Grave No. 2081
Lane, John P. Private	22	June 23, 1861, Camp Walker, Corinth, Mississippi	Co. E, 18th Mississippi Infantry	May 6, 1864, Wilderness, Virginia	Point Lookout, Maryland, transferred to Elmira Prison, NY, August 14, 1864	Oath of Allegiance June 14, 1865
Lane, Patrick Private	Unk	July 1, 1862, Edgecombe County, North Carolina	Co. E, 33rd North Carolina Infantry	May 6, 1864, Wilderness, Virginia	Point Lookout, Maryland, transferred to Elmira Prison, NY, August 14, 1864	Oath of Allegiance June 14, 1865
Lane, Richard Corporal	36	September 11, 1862, Wake County, North Carolina	Co. F, 8th North Carolina Infantry	June 1, 1864, Cold Harbor, Virginia	Point Lookout, Maryland, transferred to Elmira Prison, NY, July 12, 1864	Exchanged February 20, 1865 at Boulware's or Cox Wharf on the James River, Virginia
Lane, Robert J. Private	Unk	Unknown	Co. B, 44th Virginia Infantry	May 12, 1864, Spotsylvania Court House, Virginia	Point Lookout, Maryland, transferred to Elmira Prison, NY, August 2, 1864	Died February 21, 1865 of Pneumonia, Grave No. 2232
Lane, Thomas J. Private	19	June 1, 1861, Dogwood Grove, North Carolina	Co. K, 3rd North Carolina Infantry	May 12, 1864, Near Spotsylvania Court House, Virginia	Point Lookout, Maryland, transferred to Elmira Prison, NY, August 14, 1864	Exchanged October 29, 1864 at Venus Point, Savannah River, GA.

Name & Rank	Age	Enlisted	Regiment and State	Where Captured	Prison	Remarks
Lane, William Private	32	May 1, 1862, South Mills, North Carolina	Co. D, 32nd North Carolina Infantry	May 10, 1864, Near Spotsylvania Court House, Virginia	Point Lookout, Maryland, transferred to Elmira Prison, NY, August 6, 1864	Exchanged 2/20/65. Died 3/3/65 of Pneumonia at Moore Hospital, Hospital No. 24, Richmond, VA.
Laney, W. Cicero Private	Unk	June 27, 1861, Whitesville, Harris County, Georgia	Co. E, 20th Georgia Infantry	May 6, 1864, Wilderness, Virginia	Old Capital Prison, Washington, DC, transferred to Elmira Prison, NY, July 14, 1864	Oath of Allegiance June 30, 1865
Langballe, F. W. Private	18	June 24, 1861, Coosawhatchie, South Carolina	Co. E, 11th South Carolina Infantry	June 24, 1864, Near Petersburg, Virginia	Point Lookout, Maryland, transferred to Elmira Prison, NY, August 18, 1864	Exchanged October 29, 1864 at Venus Point, Savannah River, GA.
Lange, J. L. Private	Unk	Unknown	Co. G, 16th Virginia Infantry	May 12, 1864, Spotsylvania Court House, Virginia	Point Lookout, Maryland, transferred to Elmira Prison, NY, August 12, 1864	Oath of Allegiance May 29, 1865
Langford, J. A. Private	Unk	August 19, 1862, Newton, Alabama	Co. F, 15th Alabama Infantry	May 6, 1864, Wilderness, Virginia	Point Lookout, Maryland, transferred to Elmira Prison, NY, August 17, 1864	Died February 6, 1865 of Variola (Smallpox) Grave No. 1922
Langley, C. A. Private	24	July 14, 1862, Mocksville, North Carolina	Co. H, 5th North Carolina Cavalry	September 22, 1863, Near Madison Court House, Virginia	Point Lookout, Maryland, transferred to Elmira Prison, NY, August 18, 1864	Exchanged October 29, 1864 at Venus Point, Savannah River, GA.
Langley, Hyman Private	29	August 10, 1861, Pitt County, North Carolina	Co. G, 8th North Carolina Infantry	June 1, 1864, Cold Harbor, Virginia	Point Lookout, Maryland, transferred to Elmira Prison, NY, July 12, 1864	Transferred for Exchanged 10/29/64 at Venus Point, Savannah River, GA.
Langley, Jeremiah R. Private	33	September 11, 1862, Calhoun, Georgia	Co. H, 16th Georgia Infantry	August 16, 1864, Front Royal, Virginia	Old Capital Prison, Washington, DC transferred to Elmira Prison, NY, August 29, 1864	Died February 25, 1865 of Variola (Smallpox), Grave No. 2285

Name & Rank	Age	Enlisted	Regiment and State	Where Captured	Prison	Remarks
Langley, William Private	Unk	April 22, 1861, Stafford Court House, Virginia	Co. J, 47th Virginia Infantry	August 8, 1863, Stafford Court House, Virginia	Point Lookout, Maryland, transferred to Elmira Prison, NY, August 18, 1864	Exchanged March 10, 1865 at Boulware's Wharf on the James River, Virginia
Langley, William H. Corporal	18	June 10, 1861, Garysburg, North Carolina	Co. E, 7th North Carolina Infantry	May 6, 1864, Wilderness, Virginia	Point Lookout, Maryland, transferred to Elmira Prison, NY, August 14, 1864	Oath of Allegiance June 12, 1865
Langlois, J. V. Private	25	September 1, 1862, New Road, Louisiana	Co. J, 2nd Louisiana Cavalry	March 30, 1864, Cane River, Louisiana	New Orleans, LA, Transferred to Elmira Prison, NY, November 19, 1864	Exchanged February 20, 1865 at Boulware's or Cox Wharf on the James River, Virginia
Langlois, John Private	Unk	September 2, 1862, Abbeville, Louisiana	Louisiana, Pointe Coupee Artillery	May 16, 1863, Champion Hill, Mississippi	Point Lookout, Maryland, transferred to Elmira Prison, NY, August 18, 1864	Exchanged February 25, 1865 at Boulware's wharf on the James River, Virginia
Langlois, Lewis Corporal	Unk	September 2, 1862, Abbeville, Louisiana	Louisiana, Pointe Coupee Artillery	May 16, 1863, Champion Hill, Mississippi	Point Lookout, Maryland, transferred to Elmira Prison, NY, August 18, 1864	Exchanged February 25, 1865 at Boulware's wharf on the James River, Virginia
Langlois, Pierre Private	Unk	June 29, 1861, New Orleans, Louisiana	Louisiana, Pointe Coupee Artillery	May 16, 1863, Champion Hill, Mississippi	Point Lookout, Maryland, transferred to Elmira Prison, NY, August 18, 1864	Exchanged February 25, 1865 at Boulware's wharf on the James River, Virginia
Lanham, John P. Private	Unk	November 1, 1862, Pack's Ferry, Virginia	Co. A, 22nd Virginia Infantry	July 15, 1864, Near Washington, DC	Old Capital Prison, Washington, DC transferred to Elmira Prison, NY, August 27, 1864	Oath of Allegiance May 17, 1865
Lanier, David Private	Unk	February 13, 1863, Kenansville, North Carolina	Co. B, 51st North Carolina Infantry	June 1, 1864, Cold Harbor, Virginia	Point Lookout, Maryland, transferred to Elmira Prison, NY, July 12, 1864	Died August 29, 1864 of Hospital Gangrene, Grave No. 58

Name & Rank	Age	Enlisted	Regiment and State	Where Captured	Prison	Remarks
Lanier, Eli Private	Unk	July 15, 1862, Duplin County, North Carolina	Co. B, 3rd North Carolina Infantry	May 12, 1864, Spotsylvania Court House, Virginia	Point Lookout, Maryland, transferred to Elmira Prison, NY, July 11, 1864	Oath of Allegiance May 29, 1865
Lanier, Lewis Private	32	June 17, 1861, Sampson County, North Carolina	Co. B, 3rd North Carolina Infantry	May 12, 1864, Near Spotsylvania, Virginia	Point Lookout, Maryland, transferred to Elmira Prison, NY, August 14, 1864	Died January 13, 1865 of Variola (Smallpox), Grave No. 1484
Lanier, R. J. Private	Unk	August 15, 1861, Natchez, Mississippi	Co. E, 4th Battalion Infantry	July 19, 1864, Rodney Parish, Louisiana	New Orleans, LA, Transferred to Elmira Prison, NY, November 19, 1864	Exchanged February 13, 1865 at Boulware's wharf on the James River, Virginia
Lanier, Thomas H. Private	Unk	February 1, 1862, Bannerman's, North Carolina	Co. K, 3rd North Carolina Infantry	May 12, 1864, Near Spotsylvania Court House, Virginia	Point Lookout, Maryland, transferred to Elmira Prison, NY, August 14, 1864	Oath of Allegiance June 27, 1865
Lanneau. W. S. Private	24	May 28, 1862, Charleston, South Carolina	Co. C, 25th South Carolina Infantry	January 15, 1865, Fort Fisher, North Carolina	January 30, 1865, Elmira Prison Camp, New York	Oath of Allegiance June 14, 1865
Lansdon, Arthur J. Private	Unk	September 5, 1862, Wacker, Alabama	Co. F, 1st Alabama Artillery	August 23, 1864, Fort Morgan, Alabama	New Orleans, Louisiana. Transferred to Elmira Prison Camp, NY, October 8, 1864	Died February 20, 1865 of Oydenia (Fluid Trapped in Tissues) Grave No. 2318
Lantz, Adam R. Private	Unk	March 1, 1864, Red Sulfur Springs, Virginia	Co. H, 17th Virginia Cavalry	July 3, 1864, Martinsburg, Near Harpers Ferry, Virginia	Old Capital Prison, Washington DC. Transferred to Elmira Prison Camp, NY, July 25, 1864.	Exchanged March 10, 1865 at Boulware's Wharf on the James River, Virginia
Lantz, Daniel Private	Unk	April 8, 1862, Camp Shenandoah, Virginia	Co. K, 25th Virginia Infantry	May 5, 1864, Mine Run, Wilderness, Virginia	Point Lookout, Maryland, transferred to Elmira Prison, NY, August 2, 1864	Died September 29, 1864 of Pneumonia, Grave No. 438. Name Lance on Headstone.
Larbin, Willis Private	Unk	Unknown	Co. H, 36th Regiment, 2nd North Carolina Artillery	January 15, 1865, Fort Fisher, North Carolina	January 30, 1865 Elmira Prison Camp, New York	Died March 18, 1865 of Unknown Disease, Grave No. 1728

Name & Rank	Age	Enlisted	Regiment and State	Where Captured	Prison	Remarks
Lard, Barney Private	Unk	Unknown	Co. C, 12th Georgia Infantry	August 20, 1864, Winchester, Virginia	Old Capital Prison, Washington, DC transferred to Elmira Prison, NY, August 27, 1864	Oath of Allegiance May 19, 1865
Laricey, O'Bryant Private	20	August 20, 1861, Ridgeville, South Carolina	Co. G, 11th South Carolina Infantry	June 18, 1864, Petersburg, Virginia	Point Lookout, Maryland, transferred to Elmira Prison, NY, July 30, 1864	Exchanged October 29, 1864 at Venus Point, Savannah River, GA.
Larmer, William Private	Unk	May 27, 1861, New Orleans, Louisiana	Co. E, 15th Louisiana Infantry	May 5, 1864, Wilderness, Virginia	Point Lookout, Maryland, transferred to Elmira Prison, NY, July 25, 1864	Oath of Allegiance May 17, 1865
Lartigue, E. J. Private	Unk	August 7, 1862, Grahamville, South Carolina	Co. G, 27th South Carolina Infantry	June 24, 1864, Near Petersburg, Virginia	Point Lookout, Maryland, transferred to Elmira Prison, NY, August 18, 1864	Transferred for Exchanged 10/29/64 at Venus Point, Savannah River, GA.
Laryc, Joseph Private	Unk	March 24, 1863, Knoxville, Tennessee	Co. G, 63rd Tennessee Infantry	June 17, 1864, Petersburg, Virginia	Point Lookout, Maryland, transferred to Elmira Prison, NY, July 30, 1864	Died October 1, 1864 of Chronic Diarrhea, Grave No. 417
Lashley, Elemuel Private	Unk	September 30, 1862, Dale County, Alabama	Co. G, 3rd Alabama Infantry	May 20, 1864, Spotsylvania Court House, Virginia	Point Lookout, Maryland, transferred to Elmira Prison, NY, July 3, 1864	Died March 24, 1865 of Variola (Smallpox), Grave No. 2448
Lashorn, William R. Private	Unk	February 22, 1862, Martinsburg, Virginia	Co. D, 2nd Virginia Infantry	May 12, 1864, Near Spotsylvania Court House, Virginia	Point Lookout, Maryland, transferred to Elmira Prison, NY, August 6, 1864	Oath of Allegiance May 15, 1865
Lassale, Bertrand Private	Unk	Unknown	Co. A, Ogden's Battalion Louisiana Cavalry	September 17, 1864, Greenville Springs, Near East Baton Rouge, Louisiana	New Orleans, Louisiana transferred to Elmira November 19, 1864.	Exchanged February 25, 1865 at Boulware's or Cox Wharf on the James River, Virginia

Name & Rank	Age	Enlisted	Regiment and State	Where Captured	Prison	Remarks
Lassiter, Everett C. Private	19	February 9, 1863, Wheelersville, North Carolina	Co. D, 32nd North Carolina Infantry	May 10, 1864, Near Spotsylvania Court House, Virginia	Point Lookout, Maryland, transferred to Elmira Prison, NY, August 6, 1864	Exchanged March 14, 1865 at Boulware's Wharf on the James River, Virginia
Lassiter, J. W. Private	19	July 16, 1862, Raleigh, North Carolina	Co. D, 5th North Carolina Infantry	May 20, 1864, Spotsylvania Court House, Virginia	Point Lookout, Maryland, transferred to Elmira Prison, NY, July 3, 1864	Exchanged March 2, 1865 at Akins Landing on the James River, Virginia
Lassiter, Jesse B. Sergeant	19	May 1, 1862, South Mills, North Carolina	Co. B, 32nd North Carolina Infantry	May 10, 1864, Near Spotsylvania Court House, Virginia	Point Lookout, Maryland, transferred to Elmira Prison, NY, August 6, 1864	Exchanged March 14, 1865 at Boulware's Wharf on the James River, Virginia
Lassiter, James H. Private	24	February 13, 1862, Winton, Hertford County, North Carolina	Co. C, 3rd Battalion North Carolina Light Artillery	January 15, 1865, Fort Fisher, North Carolina	February 1, 1865, Elmira Prison Camp, New York	Oath of Allegiance June 12, 1865
Lassiter, John F. Private	19	January 28, 1862, Winton, Hertford County, North Carolina	Co. C, 3rd Battalion North Carolina Light Artillery	January 15, 1865, Fort Fisher, North Carolina	February 1, 1865, Elmira Prison Camp, New York	Oath of Allegiance June 12, 1865
Lassiter, John R. Private	28	March 6, 1862, Newton Grove, North Carolina	Co H, 20th North Carolina Infantry	May 10, 1864, Near Spotsylvania Court House, Virginia	Point Lookout, Maryland, transferred to Elmira Prison, NY, August 14, 1864	Exchanged March 14, 1865 at Boulware's Wharf on the James River, Virginia
Lassiter, Leroy Private	33	January 28, 1862, Winton, Hertford County, North Carolina	Co. C, 3rd Battalion North Carolina Light Artillery	January 15, 1865, Fort Fisher, North Carolina	February 1, 1865, Elmira Prison Camp, New York	Oath of Allegiance June 12, 1865
Lassiter, Richard Private	19	April 15, 1862, St. John's, Hertford County, North Carolina	Co. C, 3rd Battalion North Carolina Light Artillery	January 15, 1865, Fort Fisher, North Carolina	February 1, 1865, Elmira Prison Camp, New York	Oath of Allegiance May 17, 1865
Lassiter, Richard T. Private	21	May 1, 1862, South Mills, North Carolina	Co. B, 32nd North Carolina Infantry	May 10, 1864, Near Spotsylvania Court House, Virginia	Point Lookout, Maryland, transferred to Elmira Prison, NY, August 6, 1864	Oath of Allegiance June 27, 1865

Name & Rank	Age	Enlisted	Regiment and State	Where Captured	Prison	Remarks
Latham, Edgar R. Private	17	April 10, 1862, Plymouth, North Carolina	Co. G, 1st North Carolina Infantry	May 12, 1864, Wilderness, Spotsylvania Court House, Virginia	Point Lookout, Maryland, transferred to Elmira Prison, NY, August 6, 1864	Exchanged March 10, 1865 at Boulware's Wharf on the James River, Virginia
Latham, William Corporal	Unk	March 6, 1861, Selma, Alabama	Co. C, 1st Battalion Alabama Artillery	August 23, 1864, Fort Morgan, Alabama	New Orleans, Louisiana transferred to Elmira Prison, NY, December 4, 1864.	Oath of Allegiance June 21, 1865
Latter, Edward V. Private	22	April 24, 1861, Bug Hill, North Carolina	Co. C, 18th North Carolina Infantry	July 29, 1864, Petersburg, Virginia	Point Lookout, Maryland, transferred to Elmira Prison, NY, August 12, 1864	Oath of Allegiance May 19, 1865
Lauck, Theodore H. Corporal	Unk	June 2, 1861, Luray, Virginia	Co. K, 10th Virginia Infantry	May 12, 1864, Spotsylvania Court House, Virginia	Point Lookout, Maryland, transferred to Elmira Prison, NY, August 2, 1864	Oath of Allegiance June 19, 1865
Laue, W. H. Private	Unk	Unknown	Co. H, 4th Georgia Infantry	July 10, 1864, Harpers Ferry, Virginia	Old Capital Prison, Washington DC. Transferred to Elmira Prison Camp, NY, July 25, 1864.	Exchanged February 20, 1865 at Boulware's or Cox Wharf on the James River, Virginia
Laughry, Edward C. Private	Unk	March 3, 1862, Alex Lea, Louisiana	Co. J, 8th Louisiana Infantry	May 12, 1864, Spotsylvania Court House, Virginia	Point Lookout, Maryland, transferred to Elmira Prison, NY, August 17, 1864	Died March 15, 1865 Phthisis Pulmonalis, Grave No. 1665. Name Loughry on Headstone.
Laun, William Private	Unk	Unknown	Co. B, 6th Virginia Infantry	July 4, 1864, Rockville, Virginia	Old Capital Prison, Washington DC. Transferred to Elmira Prison Camp, NY, July 25, 1864.	Oath of Allegiance May 19, 1865
Launey, Arthur R. Private	Unk	June 4, 1861, Camp Moore, Louisiana	Co. C, 6th Louisiana Infantry	May 5, 1864, Wilderness, Virginia	Point Lookout, Maryland, transferred to Elmira Prison, NY, August 17, 1864	Exchanged March 10, 1865 at Boulware's Wharf on the James River, Virginia

Name & Rank	Age	Enlisted	Regiment and State	Where Captured	Prison	Remarks
Laurent, A. Sergeant	39	February 9, 1863, Port Hudson, Louisiana	Co. B, 4th Louisiana Infantry	October 3, 1864, West Baton Rouge, Louisiana	New Orleans, Louisiana transferred to Elmira November 19, 1864.	Exchanged February 25, 1865 at Boulware's or Cox Wharf on the James River, Virginia
Lavall, Patrick Private	Unk	January 8,1862 Monticello, Florida	Co. E, 5th Florida Infantry	May 31, 1864, Gaines Farm Cold Harbor, Virginia	Point Lookout, Maryland, transferred to Elmira Prison, NY, July 12, 1864	Oath of Allegiance May 19, 1865
Lavender, Henry L. Private	Unk	March 18, 1864, Botetouch, Virginia	Co. A, 14th Virginia Infantry	May 31, 1864, Cold Harbor, Virginia	Point Lookout, Maryland, transferred to Elmira Prison, NY, July 23, 1864	Died September 20, 1864 of Chronic Diarrhea, Grave No. 346
Lavender, Robert Private	Unk	April 15, 1862, Richmond, Virginia	Co. D, 5th Virginia Cavalry	June 8, 1864, Chickahominy, Cold Harbor, Virginia	Point Lookout, Maryland, transferred to Elmira Prison, NY, July 25, 1864	Died February 8, 1865 of Chronic Diarrhea, Grave No. 1937. 4th Cavalry on Headstone.
Lawhon, James Private	39	November 6, 1861, Duplin County, North Carolina	Co. A, 36th Regiment North Carolina Artillery	January 15, 1865, Fort Fisher, North Carolina	February 1, 1865, Elmira Prison Camp, New York	Died April 10, 1865 of Chronic Diarrhea, Grave No. 2670
Lawhorn, William P. Private	Unk	May 27, 1861, Buckhannon, Virginia	Co. B, 25th Virginia Infantry	May 12, 1864, Spotsylvania Court House, Virginia	Point Lookout, Maryland, transferred to Elmira Prison, NY, July 30, 1864	Transferred for Exchange 10/11/64. Died January 13, 1865 of Chronic Diarrhea.
Lawrence, Allen Private	33	July 15, 1862, Raleigh, North Carolina	Co. G, 1st North Carolina Infantry	May 12, 1864, Wilderness, Spotsylvania Court House, Virginia	Point Lookout, Maryland, transferred to Elmira Prison, NY, August 6, 1864	Died September 6, 1864 of Meningitis, Grave No. 240
Lawrence, James M. Private	26	January 1, 1862, Newbern, Craven County, North Carolina	Co. F, 36th Regiment North Carolina Artillery	January 15, 1865, Fort Fisher, North Carolina	February 1, 1865, Elmira Prison Camp, New York	Died April 23, 1865 of Pneumonia, Grave No. 1403

Name & Rank	Age	Enlisted	Regiment and State	Where Captured	Prison	Remarks
Lawrence, John W. Private	Unk	July 17, 1862, Wake County, North Carolina	Co. E, 56th North Carolina Infantry	June 17, 1864, Petersburg, Virginia	Point Lookout, Maryland, transferred to Elmira Prison, NY, July 30, 1864	Oath of Allegiance July 3, 1865
Lawrence, John W. Private	Unk	October 8, 1862, Paris, Virginia	Co. A, 6th Virginia Cavalry	July 24, 1864, Berlin, Virginia	Old Capital Prison, Washington, DC, transferred to Elmira Prison, NY, August 12, 1864	Died December 3, 1864 of Pneumonia, Grave No. 887
Lawrence, Peter Private	24	April 25, 1861, Snow Hill, North Carolina	Co. A, 3rd North Carolina Infantry	May 12, 1864, Near Spotsylvania, Virginia	Point Lookout, Maryland, transferred to Elmira Prison, NY, August 14, 1864	Exchanged March 10, 1865 at Boulware's Wharf on the James River, Virginia
Lawrence, W. B. Private	23	July 15, 1862, Raleigh, North Carolina	Co. G, 1st North Carolina Infantry	May 12, 1864, Spotsylvania Court House, Virginia	Point Lookout, Maryland, transferred to Elmira Prison, NY, August 6, 1864	Died March 4, 1865 of Diarrhea, Grave No. 1986
Laws, Coffey Private	23	May 31, 1861, Raleigh, North Carolina	Co. B, 1st North Carolina Infantry	May 12, 1864, Spotsylvania Court House, Virginia	Point Lookout, Maryland, transferred to Elmira Prison, NY, August 6, 1864	Exchanged October 29, 1864 at Venus Point, Savannah River, GA.
Lawson, Allen Private	25	December 1, 1862, Francisco, Stokes County, North Carolina	Co. A, 2nd Battalion North Carolina Infantry	May 12, 1864, Spotsylvania Court House, Virginia	Point Lookout, Maryland, transferred to Elmira Prison, NY, July 3, 1864	Oath of Allegiance June 19, 1865
Lawson, Alva Corporal	19	October 7, 1861, Lumberton, North Carolina	Co. D, 18th North Carolina Infantry	May 12, 1864, Spotsylvania Court House, Virginia	Point Lookout, Maryland, transferred to Elmira Prison, NY, August 6, 1864	Oath of Allegiance June 19, 1865
Lawson, Clifton M. Private	Unk	June 22, 1861, Wytheville, Virginia	Co. K, 50th Virginia Infantry	May 12, 1864, Spotsylvania Court House, Virginia	Point Lookout, Maryland, transferred to Elmira Prison, NY, August 2, 1864	Transferred for Exchange 10/11/64. Died 10/18/64 of Unknown Causes at US Army Hospital, Baltimore, MD.

Name & Rank	Age	Enlisted	Regiment and State	Where Captured	Prison	Remarks
Lawson, Green A. Private	Unk	September 21, 1861, Lowndes County, Georgia	Co. H, 26th Georgia Infantry	May 20, 1864, Spotsylvania Court House, Virginia	Point Lookout, Maryland, transferred to Elmira Prison, NY, July 3, 1864	Exchanged October 29, 1864 at Venus Point, Savannah River, GA.
Lawson, James W. Private	Unk	December 10, 1862, Macon, Georgia	Captain Slaten's Battery Georgia Artillery	June 17, 1864, Petersburg, Virginia	Point Lookout, Maryland, transferred to Elmira Prison, NY, July 25, 1864	Died March 13, 1865 of Variola (Smallpox), Grave No. 2437
Lawson, James W. Private	25	March 3, 1863, Stokes County, North Carolina	Co. D, 52nd North Carolina Infantry	June 13, 1864, Chickahom-iny, Louisa Court, Virginia	Point Lookout, Maryland, transferred to Elmira Prison, NY, July 23, 1864	Oath of Allegiance May 29, 1865
Lawson, John C. Private	18	April 23, 1861, Gloucester Court House, Virginia	Co. B, 26th Virginia Infantry	June 15, 1864, Near Petersburg, Virginia	Point Lookout, Maryland, transferred to Elmira Prison, NY, July 12, 1864	Oath of Allegiance June 21, 1865
Lawson, Joseph H. Private	22	April 23, 1861, Gloucester Court House, Virginia	Co. B, 26th Virginia Infantry	June 15, 1864, Near Petersburg, Virginia	Point Lookout, Maryland, transferred to Elmira Prison, NY, July 12, 1864	Exchanged March 10, 1865 at Boulware's Wharf on the James River, Virginia
Lawson, Rowan C. Private	23	April 23, 1861, Gloucester Court House, Virginia	Co. B, 26th Virginia Infantry	June 15, 1864, Petersburg, Virginia	Point Lookout, Maryland, transferred to Elmira Prison, NY, July 12, 1864	Exchanged March 10, 1865 at Boulware's Wharf on the James River, Virginia
Lawson, William Private	Unk	Unknown	Co. K, 10th Regiment, 1st North Carolina Artillery	January 15, 1865, Fort Fisher, North Carolina	January 30, 1865, Elmira Prison Camp, New York	Died February 20, 1865 of Diarrhea, Grave No. 2320
Lawson, William R. S. Sergeant	25	January 20, 1862, Darlington, South Carolina	Co. H, 21st South Carolina Infantry	January 15, 1865, Fort Fisher, North Carolina	January 30, 1865, Elmira Prison Camp, New York	Oath of Allegiance July 11, 1865
Laxton, Thomas W. Private	19	May 31, 1861, Raleigh, North Carolina	Co. B, 1st North Carolina Infantry	May 12, 1864, Spotsylvania Court House, Virginia	Point Lookout, Maryland, transferred to Elmira Prison, NY, August 6, 1864	Died March 8, 1865 of Chronic Diarrhea, Grave No. 2363

Name & Rank	Age	Enlisted	Regiment and State	Where Captured	Prison	Remarks
Lay, C. H. Private	32	March 15, 1862, Charleston, South Carolina	Co. C, 27th South Carolina Infantry	May 16, 1864, Near Drury's Bluff, Virginia	Point Lookout, Maryland, transferred to Elmira Prison, NY, July 23, 1864	Oath of Allegiance February 9, 1865. Early Release per Lincoln's Proclamation, 12/8/1863.
Layfield, Urba Hugh Private	Unk	July 4, 1861, Hamilton, Georgia	Co. C, 35th Georgia Infantry	May 5, 1864, Wilderness, Virginia	Point Lookout, Maryland, transferred to Elmira Prison, NY, August 17, 1864	Oath of Allegiance July 7, 1865
Layman, Preston Private	Unk	June 14, 1862, Port Republic, Virginia	Co. G, 10th Virginia Infantry	May 12, 1864, Spotsylvania Court House, Virginia	Point Lookout, Maryland, transferred to Elmira Prison, NY, August 2, 1864	Oath of Allegiance June 27, 1865
Layne, James D. Private	21	June 15, 1861, Washington, Virginia	Co. F, 48th Virginia Infantry	May 12, 1864, Spotsylvania Court House, Virginia	Point Lookout, Maryland, transferred to Elmira Prison, NY, August 2, 1864	Oath of Allegiance June 14, 1865
Layton, Charles Private	19	February 24, 1862, Greensboro, North Carolina	Co. C, 45th North Carolina Infantry	July 13, 1864, Silver Springs, Maryland. Gunshot Wound of Back Near Spine.	Old Capital Prison, Washington, DC transferred to Elmira Prison, NY, August 27, 1864	Oath of Allegiance July 3, 1865
Layton, Samuel L. Private	Unk	April 15, 1863, Harrisonburg, Virginia	Co. C, 6th Virginia Cavalry	May 12, 1864, Yellow Tavern, Hanover County, Virginia	Point Lookout, Maryland, transferred to Elmira Prison, NY, August 17, 1864	Oath of Allegiance June 19, 1865
Lazenby, Joshua Private	Unk	Unknown	Co. J, 61st Alabama Infantry	May 12, 1864, Spotsylvania Court House, Virginia. Gunshot Wound Left Thigh.	Old Capital Prison, Washington, DC transferred to Elmira Prison, NY, August 27, 1864	Oath of Allegiance May 17, 1865
Lea, James B. Private	Unk	July 17, 1861, Navarro County, Texas	Co. J, 4th Texas Infantry	May 10, 1864, Spotsylvania Court House, Virginia	Point Lookout, Maryland, transferred to Elmira Prison, NY, August 17, 1864	Oath of Allegiance May 15, 1865

Name & Rank	Age	Enlisted	Regiment and State	Where Captured	Prison	Remarks
Lea, William W. Private	27	March 7, 1862, Fort Pillow, Tennessee	Co. B, 1st Jackson's Tennessee Heavy Artillery	August 23, 1864, Fort Morgan, Alabama.	New Orleans, Louisiana transferred to Elmira Prison, NY, December 4, 1864.	Died February 6, 1865 of Pneumonia, Grave No. 1903. Headstone has Lear.
Leach, Hugh C. Private	Unk	March 16, 1863, Randolph County, North Carolina	Co. F, 10th Regiment, 1st North Carolina Artillery	January 15, 1865, Fort Fisher, North Carolina	January 30, 1865, Elmira Prison Camp, New York	Died April 30, 1865 of Diarrhea, Grave No. 2591
Leach, M. Sergeant	23	Unknown	Co. B, Ogden's Louisiana Cavalry	June 24, 1864, Ascension Parish, Louisiana	New Orleans, LA, Transferred to Elmira Prison, NY, November 19, 1864	Oath of Allegiance June 14, 1865
Leach, William Private	29	February 12, 1863, South Carolina	Co. E, 7th Battalion South Carolina Infantry	August 21, 1864, Weldon Railroad, Virginia. Gunshot Wound Neck.	Old Capital Prison, Washington, DC. Transferred to Elmira Prison Camp, NY, December 17, 1864.	Died July 20, 1865 of Unknown Disease, Grave No. 2868
Leachman, James L. Private	Unk	June 13, 1861, Camp McDonald, Georgia	Co. C, 18th Georgia Infantry	June 1, 1864, Cold Harbor, Virginia	Point Lookout, Maryland, transferred to Elmira Prison, NY, July 17, 1864	Exchanged October 29, 1864 at Venus Point, Savannah River, GA.
Leaird, Thomas L. Private	Unk	February 15, 1863, Coosawhatchie, South Carolina	Co. G, 27th South Carolina Infantry	June 24, 1864, Near Petersburg, Virginia	Point Lookout, Maryland, transferred to Elmira Prison, NY, August 18, 1864	Oath of Allegiance July 11, 1865
Leake, Edward Private	20	June 18, 1861, Sperryville, Virginia	Co. K, 49th Virginia Infantry	May 30, 1864, Cold Harbor, Virginia. Gunshot wound Severe Thigh and Heel.	Old Capital Prison, Washington, DC, transferred to Elmira December 17, 1864	Exchanged February 13, 1865 at Boulware's Wharf on the James River, Virginia
Leanord, Leroy A. Sergeant	Unk	July 25, 1862, Delps Muster Ground, Carroll County, Virginia	Co. C, 29th, Virginia Infantry	June 1, 1864, Gaines Mill Cold Harbor, Virginia	Point Lookout, Maryland, transferred to Elmira Prison, NY, July 12, 1864	Oath of Allegiance July 3, 1865

Name & Rank	Age	Enlisted	Regiment and State	Where Captured	Prison	Remarks
Leap, William E. Sergeant	Unk	October 13, 1861, Mobile, Alabama	Co. B, 21st Alabama Infantry	August 8, 1864, Fort Gaines, Alabama	Steam Press No. 4 New Orleans, Louisiana transferred to Elmira Prison, NY, October 8, 1864.	Oath of Allegiance January 12, 1865. Early Release per Lincoln's Proclamation, 12/8/1863.
Lear, J. L. J. W. Private	Unk	August 19, 1861, Bethel, Tennessee	Co. A, Jackson's 1st Regiment, Tennessee Heavy Artillery	August 23, 1864, Fort Morgan, Alabama	New Orleans, Louisiana transferred to Elmira Prison, NY, December 4, 1864.	No Further Information Available.
Lear, John T. Private	30	June 7, 1861, Camp Moore, Louisiana	Co. D, 7th Louisiana Infantry	May 11, 1864, Near Spotsylvania Court House, Virginia	Point Lookout, Maryland, transferred to Elmira Prison, NY, August 17, 1864	Oath of Allegiance May 29, 1865
Leary, Lemuel Private	18	October 9, 1861, Enfield, Halifax County, North Carolina	Co. F, 36th Regiment North Carolina Artillery	January 15, 1865, Fort Fisher, North Carolina	February 1, 1865, Elmira Prison Camp, New York	Exchanged March 2, 1865 at Boulware's Wharf on the James River, Virginia
Leathers, William L. Private	36	August 19, 1861, Camp Pulaski, Louisiana	Co. G, 15th Louisiana Infantry	May 12, 1864, Spotsylvania Court House, Virginia	Point Lookout, Maryland, transferred to Elmira Prison, NY, July 25, 1864	Died October 31, 1864 of Pneumonia, Grave No. 738
Leblanc, Euphemond Private	19	March 15, 1862, Saint Martin Parish, Louisiana	Co. C, 8th Louisiana Infantry	May 12, 1864, Spotsylvania Court House, Virginia	Point Lookout, Maryland, transferred to Elmira Prison, NY, August 17, 1864	Exchanged February 25, 1865 at Boulware's or Cox Wharf on the James River, Virginia
Ledbetter, A. L. Private	Unk	March 4, 1862, Jonesboro, North Carolina	Co. C, 3rd North Carolina Infantry	May 12, 1864, Near Spotsylvania Court House, Virginia	Point Lookout, Maryland, transferred to Elmira Prison, NY, August 14, 1864	Exchanged March 10, 1865 at Boulware's Wharf on the James River, Virginia
Ledbetter, Jonathan Sergeant	20	July 25, 1861, Tullahoma, Tennessee	Co. K, 25th Tennessee Infantry	June 17, 1864, Near Petersburg, Virginia	Point Lookout, Maryland, transferred to Elmira Prison, NY, July 30, 1864	Exchanged February 25, 1865 at Boulware's or Cox Wharf on the James River, Virginia

Name & Rank	Age	Enlisted	Regiment and State	Where Captured	Prison	Remarks
Ledbetter, Louis Private	Unk	May 7, 1861, Calhoun, Tennessee	Co. G, 3rd Tennessee, Lillard's Mounted Infantry	May 17, 1863, Big Black, Mississippi	Point Lookout, Maryland, transferred to Elmira Prison, NY, August 18, 1864	Exchanged February 25, 1865 at Boulware's wharf on the James River, Virginia
Ledford, Rufus Private	21	August 3, 1861, Lincolnton, North Carolina	Co. D, 1st North Carolina Infantry	May 12, 1864, Spotsylvania Court House, Virginia	Point Lookout, Maryland, transferred to Elmira Prison, NY, August 6, 1864	Oath of Allegiance June 27, 1865
Ledford, Soloman Private	33	July 4, 1861, Madison County, North Carolina	Co. H, 2nd Battalion North Carolina Infantry	May 10, 1864, Near Spotsylvania County Court House, Virginia	Point Lookout, Maryland, transferred to Elmira Prison, NY, August 14, 1864	Exchanged March 14, 1865 at Boulware's Wharf on the James River, Virginia
Lee, Benjamin M. Private	Unk	October 15, 1863, Charleston, South Carolina	Co. A, 25th South Carolina Infantry	January 15, 1865, Fort Fisher, North Carolina	January 30, 1865, Elmira Prison Camp, New York	Oath of Allegiance June 30, 1865
Lee, Bryant Q. Private	30	April 26, 1862, Lee's Mills, Leesburg, Virginia	Co. H, 18th Mississippi Infantry	July 27, 1864, Deep Bottom, Virginia	Point Lookout, Maryland, transferred to Elmira Prison, NY, August 12, 1864	Oath of Allegiance June 16, 1865
Lee, David J. Private	Unk	October 1, 1864, Loudoun County, Virginia	Co. A, 35th Battalion Virginia Cavalry	February 16, 1865, Farquier County, Virginia	Old Capital Prison, Washington, DC, transferred to Elmira Prison, NY, May 12, 1865.	Oath of Allegiance July 7, 1865
Lee, David L. Private	Unk	January 15, 1864, Petersburg, Virginia	Co. E, 51st North Carolina Infantry	June 1, 1864, Cold Harbor, Virginia	Point Lookout, Maryland, transferred to Elmira Prison, NY, July 12, 1864	Died September 20, 1864 of Chronic Diarrhea, Grave No. 345
Lee, Harry Private	Unk	July 15, 1862, Raleigh, North Carolina	Co. C, 5th North Carolina Infantry	May 12, 1864, Spotsylvania Court House, Virginia	Point Lookout, Maryland, transferred to Elmira Prison, NY, August 6, 1864	Died January 10, 1865 of Pneumonia, Grave No. 1497

Name & Rank	Age	Enlisted	Regiment and State	Where Captured	Prison	Remarks
Lee, J. W. Private	Unk	May 25, 1862, Camp Moore, Louisiana	Co. E, 3rd Louisiana Cavalry	October 6, 1864, Clinton, Louisiana	New Orleans, Louisiana transferred to Elmira November 19, 1864.	Exchanged February 25, 1865 at Boulware's or Cox Wharf on the James River, Virginia
Lee, James H. Private	28	July 23, 1861, Staunton, Virginia	Co. H, 52nd Virginia Infantry	May 31, 1864, Mechanicsville, Virginia	Point Lookout, Maryland, transferred to Elmira Prison, NY, July 9, 1864	Oath of Allegiance June 30, 1865
Lee, James M. Private	Unk	February 25, 1864, Appomattox County, Virginia	Co. I, 42nd Virginia Infantry	May 12, 1864, Near Spotsylvania Court House, Virginia	Point Lookout, Maryland, transferred to Elmira Prison, NY, August 6, 1864	Exchanged October 29, 1864 at Venus Point, Savannah River, GA.
Lee, John H. Private	Unk	June 12, 1862, Raleigh, North Carolina	Co. E, 24th North Carolina Infantry	June 17, 1864, Petersburg, Virginia	Point Lookout, Maryland, transferred to Elmira Prison, NY, July 30, 1864	Died December 11, 1864 of Disease of Heart, Grave No. 1050
Lee, John W. Private	18	February 25, 1862, Lew's Store, Halifax County, North Carolina	Co. J, 12th North Carolina Infantry	May 12, 1864, Spotsylvania Court House, Virginia. Gunshot Wounds Right Side and Forearm.	Old Capital Prison, Washington, DC transferred to Elmira Prison, NY, August 27, 1864	Exchanged February 25, 1865 at Boulware's or Cox Wharf on the James River, Virginia
Lee, Joseph M. Private	Unk	March 1, 1864, Dorchester, Georgia	Co. H, 7th Georgia Cavalry	June 11, 1864, Trevilian Station, Louisa Court House, Virginia	Point Lookout, Maryland, transferred to Elmira Prison, NY, July 12, 1864	Exchanged October 29, 1864 at Venus Point, Savannah River, GA.
Lee, L. D. Private	Unk	Unknown	Co. A, 1st Alabama Artillery	August 23, 1864, Fort Morgan, Alabama	New Orleans, Louisiana. Transferred to Elmira Prison Camp, NY, October 8, 1864	Died May 15, 1865 of Unknown Disease, Grave No. 2805
Lee, Richard L. Private	44	Unknown	Co. B, Hood's Battalion, Virginia Reserves	June 15, 1864, Petersburg, Virginia	Point Lookout, Maryland, transferred to Elmira Prison, NY, July 30, 1864	Died February 26, 1865 of Chronic Diarrhea, Grave No. 2155

Name & Rank	Age	Enlisted	Regiment and State	Where Captured	Prison	Remarks
Lee, Robert A. Private	Unk	March 25, 1862, Camp Campbell, Virginia	Co. J, 2nd Virginia Cavalry	June 3, 1864, Gaines Mill Cold Harbor, Virginia	Point Lookout, Maryland, transferred to Elmira Prison, NY, July 17, 1864	Exchanged March 10, 1865 at Boulware's Wharf on the James River, Virginia
Lee, W. J. Private	Unk	April 27, 1862, Pee Dee Bridge, South Carolina	Co. K, 21st South Carolina Infantry	January 15, 1865, Fort Fisher, North Carolina	January 30, 1865, Elmira Prison Camp, New York	Oath of Allegiance July 11, 1865
Lee, Walter A. Corporal	18	July 15, 1862, Raleigh, North Carolina	Co. G, 55th North Carolina Infantry	May 12, 1864, Spotsylvania Court House, Virginia	Point Lookout, Maryland, transferred to Elmira Prison, NY, August 2, 1864	Oath of Allegiance June 12, 1865
Lee, Washington G. Private	18	July 10, 1863, Belle Isle, Virginia	Co. G, 45th North Carolina Infantry	May 10, 1864, Spotsylvania Court House, Virginia	Point Lookout, Maryland, transferred to Elmira Prison, NY, August 6, 1864	Oath of Allegiance June 27, 1865
Lee, William Private	Unk	February 7, 1863, Sampson County, North Carolina	Co. K, 51st North Carolina Infantry	June 1, 1864, Cold Harbor, Virginia	Transferred From Point Lookout Prison, MD, July 12, 1864. Train Never Arrived at Elmira Prison Camp, NY.	Died July 15, 1864 in Train Wreck at Shohola, Pennsylvania.
Lee, William A. Corporal	Unk	September 9, 1861, Eden Station, Georgia	Co. H, 61st Georgia Infantry	May 12, 1864, Spotsylvania Court House, Virginia	Point Lookout, Maryland, transferred to Elmira Prison, NY, July 25, 1864	Died September 20, 1864 of Scorbutus (Scurvy), Grave No. 330
Lee, Young N. Corporal	23	April 3, 1862, Johnston County, North Carolina	Co. G, 55th North Carolina Infantry	May 12, 1864, Spotsylvania Court House, Virginia	Point Lookout, Maryland, transferred to Elmira Prison, NY, August 2, 1864	Died February 4, 1865 of Variola (Smallpox), Grave No. 1737
Legg, M. W. Private	22	September 1, 1861, Cleveland, Tennessee	Co. H, 63rd Tennessee Infantry	June 17, 1864, Petersburg, Virginia	Point Lookout, Maryland, transferred to Elmira Prison, NY, July 30, 1864	Exchanged February 25, 1865 at Boulware's or Cox Wharf on the James River, Virginia
Leggett, Andrew J. Private	Unk	April 4, 1862, Bennettsville, South Carolina	Co. F, 21st South Carolina Infantry	January 15, 1865, Fort Fisher, North Carolina	January 30, 1865, Elmira Prison Camp, New York	Oath of Allegiance June 14, 1865

Name & Rank	Age	Enlisted	Regiment and State	Where Captured	Prison	Remarks
Legrand, Hosmar Private	Unk	September 14, 1863, Fort Fisher, North Carolina	Co. J, 36th Regiment North Carolina Artillery	January 15, 1865, Fort Fisher, North Carolina	February 1, 1865, Elmira Prison Camp, New York	Died March 8, 1865 of Chronic Diarrhea-Typhoid Fever on Steamer to be Exchanged.
Legrand, Julius E. Private	19	March 8, 1864, Fort Fisher, North Carolina	Co. J, 36th Regiment North Carolina Artillery	January 15, 1865, Fort Fisher, North Carolina	February 1, 1865, Elmira Prison Camp, New York	Exchanged March 2, 1865. Died March 10, 1865 of Chronic Diarrhea-Typhoid Fever at Wayside Hospital No. 9, Richmond, VA.
Lehan, John Private	Unk	April 10, 1862, Harrisonburg, Virginia	Co. C, 10th Virginia Infantry	August 13, 1864, Charlestown, Virginia	Old Capital Prison, Washington, DC transferred to Elmira Prison, NY, August 29, 1864	Oath of Allegiance May 19, 1865
Lehue, Benjamin W. Private	28	May 14, 1862, Fort St. Phillips, Brunswick County, North Carolina	Co. G, 36th Regiment North Carolina Artillery	January 15, 1865, Fort Fisher, North Carolina	February 1, 1865, Elmira Prison Camp, New York	Exchanged March 2, 1865 at Boulware's Wharf on the James River, Virginia
Leigh, John W. Private	Unk	May 13, 1862, New Kent, Virginia	Co. A, 26th Virginia Infantry	June 15, 1863, Petersburg, Virginia	Point Lookout, Maryland, transferred to Elmira Prison, NY, July 12,1864	Exchanged October 29, 1864 at Venus Point, Savannah River, GA. Died November 12, 1864. Buried at Port Royal, South Carolina.
Leigh, Thomas H. Sergeant	21	May 20, 1861, Louisburg, North Carolina	Co. K, 32nd North Carolina Infantry	May 10, 1864, Near Spotsylvania Court House, Virginia	Point Lookout, Maryland, transferred to Elmira Prison, NY, August 6, 1864	Oath of Allegiance June 16, 1865
Lejeune, John Private	19	March 3, 1862, Saint Landry Parish, Louisiana	Co. C, 6th Louisiana Infantry	May 5, 1864, Wilderness, Virginia	Point Lookout, Maryland, transferred to Elmira Prison, NY, August 17, 1864	Exchanged February 13, 1865 at Boulware's wharf on the James River, Virginia

Name & Rank	Age	Enlisted	Regiment and State	Where Captured	Prison	Remarks
Lemly, Benjamin Private	Unk	Unknown	Co. H, 23rd North Carolina Infantry	July 14, 1863, Falling Waters, Maryland	Point Lookout, Maryland, transferred to Elmira Prison, NY, August 18, 1864	Exchanged March 10, 1865 at Boulware's Wharf on the James River, Virginia
Lemoine, John H. Private	Unk	May 22, 1861, Warsaw, Virginia	Co. B, 40th Virginia Infantry	May 6, 1864, Wilderness, Virginia	Point Lookout, Maryland, transferred to Elmira Prison, NY, August 14, 1864	Oath of Allegiance June 23, 1865
Lemon, Alexander Private	27	May 7, 1862, Fort St. Phillips, Brunswick County, North Carolina	Co. G, 36th Regiment North Carolina Artillery	January 15, 1865, Fort Fisher, North Carolina	February 1, 1865, Elmira Prison Camp, New York	Oath of Allegiance June 12, 1865
Lemon, William H. Private	Unk	Unknown	Co. J, Harrison's 3rd Louisiana Cavalry	October 6, 1864, Near Hampton's Ferry, Louisiana	New Orleans, Louisiana transferred to Elmira November 19, 1864.	Died January 8, 1865 of Inflammatory Rheumatism, Grave No. 1220
Lemons, John A. Private	Unk	March 23, 1863, Union County, North Carolina	Co. F, 10th Regiment, 1st North Carolina Artillery	January 15, 1865, Fort Fisher, North Carolina	January 30, 1865, Elmira Prison Camp, New York	Died May 20, 1865 of Pneumonia, Grave No. 2939. Headstone has James A. Lemmons.
Lender, Francis Private	20	June 23, 1861, Camp Moore, Louisiana	Co. B, 2nd Louisiana Infantry	May 12, 1864, Spotsylvania Court House, Virginia	Point Lookout, Maryland, transferred to Elmira Prison, NY, August 17, 1864	Exchanged February 25, 1865 at Boulware's or Cox Wharf on the James River, Virginia
Lentz, John D. Private	22	March 3, 1862, Salisbury, North Carolina	Co. C, 42nd North Carolina Infantry	June 3, 1864, Cold Harbor, Virginia	Point Lookout, Maryland, transferred to Elmira Prison, NY, July 12, 1864	Died February 18, 1865 of Pneumonia, Grave No. 2354
Lentz, Mathias Private	33	September 6, 1862, Camp Hill, North Carolina	Co. C, 18th North Carolina Infantry	May 6, 1864, Wilderness, Virginia	Point Lookout, Maryland, transferred to Elmira Prison, NY, August 14, 1864	Died September 18, 1864 of Chronic Diarrhea, Grave No. 155

Name & Rank	Age	Enlisted	Regiment and State	Where Captured	Prison	Remarks
Lentz, Peter E. Private	18	February 9, 1863, Salisbury, North Carolina	Co. C, 42nd North Carolina Infantry	June 3, 1864, Cold Harbor, Virginia	Point Lookout, Maryland, transferred to Elmira Prison, NY, July 12, 1864	Oath of Allegiance May 19, 1865
Leon, Lewis Private	20	April 12, 1862, Charlotte, North Carolina	Co. B, 53rd North Carolina Infantry	May 8, 1864, Wilderness, Virginia	Point Lookout, Maryland, transferred to Elmira Prison, NY, July 25, 1864	Oath of Allegiance February 3, 1865
Leonard, Asa Corporal	34	May 16, 1862, Fort St. Phillips, Brunswick County, North Carolina	Co. G, 36th Regiment North Carolina Artillery	January 15, 1865, Fort Fisher, North Carolina	February 1, 1865, Elmira Prison Camp, New York	Oath of Allegiance July 7, 1865
Leonard, Caswell Private	18	March 19, 1864, Taylorsville, Virginia	Co. A, 23rd North Carolina Infantry	May 12, 1864, Spotsylvania, Virginia. Gunshot Wound Left Leg.	Old Capital Prison, Washington, DC, transferred to Elmira December 17, 1864	Exchanged February 13, 1865 at Boulware's Wharf on the James River, Virginia
Leonard, David Private	21	April 20, 1861, Holmesville, Mississippi	Co. E, 16th Mississippi Infantry	May 24, 1864, Hanover Junction, Virginia	Point Lookout, Maryland, transferred to Elmira Prison, NY, July 12, 1864	Oath of Allegiance May 29, 1865
Leonard, Lorenzo D. Private	Unk	March 7, 1864, Camp Terrell, Virginia	Co. B, 45th North Carolina Infantry	May 10, 1864, Spotsylvania Court House, Virginia	Point Lookout, Maryland, transferred to Elmira Prison, NY, August 6, 1864	Died March 7, 1865 of Chronic Diarrhea, Grave No. 2380
Leonard, Patrick Private	35	October 24, 1861, Corpus Christi, Texas	Co. C, 8th Texas Infantry	December 2, 1863, Aranzas Pass, Louisiana	New Orleans, LA, Transferred to Elmira Prison, NY, November 19, 1864	Oath of Allegiance May 13, 1865
Leopard, William P. Private	Unk	July 16, 1861, Lawrenceville, Georgia	Co. J, 16th Georgia Infantry	August 16, 1864, Front Royal, Virginia	Old Capital Prison, Washington, DC transferred to Elmira Prison, NY, August 29, 1864	Oath of Allegiance May 17, 1865

Name & Rank	Age	Enlisted	Regiment and State	Where Captured	Prison	Remarks
Leppard, A. L. Private	32	November 10, 1862, Newton, North Carolina	Co. E, 32nd North Carolina Infantry	May 10, 1864, Wilderness, Virginia	Point Lookout, Maryland, transferred to Elmira Prison, NY, August 6, 1864	Oath of Allegiance June 23, 1865
Lequeux, W. B. Private	Unk	July 28, 1863, Charleston, South Carolina	Co. J, 27th South Carolina Infantry	June 24, 1864, Petersburg, Virginia	Point Lookout, Maryland, transferred to Elmira Prison, NY, August 14, 1864	Died September 6, 1864 of Chronic Diarrhea, Grave No. 246
Lesesne, James Private	17	May 25, 1864, Fort Holmes, Brunswick County, North Carolina	Co. K, 40th Regiment, 3rd North Carolina Artillery	January 15, 1865, Fort Fisher, North Carolina	February 1, 1865, Elmira Prison Camp, New York	Oath of Allegiance June 12, 1865
Lesesne, Paul Private	17	December 4, 1862, Fort Fisher, North Carolina	Co. K, 40th Regiment, 3rd North Carolina Artillery	January 15, 1865, Fort Fisher, North Carolina	February 1, 1865, Elmira Prison Camp, New York	Exchanged March 14, 1865 at Boulware's Wharf on the James River, Virginia
Leslie, Erasmus M. Private	Unk	May 10, 1862, Meriwether County, Georgia	Co. A, 60th Georgia Infantry	May 20, 1864, Spotsylvania Court House, Virginia	Point Lookout, Maryland, transferred to Elmira Prison, NY, July 3, 1864	Exchanged March 10, 1865 at Boulware's Wharf on the James River, Virginia
Leslie, E. P. Private	Unk	Unknown	Co. K, 1st North Carolina Infantry	Unknown	Unknown	Died February 24, 1865 of Unknown Disease, Grave No. 2272
Leslie, Lewis Private	20	August 5, 1861, Lynchburg, Virginia	Co. K, 16th Mississippi Infantry	August 21, 1864, Weldon Railroad, Near Davis House, Near Petersburg, VA. Gunshot Wound Left Arm.	Old Capital Prison, Washington, DC transferred to Elmira Prison, NY, August 27, 1864	Exchanged March 2, 1865 at Akins Landing on the James River, Virginia
Lessenberry, William Private	21	May 3, 1862, Jonesboro, Tennessee	Co. D, 63rd Tennessee Infantry	June 17, 1864, Near Petersburg, Virginia	Point Lookout, Maryland, transferred to Elmira Prison, NY, July 30, 1864	Exchanged March 2, 1865 at Akins Landing on the James River, Virginia

Name & Rank	Age	Enlisted	Regiment and State	Where Captured	Prison	Remarks
Lester, J. H. Private	Unk	Unknown	Co. G, 15th Alabama Infantry	May 12, 1864, Spotsylvania Court House, Virginia	Point Lookout, Maryland, transferred to Elmira Prison, NY, July 30, 1864	Exchanged March 14, 1865 at Boulware's Wharf on the James River, Virginia
Lester, John H. Private	Unk	April 15, 1864, Macon County, Georgia	Co. J, 7th Georgia Cavalry	June 11, 1864, Trevilian Station, Louisa Court House, Virginia	Point Lookout, Maryland, transferred to Elmira Prison, NY, July 25, 1864	Transferred for Exchange 10/11/64. Died 10/26/64 of Chronic Diarrhea at Point Lookout Prison, MD.
Lester, William A. Private	35	March 11, 1862, Spring Garden, North Carolina	Co. D, 45th North Carolina Infantry	May 19, 1864, Spotsylvania Court House, Virginia. Gunshot Right Arm.	Old Capital Prison, Washington, DC, transferred to Elmira Prison, NY, August 12, 1864	Exchanged October 29, 1864 at Venus Point, Savannah River, GA.
Lester, William E. Private	Unk	March 9, 1862, Fort Nelson, Virginia	Co. J, 6th Virginia Cavalry	August 7, 1863, Warrenton, Virginia	Point Lookout, Maryland, transferred to Elmira Prison, NY, August 18, 1864	Oath of Allegiance May 17, 1865
Levy, Henry Private	21	February 27, 1862, Tallahassee, Florida	Co. C, 5th Florida Infantry	May 12, 1864, Spotsylvania Court House, Virginia	Point Lookout, Maryland, transferred to Elmira Prison, NY, July 30, 1864	Oath of Allegiance June 16, 1865
Lewallen, Zimri A. Corporal	22	March 11, 1862, Asheboro, North Carolina	Co. F, 2nd Battalion North Carolina Infantry	July 13, 1864, Near Washington, DC	Old Capital Prison, Washington DC. Transferred to Elmira Prison Camp, NY July 25, 1864.	Oath of Allegiance May 29, 1865
Lewellen, B. F. Private	Unk	May 11, 1862, Marion, South Carolina	Co. D, 6th South Carolina Cavalry	June 11, 1864, Trevilian Station, Louisa Court House, Virginia	Point Lookout, Maryland, transferred to Elmira Prison, NY, July 25, 1864	Died 9/1/1864 of Phthisis Pulmonalis, Grave No. 71. Name B. F. Lewallen 8th South Carolina on Headstone.

Name & Rank	Age	Enlisted	Regiment and State	Where Captured	Prison	Remarks
Lewellen, G. W. Private	Unk	January 27, 1862, Port Pillow, Tennessee	Co. A, Jackson's 1st Regiment, Tennessee Heavy Artillery	August 23, 1864, Fort Morgan, Alabama	New Orleans, Louisiana transferred to Elmira Prison, NY, December 4, 1864.	Died December 19, 1864 of Pneumonia, Grave No. 1069. Headstone has G. M. Lewallen.
Lewey, George Private	18	July 20, 1863, Belle Isle, Virginia	Co. G, 45th North Carolina Infantry	May 10, 1864, Spotsylvania Court House, Virginia	Point Lookout, Maryland, transferred to Elmira Prison, NY, August 6, 1864	Oath of Allegiance May 29, 1865
Lewis, A. Private	20	January 1, 1862, Camp Stevens, South Carolina	Co. D, 18th North Carolina Infantry	May 12, 1864, Spotsylvania Court House, Virginia	Point Lookout, Maryland, transferred to Elmira Prison, NY, August 6, 1864	Oath of Allegiance June 21, 1865
Lewis, Alexander J. Private	23	April 16, 1862, Fort St. Philips, Brunswick County, North Carolina	Co. G, 36th Regiment North Carolina Artillery	January 15, 1865, Fort Fisher, North Carolina	February 1, 1865, Elmira Prison Camp, New York	Exchanged February 20, 1865. Died March 20, 1865 of Pneumonia at General Hospital No. 8, Raleigh, North Carolina
Lewis, Benjamin W. Private	22	December 11, 1861, Monticello, Florida	Co. A, 5th Florida Infantry	May 12, 1864, Spotsylvania Court House, Virginia	Point Lookout, Maryland, transferred to Elmira Prison, NY, August 12, 1864	Exchanged March 14, 1865 at Boulware's Wharf on the James River, Virginia
Lewis, C. Private	Unk	August 10, 1863, Meridian, Tennessee	Co. A, Jackson's 1st Regiment, Tennessee Heavy Artillery	August 23, 1864, Fort Morgan, Alabama	New Orleans, Louisiana transferred to Elmira Prison, NY, December 4, 1864.	Exchanged February 25, 1865 at Boulware's or Cox Wharf on the James River, Virginia
Lewis, C. C. Private	Unk	November 1, 1862, Winchester, Virginia	Co. F, 2nd Louisiana Infantry	June 1, 1864, Newtown, Wilderness, Virginia	Point Lookout, Maryland, transferred to Elmira Prison, NY, August 17, 1864	Exchanged February 25, 1865 at Boulware's or Cox Wharf on the James River, Virginia

Name & Rank	Age	Enlisted	Regiment and State	Where Captured	Prison	Remarks
Lewis, Charles W. Private	Unk	January 18, 1864, Quitman County, Georgia	Co. F, 61st Georgia Infantry	May 12, 1864, Spotsylvania Court House, Virginia	Point Lookout, Maryland, transferred to Elmira Prison, NY, July 30, 1864	Died August 25, 1864 of Chronic Diarrhea, Grave No. 107
Lewis, Daniel M. Private	22	January 1, 1862, Georgetown, South Carolina	Co. A, 21st South Carolina Infantry	June 24, 1864, Near Petersburg, Virginia	Point Lookout, Maryland, transferred to Elmira Prison, NY, August 18, 1864	Died March 18, 1865 of Diarrhea, Grave No. 1731. Headstone has D. W. Lewis, 2nd SC.
Lewis, David Private	Unk	February 14, 1864, Caldwell County, North Carolina	Co. G, 22nd North Carolina Infantry	May 24, 1864, Hanover Junction, Virginia	Point Lookout, Maryland, transferred to Elmira Prison, NY, July 12, 1864	Died July 31, 1864 of Remittent Fever, Grave No. 144
Lewis, Edward S. Sergeant	Unk	September 6, 1861, Lumberton, North Carolina	Co. E, 31st North Carolina Infantry	June 1, 1864, Gaines Farm Cold Harbor, Virginia	Point Lookout, Maryland, transferred to Elmira Prison, NY, July 12, 1864	Died September 15, 1864 of Pneumonia, Grave No. 303
Lewis, G. N. Jr. Private	25	June 6, 1861, Greenville, Butler County, Alabama	Co. G, 9th Alabama Infantry	May 6, 1864, Wilderness, Virginia	Point Lookout, Maryland, transferred to Elmira Prison, NY, August 17, 1864	Died February 6, 1865 of Pneumonia, Grave No. 1920
Lewis, G. W. Private	Unk	December 31, 1861, Lexington, South Carolina	Co. G, 27th South Carolina Infantry	June 18, 1864, Near Petersburg, Virginia	Point Lookout, Maryland, transferred to Elmira Prison, NY, July 30, 1864	Exchanged March 14, 1865 at Boulware's Wharf on the James River, Virginia
Lewis, Gaines Private	28	July 23, 1863, Fort Branch, Martin County, North Carolina	Co. G, 40th Regiment, 3rd North Carolina Artillery	January 15, 1865, Fort Fisher, North Carolina	January 30, 1865 Elmira Prison Camp, New York	Exchanged February 20, 1865 at Boulware's or Cox Wharf on the James River, Virginia
Lewis, George D. Private	Unk	June 9, 1861, Jones County, Georgia	Co. B, 12th Georgia Infantry	May 10, 1864, Spotsylvania Court House, Virginia	Point Lookout, Maryland, transferred to Elmira Prison, NY, July 30, 1864	Exchanged October 29, 1864 at Venus Point, Savannah River, GA.

Name & Rank	Age	Enlisted	Regiment and State	Where Captured	Prison	Remarks
Lewis, George F. Private	Unk	September 22, 1862, Waynesville, Georgia	Co. G, 7th Georgia Cavalry	June 11, 1864, Trevilian Station, Louisa Court House, Virginia	Point Lookout, Maryland, transferred to Elmira Prison, NY, July 25, 1864	Died March 13, 1865 of Chronic Diarrhea, Grave No. 1820.
Lewis, George S. Private	Unk	April 20, 1861, Lexington, Virginia	Co. H, 4th Virginia Infantry	May 12, 1864, Spotsylvania Court House, Virginia	Point Lookout, Maryland, transferred to Elmira Prison, NY, August 2, 1864	Transferred for Exchange 10/11/64. Died 10/17/64 of Unknown Disease at US Army Hospital Baltimore, MD
Lewis, Green W. Private	Unk	June 11, 1861, Drayton, Georgia	Co. F, 12th Georgia Infantry	May 6, 1864, Wilderness, Virginia	Point Lookout, Maryland, transferred to Elmira Prison, NY, August 14, 1864	Oath of Allegiance June 21, 1865
Lewis, H. B. Private	Unk	May 16, 1861, Columbia, North Carolina	Co. A, 32nd North Carolina Infantry	May 10, 1864, Near Spotsylvania Court House, Virginia	Point Lookout, Maryland, transferred to Elmira Prison, NY, August 6, 1864	Oath of Allegiance June 14, 1865
Lewis, James Private	18	July 14, 1862, Wilmington, North Carolina	Co. C, 61st North Carolina Infantry	June 16, 1864, Petersburg, Virginia	Point Lookout, Maryland, transferred to Elmira Prison, NY, July 25, 1864	Exchanged March 14, 1865 at Boulware's Wharf on the James River, Virginia
Lewis, James H. Private, Fifer	19	January 7, 1862, Camp Bee, Weldon, Halifax County, North Carolina	Co K, 1st North Carolina Infantry	May 12, 1864, Spotsylvania Court House, Virginia	Point Lookout, Maryland, transferred to Elmira Prison, NY, August 6,1864	Oath of Allegiance July 11, 1865
Lewis, James P. Private	Unk	June 23, 1861, Camp Moore, Louisiana	Co. G, 8th Louisiana Infantry	May 12, 1864, Spotsylvania Court House, Virginia	Point Lookout, Maryland, transferred to Elmira Prison, NY, August 17, 1864	Exchanged October 29, 1864 at Venus Point, Savannah River, GA.
Lewis, Jesse H. Private	18	November 4, 1861, Randolph County, North Carolina	Co. H, 38th North Carolina Infantry	July 14, 1863, Falling Waters, Maryland	Point Lookout, Maryland, transferred to Elmira Prison, NY, August 18, 1864	Died October 19, 1864 of Chronic Diarrhea, Grave No. 534

Name & Rank	Age	Enlisted	Regiment and State	Where Captured	Prison	Remarks
Lewis, John Private	28	June 19, 1861, New Orleans, Louisiana	Co. F, 14th Louisiana Infantry	May 12, 1864, Spotsylvania Court House, Virginia	Point Lookout, Maryland, transferred to Elmira Prison, NY, July 25, 1864	Oath of Allegiance May 17, 1865
Lewis, John Private	Unk	September 1, 1863, Place Unknown	Co. D, 12th Virginia Cavalry	July 15, 1863, Harper's Ferry, Virginia	Point Lookout, Maryland, transferred to Elmira Prison, NY, August 18, 1864	Exchanged March 14, 1865 at Boulware's Wharf on the James River, Virginia
Lewis, John W. Private	Unk	September 22, 1862, Waynesville, Georgia	Co. G, 7th Georgia Cavalry	June 11, 1864, Trevilian Station, Louisa Court House, Virginia	Point Lookout, Maryland, transferred to Elmira Prison, NY, July 25, 1864	Oath of Allegiance May 29, 1865
Lewis, Nathan Private	18	May 17, 1861, Lower Black River District, North Carolina	Co. E, 18th North Carolina Infantry	May 12, 1864, Spotsylvania Court House, Virginia	Point Lookout, Maryland, transferred to Elmira Prison, NY, August 6, 1864	Died September 24, 1864 of Chronic Diarrhea, Grave No. 463
Lewis, Nathan H. Private	18	June 5, 1861, Asheboro, North Carolina	Co. I, 22nd North Carolina Infantry	May 24, 1864, Hanover Junction, Virginia	Point Lookout, Maryland, transferred to Elmira Prison, NY, July 11, 1864	Oath of Allegiance May 19, 1865
Lewis, Posar Private	Unk	July 1, 1863, Spartanburg, South Carolina	Co. J, 27th South Carolina Infantry	June 24, 1864, Near Petersburg, Virginia	Point Lookout, Maryland, transferred to Elmira Prison, NY, August 18, 1864	No Additional Information.
Lewis, R. E. Private	Unk	Unknown	Co. D, 12th Georgia Infantry	May 10, 1864, Beaver Dam Station, Virginia	Point Lookout, Maryland, transferred to Elmira Prison, NY, August 17, 1864. Ward 43.	Died January 29, 1865 of Variola (Smallpox), Grave No. 1797
Lewis, R. S. Private	Unk	April 27, 1861, Wetumpha, Alabama	Co. J, 3rd Alabama Infantry	May 12, 1864, Spotsylvania Court House, Virginia	Point Lookout, Maryland, transferred to Elmira Prison, NY, July 12, 1864	Oath of Allegiance June 16, 1865
Lewis, Robert C. Sergeant	18	August 15, 1861, Camp Wyatt, North Carolina	Co. C, 18th North Carolina Infantry	July 29, 1864, Gravel Hill, Petersburg, Virginia	Point Lookout, Maryland, transferred to Elmira Prison, NY, August 12, 1864	Oath of Allegiance June 12, 1865

Name & Rank	Age	Enlisted	Regiment and State	Where Captured	Prison	Remarks
Lewis, Robert S. Private	Unk	April 27, 1861, Wetumpka, Alabama	Co. J, 3rd Alabama Infantry	May 12, 1864, Spotsylvania Court House, Virginia	Point Lookout, Maryland, transferred to Elmira Prison, NY, August 12, 1864	Oath of Allegiance June 16, 1865
Lewis, Samuel H. Private	Unk	November 1, 1863, Clinton, Louisiana	Co. A, Miles Legion Louisiana	September 9, 1864, Near Homer, Louisiana	New Orleans, LA, Transferred to Elmira Prison, NY, November 19, 1864	Exchanged February 25, 1865 at Boulware's or Cox Wharf on the James River, Virginia
Lewis, Thomas Private	Unk	December 31, 1861, Lexington, South Carolina	Co. G, 27th South Carolina Infantry	June 24, 1864, Near Petersburg, Virginia	Point Lookout, Maryland, transferred to Elmira Prison, NY, August 18, 1864	Oath of Allegiance July 3, 1865
Lewis, Thomas Private	Unk	Unknown	Not Assigned to a Regiment	June 15, 1864, Caroline County, Virginia	Point Lookout, Maryland, transferred to Elmira Prison, NY, July 25, 1864	Transferred For Exchange October 11, 1864 to Point Lookout Prison Camp, MD. Nothing Further.
Lewis, Thomas L. Private	Unk	June 11, 1861, Drayton, Georgia	Co. F, 12th Georgia Infantry	May 10, 1864, Spotsylvania Court House, Virginia	Point Lookout, Maryland, transferred to Elmira Prison, NY, July 25, 1864	Oath of Allegiance June 21, 1865
Lewis, Willard Private	Unk	Unknown	Co. B, Hood's Battalion, Virginia Reserves	June 15, 1864, Petersburg, Virginia	Point Lookout, Maryland, transferred to Elmira Prison, NY, July 30, 1864	Died August 30, 1864 of Remittent Fever, Grave No. 59
Lewis, William Private	Unk	March 1, 1864, Camp Holmes, North Carolina	Co. B, 22nd North Carolina Infantry	May 24, 1864, Hanover Junction, Virginia	Point Lookout, Maryland, transferred to Elmira Prison, NY, July 11, 1864	Died September 7, 1864 of Chronic Diarrhea & Scurvy, Grave No. 217
Lewis, William E. Private	Unk	October 6, 1863, Goldsboro, North Carolina	Co. F, 10th Regiment, 1st North Carolina Artillery	January 15, 1865, Fort Fisher, North Carolina	January 30, 1865, Elmira Prison Camp, New York	Oath of Allegiance May 19, 1865

Name & Rank	Age	Enlisted	Regiment and State	Where Captured	Prison	Remarks
Lewis, William L. Private	19	April 17, 1861, Alexandria, Virginia	Co. E, 17th Virginia Infantry	July 21, 1863, Manassas Gap, Virginia	Point Lookout, Maryland, transferred to Elmira Prison, NY, August 18, 1864	Exchanged March 10, 1865 at Boulware's Wharf on the James River, Virginia
Licklider, Joseph S. Private	20	August 8, 1862, Manassas, Virginia	Co. D, 12th Virginia Cavalry	August 2, 1864, Shepherds-town Virginia	Old Capital Prison, Washington, DC, transferred to Elmira Prison, NY, August 12, 1864	Exchanged October 29, 1864 at Venus Point, Savannah River, GA.
Liddon, David S. Private	21	April 22, 1861, Washington, North Carolina	Co. K, 10th Regiment, 1st North Carolina Artillery	January 15, 1865, Fort Fisher, North Carolina	January 30, 1865, Elmira Prison Camp, New York	Oath of Allegiance May 29, 1865
Lide, Robert T. Private	Unk	February 24, 1863, Chesterfield, South Carolina	Co. D, 21st South Carolina Infantry	January 15, 1865, Fort Fisher, North Carolina	January 30, 1865, Elmira Prison Camp, New York	Oath of Allegiance July 7, 1865
Liffage, Theodore M. Sergeant	30	December 29, 1861, Williamsburg, South Carolina	Co. K, 25th South Carolina Infantry	January 15, 1865, Fort Fisher, North Carolina	January 30, 1865, Elmira Prison Camp, New York	Died April 3, 1865 of Diarrhea, Grave No. 2567. Headstone has F. M. Lifarge.
Liggett, Charles T. Private	Unk	April 18, 1861, Harrisonburg, Virginia	Co. B, 10th Virginia Infantry	May 12, 1864, Spotsylvania Court House, Virginia	Point Lookout, Maryland, transferred to Elmira Prison, NY, August 2, 1864	Oath of Allegiance June 27, 1865
Light, Nelson Private	29	October 1, 1862, Raleigh, North Carolina	Co. J, 32nd North Carolina Infantry	May 10, 1864, Spotsylvania, Virginia	Point Lookout, Maryland, transferred to Elmira Prison, NY, July 26,1864	Oath of Allegiance May 29, 1865
Light, W. T. S. Private	Unk	April 9, 1862, Haynesville, Alabama	Co. K, 5th Alabama Infantry	July 10, 1864, Frederick, Maryland	Old Capital Prison, Washington DC. Transferred to Elmira Prison Camp, NY, July 25, 1864.	Oath of Allegiance July 7, 1865

Name & Rank	Age	Enlisted	Regiment and State	Where Captured	Prison	Remarks
Lightner, Thomas R. Private	Unk	April 15, 1864, Sumerville Ford, Virginia	Co. I, 52nd Virginia Infantry	May 31, 1864, Mechanics-ville, Virginia	Point Lookout, Maryland, transferred to Elmira Prison, NY, July 9, 1864	Died December 5, 1864 of Chronic Diarrhea, Grave No. 1019
Liles, Henry H. Private	Unk	September 22, 1862, Waynesville, Georgia	Co. G, 7th Georgia Cavalry	June 11, 1864, Trevilian Station, Louisa Court House, Virginia	Point Lookout, Maryland, transferred to Elmira Prison, NY, July 25, 1864	Died September 30, 1864 of Chronic Diarrhea, Grave No. 406
Liles, Henry H. Private	38	February 22, 1862, Halifax County, North Carolina	Co. F, 43rd North Carolina Infantry	July 13, 1864, Silver Springs, Maryland	Old Capital Prison, Washington, DC, transferred to Elmira Prison, NY, August 12, 1864	Died October 3, 1864 of Chronic Diarrhea, Grave No. 619
Lillard, Richard Private	35	February 27, 1862, Reidsville, Rockingham County, North Carolina	Co. G, 45th North Carolina Infantry	May 10, 1864, Spotsylvania Court House, Virginia	Point Lookout, Maryland, transferred to Elmira Prison, NY, August 6, 1864	Died September 27, 1864 of Chronic Diarrhea, Grave No. 443
Lilleston, Alfred J. Private	Unk	April 1, 1863, White House, Virginia	Co. F, 46th Virginia Infantry	March 18, 1864, Accomac County, Virginia	Point Lookout, Maryland, transferred to Elmira Prison, NY, July 23, 1864	Oath of Allegiance December 5, 1864. Early Release per Lincoln's Proclamation, 12/8/1863.
Lilley, Hugh B. Private	Unk	April 18, 1861, McGaheysville, Virginia	Co. E, 10th Virginia Infantry	May 12, 1864, Spotsylvania Court House, Virginia	Point Lookout, Maryland, transferred to Elmira Prison, NY, August 2, 1864	Oath of Allegiance June 27, 1865
Lilliston, Calvin T. Private	Unk	September 22, 1862, New Hope, Virginia	Co. C, 24th Virginia Cavalry	July 29, 1864, Petersburg, Virginia	Point Lookout, Maryland, transferred to Elmira Prison, NY, August 12, 1864	Exchanged 3/2/65. Died 3/12/65 of Acute Diarrhea at Wayside Hospital No. 9, Richmond, VA.
Lilly, Atlas Dargan Private	Unk	March 15, 1864, Orange County Court House, Virginia	Co. C, 14th North Carolina Infantry	May 8, 1864, Wilderness, Virginia	Point Lookout, Maryland, transferred to Elmira Prison, NY, July 23, 1864	Oath of Allegiance May 29, 1865

Name & Rank	Age	Enlisted	Regiment and State	Where Captured	Prison	Remarks
Lilly, Joseph S. Private	18	October 8, 1861, Hamilton, Martin County, North Carolina	Co. F, 31st North Carolina Infantry	June 1, 1864, Gaines Farm Cold Harbor, Virginia	Point Lookout, Maryland, transferred to Elmira Prison, NY, July 12, 1864	Died November 24, 1864 of Pneumonia, Grave No. 910
Lilly, Thomas C. Private	Unk	January 8, 1863, Saluda, Virginia	Co. D, 24th Virginia Cavalry	July 29, 1864, Petersburg, Virginia	Point Lookout, Maryland, transferred to Elmira Prison, NY, August 12, 1864	Oath of Allegiance July 7, 1865
Lilly, William B. Private	18	September 20, 1861, Washington, North Carolina	Co. F, 10th Regiment, 1st North Carolina Artillery	January 15, 1865, Fort Fisher, North Carolina	January 30, 1865, Elmira Prison Camp, New York	Oath of Allegiance July 19, 1865
Lime, William Private	Unk	Unknown	Co. J, 36th Regiment, 2nd North Carolina Artillery	January 15, 1865, Fort Fisher, North Carolina	January 30, 1865 Elmira Prison Camp, New York	Died May 31, 1865 of Unknown Disease, Grave No. 2595
Limehouse, R. J. Private	Unk	July 11, 1862, Cheeha, South Carolina	Co. C, 5th South Carolina Cavalry	May 13, 1864, Near Drury's Bluff, Virginia	Point Lookout, Maryland, transferred to Elmira Prison, NY, July 25, 1864	Oath of Allegiance June 19, 1865
Linbecker, C. M. Private	Unk	February 25, 1862, C. Parsons, Texas	Co. E, 12th Texas Cavalry	October 20, 1864, Pointe Coupee, Louisiana	New Orleans, Louisiana transferred to Elmira November 19, 1864.	Died January 2, 1865 of Variola (Smallpox). Grave No. 1338
Lincoln, Josiah Private	27	June 9, 1861, Camp Moore, New Orleans, Louisiana	Co. J, 15th Louisiana Infantry	May 12, 1864, Spotsylvania Court House, Virginia	Point Lookout, Maryland, transferred to Elmira Prison, NY, July 25, 1864	Exchanged February 20, 1865 at Boulware's or Cox Wharf on the James River, Virginia
Linder, Berrien B. Corporal	Unk	July 9, 1861, Dublin, Georgia	Co. H, 14th Georgia Infantry	May 12, 1864, Spotsylvania Court House, Virginia	Point Lookout, Maryland, transferred to Elmira Prison, NY, July 30, 1864	Oath of Allegiance July 19, 1865
Linder, Robert Private	45	July 22, 1861, Camp Moore, Louisiana	Co. K, 10th Louisiana Infantry	May 12, 1864, Spotsylvania Court House, Virginia	Point Lookout, Maryland, transferred to Elmira Prison, NY, July 25, 1864	Oath of Allegiance May 21, 1865

Name & Rank	Age	Enlisted	Regiment and State	Where Captured	Prison	Remarks
Lindsay, Augustus Private	Unk	May 6, 1862, Marietta, Georgia	Philips Legion, Georgia Infantry	June 1, 1864, Cold Harbor, Virginia	Point Lookout, Maryland, transferred to Elmira Prison, NY, July 12, 1864	Died October 20, 1864 of Chronic Diarrhea, Grave No. 745
Lindsay, J. W. Private	Unk	October 2, 1863, Cleveland County, North Carolina	Co. F, 56th North Carolina Infantry	June 17, 1864, Petersburg, Virginia	Point Lookout, Maryland, transferred to Elmira Prison, NY, July 30, 1864	Died October 12, 1864 of Chronic Diarrhea and Scorbutus (Scurvy), Grave No. 572
Lindsay, O. L. Private	20	January 8, 1863, Camp Whatley, South Carolina	Co. B, 1st South Carolina Cavalry	July 29, 1864, Petersburg, Virginia	Point Lookout, Maryland, transferred to Elmira Prison, NY, August 12, 1864	Oath of Allegiance June 16, 1865
Lindsey, James R. Sergeant	26	February 27, 1862, Reidsville, Rockingham County, North Carolina	Co. G, 45th North Carolina Infantry	May 10, 1864, Spotsylvania Court House, Virginia	Point Lookout, Maryland, transferred to Elmira Prison, NY, August 6, 1864	Oath of Allegiance June 14, 1865
Lindsey, John H. Private	27	July 22, 1861, Camp Moore, Louisiana	Co. K, 10th Louisiana Infantry	August 17, 1864, Winchester, Virginia	Old Capital Prison, Washington, DC transferred to Elmira Prison, NY, August 29, 1864	Exchanged February 25, 1865 at Boulware's or Cox Wharf on the James River, Virginia
Lindsey, William T. Private	Unk	May 20, 1861, Nashville, Tennessee	Co. K, 7th Tennessee Infantry	June 2, 1864, Near Talapatomoy Creek, Cold Harbor, Virginia	Point Lookout, Maryland, transferred to Elmira Prison, NY, July 12, 1864	Exchanged October 29, 1864 at Venus Point, Savannah River, GA.
Line, William F. Private	22	Unknown	Co. A, 1st Tennessee Cavalry	August 7, 1864, Maryland Heights, Maryland	Old Capital Prison, Washington, DC, transferred to Elmira Prison, NY, August 12, 1864	Oath of Allegiance May 2, 1865 Early Release per Lincoln's Proclamation, 12/8/1863.
Linebarger, Avery P. Corporal	18	March 15, 1862, Newton, North Carolina	Co. B, 28th North Carolina Infantry	July 21, 1864, Deep Bottom, Virginia	Point Lookout, Maryland, transferred to Elmira Prison, NY, August 18, 1864	Died September 21, 1864 of Typhoid Fever, Grave No. 494

Name & Rank	Age	Enlisted	Regiment and State	Where Captured	Prison	Remarks
Lineberry, Orrin A. Corporal	Unk	April 3, 1862, Saltville, Virginia	Co. F, 29th, Virginia Infantry	June 1, 1864, Gaines Mill Cold Harbor, Virginia	Point Lookout, Maryland, transferred to Elmira Prison, NY, July 12, 1864	Exchanged on the James River, Virginia February 14, 1865
Lingamfelter, Walter H. Sergeant	30	April 19, 1864, Hedgesville, Virginia	Co. E, 2nd Virginia Infantry	July 9, 1864, Frederick, Maryland	Old Capital Prison, Washington DC. Transferred to Elmira Prison Camp, NY, July 25, 1864.	Exchanged October 29, 1864 at Venus Point, Savannah River, GA.
Lingerfelt, Daniel Private	25	July 4, 1862, Lincolnton, North Carolina	Co. G, 57th North Carolina Infantry	May 16, 1864, Near Drury's Bluff, Virginia	Point Lookout, Maryland, transferred to Elmira Prison, NY, August 17, 1864	Exchanged October 29, 1864 at Venus Point, Savannah River, GA.
Linhoss, David H. Private	Unk	April 18, 1861, Harrisonburg, Virginia	Co. D, 10th Virginia Infantry	May 12, 1864, Spotsylvania Court House, Virginia	Point Lookout, Maryland, transferred to Elmira Prison, NY, August 2, 1864	Transferred for Exchanged 10/29/64 at Venus Point, Savannah River, GA.
Lining, John D. Private	Unk	January 13, 1864, James Island, South Carolina	Co. A, 27th South Carolina Infantry	June 18, 1864, Near Petersburg, Virginia	Point Lookout, Maryland, transferred to Elmira Prison, NY, July 30, 1864	Exchanged March 10, 1865 at Boulware's Wharf on the James River, Virginia
Link, John Private	21	July 20, 1862, Camp Holmes, Raleigh, North Carolina	Co. E, 35th North Carolina Infantry	June 17, 1864, Petersburg, Virginia	Point Lookout, Maryland, transferred to Elmira Prison, NY, July 30, 1864	Oath of Allegiance July 3, 1865
Linkons, John A. Private	34	March 20, 1864, Dublin, Virginia	Co. C, 4th Virginia Infantry	May 5, 1864, Wilderness, Virginia	Point Lookout, Maryland, transferred to Elmira Prison, NY, July 25, 1864	Transferred for Exchanged 10/29/64 at Venus Point, Savannah River, GA.
Linkous, Edwin J. Private	Unk	July 16, 1861, Blacksburg, Virginia	Co. L, 4th Virginia Infantry	May 12, 1864, Near Spotsylvania Court House, Virginia	Point Lookout, Maryland, transferred to Elmira Prison, NY, August 2, 1864	Oath of Allegiance June 19, 1865
Linsey, E. R. Landsman-Sailor	Unk	Unknown	Confederate States Navy	January 15, 1865, Fort Fisher, North Carolina	February 1, 1865, Elmira Prison Camp, New York	Died March 8, 1865 of Pneumonia, Grave No. 2773

Name & Rank	Age	Enlisted	Regiment and State	Where Captured	Prison	Remarks
Lintinger, John Corporal	17	June 7, 1861, Camp Moore, Louisiana	Co. K, 7th Louisiana Infantry	May 11, 1864, Spotsylvania Court House, Virginia	Point Lookout, Maryland, transferred to Elmira Prison, NY, August 17, 1864	Exchanged October 29, 1864 at Venus Point, Savannah River, GA..
Lipscomb, Winfield T. Sergeant	22	May 2, 1862, Guineas, Virginia	Co. J, 5th Virginia Cavalry	May 11, 1864, Henrico County, Virginia	Point Lookout, Maryland, transferred to Elmira Prison, NY, August 17, 1864	Exchanged October 29, 1864 at Venus Point, Savannah River, GA.
Litchfield, Joseph Private	24	August 1, 1861, Coinjock, Currituck County, North Carolina	Co. B, 8th North Carolina Infantry	June 1, 1864, Cold Harbor, Virginia	Point Lookout, Maryland, transferred to Elmira Prison, NY, July 12, 1864	Died April 29, 1865 of Smallpox, Grave No. 2733
Litchfield, Orson Private	25	July 18, 1862, Columbus, Georgia	Co. D, 7th Confederate Cavalry	April 27, 1864, Bogue Bank, North Carolina	Point Lookout, Maryland, transferred to Elmira Prison, NY, July 23, 1864	Oath of Allegiance May 15, 1865
Litchfield, Thomas Private	22	August 1, 1861, Coinjock, Currituck County, North Carolina	Co. B, 8th North Carolina Infantry	June 1, 1864, Cold Harbor, Virginia	Point Lookout, Maryland, transferred to Elmira Prison, NY, July 17, 1864	Exchanged October 29, 1864 at Venus Point, Savannah River, GA.
Lites, James C. Private	26	July 20, 1861, Camp Pickens, Anderson District, South Carolina	Co. B, 1st South Carolina Infantry	July 14, 1863, Falling Waters, Maryland	Point Lookout, Maryland, transferred to Elmira Prison, NY, August 18, 1864	Exchanged March 10, 1865 at Boulware's Wharf on the James River, Virginia
Litten, Elihu Private	Unk	November 10, 1862, Hillsboro, Tennessee	Co. E, 44th Tennessee Infantry	June 17, 1864, Petersburg, Virginia	Point Lookout, Maryland, transferred to Elmira Prison, NY, July 23, 1864	Oath of Allegiance May 15, 1865
Little, Calvin A. Corporal	19	August 14, 1861, Catawba Station, North Carolina	Co. E, 32nd North Carolina Infantry	May 10, 1864, Wilderness, Virginia	Point Lookout, Maryland, transferred to Elmira Prison, NY, August 6, 1864	Oath of Allegiance June 21, 1865
Little, John W. Private	Unk	June 15, 1861, Entonton, Georgia	Co. G, 12th Georgia Infantry	May 6, 1864, Wilderness, Virginia	Point Lookout, Maryland, transferred to Elmira Prison, NY, August 14, 1864	Oath of Allegiance June 21, 1865

Name & Rank	Age	Enlisted	Regiment and State	Where Captured	Prison	Remarks
Little, Junius Pinkney Private	Unk	August 13, 1861, Newton, North Carolina	Co. C, 28th North Carolina Infantry	May 10, 1864, Near Spotsylvania, Virginia	Point Lookout, Maryland, transferred to Elmira Prison, NY, August 14, 1864	Oath of Allegiance June 16, 1865
Little, Pleasant M. Private	25	March 20, 1862, Union County, North Carolina	Co. J, 53rd North Carolina Infantry	May 11, 1864, Spotsylvania Court House, Virginia	Old Capital Prison, Washington DC. Transferred to Elmira Prison Camp NY July 25, 1864.	Exchanged March 2, 1865 at Akins Landing on the James River, Virginia
Little, Robert Augustus Private	31	May 30, 1863, Tarboro, Edgecombe County, North Carolina	Co. D, 13th Battalion, North Carolina Light Artillery	January 15, 1865, Fort Fisher, North Carolina	February 1, 1865, Elmira Prison Camp, New York	Died March 20, 1865 of Chronic Diarrhea, Grave No. 1577
Little, Thomas Private	Unk	June 10, 1861, Morgan, Georgia	Co. D, 12th Georgia Infantry	May 10, 1864, Spotsylvania Court House, Virginia	Point Lookout, Maryland, transferred to Elmira Prison, NY, July 30, 1864	Exchanged March 2, 1865 at Akins Landing on the James River, Virginia
Little, Thomas E. Private	23	September 9, 1861, Camp Macon, Pitt County, North Carolina	Co. G, 8th North Carolina Infantry	June 1, 1864, Cold Harbor, Virginia	Point Lookout, Maryland, transferred to Elmira Prison, NY, July 12, 1864	Exchanged February 20, 1865 at Boulware's or Cox Wharf on the James River, Virginia
Little, William Private	36	September 22, 1861, Camp Macon, Pitt County, North Carolina	Co. G, 8th North Carolina Infantry	June 1, 1864, Cold Harbor, Virginia	Point Lookout, Maryland, transferred to Elmira Prison, NY, July 12, 1864	Oath of Allegiance July 3, 1865
Little, William P. Private	Unk	Unknown	Co. J, 53rd North Carolina Infantry	May 11, 1864, Spotsylvania Court House, Virginia	Old Capital Prison, Washington DC. Transferred to Elmira Prison Camp, NY, July 25, 1864.	Died February 5, 1865 of Chronic Diarrhea, Grave No. 1896
Little, William S. Private	18	February 25, 1863, Newton, North Carolina	Co. E, 32nd North Carolina Infantry	May 10, 1864, Wilderness, Virginia	Point Lookout, Maryland, transferred to Elmira Prison, NY, August 6, 1864	Oath of Allegiance June 27, 1865

Name & Rank	Age	Enlisted	Regiment and State	Where Captured	Prison	Remarks
Littlejohn, Salathiel Private	Unk	November 1, 1863, Union, South Carolina	Co. J, 6th South Carolina Cavalry	June 11, 1864, Trevilian Station, Louisa Court House, Virginia	Point Lookout, Maryland, transferred to Elmira Prison, NY, July 25, 1864	Died December 15, 1864 of Pneumonia, Grave No. 1115
Littlejohn, W. E. S. Private	Unk	August 20, 1863, Charleston, South Carolina	Co. B, 27th South Carolina Infantry	June 24, 1864, Near Petersburg, Virginia	Point Lookout, Maryland, transferred to Elmira Prison, NY, August 18, 1864	Exchanged February 20, 1865. Died March 6, 1865 of Chronic Diarrhea at Hospital No. 9, Richmond, Va.
Lively, Jasper Private	Unk	January 14, 1862, Camp Walsh, South Carolina	Co. J, Holcombe Legion, South Carolina Infantry	May 7, 1864, Stony Creek, Virginia	Point Lookout, Maryland, transferred to Elmira Prison, NY, August 17, 1864	Died August 30, 1864 of Chronic Diarrhea, Grave No. 97. Headstone has Initials G. J.
Lively, Joseph A. Soloman, Private	Unk	September 4, 1863, Camp Sam Jones, Virginia	Co. H, 26th Battalion, Virginia Infantry	June 3, 1864, Gaines Farm Cold Harbor, Virginia	Point Lookout, Maryland, transferred to Elmira Prison, NY, July 17, 1864	Transferred for Exchange 10/11/64. Died 10/19/64 at U. S. Army Hospital, Baltimore, MD
Livengood, Abs Private	31	July 4, 1862, Winston, North Carolina	Co. D, 57th North Carolina Infantry	May 24, 1864, Hanover Junction, Virginia	Point Lookout, Maryland, transferred to Elmira Prison, NY, July 12, 1864	Exchanged October 29, 1864 at Venus Point, Savannah River, GA.
Livingston, Alexander S. Corporal	32	September 15, 1862, Camp Mangum, Raleigh, North Carolina	Co. B, 31st North Carolina Infantry	June 1, 1864, Cold Harbor, Virginia	Point Lookout, Maryland, transferred to Elmira Prison, NY, July 12, 1864	Exchanged February 20, 1865 at Boulware's or Cox Wharf on the James River, Virginia
Livingston, J. H. Private	Unk	Unknown	Co. H, 48th Alabama Infantry	May 6, 1864, Wilderness, Virginia	Point Lookout, Maryland, transferred to Elmira Prison, NY, August 17, 1864	Oath of Allegiance June 14, 1865
Livingston, Peter Private	Unk	April 26, 1862, Cross Roads, Camp Holmes, North Carolina	Co. D, 51st North Carolina Infantry	June 1, 1864, Cold Harbor, Virginia	Point Lookout, Maryland, transferred to Elmira Prison, NY, July 12, 1864	Exchanged March 10, 1865 at Boulware's Wharf on the James River, Virginia

Name & Rank	Age	Enlisted	Regiment and State	Where Captured	Prison	Remarks
Lloyd, Bunk Private	16	September 1, 1861, Orange County, North Carolina	Co. G, 28th North Carolina Infantry	May 10, 1864, Near Spotsylvania Court House, Virginia	Point Lookout Prison Camp, Maryland. Transferred to Elmira Prison Camp, New York August 6, 1864	Died October 20, 1864 of Typhoid Fever, Grave No. 531
Lloyd, Henry Private	18	March 5, 1864, Orange County, North Carolina	Co. G, 33rd North Carolina Infantry	May 10, 1864, Near Spotsylvania, Virginia	Point Lookout, Maryland, transferred to Elmira Prison, NY, August 14, 1864	Exchanged March 2, 1865 at Akins Landing on the James River, Virginia
Lloyd, Henry W. Private	Unk	March 24, 1864, Orange County, North Carolina	Co. G, 33rd North Carolina Infantry	May 10, 1864, Near Spotsylvania, Virginia	Point Lookout, Maryland, transferred to Elmira Prison, NY, August 14, 1864	Exchanged October 29, 1864 at Venus Point, Savannah River, GA.
Lloyd, John Private	22	May 9, 1864, Richmond, Virginia	Co. F, 1st Maryland Cavalry	July 12, 1864, Near Washington, DC	Old Capital Prison, Washington DC. Transferred to Elmira Prison Camp, NY, July 25, 1864.	Exchanged March 10, 1865 at Boulware's Wharf on the James River, Virginia
Lloyd, Lucius J. Sergeant	18	December 20, 1861, Orange County, North Carolina	Co. K, 28th North Carolina Infantry	May 12, 1864, Spotsylvania Court House, Virginia	Point Lookout, Maryland, transferred to Elmira Prison, NY, August 12, 1864	Exchanged October 29, 1864 at Venus Point, Savannah River, GA.
Lloyd, Samuel C. Private	Unk	July 8, 1862, Hillsboro, North Carolina	Co. F, 33rd North Carolina Infantry	May 10, 1864, Near Spotsylvania, Virginia	Point Lookout, Maryland, transferred to Elmira Prison, NY, August 14, 1864	Oath of Allegiance June 27, 1865
Lloyd, Thomas Private	Unk	September 1, 1862, Richmond, Virginia	Co. E, 44th Virginia Infantry	May 12, 1864, Spotsylvania Court House, Virginia	Point Lookout Prison Camp, Maryland. Transferred to Elmira Prison Camp, New York August 2, 1864	Died October 27, 1864 of Chronic Diarrhea, Grave No. 723. Name Floyd on Headstone.
Locke, Robert A. Sergeant	18	January 1, 1862, Springfield, Missouri	Co. J, 1st Missouri Cavalry	May 17, 1863, Big Black Bridge, Champion Hill, Mississippi	Point Lookout, Maryland, transferred to Elmira Prison, NY, August 18, 1864	Exchanged February 13, 1865 at Boulware's wharf on the James River, Virginia

Name & Rank	Age	Enlisted	Regiment and State	Where Captured	Prison	Remarks
Lockemy, Resin Private	28	July 6, 1863, Fort Caswell, Brunswick County, North Carolina	Co. D, 36th Regiment North Carolina Artillery	January 15, 1865, Fort Fisher, North Carolina	February 1, 1865, Elmira Prison Camp, New York	Died March 13, 1865 of Pneumonia, Grave No. 2423. Headstone has R. Lockenna.
Lockett, James H. Private	Unk	Unknown	Co. B, Hood's Battalion, Virginia Reserves	June 15, 1864, Petersburg, Virginia	Point Lookout, Maryland, transferred to Elmira Prison, NY, July 30, 1864	Died November 15, 1864 of Chronic Diarrhea, Grave No. 803
Lockett, John W. Private	Unk	Unknown	Co. B, Hood's Battalion, Virginia Reserves	June 15, 1864, Petersburg, Virginia	Point Lookout, Maryland, transferred to Elmira Prison, NY, July 30, 1864	Oath of Allegiance June 19, 1865
Lockoma, Rueben O. Private	Unk	March 4, 1863, Calhoun County, Georgia	Co. B, 51st Georgia Infantry	June 3, 1864, Gaines Farm Cold Harbor, Virginia	Point Lookout, Maryland, transferred to Elmira Prison, NY, July 12, 1864	Died August 21, 1864 of Paraplegia, Grave No. 110
Lockrema, Daniel Private	30	Unknown	Co. D, 36th Regiment North Carolina Artillery	January 15, 1865, Fort Fisher, North Carolina	February 1, 1865, Elmira Prison Camp, New York	Died April 29, 1865 of Typhoid Fever, Grave No. 2729. headstone has D. Lockrana
Lockwood, William L. C. Private	Unk	May 6, 1861, Montgomery, Alabama	Co. H, 6th Alabama Infantry	July 13, 1864, Silver Springs, Near Washington, DC. Gunshot Wound Right Chest Under Arm Pit.	Old Capital Prison, Washington, DC transferred to Elmira Prison, NY, August 27, 1864	Exchanged March 14, 1865 at Boulware's Wharf on the James River, Virginia
Loftin, Isaac N. Private	Unk	April 20, 1864, Fort Holmes, North Carolina	Co. G, 40th Regiment, 3rd North Carolina Artillery	January 15, 1865, Fort Fisher, North Carolina	January 30, 1865 Elmira Prison Camp, New York	Died March 30, 1865 of Diarrhea, Grave No. 2534. Headstone has J. H. Lofton.

Name & Rank	Age	Enlisted	Regiment and State	Where Captured	Prison	Remarks
Logan, Arthur Private	Unk	April 14, 1863, Atlanta, Georgia	Co. C, 64th Georgia Infantry	August 16, 1864, New Market, Virginia	Old Capital Prison, Washington, DC transferred to Elmira Prison, NY, August 29, 1864	Oath of Allegiance June 21, 1865
Logan, David W. Private	30	April 12, 1862, Goat Island, South Carolina	Co. C, 25th South Carolina Infantry	August 21, 1864, Petersburg, Virginia. Gunshot Wound Left Leg, Below Knee.	Old Capital Prison, Washington, DC, transferred to Elmira Prison, NY, December 17, 1864	Oath of Allegiance July's 13, 1865
Logan, Francis Private	Unk	March 19, 1862, Camp Blair, South Carolina	Co. F, Holcombe Legion, South Carolina	May 8, 1864, Jarrett's Depot, Virginia	Point Lookout, Maryland, transferred to Elmira Prison, NY, August 17, 1864	Died March 3, 1865 of Pneumonia, Grave No. 1997
Logan, John A. Private	Unk	August 19, 1863, Camp Instruction, Virginia	Co. L, 26th Battalion, Virginia Infantry	June 3, 1864, Gaines Farm Cold Harbor, Virginia	Point Lookout, Maryland, transferred to Elmira Prison, NY, July 17, 1864	Oath of Allegiance July 3, 1865
Logan, Leonidas Marion Private	18	May 1, 1861, Shelby, North Carolina	Co. E, 12th North Carolina Infantry	May 12, 1864, Near Spotsylvania, Virginia	Point Lookout, Maryland, transferred to Elmira Prison, NY, August 14, 1864	Oath of Allegiance June 16, 1865
Logan, Robert A. Private	Unk	September 7, 1864, Virginia	Co. I, 26th Battalion Virginia Infantry	June 3, 1864, Gaines Farm, Cold Harbor, Virginia	Point Lookout, Maryland, transferred to Elmira Prison, NY, July 17,1864	Exchanged October 29, 1864 at Venus Point, Savannah River, GA.
Logan, Theophilus F. Corporal	Unk	April 1, 1862, Americus, Georgia	Co. K, 9th Georgia Infantry	May 6, 1864, Wilderness, Virginia	Point Lookout, Maryland, transferred to Elmira Prison, NY, August 14, 1864	Oath of Allegiance June 14, 1865
Logensuhl, J. J. Seaman	Unk	Unknown	Confederate States Steamer Bomb Shell	May 5, 1864, Albemarle Sound, North Carolina	Point Lookout, Maryland, transferred to Elmira Prison, NY, July 23, 1864	Oath of Allegiance April 17, 1865

Name & Rank	Age	Enlisted	Regiment and State	Where Captured	Prison	Remarks
Loggins, John D. Private	21	May 28, 1861, Camp Walker, Corinth, Mississippi	Co. C, 18th Mississippi Infantry	May 6, 1864, Wilderness, Virginia	Point Lookout, Maryland, transferred to Elmira Prison, NY, August 14, 1864	Oath of Allegiance June 19, 1865
Logic, George Private	25	February 26, 1861, Mobile, Alabama	Co. B, 1st Battalion Alabama Artillery	August 23, 1864, Fort Morgan, Alabama	New Orleans, Louisiana transferred to Elmira Prison, NY, December 4, 1864.	Oath of Allegiance May 19, 1865
Lomas, William Private	19	October 31, 1863, Battery Marshall, South Carolina	Co. C, 7th Battalion South Carolina Infantry	August 21, 1864, Weldon Railroad, Virginia. Gunshot Wound Left Leg.	Old Capital Prison, Washington, DC. Transferred to Elmira Prison Camp, NY, March 3, 1865.	Died March 28, 1865 of Hospital Gangrene, Grave No. 2523
Long, Alexander Private	20	October 19, 1861, Elizabethtown, Bladen County, North Carolina	Co. J, 36th Regiment North Carolina Artillery	January 15, 1865, Fort Fisher, North Carolina	February 1, 1865, Elmira Prison Camp, New York	Oath of Allegiance July 11, 1865
Long, Andrew D. Private	Unk	March 14, 1862, Rhudes Hall, Virginia	Co. A, 5th Virginia Infantry	May 12, 1864, Spotsylvania Court House, Virginia. Gunshot Wound of Back, Left Shoulder.	Old Capital Prison, Washington DC. Transferred to Elmira Prison Camp, NY, July 25, 1864.	Exchanged March 14, 1865 at Boulware's Wharf on the James River, Virginia
Long, Charles R. Private	20	December 21, 1863, Camp Elzey, South Carolina	Co. C, 7th South Carolina Cavalry	May 30, 1864, Old Church, Cold Harbor, Virginia. Gunshot Wound of Chest.	Old Capital Prison, Washington DC. Transferred to Elmira Prison Camp, NY, July 25, 1864.	Exchanged October 29, 1864 at Venus Point, Savannah River, GA.
Long, Daniel M. Private	Unk	February 2, 1863, Camp Whiting, Wilmington, North Carolina	Co. G, 51st North Carolina Infantry	June 1, 1864, Gaines Mill Cold Harbor, Virginia	Point Lookout, Maryland, transferred to Elmira Prison, NY, July 12, 1864	Oath of Allegiance June 21, 1865
Long, Ezra Private	Unk	September 17, 1863, Raleigh, North Carolina	Co. J, 14th North Carolina Infantry	June 10, 1864, Spotsylvania, Virginia	Point Lookout, Maryland, transferred to Elmira Prison, NY, July 25, 1864	Died August 31, 1864 of Chronic Diarrhea, Grave No. 94

Name & Rank	Age	Enlisted	Regiment and State	Where Captured	Prison	Remarks
Long, F. H. G. Private	Unk	Unknown	Co. A, Captain Norwood's Home Guard Florida	September 27, 1864, Marianna, Florida	New Orleans, Louisiana transferred to Elmira November 19, 1864.	Oath of Allegiance December 14, 1864 Due to Debility. Early Release Granted by Commissary General of Prisoners.
Long, Hardie Private	19	September 25, 1861, Camp Branch, Roxboro, North Carolina	Co. E, 35th North Carolina Infantry	June 17, 1864, Petersburg, Virginia	Point Lookout, Maryland, transferred to Elmira Prison, NY, July 30, 1864	Died April 22, 1865 of Chronic Diarrhea, Grave No. 1394
Long, Isaac N. Private	Unk	March 25, 1862, Rockingham County, Virginia	Co. C, 11th Virginia Cavalry	August 2, 1864, Halltown, Virginia	Old Capital Prison, Washington, DC, transferred to Elmira Prison, NY, August 12, 1864	Exchanged March 10, 1865 at Boulware's Wharf on the James River, Virginia
Long, Isaiah Private	26	August 15, 1862, Statesville, North Carolina	Co. B, 37th North Carolina Infantry	May 12, 1864, Near Spotsylvania Court House, Virginia	Point Lookout, Maryland, transferred to Elmira Prison, NY, August 14, 1864	Exchanged March 2, 1865 at Akins Landing on the James River, Virginia
Long, James Private	26	October 4, 1862, Cleveland, Tennessee	Co. H, 63rd Tennessee Infantry	June 17, 1864, Petersburg, Virginia	Point Lookout, Maryland, transferred to Elmira Prison, NY, July 30, 1864	Died 11/24/64 of Pneumonia, Grave No. 923. Name Samuel on Headstone.
Long, John Private	21	July 15, 1862, Forsythe County, North Carolina	Co. G, 33rd North Carolina Infantry	May 12, 1864, Wilderness, Virginia	Point Lookout, Maryland, transferred to Elmira Prison, NY, August 14, 1864	Oath of Allegiance June 23, 1865
Long, John H. Private	Unk	July 15, 1862, Forsyth County, North Carolina	Co. G, 33rd North Carolina Infantry	May 12, 1864, Near Spotsylvania Court House, Virginia	Point Lookout, Maryland, transferred to Elmira Prison, NY, August 14, 1864	Oath of Allegiance June 23, 1865
Long, John J. Private	21	April 24, 1861, Bug Hill, North Carolina	Co. C, 18th North Carolina Infantry	May 12, 1864, Spotsylvania Court House, Virginia	Point Lookout, Maryland, transferred to Elmira Prison, NY, August 6, 1864	Died March 22, 1865 of Pneumonia, Grave No. 1510

Name & Rank	Age	Enlisted	Regiment and State	Where Captured	Prison	Remarks
Long, John J. Corporal	30	August 12, 1862, Woodstock, Virginia	Co. K, 12th Virginia Cavalry	September 14, 1863, Near Culpepper, Virginia	Point Lookout, Maryland, transferred to Elmira Prison, NY, August 18, 1864	Exchanged March 10, 1865 at Boulware's Wharf on the James River, Virginia
Long, John M. Private	Unk	Unknown	Co. H, 50th Virginia Infantry	May 12, 1864, Spotsylvania Court House, Virginia	Point Lookout, Maryland, transferred to Elmira Prison, NY, August 2, 1864	Exchanged October 29, 1864 at Venus Point, Savannah River, GA.
Long, John R. Sergeant	21	January 14, 1862, Springfield, Missouri	Co. D, 3rd Missouri Cavalry	May 17, 1863, Black River Bridge, Mississippi	Point Lookout, Maryland, transferred to Elmira Prison, NY, July 25, 1864	Oath of Allegiance 11/29/64. Early Release per Lincoln's Proclamation, 12/8/1863.
Long, Joseph Private	18	November 14, 1862, Edgecombe County, North Carolina	Co. K, 15th North Carolina Infantry	June 2, 1864, Old Church Cold Harbor, Virginia	Point Lookout, Maryland, transferred to Elmira Prison, NY, July 17, 1864	Died March 2, 1865 of Pneumonia, Grave No. 2009
Long, Joseph Private	Unk	July 1, 1862, Columbus County, North Carolina	Co. H, 33rd North Carolina Infantry	May 13, 1864, Near Spotsylvania, Virginia	Point Lookout, Maryland, transferred to Elmira Prison, NY, August 14, 1864	Died December 9, 1864 of Chronic Diarrhea, Grave No. 1169
Long, Lillington D. Private	35	February 3, 1862, Elizabethtown, Bladen County, North Carolina	Co. J, 36th Regiment North Carolina Artillery	January 15, 1865, Fort Fisher, North Carolina	February 1, 1865, Elmira Prison Camp, New York	Exchanged February 20, 1865. Died April 2, 1865 of Unknown Disease at Howard's Grove Hospital, Richmond, VA.
Long, Nicholas A. Private	30	Unknown	Co. A, Captain Norwood's Home Guard Florida	September 27, 1864, Marianna, Florida	New Orleans, Louisiana transferred to Elmira November 19, 1864.	Oath of Allegiance December 16, 1864 Early Release by, Commissary General of Prisoners.
Long, Robert Private	Unk	April 19, 1861, Harrisonburg, Virginia	Co. B, 10th Virginia Infantry	May 12, 1864, Spotsylvania Court House, Virginia	Point Lookout, Maryland, transferred to Elmira Prison, NY, August 2, 1864	Died April 22, 1865 of Variola (Smallpox), Grave No. 1393

Name & Rank	Age	Enlisted	Regiment and State	Where Captured	Prison	Remarks
Long, Samuel Private	31	March 10, 1863, Salem, North Carolina	Co. G, 2nd Battalion North Carolina Infantry	July 5, 1863, Gettysburg, Pennsylvania	Point Lookout, Maryland, transferred to Elmira Prison, NY, July 23, 1864	Died April 6, 1865 of Chronic Diarrhea, Grave No. 2629
Long, Thomas Private	Unk	Unknown	Co. C, 5th North Carolina Infantry	May 24, 1864, Wilson's Landing Near City Point, Virginia	Point Lookout, Maryland, transferred to Elmira Prison, NY, July 23, 1864	Oath of Allegiance May 13, 1865
Long, Uriah Jeptha Private	18	August 14, 1861, Newton, North Carolina	Co. E, 32nd North Carolina Infantry	May 10, 1864, Wilderness, Virginia	Point Lookout, Maryland, transferred to Elmira Prison, NY, August 6, 1864	Oath of Allegiance June 23, 1865
Long, Virgil Private	Unk	Unknown	Co. F, 4th Virginia Infantry	May 12, 1864, Spotsylvania Court House, Virginia	Point Lookout, Maryland, transferred to Elmira Prison, NY, August 2, 1864. Ward No. 39	Died August 5, 1864 of Chronic Valvular Disease of the Heart, Grave No. 142
Long, William C. Private	Unk	August's 21, 1862, Rappahannock River, Virginia	Co. C, 10th Virginia Infantry	May 12, 1864, Spotsylvania Court House, Virginia	Point Lookout, Maryland, transferred to Elmira Prison, NY, August 2, 1864	Exchanged March 2, 1865 at Akins Landing on the James River, Virginia
Long, William E. Private	Unk	October 24, 1863, Camp Holmes, North Carolina	Co. C, 18th North Carolina Infantry	May 12, 1864, Spotsylvania Court House, Virginia	Point Lookout, Maryland, transferred to Elmira Prison, NY, August 6, 1864	Died October 3, 1864 of Chronic Diarrhea, Grave No. 612
Long, William G. Private	Unk	Unknown	Co. D, 33rd North Carolina Infantry	May 17, 1864, Spotsylvania Court House, Virginia	Point Lookout, Maryland, transferred to Elmira Prison, NY, July 12, 1864	Oath of Allegiance May 12, 1865
Longacre, J. E. Corporal	22	June 6, 1861, Lynchburg, Virginia	Co. E, 63rd Tennessee Infantry	June 17, 1864, Near Petersburg, Virginia	Point Lookout, Maryland, transferred to Elmira Prison, NY, July 30, 1864	Oath of Allegiance July 3, 1865

Name & Rank	Age	Enlisted	Regiment and State	Where Captured	Prison	Remarks
Longest, John T. Private	35	June 13, 1861, Clarkson, Virginia	Co. J, 26th North Carolina Infantry	June 17, 1864, Near Petersburg, Virginia	Point Lookout, Maryland, transferred to Elmira Prison, NY, July 30, 1864	Died January 5, 1865 of Pneumonia, Grave No. 1254
Longley, Charles W. Private	Unk	April 18, 1861, Harrisonburg, Virginia	Co. D, 10th Virginia Infantry	May 12, 1864, Spotsylvania Court House, Virginia	Point Lookout, Maryland, transferred to Elmira Prison, NY, August 2, 1864	Died October 2, 1864 of Chronic Diarrhea, Grave No. 420. Name Langley on Headstone.
Looker, William P. Private	Unk	April 16, 1862, Rudes Hill, Virginia	Co. F, 2nd Virginia Infantry	May 12, 1864, Near Spotsylvania Court House, Virginia	Point Lookout, Maryland, transferred to Elmira Prison, NY, August 2, 1864	Oath of Allegiance June 27, 1865
Looper, James Private	Unk	June 1, 1863, Rocky Mount, North Carolina	Co. C, 8th North Carolina Infantry	June 1, 1864, Cold Harbor, Virginia	Point Lookout, Maryland, transferred to Elmira Prison, NY, July 17,1864	Oath of Allegiance July 3, 1865
Lord, Albert Private	Unk	December 15, 1861, Monticello, Florida	Co. A, 5th Florida Infantry	May 12, 1864, Spotsylvania Court House, Virginia	Point Lookout, Maryland, transferred to Elmira Prison, NY, August 12, 1864	Exchanged October 29, 1864 at Venus Point, Savannah River, GA.
Lord, Zachariah Corporal	Unk	December 11, 1861, Monticello, Florida	Co. A, 5th Florida Infantry	May 12, 1864, Spotsylvania Court House, Virginia	Point Lookout, Maryland, transferred to Elmira Prison, NY, August 12, 1864	Exchanged March 14, 1865 at Boulware's Wharf on the James River, Virginia
Lore, David Private	42	March 31, 1863, Newton, North Carolina	Co. E, 32nd North Carolina Infantry	May 10, 1864, Wilderness, Virginia	Point Lookout, Maryland, transferred to Elmira Prison, NY, August 6, 1864	Oath of Allegiance June 21, 1865
Loth, William Private	Unk	Unknown	Co. I, 5th Arsenal Battalion, Local Defense, Infantry	June 12, 1864, Bottoms Bridge, Chickahominy River, Virginia	Point Lookout, Maryland, transferred to Elmira Prison, NY, July 23, 1864	Oath of Allegiance May 29, 1865

Name & Rank	Age	Enlisted	Regiment and State	Where Captured	Prison	Remarks
Lothrop, William H. Private	25	October 2, 1862, Raleigh, North Carolina	Co. E, 28th North Carolina Infantry	July 29, 1864, Petersburg, Virginia	Point Lookout, Maryland, transferred to Elmira Prison, NY, August 12, 1864	Transferred for Exchange 10/11/64. Died 12/19/64 of Chronic Diarrhea at US Army Hospital, Baltimore, MD.
Lott, John M. Sergeant	20	August 12, 1861, Camp Butler, South Carolina	Co. B, 14th South Carolina Infantry	July 29, 1864, Petersburg, Virginia	Point Lookout, Maryland, transferred to Elmira Prison, NY, August 12, 1864	Oath of Allegiance June 19, 1865
Lott, W. L. Private	Unk	August 13, 1863, Center Hill, Georgia	Co. B, 16th Georgia Infantry	June 1, 1864, Gaines Farm Cold Harbor, Virginia	Point Lookout, Maryland, transferred to Elmira Prison, NY, July 12, 1864	Oath of Allegiance July 7, 1865
Lotzen, H. L. Sergeant	Unk	October 22, 1862 Charleston, South Carolina	Co. K, 27th South Carolina Infantry	June 24, 1864, Near Petersburg, Virginia	Point Lookout, Maryland, transferred to Elmira Prison, NY, July 25, 1864	Oath of Allegiance May 17, 1865
Loucus, John Private	22	June 19, 1861, Encampment Abingdon, Virginia	Co. C, 48th Virginia Infantry	May 12, 1864, Spotsylvania Court House, Virginia	Old Capital Prison, Washington DC. Transferred to Elmira Prison Camp, NY, July 25, 1864.	Oath of Allegiance June 27, 1865
Loudermilk, J. Private	Unk	Unknown	Co. C, 5th North Carolina Infantry	July 12, 1864, Near Washington, DC	Old Capital Prison, Washington DC. Transferred to Elmira Prison Camp, NY, July 25, 1864.	Exchanged March 10, 1865 at Boulware's Wharf on the James River, Virginia
Loudermilk, W. Private	Unk	July 1, 1862, Georgia	Co. C, Phillips Legion, Georgia	June 2, 1864, Gaines Farm Cold Harbor, Virginia	Point Lookout, Maryland, transferred to Elmira Prison, NY, July 12, 1864	Oath of Allegiance July 11, 1865
Loudin, William R. Private	Unk	May 27, 1861, Buckhannon, Virginia	Co. B, 25th Virginia Infantry	May 12, 1864, Spotsylvania Court House, Virginia	Point Lookout, Maryland, transferred to Elmira Prison, NY, July 30, 1864	Oath of Allegiance June 23, 1865

Name & Rank	Age	Enlisted	Regiment and State	Where Captured	Prison	Remarks
Loudoun, H. S. Private	32	May 16, 1862, Charleston, South Carolina	Co. J, 25th South Carolina Infantry	January 15, 1865, Fort Fisher, North Carolina	January 30, 1865, Elmira Prison Camp, New York	Exchanged March 14, 1865 at Boulware's Wharf on the James River, Virginia
Lough, Augustus B. Private	Unk	June 24, 1861, Beverly, Virginia	Co. G, 25th Virginia Infantry	May 6, 1864, Wilderness, Virginia	Old Capital Prison, Washington, DC, transferred to Elmira Prison, NY, July 14, 1864	Oath of Allegiance June 23, 1865
Lough, Francis M. Private	Unk	June 24, 1861, Beverly, Virginia	Co. G, 25th Virginia Infantry	May 6, 1864, Wilderness, Virginia	Old Capital Prison, Washington, DC, transferred to Elmira Prison, NY, July 14, 1864	Oath of Allegiance June 19, 1865
Lough, John W. Corporal	18	April 5, 1862, Camp Shenandoah, Virginia	Co. E, 25th Virginia Infantry	May 12, 1864, Spotsylvania Court House, Virginia	Point Lookout, Maryland, transferred to Elmira Prison, NY, August 12, 1864	Exchanged October 29, 1864 at Venus Point, Savannah River, GA.
Louisiana, Joseph Private	Unk	January 5, 1862, Monticello, Florida	Co. A, 5th Florida Infantry	May 12, 1864, Spotsylvania Court House, Virginia	Point Lookout, Maryland, transferred to Elmira Prison, NY, August 12, 1864	Exchanged March 14, 1865 at Boulware's Wharf on the James River, Virginia
Louzader, John L. Private	27	May 13, 1862, Fetterman, Virginia	Co. A, 25th Virginia Infantry	May 12, 1864, Spotsylvania, Virginia	Point Lookout, Maryland, transferred to Elmira Prison, NY, July 23, 1864	Oath of Allegiance May 19, 1865
Louzader, William G. Private	16	July 1, 1862 Richmond, Virginia	Co. A, 25th Virginia Infantry	May 5, 1864, Wilderness, Virginia	Point Lookout, Maryland, transferred to Elmira Prison, NY, July 23, 1864	Oath of Allegiance May 19, 1865
Love, Andrew F. Private	Unk	March 4, 1862, Calhoun, Georgia	Co. D, 21st Georgia Infantry	July 8, 1864, Harpers Ferry, Virginia	Old Capital Prison, Washington DC. Transferred to Elmira Prison Camp, NY, July 25, 1864.	Oath of Allegiance June 19, 1865

Name & Rank	Age	Enlisted	Regiment and State	Where Captured	Prison	Remarks
Love, Harvey W. Private	Unk	March 26, 1862, Jonesville, Lee County, Virginia	Co. E, 37th Virginia Infantry	May 12, 1864, Spotsylvania Court House, Virginia	Point Lookout, Maryland, transferred to Elmira Prison, NY, August 2, 1864	Exchanged March 14, 1865 at Boulware's Wharf on the James River, Virginia
Love, Heartford S. Private	46	September 8, 1862, Statesville, North Carolina	Co. A, 18th North Carolina Infantry	May 6, 1864, Wilderness, Virginia	Point Lookout, Maryland, transferred to Elmira Prison, NY, August 14, 1864	Died December 16, 1864 of Pneumonia, Grave No. 1059
Love, John F. Private	Unk	January 1, 1862, Georgia	Co. C, Phillips Legion, Georgia	June 1, 1864, Gaines Farm Cold Harbor, Virginia	Point Lookout, Maryland, transferred to Elmira Prison, NY, July 12, 1864	Exchanged February 20, 1865 at Boulware's or Cox Wharf on the James River, Virginia
Love, Robert A. Private	24	September 15, 1861, Red Springs, Robeson County, North Carolina	Co. E, 40th Regiment, 3rd North Carolina Artillery	January 15, 1865, Fort Fisher, North Carolina	February 1, 1865, Elmira Prison Camp, New York	Exchanged March 2, 1865 at Boulware's Wharf on the James River, Virginia
Love, Thomas J. Sergeant	Unk	September 19, 1861, Red Springs, Robeson County, North Carolina	Co. E, 40th Regiment, 3rd North Carolina Artillery	January 15, 1865, Fort Fisher, North Carolina	February 1, 1865, Elmira Prison Camp, New York	Exchange March 2, 1865. Died March 15, 1865 of Chronic Diarrhea at General Hospital No. 8, Raleigh, NC
Lovelace, William F. Private	23	May 28, 1861, Raleigh, North Carolina	Co. G, 22nd North Carolina Infantry	May 23, 1864, Chickahominy, Cold Harbor, Virginia	Point Lookout, Maryland, transferred to Elmira Prison, NY, July 12, 1864	Died November 25, 1864 of Pleuro Pneumonia, Grave No. 909
Loven, Robert S. Private	45	June 25, 1861, Mathias Point, Virginia	Co. H, 30th Virginia Infantry	April 1, 1865, Southside Railroad, Virginia. Gunshot Wound Right Arm.	Old Capital Prison, Washington, DC, transferred to Elmira Prison, NY, May 12, 1865.	Oath of Allegiance July 7, 1865
Lovett, Henry Private	23	July 3, 1861, Lumberton, North Carolina	Co. D, 18th North Carolina Infantry	May 12, 1864, Spotsylvania Court House, Virginia	Point Lookout, Maryland, transferred to Elmira Prison, NY, August 12, 1864	Died April 3, 1865 of Variola (Smallpox) Grave No. 2576

Name & Rank	Age	Enlisted	Regiment and State	Where Captured	Prison	Remarks
Lovett, James M. Private	Unk	May 15, 1862, Savannah, Georgia	Co. B, 7th Georgia Cavalry	June 11, 1864, Trevilian Station, Louisa Court House, Virginia	Point Lookout, Maryland, transferred to Elmira Prison, NY, July 25, 1864	Died September 1, 1864 of Chronic Diarrhea, Grave No. 88
Lovett, Samuel W. Private	21	March 9, 1862, High Point, North Carolina	Co. K, 45th North Carolina Infantry	May 20, 1864, Spotsylvania Court House, Virginia	Point Lookout, Maryland, transferred to Elmira Prison, NY, July 6, 1864	Exchanged February 20, 1865 at Boulware's or Cox Wharf on the James River, Virginia
Lovette, Aaron Private	Unk	May 11, 1862, Bethesda, Georgia	Co. C, 61st Georgia Infantry	May 12, 1864, Spotsylvania Court House, Virginia	Point Lookout, Maryland, transferred to Elmira Prison, NY, July 30, 1864	Exchanged October 29, 1864 at Venus Point, Savannah River, GA.
Loving, Albert G. Private	Unk	February 10, 1863, Nelson County, Virginia	Co. B, 8th Virginia Cavalry	July 3, 1864, Jefferson County, Virginia	Old Capital Prison, Washington DC. Transferred to Elmira Prison Camp, NY, July 25, 1864.	Exchanged March 14, 1865 at Boulware's Wharf on the James River, Virginia
Loving, Joseph F. Private	Unk	May 23, 1861, Trevilians, Virginia	Co. D, 23rd Virginia Infantry	May 12, 1864, Spotsylvania Court House, Virginia	Old Capital Prison, Washington DC. Transferred to Elmira Prison Camp, NY, July 25, 1864.	Died March 12, 1865 of rheumatic Pinaditis, Grave No. 1847. Headstone has Joseph T. Loring.
Lovins, William W. Private	18	March 7, 1862, Rockingham County, North Carolina	Co. E, 45th North Carolina Infantry	May 20, 1864, Spotsylvania Court House, Virginia	Point Lookout, Maryland, transferred to Elmira Prison, NY, July 6, 1864	Exchanged March 14, 1864 on the James River, Virginia
Low, James D. Private	Unk	July 3, 1861, Lynchburg, Virginia	Co. G, 42nd Virginia Infantry	July 16, 1864, Loudoun County, Virginia	Old Capital Prison, Washington DC. Transferred to Elmira Prison Camp, NY, July 25, 1864.	Oath of Allegiance May 19, 1865
Low, L. H. Private	Unk	January 1, 1862, Adam's Run, South Carolina	Co. C, Holcombe's Legion, South Carolina	May 11, 1864, Petersburg and Richmond Turnpike, Virginia	Point Lookout, Maryland, transferred to Elmira Prison, NY, August 17, 1864	Oath of Allegiance June 28, 1865

Name & Rank	Age	Enlisted	Regiment and State	Where Captured	Prison	Remarks
Low, Wilson M. Private	25	March 12, 1862, Brush Valley, Louisiana	Co. H, 9th Louisiana Infantry	May 12, 1864, Spotsylvania Court House, Virginia	Point Lookout, Maryland, transferred to Elmira Prison, NY, August 17, 1864	Exchanged February 13, 1865 at Boulware's wharf on the James River, Virginia
Lowder, Daniel Corporal	28	March 25, 1862, Albemarle, North Carolina	Co. J, 52nd North Carolina Infantry	July 14, 1863, Falling Waters, Maryland	Point Lookout, Maryland, transferred to Elmira Prison, NY, August 18, 1864	Exchanged March 10, 1865 at Boulware's Wharf on the James River, Virginia
Lowder, H. S. Private	31	May 16, 1862, Georgetown, South Carolina	Co. I, 25th South Carolina Infantry	January 15, 1865, Fort Fisher, North Carolina	January 30, 1865, Elmira Prison Camp, New York	Exchanged March 14, 1865 at Boulware's Wharf on the the James River, Virgina
Lowder, Jacob A. Private	25	March 24, 1862, Salisbury, North Carolina	Co. C, 42nd North Carolina Infantry	June 3, 1864, Gaines Farm Cold Harbor, Virginia	Point Lookout, Maryland, transferred to Elmira Prison, NY, July 12, 1864	Oath of Allegiance July 3, 1865
Lowder, James O. Private	29	May 28, 1862, Charleston, South Carolina	Co. J, 25th South Carolina Infantry	January 15, 1865, Fort Fisher, North Carolina	January 30, 1865, Elmira Prison Camp, New York	Oath of Allegiance July 3, 1865
Lowder, John M. Private	Unk	March 7, 1861, Albemarle, North Carolina	Co. K, 28th North Carolina Infantry	May 6, 1864, Wilderness, Virginia	Point Lookout, Maryland, transferred to Elmira Prison, NY, August 14, 1864	Oath of Allegiance June 23, 1865
Lowe, Daniel Private	18	August 14, 1862, Chesterfield County, Virginia	Co. E, 52nd North Carolina Infantry	May 12, 1864, Spotsylvania Court House, Virginia	Point Lookout, Maryland, transferred to Elmira Prison, NY, August 12, 1864	Exchanged February 20, 1865 at Boulware's or Cox Wharf on the James River, Virginia
Lowe, Erastus P. Corporal	Unk	April 29, 1862, White Sulfur Springs, Virginia	Co. F, 26th Battalion, Virginia Infantry	June 3, 1864, Gaines Farm Cold Harbor, Virginia	Point Lookout, Maryland, transferred to Elmira Prison, NY, July 17, 1864	Oath of Allegiance July 3, 1865
Lowe, James A. Private	Unk	June 11, 1861, Drayton, Georgia	Co. F, 12th Georgia Infantry	May 10, 1864, Spotsylvania Court House, Virginia	Point Lookout, Maryland, transferred to Elmira Prison, NY, July 25, 1864	Died March 11, 1865 of Variola (Smallpox), Grave No. 1851

Name & Rank	Age	Enlisted	Regiment and State	Where Captured	Prison	Remarks
Lowe, James L. Private	Unk	Unknown	Co. D, 24th North Carolina Infantry	June 17, 1864, Petersburg, Virginia	Point Lookout, Maryland, transferred to Elmira Prison, NY, July 30, 1864	Exchanged 2/20/65. Died 2/22/65 of Chronic Diarrhea at US Army Hospital, Baltimore, MD
Lowe, John D. Private	24	April 9, 1862, Lawrenceville, Georgia	Co. E, Cobb's Legion Georgia	May 12, 1864, Spotsylvania Court House, Virginia	Point Lookout, Maryland, transferred to Elmira Prison, NY, August 12, 1864	Died May 3, 1865 of Chronic Diarrhea, Grave No. 2755
Lowe, Levi A. Private	26	May 27, 1861, Logan County Court House, Virginia	Co. E, 4th Virginia Infantry	May 12, 1864, Spotsylvania Court House, Virginia	Point Lookout, Maryland, transferred to Elmira Prison, NY, July 25, 1864	Oath of Allegiance June 19, 1865
Lowe, Lorenzo G. Private	27	June 12, 1861, Red Sulfur Springs, Virginia	Co. F, 26th Battalion, Virginia Infantry	May 31, 1864, Chickahominy, Cold Harbor, Virginia	Point Lookout, Maryland, transferred to Elmira Prison, NY, July 12, 1864	Exchanged February 25, 1864 on the James River, Virginia
Lowe, Thomas G. Private	22	June 12, 1861, Red Sulfur Springs, Virginia	Co. F, 26th Battalion Virginia Infantry	June 3, 1864, Gaines Farm Cold Harbor, Virginia	Point Lookout, Maryland, transferred to Elmira Prison, NY, July 17, 1864	Exchanged February 20, 1865 at Boulware's or Cox Wharf on the James River, Virginia
Lowe, William Private	Unk	Unknown	Co. D, 24th North Carolina Infantry	June 17, 1864, Petersburg, Virginia	Point Lookout, Maryland, transferred to Elmira Prison, NY, July 30, 1864	Died September 5, 1864 of Typhoid Fever, Grave No. 237
Lowe, William D. Private	Unk	March 9, 1864, Macon, Georgia	Co. H, 49th Georgia Infantry	May 6, 1864, Wilderness, Virginia	Point Lookout, Maryland, transferred to Elmira Prison, NY, August 14, 1864	Oath of Allegiance June 30, 1865
Lowe, William T. Private	27	September 15, 1862, Statesville, North Carolina	Co. B, 37th North Carolina Infantry	May 6, 1864, Wilderness, Virginia	Point Lookout, Maryland, transferred to Elmira Prison, NY, August 14, 1864	Oath of Allegiance June 23, 1865

Name & Rank	Age	Enlisted	Regiment and State	Where Captured	Prison	Remarks
Lowery, Albert P. Private	19	April 26, 1861, Townsville, North Carolina	Co. B, 12th North Carolina Infantry	May 20, 1864, Spotsylvania Court House, Virginia	Point Lookout, Maryland, transferred to Elmira Prison, NY, July 3, 1864	Oath of Allegiance June 21, 1865
Lowery, Asa D. Sergeant	Unk	May 23, 1861, Coffee County, Alabama	Co. F, 12th Alabama Infantry	May 13, 1864, Spotsylvania Court House, Virginia	Point Lookout, Maryland, transferred to Elmira Prison, NY, August 17, 1864	Oath of Allegiance June 14, 1865
Lowery, Hugh K. Private	Unk	March 1, 1863, Sweetwater, Monroe County, Tennessee	Co. D, 62nd Tennessee Mounted Infantry	May 17, 1863, Big Black, Mississippi	Point Lookout, MD, transferred to Elmira Prison, NY, July 23, 1864.	Oath of Allegiance May 29, 1865
Lowman, James D. Private	Unk	December 8, 1862, Winchester, Virginia	Co. G, 11th Virginia Cavalry	September 22, 1863, Near Madison Court House, Virginia	Point Lookout, Maryland, transferred to Elmira Prison, NY, August 18, 1864	Exchanged October 29, 1864 at Venus Point, Savannah River, GA.
Lowman, Joshua Private	Unk	June 14, 1864, Raleigh, North Carolina	Co. E, 2nd North Carolina Infantry	July 12, 1864, Frederick, Maryland	Old Capital Prison, Washington DC. Transferred to Elmira Prison Camp, NY, July 25, 1864.	Died February 18, 1865 of Chronic Diarrhea, Grave No. 2342. Headstone has Joseph Larman.
Lowman, William H. R. Private	Unk	May 21, 1861, Brownsburg, Virginia	Co. H, 25th Virginia Infantry	May 6, 1864, Wilderness, Virginia	Old Capital Prison, Washington, DC, transferred to Elmira Prison, NY, July 14, 1864	Oath of Allegiance June 23, 1865
Lowrance, J. K. P. Private	Unk	September 7, 1862, Murfreesboro, Tennessee	Co. B, 17th Tennessee Infantry	June 17, 1864, Petersburg, Virginia	Point Lookout, Maryland, transferred to Elmira Prison, NY, July 30, 1864	Exchanged February 25, 1865 at Boulware's or Cox Wharf on the James River, Virginia

Name & Rank	Age	Enlisted	Regiment and State	Where Captured	Prison	Remarks
Lowrimore, H. L. Private	32	December 20, 1861, Camp Harllee, Britton's Neck, South Carolina	Co. J, 21st South Carolina Infantry	June 24, 1864, Petersburg, Virginia	Point Lookout, Maryland, transferred to Elmira Prison, NY, August 18, 1864	Transferred For Exchange October 11, 1864 to Point Lookout Prison, MD. Died October 22, 1864 of Unknown Causes at Point Lookout Prison, Maryland.
Lowry, Calvin Corporal	35	July 1, 1862, Chesterfield, South Carolina	Co. K, 6th South Carolina Cavalry	June 11, 1864, Trevilian Station, Louisa Court House, Virginia	Point Lookout, Maryland, transferred to Elmira Prison, NY, July 25, 1864	Died August 30, 1864 of Chronic Diarrhea, Grave No. 96
Lowry, William B. Private	Unk	April 22, 1861, Stafford Court House, Virginia	Co. J, 47th Virginia Infantry	August 9, 1863, Stafford Court House, Virginia	Point Lookout, Maryland, transferred to Elmira Prison, NY, August 18, 1864	Oath of Allegiance June 19, 1865. Refused to be Exchanged March 14, 1865.
Loy, Maben Private	28	November 10, 1862, Camp Holmes, Raleigh, North Carolina	Co. F, 32nd North Carolina Infantry	May 10, 1864, Spotsylvania Court House, Virginia	Point Lookout, Maryland, transferred to Elmira Prison, NY, July 23, 1864	Oath of Allegiance May 29, 1865
Loy, Milton Private	30	July 15, 1862, Raleigh, North Carolina	Co. E, 1st North Carolina Infantry	May 12, 1864, Spotsylvania Court House, Virginia	Point Lookout, Maryland, transferred to Elmira Prison, NY, August 6, 1864	Oath of Allegiance June 14, 1865
Loyal, Thomas Private	20	July 29, 1861, Livingston, Tennessee	Co. C, 25th Tennessee Infantry	May 16, 1864, Near Drury's Bluff, Virginia	Point Lookout, Maryland, transferred to Elmira Prison, NY, August 17, 1864	Exchanged February 25, 1865 at Boulware's or Cox Wharf on the James River, Virginia
Loyd, J. B. Private	17	May 27, 1863, Chatham County, North Carolina	Co. D, 61st North Carolina Infantry	August 27, 1863, Battery Wagner, Morris Island, South Carolina	Point Lookout, Maryland, transferred to Elmira Prison, NY, August 18, 1864	Exchanged October 29, 1864 at Venus Point, Savannah River, GA.

Name & Rank	Age	Enlisted	Regiment and State	Where Captured	Prison	Remarks
Loyd, James W. Private	19	January 21, 1862, Rolesville, North Carolina	Co. I, 1st North Carolina Infantry	May 12, 1864, Spotsylvania, Virginia	Point Lookout Prison Camp, Maryland. Transferred to Elmira Prison, August 6, 1864	Died December 30, 1864 of Pneumonia, Grave No. 1323
Lucas, Edmond M. Private	Unk	June 4, 1861, Camp Moore, Louisiana	Co. G, 6th Louisiana Infantry	May 5, 1864, Wilderness, Virginia	Point Lookout, Maryland, transferred to Elmira Prison, NY, August 17, 1864	Oath of Allegiance May 10, 1865
Lucas, Henry Private	37	February 9, 1863, Clinton, Sampson County, North Carolina	Co. D, 36th Regiment North Carolina Artillery	January 15, 1865, Fort Fisher, North Carolina	February 1, 1865, Elmira Prison Camp, New York	Exchanged March 14, 1865 at Boulware's Wharf on the James River, Virginia
Lucas, J. T. Private	Unk	March 20, 1863, Goldsboro, North Carolina	Co. F, 10th Regiment, 1st North Carolina Artillery	January 15, 1865, Fort Fisher, North Carolina	January 30, 1865, Elmira Prison Camp, New York	Died April 15, 1865 of Chronic Diarrhea, Grave No. 2711. Headstone has J. F. Lucas.
Lucas, Jesse Private	19	February 14, 1862, Black Creek, North Carolina	Co. C, 43rd North Carolina Infantry	May 25, 1864, Hanover Junction, Virginia	Point Lookout, Maryland, transferred to Elmira Prison, NY, July 11, 1864	Oath of Allegiance June 30, 1865
Lucas, Jesse B. Private	25	May 21, 1861, Gloucester Point, Virginia	Co. A, 26th Virginia Infantry	June 15, 1864, Petersburg, Virginia	Point Lookout, Maryland, transferred to Elmira Prison, NY, July 12, 1864	Exchanged February 13, 1864 on the James River, Virginia
Lucas, Joel Private	Unk	July 31, 1863, Garysburg, North Carolina	Co. D, 24th North Carolina Infantry	June 17, 1864, Near Petersburg, Virginia	Point Lookout, Maryland, transferred to Elmira Prison, NY, July 30, 1864	Exchanged October 29, 1864 at Venus Point, Savannah River, GA.
Lucas, John Private	32	May 15, 1862, Halifax County, North Carolina	Co. D, 24th North Carolina Infantry	June 17, 1864, Petersburg, Virginia	Point Lookout, Maryland, transferred to Elmira Prison, NY, July 30, 1864	Oath of Allegiance July 7, 1865

Name & Rank	Age	Enlisted	Regiment and State	Where Captured	Prison	Remarks
Lucas, John F. Private	Unk	June 4, 1861, Brownsburg, Virginia	Co. H, 25th Virginia Infantry	May 6, 1864, Wilderness, Virginia	Old Capital Prison, Washington, DC, transferred to Elmira Prison, NY, July 14, 1864	Oath of Allegiance June 23, 1865
Lucas, John H. Corporal	Unk	August 3, 1861, Staunton, Virginia	Co. D, 5th Virginia Infantry	May 20, 1864, Spotsylvania Court House, Virginia	Point Lookout Prison Camp, Maryland. Transferred to Elmira Prison Camp, NY, July 6, 1864	Died May 30, 1865 of Dropsy From Hepatic Fatty Liver Disease, Grave No. 2908
Lucas, Rufus Private	Unk	March 15, 1862, Scottsville, Alabama	Co. B, 44th Alabama Infantry	May 5, 1864, Wilderness, Virginia	Point Lookout, Maryland, transferred to Elmira Prison, NY, July 11, 1864	Oath of Allegiance June 14, 1865
Lucas, Stephen Private	21	October 22, 1861, Clinton, North Carolina	Co. D, 38th North Carolina Infantry	May 6, 1864, Wilderness, Virginia	Point Lookout, Maryland, transferred to Elmira Prison, NY, August 14, 1864	Oath of Allegiance June 27, 1865
Lucas, Thomas Private	Unk	March 6, 1862, Luray, Virginia	Co. K, 10th Virginia Infantry	May 12, 1864, Spotsylvania Court House, Virginia	Point Lookout, Maryland, transferred to Elmira Prison, NY, August 2, 1864	Oath of Allegiance June 27, 1865
Luck, E. E. Sergeant	20	November 4, 1861, Randolph County, North Carolina	Co. H, 38th North Carolina Infantry	May 30, 1864, Mechanics-ville, Virginia	Point Lookout, Maryland, transferred to Elmira Prison, NY, July 12, 1864	Oath of Allegiance June 16, 1865
Lucky, David Private	34	March 23, 1862, Capt. Lowe's, North Carolina	Co. G, 52nd North Carolina Infantry	May 12, 1864, Spotsylvania Court House, Virginia	Point Lookout, Maryland, transferred to Elmira Prison, NY, August 12, 1864	Died February 28, 1865 of Chronic Diarrhea, Grave No. 2161
Ludwick, Siar F. Private	19	July 7, 1862, Charlotte, North Carolina	Co. K, 5th North Carolina Cavalry	May 31, 1864, Hanover Court House, Virginia	Point Lookout, Maryland, transferred to Elmira Prison, NY, July 12, 1864	Oath of Allegiance June 30, 1865

Name & Rank	Age	Enlisted	Regiment and State	Where Captured	Prison	Remarks
Ludwig, Henry P. Corporal	Unk	April 16, 1862, Rudes Hill, Virginia	Co. E, 2nd Virginia Infantry	May 12, 1864, Near Spotsylvania Court House, Virginia	Point Lookout, Maryland, transferred to Elmira Prison, NY, August 6, 1864	Oath of Allegiance June 27, 1865
Luffman, William Private	Unk	March 14, 1864, Camp Vance, North Carolina	Co. F, 37th North Carolina Infantry	May 12, 1864, Near Spotsylvania Court House, Virginia	Point Lookout, Maryland, transferred to Elmira Prison, NY, August 14, 1864	Died November 29, 1864 of Pleuro-Pneumonia, Grave No. 982. Name Laffman on Headstone.
Lugenbuhl, Peter Private	Unk	Unknown	Co. A, Captain Hutton's Co. Crescent Louisiana Artillery	March 14, 1864, Fort DeRussy, Louisiana	New Orleans, LA, Transferred to Elmira Prison, NY, November 19, 1864	Oath of Allegiance May 17, 1865
Lumbley, William L. Private	Unk	August 10, 1861, Wake County, North Carolina	Co. D, 30th North Carolina Infantry	May 20, 1864, Spotsylvania Court House, Virginia	Point Lookout, Maryland, transferred to Elmira Prison, NY, July 3, 1864	Oath of Allegiance June 19, 1865
Lumley, William F. Private	27	July 28, 1861, Cedar Fork, North Carolina	Co. G, 7th North Carolina Infantry	July 29, 1864, Petersburg, Virginia	Point Lookout, Maryland, transferred to Elmira Prison, NY, August 12, 1864	Died October 11, 1864 of Chronic Diarrhea, Grave No. 581
Lumpkin, James F. Private	Unk	September 20, 1862, Camp Watts, Alabama	Co. G, 6th Alabama Infantry	May 20, 1864, Spotsylvania Court House, Virginia	Point Lookout, Maryland, transferred to Elmira Prison, NY, July 3, 1864	Oath of Allegiance July 7, 1865
Lumpkin, Theodore F. Private	Unk	January 12, 1863, Chaffin's Bluff, Virginia	Co. K, 34th Virginia Infantry	June 16, 1864, Petersburg, Virginia	Point Lookout, Maryland, transferred to Elmira Prison, NY, July 12, 1864	Exchanged October 29, 1864 at Venus Point, Savannah River, GA.
Lumpkin, Troy G. Private	Unk	March 1, 1863, Camp Prichard, South Carolina	Co. B, 4th South Carolina Cavalry	June 11, 1864, Trevilian Station, Louisa Court House, Virginia	Point Lookout, Maryland, transferred to Elmira Prison, NY, July 25, 1864	Exchanged March 14, 1865 at Boulware's Wharf on the James River, Virginia

Name & Rank	Age	Enlisted	Regiment and State	Where Captured	Prison	Remarks
Lumsden, B. T. Private	Unk	April 28, 1863, Macon, Georgia	Co. B, 64th Georgia Infantry	June 17, 1864, Petersburg, Virginia	Point Lookout, Maryland, transferred to Elmira Prison, NY, July 30, 1864	Exchanged October 29, 1864 at Venus Point, Savannah River, GA.
Lumsden, George A. Corporal	21	May 31, 1861, Middle Sound, North Carolina	Co. E, 1st North Carolina Infantry	May 12, 1864, Near Spotsylvania Court House, Virginia	Point Lookout, Maryland, transferred to Elmira Prison, NY, July 23, 1864	Oath of Allegiance May 13, 1865
Lumsden, William C. Private	Unk	March 14, 1862, Petersburg, Virginia	Co. A, 9th Virginia Infantry	June 15, 1864, Petersburg, Virginia	Point Lookout, Maryland, transferred to Elmira Prison, NY, July 30, 1864	Transferred for Exchanged 10/29/64 at Venus Point, Savannah River, GA.
Lunford, David C. Private	Unk	July 20, 1862, Camp Holmes, Raleigh, North Carolina	Co. E, 35th North Carolina Infantry	June 17, 1864, Petersburg, Virginia	Point Lookout, Maryland, transferred to Elmira Prison, NY, July 30, 1864	Oath of Allegiance May 14, 1865
Lunford, Samuel S. Sergeant	23	May 18, 1861, Edenton, North Carolina	Co. G, 1st North Carolina Infantry	May 12, 1864, Spotsylvania Court House, Virginia	Point Lookout, Maryland, transferred to Elmira Prison, NY, August 6, 1864	Oath of Allegiance June 12, 1865
Lunsford, James R. Private	27	September 23, 1863, Camp Holmes, North Carolina	Co. C, 30th North Carolina Infantry	May 12, 1864, Near Spotsylvania Court House, Virginia	Point Lookout, Maryland, transferred to Elmira Prison, NY, August 14, 1864	Oath of Allegiance May 29, 1865
Lunsford, Jesse A. Corporal	Unk	November 15, 1863, Greenville, North Carolina	Co. H, 24th North Carolina Infantry	June 17, 1864, Petersburg, Virginia	Point Lookout, Maryland, transferred to Elmira Prison, NY, July 30, 1864	Died January 23, 1865 of Remittent Fever, Grave No. 1612. Name Joseph A. Lumesford on Headstone.
Lush, Michael Private	33	June 4, 1861, Camp Moore, New Orleans, Louisiana	Co. G, 6th Louisiana Infantry	May 5, 1864, Wilderness, Virginia	Point Lookout, Maryland, transferred to Elmira Prison, NY, July 25, 1864	Oath of Allegiance May 19, 1865

Name & Rank	Age	Enlisted	Regiment and State	Where Captured	Prison	Remarks
Lusk, D. H. Corporal	Unk	January 23, 1863, Oline Branch, Louisiana	Co. G, 14th Confederate States Cavalry	May 15, 1864, Near Port Hudson, Louisiana	New Orleans, Louisiana transferred to Elmira November 19, 1864.	Exchanged February 25, 1865 at Boulware's or Cox Wharf on the James River, Virginia
Luther, Jesse M. Private	23	August 1, 1861, Troy, North Carolina	Co. E, 28th North Carolina Infantry	July 29, 1864, Petersburg, Virginia	Point Lookout, Maryland, transferred to Elmira Prison, NY, August 12, 1864	Exchanged March 14, 1865 at Boulware's Wharf on the James River, Virginia
Luther, Josiah Private	Unk	March 18, 1862, Randolph County, North Carolina	Co. L, 22nd North Carolina Infantry	July 14, 1863, Falling Waters, Maryland	Point Lookout, Maryland, transferred to Elmira Prison, NY, August 18, 1864	Exchanged March 10, 1865 at Boulware's Wharf on the James River, Virginia
Lyerly, Alexander M. Private	17	September 11, 1863, Salisbury, North Carolina	Co. K, 8th North Carolina Infantry	May 31, 1864, Cold Harbor, Virginia	Point Lookout, Maryland, transferred to Elmira Prison, NY, July 12, 1864	Oath of Allegiance June 30, 1865
Lyle, James Private	Unk	January 14, 1862, Camp Hampton, Columbia, South Carolina	Co. D, 17th South Carolina Infantry	July 30, 1864, Petersburg, Virginia	Point Lookout, Maryland, transferred to Elmira Prison, NY, August 12, 1864	Died December 10, 1864 of Chronic Diarrhea, Grave No. 1154
Lyle, Joseph H. Private	Unk	June 22, 1861, Henry County, Virginia	Co. F, 42nd Virginia Infantry	May 12, 1864, Near Spotsylvania Court House, Virginia	Point Lookout, Maryland, transferred to Elmira Prison, NY, August 6, 1864	Oath of Allegiance June 27, 1865
Lyles, Preston Private	24	July 9, 1861, Weldon, North Carolina	Co K, 1st North Carolina Infantry	May 12, 1864, Spotsylvania Court House, Virginia	Point Lookout, Maryland, transferred to Elmira Prison, NY, August 6,1864	Died February 24, 1865 of Chronic Diarrhea, Grave No. 2272. Headstone has E. P. Leslie.
Lynch, Ahijah Oliver Private	22	September 2, 1861, Rutherford County, North Carolina	Co. C, 34th North Carolina Infantry	July 14, 1863, Falling Waters, Maryland	Point Lookout, Maryland, transferred to Elmira Prison, NY, August 18, 1864	Exchanged March 10, 1865 at Boulware's Wharf on the James River, Virginia

Name & Rank	Age	Enlisted	Regiment and State	Where Captured	Prison	Remarks
Lynch, Elijah Private	29	July 2, 1861, Weldon, North Carolina	Co. K, 1st North Carolina Infantry	May 12, 1864, Spotsylvania, Virginia	Point Lookout Prison Camp, Maryland. Transferred to Elmira Prison Camp, New York, August 6, 1864	Died September 11, 1864 of Epilepsy, Grave No. 252
Lynch, F. Sergeant	Unk	Date Unknown, Charleston, South Carolina	Co. J, 27th South Carolina Infantry	June 24, 1864, Near Petersburg, Virginia	Point Lookout, Maryland, transferred to Elmira Prison, NY, August 18, 1864	Exchanged October 29, 1864 at Venus Point, Savannah River, GA.
Lynch, G. W. Private	Unk	January 28, 1862, McClellans-ville, South Carolina	Co. J, 26th South Carolina Infantry	July 30, 1864, Petersburg, Virginia	Point Lookout, Maryland, transferred to Elmira Prison, NY, August 12, 1864	Died September 16, 1864 of Chronic Diarrhea, Grave No. 296
Lynch, John Private	35	June 5, 1861, Memphis, Tennessee	Co. B, 1st Jackson's Tennessee Heavy Artillery	August 23, 1864, Fort Morgan, Alabama.	New Orleans, Louisiana transferred to Elmira Prison, NY, December 4, 1864.	Exchanged March 10, 1865 at Boulware's Wharf on the James River, Virginia
Lynch, John S. Private	33	May 1, 1863, Harrisonburg, Virginia	2nd Battery Maryland Artillery	July 11, 1864, Frederick, Maryland	Old Capital Prison, Washington DC. Transferred to Elmira Prison Camp, NY, July 25, 1864.	Exchanged October 29, 1864 at Venus Point, Savannah River, GA.
Lynch, Philip Private	25	July 2, 1861, Sunflower County, Mississippi	Co. J, 21st Mississippi Infantry	July 8, 1864, Spotsylvania Court House, Virginia. Gunshot Wound of Back.	Old Capital Prison, Washington DC. Transferred to Elmira Prison Camp, NY, July 25, 1864.	Exchanged October 29, 1864 at Venus Point, Savannah River, GA.
Lynch, T. C. Private	Unk	Unknown	Co. J, 24th South Carolina Infantry	June 25, 1864, Near Petersburg, Virginia	Unknown	Transferred for Exchange October 11, 1864. No Further Information.
Lynn, E. J. Private	Unk	November 18, 1861, College Green, Columbia, South Carolina	Co. A, 17th South Carolina Infantry	July 30, 1864, Petersburg, Virginia	Point Lookout, Maryland, transferred to Elmira Prison, NY, August 12, 1864	Oath of Allegiance July 3, 1865

Name & Rank	Age	Enlisted	Regiment and State	Where Captured	Prison	Remarks
Lynn, Franklin C. Private	36	March 8, 1861, Montgomery, Alabama	Co. D, 1st Battalion Alabama Artillery	August 23, 1864, Fort Morgan, Alabama	Steam Press No. 4, New Orleans, Louisiana transferred to Elmira Prison, NY, October 8, 1864.	Died December 12, 1864 of Chronic Diarrhea, Grave No. 1142
Lynn, Jacob Private	Unk	July 17, 1861, Center Hall, Georgia	Co. B, 16th Georgia Infantry	June 1, 1864, Cold Harbor, Virginia	Point Lookout, Maryland, transferred to Elmira Prison, NY, July 12, 1864	Exchanged March 14, 1865 at Boulware's Wharf on the James River, Virginia
Lynn, James W. Private	Unk	Unknown	Co. K, 12th Virginia Cavalry	September 22, 1863, Near Culpepper, Virginia	Point Lookout, Maryland, transferred to Elmira Prison, NY, August 18, 1864	Died October 16, 1864 of Remittent Fever, Grave No. 560
Lynn, Thomas E. Private	Unk	September 30, 1862, Charleston, Virginia	Co. F, 26th Battalion, Virginia Infantry	May 31, 1864, Cold Harbor, Virginia	Point Lookout, Maryland, transferred to Elmira Prison, NY, July 12, 1864	Oath of Allegiance May 15, 1865
Lyon, Jacob A. Private	Unk	June 25, 1861, Wytheville, Virginia	Co. I, 50th Virginia Infantry	May 12, 1864, Spotsylvania Court House, Virginia	Point Lookout, Maryland, transferred to Elmira Prison, NY, August 2, 1864	Oath of Allegiance June 27, 1865
Lyon, James V. Private	Unk	March 25, 1862, Scott County, Virginia	Co. A, 48th Virginia Infantry	May 12, 1864 Spotsylvania Court House, Virginia	Point Lookout, Maryland, transferred to Elmira Prison, NY, August 2, 1864	Exchanged March 14, 1865 at Boulware's Wharf on the James River, Virginia
Lyon, Stephen Private	Unk	July 21, 1862, Pulaski, Virginia	Co. L, 26th Battalion, Virginia Infantry	June 3, 1864, Gaines Farm Cold Harbor, Virginia	Point Lookout, Maryland, transferred to Elmira Prison, NY, July 17, 1864	Exchanged February 13, 1865 at Boulware's wharf on the James River, Virginia
Lyons, Charles T. Private	Unk	September 22, 1862, Waynesville, Georgia	Co. G, 7th Georgia Cavalry	June 11, 1864, Trevilian Station, Louisa Court House, Virginia	Point Lookout, Maryland, transferred to Elmira Prison, NY, July 25, 1864	Died March 2, 1865 of Variola (Smallpox) Grave No. 2017

Name & Rank	Age	Enlisted	Regiment and State	Where Captured	Prison	Remarks
Lyons, Enos Private	21	May 18, 1861, Huntersville, Virginia	Co. I, 25th Virginia Infantry	May 12, 1864, Spotsylvania Court House, Virginia	Point Lookout, Maryland, transferred to Elmira Prison, NY, August 12, 1864	Oath of Allegiance May 29, 1865
Lytle, John A. Private	40	January 2, 1862, Newton, North Carolina	Co. E, 32nd North Carolina Infantry	May 10, 1864, Wilderness, Virginia	Point Lookout, Maryland, transferred to Elmira Prison, NY, August 6, 1864	Oath of Allegiance June 27, 1865
Lytz, James K. Private	Unk	February 23, 1864, Dublin Depot, Virginia	Co. L, 26th Battalion, Virginia Infantry	June 3, 1864, Gaines Farm Cold Harbor, Virginia	Point Lookout, Maryland, transferred to Elmira Prison, NY, July 17, 1864	Exchanged October 29, 1864 at Venus Point, Savannah River, GA.

Name & Rank	Age	Enlisted	Regiment and State	Where Captured	Prison	Remarks
Mabe, Isaac Sergeant	18	Unknown	Co. F, 2nd Battalion North Carolina Infantry	May 12, 1864, Near Spotsylvania County Court House, Virginia	Point Lookout, Maryland, transferred to Elmira Prison, NY, August 14, 1864	Died August 27, 1864 of Chronic Diarrhea, Grave No. 105
Mabe, Samuel N. Private	Unk	June 22, 1861, Wytheville, Virginia	Co. K, 50th Virginia Infantry	May 12, 1864, Spotsylvania Court House, Virginia	Point Lookout, Maryland, transferred to Elmira Prison, NY, August 2, 1864	Died May 1, 1865 of Pneumonia, Grave No. 2738
Mabie, Jessie Private	Unk	Unknown	Co. K, 58th Alabama Infantry	May 23, 1864, Hanover Junction, Virginia	Point Lookout, Maryland, transferred to Elmira Prison, NY, July 23, 1864	Oath of Allegiance June 30, 1865
Mabry, John B. Corporal	28	February 25, 1862, Lew's Store, North Carolina	Co. G, 12th North Carolina Infantry	May 12, 1864, Near Spotsylvania, Virginia	Point Lookout, Maryland, transferred to Elmira Prison, NY, August 14, 1864	Died September 21, 1864 of Chronic Diarrhea, Grave No. 331. Name J. B. Mabree on Headstone.

Name & Rank	Age	Enlisted	Regiment and State	Where Captured	Prison	Remarks
Mabry, Thomas W. Private	Unk	March 26, 1863, Athens, Georgia	Co. D, Cobb's Legion, Georgia	August 16, 1864, Front Royal, Virginia	Old Capital Prison, Washington, DC transferred to Elmira Prison, NY, August 29, 1864	Exchanged March 2, 1865 at Akins Landing on the James River, Virginia
Macauley, John Private	Unk	August 13, 1861, Staunton, Virginia	Co. G, 5th Virginia Infantry	May 20, 1864, Spotsylvania Court House, Virginia	Point Lookout, Maryland, transferred to Elmira Prison, NY, July 3, 1864	Exchanged March 10, 1865 at Boulware's Wharf on the James River, Virginia
Mace, Abraham Private	18	February 29, 1863, Morganton, North Carolina	Co. B, 11th North Carolina Infantry	July 14, 1863, Falling Waters, Maryland	Point Lookout, Maryland, transferred to Elmira Prison, NY, August 18, 1864	Died September 16, 1864 of Typhoid-Pneumonia, Grave No. 305
Mace, John M. Private	20	May 23, 1861, Lincolnton, Lincoln County, North Carolina	Co. B, 23rd North Carolina Infantry	July 16, 1864, Poolesville, Maryland	Old Capital Prison, Washington DC. Transferred to Elmira Prison Camp New York July 25, 1864.	Oath of Allegiance May 19, 1865
Mack, George T. Sergeant	Unk	July 1, 1861, New Orleans, Louisiana	Co. H, 14th Louisiana Infantry	May 12, 1864, Spotsylvania Court House, Virginia	Point Lookout, Maryland, transferred to Elmira Prison, NY, July 25, 1864	Oath of Allegiance June 21, 1865
Mackey, Robert A. Private	23	August 28, 1862, Camp Hill, North Carolina	Co. J, 28th North Carolina Infantry	May 12, 1864, Spotsylvania, Virginia	Old Capital Prison, Washington, DC, transferred to Elmira Prison, NY, December 17, 1864	Oath of Allegiance June 12, 1865
MacKinnan, G. W. Private	Unk	July 10, 1861, Auburn, Alabama	Co. F, 12th Alabama Infantry	May 8, 1864, wilderness, Virginia	Point Lookout, Maryland, transferred to Elmira Prison, NY, August 17, 1864	Exchanged March 14, 1865 at Boulware's Wharf on the James River, Virginia
Mackubbin, Edmund H. Private	Unk	June 1, 1862, Richmond, Virginia	Co. K, 1st Virginia Cavalry	July 15, 1864, Wheatland, Virginia	Old Capital Prison, Washington DC. Transferred to Elmira Prison Camp, NY, July 25, 1864.	Oath of Allegiance May 17, 1865

Name & Rank	Age	Enlisted	Regiment and State	Where Captured	Prison	Remarks
Macon, Isaac Private	24	July 16, 1862, Raleigh, North Carolina	Co. E, 14th North Carolina Infantry	June 10, 1864, Spotsylvania, Virginia	Point Lookout, Maryland, transferred to Elmira Prison, NY, July 25, 1864	Oath of Allegiance June 12, 1865
Macon, John A. Private	23	May 20, 1861, Louisburg, North Carolina	Co. K, 32nd North Carolina Infantry	May 10, 1864, Near Spotsylvania Court House, Virginia	Point Lookout, Maryland, transferred to Elmira Prison, NY, August 6, 1864	Exchanged October 29, 1864 at Venus Point, Savannah River, GA.
Madden, Edward Private	25	June 7, 1861, Camp Moore, Louisiana	Co. I, 7th Louisiana Infantry	May 12, 1864, Spotsylvania Court House, Virginia	Point Lookout, Maryland, transferred to Elmira Prison, NY, August 17, 1864	Exchanged February 25, 1865 at Boulware's or Cox Wharf on the James River, Virginia
Madden, John C. Private	Unk	March 1, 1862, Vernon, Louisiana	Co. M, 12th Louisiana Infantry	May 16, 1863, Baker's Creek, Champion Hill, Mississippi	Point Lookout, Maryland, transferred to Elmira Prison, NY, August 18, 1864	Exchanged February 25, 1865 at Boulware's wharf on the James River, Virginia
Maddox, Francis A. Corporal	Unk	June 15, 1861, Eatonton, Georgia	Co. G, 12th Georgia Infantry	May 10, 1864, Spotsylvania Court House, Virginia	Point Lookout, Maryland, transferred to Elmira Prison, NY, July 30, 1864	Oath of Allegiance June 16, 1865
Maddox, Isham Private	Unk	March 4, 1862, Perry, Georgia	Co. H, 45th Georgia Infantry	May 6, 1864, Wilderness, Virginia	Point Lookout, Maryland, transferred to Elmira Prison, NY, August 14, 1864	Died February 28, 1865 of Diarrhea, Grave No. 2126
Maddox, Robert Private	Unk	March 5, 1862, Lynchburg, Virginia	Co. I, 42nd Virginia Infantry	May 12, 1864, Near Spotsylvania Court House, Virginia	Point Lookout, Maryland, transferred to Elmira Prison, NY, August 6, 1864	Exchanged February 20, 1865 at Boulware's or Cox Wharf on the James River, Virginia
Maddy, Thaddeus R. Sergeant	21	June 12, 1861, Red Sulfur Springs, Virginia	Co. F, 26th Battalion, Virginia Infantry	June 3, 1864, Gaines Farm Cold Harbor, Virginia	Point Lookout, Maryland, transferred to Elmira Prison, NY, July 17, 1864	Exchanged October 29, 1864 at Venus Point, Savannah River, GA.

Name & Rank	Age	Enlisted	Regiment and State	Where Captured	Prison	Remarks
Madra, George A. Private	18	August 31, 1861, Crab Tree, Raleigh, North Carolina	Co. F, 30th North Carolina Infantry	May 20, 1864, Spotsylvania Court House, Virginia	Point Lookout, Maryland, transferred to Elmira Prison, NY, July 3, 1864	Oath of Allegiance June 19, 1865
Madray, John L. Private	21	August 1, 1861, Waynesboro, Georgia	Co. D, Cobb's Legion, Georgia	August 16, 1864, Front Royal, Virginia	Old Capital Prison, Washington, DC transferred to Elmira Prison, NY, August 29, 1864	Died March 24, 1865 of Diarrhea, Grave No. 2445
Madry, David Private	29	May 14, 1862, Wilmington, North Carolina	Co. D, 43rd North Carolina Infantry	March 25, 1865, Petersburg, Virginia. Gunshot Wound Left Foot.	Old Capital Prison, Washington, DC, transferred to Elmira Prison, NY, May 12, 1865.	Oath of Allegiance July 7, 1865
Magan, David Private	Unk	Unknown	Capt. W. H. Chapman's Battery, Virginia Light Artillery	July 11, 1864, Frederick, Maryland	Old Capital Prison, Washington DC. Transferred to Elmira Prison Camp New York July 25, 1864.	Oath of Allegiance May 19, 1865
Magruder, William H. Sergeant	Unk	April 18, 1861, Marion, Virginia	Co. D, 4th Virginia Infantry	May 12, 1864 Spotsylvania Court House, Virginia	Point Lookout, Maryland, transferred to Elmira Prison, NY, August 2, 1864	Transferred For Exchange October 11, 1864 to Point Lookout Prison Camp, MD. Nothing Further.
Maguire, John Private	Unk	February 15, 1861, Mobile, Alabama	Co. A, 1st Battalion Alabama Artillery	August 23, 1864, Fort Morgan, Alabama	New Orleans, Louisiana transferred to Elmira Prison, NY, December 4, 1864.	Oath of Allegiance May 17, 1865
Maguire, Joseph E. Private	Unk	May 30, 1864, H. Junction, Virginia	Co. D, 1st Maryland Cavalry	July 8, 1864, Boonsboro, Maryland	Old Capital Prison, Washington DC. Transferred to Elmira Prison Camp New York July 25, 1864.	Exchanged February 25, 1865 at Boulware's or Cox Wharf on the James River, Virginia
Maguire, William Private	27	January 27, 1862, Covington, Tennessee	Co. A, 1st Jackson's Tennessee Heavy Artillery	August 23, 1864, Fort Morgan, Alabama.	New Orleans, Louisiana transferred to Elmira Prison, NY, December 4, 1864.	Died March 21, 1865 of Pneumonia, Grave No. 1535

Name & Rank	Age	Enlisted	Regiment and State	Where Captured	Prison	Remarks
Mahan, Lewis C. Private	Unk	July 7, 1861, Richmond, Virginia	Co. J, 21st Virginia Infantry	May 12, 1864, Near Spotsylvania Court House, Virginia	Point Lookout, Maryland, transferred to Elmira Prison, NY, August 6, 1864	Exchanged February 13, 1865 at Boulware's wharf on the James River, Virginia
Mahanes, James H. Private	22	July 6, 1861, Winchester, Virginia	Co. C, 30th Virginia Infantry	April 9, 1865, Appomattox Court House, Virginia. Gunshot Wound Right Shoulder.	Old Capital Prison, Washington, DC, transferred to Elmira Prison, NY, May 12, 1865.	Oath of Allegiance July 3, 1865
Mahon, Patrick Private	Unk	July 22, 1861, Camp Moore, Louisiana	Co. B, 10th Louisiana Infantry	May 5, 1864, Wilderness, Virginia	Point Lookout, Maryland, transferred to Elmira Prison, NY, July 25, 1864	Oath of Allegiance May 15, 1865
Mahoner, L. Private	Unk	Unknown	Co. A, 1st Tennessee Heavy Artillery	August 23, 1864, Fort Morgan, Alabama	Fort Columbus, NY Harbor. Transferred to Elmira Prison, NY, December 5, 1865	He Died March 18, 1865 of Pneumonia, Grave No. 1724. Headstone has A. Mahones.
Mahoney, Cornelius Sergeant	30	July 22, 1861, Camp Moore, Louisiana	Co. J, 10th Louisiana Infantry	May 12, 1864, Near Spotsylvania Court House, Virginia	Point Lookout, Maryland, transferred to Elmira Prison, NY, July 23, 1864	Oath of Allegiance May 14, 1865
Mahoney, Jerry Private	26	June 5, 1861, Memphis, Tennessee	Co. B, 1st Jackson's Tennessee Heavy Artillery	August 23, 1864, Fort Morgan, Alabama.	New Orleans, Louisiana transferred to Elmira Prison, NY, December 4, 1864.	Exchanged March 10, 1865 at Boulware's Wharf on the James River, Virginia
Mahoney, John H. Private	Unk	July 2, 1861, New Orleans, Louisiana	Co. H, 14th Louisiana Infantry	May 12, 1864, Spotsylvania Court House, Virginia	Point Lookout, Maryland, transferred to Elmira Prison, NY, July 25, 1864	Exchanged March 2, 1865 at Akins Landing on the James River, Virginia
Maiden, William F. Corporal	Unk	Unknown	Co. B, 48th Virginia Infantry	May 12, 1864, Spotsylvania Court House, Virginia	Point Lookout, Maryland, transferred to Elmira Prison, NY, August 12, 1864	Oath of Allegiance July 11, 1865

Name & Rank	Age	Enlisted	Regiment and State	Where Captured	Prison	Remarks
Maines, W. Private	Unk	Unknown	Co. C, 58th North Carolina Infantry	June 1, 1864, Gaines Mill Cold Harbor, Virginia	Point Lookout, Maryland, transferred to Elmira Prison, NY, July 12, 1864	Exchanged March 2, 1865 at Akins Landing on the James River, Virginia
Mains, R. A. Private	Unk	Unknown	Co. A, 6th Alabama Infantry	May 20, 1864, Spotsylvania Court House, Virginia	Point Lookout, Maryland, transferred to Elmira Prison, NY, July 3, 1864	Exchanged February 25, 1865 at Boulware's or Cox Wharf on the James River, Virginia
Mainwarring, George Sergeant	Unk	May 21, 1861, Brownsburg, Virginia	Co. H, 25th Virginia Infantry	May 5, 1864, Wilderness, Virginia	Point Lookout, Maryland, transferred to Elmira Prison, NY, August 2, 1864	Oath of Allegiance June 16, 1865
Maize, George T. Private	Unk	June 22, 1861, Wytheville, Virginia	Co. K, 50th Virginia Infantry	May 5, 1864, Wilderness, Virginia	Point Lookout, Maryland, transferred to Elmira Prison, NY, August 17, 1864	Died April 13, 1865 of Pneumonia, Grave No. 2695. Name G. W. Maze on Headstone.
Makemson, William Private	27	August 24, 1861, Poplar Springs, Hall County, Georgia	Co. J, 24th Georgia Infantry	June 1, 1864, Cold Harbor, Virginia	Point Lookout, Maryland, transferred to Elmira Prison, NY, July 12, 1864	Oath of Allegiance July 7, 1865
Maks, J. C. Sergeant	Unk	Unknown	Co. A, 24th Georgia Infantry	June 1, 1864, Cold Harbor, Virginia	Point Lookout, Maryland, transferred to Elmira Prison, NY, July 12, 1864	Exchanged October 29, 1864 at Venus Point, Savannah River, GA.
Mal, H. Private	Unk	Unknown	Co. B, 22nd Virginia Infantry	June 1, 1864, Cold Harbor, Virginia	Point Lookout, Maryland, transferred to Elmira Prison, NY, July 12, 1864	Transferred for Exchange October 11, 1864. No Additional Information.
Malett, William B. Private	Unk	August 14, 1863, Lake City, Florida	Co. E, 9th Florida Infantry	July 2, 1864, Petersburg, Virginia	Point Lookout, Maryland, transferred to Elmira Prison, NY, July 23, 1864	Oath of Allegiance May 17, 1865

Name & Rank	Age	Enlisted	Regiment and State	Where Captured	Prison	Remarks
Mallard, John W. Private	20	August 28, 1861, Teachey's, North Carolina	Co. E, 30th North Carolina Infantry	May 12, 1864, Near Spotsylvania Court House, Virginia	Point Lookout, Maryland, transferred to Elmira Prison, NY, August 14, 1864	Exchanged March 14, 1865 at Boulware's Wharf on the James River, Virginia
Mallette, Jasper Private	Unk	June 9, 1861, Bibb County, Georgia	Co. H, 12th Georgia Infantry	May 10, 1864, Spotsylvania Court House, Virginia	Point Lookout, Maryland, transferred to Elmira Prison, NY, July 30, 1864	Oath of Allegiance June 16, 1865
Mallison, David B. Private	17	January 1, 1863, Wilmington, North Carolina	Co. K, 10th Regiment, 1st North Carolina Artillery	January 15, 1865, Fort Fisher, North Carolina	January 30, 1865, Elmira Prison Camp, New York	Oath of Allegiance May 19, 1865
Mallory, James D. Private	21	August 15, 1861, Union City, Tennessee	Co. G, 14th Mississippi Infantry	May 16, 1862, Champion Hill, Mississippi	Point Lookout, Maryland, transferred to Elmira Prison, NY, August 18, 1864	Exchanged March 10, 1865 at Boulware's wharf on the James River, Virginia
Malloy, Edward Private	29	May 9, 1862, Robeson County, North Carolina	Co. D, 1st Battalion North Carolina Heavy Artillery	January 15, 1865, Fort Fisher, North Carolina	February 1, 1865, Elmira Prison Camp, New York	Died April 19, 1865 of Chronic Diarrhea, Grave No. 1369. Headstone has E. Melloy.
Malone, Albert A. Sergeant	25	March 5, 1862, Yanceyville, North Carolina	Co. I, 45th North Carolina Infantry	May 10, 1864, Spotsylvania Court House, Virginia	Point Lookout Prison Camp, Maryland. Transferred to Elmira Prison Camp, NY August 6, 1864	Died August 28, 1864 of Chronic Diarrhea, Grave No. 100
Malone, James Private	18	October 4, 1862, Zollicoffer, Tennessee	Co. K, 61st Tennessee Mounted Infantry	May 17, 1863, Big Black, Mississippi	Point Lookout, Maryland, transferred to Elmira Prison, NY, July 25, 1864	Oath of Allegiance May 17, 1865
Malone, Patrick Private	Unk	March 15, 1862, Charleston, South Carolina	Co. C, 27th South Carolina Infantry	June 24, 1864, Near Petersburg, Virginia	Point Lookout, Maryland, transferred to Elmira Prison, NY, July 23, 1864	Died November 20, 1864 of Chronic Diarrhea, Grave No. 941.

Name & Rank	Age	Enlisted	Regiment and State	Where Captured	Prison	Remarks
Malone, R. C. Private	Unk	Unknown	Co. A, Jackson's 1st Regiment, Tennessee Heavy Artillery	August 23, 1864, Fort Morgan, Alabama	New Orleans, Louisiana transferred to Elmira Prison, NY, December 4, 1864.	Exchanged February 25, 1865 at Boulware's or Cox Wharf on the James River, Virginia
Malone, S. C. Private	24	June 4, 1861, Athens, Georgia	Co. E, 9th Alabama Infantry	May 6, 1864, Wilderness, Virginia	Point Lookout, Maryland, transferred to Elmira Prison, NY, August 17, 1864	Escaped October 7, 1864 by Tunneling Under Fence.
Malone, Zihman Private	21	February 27, 1862, Reidsville, Rockingham County, North Carolina	Co. E, 45th North Carolina Infantry	May 10, 1864, Spotsylvania Court House, Virginia	Point Lookout, Maryland, transferred to Elmira Prison, NY, August 6, 1864	Died April 6, 1865 of Variola (Smallpox), Grave No. 2648
Maloney, John Private	28	April 28, 1861, New Orleans, Louisiana	Co. D, 1st Louisiana Infantry	May 20, 1864, Spotsylvania Court House, Virginia	Point Lookout, Maryland, transferred to Elmira Prison, NY, July 3, 1864	Exchanged February 25, 1865 at Boulware's or Cox Wharf on the James River, Virginia
Maloy, John A. Private	Unk	May 8, 1862, Georgia	Co. F, 3rd Battalion Georgia Sharp Shooters	August 16, 1864, Front Royal, Virginia	Old Capital Prison, Washington, DC transferred to Elmira Prison, NY, August 29, 1864	No Additional Information
Maloy, Michael Private	Unk	Unknown	Co. A, 1st Jackson's Tennessee Heavy Artillery	August 23, 1864, Fort Morgan, Alabama.	New Orleans, Louisiana transferred to Elmira Prison, NY, December 4, 1864.	Oath of Allegiance May 15, 1865
Malpass, Owen M. Private	16	March 1, 1862, Piney Woods, North Carolina	Co. A, 51st North Carolina Infantry	June 3, 1864, Gaines Mill Cold Harbor, Virginia	Point Lookout, Maryland, transferred to Elmira Prison, NY, July 12, 1864	Died September 29, 1864 of Chronic Diarrhea Grave No. 431
Malpass, Thaddeus D. Private	23	May 17, 1861, Lower Black River District, North Carolina	Co. F, 18th North Carolina Infantry	May 12, 1864, Spotsylvania Court House, Virginia	Point Lookout, Maryland, transferred to Elmira Prison, NY, July 17, 1864	Exchanged March 14, 1865 at Boulware's Wharf on the James River, Virginia

Name & Rank	Age	Enlisted	Regiment and State	Where Captured	Prison	Remarks
Manberet, Amielee Private	Unk	March 5, 1862, New Orleans, Louisiana	Captain Homes' Battery Louisiana Light Artillery	August 25, 1864, Near Clinton, Louisiana	New Orleans, LA, Transferred to Elmira Prison, NY, November 19, 1864	Exchanged March 14, 1865 at Boulware's Wharf on the James River, Virginia
Manchino, Fortunato Private	18	July 22, 1861, Camp Moore, Louisiana	Co. J, 10th Louisiana Infantry	May 12, 1864, Spotsylvania Court House, Virginia	Point Lookout, Maryland, transferred to Elmira Prison, NY, July 25, 1864	Oath of Allegiance May 13, 1865
Maner, William T. Private	16	March 29, 1862, Samson County, North Carolina	Co. I, 51st North Carolina Infantry	June 1, 1864, Gaines Mill, Cold Harbor, Virginia	Point Lookout, Maryland, transferred to Elmira Prison, NY, July 17, 1864	Exchanged March 2, 1865 at Boulware's Wharf on the James River, Virginia
Maners, Hammet J. Private	18	March 25, 1862, Albemarle, North Carolina	Co. J, 52nd North Carolina Infantry	July 14, 1863, Falling Waters, Maryland	Point Lookout, Maryland, transferred to Elmira Prison, NY, August 18, 1864	Transferred for Exchanged 10/29/64 at Venus Point, Savannah River, GA.
Manes, Matthew Private	Unk	May 27, 1863, Chatham County, North Carolina	Co. D, 61st North Carolina Infantry	August 27, 1863, Battery Wagner, Morris Island, South Carolina	Point Lookout, Maryland, transferred to Elmira Prison, NY, August 18, 1864	Exchanged October 29, 1864 at Venus Point, Savannah River, GA.
Maness, Thomas Milton Private	28	April 16, 1862, Monroe, North Carolina	Co. B, 43rd North Carolina Infantry	July 12, 1864, Near Washington, DC	Old Capital Prison, Washington DC. Transferred to Elmira Prison Camp New York July 25, 1864.	Died October 22, 1864 of Chronic Diarrhea, Grave No. 864. Headstone has McManiss.
Maness, Thomas S. Private	18	June 3, 1861, Carthage, North Carolina	Co. H, 23rd South Carolina Infantry	June 12, 1864, Chickahominy, Virginia	Point Lookout, Maryland, transferred to Elmira Prison, NY, July 30, 1864	Oath of Allegiance May 29, 1865
Manley, Hector D. Private	Unk	April 1, 1861, Lacy's Store, Virginia	Co. B, 44th Virginia Infantry	May 12, 1864, Spotsylvania Court House, Virginia	Point Lookout, Maryland, transferred to Elmira Prison, NY, August 2, 1864	Exchanged March 14, 1865 at Boulware's Wharf on the James River, Virginia

Name & Rank	Age	Enlisted	Regiment and State	Where Captured	Prison	Remarks
Manley, William H. Private	46	May 9, 1861, Charles City Court House, Virginia	Co. D, 3rd Virginia Cavalry	May 12, 1864, Spotsylvania Court House, Virginia	Point Lookout, Maryland, transferred to Elmira Prison, NY, July 17,1864	Exchanged March 2, 1865 at Akins Landing on the James River, Virginia
Manly, Robert Private	29	July 20, 1861, Camp Picken's, South Carolina	Co, F, Orr's Rifles 1st South Carolina Infantry	May 24, 1864, Beaver Dam Station, Virginia	Point Lookout, Maryland, transferred to Elmira Prison, NY, July 12, 1864	Oath of Allegiance June 23, 1865
Mann, Henry A. Private	Unk	Unknown	Co. B, 6th North Carolina Infantry	May 30, 1864, Mechanics-ville, Virginia	Point Lookout, Maryland, transferred to Elmira Prison, NY, July 12, 1864	Oath of Allegiance May 29, 1865
Mann, Johnson Private	Unk	November 19, 1862, Chatham County, North Carolina	Co. D, 61st North Carolina Infantry	August 26, 1863, Battery Wagner, Morris Island, South Carolina	Point Lookout, Maryland, transferred to Elmira Prison, NY, August 18, 1864	Exchanged March 10, 1865 at Boulware's Wharf on the James River, Virginia
Mann, T. W. Sergeant	Unk	June 12, 1861, Red Sulfur Springs, Virginia	Co. F, 26th Battalion Virginia Infantry	June 3, 1864, Gaines Farm Cold Harbor, Virginia	Point Lookout, Maryland, transferred to Elmira Prison, NY, July 17, 1864	Oath of Allegiance July 3, 1865
Mann, William R. Private	Unk	May 18, 1861, Lisbon, Virginia	Co. C, 42nd Virginia Infantry	May 12, 1864, Spotsylvania Court House, Virginia	Point Lookout, Maryland, transferred to Elmira Prison, NY, August 2,1864	Died March 7, 1865 of Variola (Smallpox), Grave No. 2388
Manning, James S. Private	38	July 15, 1862, Raleigh, North Carolina	Co. H, 33rd North Carolina Infantry	May 6, 1864, Wilderness, Virginia	Point Lookout, Maryland, transferred to Elmira Prison, NY, August 12, 1864	Died February 1, 1865 of Variola (Smallpox), Grave No. 1781
Manning, Louis E. Private	38	July 3, 1861, Brunswick County, North Carolina	Co. C, 8th North Carolina Infantry	May 30, 1864, Cold Harbor, Virginia	Old Capital Prison, Washington, DC, transferred to Elmira Prison Camp, NY, December 17, 1864	Oath of Allegiance June 30, 1865

Name & Rank	Age	Enlisted	Regiment and State	Where Captured	Prison	Remarks
Manning, Matthew Private	Unk	February 15, 1863, Buckner's Neck, Virginia	Co. D, 25th Virginia Infantry	May 12, 1864, Spotsylvania Court House, Virginia	Point Lookout, Maryland, transferred to Elmira Prison, NY, August 2, 1864	Oath of Allegiance June 27, 1865
Manning, Wallace Private	34	October 8, 1861, Martin County, North Carolina	Co. F, 31st North Carolina Infantry	June 1, 1864, Gaines Mill, Cold Harbor, Virginia	Transferred From Point Lookout Prison, MD, July 12, 1864. Train Never Arrived at Elmira Prison Camp, NY.	Died July 15, 1864 in Train Wreck at Shohola, Pennsylvania.
Mansel, Edmund Private	Unk	July 14, 1862, Camp Randolph, Georgia	Co. J, 26th Georgia Infantry	May 20, 1864, Spotsylvania Court House, Virginia	Point Lookout, Maryland, transferred to Elmira Prison, NY, July 3, 1864	Oath of Allegiance June 30, 1865
Mantle, Henry Private	Unk	May 10, 1861, Richmond, Virginia	Co. C, 38th Battalion, Virginia Light Artillery	June 3, 1864, Gaines Farm Cold Harbor, Virginia	Point Lookout, Maryland, transferred to Elmira Prison, NY, July 12, 1864	Oath of Allegiance May 13, 1865
Marable, George P. Sergeant	Unk	April 26, 1864, West Point, Georgia	Co. D, 4th Georgia Infantry	July 12, 1864, Near Washington, DC	Old Capital Prison, Washington DC. Transferred to Elmira Prison Camp New York July 25, 1864.	Exchanged March 10, 1865 at Boulware's Wharf on the James River, Virginia
Marcantel, Maxile Private	24	July 22, 1861, Camp Moore, Louisiana	Co. K, 10th Louisiana Infantry	May 12, 1864, Spotsylvania Court House, Virginia	Point Lookout, Maryland, transferred to Elmira Prison, NY, July 25, 1864	Exchanged February 25, 1865 at Boulware's or Cox Wharf on the James River, Virginia
Marchand, Alexander Private	19	June 19, 1861, Camp Moore, Louisiana	Co. K, 8th Louisiana Infantry	May 12, 1864, Spotsylvania Court House, Virginia	Point Lookout, Maryland, transferred to Elmira Prison, NY, August 17, 1864	Exchanged February 25, 1865 at Boulware's or Cox Wharf on the James River, Virginia

Name & Rank	Age	Enlisted	Regiment and State	Where Captured	Prison	Remarks
Marchant, Abraham Private	24	July 23, 1861, Matthews Court House, Virginia	Co. F, 5th Virginia Cavalry	May 11, 1864, Yellow Tavern, Hanover County, Virginia	Point Lookout, Maryland, transferred to Elmira Prison, NY, August 17, 1864	Exchanged February 20, 1865. Died March 18, 1865 of Unknown Causes at Howard's Grove Hospital, Richmond, VA.
Marcom, William W. Private	20	September 2, 1861, Orange County Court House, North Carolina	Co. G, 28th North Carolina Infantry	May 6, 1864, Wilderness, Virginia	Point Lookout, Maryland, transferred to Elmira Prison, NY, August 14, 1864	Oath of Allegiance June 27, 1865
Marion, Taylor J. Private	Unk	July 28, 1863, Pritchard, South Carolina	Co. B, 4th South Carolina Cavalry	May 30, 1864, Old Church, Cold Harbor, Virginia	Point Lookout, Maryland, transferred to Elmira Prison, NY, July 12, 1864	Oath of Allegiance June 21, 1865
Market, Benjamin F. Private	Unk	September 12, 1861, Americus, Georgia	Co. A, 12th Georgia Infantry	May 10, 1864, Spotsylvania Court House, Virginia	Point Lookout, Maryland, transferred to Elmira Prison, NY, July 30, 1864	Oath of Allegiance June 16, 1865
Markey, James Private	25	June 7, 1861, Camp Moore, New Orleans, Louisiana	Co. C, 7th Louisiana Infantry	May 11, 1864, Spotsylvania Court House, Virginia	Point Lookout, Maryland, transferred to Elmira Prison, NY, August 17, 1864	Exchanged February 13, 1865 at Boulware's wharf on the James River, Virginia
Marlain, William T. Private	17	January 6, 1865, Robeson County, North Carolina	Co. D, 1st Battalion North Carolina Heavy Artillery	January 15, 1865, Fort Fisher, North Carolina	February 1, 1865, Elmira Prison Camp, New York	Oath of Allegiance May 17, 1865
Marler, Jesse J. Private	Unk	September 20, 1863, Goldsboro, North Carolina	Co. K, 10th Regiment, 1st North Carolina Artillery	January 15, 1865, Fort Fisher, North Carolina	January 30, 1865, Elmira Prison Camp, New York	Oath of Allegiance June 23, 1865
Marler, Joseph F. Private	34	June 18, 1861, East Bend, North Carolina	Co. F, 28th North Carolina Infantry	May 6, 1864, Wilderness, Virginia	Point Lookout, Maryland, transferred to Elmira Prison, NY, July 25, 1864	Died February 25, 1865 of Pneumonia, Grave No. 2292

Name & Rank	Age	Enlisted	Regiment and State	Where Captured	Prison	Remarks
Marler, Nathan Private	21	April 25, 1861, Snow Hill, North Carolina	Co. A, 3rd North Carolina Infantry	May 12, 1864, Spotsylvania Court House, Virginia	Point Lookout, Maryland, transferred to Elmira Prison, NY, July 3, 1864	Died January 9, 1865 of Variola (Smallpox), Grave No. 1225. Name Marlow on Headstone.
Marlon, Josephus Private	18	September 15, 1861, Allegheny County, North Carolina	Co. K, 37th North Carolina Infantry	May 12, 1864, Near Spotsylvania Court House, Virginia	Point Lookout, Maryland, transferred to Elmira Prison, NY, August 14, 1864	Died February 26, 1865 of Pneumonia, Grave No. 2282
Marlow, Robert Private	Unk	September 12, 1862, Knoxville, Maryland	Co. G, Ashby's 7th Regiment Virginia Cavalry	July 18, 1864, Percersville, Loudoun County, Virginia	Old Capital Prison, Washington, DC, transferred to Elmira Prison, NY, August 12, 1864	Oath of Allegiance May 17, 1865
Marmaduke, Luther Private	23	June 18, 1861, Winchester, Virginia	Co. B, 2nd Virginia Infantry	May 12, 1864, Spotsylvania Court House, Virginia	Point Lookout, Maryland, transferred to Elmira Prison, NY, August 2, 1864	Died October 1, 1864 of Typhoid Fever, Grave No. 616. Headstone has First Name A.
Maroney, Charles B. Private	Unk	February 1, 1863, Charleston, South Carolina	Co. A, 21st Battalion Georgia Cavalry	June 11, 1864, Trevilian Station, Louisa Court House, Virginia	Point Lookout, Maryland, transferred to Elmira Prison, NY, July 23, 1864	Oath of Allegiance May 15, 1865
Maroney, Samuel S. Corporal	Unk	November 18, 1861, Columbia, South Carolina	Co. A, 18th South Carolina Infantry	July 30, 1864, Battle of the Crater, Petersburg, Virginia	Point Lookout, Maryland, transferred to Elmira Prison, NY, August 12, 1864	Exchanged March 2, 1865 at Akins Landing on the James River, Virginia
Marquis, James Private	22	April 18, 1861, Harper's Ferry, Virginia	Co. H, 2nd Virginia Infantry	May 12, 1864, Near Spotsylvania Court House, Virginia	Point Lookout, Maryland, transferred to Elmira Prison, NY, August 6, 1864	Transferred for Exchanged 10/29/64 at Venus Point, Savannah River, GA.
Marr, John R. Private	Unk	February 3, 1864, Danville, Virginia	Co. D, 45th North Carolina Infantry	May 24, 1864, Near Hanover Junction, Virginia	Point Lookout, Maryland, transferred to Elmira Prison, NY, July 12, 1864	Died October 9, 1864 of Typhoid Fever, Grave No. 667

Name & Rank	Age	Enlisted	Regiment and State	Where Captured	Prison	Remarks
Marriman, William Private	Unk	Unknown	Co. C, 1st Battalion Alabama Artillery	August 23, 1864, Fort Morgan, Alabama	New Orleans, Louisiana transferred to Elmira Prison, NY, December 4, 1864.	Died March 13, 1865 of Diarrhea, Grave No. 1823. Headstone has William Merriman.
Marron, Peter H. Sergeant	21	April 17, 1861, Christiansburg, Virginia	Co. G, 4th Virginia Infantry	May 12, 1864, Spotsylvania Court House, Virginia	Point Lookout, Maryland, transferred to Elmira Prison, NY, August 2, 1864	Exchanged March 10, 1865 at Boulware's Wharf on the James River, Virginia
Marsh, John W. Private	18	March 10, 1864, Camp Holmes, Raleigh, North Carolina	Co. B, 32nd North Carolina Infantry	May 10, 1864, Spotsylvania Court House, Virginia. Gunshot Wound Left Arm. Arm Amputated.	Old Capital Prison, Washington, DC, transferred to Elmira Prison, NY, March 27, 1865.	Oath of Allegiance June 12, 1865
Marsh, Neill Private	40	September 20, 1863, Cumberland County, North Carolina	Co. B, 36th 2nd North Carolina Artillery	January 15, 1865, Fort Fisher, North Carolina	February 1, 1865, Elmira Prison Camp, New York	Exchanged March 2, 1865. Died March 19, 1865 of Typhoid-Pneumonia at Pettigrew Hospital, Raleigh, North Carolina.
Marsh, Samuel Private	19	June 18, 1861, Randolph County, North Carolina	Co. L, 22nd North Carolina Infantry	May 24, 1864, Near Hanover Junction, Virginia	Point Lookout, Maryland, transferred to Elmira Prison, NY, July 12, 1864	Oath of Allegiance August 8, 1865
Marshall, Andrew M. Private	44	August 18, 1863, Fort Branch, Martin County, North Carolina	Co. G, 40th Regiment, 3rd North Carolina Artillery	January 15, 1865, Fort Fisher, North Carolina	January 30, 1865 Elmira Prison Camp, New York	Oath of Allegiance June 12, 1865
Marshall, George F. Private	16	April 1, 1862, Rapidan, Virginia	Co. D, 34th Virginia Infantry	June 17, 1864, Petersburg, Virginia	Point Lookout, Maryland, transferred to Elmira Prison, NY, July 30, 1864	Oath of Allegiance July 7, 1865
Marshall, George W. Private	20	May 27, 1861, Wilson, North Carolina	Co. B, 2nd North Carolina Infantry	May 30, 1864, Old Church, Cold Harbor, Virginia	Point Lookout, Maryland, transferred to Elmira Prison, NY, July 17, 1864	Oath of Allegiance June 30, 1865

Name & Rank	Age	Enlisted	Regiment and State	Where Captured	Prison	Remarks
Marshall, John Private	19	June 3, 1861, Raleigh Court House, Virginia	Co. C, 36th Virginia Infantry	July 7, 1864, Harpers Ferry, Virginia	Old Capital Prison, Washington DC. Transferred to Elmira Prison Camp New York July 25, 1864.	Oath of Allegiance May 19, 1865
Marshall, John H. Private	Unk	April 18, 1861, Conrad's Store, Virginia	Co. I, 10th Virginia Infantry	May 12, 1864, Spotsylvania Court House, Virginia	Point Lookout, Maryland, transferred to Elmira Prison, NY, August 2, 1864	Died March 15, 1865 of Variola (Smallpox), Grave No. 1688
Marshall, John H. Private	Unk	December 18, 1861, Little Plymouth, Virginia	Co. G, 26th Virginia Infantry	June 15, 1864, Petersburg, Virginia	Point Lookout, Maryland, transferred to Elmira Prison, NY, July 30, 1864	Died October 16, 1864 of Pneumonia, Grave No. 558
Marshall, John R. Sergeant Major	Unk	December 30, 1861, Camp Weakly, Nashville, Tennessee	Co. J, 44th Tennessee Infantry	June 17, 1864, Petersburg, Virginia	Point Lookout, Maryland, transferred to Elmira Prison, NY, July 30, 1864	Exchanged February 25, 1865 at Boulware's or Cox Wharf on the James River, Virginia
Marshall, M. R. Private	Unk	December 10, 1862, Vicksburg, Mississippi	Co. A, Jackson's 1st Regiment, Tennessee Heavy Artillery	August 23, 1864, Fort Morgan, Alabama	New Orleans, Louisiana transferred to Elmira Prison, NY, December 4, 1864.	Exchanged February 25, 1865 at Boulware's or Cox Wharf on the James River, Virginia
Marshall, Robert Private	Unk	May 15, 1862, Camp Harris, Tennessee	Co. G, 17th Tennessee Infantry	June 17, 1864, Petersburg, Virginia	Point Lookout, Maryland, transferred to Elmira Prison, NY, July 30, 1864	Exchanged February 25, 1865 at Boulware's or Cox Wharf on the James River, Virginia
Marshall, Robert A. Private	31	March 19, 1862, Van Buren, Virginia	Co. D, 25th Virginia Infantry	May 12, 1864, Spotsylvania Court House, Virginia	Point Lookout, Maryland, transferred to Elmira Prison, NY, August 2, 1864	Exchanged March 10, 1865 at Boulware's Wharf on the James River, Virginia
Marshall, Robert A. M. Corporal	Unk	October 1, 1862, Snickersville, Virginia	Co. G, 6th Virginia Cavalry	May 11, 1864, Yellow Tavern, Hanover County, Virginia	Point Lookout, Maryland, transferred to Elmira Prison, NY, August 17, 1864	Died March 4, 1865 of Pneumonia, Grave No. 1976

Name & Rank	Age	Enlisted	Regiment and State	Where Captured	Prison	Remarks
Marshall, Robert F. Private	Unk	June 1, 1863, Hamilton Crossing, Virginia	Co. I, 10th Virginia Infantry	May 12, 1864, Spotsylvania Court House, Virginia	Point Lookout, Maryland, transferred to Elmira Prison, NY, August 2, 1864	Died September 9, 1864 of Laryngitis, Grave No. 200
Marshall, Warren William Sergeant	Unk	June 11, 1861, Hevener's Store, Virginia	Co. F, 25th Virginia Infantry	May 5, 1864, Wilderness, Virginia	Point Lookout, Maryland, transferred to Elmira Prison, NY, August 14, 1864	Oath of Allegiance June 27, 1865
Marshall, William Private	Unk	February 13, 1864, Camp Holmes, North Carolina	Co. H, 13th North Carolina Infantry	May 6, 1864, Wilderness, Virginia	Point Lookout, Maryland, transferred to Elmira Prison, NY, August 14, 1864	Died August 22, 1864 of Chronic Diarrhea, Grave No. 29
Marshall, William D. Corporal	16	July 18, 1861, Camp Howard, North Carolina	Co. C, 30th North Carolina Infantry	May 12, 1864, Near Spotsylvania Court House, Virginia	Point Lookout, Maryland, transferred to Elmira Prison, NY, August 14, 1864	Oath of Allegiance June 23, 1865
Marshburn, Hosea Q. Private	Unk	March 23, 1862, Duplin County, North Carolina	Co. B, 3rd North Carolina Infantry	May 12, 1864, Near Spotsylvania County Court House, Virginia	Point Lookout, Maryland, transferred to Elmira Prison, NY, August 14, 1864	Exchanged October 29, 1864 at Venus Point, Savannah River, GA.
Marsteller, Lewis A. Private	24	April 23, 1861, Brentsville, Virginia	Co. A, 4th Virginia Cavalry	August 22, 1863, Prince William County, Virginia	Point Lookout, Maryland, transferred to Elmira Prison, NY, August 18, 1864	Exchanged October 29, 1864 at Venus Point, Savannah River, GA.
Marten, Davis Private	Unk	Unknown	No Co., 2nd Louisiana Cavalry	September 22, 1864, Bayou Alabama, Louisiana	New Orleans, Louisiana transferred to Elmira November 19, 1864.	Died March 21, 1865 of Bronchitis, Grave No. 1530. Headstone has David Martin.
Martin, A. A. Civilian	Unk	Louisiana	Citizen of Louisiana	October 22, 1864, Pointe Coupee, Louisiana	New Orleans, Louisiana transferred to Elmira November 19, 1864.	Exchanged February 20, 1865 at Boulware's or Cox Wharf on the James River, Virginia

Name & Rank	Age	Enlisted	Regiment and State	Where Captured	Prison	Remarks
Martin, Alfred Private	Unk	March 10, 1861, Athens, Texas	Co. K, 4th Texas Infantry	May 12, 1864, Spotsylvania Court House, Virginia	Point Lookout, Maryland, transferred to Elmira Prison, NY, July 30, 1864	Died September 30, 1864 of Chronic Diarrhea, Grave No. 401
Martin, Allen M. Private	Unk	October 8, 1862, Charleston, Virginia	Co. D, 22nd Virginia Infantry	June 3, 1864, Gaines Farm Cold Harbor, Virginia	Point Lookout, Maryland, transferred to Elmira Prison, NY, July 12, 1864	Oath of Allegiance June 21, 1865
Martin, Benjamin F. Sergeant	19	August 17, 1861, Lightwood Knot Springs, Near Columbia, South Carolina	Co. E, 14th South Carolina Infantry	July 29, 1864, Petersburg, Virginia	Point Lookout, Maryland, transferred to Elmira Prison, NY, August 12, 1864	Exchanged March 14, 1865 at Boulware's Wharf on the James River, Virginia
Martin, Charles F. Private	33	May 17, 1862, Gainesville, Florida	Co. F, 2nd Florida Cavalry	May 12, 1863, Big Black, Mississippi	Point Lookout, Maryland, transferred to Elmira Prison, NY, August 18, 1864	Exchanged October 29, 1864 at Venus Point, Savannah River, GA.
Martin, Charles S. Private	18	August 31, 1861, Lincolnton, North Carolina	Co. E, 34th North Carolina Infantry	May 6, 1864, Wilderness, Virginia	Point Lookout, Maryland, transferred to Elmira Prison, NY, August 14, 1864	Oath of Allegiance May 19, 1865
Martin, Christopher Private	Unk	June 9, 1861, Bibb County, Georgia	Co. H, 12th Georgia Infantry	May 10, 1864, Spotsylvania Court House, Virginia	Point Lookout, Maryland, transferred to Elmira Prison, NY, July 30, 1864	Exchanged March 14, 1865 at Boulware's Wharf on the James River, Virginia
Martin, Daniel B. Private	Unk	July 20, 1863, C. S. Jones, Virginia	Co. C, 26th Battalion, Virginia Infantry	June 3, 1864, Gaines Farm Cold Harbor, Virginia	Point Lookout, Maryland, transferred to Elmira Prison, NY, July 17, 1864	Died September 23, 1864 of Chronic Diarrhea, Grave No. 467
Martin, Edward T. Private	24	April 20, 1861, Greensboro, Alabama	Co. D, 5th Alabama Infantry	May 5, 1864, Wilderness, Virginia	Old Capital Prison, Washington DC. Transferred to Elmira Prison Camp New York July 25, 1864.	Oath of Allegiance June 14, 1865

Name & Rank	Age	Enlisted	Regiment and State	Where Captured	Prison	Remarks
Martin, G. W. Private	Unk	June 12, 1862, Hall County, Georgia	Co. C, 7th Georgia Cavalry	June 11, 1864, Trevilian Station, Louisa Court House, Virginia	Point Lookout, Maryland, transferred to Elmira Prison, NY, July 25, 1864	Died September 29, 1864 of Chronic Diarrhea, Grave No. 439.
Martin, Harmon Sergeant	22	July 29, 1861, Madison, Georgia	Co. G, Cobb's Legion Georgia	August 16, 1864, Front Royal, Virginia	Old Capital Prison, Washington, DC transferred to Elmira Prison, NY, August 29, 1864	Oath of Allegiance July 7, 1865
Martin, Hugh Private	Unk	Unknown	Co. C, 23rd Virginia Cavalry	July 12, 1864, Near Washington, DC	Old Capital Prison, Washington DC. Transferred to Elmira Prison Camp New York July 25, 1864.	Exchanged March 14, 1865 at Boulware's Wharf on the James River, Virginia
Martin, J. Private	Unk	February 1, 1864, Greenville, Alabama	Co. H, 59th Alabama Infantry	June 17, 1864, Petersburg, Virginia	Point Lookout, Maryland, transferred to Elmira Prison, NY, July 12, 1864. Ward No. 20	Died August 12, 1864 of Chronic Diarrhea, Grave No. 16
Martin, Jackson M. Sergeant	19	May 3, 1861, Wentworth, North Carolina	Co. H, 13th North Carolina Infantry	May 6, 1864, Wilderness, Virginia	Point Lookout, Maryland, transferred to Elmira Prison, NY, August 14, 1864	Exchanged October 29, 1864 at Venus Point, Savannah River, GA.
Martin, James F. Private	Unk	April 15, 1862, Yorktown, Virginia	Co. G, 49th Virginia Infantry	July 4, 1863, Gettysburg, Pennsylvania	Point Lookout, Maryland, transferred to Elmira Prison, NY, August 18, 1864	Oath of Allegiance June 16, 1865
Martin, James G. Private	Unk	July 22, 1861, Davis Barracks, Virginia	Co. G, 49th Virginia Infantry	August 10, 1864, Berryville, Virginia	Old Capital Prison, Washington, DC transferred to Elmira Prison, NY, August 29, 1864	Exchanged March 14, 1865 at Boulware's Wharf on the James River, Virginia
Martin, James L. Private	16	July 20, 1861, Rocky River, Cabarrus County, North Carolina	Co. H, 7th North Carolina Infantry	July 21, 1864, Deep Bottom, Virginia	Point Lookout, Maryland, transferred to Elmira Prison, NY, August 18, 1864	Oath of Allegiance June 12, 1865

Name & Rank	Age	Enlisted	Regiment and State	Where Captured	Prison	Remarks
Martin, John Private	Unk	October 30, 1862, South Santee, South Carolina	Co. D, 4th South Carolina Cavalry	June 11, 1864, Trevilian Station, Louisa Court House, Virginia	Point Lookout, Maryland, transferred to Elmira Prison, NY, July 25, 1864	Oath of Allegiance July 3, 1865
Martin, John Private	39	April 15, 1862, Charleston, South Carolina	Co. E, 25th South Carolina Volunteers	January 15, 1865, Fort Fisher, North Carolina. Wounded.	January 30, 1865, Elmira Prison Camp, New York	Oath of Allegiance May 17, 1865
Martin, John B. Sergeant	31	October 16, 1861, Yadkinville, North Carolina	Co. B, 38th North Carolina Infantry	May 6, 1864, Wilderness, Virginia	Point Lookout, Maryland, transferred to Elmira Prison, NY, August 14, 1864	Oath of Allegiance May 29, 1865
Martin, John G. Private	20	June 1, 1861, Richmond County, North Carolina	Co. F, 18th North Carolina Infantry	May 12, 1864, Spotsylvania Court House, Virginia	Point Lookout, Maryland, transferred to Elmira Prison, NY, August 6, 1864	Oath of Allegiance June 12, 1865
Martin, John M. Private	Unk	May 15, 1862, Atlanta, Georgia	Co. J, 38th Georgia Infantry	May 20, 1864, Spotsylvania Court House, Virginia	Point Lookout, Maryland, transferred to Elmira Prison, NY, July 3, 1864	Died October 24, 1864 of Chronic Diarrhea, Grave No. 711
Martin, John T. Private	36	February 28, 1862, Fayetteville, North Carolina	Co. G, 33rd North Carolina Infantry	May 6, 1864, Wilderness, Virginia	Old Capital Prison, Washington, DC, transferred to Elmira Prison, NY, July 14, 1864	Exchanged October 29, 1864 at Venus Point, Savannah River, GA.
Martin, John W. Sergeant	Unk	May 15, 1862, Savannah, Georgia	Co. B, 7th Georgia Cavalry	June 11, 1864, Trevilian Station, Louisa Court House, Virginia	Point Lookout, Maryland, transferred to Elmira Prison, NY, July 25, 1864	Oath of Allegiance July 11, 1865
Martin, John W. Private	19	August 17, 1862, Raleigh, North Carolina	Co. I, 18th North Carolina Infantry	May 25, 1864, Cold Harbor, Virginia	Point Lookout, Maryland, transferred to Elmira Prison, NY, July 11, 1864	Oath of Allegiance June 30, 1865
Martin, Joseph P. Private	Unk	March 1, 1863, Liberty, Virginia	Co. C, 42nd Virginia Infantry	May 12, 1864, Spotsylvania Court House, Virginia	Point Lookout, Maryland, transferred to Elmira Prison, NY, August 2, 1864	Exchanged March 14, 1865 at Boulware's Wharf on the James River, Virginia

Name & Rank	Age	Enlisted	Regiment and State	Where Captured	Prison	Remarks
Martin, Joseph S. Private	Unk	Unknown	Co. A, 7th Alabama Cavalry	August 27, 1864, Milton, Walton County, Florida	New Orleans, LA, Transferred to Elmira Prison, NY, November 19, 1864	Died November 29, 1864 of Pneumonia, Grave No. 1003
Martin, Joseph V. Sergeant	18	May 1, 1862, South Mills, North Carolina	Co. C, 32nd North Carolina Infantry	May 10, 1864, Near Spotsylvania Court House, Virginia	Point Lookout, Maryland, transferred to Elmira Prison, NY, August 6, 1864	Oath of Allegiance June 27, 1865
Martin, Luther Sergeant Major	45	February 9, 1861, Montgomery, Alabama	Field and Staff, 1st Alabama Artillery	August 23, 1864, Fort Morgan, Alabama.	New Orleans, Louisiana transferred to Elmira Prison, NY, December 4, 1864.	Oath of Allegiance June 14, 1865
Martin, M. S. Private	Unk	August 30, 1862, Hartwell, Georgia	Co. C, 16th Georgia Infantry	June 1, 1864, Gaines Farm Cold Harbor, Virginia	Point Lookout, Maryland, transferred to Elmira Prison, NY, July 12, 1864	Oath of Allegiance June 16, 1865
Martin, Milton V. Sergeant	23	May 3, 1861, Wentworth, North Carolina	Co. H, 13th North Carolina Infantry	May 6, 1864, Wilderness, Virginia	Point Lookout, Maryland, transferred to Elmira Prison, NY, August 14, 1864	Exchanged March 10, 1865 at Boulware's Wharf on the James River, Virginia
Martin, Philip Private	Unk	December 28, 1861, Camp Hampton, South Carolina	Co. G, 7th Battalion South Carolina Infantry	May 16, 1864, Near Drury's Bluff, Virginia	Point Lookout, Maryland, transferred to Elmira Prison, NY, August 17, 1864	Oath of Allegiance June 27, 1865
Martin, R. C. Private	Unk	April 9, 1864, Fort McAllister, Georgia	Co. H, 7th Georgia Cavalry	June 11, 1864, Trevilian Station, Louisa Court House, Virginia	Point Lookout, Maryland, transferred to Elmira Prison, NY, July 25, 1864	Died November 10, 1864 of Pneumonia, Grave No. 828
Martin, Riley T. Private	Unk	March 16, 1864, Camp Taylor, Georgia	Co. D, 12th Georgia Infantry	May 10, 1864, Spotsylvania Court House, Virginia	Point Lookout, Maryland, transferred to Elmira Prison, NY, July 30, 1864	Transferred For Exchange October 11, 1864 to Point Lookout Prison Camp, MD. Nothing Further.
Martin, Robert H. Private	Unk	May 5, 1862, Camp Holmes, New Hanover, North Carolina	Co. E, 51st North Carolina Infantry	June 1, 1864, Cold Harbor, Virginia	Point Lookout, Maryland, transferred to Elmira Prison, NY, July 12, 1864	Died August 25, 1864 of Chronic Diarrhea, Grave No. 42

Name & Rank	Age	Enlisted	Regiment and State	Where Captured	Prison	Remarks
Martin, Simeon Private	Unk	September 21, 1863, Lewisburg, Virginia	Co. A, 26th Battalion, Virginia Infantry	June 3, 1864, Gaines Farm Cold Harbor, Virginia	Point Lookout, Maryland, transferred to Elmira Prison, NY, July 17, 1864	Exchanged 2/13/65. Died 3/10/65 of Chronic Diarrhea at Chimborazo Hospital No. 2, Richmond, VA.
Martin, Thomas A. Corporal	21	January 1, 1862, Yadkinville, North Carolina	Co. B, 38th North Carolina Infantry	May 6, 1864, Wilderness, Virginia	Point Lookout, Maryland, transferred to Elmira Prison, NY, August 14, 1864	Oath of Allegiance May 19, 1865
Martin, Thomas Y. Private	Unk	June 10, 1861, Morgan, Georgia	Co. D, 12th Georgia Infantry	May 10, 1864, Spotsylvania Court House, Virginia	Point Lookout, Maryland, transferred to Elmira Prison, NY, July 30, 1864	Oath of Allegiance June 16, 1865
Martin, William Private	Unk	November 18, 1861, College Green, Columbia, South Carolina	Co. A, 17th South Carolina Infantry in an	July 30, 1864, Petersburg, Virginia	Point Lookout, Maryland, transferred to Elmira Prison, NY, August 12, 1864	Oath of Allegiance June 19, 1865
Martin, William A. Private	Unk	July 11, 1861, Athens, Georgia	Co. C, 3rd Battalion Georgia Sharp Shooters	August 16, 1864, Front Royal, Virginia	Old Capital Prison, Washington, DC transferred to Elmira Prison, NY, August 29, 1864	Oath of Allegiance June 21, 1865
Martin, William A. Private	32	October 4, 1862, Drury's Bluff, Virginia	Co. A, 45th North Carolina Infantry	July 13, 1864, Near Washington, DC	Old Capital Prison, Washington DC. Transferred to Elmira Prison Camp New York July 25, 1864.	Oath of Allegiance May 17, 1865
Martin, William A. Private	Unk	June 2, 1862, Luray, Virginia	Co. K, 10th Virginia Infantry	May 12, 1864, Spotsylvania Court House, Virginia	Point Lookout, Maryland, transferred to Elmira Prison, NY, August 2, 1864	Oath of Allegiance June 19, 1865
Martin, William G. Private	Unk	June 14, 1861, Elamsville, Virginia	Co. D, 51st Virginia Infantry	July 16, 1864, Snickers Gap, Loudoun County, Virginia	Old Capital Prison, Washington DC. Transferred to Elmira Prison Camp New York July 25, 1864.	Oath of Allegiance May 29, 1865

Name & Rank	Age	Enlisted	Regiment and State	Where Captured	Prison	Remarks
Martin, William H. Private	Unk	Unknown	Co. D, 12th Georgia Infantry	May 10, 1864, Spotsylvania Court House, Virginia	Point Lookout, Maryland, transferred to Elmira Prison, NY, July 30, 1864	Died September 26, 1864 of Chronic Diarrhea, Grave No. 364
Martin, William H. Private	19	March 8, 1862, Rockingham County, North Carolina	Co. G, 45th North Carolina Infantry	May 10, 1864, Spotsylvania Court House, Virginia	Point Lookout, Maryland, transferred to Elmira Prison, NY, August 6, 1864	Died March 11, 1865 of Chronic Diarrhea, Grave No. 1844
Martin, William R. Corporal	Unk	March 4, 1863, Wilmington, North Carolina	Co. H, 23rd South Carolina Infantry	June 17, 1864, Near Petersburg, Virginia	Point Lookout, Maryland, transferred to Elmira Prison, NY, July 30, 1864	Transferred for Exchanged 10/29/64 at Venus Point, Savannah River, GA.
Martindale, Henry H. Private	18	May 21, 1861, Raleigh, North Carolina	Co. K, 14th North Carolina Infantry	July 16, 1864, Near Harpers Ferry, Loudoun County, Virginia	Old Capital Prison, Washington DC. Transferred to Elmira Prison Camp New York July 25, 1864.	Exchanged February 25, 1865 at Boulware's or Cox Wharf on the James River, Virginia
Mason, C. R. Sergeant	Unk	February 1, 1864, Staunton, Virginia	Co. E, 5th Virginia Cavalry	April 12, 1865, City Point, Virginia	Old Capital Prison, Washington, DC, transferred to Elmira Prison, NY, May 12, 1865.	Oath of Allegiance July 7, 1865
Mason, E. L. Private	Unk	April 28, 1862, Marietta, Georgia	Co. M, Phillips Legion, Georgia	July 29, 1864, Petersburg, Virginia	Point Lookout, Maryland, transferred to Elmira Prison, NY, August 12, 1864	Oath of Allegiance July 7, 1865
Mason, J. M. Private	Unk	Unknown	Co. A, Jackson's 1st Regiment, Tennessee Heavy Artillery	August 23, 1864, Fort Morgan, Alabama	New Orleans, Louisiana transferred to Elmira Prison, NY, December 4, 1864.	Oath of Allegiance July 11, 1865
Mason, James Private	19	August 23, 1861, Camp Trousdale, Tennessee	Co. D, 23rd Tennessee Infantry	June 17, 1864, Petersburg, Virginia	Point Lookout, Maryland, transferred to Elmira Prison, NY, July 30, 1864	Exchanged February 25, 1865 at Boulware's or Cox Wharf on the James River, Virginia

Name & Rank	Age	Enlisted	Regiment and State	Where Captured	Prison	Remarks
Mason, James A. Private	20	March 25, 1862, Albemarle, North Carolina	Co. J, 52nd North Carolina Infantry	May 12, 1864, Spotsylvania Court House, Virginia	Point Lookout, Maryland, transferred to Elmira Prison, NY, August 12, 1864	Exchanged February 20, 1865 at Boulware's or Cox Wharf on the James River, Virginia
Mason, Joseph John Private	Unk	August 7, 1861, Jones County, Georgia	Co. B, 12th Georgia Infantry	May 10, 1864, Spotsylvania Court House, Virginia	Point Lookout, Maryland, transferred to Elmira Prison, NY, July 30, 1864	Exchanged October 29, 1864 at Venus Point, Savannah River, GA.
Mason, Levi H. Private	22	May 8, 1862, Camp Hill, Stanley County, North Carolina	Co. F, 5th North Carolina Infantry	May 6, 1864, Wilderness, Virginia	Point Lookout, Maryland, transferred to Elmira Prison, NY, July 30, 1864	Oath of Allegiance May 15, 1865
Mason, Ralph Private	22	May 27, 1861, Troy, Montgomery County, North Carolina	Co. C, 23rd North Carolina Infantry	May 12, 1864, Near Spotsylvania Court House, Virginia	Point Lookout Prison, Maryland. Transferred to Elmira Prison Camp New York August 14, 1864.	Exchanged October 29, 1864 at Venus Point, Savannah River, GA.
Mason, S. E. Private	Unk	April 28, 1861, New Orleans, Louisiana	Co. A, 1st Louisiana Infantry	May 12, 1864, Spotsylvania Court House, Virginia	Point Lookout, Maryland, transferred to Elmira Prison, NY, August 17, 1864	Exchanged February 13, 1865 at Boulware's wharf on the James River, Virginia
Mason, William B. Private	33	August 8, 1862, Statesville, North Carolina	Co. D, 7th North Carolina Infantry	May 6, 1864, Wilderness, Virginia	Point Lookout, Maryland, transferred to Elmira Prison, NY, August 14, 1864	Oath of Allegiance June 12, 1865
Mass, Lewis F. Private	Unk	April 15, 1862, Richmond, Virginia	Co. D, 5th Virginia Cavalry	May 11, 1864, Yellow Tavern, Hanover County, Virginia	Point Lookout, Maryland, transferred to Elmira Prison, NY, August 17, 1864	Oath of Allegiance June 27, 1865
Massee, William Y. Private	Unk	June 2, 1861, Centerville, Virginia	Co. H, 26th North Carolina Infantry	June 17, 1864, Near Petersburg, Virginia	Point Lookout, Maryland, transferred to Elmira Prison, NY, July 30, 1864	Exchanged March 14, 1865 at Boulware's Wharf on the James River, Virginia

Name & Rank	Age	Enlisted	Regiment and State	Where Captured	Prison	Remarks
Massey, Able C. Corporal	Unk	July 9, 1861, Isabella, Worth County, Georgia	Co. G, 14th Georgia Infantry	May 12, 1864, Spotsylvania Court House, Virginia	Point Lookout, Maryland, transferred to Elmira Prison, NY, July 30, 1864	Died December 17, 1864 of Pneumonia, Grave No. 1274
Massey, Daniel W. Private	29	March 18, 1862, Mocksville, Davie County, North Carolina	Co. E, 42nd North Carolina Infantry	June 1, 1864, Gaines Farm Cold Harbor, Virginia	Point Lookout, Maryland, transferred to Elmira Prison, NY, July 12, 1864	Exchanged February 20, 1865 at Boulware's or Cox Wharf on the James River, Virginia
Massey, F. M. Private	Unk	March 13, 1862, Hamer, Banks County, Georgia	Co. A, 24th Georgia Infantry	June 1, 1864, Cold Harbor, Virginia	Point Lookout, Maryland, transferred to Elmira Prison, NY, July 12, 1864	Exchanged October 29, 1864 at Venus Point, Savannah River, GA.
Massey, Joseph Private	Unk	September 7, 1862, Walker, Choctaw County, Alabama	Co. E, 1st Battalion Alabama Artillery	August 23, 1864, Fort Morgan, Alabama	New Orleans, Louisiana transferred to Elmira Prison, NY, December 4, 1864.	Died January 23, 1865 of Variola (Smallpox), Grave No. 1596
Massey, S. E. Private	Unk	August 11, 1861, Gwinnett County, Georgia	Co. A, 16th Georgia Infantry	August 16, 1864, Front Royal, Virginia	Old Capital Prison, Washington, DC transferred to Elmira Prison, NY, August 29, 1864	Died February 18, 1865 of Variola (Smallpox), Grave No. 2343
Massingale, Robert H. Private	33	September 17, 1862, Raleigh, North Carolina	Co. K, 30th North Carolina Infantry	May 30, 1864 Mechanics-ville, Virginia	Point Lookout, Maryland, transferred to Elmira Prison, NY, July 12, 1864	Oath of Allegiance May 29, 1865
Masters, Charles H. Sergeant	Unk	May 18, 1861, Franklin, Virginia	Co. K, 25th Virginia Infantry	May 5, 1864, Wilderness, Virginia	Point Lookout, Maryland, transferred to Elmira Prison, NY, August 14, 1864	Exchanged March 10, 1865 at Boulware's Wharf on the James River, Virginia
Masters, William E. Private	27	May 14, 1861, Franklin, Virginia	Co. E, 25th Virginia Infantry	May 6, 1864, Wilderness, Virginia	Old Capital Prison, Washington, DC, transferred to Elmira Prison, NY, July 14, 1864	Oath of Allegiance June 23, 1865

Name & Rank	Age	Enlisted	Regiment and State	Where Captured	Prison	Remarks
Matheney, Joseph Private	Unk	April 24, 1864, Bath., Virginia	Co. A, 6th Virginia Infantry	July 30, 1864, Petersburg, Virginia	Point Lookout, Maryland, transferred to Elmira Prison, NY, August 12, 1864	Died 9/18/64 of Chronic Diarrhea, Grave No. 313. Name McFeney, 63rd Regiment on Headstone.
Mathers, William Private	30	May 20, 1861, Mobile, Alabama	Co. J, 8th Alabama Infantry	June 30, 1864, Near Petersburg, Virginia	Point Lookout, Maryland, transferred to Elmira Prison, NY, July 26,1864	Oath of Allegiance January 24, 1865. Early Release per Lincoln's Proclamation, 12/8/1863.
Mathews, Abram Private	18	June 23, 1863, Staunton, Virginia	Co. A, 52nd Virginia Infantry	May 28, 1864, Old Church, Virginia. Gunshot Wound Right Forearm.	Old Capital Prison, Washington, DC transferred to Elmira Prison, NY, August 29, 1864	Exchanged October 29, 1864 at Venus Point, Savannah River, GA.
Mathews, Archibald B. Private	18	May 15, 1863, Fort Caswell, Brunswick County, North Carolina	Co. E, 40th Regiment, 3rd North Carolina Artillery	January 15, 1865, Fort Fisher, North Carolina	February 1, 1865, Elmira Prison Camp, New York	Died February 10, 1865 of Pneumonia, Grave No. 2090
Mathews, Charles M. Private	16	January 15, 1862, Williamsburg, South Carolina	Co. K, 25th South Carolina Infantry	January 15, 1865, Fort Fisher, North Carolina	January 30, 1865, Elmira Prison Camp, New York	Oath of Allegiance August 7, 1865
Mathews, Daniel W. Private	Unk	March 1, 1862, Vernon, Louisiana	Co. M, 12th Louisiana Infantry	May 16, 1863, Baker's Creek, Champion Hill, Mississippi	Point Lookout, Maryland, transferred to Elmira Prison, NY, August 18, 1864	Exchanged October 29, 1864 at Venus Point, Savannah River, GA.
Mathews, David Private	Unk	July 16, 1861, Staunton, Virginia	Co. A, 52nd Virginia Infantry	May 30, 1864 Mechanics-ville, Virginia	Point Lookout, Maryland, transferred to Elmira Prison, NY, July 9, 1864	Exchanged March 14, 1865 at Boulware's Wharf on the James River, Virginia
Mathews, J. Corporal	Unk	Unknown	Co, B, 22nd Alabama Infantry	June 3, 1864, Gaines Mill Cold Harbor, Virginia	Point Lookout, Maryland, transferred to Elmira Prison, NY, July 17, 1864	Transferred for Exchange October 11, 1864. Nothing Further.
Mathews, J. M. Private	20	April 12, 1862, Battery Island, South Carolina	Co. C, 25th South Carolina Infantry	January 15, 1865, Fort Fisher, North Carolina	January 30, 1865, Elmira Prison Camp, New York	Oath of Allegiance July 11, 1865

Name & Rank	Age	Enlisted	Regiment and State	Where Captured	Prison	Remarks
Mathews, J. W. Private	Unk	Unknown	Co. A, 52nd Virginia Infantry	May 30, 1864 Mechanics-ville, Virginia	Point Lookout, Maryland, transferred to Elmira Prison, NY, July 9, 1864	Transferred for Exchange October 11, 1864. Nothing Further.
Mathews, John A. Private	Unk	January 1, 1862, Camp Hampton, Columbia, South Carolina	Co. G, 18th South Carolina Infantry	July 30, 1864, Petersburg, Virginia	Point Lookout, Maryland, transferred to Elmira Prison, NY, August 12, 1864	Died May 2, 1865 of Chronic Diarrhea, Grave No. 2743
Mathews, W. J. Private	Unk	May 3, 1862, Myersville, South Carolina	Co. H, 25th South Carolina Infantry	January 15, 1865, Fort Fisher, North Carolina	January 30, 1865, Elmira Prison Camp, New York	Died April 7, 1865 of Variola (Smallpox), Grave No. 2649
Mathews, William Private	Unk	Unknown	1st Florida Reserves Infantry	July 27, 1864, New Orleans, Louisiana	New Orleans, Louisiana transferred to Elmira November 19, 1864.	Died December 24, 1864 of Chronic Diarrhea, Grave No. 1104
Mathews, William Private	Unk	April 22, 1861, Leesburg, Virginia	Co. K, 6th Virginia Cavalry	June 26, 1864, Leesburg, Virginia	Old Capital Prison, Washington DC. Transferred to Elmira Prison Camp New York July 25, 1864.	Oath of Allegiance June 14, 1865
Mathews, William A. Private	19	July 4, 1861, Weldon, Halifax County, North Carolina	Co K, 1st North Carolina Infantry	May 12, 1864, Spotsylvania Court House, Virginia	Point Lookout, Maryland, transferred to Elmira Prison, NY, August 6,1864	Oath of Allegiance June 27, 1865
Mathews, William A. Private	Unk	March 17, 1862, Ridgeway, Virginia	Co. A, 42nd Virginia Infantry	July 9, 1864, Near Harpers Ferry, Virginia	Old Capital Prison, Washington DC. Transferred to Elmira Prison Camp New York July 25, 1864.	Oath of Allegiance June 21, 1865
Mathias, Jesse M. Private	Unk	December 18, 1861, Lexington, South Carolina	Co. F, 5th South Carolina Cavalry	June 11, 1864, Trevilian Station, Louisa Court House, Virginia	Point Lookout, Maryland, transferred to Elmira Prison, NY, July 25, 1864	Exchanged March 2, 1865 at Akins Landing on the James River, Virginia
Mathis, Luther R.	28	March 6, 1862, Wilmington, North Carolina	Co. C, 51st North Carolina Infantry	June 16, 1864, Near Petersburg, Near Bermuda Hundred, Virginia	Point Lookout, Maryland, transferred to Elmira Prison, NY, July 12, 1864	Exchanged February 13, 1865 at Boulware's wharf on the James River, Virginia

Name & Rank	Age	Enlisted	Regiment and State	Where Captured	Prison	Remarks
Mathis, Moses Private	Unk	May 1, 1862, Sandersville, Georgia	Co. E, 12th Georgia Light Artillery	July 8, 1864, Harpers Ferry, Virginia	Old Capital Prison, Washington DC. Transferred to Elmira Prison Camp New York July 25, 1864.	Oath of Allegiance May 29, 1865
Mathus, William M. Private	Unk	January 8, 1862, Camp Hampton, Spartanburg, South Carolina	Co. K, 18th South Carolina Infantry	July 30, 1864, Petersburg, Virginia	Point Lookout, Maryland, transferred to Elmira Prison, NY, August 12, 1864	Died September 15, 1864 of Chronic Diarrhea, Grave No. 282. Name Mathews on Headstone.
Matthews, Andrew J. Private	Unk	April 1, 1861, Lacy's Store, Virginia	Co. B, 44th Virginia Infantry	May 12, 1864, Spotsylvania Court House, Virginia	Point Lookout, Maryland, transferred to Elmira Prison, NY, August 2, 1864	Exchanged March 14, 1865 at Boulware's Wharf on the James River, Virginia
Matthews, Benjamin H. Private	Unk	June 15, 1861, Macon, Georgia	Co. B, 12th Georgia Infantry	May 10, 1864, Spotsylvania Court House, Virginia	Point Lookout, Maryland, transferred to Elmira Prison, NY, July 30, 1864	Died April 8, 1865 of Chronic Diarrhea, Grave No. 2643
Matthews, C. A. Private	Unk	April 1, 1861, Lacy's Store, Virginia	Co. B, 44th Virginia Infantry	May 12, 1864, Spotsylvania Court House, Virginia	Point Lookout, Maryland, transferred to Elmira Prison, NY, August 2, 1864	Oath of Allegiance June 27, 1865
Matthews, Charles W. Private	Unk	Unknown	Co. B, 35th Battalion Virginia Cavalry	July 30, 1864, Potomac River, Virginia	Old Capital Prison, Washington, DC, transferred to Elmira Prison, NY, August 12, 1864	Exchanged March 10, 1865 at Boulware's Wharf on the James River, Virginia
Matthews, Edwin J. Private	18	February 26, 1862, Fayetteville, North Carolina	Co. C, 36th 2nd North Carolina Artillery	January 15, 1865, Fort Fisher, North Carolina	February 1, 1865, Elmira Prison Camp, New York	Died March 17, 1865 of Pneumonia, Grave No. 1555
Matthews, Francis M. Sergeant	Unk	April 1, 1861, Lacy's Store, Virginia	Co. B, 44th Virginia Infantry	May 12, 1864, Spotsylvania Court House, Virginia	Point Lookout, Maryland, transferred to Elmira Prison, NY, August 2, 1864	Exchanged March 2, 1865 at Akins Landing on the James River, Virginia
Matthews, J. W. Private	Unk	Unknown	Co. A, 52nd Virginia Infantry	Unknown	Unknown	Died May 23, 1865 of Unknown Disease, Grave No. 2928

Name & Rank	Age	Enlisted	Regiment and State	Where Captured	Prison	Remarks
Matthews, Jacob M. Private	22	February 26, 1862, Fayetteville, Cumberland County, North Carolina	Co. C, 36th 2nd North Carolina Artillery	January 15, 1865, Fort Fisher, North Carolina	February 1, 1865, Elmira Prison Camp, New York	Died April 19, 1865 of Variola (Smallpox), Grave No. 1370
Matthews, John Private	40	June 26, 1861, Manchester, North Carolina	Co. C, 7th North Carolina Infantry	July 29, 1864, Petersburg, Virginia	Point Lookout, Maryland, transferred to Elmira Prison, NY, August 12, 1864	Died May 3, 1865 of Chronic Diarrhea, Grave No. 2750. Joel on Headstone.
Matthews, John Allen Musician Private	28	February 20, 1862, Lillington, Hartnett County, North Carolina	Co. C, 36th 2nd North Carolina Artillery	January 15, 1865, Fort Fisher, North Carolina	February 1, 1865, Elmira Prison Camp, New York	Oath of Allegiance June 12, 1865
Matthews, John R. Private	24	March 8, 1863, Fort Caswell, Brunswick County, North Carolina	Co. D, 36th 2nd North Carolina Artillery	January 15, 1865, Fort Fisher, North Carolina	February 1, 1865, Elmira Prison Camp, New York	Exchanged March 2, 1865 at Boulware's Wharf on the James River, Virginia
Matthews, Neill A. Private	18	December 12, 1862, Fort Fisher, New Hanover County, North Carolina	Co. C, 36th 2nd North Carolina Artillery	January 15, 1865, Fort Fisher, North Carolina	February 1, 1865, Elmira Prison Camp, New York	Oath of Allegiance June 12, 1865
Matthews, William H. Private	26	February 26, 1862, Lillington, Hartnett County, North Carolina	Co. C, 36th 2nd North Carolina Artillery	January 15, 1865, Fort Fisher, North Carolina	February 1, 1865, Elmira Prison Camp, New York	Died March 27, 1865 of Variola (Smallpox), Grave No. 2471
Matthias, Elsy Private	33	June 26, 1861, Plymouth, North Carolina	Co. G, 1st North Carolina Infantry	May 12, 1864, Wilderness, Spotsylvania Court House, Virginia	Point Lookout, Maryland, transferred to Elmira Prison, NY, August 6, 1864	Died December 29, 1864 of Pneumonia, Grave No. 1308
Matthias, Jesse Private	31	September 6, 1862, Caldwell County, North Carolina	Co. G, 33rd North Carolina Infantry	May 12, 1864, Near Spotsylvania Court House, Virginia	Point Lookout, Maryland, transferred to Elmira Prison, NY, August 14, 1864	Oath of Allegiance June 12, 1865
Matthis, Neill Private	37	November 15, 1863, Harnett County, North Carolina	3rd Co. B, 36th Regiment North Carolina, 2nd Artillery	January 15, 1865, Fort Fisher, North Carolina	February 1, 1865, Elmira Prison Camp, New York	Oath of Allegiance July 7, 1865

Name & Rank	Age	Enlisted	Regiment and State	Where Captured	Prison	Remarks
Matthis, Timothy Private	Unk	May 14, 1862, Nashville, Georgia	Co. J, 50th Georgia Infantry	May 24, 1864, Hanover Junction, Virginia	Point Lookout, Maryland, transferred to Elmira Prison, NY, August 12, 1864	Oath of Allegiance June 21, 1865
Mattox, Houston Private	Unk	August 11, 1862, Lafayette, Georgia	Co. H, 23rd Georgia Infantry	June 18, 1864, Near Petersburg, Virginia	Point Lookout, Maryland, transferred to Elmira Prison, NY, July 23, 1864	Oath of Allegiance May 15, 1865
Mattox, John Private	23	August 11, 1862, Lafayette, Georgia	Co. H, 23rd Georgia Infantry	June 18, 1864, Petersburg, Virginia. Gunshot Fracture Left Elbow. Arm Amputated.	Old Capital Prison, Washington, DC transferred to Elmira Prison, NY, August 27, 1864	Exchanged February 20, 1865 at Boulware's or Cox Wharf on the James River, Virginia
Mauch, John C. Sergeant	Unk	April 18, 1861, Harrisonburg, Virginia	Co. B, 10th Virginia Infantry	May 12, 1864, Spotsylvania Court House, Virginia	Point Lookout, Maryland, transferred to Elmira Prison, NY, August 2, 1864	Oath of Allegiance June 27, 1865
Maudlin, Rufus S. Private	Unk	May 5, 1862, Hawkinsville, Georgia	Co. F, 31st Georgia Infantry	July 12, 1864, Near Washington, DC	Old Capital Prison, Washington DC. Transferred to Elmira Prison Camp New York July 25, 1864.	Exchanged February 13, 1865 at Boulware's wharf on the James River, Virginia
Maughan, Patrick Private	29	May 7, 1861, New Orleans, Louisiana	Co. K, 5th Louisiana Infantry	May 5, 1864, Wilderness, Virginia	Point Lookout, Maryland, transferred to Elmira Prison, NY, August 17, 1864	Oath of Allegiance May 19, 1865
Maulden, James A. Private	22	August 24, 1861, Lawrenceville, Georgia	Co. F, 24th Georgia Infantry	June 1, 1864, Cold Harbor, Virginia	Point Lookout, Maryland, transferred to Elmira Prison, NY, July 12, 1864	Died January 8, 1865 of Variola (Smallpox), Grave No. 1223
Maull, John Fox Sergeant	18	July 1, 1861, Selma, Alabama	Jeff Davis Alabama Artillery	May 5, 1864, Wilderness, Virginia	Point Lookout, Maryland, transferred to Elmira Prison, NY, August 17, 1864	Escaped October 7, 1864 by Tunneling under Fence.

Name & Rank	Age	Enlisted	Regiment and State	Where Captured	Prison	Remarks
Mauney, Manassas P. Private	20	August 12, 1862, Statesville, North Carolina	Co. D, 37th North Carolina Infantry	July 29, 1864, Gravel Hill, Near Petersburg, Virginia	Point Lookout, Maryland, transferred to Elmira Prison, NY, August 12, 1864	Oath of Allegiance May 29, 1865
Maverly, George W. Private	Unk	June 22, 1861, Henry County, Virginia	Co. F, 42nd Virginia Infantry	May 12, 1864, Near Spotsylvania Court House, Virginia	Point Lookout, Maryland, transferred to Elmira Prison, NY, August 6, 1864	Transferred for Exchange 10/11/64. Died 11/5/64 of Chronic Diarrhea at US Army Hospital, Baltimore MD.
Maxey, B. A. Private	Unk	March 3, 1862, Lexington, Georgia	Co. K, 8th Georgia Infantry	May 6, 1864, Wilderness, Virginia	Point Lookout, Maryland, transferred to Elmira Prison, NY, August 14, 1864	Exchanged February 13, 1865 at Boulware's Wharf on the James River, Virginia
Maxey, Obadiah H. Private	Unk	May 19, 1864, Amelia County, Virginia	Co. G, 6th Virginia Infantry	July 30, 1864, Malvern Hill, Virginia	Point Lookout, Maryland, transferred to Elmira Prison, NY, August 12, 1864	Died October 10, 1864 of Chronic Diarrhea, Grave No. 685. Name Maney on Headstone.
Maxwell, Daniel L. Private	Unk	April 28, 1862, Bainbridge, Georgia	Co. F, 50th Georgia Infantry	June 4, 1864, Gaines Mill Cold Harbor, Virginia	Point Lookout, Maryland, transferred to Elmira Prison, NY, July 12, 1864	Oath of Allegiance June 23, 1865
Maxwell, John D. Private	Unk	May 15, 1861, Montgomery, Alabama	Co. H, 6th Alabama Infantry	July 6, 1863, Gettysburg, Pennsylvania	Point Lookout, Maryland, transferred to Elmira Prison, NY, August 18, 1864	Exchanged March 2, 1865 at Akins Landing on the James River, Virginia
Maxwell, John T. Private	22	April 25, 1861, Twiggs County, Georgia	Co. C, 4th Georgia Infantry	July 16, 1864, Poolesville, Maryland	Old Capital Prison, Washington DC. Transferred to Elmira Prison Camp New York July 25, 1864.	Died October 30, 1864 of Typhoid Fever, Grave No. 733
Maxwell, Whitford Private	35	June 16, 1864, Camp Wyatt, New Hanover County, North Carolina	Co. D, 36th 2nd North Carolina Artillery	January 15, 1865, Fort Fisher, North Carolina	February 1, 1865, Elmira Prison Camp, New York	Died March 11, 1865 of Chronic Diarrhea, Grave No. 1835

Name & Rank	Age	Enlisted	Regiment and State	Where Captured	Prison	Remarks
Maxwell, William, Sergeant	Unk	March 4, 1862, Bainbridge, Georgia	Co. F, 50th Georgia Infantry	June 1, 1864, Gaines Mill Cold Harbor, Virginia	Point Lookout, Maryland, transferred to Elmira Prison, NY, July 12, 1864	Exchanged February 20, 1865 at Boulware's or Cox Wharf on the James River, Virginia
Maxwell, William S., Private	35	March 15, 1864, Camp Wyatt, New Hanover County, North Carolina	Co. D, 36th 2nd North Carolina Artillery	January 15, 1865, Fort Fisher, North Carolina	February 1, 1865, Elmira Prison Camp, New York	Exchanged March 14, 1865 at Boulware's Wharf on the James River, Virginia
May, James L., Private	Unk	April 25, 1862, Fredericksburg, Virginia	Co. H, 40th Virginia Infantry	May 6, 1864, Wilderness, Virginia	Point Lookout, Maryland, transferred to Elmira Prison, NY, August 14, 1864	Exchanged February 13, 1865 at Boulware's Wharf on the James River, Virginia
May, John C., Private	Unk	December 30, 1861, Nashville, Tennessee	Co. I, 44th Tennessee Infantry	June 17, 1864, Petersburg, Virginia	Point Lookout, Maryland, transferred to Elmira Prison, NY, July 30, 1864	Oath of Allegiance March 22, 1865. Early Release per Lincoln's Proclamation, 12/8/1863.
May, John H., Private	19	April 20, 1862, Camp Holmes, North Carolina	Co. C, 28th North Carolina Infantry	May 20, 1864, Spotsylvania Court House, Virginia	Point Lookout, Maryland, transferred to Elmira Prison, NY, July 3, 1864	Exchanged October 29, 1864 at Venus Point, Savannah River, GA.
May, John R., Private	Unk	March 13, 1863, Frankfort, Virginia	Co. E, 19th Virginia Cavalry	July 15, 1864, Harpers Ferry, Virginia	Old Capital Prison, Washington DC. Transferred to Elmira Prison Camp New York July 25, 1864.	Died November 29, 1864 of Pneumonia, Grave No. 904
May, Oliver H. P., Private	Unk	June 9, 1861, Jones County, Georgia	Co. B, 12th Georgia Infantry	May 6, 1864, Wilderness, Virginia	Point Lookout, Maryland, transferred to Elmira Prison, NY, August 14, 1864	Exchanged March 14, 1865 at Boulware's Wharf on the James River, Virginia
May, Patrick F., Sergeant	18	February 22, 1862, Charleston, South Carolina	Co. E, 25th South Carolina Infantry	January 15, 1865, Fort Fisher, North Carolina	January 30, 1865, Elmira Prison Camp, New York	Oath of Allegiance May 17, 1865

Name & Rank	Age	Enlisted	Regiment and State	Where Captured	Prison	Remarks
May, William J. Private	Unk	March 13, 1863, Frankfort, Virginia	Co. E, 19th Virginia Cavalry	July 15, 1864, Harpers Ferry, Virginia	Old Capital Prison, Washington DC. Transferred to Elmira Prison Camp New York July 25, 1864.	Oath of Allegiance May 15, 1865
Maybe, William L. Private	Unk	June 25, 1861, Wytheville, Virginia	Co. I, 50th Virginia Infantry	May 12, 1864, Spotsylvania Court House, Virginia	Point Lookout, Maryland, transferred to Elmira Prison, NY, August 2, 1864	Oath of Allegiance June 27, 1865
Mayberry, A. Z. Corporal	Unk	April 13, 1861, Limestone Springs, South Carolina	Co. M, 1st Palmetto Sharp Shooters, South Carolina	June 1, 1864, Cold Harbor, Virginia	Point Lookout, Maryland, transferred to Elmira Prison, NY, July 12, 1864	Oath of Allegiance June 21, 1865
Mayberry, Forster Private	26	December 17, 1861, Unionville, South Carolina	Co. C, 18th South Carolina Infantry	July 30, 1864, Petersburg, Virginia	Point Lookout, Maryland, transferred to Elmira Prison, NY, August 12, 1864	Transferred for Exchange 10/11/64. Died 10/23/64 of Chronic Diarrhea at Point Lookout, MD.
Mayers, J. E. Private	Unk	July 12, 1861, Staunton, Virginia	Co. A, 52nd Virginia Infantry	May 30, 1864 Mechanics-ville, Virginia	Point Lookout, Maryland, transferred to Elmira Prison, NY, July 9, 1864	Died June 29, 1865 of Chronic Diarrhea, Grave No. 2829
Mayes, Joseph Private	31	August 27, 1862, Raleigh, North Carolina	Co. I, 18th North Carolina Infantry	May 12, 1864, Spotsylvania, Virginia	Point Lookout Prison Camp, Maryland. Transferred to Elmira Prison Camp, NY, July 6, 1864	Died June 30, 1865 of Pneumonia, Grave No. 2832. Headstone has James M. Maze.
Mayfield, M. L. Private	Unk	June 16, 1864, Columbia, South Carolina	Co. C, 22nd South Carolina Infantry	July 30, 1864, Petersburg, Virginia	Point Lookout, Maryland, transferred to Elmira Prison, NY, August 12, 1864	Exchanged March 14, 1865 at Boulware's Wharf on the James River, Virginia
Mayfield, T. J. Private	Unk	May 11, 1861, New Orleans, Louisiana	Co. K, 2nd Louisiana Infantry	May 12, 1864, Spotsylvania Court House, Virginia	Point Lookout, Maryland, transferred to Elmira Prison, NY, August 17, 1864	Died August 20, 1864 of Chronic Diarrhea, Grave No. 504

Name & Rank	Age	Enlisted	Regiment and State	Where Captured	Prison	Remarks
Maynard, W. H. Private	34	February 10, 1862, Raleigh, North Carolina	Co. C, 47th North Carolina Infantry	July 14, 1863, Falling Waters, Maryland	Point Lookout, Maryland, transferred to Elmira Prison, NY, August 18, 1864	Died February 5, 1865 of Variola (Smallpox), Grave No. 1904
Mays, Andrew A. Private	Unk	October 1, 1862, Lewisburg, Virginia	Co. D, 14th Virginia Cavalry	July 16, 1864, Near Harpers Ferry, Loudoun County, Virginia	Old Capital Prison, Washington DC. Transferred to Elmira Prison Camp New York July 25, 1864.	Died October 13, 1864 of Diphtheria, Grave No. 699
Mays, Crafford S. Private	Unk	May 14, 1862, Jefferson, Jackson County, Georgia	Co. H, 13th Georgia Cavalry	July 23, 1864, Martinsburg, Virginia	Old Capital Prison, Washington, DC, transferred to Elmira Prison, NY, August 12, 1864	Exchanged March 14, 1865 at Boulware's Wharf on the James River, Virginia
Mays, Green J. Private	Unk	August 18, 1861, Camp Moore, Louisiana	Co. M, 12th Louisiana Infantry	May 16, 1863, Baker's Creek, Champion Hill, Mississippi	Point Lookout, Maryland, transferred to Elmira Prison, NY, August 18, 1864	Died December 30, 1864 of Chronic Diarrhea, Grave No. 1317
Mays, James M. Private	Unk	March 1, 1862, Richmond, Virginia	Co. D, 5th Virginia Cavalry	May 11, 1864, Yellow Tavern, Hanover County, Virginia	Point Lookout, Maryland, transferred to Elmira Prison, NY, August 17, 1864	Died March 28, 1865 of Diarrhea, Grave No. 2521. Headstone has Mayo.
Mayson, Benjamin W. Private	18	August 25, 1861, Camp Butler, South Carolina	Co. K, 14th South Carolina Infantry	July 29, 1864, Petersburg, Virginia	Point Lookout, Maryland, transferred to Elmira Prison, NY, August 12, 1864	Oath of Allegiance May 29, 1865
McAfee, T. R. Private	Unk	July 24, 1861, Clarksville, Georgia	Co. E, 16th Georgia Infantry	August 16, 1864, Front Royal, Virginia	Old Capital Prison, Washington, DC transferred to Elmira Prison, NY, August 29, 1864	Oath of Allegiance July 11, 1865
McAlexander, Joel Private	Unk	June 22, 1861, Wytheville, Virginia	Co. K, 50th Virginia Infantry	May 12, 1864, Spotsylvania Court House, Virginia	Point Lookout, Maryland, transferred to Elmira Prison, NY, August 2, 1864	Exchanged February 20, 1865 at Boulware's or Cox Wharf on the James River, Virginia

Name & Rank	Age	Enlisted	Regiment and State	Where Captured	Prison	Remarks
McAlhany, James D. Private	18	September 1, 1863, Green Pond, South Carolina	Co. G, 4th South Carolina Cavalry	May 28, 1864, Old Church, Cold Harbor, Virginia. Gunshot Wound Right Shoulder.	Old Capital Prison, Washington, DC, transferred to Elmira Prison, NY, December 17, 1864	Oath of Allegiance June 21, 1865
McAnear, John Private	Unk	July 8, 1861, Decatur, Alabama	Co. I, 12th Alabama Infantry	May 12, 1864, Spotsylvania Court House, Virginia	Point Lookout, Maryland, transferred to Elmira Prison, NY, August 17, 1864	Died December 15, 1864 of Pneumonia, Grave No. 1113
McArthur, Adam H. Private	Unk	Unknown	Co. D, 2nd Texas Cavalry	May 15, 1864, Louisiana	New Orleans, Louisiana transferred to Elmira November 19, 1864.	Oath of Allegiance May 17, 1865 per Commissary General of Prisoners.
McArthur, John J. Private	37	February 28, 1863, Johnsonville, North Carolina	Co. C, 35th North Carolina Infantry	June 17, 1864, Petersburg, Virginia	Point Lookout, Maryland, transferred to Elmira Prison, NY, July 30, 1864	Exchanged October 29, 1864 at Venus Point, Savannah River, GA.
McArthur, Robert E. Private	Unk	September 12, 1861, Galveston, Texas	Co. H, 2nd Texas Infantry	May 22, 1862, Near Vicksburg, Mississippi	Point Lookout, Maryland, transferred to Elmira Prison, NY, August 18, 1864	Oath of Allegiance June 14, 1865
McBrayer, George W. Private	Unk	May 8, 1862, Cumming, Georgia	Co. E, 14th Georgia Infantry	May 12, 1864, Spotsylvania Court House, Virginia	Point Lookout, Maryland, transferred to Elmira Prison, NY, August 12, 1864	Exchanged 3/2/65. Died 5/7/65 of Typhoid Fever at Jackson Hospital, Richmond, VA.
McBride, Alexander Sergeant	25	March 5, 1862, Reidsville, Rockingham County, North Carolina	Co. G, 45th North Carolina Infantry	May 10, 1864, Spotsylvania Court House, Virginia	Point Lookout, Maryland, transferred to Elmira Prison, NY, August 6, 1864	Died February 18, 1865 of Variola (Smallpox), Grave No. 2345
McBride, James Private	25	March 15, 1862, New Orleans, Louisiana	Co. G, 5th Louisiana Infantry	May 5, 1864, Wilderness, Virginia	Point Lookout, Maryland, transferred to Elmira Prison, NY, July 25, 1864	Oath of Allegiance May 29, 1865

Name & Rank	Age	Enlisted	Regiment and State	Where Captured	Prison	Remarks
McBride, John T. Private	Unk	February 27, 1862, Monroe, Louisiana	Co. M, 12th Louisiana Infantry	May 16, 1863, Baker's Creek, Champion Hill, Mississippi	Point Lookout, Maryland, transferred to Elmira Prison, NY, August 18, 1864	Exchanged February 25, 1865 at Boulware's wharf on the James River, Virginia
McBride, Samuel S. Sergeant	18	September 3, 1861, Abbeville District, Doris Mines, South Carolina	Co. K, 15th South Carolina Infantry	July 29, 1864, Petersburg, Virginia	Point Lookout, Maryland, transferred to Elmira Prison, NY, August 12, 1864	Exchanged October 29, 1864 at Venus Point, Savannah River, GA.
McCafferty, Anthony B. Private	Unk	July 29, 1861, Fredonia, Alabama	Co. C, 14th Alabama Infantry	May 24, 1864, North Anna River, Hanover Junction, Virginia	Point Lookout, Maryland, transferred to Elmira Prison, NY, July 11, 1864	Oath of Allegiance June 19, 1865
McCaleb, Thomas Sergeant	Unk	May 4, 1864, Petersburg, Virginia	Co. A, 3rd Battalion Virginia Reserves	June 9, 1864, Near Petersburg, Virginia	Point Lookout, Maryland, transferred to Elmira Prison, NY, July 23, 1864	Oath of Allegiance November 30, 1864. Early Release per Lincoln's Proclamation, 12/8/1863.
McCalister, E. Private	Unk	May 14, 1862, Myers Mill, South Carolina	Co. H, 25th South Carolina Infantry	January 15, 1865, Fort Fisher, North Carolina	January 30, 1865, Elmira Prison Camp, New York	Died April 20, 1865 of Variola (Smallpox), Grave No. 1378
McCall, Barnabus Private	Unk	May 12, 1862, Marion, South Carolina	Co. L, 21st South Carolina Infantry	January 15, 1865, Fort Fisher, North Carolina	January 30, 1865, Elmira Prison Camp, New York	Oath of Allegiance July 7, 1865
McCall, Charles N. Private	34	October 25, 1861, Mecklenburg County, North Carolina	Co. H, 35th North Carolina Infantry	June 17, 1864, Petersburg, Virginia	Point Lookout, Maryland, transferred to Elmira Prison, NY, July 30, 1864	Exchanged October 29, 1864 at Venus Point, Savannah River, GA.
McCall, James Private	26	May 15, 1862, Camp McIntosh, Lenoir County, North Carolina	Co. D, 1st North Carolina Infantry	May 12, 1864, Near Spotsylvania Court House, Virginia	Point Lookout Prison, Maryland. Transferred to Elmira Prison Camp New York August 6, 1864.	Oath of Allegiance June 14, 1865
McCall, Neil Private	Unk	July 18, 1862, Cumberland County, North Carolina	Co. C, 3rd North Carolina Infantry	May 10, 1864, Near Spotsylvania County Court House, Virginia	Point Lookout, Maryland, transferred to Elmira Prison, NY, August 14, 1864	Died December 15, 1864 of Pneumonia, Grave No. 1063

Name & Rank	Age	Enlisted	Regiment and State	Where Captured	Prison	Remarks
McCall, O. P. Private	Unk	Unknown	Co. H, 48th Georgia Infantry	May 6, 1864, Wilderness, Virginia	Point Lookout, Maryland, transferred to Elmira Prison, NY, August 14, 1864	Died March 13, 1865 of Chronic Diarrhea. No Grave in Woodlawn Cemetery.
McCallum, Angus Private	30	March 3, 1863, Carthage, North Carolina	Co. D, 49th North Carolina Infantry	June 2, 1864, Bermuda Hundred, Virginia	Point Lookout, Maryland, transferred to Elmira Prison, NY, July 12, 1864	Died August 14, 1864, Grave No. 128
McCampbell, Andrew W. Private	Unk	Unknown	Co. A, 1st Maryland Cavalry	July 10, 1864, Frederick, Maryland	Old Capital Prison, Washington DC. Transferred to Elmira Prison Camp New York July 25, 1864.	Exchanged February 13, 1865 at Boulware's wharf on the James River, Virginia
McCampbell, Samuel J. Private	Unk	April 18, 1861, Lexington, Virginia	Co. H, 27th Virginia Infantry	August 12, 1864, Newton, Virginia	Old Capital Prison, Washington, DC transferred to Elmira Prison, NY, August 29, 1864	Oath of Allegiance July 26, 1865
McCandless, Clarey Private	Unk	August 22, 1863, Floyd Court House, Virginia	Co. G, 21st Virginia Cavalry	July 8, 1864, Near Harpers Ferry, Virginia	Old Capital Prison, Washington DC. Transferred to Elmira Prison Camp New York July 25, 1864.	Oath of Allegiance July 19, 1865
McCandlish, Robert Private	Unk	May 4, 1864, Petersburg, Virginia	Co. B, 3rd Archer's Battalion, Virginia Reserves Infantry	June 9, 1864, Petersburg, Virginia	Point Lookout, Maryland, transferred to Elmira Prison, NY, July 12,1864	Exchanged October 29, 1864 at Venus Point, Savannah River, GA.
McCandlish, William T. Private	Unk	May 4, 1864, Petersburg, Virginia	Co. B, 3rd Archer's Battalion, Virginia Reserves Infantry	June 9, 1864, Petersburg, Virginia	Point Lookout, Maryland, transferred to Elmira Prison, NY, July 12,1864	Exchanged October 29, 1864 at Venus Point, Savannah River, GA.
McCann, Andrew J. Private	25	August 1, 1861, Waynesboro, Georgia	Co. E, Cobb's Legion, Georgia	August 16, 1864, Front Royal, Virginia	Old Capital Prison, Washington, DC transferred to Elmira Prison, NY, August 29, 1864	Died March 12, 1865 of Diarrhea, Grave No. 2424

Name & Rank	Age	Enlisted	Regiment and State	Where Captured	Prison	Remarks
McCann, Avery Fleming Private	28	August 1, 1861, Waynesboro, Georgia	Co. E, Cobb's Legion, Georgia	June 2, 1864, Gaines Mill Cold Harbor, Virginia	Point Lookout, Maryland, transferred to Elmira Prison, NY, July 12, 1864	Died December 6, 1864 of Chronic Diarrhea, Grave No. 1188
McCants, John H. Private	Unk	March 15, 1861, Pineville, Alabama	Co. C, 5th Alabama Infantry	May 5, 1864, Wilderness, Virginia	Point Lookout, Maryland, transferred to Elmira Prison, NY, August 17, 1864	Exchanged October 29, 1864 at Venus Point, Savannah River, GA.
McCarquedale, Malcolm Private	Unk	May 23. 1863, Cumberland County, North Carolina	Co. I, 51st North Carolina Infantry	June 1, 1864, Cold Harbor, Virginia	Transferred From Point Lookout Prison, MD, July 12, 1864. Train Never Arrived at Elmira Prison Camp, NY.	Died July 15, 1864 in Train Wreck at Shohola, Pennsylvania.
McCarron, John Sergeant	27	May 20, 1861, Mobile, Alabama	Co. J, 8th Alabama Infantry	May 6, 1864, Wilderness, Virginia	Point Lookout, Maryland, transferred to Elmira Prison, NY, August 17, 1864	Exchanged October 29, 1864 at Venus Point, Savannah River, GA.
McCarter, John C. Sergeant	Unk	January 1, 1862, Camp Hampton, Columbia, South Carolina	Co. H, 18th South Carolina Infantry	July 30, 1864, Petersburg, Virginia	Point Lookout, Maryland, transferred to Elmira Prison, NY, August 12, 1864	Exchanged March 14, 1865 at Boulware's Wharf on the James River, Virginia
McCarter, William B. Corporal	Unk	March 20, 1862, Elk Creek, Virginia	Co. F, 4th Virginia Infantry	May 12, 1864, Spotsylvania Court House, Virginia	Point Lookout, Maryland, transferred to Elmira Prison, NY, August 2, 1864	Oath of Allegiance June 19, 1865
McCarthy, C. Private	Unk	Unknown	Unassigned	July 4, 1864, Alexander County, Virginia	Old Capital Prison, Washington DC. Transferred to Elmira Prison Camp New York July 25, 1864.	Dropped from Roles as a Prisoner and Taken Up as a Deserter.
McCarthy, Thomas Private	Unk	July 1, 1861, New Orleans, Louisiana	Co. A, 14th Louisiana Infantry	May 20, 1864, Spotsylvania Court House, Virginia	Point Lookout, Maryland, transferred to Elmira Prison, NY, July 3, 1864	Exchanged February 20, 1865 at Boulware's or Cox Wharf on the James River, Virginia

Name & Rank	Age	Enlisted	Regiment and State	Where Captured	Prison	Remarks
McCarty, Fletcher M. Private	Unk	February 1, 1864, Macon County, Alabama	Co. A, 61st Alabama Infantry	May 12, 1864, Spotsylvania Court House, Virginia	Point Lookout, Maryland, transferred to Elmira Prison, NY, July 30, 1864	Exchanged October 29, 1864 at Venus Point, Savannah River, GA.
McCarty, John Private	32	June 7, 1861, Camp Moore, Near Tanipahoa, Louisiana	Co. F, 7th Louisiana Infantry	May 5, 1864, Wilderness, Virginia	Point Lookout, Maryland, transferred to Elmira Prison, NY, August 17, 1864	Oath of Allegiance May 29, 1865
McCarver, Alexander Private	25	February 4, 1862, Charlotte, North Carolina	Co. D, 42nd North Carolina Infantry	June 2, 1864, Cold Harbor, Virginia	Point Lookout, Maryland, transferred to Elmira Prison, NY, July 12, 1864	Oath of Allegiance May 29, 1865
McCaskill, Francis M. Private	18	April 29, 1863, Montgomery County, North Carolina	Co. B, 36th 2nd North Carolina Artillery	January 15, 1865, Fort Fisher, North Carolina	February 1, 1865, Elmira Prison Camp, New York	Oath of Allegiance July 11, 1865
McCaskill, John C. Private	40	July 30, 1863, Fort Branch, Martin County North Carolina	Co. G, 40th Regiment, 3rd North Carolina Artillery	January 15, 1865, Fort Fisher, North Carolina	February 1, 1865, Elmira Prison Camp, New York	Died March 18, 1865 of Rheumatism, Grave No. 1553
McCauley, John Private	Unk	December 19, 1862, Fort Caswell, Brunswick County, North Carolina	Co. D, 36th 2nd North Carolina Artillery	January 15, 1865, Fort Fisher, North Carolina	February 1, 1865, Elmira Prison Camp, New York	Exchanged March 2, 1865 at Boulware's Wharf on the James River, Virginia
McChein, R. Private	Unk	Unknown	Co. J, 2nd Louisiana Cavalry	September 29, 1864, Point Coupee Parish, Louisiana	New Orleans, Louisiana transferred to Elmira November 19, 1864.	Exchanged February 25, 1865 at Boulware's or Cox Wharf on the James River, Virginia
McClamroch, L. M. Private	Unk	September 3, 1862, Mocksville, North Carolina	Co. H, 7th Confederate Cavalry	May 6, 1864, Proctor's Bridge, Virginia	Point Lookout, Maryland, transferred to Elmira Prison, NY, August 17, 1864	Oath of Allegiance June 23, 1865
McClanahan, E. K. Private	Unk	December 9, 1861, Camp Trousdale, Tennessee	Co. K, 44th Tennessee Infantry	June 17, 1864, Petersburg, Virginia	Point Lookout, Maryland, transferred to Elmira Prison, NY, July 30, 1864	Oath of Allegiance May 19, 1865

Name & Rank	Age	Enlisted	Regiment and State	Where Captured	Prison	Remarks
McClanahan, Rueben G. Sergeant	Unk	December 9, 1861, Camp Trousdale, Tennessee	Co. K, 44th Tennessee Infantry	June 17, 1864, Petersburg, Virginia	Point Lookout, Maryland, transferred to Elmira Prison, NY, July 30, 1864	Oath of Allegiance May 19, 1865
McClary, D. S. Private	Unk	April 5, 1864, James Island, South Carolina	Co. C, 25th South Carolina Infantry	January 15, 1865, Fort Fisher, North Carolina	January 30, 1865, Elmira Prison Camp, New York	Oath of Allegiance July 11, 1865
McClellan, E. Private	Unk	Unknown	Co. J, 12th Georgia Infantry	May 6, 1864, Wilderness, Virginia	Point Lookout, Maryland, transferred to Elmira Prison, NY, August 14, 1864	Oath of Allegiance June 14, 1865
McClellan, E. T. Private	25	Unknown	Co. C, 49th North Carolina Infantry	April 1, 1865, South Side Railroad, Virginia. Saber Gash on Head	Old Capital Prison, Washington, DC, transferred to Elmira Prison, NY, May 2, 1865.	Oath of Allegiance July 11, 1865
McClellan, T. P. Private	Unk	July 15, 1861, Elberton, Georgia	Co. F, Holcombe Legion, South Carolina	May 8, 1864, Jarrett's Depot, Virginia	Point Lookout, Maryland, transferred to Elmira Prison, NY, August 17, 1864	Exchanged March 2, 1865 at Akins Landing on the James River, Virginia
McClellan, William P. Sergeant	23	December 28, 1861, Camp Hampton, South Carolina	Co. F, Holcombe Legion, South Carolina	May 8, 1864, Jarrett's Depot, Virginia	Point Lookout, Maryland, transferred to Elmira Prison, NY, August 17, 1864	Died October 11, 1861 of Typhoid Fever, Grave No. 579. Headstone has McClennan.
McClelland, Robert Private	Unk	December 15, 1862, Charleston, South Carolina	Co. B, 7th Georgia Cavalry	June 11, 1864, Trevilian Station, Louisa Court House, Virginia	Point Lookout, Maryland, transferred to Elmira Prison, NY, July 25, 1864	Died November 21, 1864 of Pneumonia, Grave No. 934. Name McClennand on Headstone.
McClelland, William A. Private	Unk	April 12, 1862, MT. Jackson, Virginia	Co. J, 4th Virginia Infantry	May 12, 1864, Near Spotsylvania Court House, Virginia	Point Lookout, Maryland, transferred to Elmira Prison, NY, August 6, 1864	Exchanged March 14, 1865 at Boulware's Wharf on the James River, Virginia
McClendon, F. P. Private	Unk	March 15, 1862, Charleston, South Carolina	Co. A, 22nd South Carolina Infantry	June 15, 1864, Petersburg, Virginia	Point Lookout, Maryland, transferred to Elmira Prison, NY, July 12, 1864	Died April 7, 1865 of Chronic Diarrhea, Grave No. 2654

Name & Rank	Age	Enlisted	Regiment and State	Where Captured	Prison	Remarks
McClendon, Joel Private	30	July 24, 1863, Fort Branch, Martin County, North Carolina	Co. G, 40th Regiment, 3rd North Carolina Artillery	January 15, 1865, Fort Fisher, North Carolina	January 30, 1865 Elmira Prison Camp, New York	Died February 18, 1865 of Remittent Fever, Grave No. 2218
McClendon, Wiley E. Private	Unk	February 27, 1862, Roanoke, Alabama	Co. J, 13th Alabama Infantry	May 12, 1864, Spotsylvania Court House, Virginia	Point Lookout, Maryland, transferred to Elmira Prison, NY, July 30, 1864	Oath of Allegiance June 19, 1865
McClintock, Charles P. Private	20	May 11, 1861, Wytheville, Virginia	Co. A, 4th Virginia Infantry	May 12, 1864, Spotsylvania Court House, Virginia	Point Lookout, Maryland, transferred to Elmira Prison, NY, August 2, 1864	Exchanged March 14, 1865 at Boulware's Wharf on the James River, Virginia
McCloud, Elisha Private	Unk	March 31, 1862, Alleghany, Virginia	Co. E, 31st Virginia Infantry	May 31, 1864, Old Church, Cold Harbor, Virginia	Point Lookout, Maryland, transferred to Elmira Prison, NY, July 11, 1864	Oath of Allegiance May 17, 1865
McCloud, John N. Private	Unk	Unknown	Co. H, 3rd North Carolina Infantry	May 12, 1864, Near Spotsylvania County Court House, Virginia	Point Lookout, Maryland, transferred to Elmira Prison, NY, August 14, 1864	Died February 3, 1865 of Variola (Smallpox), Grave No. 1743
McClure, Nathaniel T. Private	23	April 28, 1861, New Orleans, Louisiana	Co. A, 1st Louisiana Infantry	May 12, 1864, Spotsylvania Court House, Virginia	Point Lookout, Maryland, transferred to Elmira Prison, NY, August 17, 1864	Died January 1, 1865 of Pneumonia, Grave No. 1333
McColl, Hugh S. Private	Unk	January 12, 1862, Bennetteville, South Carolina	Co. E, 4th South Carolina Cavalry	May 28, 1864, Hall's Shop, Virginia	Point Lookout, Maryland, transferred to Elmira Prison, NY, July 12, 1864	Died October 10, 1864 of Phthisis Pulmonalis, Grave No. 680
McCollough, Milas F. S. Sergeant	28	Unknown	Co. G, 18th South Carolina Infantry	July 30, 1864, Petersburg, Virginia	Point Lookout, Maryland, transferred to Elmira Prison, NY, August 12, 1864	Oath of Allegiance July 3, 1865
McCollum, Rueben W. Private	22	October 23, 1862, Drury's Bluff, Virginia	Co. E, 45th North Carolina Infantry	May 10, 1864, Spotsylvania Court House, Virginia	Point Lookout, Maryland, transferred to Elmira Prison, NY, August 6, 1864	Exchanged February 20, 1865 at Boulware's or Cox Wharf on the James River, Virginia

Name & Rank	Age	Enlisted	Regiment and State	Where Captured	Prison	Remarks
McCombs, John Private	Unk	August 28, 1862, Talladega, Alabama	Co. I, 12th Alabama Infantry	May 13, 1864, Spotsylvania Court House, Virginia	Point Lookout, Maryland, transferred to Elmira Prison, NY, August 17, 1864	Exchanged February 20, 1865 at Boulware's or Cox Wharf on the James River, Virginia
McCombs, Morgan Private	Unk	December 18, 1863, Camp Just., South Carolina	Co. K, 18th South Carolina Infantry	July 30, 1864, Petersburg, Virginia	Point Lookout, Maryland, transferred to Elmira Prison, NY, August 12, 1864	Died September 4, 1864 of Chronic Diarrhea, Grave No. 73
McCook, Jacob R. Corporal	Unk	May 14, 1862, Irwinville, Georgia	Co. F, 49th Georgia Infantry	May 6, 1864, Wilderness, Virginia	Point Lookout, Maryland, transferred to Elmira Prison, NY, August 14, 1864	Exchanged February 13, 1865 at Boulware's wharf on the James River, Virginia
McCord, J. L. Private	Unk	December 28, 1861, Camp Hampton Legion, South Carolina	Co. F, Holcombe Legion, South Carolina	May 8, 1864, Jarrett's Depot, Virginia	Point Lookout, Maryland, transferred to Elmira Prison, NY, August 17, 1864	Oath of Allegiance June 21, 1865
McCord, M. P. Sergeant	Unk	May 11, 1861, New Orleans, Louisiana	Co. G, 2nd Louisiana Infantry	May 12, 1864, Spotsylvania Court House, Virginia	Point Lookout, Maryland, transferred to Elmira Prison, NY, August 14, 1864	Exchanged February 25, 1865 at Boulware's or Cox Wharf on the James River, Virginia
McCorkle, J. F. Private	Unk	April 20, 1862, Marion Court House, South Carolina	Co. B, 25th South Carolina Infantry	January 15, 1865, Fort Fisher, North Carolina	January 30, 1865, Elmira Prison Camp, New York	Oath of Allegiance July 7, 1865
McCormack, Dominick Private	Unk	March 2, 1862, Greenbrier County, Virginia	Co. F, 23rd Virginia Infantry	July 14, 1864, Frederick, Maryland	Old Capital Prison, Washington DC. Transferred to Elmira Prison Camp New York July 25, 1864.	Oath of Allegiance September 12, 1864 by Orders of Commissary General of Prisoners.
McCormick, Aaron F. Private	32	January 15, 1862, High Point, North Carolina	Co. K, 45th North Carolina Infantry	May 19, 1864, Spotsylvania Court House, Virginia	Point Lookout, Maryland, transferred to Elmira Prison, NY, July 3, 1864	Exchanged March 2, 1865 at Akins Landing on the James River, Virginia

Name & Rank	Age	Enlisted	Regiment and State	Where Captured	Prison	Remarks
McCormick, Duncan Private	19	September 17, 1861, Red Springs, Robison County, North Carolina	Co. E, 40th 3rd North Carolina Artillery	January 15, 1865, Fort Fisher, North Carolina	February 1, 1865, Elmira Prison Camp, New York	Died July 21, 1865 of Unknown Disease, Grave No. 2867
McCormick, James Private	30	June 7, 1861, Camp Moore, Near Tanipahoa, Louisiana	Co. F, 7th Louisiana Infantry	May 11, 1864, Spotsylvania Court House, Virginia	Point Lookout, Maryland, transferred to Elmira Prison, NY, August 17, 1864	Exchanged February 13, 1865 at Boulware's Wharf on the James River, Virginia
McCormick, Michael Private	40	June 4, 1861, Camp Moore, Louisiana	Co. F, 6th Louisiana Infantry	May 5, 1864, Wilderness, Virginia	Point Lookout, Maryland, transferred to Elmira Prison, NY, August 17, 1864	Oath of Allegiance May 29, 1865
McCormick, William Private	Unk	April 26, 1861, West Point, Georgia	Co. D, 4th Georgia Infantry	May 5, 1864, Wilderness, Virginia	Point Lookout, Maryland, transferred to Elmira Prison, NY, July 23, 1864	Oath of Allegiance May 13, 1865
McCorquodala, Ephraim A. Private	25	August 1, 1861, Galveston, Texas	Co. L, 1st Texas Infantry	July 5, 1863, Cashtown, Pennsylvania	Point Lookout, Maryland, transferred to Elmira Prison, NY, August 18, 1864	Transferred for Exchanged 10/29/64 at Venus Point, Savannah River, GA.
McCotter, Thomas Y. Private	20	May 29, 1861, Newbern, North Carolina	Co. J, 2nd North Carolina Infantry	July 12, 1864, Near Washington, DC	Old Capital Prison, Washington DC. Transferred to Elmira Prison Camp New York July 25, 1864.	Exchanged March 10, 1865 at Boulware's Wharf on the James River, Virginia
McCown, William M. Private	Unk	April 23, 1861, Brownsburg, Virginia	Co. H, 25th Virginia Infantry	May 5, 1864, Wilderness, Virginia	Point Lookout, Maryland, transferred to Elmira Prison, NY, August 2, 1864	Exchanged March 10, 1865 at Boulware's Wharf on the James River, Virginia
McCoy, Edgar T. Sergeant	Unk	June 24, 1861, Beverly, Virginia	Co. G, 25th Virginia Infantry	May 6, 1864, Wilderness, Virginia	Old Capital Prison, Washington, DC, transferred to Elmira Prison, NY, July 14, 1864	Oath of Allegiance June 23, 1865

Name & Rank	Age	Enlisted	Regiment and State	Where Captured	Prison	Remarks
McCoy, James E. Private	Unk	May 13, 1862, New Kent, Virginia	Co. A, 26th Virginia Infantry	June 15, 1864, Near Petersburg, Virginia	Point Lookout, Maryland, transferred to Elmira Prison, NY, July 12, 1864	Oath of Allegiance July 3, 1865
McCoy, Joseph W. Private	Unk	November 21, 1862, Elkton, Tennessee	Co. A, 3rd Tennessee Infantry	May 12, 1863, Raymond, Mississippi	Point Lookout, Maryland, transferred to Elmira Prison, NY, August 18, 1864	Exchanged February 25, 1865 at Boulware's wharf on the James River, Virginia
McCoy, Joshua F. Sergeant	Unk	Unkown	Co. A, 66th North Carolina Infantry	September 19, 1863, Big Black, Mississippi	Point Lookout, Maryland, transferred to Elmira Prison, NY, August 18, 1864	Exchanged October 29, 1864 at Venus Point, Savannah River, GA.
McCoy, M. H. Private	Unk	March 11, 1863, Richmond, Virginia	Co. B, 4th Virginia Cavalry	September 19, 1863, Germania Ford, Virginia	Point Lookout, Maryland, transferred to Elmira Prison, NY, August 18, 1864	Exchanged March 10, 1865 at Boulware's Wharf on the James River, Virginia
McCoy, Malachi Private	17	May 30, 1861, Camden County, North Carolina	Co. B, 32nd North Carolina Infantry	May 10, 1864, Spotsylvania Court House, Virginia	Old Capital Prison, Washington DC. Transferred to Elmira Prison Camp New York July 25, 1864.	Oath of Allegiance May 17, 1865
McCoy, William Corporal	Unk	June 1, 1863, Tallapoosa County, Alabama	Co. C, 61st Alabama Infantry	May 12, 1864, Spotsylvania Court House, Virginia	Point Lookout, Maryland, transferred to Elmira Prison, NY, July 30, 1864	Oath of Allegiance June 19, 1865
McCrackin, John V. Private	21	June 11, 1861, Cobb County, Georgia	Co. C, Phillips Legion, Georgia	June 2, 1864, Gaines Farm Cold Harbor, Virginia	Point Lookout, Maryland, transferred to Elmira Prison, NY, July 12, 1864	Oath of Allegiance June 16, 1865
McCrary, John C. Corporal	Unk	May 13, 1861, Harrisonburg, Virginia	Co. B, 10th Virginia Infantry	May 12, 1864, Spotsylvania Court House, Virginia	Point Lookout, Maryland, transferred to Elmira Prison, NY, August 2, 1864	Exchanged March 2, 1865 at Akins Landing on the James River, Virginia

Name & Rank	Age	Enlisted	Regiment and State	Where Captured	Prison	Remarks
McCraw, W. M. Private	Unk	September 21, 1862, Jefferson County, Alabama	Co. A, 21st Alabama Infantry	August 23, 1864, Fort Morgan, Alabama	Steam Press No. 4 New Orleans, Louisiana transferred to Elmira Prison, NY, October 8, 1864.	Died February 2, 1865 of Pneumonia, Grave No. 1749
McCray, Charles E. Corporal	Unk	February 16, 1862, Camp Allegheny, Virginia	Co. G, 25th Virginia Infantry	May 5, 1864, Wilderness, Virginia	Point Lookout, Maryland, transferred to Elmira Prison, NY, August 14, 1864	Exchanged February 13, 1865 at Boulware's wharf on the James River, Virginia
McCray, Evan D. Corporal	Unk	June 13, 1861, Conrad's, Virginia	Co. G, 25th Virginia Infantry	May 5, 1864, Wilderness, Virginia	Point Lookout, Maryland, transferred to Elmira Prison, NY, August 14, 1864	Oath of Allegiance June 27, 1865
McCray, William Joseph Private	18	August 10, 1863, Alamance County, North Carolina	Co. J, 57th North Carolina Infantry	July 12, 1864, Near Washington, DC	Old Capital Prison, Washington DC. Transferred to Elmira Prison Camp New York July 25, 1864.	Oath of Allegiance May 15, 1865
McCrea, J. A. Private	Unk	February 3, 1862, Georgetown, South Carolina	Co. J, 4th South Carolina Cavalry	June 11, 1864, Trevilian Station, Louisa Court House, Virginia	Point Lookout, Maryland, transferred to Elmira Prison, NY, July 25, 1864	Oath of Allegiance June 14, 1865
McCroray, Edward F. Private	51	February 21, 1863, Kinston, North Carolina	Co. I, 45th North Carolina Infantry	May 10, 1864, Spotsylvania Court House, Virginia	Point Lookout, Maryland, transferred to Elmira Prison, NY, August 6, 1864	Exchanged October 29, 1864 at Venus Point, Savannah River, GA.
McCullin, Arin Private	34	July 23, 1862, North Carolina	Co. G, 3rd North Carolina Infantry	May 12, 1864, Near Spotsylvania County Court House, Virginia	Point Lookout, Maryland, transferred to Elmira Prison, NY, August 14, 1864	Exchanged March 2, 1865 at Akins Landing on the James River, Virginia
McCulloch, E. Landsman	Unk	Unknown	Confederate States Navy	May 5, 1864, Albemarle Sound on Steamer CSS Bombshell	Point Lookout, Maryland, transferred to Elmira Prison, NY, August 17, 1864	Oath of Allegiance June 16, 1865

Name & Rank	Age	Enlisted	Regiment and State	Where Captured	Prison	Remarks
McCullough, John Private	Unk	January 20, 1862, Camp Hampton, South Carolina	Co. B, 4th South Carolina Cavalry	June 11, 1864, Trevilian Station, Louisa Court House, Virginia	Point Lookout, Maryland, transferred to Elmira Prison, NY, July 25, 1864	Died August 15, 1864 of Chronic Diarrhea. Grave No. 25
McCullough, Thomas Corporal	Unk	January 20, 1862, Camp Hampton, South Carolina	Co. B, 4th South Carolina Cavalry	June 11, 1864, Trevilian Station, Louisa Court House, Virginia	Point Lookout, Maryland, transferred to Elmira Prison, NY, July 25, 1864	Died August 18, 1864 of Scorbutus (Scurvy), Grave No. 121
McCullough, William A. Private	Unk	August 23, 1861, Camp Trousdale, Tennessee	Co. H, 23rd Tennessee Infantry	June 17, 1864, Petersburg, Virginia	Point Lookout, Maryland, transferred to Elmira Prison, NY, July 30, 1864	Died January 31, 1865 of Chronic Diarrhea, Grave No. 1784
McCumber, Florney Noah Private	24	May 27, 1861, Wilmington, North Carolina	Co. D, 3rd North Carolina Infantry	May 12, 1864, Near Spotsylvania County Court House, Virginia	Point Lookout, Maryland, transferred to Elmira Prison, NY, August 14, 1864	Exchanged February 13, 1865 at Boulware's wharf on the James River, Virginia
McCumber, Orrin Private	23	May 27, 1861, Wilmington, North Carolina	Co. D, 3rd North Carolina Infantry	May 12, 1864, Near Spotsylvania County Court House, Virginia	Point Lookout, Maryland, transferred to Elmira Prison, NY, August 14, 1864	Oath of Allegiance June 27, 1865
McCurry, M. Rufus Private	Unk	March 12, 1862, Athens, Georgia	Co. H, Cobb's Legion Georgia Infantry	June 11, 1864, Trevilian Station, Louisa Court House, Virginia	Point Lookout, Maryland, transferred to Elmira Prison, NY, July 25, 1864	Died October 11, 1864 of Chronic Diarrhea, Grave No. 580
McCurry, T. W. Private	Unk	Unknown	Co. A, 16th Georgia Infantry	June 1, 1864, Gaines Farm Cold Harbor, Virginia	Transferred From Point Lookout Prison, MD, July 12, 1864. Train Never Arrived at Elmira Prison Camp, NY.	Died July 15, 1864 in Train Wreck at Shohola, Pennsylvania.
McCurry, W. E. Private	Unk	May 10, 1862, Savannah, Georgia	Co. F, 38th Georgia Infantry	May 20, 1864, Spotsylvania Court House, Virginia	Point Lookout, Maryland, transferred to Elmira Prison, NY, July 3, 1864	Oath of Allegiance June 30, 1865

Name & Rank	Age	Enlisted	Regiment and State	Where Captured	Prison	Remarks
McCutchan, John F. Corporal	Unk	July 6, 1861, Rich Mountain, Virginia	Co. H, 25th Virginia Infantry	May 5, 1864, Wilderness, Virginia	Point Lookout, Maryland, transferred to Elmira Prison, NY, August 14, 1864	Oath of Allegiance June 19, 1865
McCutchan, Joseph H. Private	Unk	August 5, 1861, Monterey, Virginia	Co. H, 25th Virginia Infantry	May 6, 1864, Wilderness, Virginia	Old Capital Prison, Washington, DC, transferred to Elmira Prison, NY, July 14, 1864	Exchanged March 14, 1865 at Boulware's Wharf on the James River, Virginia
McCutchen, T. Jay Private	Unk	August 9, 1863, McPherson-ville, South Carolina	Co. J, 4th South Carolina Cavalry	June 11, 1864, Trevilian Station, Louisa Court House, Virginia	Point Lookout, Maryland, transferred to Elmira Prison, NY, July 25, 1864	Oath of Allegiance June 16, 1865
McDaniel, Archibald A. Private	16	December 31, 1861, Springfield, Missouri	Co. F, 1st Missouri Cavalry	May 17, 1863, Big Black Bridge, Champion Hill, Mississippi	Point Lookout, Maryland, transferred to Elmira Prison, NY, August 18, 1864	Transferred For Exchange October 11, 1864 to Point Lookout Prison Camp, MD. Nothing Further.
McDaniel, Charles Private	Unk	March 8, 1862, Rapides Parish, Louisiana	Co. H, 8th Louisiana Infantry	May 12, 1864, Spotsylvania Court House, Virginia	Point Lookout, Maryland, transferred to Elmira Prison, NY, August 17, 1864	Died January 5, 1865 of Variola (Smallpox), Grave No. 1245
McDaniel, Charles L. Private	Unk	April 18, 1862, Amherst County Court House, Virginia	Co. F, 50th Virginia Infantry	May 12, 1864, Spotsylvania Court House, Virginia	Point Lookout, Maryland, transferred to Elmira Prison, NY, July 30, 1864	Oath of Allegiance June 19, 1865
McDaniel, E. B. Private	Unk	April 30, 1864, Sullivan's Island, Georgia	Co. N, 38th Georgia Infantry	June 3, 1864, Cold Harbor, Virginia	Point Lookout, Maryland, transferred to Elmira Prison, NY, July 12, 1864	Exchange March 14, 1865 at Boulware's Wharf on the James River, Virginia
McDaniel, E. M. Sergeant	Unk	August 11, 1861, Gwinnett, Georgia	Co. H, 16th Georgia Infantry	June 1, 1864, Cold Harbor, Virginia	Point Lookout, Maryland, transferred to Elmira Prison, NY, July 12, 1864	Oath of Allegiance June 16, 1865

Name & Rank	Age	Enlisted	Regiment and State	Where Captured	Prison	Remarks
McDaniel, Isaac Private	26	May 30, 1861, Camden County, North Carolina	Co. B, 32nd North Carolina Infantry	May 10, 1864, Near Spotsylvania Court House, Virginia	Point Lookout, Maryland, transferred to Elmira Prison, NY, August 6, 1864	Died February 14, 1865 of Chronic Diarrhea, Grave No. 2169. Name John McDonald on Headstone.
McDaniel, J. R. Private	23	December 20, 1861, Brittons Neck, South Carolina	Co. J, 21st South Carolina Infantry	January 15, 1865, Fort Fisher, North Carolina	January 30, 1865, Elmira Prison Camp, New York	Died June 11, 1865 of Pneumonia, Grave No. 2885
McDaniel, James Private	Unk	September 5, 1861, Luka, Mississippi	Co. K, 2nd Mississippi Infantry	June 11, 1864, Trevilian Station, Louisa Court House, Virginia	Point Lookout, Maryland, transferred to Elmira Prison, NY, July 25, 1864	Oath of Allegiance May 17, 1865
McDaniel, John P. Corporal	Unk	July 16, 1861, Winchester, Virginia	Co. D, 2nd Virginia Infantry	May 12, 1864, Near Spotsylvania Court House, Virginia	Point Lookout, Maryland, transferred to Elmira Prison, NY, August 6, 1864	Exchanged March 2, 1865 at Akins Landing on the James River, Virginia
McDaniel, Nathan Private	20	June 15, 1861, Mocksville, North Carolina	Co. G, 4th North Carolina Infantry	July 9, 1864, Harpers Ferry, Virginia	Old Capital Prison, Washington DC. Transferred to Elmira Prison Camp New York July 25, 1864.	Oath of Allegiance May 29, 1865
McDaniel, Simeon Private	Unk	Unknown	Co. G, 19th Georgia Infantry	August 19, 1864, Weldon Railroad, Near Petersburg, Virginia. Gunshot Wound Left Foot.	Old Capital Prison, Washington, DC transferred to Elmira Prison, NY, August 27, 1864	Exchanged March 14, 1865 at Boulware's Wharf on the James River, Virginia
McDaniel, Thomas Private	Unk	May 15, 1862, Lenoir County, North Carolina	Co. E, 3rd North Carolina Cavalry	May 27, 1864, Nelson's Ford, Virginia	Point Lookout, Maryland, transferred to Elmira Prison, NY, July 12, 1864	Died August 30, 1864 of Chronic Diarrhea, Grave No. 53. Name McDonald on Headstone.
McDaniel, W. M. Corporal	Unk	August 24, 1861, Lawrenceville, Georgia	Co. F, 24th Georgia Infantry	June 1, 1864, Cold Harbor, Virginia	Point Lookout, Maryland, transferred to Elmira Prison, NY, July 12, 1864	Died June 14, 1865 of Variola (Smallpox), Grave No. 2881

Name & Rank	Age	Enlisted	Regiment and State	Where Captured	Prison	Remarks
McDaniel, William Private	Unk	June 8, 1861, Mobile County, Alabama	Co. G, 12th Alabama Infantry	May 6, 1864, Wilderness, Virginia	Point Lookout, Maryland, transferred to Elmira Prison, NY, August 17, 1864	Died March 11, 1865 of Chronic Diarrhea, Grave No. 1846
McDaniel, William A. Private	Unk	April 18, 1862, Amherst County Court House, Virginia	Co. F, 50th Virginia Infantry	May 12, 1864, Spotsylvania Court House, Virginia	Point Lookout, Maryland, transferred to Elmira Prison, NY, July 30, 1864	Oath of Allegiance June 23, 1865
McDaniel, William H. Private	20	May 6, 1862, Atlanta, Georgia	Co. B, Cobb's Legion, Georgia	May 13, 1864, King George County, Virginia	Point Lookout, Maryland, transferred to Elmira Prison, NY, July 3, 1864	Oath of Allegiance June 21, 1865
McDaniel, William L. Private	44	August 1, 1863, Fort Branch, Martin County, North Carolina	Co. G, 40th Regiment, 3rd North Carolina Artillery	January 15, 1865, Fort Fisher, North Carolina	January 30, 1865 Elmira Prison Camp, New York	Oath of Allegiance June 12, 1865
McDermott, Charles Sergeant	Unk	July 1, 1861, New Orleans, Louisiana	Co. H, 14th Louisiana Infantry	May 12, 1864, Spotsylvania Court House, Virginia	Point Lookout, Maryland, transferred to Elmira Prison, NY, July 25, 1864	Oath of Allegiance May 29, 1865
McDonald, Archibald Private	41	April 9, 1862, Cumberland County, North Carolina	Co. A, 51st North Carolina Infantry	June 1, 1864, Cold Harbor, Virginia	Point Lookout, Maryland, transferred to Elmira Prison, NY, July 12, 1864	Exchanged October 29, 1864, at Venus Point, Savannah River, GA.
McDonald, Archibald N. Private	23	April 5, 1862, Lumber Bridge, North Carolina	Co. D, 51st North Carolina Infantry	June 1, 1864, Cold Harbor, Virginia	Point Lookout, Maryland, transferred to Elmira Prison, NY, July 12, 1864	Oath of Allegiance July 3, 1865
McDonald, Benjamin F. Private	Unk	May 26, 1861, Baldwyn, Mississippi	Co. K, 19th Mississippi Infantry	July 29, 1864, Petersburg, Virginia	Point Lookout, Maryland, transferred to Elmira Prison, NY, August 12, 1864	Oath of Allegiance May 29, 1865
McDonald, D. S. Private	Unk	Unknown	Co. K, 3rd Georgia Infantry	July 4, 1863, Fredericksburg, Virginia	Point Lookout, Maryland, transferred to Elmira Prison, NY, August 17, 1864	Died March 23, 1865 of Cause Unknown, Grave No. 2442

Name & Rank	Age	Enlisted	Regiment and State	Where Captured	Prison	Remarks
McDonald, Daniel K. Private	Unk	Unknown	Co. C, 1st Reserves Florida Infantry	September 23, 1864, Euchee Anna, Florida	New Orleans, Louisiana transferred to Elmira November 19, 1864.	Died January 25, 1865 of Apoplexy (Cerebral Hemorrhage or Stroke) Grave No. 1623
McDonald, Daniel P. Private	21	September 12, 1861, Carthage, North Carolina	Co. C, 35th North Carolina Infantry	June 17, 1864, Petersburg, Virginia	Point Lookout, Maryland, transferred to Elmira Prison, NY, July 30, 1864	Exchanged March 14, 1865 at Boulware's Wharf on the James River, Virginia
McDonald, Elias A. Private	Unk	February 25, 1861, Selma, Alabama	Co. A, 1st Battalion Alabama Artillery	August 23, 1864, Fort Morgan, Alabama	New Orleans, Louisiana transferred to Elmira Prison, NY, December 4, 1864.	Oath of Allegiance July 7, 1865
McDonald, Floyd Private	Unk	October 9, 1862, Tazwell, Virginia	Co. J, 16th Virginia Cavalry	July 10, 1864, Frederick, Maryland	Old Capital Prison, Washington DC. Transferred to Elmira Prison Camp New York July 25, 1864.	Died February 11, 1865 of Pneumonia, Grave No. 2085
McDonald, Franklin M. Private	Unk	April 23, 1864, Petersburg, Virginia	Co. F, 51st North Carolina Infantry	June 1, 1864, Cold Harbor, Virginia	Point Lookout, Maryland, transferred to Elmira Prison, NY, July 12, 1864	Transferred for Exchange 10/11/64. Died 10/27/64 of Chronic Diarrhea at Point Lookout, MD.
McDonald, J. C. Private	Unk	July 13, 1861, Hartwell, Georgia	Co. C, 16th Georgia Infantry	August 16, 1864, Front Royal, Virginia	Old Capital Prison, Washington, DC transferred to Elmira Prison, NY, August 29, 1864	Died May 1, 1865 of Pneumonia, Grave No. 2735. Headstone has VA not GA.
McDonald, John C. Private	Unk	June 1, 1864, Tazewell County, Virginia	Co. J, 16th Virginia Infantry	July 10, 1864, Frederick, Maryland	Old Capital Prison, Washington, DC, transferred to Elmira Prison, NY, July 23, 1864	Transferred for Exchange 10/11/1864. Died 11/23/64 of Chronic Diarrhea at Point Lookout, MD.
McDonald, John E. Private	Unk	September 20, 1861, Camp Harmon, Virginia	Co. E, 4th Virginia Infantry	May 12, 1864, Near Spotsylvania Court House, Virginia	Point Lookout, Maryland, transferred to Elmira Prison, NY, August 2, 1864	Exchanged October 29, 1864, at Venus Point, Savannah River, GA.

Name & Rank	Age	Enlisted	Regiment and State	Where Captured	Prison	Remarks
McDonald, Malcolm Private	20	May 1, 1861, Elizabethtown, North Carolina	Co. K, 18th North Carolina Infantry	July 29, 1864, Petersburg, Virginia	Point Lookout, Maryland, transferred to Elmira Prison, NY, August 12, 1864	Oath of Allegiance June 12, 1865
McDonald, Peter Private	24	April 5, 1862, Camp Shenandoah, Virginia	Co. E, 25th Virginia Infantry	May 12, 1864, Spotsylvania Court House, Virginia	Point Lookout, Maryland, transferred to Elmira Prison, NY, August 12, 1864	Oath of Allegiance June 30, 1865
McDonald, R. B. Private	Unk	December 16, 1863, Grove Hill, Alabama	Co. F, 1st Battalion Alabama Artillery	August 23, 1864, Fort Morgan, Alabama	Steam Press No. 4 New Orleans, Louisiana transferred to Elmira Prison, NY, October 8, 1864.	Exchanged February 20, 1865 at Boulware's or Cox Wharf on the James River, Virginia
McDonald, Thomas Private	26	June 19, 1861, Camp Pulaski, Near New Orleans, Louisiana	Co. F, 14th Louisiana Infantry	July 10, 1864, Frederick, Maryland	Old Capital Prison, Washington DC. Transferred to Elmira Prison Camp New York July 25, 1864.	Oath of Allegiance May 13, 1865
McDonald, William Private	Unk	Unknown	Co. B, 27th South Carolina Infantry	June 24, 1864, Near Petersburg, Virginia	Point Lookout, Maryland, transferred to Elmira Prison, NY, August 18, 1864	Exchanged February 25, 1865 at Boulware's or Cox Wharf on the James River, Virginia
McDonald, William J. Private	Unk	August 18, 1861, Camp Moore, Louisiana	Co. C, 12th Louisiana Infantry	May 16, 1863, Baker's Creek, Champion Hill, Mississippi	Point Lookout, Maryland, transferred to Elmira Prison, NY, August 18, 1864	Exchanged October 29, 1864, at Venus Point, Savannah River, GA.
McDonnel, D. L. Private	Unk	Unknown	Co. K, 3rd Georgia Cavalry	July 4, 1864, Frederick, Maryland	Point Lookout, Maryland, transferred to Elmira Prison, NY, August 17, 1864	Died March 23, 1865 of Chronic Diarrhea, Grave No. 2442. Headstone has McDonald, D. S.
McDonough, James Private	Unk	Unknown	Co. B, 12th Virginia Cavalry	July 12, 1864, Jefferson County, Virginia	Old Capital Prison, Washington DC. Transferred to Elmira Prison Camp New York July 25, 1864.	Died August 14, 1864 of Remittent Fever, Grave No. 126

Name & Rank	Age	Enlisted	Regiment and State	Where Captured	Prison	Remarks
McDougal, Neill G. Private	Unk	August 25, 1862, Richmond, Virginia	Co. A, 3rd Battalion Georgia Sharp Shooters	August 16, 1864, Front Royal, Virginia	Old Capital Prison, Washington, DC transferred to Elmira Prison, NY, August 29, 1864	Oath of Allegiance June 19, 1865
McDowell, James M. Private	24	March 4, 1862, Ashboro, North Carolina	Co. I, 22nd North Carolina Infantry	May 30, 1864 Mechanics-ville, Virginia	Point Lookout, Maryland, transferred to Elmira Prison, NY, July 11, 1864	Oath of Allegiance May 29, 1865
McDuff, Henry S. Private	Unk	August 5, 1861, Danielsville, Georgia	Co. D, 16th Georgia Infantry	June 1, 1864, Gaines Farm Cold Harbor, Virginia	Point Lookout, Maryland, transferred to Elmira Prison, NY, July 12, 1864	Oath of Allegiance May 29, 1865
McDuffee, William J. Private	20	April 30, 1861, Elizabethtown, North Carolina	Co. K, 18th North Carolina Infantry	May 12, 1864, Spotsylvania Court House, Virginia	Point Lookout, Maryland, transferred to Elmira Prison, NY, August 6, 1864	Oath of Allegiance June 12, 1865
McDuffie, Daniel K. Private	21	July 16, 1862, Fort St. Phillips, North Carolina	Co. K, 40th Regiment, 3rd North Carolina Artillery	January 15, 1865, Fort Fisher, North Carolina	February 1, 1865, Elmira Prison Camp, New York	Exchanged March 2, 1865 at Boulware's Wharf on the James River, Virginia
McDuffie, Henry F. Private	18	July 16, 1862, Fort St. Philips, North Carolina	Co. K, 40th Regiment, 3rd North Carolina Artillery	January 15, 1865, Fort Fisher, North Carolina	February 1, 1865 Elmira Prison Camp, New York	Died February 20, 1865 of Unknown Disease on Boat to be Exchanged.
McEachearn, John A. Private	Unk	October 11, 1861, Fayetteville, Georgia	Co. C, 53rd Georgia Infantry	June 1, 1864, Gaines Mill Cold Harbor, Virginia	Point Lookout, Maryland, transferred to Elmira Prison, NY, July 17,1864	Oath of Allegiance July 7, 1865
McEachern, James W. Private	20	September 23, 1861, Camp Lamar, Georgia	Co. F, 61st Georgia Infantry	May 12, 1864, Spotsylvania Court House, Virginia	Point Lookout, Maryland, transferred to Elmira Prison, NY, July 30, 1864	Oath of Allegiance June 16, 1865
McEachin, Milton E. Private	17	June 1, 1861, Richmond County, North Carolina	Co. F, 18th North Carolina Infantry	May 12, 1864, Spotsylvania Court House, Virginia	Point Lookout, Maryland, transferred to Elmira Prison, NY, August 6, 1864	Oath of Allegiance June 12, 1865

Name & Rank	Age	Enlisted	Regiment and State	Where Captured	Prison	Remarks
McEarin, A. N. Sergeant	Unk	Unknown	Co. D, 49th Virginia Infantry	May 30, 1864, Gaines Mill Cold Harbor, Virginia	Point Lookout, Maryland, transferred to Elmira Prison, NY, July 11, 1864	Exchanged March 14, 1865 at Boulware's Wharf on the James River, Virginia
McElmurray, Andrew J. Private	Unk	February 23, 1862, Schley County, Georgia	Co. A, 27th Georgia Infantry	June 16, 1864, Petersburg, Virginia	Point Lookout, Maryland, transferred to Elmira Prison, NY, July 30, 1864	Oath of Allegiance June 16, 1865
McElreath, Miller J. Private	Unk	May 10, 1862, Cartersville, Georgia	Co. K, 60th Georgia Infantry	May 20, 1864, Spotsylvania Court House, Virginia	Point Lookout, Maryland, transferred to Elmira Prison, NY, July 3, 1864	Exchanged March 10, 1865 at Boulware's Wharf on the James River, Virginia
McElveen, J. F. Private	Unk	April 15, 1864, Charleston, South Carolina	Co. H, 26th South Carolina Infantry	July 30, 1864, Petersburg, Virginia	Point Lookout, Maryland, transferred to Elmira Prison, NY, August 12, 1864	Exchanged March 14, 1865 at Boulware's Wharf on the James River, Virginia
McEnnany, Nicholas Private	24	June 19, 1861, Camp Moore, Louisiana	Co. A, 8th Louisiana Infantry	May 12, 1864, Spotsylvania Court House, Virginia	Point Lookout, Maryland, transferred to Elmira Prison, NY, August 17, 1864	Oath of Allegiance May 29, 1865
McEver, Christopher C. Sergeant	Unk	July 20, 1861, Jefferson, Georgia	Co. G, 16th Georgia Infantry	June 1, 1864, Gaines Farm Cold Harbor, Virginia	Point Lookout, Maryland, transferred to Elmira Prison, NY, July 12, 1864	Oath of Allegiance June 16, 1865
McEwen, Archibald Daniel Corporal	23	May 6, 1862, Elizabethtown, Bladen County, North Carolina	Co. K, 40th Regiment, 3rd North Carolina Artillery	January 15, 1865, Fort Fisher, North Carolina	February 1, 1865, Elmira Prison Camp, New York	Oath of Allegiance June 12, 1865. Died June 19, 1865 of Chronic Diarrhea at Manchester, Virginia
McFadden, R. M. Corporal	Unk	November 18, 1861, College Green, Columbia, South Carolina	Co. A, 17th South Carolina Infantry	July 30, 1864, Petersburg, Virginia	Point Lookout, Maryland, transferred to Elmira Prison, NY, August 12, 1864	Oath of Allegiance June 16, 1865

Name & Rank	Age	Enlisted	Regiment and State	Where Captured	Prison	Remarks
McFarland, Henry C. Private	Unk	September 13, 1862, Loudoun County, Virginia	Co. A, 35th Battalion Virginia Cavalry	September 19, 1863, Germania Ford, Virginia	Point Lookout, Maryland, transferred to Elmira Prison, NY, August 18, 1864	Exchanged March 10, 1865 at Boulware's Wharf on the James River, Virginia
McFarland, William A. Sergeant	24	June 17, 1861, Front Royal, Virginia	Co. D, 49th Virginia Infantry	May 30, 1864, Gaines Mill Cold Harbor, Virginia	Point Lookout, Maryland, transferred to Elmira Prison, NY, July 11, 1864	Exchanged March 14, 1865 at Boulware's Wharf on the James River, Virginia
McFeeley, James G. Private	Unk	May 5, 1862, Charleston, South Carolina	Co. H, 25th South Carolina Infantry	January 15, 1865, Fort Fisher, North Carolina	January 30, 1865, Elmira Prison Camp, New York	Oath of Allegiance May 17, 1865
McGahee, Samuel Private	Unk	July 29, 1863, Decatur, Georgia	Co. G, 38th Georgia Infantry	May 20, 1864, Spotsylvania Court House, Virginia	Point Lookout, Maryland, transferred to Elmira Prison, NY, July 3, 1864	Died May 4, 1865 of General Debility, Grave No. 2759
McGarrity, Richard Private	40	June 7, 1861, Camp Moore, Louisiana	Co. B, 7th Louisiana Infantry	May 5, 1864, Wilderness, Virginia	Point Lookout, Maryland, transferred to Elmira Prison, NY, August 17, 1864	Exchanged October 29, 1864, at Venus Point, Savannah River, GA..
McGee, Allison Private	27	August 10, 1862, Dobson, North Carolina	Co. B, 2nd Battalion North Carolina Infantry	July 3, 1863, Gettysburg, Pennsylvania yeah	Point Lookout Prison Camp, Maryland. Transferred to Elmira Prison Camp, New York August 18, 1864	Died October 1, 1864 of Pneumonia And Erysipelas, Grave No. 411
McGee, Anderson Private	Unk	April 3, 1862, Saltville, Virginia	Co. F, 29th, Virginia Infantry	June 1, 1864, Gaines Mill Cold Harbor, Virginia	Point Lookout, Maryland, transferred to Elmira Prison, NY, July 12, 1864	Oath of Allegiance July 3, 1865
McGee, Henry W. Private	46	October 1, 1863, Richmond, Virginia	Co. I, 3rd Virginia Infantry, Local Defense	July 29, 1864, Deserted to Union Lines, Petersburg, Virginia	Point Lookout, Maryland, transferred to Elmira Prison, NY, August 12, 1864	Oath of Allegiance November 30, 1864. Early Release per Lincoln's Proclamation, 12/8/1863.

Name & Rank	Age	Enlisted	Regiment and State	Where Captured	Prison	Remarks
McGee, Isaac Private	25	August 15, 1862, Iredell County, North Carolina	Co. J, 37th North Carolina Infantry	May 8, 1864, Spotsylvania Court House, Virginia	Point Lookout, Maryland, transferred to Elmira Prison, NY, August 12, 1864	Died December 17, 1864 of Pneumonia, Grave No. 1130
McGee, John W. Private	Unk	February 29, 1864, Dorchester, Georgia	Co. B, 7th Georgia Cavalry	June 11, 1864, Trevilian Station, Louisa Court House, Virginia	Point Lookout, Maryland, transferred to Elmira Prison, NY, July 25, 1864	Died September 16, 1864 of Remittent Fever. Grave No. 159
McGee, Judson Private	Unk	Unknown	Co. I, 22nd South Carolina Infantry	July 30, 1864, Petersburg, Virginia	Point Lookout, Maryland, transferred to Elmira Prison, NY, August 12, 1864	Oath of Allegiance May 19, 1865
McGhee, W. H. Private	19	October 19, 1861, Elizabethtown, Bladen County, North Carolina	Co. J, 36th 2nd North Carolina Artillery	January 15, 1865, Fort Fisher, North Carolina	February 1, 1865, Elmira Prison Camp, New York	Exchanged March 14, 1865 at Boulware's Wharf on the James River, Virginia
McGill, Thomas H. Private	Unk	July 12, 1861, Madison Court House, Virginia	Co. C, 4th Virginia Cavalry	June 26, 1864, Leesburg, Virginia	Old Capital Prison, Washington DC. Transferred to Elmira Prison Camp New York July 25, 1864.	Exchanged March 14, 1865 at Boulware's Wharf on the James River, Virginia
McGilligan, Thomas Private	Unk	May 8, 1862, Augusta, Georgia	Co. A, 7th Georgia Cavalry	June 11, 1864, Trevilian Station, Louisa Court House, Virginia	Point Lookout, Maryland, transferred to Elmira Prison, NY, July 23, 1864	Oath of Allegiance May 15, 1865
McGimsey, John W. Private	22	October 7, 1861, Morganton, North Carolina	Co. F, 3rd North Carolina Cavalry	May 27, 1864, Hanover Town, Virginia	Point Lookout, Maryland, transferred to Elmira Prison, NY, July 12, 1864	Died September 4, 1864 of Chronic Diarrhea, Grave No. 234
McGivey, Patrick Private	Unk	Unknown	Co. K, 10th Tennessee Infantry	May 16, 1863, Big Black, Mississippi	Point Lookout, Maryland, transferred to Elmira Prison, NY, July 25, 1864	Oath of Allegiance May 17, 1865

Name & Rank	Age	Enlisted	Regiment and State	Where Captured	Prison	Remarks
McGlaughlin, Hugh P. M. Corporal	Unk	May 18, 1861, Huntersville, Virginia	Co. I, 25th Virginia Infantry	May 12, 1864, Spotsylvania Court House, Virginia	Point Lookout, Maryland, transferred to Elmira Prison, NY, August 12, 1864	Exchanged March 2, 1865 at Akins Landing on the James River, Virginia
McGlaughlin, Robert W. Private	Unk	June 11, 1861, Heveners, Virginia	Co. E, 31st Virginia Infantry	May 12, 1864, Spotsylvania Court House, Virginia	Point Lookout, Maryland, transferred to Elmira Prison, NY, July 23, 1864	Died November 8, 1864 of Chronic Diarrhea, Grave No. 832. Name McLaughlin on Headstone
McGlawhorn, Alfred Private	22	July 15, 1862, Raleigh, North Carolina	Co. D, 3rd North Carolina Infantry	May 12, 1864, Near Spotsylvania County Court House, Virginia	Point Lookout, Maryland, transferred to Elmira Prison, NY, August 14, 1864	Oath of Allegiance June 19, 1865
McGlawhorn, Luke Private	23	July 15, 1862, Raleigh, North Carolina	Co. D, 3rd North Carolina Infantry	May 10, 1864, Near Spotsylvania Court House, Virginia	Point Lookout, Maryland, transferred to Elmira Prison, NY, August 14, 1864	Oath of Allegiance July 3, 1865
McGowan, Charles B. Private	Unk	July 15, 1862, Duplin County, North Carolina	Co. B, 3rd North Carolina Infantry	May 12, 1864, Near Spotsylvania County Court House, Virginia	Point Lookout, Maryland, transferred to Elmira Prison, NY, August 14, 1864	Transferred for Exchange 10/11/64. Died 10/31/64 of Unknown Causes at Fort Monroe, VA.
McGowan, Owen Private	Unk	September 23, 1861, Flint Hill, South Carolina	Co. C, 7th South Carolina Infantry	May 23, 1864, North Anna, Hanover Junction, Virginia	Point Lookout, Maryland, transferred to Elmira Prison, NY, July 23, 1864	Oath of Allegiance May 29, 1865
McGrady, Henderson Private	Unk	Unknown	Co. D, 50th Virginia Infantry	May 12, 1864, Spotsylvania Court House, Virginia	Point Lookout, Maryland, transferred to Elmira Prison, NY, August 2, 1864	Oath of Allegiance June 30, 1865
McGrady, John W. Private	Unk	June 1, 1864, Carroll, Virginia	Co. F, 25th Virginia Cavalry	July 6, 1864, Harpers Ferry, Virginia	Old Capital Prison, Washington DC. Transferred to Elmira Prison Camp New York July 25, 1864.	Transferred For Exchange October 11, 1864. Died October 27, 1864 of Chronic Diarrhea at Point Lookout Prison, MD.

Name & Rank	Age	Enlisted	Regiment and State	Where Captured	Prison	Remarks
McGregor, Benjamin F. Private	18	January 23, 1863, Fort Caswell, Brunswick County, North Carolina	Co. E, 40th Regiment, 3rd North Carolina Artillery	January 15, 1865, Fort Fisher, North Carolina	February 1, 1865, Elmira Prison Camp, New York	Oath of Allegiance June 12, 1865
McGregor, Martin V. Private	Unk	May 12, 1862, Gordonville, Virginia	Co. F, 18th North Carolina Infantry	May 12, 1864, Spotsylvania Court House, Virginia	Point Lookout, Maryland, transferred to Elmira Prison, NY, August 6, 1864	Oath of Allegiance June 12, 1865
McGriff, Francis M. Private	Unk	September 7, 1861, Camp Bartow, Virginia	Co. B, 7th Georgia Infantry	May 6, 1864, Wilderness, Virginia	Old Capital Prison, Washington DC. Transferred to Elmira Prison Camp New York July 25, 1864.	Exchanged March 14, 1865 at Boulware's Wharf on the James River, Virginia
McGuggin, Bernard Private	Unk	Unknown	Co. E, 1st Maryland Infantry	July 15, 1864, Leasburg, Virginia. Deserted to Union Lines.	Old Capital Prison, Washington, DC, transferred to Elmira Prison, NY, August 12, 1864	Oath of Allegiance February 13, 1865. Early Release per Lincoln's Proclamation, 12/8/1863.
McGuire, William Private	30	July 12, 1861, Camp Moore, Louisiana	Co. A, 10th Louisiana Infantry	May 12, 1864, Spotsylvania Court House, Virginia	Point Lookout, Maryland, transferred to Elmira Prison, NY, July 25, 1864	Oath of Allegiance May 29, 1865
McHatton, Robert E. Private	Unk	August 8, 1861, Baton Rouge, Louisiana	Co. B, Point Coupe Louisiana Artillery	October 7, 1864, Osyka, Mississippi	New Orleans, Louisiana transferred to Elmira November 19, 1864.	Exchanged February 13, 1865 at Boulware's Wharf on the James River, Virginia
McHethey, R. Private	Unk	Unknown	Co. E, Gober's Regiment Louisiana Cavalry	October 6, 1864, Clinton, Louisiana	New Orleans, Louisiana transferred to Elmira November 19, 1864.	Exchanged February 25, 1865 at Boulware's or Cox Wharf on the James River, Virginia
McIlvane, J. H. Private	Unk	January 1, 1862, Darlington District, South Carolina	Co. B, 21st South Carolina Infantry	January 15, 1865, Fort Fisher, North Carolina	January 30, 1865, Elmira Prison Camp, New York	Oath of Allegiance July 7, 1865

Name & Rank	Age	Enlisted	Regiment and State	Where Captured	Prison	Remarks
McIlwain, William Private	Unk	August 4, 1863, Abbeville Court House, South Carolina	Co. F, Holcombe Legion, South Carolina	May 8, 1864, Jarrett's Depot, Virginia	Point Lookout, Maryland, transferred to Elmira Prison, NY, August 17, 1864	Died January 2, 1865 of Chronic Diarrhea, Grave No. 1345
McInnerney, Patrick W. Private	26	May 18, 1861, Mobile, Alabama	Co. C, 8th Alabama Infantry	May 6, 1864, Wilderness, Virginia	Point Lookout, Maryland, transferred to Elmira Prison, NY, August 17, 1864	Oath of Allegiance May 15, 1865
McIntire, Elisha Private	Unk	May 25, 1864, Camp Vance, North Carolina	Co. D, 54th North Carolina Infantry	July 8, 1864, Harpers Ferry, Virginia	Old Capital Prison, Washington DC. Transferred to Elmira Prison Camp New York July 25, 1864.	Oath of Allegiance July 3, 1865
McIntire, Frank P. Sergeant	18	June 11, 1861, Lillington, North Carolina	Co. C, 1st North Carolina Infantry	May 12, 1864, Spotsylvania Court House, Virginia	Point Lookout, Maryland, transferred to Elmira Prison, NY, August 6, 1864	Exchanged October 29, 1864, at Venus Point, Savannah River, GA.
McIntire, John F. Corporal	25	April 18, 1861, Martinsburg, Virginia	Co. C, 2nd Virginia Infantry	May 12, 1864, Near Spotsylvania Court House, Virginia	Point Lookout, Maryland, transferred to Elmira Prison, NY, August 6, 1864	Exchanged October 29, 1864, at Venus Point, Savannah River, GA.
McIntosh, David G. Sergeant	26	September 10, 1861, Jonesboro, North Carolina	Co. J, 30th North Carolina Infantry	May 20, 1864, Spotsylvania Court House, Virginia	Point Lookout, Maryland, transferred to Elmira Prison, NY, July 3, 1864	Oath of Allegiance June 30, 1865
McIntosh, Daniel R. Private	Unk	April 12, 1864, Camp Holmes, North Carolina	Co. K, 10th Regiment, 1st North Carolina Artillery	January 15, 1865, Fort Fisher, North Carolina	January 30, 1865, Elmira Prison Camp, New York	Died April 2, 1865 of Diarrhea, Grave No. 2586. Headstone has Daniel McJosh.
McIntosh, John W. Private	Unk	March 19, 1862, Auburn, Alabama	Co. F, 12th Alabama Infantry	May 12, 1864, Spotsylvania Court House, Virginia	Point Lookout, Maryland, transferred to Elmira Prison, NY, August 17, 1864	Oath of Allegiance June 21, 1865
McIntosh, Neill Sergeant	Unk	June 6, 1861, Carthage, North Carolina	Co. H, 26th North Carolina Infantry	May 12, 1864, Spotsylvania Court House, Virginia	Point Lookout, Maryland, transferred to Elmira Prison, NY, July 30, 1864	Oath of Allegiance June 21, 1865

Name & Rank	Age	Enlisted	Regiment and State	Where Captured	Prison	Remarks
McIntyre, Dugald Private	33	April 21, 1862, Cumberland County, North Carolina	Co. I, 51st North Carolina Infantry	June 1, 1864, Cold Harbor, Virginia	Point Lookout, Maryland, transferred to Elmira Prison, NY, July 12, 1864	Exchanged October 29, 1864, at Venus Point, Savannah River, GA.
McIntyre, Isaiah Private	22	September 7, 1861, Albemarle, North Carolina	Co. K, 28th North Carolina Infantry	May 12, 1864, Near Spotsylvania Court House, Virginia	Point Lookout, Maryland, transferred to Elmira Prison, NY, August 14, 1864	Oath of Allegiance June 7, 1865
McIntyre, John T. Sergeant Major	Unk	May 12, 1862, Bennettsville, South Carolina	Co. F, 21st South Carolina Infantry	January 15, 1865, Fort Fisher, North Carolina	January 30, 1865, Elmira Prison Camp, New York	Died March 5, 1865 of Chronic Diarrhea, Grave No. 2413
McIntyre, W. Duncan Musician Private	Unk	February 6, 1863, Wilmington, North Carolina	Co. F, 10th Regiment, 1st North Carolina Artillery	January 15, 1865, Fort Fisher, North Carolina	January 30, 1865, Elmira Prison Camp, New York	Oath of Allegiance May 15, 1865
McIntyre, William H. Private	Unk	Unknown	Co. B, 1st Maryland Cavalry	October 27, 1864, Fauquier County, Virginia	Old Capital Prison, Washington, DC, transferred to Elmira Prison, NY, December 17, 1864	Exchanged March 2, 1865 at Boulware's Wharf on the James River, Virginia
McIver, David A. Private	Unk	April 11, 1862, Coles Island, South Carolina	Co. F, 25th South Carolina Infantry	January 15, 1865, Fort Fisher, North Carolina	January 30, 1865, Elmira Prison Camp, New York	Exchanged March 2, 1865 at Boulware's Wharf on the James River, Virginia
McKay, Archibald P. Private	23	June 1, 1861, Richmond County, North Carolina	Co. F, 18th North Carolina Infantry	May 12, 1864, Spotsylvania Court House, Virginia	Point Lookout, Maryland, transferred to Elmira Prison, NY, August 6, 1864	Died October 30, 1864 of Chronic Diarrhea, Grave No. 736
McKay, John L. Private	18	July 22, 1863, Fort Fisher, North Carolina	Co. K, 40th 3rd North Carolina Artillery	January 15, 1865, Fort Fisher, North Carolina	February 1, 1865, Elmira Prison Camp, New York	Exchanged March 14, 1865 at Boulware's Wharf on the James River, Virginia
McKay, Malcom G. Private	22	August 1, 1861, Camp Wyatt, Wilmington, North Carolina	Co. F, 18th North Carolina Infantry	May 12, 1864, Spotsylvania Court House, Virginia	Point Lookout, Maryland, transferred to Elmira Prison, NY, August 6, 1864	Exchanged October 29, 1864, at Venus Point, Savannah River, GA.

Name & Rank	Age	Enlisted	Regiment and State	Where Captured	Prison	Remarks
McKay, Thomas A. Private	Unk	May 14, 1862, Johnson's Station, Reidsville, Georgia	Co. H, 61st Georgia Infantry	May 12, 1864, Spotsylvania Court House, Virginia	Point Lookout, Maryland, transferred to Elmira Prison, NY, July 30, 1864	Oath of Allegiance June 16, 1865
McKee, Daniel B. Private	16	May 10, 1862, Wilmington, North Carolina	Co. H, 36th 2nd North Carolina Artillery	January 15, 1865, Fort Fisher, North Carolina	February 1, 1865, Elmira Prison Camp, New York	Exchanged February 20, 1865 at Boulware's or Cox Wharf on the James River, Virginia
McKee, James Corporal	Unk	July 26, 1861, Brockville, Alabama	Co. K, 13th Alabama Infantry	May 5, 1864, Wilderness, Virginia	Point Lookout, Maryland, transferred to Elmira Prison, NY, August 14, 1864	Exchanged March 2, 1865 at Akins Landing on the James River, Virginia
McKeel, William Private	19	March 7, 1863, Alamance County, North Carolina	Co. J, 8th North Carolina Infantry	June 1, 1864, Cold Harbor, Virginia	Point Lookout, Maryland, transferred to Elmira Prison, NY, July 12, 1864	Exchanged February 13, 1865 at Boulware's wharf on the James River, Virginia
McKeel, William H. Private	Unk	November 8, 1861, Camp Cheatum, Tennessee	Co. G, 23rd Tennessee Infantry	June 17, 1864, Petersburg, Virginia	Point Lookout, Maryland, transferred to Elmira Prison, NY, July 30, 1864	Exchanged February 13, 1865 at Boulware's wharf on the James River, Virginia
McKellar, John C. Sergeant	21	May 18, 1861, Lumberton, North Carolina	Co. D, 1st North Carolina Infantry	May 12, 1864, Spotsylvania Court House, Virginia	Point Lookout, Maryland, transferred to Elmira Prison, NY, August 6, 1864	Oath of Allegiance June 30, 1865
McKelvey, H. A. Private	19	November 1, 1863, Charleston, South Carolina	Co. K, Holcombe Legion, South Carolina Infantry	May 7, 1864, Stony Creek, Virginia	Point Lookout, Maryland, transferred to Elmira Prison, NY, August 17, 1864	Exchanged October 29, 1864. Died of Chronic Diarrhea December 28, 1864 at 1st Division Hospital, 20th A. C., Savannah, GA.

Name & Rank	Age	Enlisted	Regiment and State	Where Captured	Prison	Remarks
McKemey, Robert A. Sergeant	Unk	July 6, 1861, Rich Mountain, Virginia	Co. H, 25th Virginia Infantry	May 12, 1864, Spotsylvania Court House, Virginia	Point Lookout, Maryland, transferred to Elmira Prison, NY, August 12, 1864	Exchanged October 29, 1864, at Venus Point, Savannah River, GA.
McKemey, William D. Private	Unk	August 5, 1861, Monterey, Virginia	Co. H, 25th Virginia Infantry	May 12, 1864, Spotsylvania Court House, Virginia	Point Lookout, Maryland, transferred to Elmira Prison, NY, August 12, 1864	Oath of Allegiance June 30, 1865
McKenna, Michael Corporal	36	May 3, 1862, Macon, Georgia	Captain Slaten's Battery Georgia Light Artillery	June 17, 1864, Petersburg, Virginia	Point Lookout, Maryland, transferred to Elmira Prison, NY, July 25, 1864	Oath of Allegiance May 17, 1865
Mckenzie, Hiram E. Private	42	July 1, 1862, Charlottesville, Virginia	2nd Battalion Maryland Artillery	May 11, 1864, Yellow Tavern, Hanover County, Virginia	Point Lookout, Maryland, transferred to Elmira Prison, NY, August 17, 1864	Exchanged February 13, 1865 at Boulware's wharf on the James River, Virginia
Mckenzie, William M. Private	Unk	December 9, 1861, Camp Hampton, South Carolina	Co. H, 17th South Carolina Infantry	July 30, 1864, Petersburg, Virginia	Point Lookout, Maryland, transferred to Elmira Prison, NY, August 12, 1864	Exchanged October 29, 1864, at Venus Point, Savannah River, GA.
McKeown, Saul S. Private	Unk	January 14, 1862, Camp Hampton, Columbia, South Carolina	Co. H, 17th South Carolina Infantry	July 30, 1864, Petersburg, Virginia	Point Lookout, Maryland, transferred to Elmira Prison, NY, August 12, 1864	Died December 9, 1864 of Pneumonia, Grave No. 1151. Name Daniel McGowen on Headstone.
McKillop, John A. Sergeant	20	May 15, 1861, Edneyville, North Carolina	Co. A, 25th North Carolina Infantry	June 17, 1864, Petersburg, Virginia	Point Lookout, Maryland, transferred to Elmira Prison, NY, July 25, 1864	Died December 27, 1864 of Pneumonia, Grave No. 1296
McKimmie, Johnson Private	Unk	June 11, 1861, Fort Gaines, Georgia	Co. D, 9th Georgia Infantry	May 6, 1864, Wilderness, Virginia	Old Capital Prison, Washington, DC, transferred to Elmira Prison, NY, July 14, 1864	Died February 10, 1865 of Variola (Smallpox), Grave No. 1952. Name J. McKenzie on Headstone.

Name & Rank	Age	Enlisted	Regiment and State	Where Captured	Prison	Remarks
McKindly, Green W. Private	Unk	October 16, 1862, White Sulfur Springs, Virginia	Co. B, 13th Georgia Infantry	August 10, 1864, Berryville, Virginia	Old Capital Prison, Washington, DC transferred to Elmira Prison, NY, August 29, 1864	Oath of Allegiance July 7, 1865
McKiney, George C. Private	26	April 5, 1864, Camp Holmes, North Carolina	Co. G, 32nd North Carolina Infantry	May 10, 1864, Spotsylvania Court House, Virginia. Gunshot Wound Right Arm.	Old Capital Prison, Washington DC. Transferred to Elmira Prison Camp New York July 25, 1864.	Oath of Allegiance May 19, 1865
McKinley, Stephen Private	Unk	March 15, 1863, Atlanta, Georgia	Co. C, 64th Georgia Infantry	August 16, 1864, New Market, Virginia	Old Capital Prison, Washington, DC transferred to Elmira Prison, NY, August 29, 1864	Died December 26, 1864 of Chronic Diarrhea, Grave No. 1287
McKinney, A. Civilian	Unk	Louisiana	Citizen of Louisiana	September 19, 1864, Tensan Parish, Louisiana	New Orleans, LA, Transferred to Elmira Prison, NY, November 19, 1864	Oath of Allegiance January 6, 1865. Early Release per Lincoln's Proclamation, 12/8/1863.
McKinney, Caleb Private	Unk	August 28, 1862, Calhoun, Georgia	Co. H, 12th Georgia Infantry	May 10, 1864, Spotsylvania Court House, Virginia	Point Lookout, Maryland, transferred to Elmira Prison, NY, July 30, 1864	Oath of Allegiance June 16, 1865
McKinney, J. B. Private	Unk	August 14, 1861, White Springs, Florida	Co. C, 24th Georgia Infantry	August 16, 1864, Front Royal, Virginia	Old Capital Prison, Washington, DC transferred to Elmira Prison, NY, August 29, 1864	Oath of Allegiance June 16, 1865
McKinney, J. W. Private	27	April 26, 1864, Decatur, Georgia	Co. M, 1st Regulars Georgia Infantry	December 21, 1864, Fort Pulaski, Savannah, Georgia.	Old Capital Prison, Washington, DC, transferred to Elmira Prison, NY, April 14, 1865.	Oath of Allegiance July 7, 1865
McKinney, Joseph Private	Unk	April 1, 1861, Lacy's Store, Virginia	Co. B, 44th Virginia Infantry	May 12, 1864, Spotsylvania Court House, Virginia	Point Lookout, Maryland, transferred to Elmira Prison, NY, August 2, 1864	Exchanged March 2, 1865 at Akins Landing on the James River, Virginia

Name & Rank	Age	Enlisted	Regiment and State	Where Captured	Prison	Remarks
McKinney, William M. Corporal	Unk	December 5, 1861, Sac River, St. Clair County, Missouri	Co. K, 1st Missouri Cavalry	May 17, 1863, Big Black Bridge, Champion Hill, Mississippi	Point Lookout, Maryland, transferred to Elmira Prison, NY, August 18, 1864	Exchanged October 29, 1864, at Venus Point, Savannah River, GA.
McKinnie, Robert Private	Unk	September 22, 1863, Holmes, North Carolina	Co. G, 40th Regiment, 3rd North Carolina Artillery	January 15, 1865, Fort Fisher, North Carolina	January 30, 1865 Elmira Prison Camp, New York	Exchanged February 20, 1865 at Boulware's or Cox Wharf on the James River, Virginia
McKinnon, Alexander D. Private	Unk	July 20, 1861, Eucheenanna, Florida	Co. D, 1st Florida Infantry	August 15, 1864, Milton, Walton County, Florida	New Orleans, LA, Transferred to Elmira Prison, NY, November 19, 1864	Oath of Allegiance May 16, 1865
McKinnon, Milton C. Private	Unk	May 22, 1861, Rose Hill, Virginia	Co. E, 37th Virginia Infantry	May 12, 1864, Spotsylvania Court House, Virginia	Point Lookout, Maryland, transferred to Elmira Prison, NY, August 2, 1864	Oath of Allegiance June 19, 1865
McKinnon, Murdock M. Private	18	June 4, 1863, Fort Caswell, Brunswick County, North Carolina	Co. E, 40th Regiment, 3rd North Carolina Artillery	January 15, 1865, Fort Fisher, North Carolina	February 1, 1865, Elmira Prison Camp, New York	Oath of Allegiance June 12, 1865
McKinnon, Nicholas B. Private	22	May 30, 1861, Rockingham, North Carolina	Co. D, 23rd North Carolina Infantry	May 20, 1864, Spotsylvania Court House, Virginia	Point Lookout, Maryland, transferred to Elmira Prison, NY, July 3, 1864	Exchanged February 13, 1865 at Boulware's wharf on the James River, Virginia
McKinnon, Robert Corporal	31	July 30, 1861, Weldon, North Carolina	Co. F, 24th North Carolina Infantry	May 16, 1864, Near Drury's Bluff, Virginia	Point Lookout Prison Camp, Maryland. Transferred to Elmira Prison, NY, August 18, 1864	Died March 7, 1865 of Diarrhea, Grave No. 2396
McKissack, Alonzo Sergeant	Unk	May 21, 1861, Camp Cheatham, Tennessee	Co. E, 3rd Tennessee Infantry	May 12, 1863, Raymond, Mississippi	Point Lookout, Maryland, transferred to Elmira Prison, NY, August 18, 1864	Exchanged February 25, 1865 at Boulware's wharf on the James River, Virginia

Name & Rank	Age	Enlisted	Regiment and State	Where Captured	Prison	Remarks
McKnight, William M. Corporal	28	April 12, 1862, Battery Island, South Carolina	Co. C, 25th South Carolina Infantry	January 15, 1865, Fort Fisher, North Carolina	January 30, 1865, Elmira Prison Camp, New York	Exchanged February 20, 1865 at Boulware's or Cox Wharf on the James River, Virginia
McLain, J. B. Private	Unk	Unknown	Co. E, 11th South Carolina Infantry	June 24, 1864, Near Petersburg, Virginia	Point Lookout, Maryland, transferred to Elmira Prison, NY, August 18, 1864	Died May 10, 1865 of Chronic Diarrhea, Grave No. 2792. Headstone has McLane.
McLamb, Isham Private	22	April 26, 1862, Clinton, North Carolina	Co. J, 46th North Carolina Infantry	May 12, 1864, Spotsylvania Court House, Virginia	Point Lookout, Maryland, transferred to Elmira Prison, NY, July 30, 1864	Exchanged February 13, 1865 at Boulware's wharf on the James River, Virginia
McLamone, John Private	Unk	Unknown	Co. B, Hood's Battalion, Virginia Reserves	June 15, 1864, Petersburg, Virginia	Point Lookout, Maryland, transferred to Elmira Prison, NY, July 30, 1864	Transferred for Exchanged 10/29/64 at Venus Point, Savannah River, GA.
McLane, Jesse J. Private	Unk	March 4, 1862, Clinton, Georgia	Co. F, 45th Georgia Infantry	May 6, 1864, Wilderness, Virginia	Old Capital Prison, Washington, DC, transferred to Elmira Prison, NY, July 14, 1864	Transferred for Exchanged 10/29/64 at Venus Point, Savannah River, GA.
McLane, John J. Private	Unk	June 11, 1861, Fort Gaines, Georgia	Co. D, 9th Georgia Infantry	May 6, 1864, Wilderness, Virginia	Old Capital Prison, Washington, DC, transferred to Elmira Prison, NY, July 14, 1864	Exchanged 10/29/64 at Venus Point, Savannah River, GA. Died 11/14/64 of Unknown Causes at Port Royal, SC.
McLane, W. Private	Unk	Unknown	No Co., 10th Battalion Louisiana Cavalry	May 15, 1864, Near Port Hudson, Louisiana	New Orleans, Louisiana transferred to Elmira November 19, 1864.	Exchanged February 13, 1865 at Boulware's wharf on the James River, Virginia

Name & Rank	Age	Enlisted	Regiment and State	Where Captured	Prison	Remarks
McLauchlin, Neil L. Private	Unk	July 15, 1862, Moore County, North Carolina	Co. B, 3rd North Carolina Infantry	May 12, 1864, Near Spotsylvania County Court House, Virginia	Point Lookout, Maryland, transferred to Elmira Prison, NY, August 14, 1864	Died August 23, 1864 of Chronic Diarrhea, Grave No. 37. Name W. S. McLaughlin on Headstone.
McLaughlin, James B. Private	Unk	May 18, 1861, Sutton, Virginia	Co. C, 25th Virginia Infantry	May 6, 1864, Wilderness, Virginia	Old Capital Prison, Washington, DC, transferred to Elmira Prison, NY, July 14, 1864	Oath of Allegiance June 23, 1865
McLaurin, John Private	41	August 18, 1863, Fort Branch, Martin County, North Carolina	Co. G, 40th Regiment, 3rd North Carolina Artillery	January 15, 1865, Fort Fisher, North Carolina	January 30, 1865 Elmira Prison Camp, New York	Died February 13, 1865 of Erysipelas, Grave No. 2065
McLaurine, George T. Private	Unk	May 21, 1861, Camp Cheatham, Tennessee	Co. B, 3rd Tennessee Infantry	May 12, 1863, Raymond, Mississippi	Point Lookout, Maryland, transferred to Elmira Prison, NY, August 18, 1864	Exchanged February 25, 1865 at Boulware's wharf on the James River, Virginia
McLean, Daniel Private	19	June 1, 1862, Richmond County, North Carolina	Co. F, 18th North Carolina Infantry	May 12, 1864 Spotsylvania Court House, Virginia	Point Lookout, Maryland, transferred to Elmira Prison, NY, August 6, 1864	Died March 5, 1865 of Chronic Diarrhea, Grave No. 1970
McLean, Malcom Private	Unk	Unknown	Co. C, 12th Georgia Infantry	May 10, 1864, Spotsylvania Court House, Virginia	Point Lookout, Maryland, transferred to Elmira Prison, NY, July 30, 1864	Transferred For Exchange October 11, 1864 to Point Lookout Prison Camp, MD. Nothing Further.
McLean, Murettus S. Sergeant	20	June 1, 1861, Richmond County, North Carolina	Co. F, 18th North Carolina Infantry	May 12, 1864, Spotsylvania Court House, Virginia	Point Lookout, Maryland, transferred to Elmira Prison, NY, August 6, 1864	Died April 5, 1865 of Chronic Diarrhea, Grave No. 2557
McLean, Oliver P. Sergeant	27	April 21, 1861, Memphis, Tennessee	Co. A, Jackson's 1st Regiment, Tennessee Heavy Artillery	August 23, 1864, Fort Morgan, Alabama	New Orleans, Louisiana transferred to Elmira Prison, NY, December 4, 1864.	Exchanged February 20, 1865 at Boulware's or Cox Wharf on the James River, Virginia

Name & Rank	Age	Enlisted	Regiment and State	Where Captured	Prison	Remarks
McLean, Weston G. Sergeant	28	February 28, 1862, Lumberton, North Carolina	Co. E, 51st North Carolina Infantry	June 1, 1864, Cold Harbor, Virginia	Point Lookout, Maryland, transferred to Elmira Prison, NY, July 12, 1864	Exchanged 2/20/65. Died 3/12/65 of Chronic Diarrhea at Jackson Hospital, Richmond, VA
McLeish, John W. Sergeant	26	February 22, 1862, Charleston, South Carolina	Co. E, 25th South Carolina Infantry	January 15, 1865, Fort Fisher, North Carolina	January 30, 1865, Elmira Prison Camp, New York	Oath of Allegiance May 29, 1865
McLellan, E. T. Private	Unk	May 1, 1862, Marion, South Carolina	Co. J, 21st South Carolina Infantry	January 15, 1865, Fort Fisher, North Carolina	January 30, 1865, Elmira Prison Camp, New York	Died March 2, 1865 of Diarrhea, Grave No. 2020. Headstone has P. See McClennan, 31st North Carolina.
McLellan, R. Civilian	Unk	Louisiana	Citizen of Louisiana	September 19, 1864, Tensan Parish, Louisiana	New Orleans, LA, Transferred to Elmira Prison, NY, November 19, 1864	Discharge from Custody February 15, 1865. Per Orders of L. C. Turner.
McLelland, Benjamin W. Private	Unk	May 1, 1862, Gloucester Point, Virginia	Co. K, 34th Virginia Infantry	June 15, 1864, Petersburg, Virginia	Point Lookout, Maryland, transferred to Elmira Prison, NY, July 12, 1864	Exchanged October 29, 1864, at Venus Point, Savannah River, GA.
McLemore, John H. Private	30	July 15, 1862, Raleigh, North Carolina	Co. E, 3rd North Carolina Infantry	May 20, 1864, Spotsylvania Court House, Virginia	Point Lookout, Maryland, transferred to Elmira Prison, NY, July 3, 1864	Oath of Allegiance July 11, 1865
McLemore, Peter J. Private	29	April 18, 1861, Blacksburg, Virginia	Co. E, 4th Virginia Infantry	May 5, 1864, Near Wilderness, Virginia	Point Lookout, Maryland, transferred to Elmira Prison, NY, July 23, 1864	Oath of Allegiance May 13, 1865
McLendon, Moses G. Private	Unk	May 10, 1862, Cartersville, Georgia	Co. K, 60th Georgia Infantry	May 20, 1864, Spotsylvania Court House, Virginia	Point Lookout, Maryland, transferred to Elmira Prison, NY, July 3, 1864	Oath of Allegiance June 30, 1865
McLeod, Daniel Private	33	April 30, 1862, Hartnett County, North Carolina	Co. C, 36th 2nd North Carolina Artillery	January 15, 1865, Fort Fisher, North Carolina	February 1, 1865, Elmira Prison Camp, New York	Oath of Allegiance June 12, 1865

Name & Rank	Age	Enlisted	Regiment and State	Where Captured	Prison	Remarks
McLeod, Neill Private	Unk	July 15, 1862, Raleigh, North Carolina	Co. E, 3rd North Carolina Infantry	May 12, 1864, Near Spotsylvania County Court House, Virginia	Point Lookout, Maryland, transferred to Elmira Prison, NY, August 14, 1864	Died December 10, 1864 of Pneumonia, Grave No. 1157. Name McCloud on Headstone.
McLeon, W. Private	Unk	June 14, 1861, Valdosta, Georgia	Co. J, 12th Georgia Infantry	May 10, 1864, Spotsylvania Court House, Virginia	Point Lookout, Maryland, transferred to Elmira Prison, NY, July 25, 1864	Exchanged February 13, 1865 at Boulware's wharf on the James River, Virginia
McLeroy, David D. Private	Unk	June 15, 1861, Eatonton, Georgia	Co. G, 12th Georgia Infantry	May 10, 1864, Spotsylvania Court House, Virginia	Point Lookout, Maryland, transferred to Elmira Prison, NY, July 30, 1864	Oath of Allegiance June 16, 1865
McLoud, John B. Private	25	September 2, 1861, Fayetteville, North Carolina	Co. E, 8th North Carolina Infantry	June 1, 1864, Gaines Mill Cold Harbor, Virginia	Point Lookout, Maryland, transferred to Elmira Prison, NY, July 12, 1864	Oath of Allegiance June 30, 1865
Mcloud, Joseph E. Private	18	September 11, 1861, Fayetteville, North Carolina	Co. E, 8th North Carolina Infantry	June 1, 1864, Gaines Mill, Cold Harbor, Virginia	Point Lookout, Maryland, transferred to Elmira Prison, NY, July 17,1864	Oath of Allegiance May 19, 1865
McMahan, Andrew J. Private	Unk	April 27, 1863, Camp Piney, Virginia	Capt. Bryan's Battery Virginia Artillery	July 12, 1864, Near Washington, DC	Old Capital Prison, Washington DC. Transferred to Elmira Prison Camp New York July 25, 1864.	Oath of Allegiance May 17, 1865
McMahan, Walter Sergeant	Unk	July 21, 1861, New Orleans, Louisiana	Co. F, 15th Louisiana Infantry	May 20, 1864, Spotsylvania Court House, Virginia	Point Lookout, Maryland, transferred to Elmira Prison, NY, July 3, 1864	Exchanged February 13, 1865 at Boulware's wharf on the James River, Virginia
McMahon, Patrick Private	22	June 7, 1861, Camp Moore, Louisiana	Co. D, 7th Louisiana Infantry	May 5, 1864, Wilderness, Virginia	Point Lookout, Maryland, transferred to Elmira Prison, NY, August 17, 1864	Oath of Allegiance May 15, 1865

Name & Rank	Age	Enlisted	Regiment and State	Where Captured	Prison	Remarks
McMannus, Jonas P. Private	28	May 17, 1861, Macon, Mississippi	Co. A, 19th Mississippi Infantry	May 10, 1864, Spotsylvania Court House, Virginia	Point Lookout, Maryland, transferred to Elmira Prison, NY, July 3, 1864	Exchanged March 2, 1865 at Akins Landing on the James River, Virginia
McMaster, J. C. Private	Unk	Unknown	Co. G, 57th North Carolina Infantry	May 30, 1864 Mechanicsville, Virginia	Point Lookout, Maryland, transferred to Elmira Prison, NY, July 12, 1864	Exchanged October 29, 1864 on the James River, Virginia
McMasters, Wesley W. Private	29	May 25, 1863, Asheboro, North Carolina	Co. G, 40th Regiment, 3rd North Carolina Artillery	January 15, 1865, Fort Fisher, North Carolina	January 30, 1865 Elmira Prison Camp, New York	Exchanged 3/2/1865, Died of Remittent Fever 3/18/1865 At Jackson Hospital, Richmond, VA, Buried in Hollywood Cemetery, VA
McMellan, Peter Private	31	September 4, 1861, Fayetteville, North Carolina	Co. E, 8th, North Carolina Infantry	June 1, 1864, Gaines Mill Cold Harbor, Virginia	Point Lookout, Maryland, transferred to Elmira Prison, NY, July 12, 1864	Died March 21, 1865 of Chronic Diarrhea, Grave No. 1525
McMellen, Edward W. Private	Unk	June 22, 1861, Wytheville, Virginia	Co. K, 50th Virginia Infantry	May 12, 1864, Spotsylvania Court House, Virginia	Point Lookout, Maryland, transferred to Elmira Prison, NY, August 2, 1864	Oath of Allegiance May 17, 1865
McMichael, Lee Private	18	February 22, 1862, Greensboro, North Carolina	Co. C, 45th North Carolina Infantry	July 12, 1864, Near Washington, DC	Old Capital Prison, Washington DC. Transferred to Elmira Prison Camp New York July 25, 1864.	Oath of Allegiance May 19, 1865
McMichael, W. R. Private	Unk	May 15, 1862, Camp Harris, Tennessee	Co. G, 17th Tennessee Infantry	June 17, 1864, Petersburg, Virginia	Point Lookout, Maryland, transferred to Elmira Prison, NY, July 30, 1864	Exchanged February 25, 1865 at Boulware's or Cox Wharf on the James River, Virginia
McMillan, Daniel Private	16	August 12, 1864, Fort Caswell, Brunswick County, North Carolina	Co. C, 3rd Battalion North Carolina Light Artillery	January 15, 1865, Fort Fisher, North Carolina	February 1, 1865, Elmira Prison Camp, New York	Exchanged February 20, 1865. Died of Unknown Disease on Route to be Exchanged.

Name & Rank	Age	Enlisted	Regiment and State	Where Captured	Prison	Remarks
McMillan, Daniel J. Private	20	March 18, 1862, Fayetteville, North Carolina	Co. D, 51st North Carolina Infantry	June 1, 1864, Cold Harbor, Virginia	Point Lookout, Maryland, transferred to Elmira Prison, NY, July 12, 1864	Died October 21, 1864 of Chronic Diarrhea, Grave No. 874
McMillan, Dugald J. Private	28	May 10, 1861, Bladen County, North Carolina	Co. H, 3rd North Carolina Infantry	May 12, 1864, Near Spotsylvania County Court House, Virginia	Point Lookout, Maryland, transferred to Elmira Prison, NY, August 14, 1864	Exchanged February 20, 1865 at Boulware's wharf on the James River, Virginia
McMillan, Wafford William Private	Unk	August 24, 1861, Habersham County, Georgia	Co. K, 24th Georgia Infantry	June 1, 1864, Cold Harbor, Virginia	Point Lookout, Maryland, transferred to Elmira Prison, NY, July 12, 1864	Died June 29, 1865 of Chronic Diarrhea, Grave No. 2827
McMillon, William M. Sergeant	Unk	May 18, 1861, Lisbon, Virginia	Co. K, 42nd Virginia Infantry	May 12, 1864, Spotsylvania Court House, Virginia	Point Lookout, Maryland, transferred to Elmira Prison, NY, August 2, 1864	Oath of Allegiance June 19, 1865
McMullen, James Civilian	Unk	Unknown	Citizen Guilford County, North Carolina	April 21, 1864, Wilmington, North Carolina	Point Lookout, Maryland, transferred to Elmira Prison, NY, July 25, 1864	Oath of Allegiance June 20, 1865
McMullen, W. Sergeant	28	July 22, 1861, Camp Moore, Louisiana	Co. A, 10th Louisiana Infantry	May 12, 1864, Spotsylvania Court House, Virginia	Point Lookout, Maryland, transferred to Elmira Prison, NY, July 25, 1864	Exchanged February 25, 1865 at Boulware's or Cox Wharf on the James River, Virginia
McMurry, Joseph D. Private	Unk	October 1, 1861, Lauderdale County, Alabama	Co. D, 9th Alabama Infantry	May 23, 1864, North Anna, Virginia	Point Lookout, Maryland, transferred to Elmira Prison, NY, July 23, 1864	Oath of Allegiance May 29, 1865
McMurtrie, Thomas B. Sergeant	Unk	July 1, 1861, Prince William County, Virginia	Co. A, 49th Virginia Infantry	May 30, 1864, Gaines Mill Cold Harbor, Virginia	Point Lookout, Maryland, transferred to Elmira Prison, NY, July 11, 1864	Oath of Allegiance June 19, 1865

Name & Rank	Age	Enlisted	Regiment and State	Where Captured	Prison	Remarks
McNabb, Richard Private	20	March 3, 1862, Madisonville, Tennessee	Co. F, 3rd Tennessee, Lillard's Mounted Infantry	May 17, 1863, Big Black, Mississippi	Point Lookout, Maryland, transferred to Elmira Prison, NY, August 18, 1864	Exchanged October 29, 1864, at Venus Point, Savannah River, GA.
McNair, Daniel P. Private	36	August 8, 1863, Robeson County, North Carolina	3rd Co. B, 36th Regiment North Carolina, 2nd Artillery	January 15, 1865, Fort Fisher, North Carolina. Wounded.	January 30, 1865, Elmira Prison Camp, New York	Died March 10, 1865 of Diarrhea, Grave No. 1881
McNair, William A. Private	Unk	February 9, 1863, Selma, Alabama	Co. F, 1st Battalion Alabama Artillery	August 23, 1864, Fort Morgan, Alabama	Steam Press No. 4 New Orleans, Louisiana transferred to Elmira Prison, NY, October 8, 1864.	Died March 18, 1865 of Diarrhea, Grave No. 1733
McNamara, John Private	Unk	March 5, 1861, Mobile, Alabama	Co. A, 1st Battalion Alabama Artillery	August 23, 1864, Fort Morgan, Alabama	New Orleans, Louisiana transferred to Elmira Prison, NY, December 4, 1864.	Oath of Allegiance May 14, 1865
McNamara, Patrick Private	26	June 7, 1861, Camp Moore, New Orleans, Louisiana	Co. C, 7th Louisiana Infantry	May 11, 1864, Spotsylvania Court House, Virginia	Point Lookout, Maryland, transferred to Elmira Prison, NY, August 17, 1864	Exchanged February 13, 1865 at Boulware's wharf on the James River, Virginia
McNaughton, James Private	Unk	Unknown	Co. D, 12th Georgia Infantry	July 24, 1864, Winchester, Virginia	Old Capital Prison, Washington, DC, transferred to Elmira Prison, NY, August 12, 1864	Oath of Allegiance May 29, 1865
McNeal, James A. Private	Unk	January 7, 1864, Mobile, Alabama	Co. E, 1st Battalion Alabama Artillery	August 23, 1864, Fort Morgan, Alabama	Steam Press No. 4, New Orleans, Louisiana transferred to Elmira Prison, NY, October 8, 1864.	Died December 20, 1864 of Chronic Diarrhea, Grave No. 1078
McNeal, James A. Private	Unk	April 5, 1864, Raleigh, North Carolina	Co. G, 12th North Carolina Infantry	May 20, 1864, Spotsylvania Court House, Virginia	Point Lookout, Maryland, transferred to Elmira Prison, NY, July 3, 1864	Exchanged March 2, 1865 at Akins Landing on the James River, Virginia

Name & Rank	Age	Enlisted	Regiment and State	Where Captured	Prison	Remarks
McNeal, James P. Private	Unk	September 18, 1862, Pike County, Alabama	Co. B, 3rd Alabama Infantry	May 20, 1864, Spotsylvania Court House, Virginia	Point Lookout, Maryland, transferred to Elmira Prison, NY, July 3, 1864	Oath of Allegiance June 30, 1865
McNeely, Robert Corporal	Unk	September 6, 1862, Coosa, Alabama	Co. E, 1st Battalion Alabama Artillery	August 23, 1864, Fort Morgan, Alabama	New Orleans, Louisiana transferred to Elmira Prison, NY, December 4, 1864.	Oath of Allegiance May 29, 1865
McNeese, William T. Private	22	July 13, 1861, Jacksonville, Florida	Co. J, 2nd Florida Infantry	May 12, 1864, Spotsylvania Court House, Virginia	Point Lookout, Maryland, transferred to Elmira Prison, NY, August 12, 1864	Died March 14, 1865 of Pneumonia, Grave No. 2433
McNeil, Franklin Purcell Private	18	April 22, 1863, Robeson County, North Carolina	Co. D, 1st Battalion North Carolina Heavy Artillery	January 15, 1865, Fort Fisher, North Carolina	February 1, 1865, Elmira Prison Camp, New York	Oath of Allegiance June 26, 1865
McNellis, Frank Corporal	26	June 25, 1861, New Orleans, Louisiana	Co. G, 14th Louisiana Infantry	May 12, 1864, Spotsylvania Court House, Virginia	Point Lookout, Maryland, transferred to Elmira Prison, NY, July 25, 1864	Oath of Allegiance March 6, 1865
McPeak, Bluford Private	Unk	June 22, 1861, Wytheville, Virginia	Co. K, 50th Virginia Infantry	May 12, 1864, Spotsylvania Court House, Virginia	Point Lookout, Maryland, transferred to Elmira Prison, NY, August 2, 1864	Exchanged October 29, 1864, at Venus Point, Savannah River, GA.
McPherson, Coleman Private	21	April 26, 1861, Columbus County, North Carolina	Co. D, 20th North Carolina Infantry	May 12, 1864, Near Spotsylvania Court House, Virginia	Point Lookout Prison, Maryland. Transferred to Elmira Prison Camp New York August 14, 1864.	Oath of Allegiance June 14, 1865
McPherson, Edgar P. Corporal	18	June 1, 1861, Richmond County, North Carolina	Co. F, 18th North Carolina Infantry	May 12, 1864, Spotsylvania Court House, Virginia	Point Lookout, Maryland, transferred to Elmira Prison, NY, August 6, 1864	Oath of Allegiance June 21, 1865

Name & Rank	Age	Enlisted	Regiment and State	Where Captured	Prison	Remarks
McPherson, Edward Private	22	April 26, 1861, Columbus County, North Carolina	Co. D, 20th North Carolina Infantry	May 12, 1864, Near Spotsylvania Court House, Virginia	Point Lookout Prison, Maryland. Transferred to Elmira Prison Camp New York August 14, 1864.	Exchanged October 29, 1864, at Venus Point, Savannah River, GA.
McPherson, John Private	Unk	July 2, 1861, New Orleans, Louisiana	Co. H, 15th Louisiana Infantry	May 12, 1864, Spotsylvania Court House, Virginia	Point Lookout, Maryland, transferred to Elmira Prison, NY, July 25, 1864	Exchanged February 13, 1865 at Boulware's wharf on the James River, Virginia
McPhual, Timothy D. Sergeant	19	March 1, 1862, R. Bridge, Lumberton, North Carolina	Co. D, 51st North Carolina Infantry	May 31, 1864 Cold Harbor, Virginia	Point Lookout, Maryland, transferred to Elmira Prison, NY, July 12, 1864	Oath of Allegiance June 14, 1865
McQuage, Alexander Private	18	February 27, 1863, Hansen County, North Carolina	Co. B, 31st North Carolina Infantry	June 1, 1864, Cold Harbor, Virginia	Transferred From Point Lookout Prison, MD, July 12, 1864. Train Never Arrived at Elmira Prison Camp, NY.	Died July 15, 1864 in Train Wreck at Shohola, Pennsylvania.
McQueen, Daniel M. Private	16	Unknown	Co. E, 40th Regiment, 3rd North Carolina Artillery	January 15, 1865, Fort Fisher, North Carolina	February 1, 1865, Elmira Prison Camp, New York	Died February 22, 1865 of Chronic Diarrhea, Grave No. 2243
McQueen, William M. Private	Unk	January 29, 1864, Notasulga, Alabama	Co. C, 1st Battalion Alabama Artillery	August 23, 1864, Fort Morgan, Alabama	New Orleans, Louisiana transferred to Elmira Prison, NY, December 4, 1864.	Exchanged February 13, 1865 at Boulware's wharf on the James River, Virginia.
McRae, Charles Sergeant	21	October 17, 1861, Marlboro District, South Carolina	Co. G, 23rd South Carolina Infantry	June 17, 1864, Near Petersburg, Virginia	Point Lookout, Maryland, transferred to Elmira Prison, NY, July 30, 1864	Exchanged October 29, 1864, at Venus Point, Savannah River, GA.
McRae, James Private	18	September 15, 1862, Camp Mangum, Raleigh, North Carolina	Co. B, 31st North Carolina Infantry	June 1, 1864, Cold Harbor, Virginia	Point Lookout, Maryland, transferred to Elmira Prison, NY, July 12, 1864	Exchanged March 10, 1865 at Boulware's Wharf on the James River, Virginia

Name & Rank	Age	Enlisted	Regiment and State	Where Captured	Prison	Remarks
McRae, V. A. Private	Unk	March 1, 1864, Wilmington, North Carolina	Co. E, 7th South Carolina Cavalry	June 13, 1864, Malvern Hill, Virginia	Point Lookout, Maryland, transferred to Elmira Prison, NY, July 30, 1864	Died March 11, 1865 of Pneumonia, Grave No. 1856
McRary, Franklin Private	21	July 8, 1862, Pfafftown, North Carolina	Co. J, 33rd North Carolina Infantry	May 6, 1864, Wilderness, Virginia	Old Capital Prison, Washington, DC, transferred to Elmira Prison, NY, July 14, 1864	Oath of Allegiance June 23, 1865
McSwain, John E. Private	Unk	March 24, 1861, Eastville, Alabama	Co. E, 13th Alabama Infantry	May 12, 1864, Spotsylvania Court House, Virginia	Point Lookout, Maryland, transferred to Elmira Prison, NY, August 2, 1864	Died April 13, 1865 of Pneumonia, Grave No. 2696
McVea, Thomas S. Private	Unk	Unknown	Co. J, 3rd Louisiana Cavalry	August 25, 1864, Near Clinton, Louisiana	New Orleans, LA, Transferred to Elmira Prison, NY, November 19, 1864	Exchanged February 13, 1865 at Boulware's wharf on the James River, Virginia
McVeigh, J. Milton Private	Unk	July 17, 1862, Charlottesville, Virginia	Co. F, 35th Battalion Virginia Cavalry	July 18, 1864, Percersville, Loudoun County, Virginia	Old Capital Prison, Washington, DC, transferred to Elmira Prison, NY, August 12, 1864	Exchanged October 29, 1864, at Venus Point, Savannah River, GA.
McVeigh, Joseph Private	Unk	Unknown	Co. H, 1st South Carolina Infantry	July 10, 1863, Morris Island, South Carolina	Point Lookout, Maryland, transferred to Elmira Prison, NY, August 18, 1864	Exchanged October 29, 1864, at Venus Point, Savannah River, GA.
McWaters, Jesse Private	Unk	January 14, 1862, Camp Hampton, South Carolina	Co. D, 17th South Carolina Infantry	July 30, 1864, Petersburg, Virginia	Point Lookout, Maryland, transferred to Elmira Prison, NY, August 12, 1864	Died November 9, 1864 of Pneumonia, Grave No. 834
McWaters, John Private	Unk	July 11, 1862, Camp Simmons, South Carolina	Co. D, 17th South Carolina Infantry	July 30, 1864, Petersburg, Virginia	Point Lookout, Maryland, transferred to Elmira Prison, NY, August 12, 1864	Died April 11, 1865 of Chronic Diarrhea, Grave No. 2676. Name McWalters on Headstone.

Name & Rank	Age	Enlisted	Regiment and State	Where Captured	Prison	Remarks
McWaters, William L. Sergeant	42	January 14, 1862, Camp Hampton, South Carolina	Co. D, 17th South Carolina Infantry	July 30, 1864, Petersburg, Virginia	Point Lookout, Maryland, transferred to Elmira Prison, NY, August 12, 1864	Exchanged February 20, 1865 at Boulware's or Cox Wharf on the James River, Virginia
McWatters, Ansil Private	Unk	January 14, 1862, Camp Hampton, South Carolina	Co. D, 17th South Carolina Infantry	July 30, 1864, Petersburg, Virginia	Point Lookout, Maryland, transferred to Elmira Prison, NY, August 12, 1864	Died February 20, 1865 of Variola (Smallpox), Grave No. 834. No Grave in Woodlawn Cemetery.
McWatters, Jesse Private	Unk	January 14, 1862, Camp Hampton, South Carolina	Co. D, 17th South Carolina Infantry	July 30, 1864, Petersburg, Virginia	Point Lookout, Maryland, transferred to Elmira Prison, NY, August 12, 1864	Died November 9, 1864 of Pneumonia, Grave No. 834. Name John on Headstone.
McWatters, John Private	Unk	July 11, 1862, Camp Simmons, South Carolina	Co. D, 17th South Carolina Infantry	July 30, 1864, Petersburg, Virginia	Point Lookout, Maryland, transferred to Elmira Prison, NY, August 12, 1864	Died April 11, 1865 of Chronic Diarrhea, Grave No. 2676
McWatters, Sumpter M. Private	Unk	January 14, 1862, Camp Hampton, South Carolina	Co. D, 17th South Carolina Infantry	July 30, 1864, Petersburg, Virginia	Point Lookout, Maryland, transferred to Elmira Prison, NY, August 12, 1864	Oath of Allegiance June 21, 1865
McWatters, William Private	Unk	February 12, 1864, Green Pond, South Carolina	Co. H, 18th South Carolina Infantry	July 30, 1864, Petersburg, Virginia	Point Lookout, Maryland, transferred to Elmira Prison, NY, August 12, 1864	Exchanged October 29, 1864, at Venus Point, Savannah River, GA.
McWilliams, William Private	Unk	April 18, 1864, Rudes Hill, Virginia	Co. B, 2nd Virginia Infantry	May 12, 1864, Near Spotsylvania Court House, Virginia	Point Lookout, Maryland, transferred to Elmira Prison, NY, August 6, 1864	Oath of Allegiance June 14, 1865
Meacham, Jackson Private	31	July 1, 1862, Rockingham, North Carolina	Co. K, 33rd North Carolina Infantry	May 6, 1864, Wilderness, Virginia	Old Capital Prison, Washington, DC, transferred to Elmira Prison, NY, July 14, 1864	Transferred for Exchange October 31, 1864. Nothing Further.

Name & Rank	Age	Enlisted	Regiment and State	Where Captured	Prison	Remarks
Meacham, John A. Private	22	April 15, 1861, Pittsboro, North Carolina	Co. J, 32nd North Carolina Infantry	May 10, 1864, Near Spotsylvania Court House, Virginia	Point Lookout, Maryland, transferred to Elmira Prison, NY, July 23, 1864	Exchanged March 14, 1864 on the James River, Virginia
Meacham, Robert C. Private	22	March 8, 1862, Richmond County, North Carolina	Co. E, 52nd North Carolina Infantry	July 14, 1863, Falling Waters, Maryland	Point Lookout, Maryland, transferred to Elmira Prison, NY, August 18, 1864	Transferred for Exchanged 10/29/64 at Venus Point, Savannah River, GA.
Meador, John A. Private	24	July 24, 1861, Bedford County, Virginia	Co. F, 58th Virginia Infantry	May 20, 1864, Spotsylvania Court House, Virginia	Point Lookout, Maryland, transferred to Elmira Prison, NY, July 3, 1864	Exchanged March 10, 1865 at Boulware's Wharf on the James River, Virginia
Meadow, Western A. Private	Unk	December 23, 1861, Camp Trousdale, Tennessee	Co. C, 44th Tennessee Infantry	June 17, 1864, Petersburg, Virginia	Point Lookout, Maryland, transferred to Elmira Prison, NY, July 23, 1864	Died March 16, 1865 of Pneumonia, Grave No. 1686
Meadows, Alen P. Private	Unk	February 22, 1863, Centerville, Virginia	Co. F, 26th Battalion Virginia Infantry	June 3, 1864, Gaines Farm Cold Harbor, Virginia	Point Lookout, Maryland, transferred to Elmira Prison, NY, July 17, 1864	Died October 19, 1864 of Chronic Diarrhea, Grave No. 529
Meadows, James W. Private	Unk	December 2, 1863, Cartersville, Georgia	Co. C, 64th Georgia Infantry	August 16, 1864, New Market, Virginia	Old Capital Prison, Washington, DC transferred to Elmira Prison, NY, August 29, 1864	Exchanged March 14, 1865 at Boulware's Wharf on the James River, Virginia
Meadows, James W. Corporal	Unk	April 29, 1862, White Sulfur Springs, Virginia	Co. F, 26th Battalion Virginia Infantry	June 3, 1864, Gaines Farm Cold Harbor, Virginia	Point Lookout, Maryland, transferred to Elmira Prison, NY, July 17, 1864	Oath of Allegiance July 3, 1865
Meadows, John H. Private	21	July 10, 1861, Halifax County, North Carolina	Co. I, 5th North Carolina Infantry	May 12, 1864, Spotsylvania Court House, Virginia	Point Lookout, Maryland, transferred to Elmira Prison, NY, August 6, 1864	Died March 11, 1865 of Diarrhea and Scurvy, Grave No. 1863

Name & Rank	Age	Enlisted	Regiment and State	Where Captured	Prison	Remarks
Meadows, John M. Private	Unk	January 20, 1864, Mount Pleasant, South Carolina	Co. G, 27th South Carolina Infantry	June 24, 1864, Near Petersburg, Virginia	Point Lookout, Maryland, transferred to Elmira Prison, NY, August 18, 1864	Oath of Allegiance June 19, 1865
Meadows, Raymond Private	19	July 1, 1861, Jacksonville, Onslow County, North Carolina	Co. G, 3rd North Carolina Infantry	May 12, 1864, Near Spotsylvania County Court House, Virginia	Point Lookout, Maryland, transferred to Elmira Prison, NY, August 14, 1864	Died October 20, 1864 of Typhoid Fever, Grave No. 524. Name Ransom Meadows on Headstone.
Meadows, William H. Private	Unk	September 23, 1861, Meadow Bluff, Georgia	Co. F, 13th Georgia Infantry	May 6, 1864, Wilderness, Virginia	Old Capital Prison, Washington, DC, transferred to Elmira Prison, NY, July 14, 1864	Oath of Allegiance June 30, 1865
Meadows, William H. Private	30	April 29, 1862, White Sulfur Springs, Virginia	Co. F, 26th Battalion Virginia Infantry	May 31, 1864, Chickahom-iny, Cold Harbor, Virginia	Point Lookout, Maryland, transferred to Elmira Prison, NY, July 12, 1864	Exchanged March 14, 1865 at Boulware's Wharf on the James River, Virginia
Meadows, William T. Private	Unk	July 9, 1861, Isabella, Worth County, Georgia	Co. F, 14th Georgia Infantry	May 12, 1864, Spotsylvania Court House, Virginia	Point Lookout, Maryland, transferred to Elmira Prison, NY, July 12, 1864	Oath of Allegiance May 17, 1865
Mears, Elihu Private	19	October 19, 1861, Elizabethtown, Bladen County, North Carolina	Co. I, 36th 2nd North Carolina Artillery	January 15, 1865, Fort Fisher, North Carolina	February 1, 1865, Elmira Prison Camp, New York	Oath of Allegiance June 12, 1865
Mears, John L. Private	20	April 25, 1861, Snow Hill, North Carolina	Co. A, 3rd North Carolina Infantry	May 12, 1864, Spotsylvania Court House, Virginia	Point Lookout, Maryland, transferred to Elmira Prison, NY, July 3, 1864	Oath of Allegiance May 29, 1865
Medlen, Daniel Corporal	40	December 28, 1861, Camp Hampton, South Carolina	Co. C, 7th Battalion South Carolina Infantry	August 21, 1864, Weldon Railroad, Near Petersburg, Virginia. Gunshot Wound Face.	DeCamp General Hospital, David's Island New York Harbor.	Died February 3, 1865 of Chronic Diarrhea, Grave No. 1747

Name & Rank	Age	Enlisted	Regiment and State	Where Captured	Prison	Remarks
Medlicott, Samuel R. Private	Unk	March 1, 1864, Camp Hunton, Virginia	Co. C, 24th Virginia Cavalry	July 28, 1864, Petersburg, Virginia	Point Lookout, Maryland, transferred to Elmira Prison, NY, August 12, 1864	Died January 30, 1865 of Variola (Smallpox), Grave No. 1790. Name Midlicott on Headstone.
Medlin, Hawkins Private	26	March 5, 1862, Rolesville, North Carolina	Co. I, 1st North Carolina Infantry	May 30, 1864, Cold Harbor, Virginia	Point Lookout, Maryland, transferred to Elmira Prison, NY, July 12, 1864	Died May 23, 1865 of Pneumonia, Grave No. 2930
Medlin, Henry L. Private	Unk	February 6, 1864, In Regiment, North Carolina	Co. G, 7th North Carolina Infantry	July 29, 1864, Petersburg, Virginia	Point Lookout, Maryland, transferred to Elmira Prison, NY, August 12, 1864	Oath of Allegiance May 29, 1865
Meek, John Sergeant	23	July 25, 1861, Tullahoma, Tennessee	Co. A, 25th Tennessee Infantry	June 17, 1864, Near Petersburg, Virginia	Point Lookout, Maryland, transferred to Elmira Prison, NY, July 30, 1864	Exchanged February 25, 1865 at Boulware's or Cox Wharf on the James River, Virginia
Meeks, Brantley Private	26	February 27, 1863, Wilmington, New Hanover County, North Carolina	Co. D, 1st Battalion North Carolina Heavy Artillery	January 15, 1865, Fort Fisher, North Carolina	February 1, 1865, Elmira Prison Camp, New York	Exchanged March 14, 1865 at Boulware's Wharf on the James River, Virginia
Meeks, D. K. Private	18	April 26, 1862, Jonesboro, Tennessee	Co. D, 63rd Tennessee Infantry	June 17, 1864, Petersburg, Virginia	Point Lookout, Maryland, transferred to Elmira Prison, NY, July 30, 1864	Exchanged February 25, 1865 at Boulware's or Cox Wharf on the James River, Virginia
Meeks, James C. Sergeant	22	August 24, 1861, Banks County, Georgia	Co. A, 24th Georgia Infantry	June 1, 1864, Cold Harbor, Virginia	Point Lookout, Maryland, transferred to Elmira Prison, NY, July 17, 1864	Exchanged 10/29/64, at Venus Point, Savannah River, GA. Died March 21, 1865 of Chronic Diarrhea at Jackson Hospital, Richmond, VA.

Name & Rank	Age	Enlisted	Regiment and State	Where Captured	Prison	Remarks
Meffin, D. B. Private	Unk	Unknown	Co. F, 61st Georgia Infantry	May 12, 1864, Spotsylvania Court House, Virginia	Point Lookout, Maryland, transferred to Elmira Prison, NY, July 30, 1864	Transferred For Exchange October 11, 1864 to Point Lookout Prison Camp, MD. Nothing Further.
Meherds, W. M. Private	Unk	Unknown	Co. K, 59th Alabama Infantry	May 31, 1864, Old Church, Cold Harbor, Virginia	Point Lookout, Maryland, transferred to Elmira Prison, NY, July 11, 1864	Oath of Allegiance May 29, 1865
Meisenheimer, Joseph T. Private	23	August 13, 1861, Concord, North Carolina	Co. F, 33rd North Carolina Infantry	May 6, 1864, Wilderness, Virginia	Point Lookout, Maryland, transferred to Elmira Prison, NY, August 14, 1864	Exchanged February 13, 1865 at Boulware's wharf on the James River, Virginia
Melan, John Private	21	April 1, 1862, New Orleans, Louisiana	Co. K, 14th Louisiana Infantry	May 12, 1864, Spotsylvania Court House, Virginia	Point Lookout, Maryland, transferred to Elmira Prison, NY, July 25, 1864	Oath of Allegiance July 11, 1865
Melcher, V. T. Private	Unk	September 7, 1861, Mount Pleasant, North Carolina	Co. H, 8th North Carolina Infantry	May 31, 1864, Cold Harbor, Virginia	Point Lookout, Maryland, transferred to Elmira Prison, NY, July 12, 1864	Exchanged March 2, 1865 at Akins Landing on the James River, Virginia
Melchor, John V. Private	30	August 8, 1862, Raleigh, North Carolina	Co. B, 5th North Carolina Infantry	May 12, 1864, Spotsylvania Court House, Virginia	Point Lookout, Maryland, transferred to Elmira Prison, NY, August 6, 1864	Oath of Allegiance June 16, 1865
Melgaard, George Sergeant	Unk	October 1, 1861, Millican, Texas	Co. E, 26 Texas Cavalry	May 18, 1864, Marksville, Louisiana	New Orleans, LA, Transferred to Elmira Prison, NY, November 19, 1864	Oath of Allegiance May 15, 1865
Mellichampe, James M. Private	22	February 24, 1862, Charleston, South Carolina	Co. A, 25th South Carolina Infantry	January 15, 1865, Fort Fisher, North Carolina	January 30, 1865, Elmira Prison Camp, New York	Died February 12, 1865 of Pneumonia, Grave No. 2052
Melton, Samuel Private	Unk	July 25, 1861, Delphs Muster Ground, Carroll County, Virginia	Co. C, 29th Virginia Infantry	June 3, 1864, Gaines Mill Cold Harbor, Virginia	Point Lookout, Maryland, transferred to Elmira Prison, NY, July 12, 1864	Exchanged February 20, 1865 at Boulware's or Cox Wharf on the James River, Virginia

Name & Rank	Age	Enlisted	Regiment and State	Where Captured	Prison	Remarks
Melton, W. M. D. Private	Unk	January 25, 1864, Darlington District, South Carolina	Co. G, 21st South Carolina Infantry	June 17, 1864, Petersburg, Virginia	Point Lookout, Maryland, transferred to Elmira Prison, NY, July 30, 1864	Died October 10, 1864 of Pneumonia, Grave No. 690
Melton, William Private	20	April 20, 1861, Columbus, North Carolina	Co. K, 16th North Carolina Infantry	May 24, 1864, North Anna, Virginia	Point Lookout, Maryland, transferred to Elmira Prison, NY, July 25, 1864	Transferred for Exchange 10/11/64. Died 10/23/64 of Unknown Disease at Point Lookout, MD.
Melts, Ransom D. Private	Unk	June 17, 1861, Rocky Mount, Virginia	Co. K, 42nd Virginia Infantry	May 12, 1864, Spotsylvania Court House, Virginia	Point Lookout, Maryland, transferred to Elmira Prison, NY, August 2, 1864	Exchanged February 25, 1865 at Boulware's or Cox Wharf on the James River, Virginia
Melvihil, Patrick Private	29	June 9, 1861, Camp Moore, New Orleans, Louisiana	Co. J, 15th Louisiana Infantry	July 12, 1864, Near Washington, DC	Old Capital Prison, Washington DC. Transferred to Elmira Prison Camp New York July 25, 1864.	Oath of Allegiance May 29, 1865
Melvin, Daniel M. Private	18	January 1, 1862, Wilmington, New Hanover, North Carolina	Co. I, 36th 2nd North Carolina Artillery	January 15, 1865, Fort Fisher, North Carolina	February 1, 1865, Elmira Prison Camp, New York	Died March 18, 1865 of Pneumonia, Grave No. 1716
Melvin, William Private	Unk	March 14, 1863, Alamance County, North Carolina	Co. L, 36th 2nd North Carolina Artillery	January 15, 1865, Fort Fisher, North Carolina	February 1, 1865, Elmira Prison Camp, New York	Died March 8, 1865 of Variola (Smallpox), Grave No. 1710
Melvin, William Marshal Private	Unk	March 14, 1863, Alamance County, North Carolina	Co. J, 36th 2nd North Carolina Artillery	January 15, 1865, Fort Fisher, North Carolina	January 30, 1865, Elmira Prison Camp, New York	Oath of Allegiance July 11, 1865
Menchew, John V. Private	Unk	February 1, 1862, Smithfield, North Carolina	Co. B, 12th Battalion North Carolina Cavalry	September 8, 1863, Big Black, Mississippi	Point Lookout, Maryland, transferred to Elmira Prison, NY, August 18, 1864	Exchanged October 29, 1864, at Venus Point, Savannah River, GA.
Menius, John Private	28	September 6, 1862, Camp Hill, North Carolina	Co. C, 18th North Carolina Infantry	May 12, 1864 Spotsylvania Court House, Virginia	Point Lookout, Maryland, transferred to Elmira Prison, NY, August 6, 1864	Died January 6, 1865 of Pneumonia, Grave No. 1232. Name Menins on Headstone.

Name & Rank	Age	Enlisted	Regiment and State	Where Captured	Prison	Remarks
Menude, John A. Corporal	Unk	March 17, 1862, Charleston, South Carolina	Co. J, 27th South Carolina Infantry	June 24, 1864, Petersburg, Virginia	Point Lookout, Maryland, transferred to Elmira Prison, NY, August 6, 1864	Transferred for Exchange 10/11/64. Died 10/25/64 of Chronic Diarrhea at Point Lookout, MD.
Mercer, Absalum Private	18	May 5, 1864, Fort Caswell, Brunswick County, North Carolina	Co. A, 36th 2nd North Carolina Artillery	January 15, 1865, Fort Fisher, North Carolina	February 1, 1865, Elmira Prison Camp, New York	Died February 20, 1865 of Unknown Disease on Route to be Exchanged.
Mercer, Calvin W. Private	24	May 14, 1862, Fort Caswell, Brunswick County, North Carolina	Co. A, 36th 2nd North Carolina Artillery	January 15, 1865, Fort Fisher, North Carolina	February 1, 1865, Elmira Prison Camp, New York	Exchanged March 2, 1865 at Boulware's Wharf on the James River, Virginia
Mercer, Chancy G. Private	17	January 9, 1864, Fort Caswell, Brunswick County, North Carolina	Co. A, 36th 2nd North Carolina Artillery	January 15, 1865, Fort Fisher, North Carolina	February 1, 1865, Elmira Prison Camp, New York	Died March 11, 1865 of Gangrene of Feet, Grave No. 1839
Mercer, Jesse W. Private	Unk	June 21, 1861, Camp McDonald, Georgia	Co. A, 18th Georgia Infantry	June 1, 1864, Cold Harbor, Virginia	Point Lookout, Maryland, transferred to Elmira Prison, NY, July 17, 1864	Exchanged March 14, 1865 at Boulware's Wharf on the James River, Virginia
Mercer, Lott Private	42	November 6, 1861, Duplin County, North Carolina	Co. A, 36th 2nd North Carolina Artillery	January 15, 1865, Fort Fisher, North Carolina	February 1, 1865, Elmira Prison Camp, New York	Exchanged February 20, 1865 at Boulware's or Cox Wharf on the James River, Virginia
Mercer, Noah J. Private	27	May 14, 1862, Fort Caswell, Brunswick County, North Carolina	Co. A, 36th 2nd North Carolina Artillery	January 15, 1865, Fort Fisher, North Carolina	February 1, 1865, Elmira Prison Camp, New York	Died March 17, 1865 of Typhoid Fever, Grave No. 1696
Mercer, Robert M. Private	25	August 28, 1861, Currituck, North Carolina	Co. B, 8th North Carolina Infantry	May 31, 1864, Cold Harbor, Virginia	Point Lookout, Maryland, transferred to Elmira Prison, NY, July 12,1864	Exchanged October 29, 1864, at Venus Point, Savannah River, GA.

Name & Rank	Age	Enlisted	Regiment and State	Where Captured	Prison	Remarks
Mercer, Saul Private	Unk	January 12, 1864, Petersburg, Virginia	Co. D, 51st North Carolina Infantry	June 1, 1864, Cold Harbor, Virginia	Point Lookout, Maryland, transferred to Elmira Prison, NY, July 12, 1864	Died July 27, 1864 of Chronic Diarrhea, Grave No. 149
Merchant, Joel Private	15	May 26, 1861, Camp Moore, New Orleans, Louisiana	Co. J, 8th Louisiana Infantry	May 12, 1864, Spotsylvania, Virginia. Gunshot Wound Both Legs.	Old Capital Prison, Washington, DC, transferred to Elmira Prison, NY, December 17, 1864	Oath of Allegiance June 30, 1865
Meredith, John Private	34	May 9, 1863, Camp Holmes, North Carolina	Co. D, 7th North Carolina Infantry	May 6, 1864, Wilderness, Virginia	Point Lookout, Maryland, transferred to Elmira Prison, NY, July 23, 1864	Died March 6, 1865 of Pneumonia, Grave No. 2373
Meridith, George W. Private	18	Unknown	Co. A, 44th Virginia Infantry	June 15, 1864, Petersburg, Virginia	Point Lookout, Maryland, transferred to Elmira Prison, NY, July 30, 1864	Oath of Allegiance July 30, 1865
Merkel, Lewis Private	Unk	June 11, 1862, Columbus, Georgia	Co. A, 7th Confederate Cavalry	June 16, 1864, Near Petersburg, Virginia	Point Lookout, Maryland, transferred to Elmira Prison, NY, July 23, 1864	Oath of Allegiance May 15, 1865
Merle, E. Private	Unk	Unknown	Co. D, 2nd Louisiana Cavalry	September 16, 1864, Stones Plantation, Louisiana	New Orleans, LA, Transferred to Elmira Prison, NY, November 19, 1864	Exchanged February 25, 1865 at Boulware's or Cox Wharf on the James River, Virginia
Merricks, Raleigh Edward Private	Unk	July 15, 1861, Giles County Court House, Virginia	Co. D, 7th Virginia Infantry	June 10, 1864, Newton, Virginia	Point Lookout, Maryland, transferred to Elmira Prison, NY, July 25, 1864	Exchanged March 14, 1865 at Boulware's Wharf on the James River, Virginia
Merrit, Alexander Private	Unk	Unknown	Co. A, Captain Norwood's Home Guard Florida	September 27, 1864, Marianna, Florida	New Orleans, Louisiana transferred to Elmira November 19, 1864.	No further Information Available.

Name & Rank	Age	Enlisted	Regiment and State	Where Captured	Prison	Remarks
Merrit, John C. Private	20	June 20, 1861, Abingdon, Virginia	Co. B, 48th Virginia Infantry	May 12, 1864 Spotsylvania Court House, Virginia	Point Lookout, Maryland, transferred to Elmira Prison, NY, August 2, 1864	Exchanged March 14, 1865 at Boulware's Wharf on the James River, Virginia
Merrit, John H. Private	20	June 20, 1861, Abingdon, Virginia	Co. B, 48th Virginia Infantry	May 12, 1864 Spotsylvania Court House, Virginia	Point Lookout, Maryland, transferred to Elmira Prison, NY, August 2, 1864	Died January 9, 1865 of Chronic Diarrhea, Grave No. 1221
Merritt, Asa Private	22	May 16, 1861, Columbia, North Carolina	Co. A, 32nd North Carolina Infantry	May 10, 1864, Near Spotsylvania Court House, Virginia	Point Lookout, Maryland, transferred to Elmira Prison, NY, August 6, 1864	Oath of Allegiance June 27, 1865
Merritt, Benjamin H. Private	20	February 4, 1862 Camp Wyatt, North Carolina	Co. G, 30th North Carolina Infantry	May 13, 1864, Spotsylvania Court House, Virginia	Point Lookout, Maryland, transferred to Elmira Prison, NY, July 3, 1864	Exchanged October 29, 1864, at Venus Point, Savannah River, GA.
Merritt, James D. Private	Unk	July 20, 1863, Georgia	Co. D, Philips' Legion Georgia Infantry	May 23, 1864, Mount Carmel Church, Virginia	Point Lookout, Maryland, transferred to Elmira Prison, NY, July 23, 1864	Oath of Allegiance May 17, 1865
Merritt, John A. Private	20	October 9, 1861, Enfield, Halifax County, North Carolina	Co. F, 36th 2nd North Carolina Artillery	January 15, 1865, Fort Fisher, North Carolina	February 1, 1865, Elmira Prison Camp, New York	Oath of Allegiance June 12, 1865
Merritt, N. B. Private	Unk	February 10, 1864, Prattville, Alabama	Co. C, 1st Battalion Alabama Artillery	August 23, 1864, Fort Morgan, Alabama	New Orleans, Louisiana transferred to Elmira Prison, NY, December 4, 1864.	Oath of Allegiance June 21, 1865
Merritt, Richard D. Private	35	April 21, 1863, Fort Phillips, Brunswick County, North Carolina	Co. E, 36th 2nd North Carolina Artillery	January 15, 1865, Fort Fisher, North Carolina	February 1, 1865, Elmira Prison Camp, New York	Exchanged March 14, 1865 at Boulware's Wharf on the James River, Virginia
Merritt, William Private	46	October 3, 1862, Camp Mangum, Raleigh, North Carolina	Co. B, 31st North Carolina Infantry	May 31, 1864, Cold Harbor, Virginia	Point Lookout, Maryland, transferred to Elmira Prison, NY, July 12, 1864	Died September 20, 1864 of Chronic Diarrhea, Grave No. 342

Name & Rank	Age	Enlisted	Regiment and State	Where Captured	Prison	Remarks
Merritt, William J. Private	21	March 27, 1862, Clinton, North Carolina	Co. B, 51st North Carolina Infantry	June 1, 1864, Cold Harbor, Virginia	Point Lookout, Maryland, transferred to Elmira Prison, NY, July 12, 1864	Exchanged February 20, 1865 at Boulware's or Cox Wharf on the James River, Virginia
Messer, Burrell S. Private	Unk	July 19, 1861, Montgomery, Alabama	Co. D, 13th Alabama Infantry	May 5, 1864, Spotsylvania Court House, Virginia	Point Lookout, Maryland, transferred to Elmira Prison, NY, July 30, 1864	Oath of Allegiance June 19, 1865
Messer, Isaac Private	Unk	April 18, 1861, Waresboro, Georgia	Co. E, 26th Georgia Infantry	May 20, 1864, Spotsylvania Court House, Virginia	Point Lookout, Maryland, transferred to Elmira Prison, NY, July 3, 1864	Oath of Allegiance June 30, 1865
Messer, Newton W. Private	Unk	October 22, 1863, Macon, Georgia	Co. B, 12th Georgia Infantry	May 10, 1864, Spotsylvania Court House, Virginia	Point Lookout, Maryland, transferred to Elmira Prison, NY, July 30, 1864	Exchanged October 29, 1864, at Venus Point, Savannah River, GA.
Messer, Thaddeus. B. Private	18	May 31, 1861, Waynesville, North Carolina	Co. C, 25th North Carolina Infantry	June 2, 1864, Bermuda Hundred, Virginia	Point Lookout, Maryland, transferred to Elmira Prison, NY, July 12, 1864	Exchanged October 29, 1864, at Venus Point, Savannah River, GA.
Messick, Robert C. Private	Unk	May 15, 1862, Camp Harris, Tennessee	Co. G, 17th Tennessee Infantry	June 17, 1864, Petersburg, Virginia	Point Lookout, Maryland, transferred to Elmira Prison, NY, July 30, 1864	Exchanged February 25, 1865 at Boulware's or Cox Wharf on the James River, Virginia
Messingale, James Private	Unk	March 1, 1864, Blakely, Alabama	Co. A, Jackson's 1st Regiment, Tennessee Heavy Artillery	August 23, 1864, Fort Morgan, Alabama	New Orleans, Louisiana transferred to Elmira Prison, NY, December 4, 1864.	Exchanged February 25, 1865 at Boulware's or Cox Wharf on the James River, Virginia
Methvin, Joseph C. Private	Unk	January 8, 1864, Americus, Georgia	Co. H, 64th Georgia Infantry	June 17, 1864, Petersburg, Virginia	Point Lookout, Maryland, transferred to Elmira Prison, NY, July 30, 1864	Died September 25, 1864 of Typhoid Fever, Grave No. 360

Name & Rank	Age	Enlisted	Regiment and State	Where Captured	Prison	Remarks
Metzger, George Private	Unk	October 13, 1861, Mobile, Alabama	Co. A, 21st Alabama Infantry	August 23, 1864, Fort Morgan, Alabama	Steam Press No. 4 New Orleans, Louisiana transferred to Elmira Prison, NY, October 8, 1864.	Oath of Allegiance May 17, 1865
Metzger, W. W. Private	Unk	May 13, 1863, Savannah, Georgia	Co. E, 7th Georgia Cavalry	June 11, 1864, Trevilian Station, Louisa Court House, Virginia	Point Lookout, Maryland, transferred to Elmira Prison, NY, July 25, 1864	Oath of Allegiance July 7, 1865
Michael, Matthew C. Private	Unk	Exact date Unknown, 1864, Monroe Draft, Virginia	Co. F, 26th Battalion, Virginia Infantry	June 3, 1864, Gaines Farm Cold Harbor, Virginia	Point Lookout, Maryland, transferred to Elmira Prison, NY, July 17, 1864	Died October 31, 1864 of Remittent Fever, Grave No. 740. Last Name Mitchell on Headstone.
Michael, Robert H. Corporal	Unk	April 16, 1862, Rudes Hill, Virginia	Co. F, 2nd Virginia Infantry	May 12, 1864, Near Spotsylvania Court House, Virginia	Point Lookout, Maryland, transferred to Elmira Prison, NY, August 6, 1864	Oath of Allegiance June 27, 1865
Michael, William R. Private	18	July 4, 1862, Salisbury, North Carolina	Co. A, 57th North Carolina Infantry	July 12, 1864, Near Washington, DC	Old Capital Prison, Washington DC. Transferred to Elmira Prison Camp New York July 25, 1864.	Exchanged March 14, 1865 at Boulware's Wharf on the James River, Virginia
Michalis, J. H. Private	24	March 15, 1862, Charleston, South Carolina	Co. C, 27th South Carolina Infantry	May 18, 1864, Near Drury's Bluff, Virginia	Point Lookout, Maryland, transferred to Elmira Prison, NY, July 23, 1864	Oath of Allegiance May 21, 1865
Michel, William G. Private	Unk	March 1, 1862, Three Creeks, Arkansas	Co. E, 3rd Arkansas Infantry	May 12, 1864, Spotsylvania Court House, Virginia	Point Lookout, Maryland, transferred to Elmira Prison, NY, July 30, 1864	Exchanged February 25, 1865 at Boulware's or Cox Wharf on the James River, Virginia
Michum, Christopher C. Private	22	August 1, 1861, Covington, Newton County, Georgia	Co. A, Cobb's Legion, Georgia	August 16, 1864, Front Royal, Virginia	Old Capital Prison, Washington, DC transferred to Elmira Prison, NY, August 29, 1864	Exchanged March 14, 1865 at Boulware's Wharf on the James River, Virginia

Name & Rank	Age	Enlisted	Regiment and State	Where Captured	Prison	Remarks
Mickle, Columbus F. Private	18	April 10, 1862, Goldsboro, Wayne County, North Carolina	Co. B, 1st North Carolina Infantry	May 12, 1864, Near Spotsylvania Court House, Virginia	Point Lookout Prison, Maryland. Transferred to Elmira Prison Camp New York August 6, 1864.	Transferred for Exchanged 10/29/64 at Venus Point, Savannah River, GA.
Mickle, Robert Private	Unk	September 18, 1863, Kershaw, South Carolina	Co. J, 6th South Carolina Cavalry	June 11, 1864, Trevilian Station, Louisa Court House, Virginia	Point Lookout, Maryland, transferred to Elmira Prison, NY, July 25, 1864	Exchanged October 29, 1864, at Venus Point, Savannah River, GA.
Mickle, S. T. Private	Unk	January 1, 1862, Camp Lee, Charleston, South Carolina	Co. A, 17th South Carolina Infantry	July 30, 1864, Petersburg, Virginia	Point Lookout, Maryland, transferred to Elmira Prison, NY, August 12, 1864	Oath of Allegiance June 21, 1865
Micund, L. M. Civilian	Unk	Registered Enemy	Citizen of Louisiana	July 27, 1864, New Orleans, Louisiana	New Orleans, Louisiana transferred to Elmira November 19, 1864.	Oath of Allegiance June 20, 1865
Middlebrook, John B. Sergeant	Unk	August 1, 1861, Covington, Georgia	Co. D, 3rd Battalion Georgia Sharp Shooters	August 16, 1864, Front Royal, Virginia	Old Capital Prison, Washington, DC transferred to Elmira Prison, NY, August 29, 1864	Oath of Allegiance May 19, 1865
Middleton, John T. Sergeant	22	July 13, 1861, Camp Anderson, Tennessee	Co. G, 23rd Tennessee Infantry	June 17, 1864, Petersburg, Virginia	Point Lookout, Maryland, transferred to Elmira Prison, NY, July 30, 1864	Exchanged February 25, 1865 at Boulware's or Cox Wharf on the James River, Virginia
Middleton, L. Private	Unk	Unknown	Co. F, 18th North Carolina Infantry	May 10, 1864, Spotsylvania Court House, Virginia	Point Lookout, Maryland, transferred to Elmira Prison, NY, August 6, 1864	Exchanged February 20, 1865 at Boulware's or Cox Wharf on the James River, Virginia.
Middleton, Martin Van Buren Private	27	December 29, 1863, Camden, Alabama	Co. E, 1st Battalion Alabama Artillery	August 23, 1864, Fort Morgan, Alabama	Steam Press No. 4, New Orleans, Louisiana transferred to Elmira Prison, NY, October 8, 1864.	Died December 6, 1864 of Chronic Diarrhea, Grave No. 1192

459

Name & Rank	Age	Enlisted	Regiment and State	Where Captured	Prison	Remarks
Midgett, T. C. Private	Unk	Unknown	Co. E, 66th North Carolina Infantry	September 8, 1863, Big Black, Mississippi	Point Lookout, Maryland, transferred to Elmira Prison, NY, August 18, 1864	Exchanged October 29, 1864, at Venus Point, Savannah River, GA.
Midyett, Daniel Private	Unk	September 9, 1861, Middleton, North Carolina	Co. F, 33rd North Carolina Infantry	May 6, 1864, Wilderness, Virginia	Old Capital Prison, Washington, DC, transferred to Elmira Prison, NY, July 14, 1864	Oath of Allegiance June 23, 1865
Milam, Benjamin K. Sergeant	21	July 27, 1861, Big Island, Virginia	Co. C, 58th Virginia Infantry	May 20, 1864, Spotsylvania Court House, Virginia	Point Lookout, Maryland, transferred to Elmira Prison, NY, July 3, 1864	Oath of Allegiance June 19, 1865
Milby, Hockaday D. Private	Unk	June 2, 1861, Centerville, Virginia	Co. H, 26th Virginia Infantry	June 17, 1864, Near Petersburg, Virginia	Point Lookout, Maryland, transferred to Elmira Prison, NY, July 30, 1864	Died February 1, 1865 of Chronic Diarrhea, Grave No. 1776
Milby, John T. Corporal	Unk	June 2, 1861, Centerville, Virginia	Co. H, 26th North Carolina Infantry	June 17, 1864, Near Petersburg, Virginia	Point Lookout, Maryland, transferred to Elmira Prison, NY, July 30, 1864	Died May 21, 1865 of Chronic Diarrhea, Grave No. 2935
Milby, Richard L. Private	Unk	March 8, 1862, Clarksburg, Virginia	Co. J, 55th Virginia Infantry	May 6, 1864, Wilderness, Virginia	Point Lookout, Maryland, transferred to Elmira Prison, NY, August 14, 1864	Oath of Allegiance June 14, 1865
Miley, George W. Private	24	June 25, 1861, Woodstock, Virginia	Co. F, 10th Virginia Infantry	May 20, 1864, Spotsylvania Court House, Virginia	Point Lookout, Maryland, transferred to Elmira Prison, NY, July 3, 1864	Exchanged February 20, 1865 at Boulware's or Cox Wharf on the James River, Virginia
Millen, G. A. Sergeant	Unk	November 18, 1861, College Green, Columbia, South Carolina	Co. A, 17th South Carolina Infantry	July 30, 1864, Petersburg, Virginia	Point Lookout, Maryland, transferred to Elmira Prison, NY, August 12, 1864	Oath of Allegiance June 30, 1865

Name & Rank	Age	Enlisted	Regiment and State	Where Captured	Prison	Remarks
Miller, A. J. Sergeant	Unk	December 5, 1861, Sac River, St. Clair County, Missouri	Co. B, 1st Missouri Cavalry	May 17, 1863, Big Black Bridge, Champion Hill, Mississippi	Point Lookout, Maryland, transferred to Elmira Prison, NY, August 18, 1864	Exchanged October 29, 1864, at Venus Point, Savannah River, GA.
Miller, A. R. Private	Unk	March 28, 1864, Staunton, Virginia	Co. D, 10th Virginia Infantry	May 12, 1864, Spotsylvania Court House, Virginia	Point Lookout, Maryland, transferred to Elmira Prison, NY, August 2, 1864	Oath of Allegiance June 27, 1865
Miller, Adam J. Private	17	April 6, 1864, Place Unknown	Co. G, 21st North Carolina Infantry	May 13, 1864, Near Fort Darling, Virginia	Point Lookout, Maryland, transferred to Elmira Prison, NY, July 25, 1864	Oath of Allegiance May 29, 1865
Miller, Alexander Private	Unk	February 13, 1862, Washington County, North Carolina	Co. D, 13th Battalion North Carolina Light Artillery	January 15, 1865, Fort Fisher, North Carolina	February 1, 1865, Elmira Prison Camp, New York	Exchanged February 20, 1865 at Boulware's or Cox Wharf on the James River, Virginia
Miller, Alexander B. Private	24	September 23, 1863, Camp Holmes, North Carolina	Co. C, 30th North Carolina Infantry	May 12, 1864, Near Spotsylvania Court House, Virginia	Point Lookout, Maryland, transferred to Elmira Prison, NY, August 14, 1864	Died April 12, 1865 of Pneumonia, Grave No. 2679
Miller, Archibald G. Private	Unk	January 30, 1863, Centerville, Virginia	Co. F, 26th Battalion, Virginia Infantry	June 3, 1864, Gaines Farm Cold Harbor, Virginia	Point Lookout, Maryland, transferred to Elmira Prison, NY, July 17, 1864	Oath of Allegiance May 15, 1865
Miller, Augustus Private	30	May 18, 1861, Edenton, North Carolina	Co. A, 1st North Carolina Infantry	May 12, 1864, Wilderness, Spotsylvania Court House, Virginia	Point Lookout, Maryland, transferred to Elmira Prison, NY, August 6, 1864	Oath of Allegiance June 14, 1865
Miller, Chancy W. Private	17	May 14, 1862, Fort Caswell, Brunswick County, North Carolina	Co. A, 36th 2nd North Carolina Artillery	January 15, 1865, Fort Fisher, North Carolina	February 1, 1865, Elmira Prison Camp, New York	Exchanged February 20, 1865 at Boulware's or Cox Wharf on the James River, Virginia

Name & Rank	Age	Enlisted	Regiment and State	Where Captured	Prison	Remarks
Miller, Charles L. Private	23	April 10, 1862, Harrisonburg, Virginia	Co. C, 10th Virginia Infantry	May 12, 1864, Spotsylvania Court House, Virginia	Point Lookout, Maryland, transferred to Elmira Prison, NY, August 14, 1864	Exchanged October 29, 1864, at Venus Point, Savannah River, GA.
Miller, Clayton Private	Unk	December 5, 1863, Charleston, South Carolina	Co. A, 21st South Carolina Infantry	January 15, 1865, Fort Fisher, North Carolina	January 30, 1865, Elmira Prison Camp, New York	Exchanged February 20, 1865 at Boulware's or Cox Wharf on the James River, Virginia
Miller, D. F. Private	19	August 8, 1862, Statesville, North Carolina	Co. H, 5th North Carolina Infantry	May 12, 1864, Spotsylvania Court House, Virginia	Point Lookout, Maryland, transferred to Elmira Prison, NY, August 6, 1864	Died August 24, 1864 of Typhoid Fever, Grave No. 41
Miller, Daniel Private	Unk	December 5, 1863, Charleston, South Carolina	Co. A, 21st South Carolina Infantry	January 15, 1865, Fort Fisher, North Carolina	January 30, 1865, Elmira Prison Camp, New York	Exchanged February 20, 1865 at Boulware's or Cox Wharf on the James River, Virginia
Miller, E. J. Private	Unk	October 30, 1862, Morris Island, South Carolina	Co. A, 21st South Carolina Infantry	June 24, 1864, Near Petersburg, Virginia	Point Lookout, Maryland, transferred to Elmira Prison, NY, August 18, 1864	Oath of Allegiance July 3, 1865
Miller, Edward C. Private	22	May 14, 1862, Zollicoffer, Sullivan County, Tennessee	Co. F, 63rd Tennessee Infantry	June 17, 1864, Petersburg, Virginia	Point Lookout, Maryland, transferred to Elmira Prison, NY, July 30, 1864	Died September 10, 1864 of Chronic Diarrhea, Grave No. 197
Miller, Edwin R. Private	30	July 26, 1861, Gallatin, Tennessee	Co. A, 23rd Tennessee Infantry	June 17, 1864, Petersburg, Virginia	Point Lookout, Maryland, transferred to Elmira Prison, NY, July 30, 1864	Exchanged February 25, 1865 at Boulware's or Cox Wharf on the James River, Virginia
Miller, Emanuel Private	Unk	March 1, 1864, Kinston, North Carolina	Co. K, 57th North Carolina Infantry	July 10, 1864, Harpers Ferry, Virginia	Old Capital Prison, Washington DC. Transferred to Elmira Prison Camp New York July 25, 1864.	Oath of Allegiance May 29, 1865

Name & Rank	Age	Enlisted	Regiment and State	Where Captured	Prison	Remarks
Miller, George A. Sergeant	22	June 25, 1861, Salisbury, North Carolina	Co. K, 5th North Carolina Infantry	May 12, 1864, Spotsylvania Court House, Virginia	Point Lookout, Maryland, transferred to Elmira Prison, NY, August 6, 1864	Oath of Allegiance June 12, 1865
Miller, George W. Private	Unk	June 23, 1861, Camp Moore, Louisiana	Co. G, 8th Louisiana Infantry	May 12, 1864, Spotsylvania Court House, Virginia	Point Lookout, Maryland, transferred to Elmira Prison, NY, July 12, 1864	Exchanged February 13, 1865 at Boulware's wharf on the James River, Virginia
Miller, George W. Private	Unk	September 14, 1861, Boone, North Carolina	Co. B, 37th North Carolina Infantry	May 12, 1864, Spotsylvania Court House, Virginia	Point Lookout, Maryland, transferred to Elmira Prison, NY, August 12, 1864	Oath of Allegiance June 19, 1865
Miller, H. H. Private	Unk	June 26, 1861, Camp McDonald, Georgia	Co. A, 3rd Battalion Georgia Sharp Shooters	August 16, 1864, Front Royal, Virginia	Old Capital Prison, Washington, DC transferred to Elmira Prison, NY, August 29, 1864	Oath of Allegiance June 16, 1865
Miller, Henry Private	24	June 5, 1861, Memphis, Tennessee	Co. L, 1st Jackson's Tennessee Heavy Artillery	August 23, 1864, Fort Morgan, Alabama.	New Orleans, Louisiana transferred to Elmira Prison, NY, December 4, 1864.	Exchanged March 10, 1865 at Boulware's Wharf on the James River, Virginia
Miller, Henry M. Private	Unk	February 1, 1864, Cedar Bluff, Alabama	Co. H, 48th Alabama Infantry	May 6, 1864, Wilderness, Virginia	Point Lookout, Maryland, transferred to Elmira Prison, NY, August 17, 1864	Died February 3, 1865 of Pneumonia, Grave No. 1759
Miller, Isham Private	20	October 9, 1862, Camp French, North Carolina	Co. A, 26th North Carolina Infantry	May 5, 1864, Wilderness, Virginia	Point Lookout, Maryland, transferred to Elmira Prison, NY, August 6, 1864	Died July 15, 1865 of Unknown Causes, Grave No. 2874. Name Joseph on Headstone.
Miller, J. Ambrose Private	Unk	June 20, 1861, Rockingham, Virginia	Co. C, 11th Virginia Cavalry	September 14, 1863, Near Culpepper Court House, Virginia	Point Lookout, Maryland, transferred to Elmira Prison, NY, August 18, 1864	Died December 15, 1864 of Chronic Diarrhea, Grave No. 1116. Headstone has Isaac A. Miller.

Name & Rank	Age	Enlisted	Regiment and State	Where Captured	Prison	Remarks
Miller, J. L. Private	Unk	Unknown	Co. A, 12th Alabama Infantry	May 20, 1864, Spotsylvania Court House, Virginia	Point Lookout, Maryland, transferred to Elmira Prison, NY, July 3, 1864	Oath of Allegiance June 20, 1865
Miller, James J. Private	29	January 10, 1862, Camp Hampton, Columbia, South Carolina	Co. I, 18th South Carolina Infantry	July 30, 1864, Petersburg, Virginia	Point Lookout, Maryland, transferred to Elmira Prison, NY, August 12, 1864	Exchanged February 13, 1865 at Boulware's wharf on the James River, Virginia
Miller, James M. Private	Unk	April 3, 1864, Newton, North Carolina	Co. F, 23rd North Carolina Infantry	May 12, 1864, Near Spotsylvania Court House, Virginia	Point Lookout, Maryland, transferred to Elmira Prison, NY, August 14, 1864	Exchanged October 29, 1864 at Venus Point, Savannah River, GA.
Miller, James S. Sergeant Major	Unk	April 21, 1861, Richmond, Virginia	Field & Staff, 10th Battalion Virginia Heavy Artillery	April 6, 1865, Sailor's Creek, Virginia	Old Capital Prison, Washington, DC, transferred to Elmira Prison, NY, May 2, 1865.	Oath of Allegiance June 21, 1865
Miller, John Private	Unk	March 25, 1863, Wilmington, North Carolina	Co. G, 22nd South Carolina Infantry	June 15, 1864, Petersburg, Virginia	Point Lookout, Maryland, transferred to Elmira Prison, NY, July 23, 1864	Died January 27, 1865 of Pneumonia, Grave No. 1648
Miller, John Calhoun Private	19	July 4, 1862, Salisbury, North Carolina	Co. A, 57th North Carolina Infantry	July 12, 1864, Near Washington, DC	Old Capital Prison, Washington DC. Transferred to Elmira Prison Camp New York July 25, 1864.	Died February 10, 1865 of Variola (Smallpox), Grave No. 2084. Headstone has Miller, Calhoun
Miller, John F. Private	31	July 16, 1861, Staunton, Virginia	Co. J, 52nd, Virginia Infantry	May 30, 1864, Mechanics-ville, Virginia	Point Lookout, Maryland, transferred to Elmira Prison, NY, July 9, 1864	Died October 2, 1864 of Chronic Diarrhea, Grave No. 623
Miller, John H. Private	Unk	April 14, 1862, Rudes Hill, Virginia	Co. K, 2nd Virginia Infantry	May 12, 1864, Spotsylvania Court House, Virginia	Point Lookout, Maryland, transferred to Elmira Prison, NY, August 2, 1864	Died January 8, 1865 of Typhoid Fever, Grave No. 1501

Name & Rank	Age	Enlisted	Regiment and State	Where Captured	Prison	Remarks
Miller, John T. Private	Unk	March 12 1862, Blacksburg, Virginia	Co. E, 4th Virginia Infantry	May 12, 1864, Near Spotsylvania Court House, Virginia	Point Lookout, Maryland, transferred to Elmira Prison, NY, August 2, 1864	Exchanged February 20, 1865 at Boulware's or Cox Wharf on the James River, Virginia
Miller, John W. Private	36	February 27, 1862, Reidsville, Rockingham County, North Carolina	Co. G, 45th North Carolina Infantry	May 10, 1864, Spotsylvania Court House, Virginia	Point Lookout, Maryland, transferred to Elmira Prison, NY, August 6, 1864	Transferred for Exchange 10/11/64. Died 11/3/64 of Chronic Diarrhea at Point Lookout, MD.
Miller, Jonathan Private	32	April 18, 1861, Martinsburg, Virginia	Co. D, 2nd Virginia Infantry	May 12, 1864, Near Spotsylvania Court House, Virginia	Point Lookout, Maryland, transferred to Elmira Prison, NY, August 6, 1864	Oath of Allegiance May 17, 1865
Miller, N. Private	Unk	Unknown	Co. A, Captain Jones' Home Guard Florida	September 27, 1864, Marianna, Florida	New Orleans, Louisiana transferred to Elmira November 19, 1864.	Died March 13, 1865 of Chronic Diarrhea, Grave No. 1828
Miller, Nathanial W. Private	32	July 18, 1862, Camp Hill, North Carolina	Co. F, 18th North Carolina Infantry	May 12, 1864, Spotsylvania Court House, Virginia	Point Lookout, Maryland, transferred to Elmira Prison, NY, July 17, 1864	Died October 11, 1864 of Chronic Diarrhea, Grave No. 694
Miller, Noah Private	Unk	April 16, 1862, Rudes Hill, Virginia	Co. K, 2nd Virginia Infantry	May 12, 1864, Spotsylvania Court House, Virginia	Old Capital Prison, Washington DC, transferred to Elmira Prison, NY, July 30, 1864	Oath of Allegiance June 30, 1865
Miller, Robert J. Private	32	February 15, 1862, Warsaw, North Carolina	Co. B, 51st North Carolina Infantry	June 1, 1864, Cold Harbor, Virginia	Point Lookout, Maryland, transferred to Elmira Prison, NY, July 12, 1864	Transferred for Exchange October 11, 1864. Died October 23, 1864 of Chronic Diarrhea at Point Lookout, MD
Miller, Robert W. Sergeant Major	Unk	December 7, 1861, Lebanon, Tennessee	Field and Staff, Jackson's 1st Regiment, Tennessee Heavy Artillery	August 23, 1864, Fort Morgan, Alabama	New Orleans, Louisiana transferred to Elmira Prison, NY, December 4, 1864.	Exchanged March 10, 1865 at Boulware's Wharf on the James River, Virginia

Name & Rank	Age	Enlisted	Regiment and State	Where Captured	Prison	Remarks
Miller, Rufus Private	32	October 6, 1862, Camp Holmes, Newton, North Carolina	Co. E, 32nd North Carolina Infantry	May 10, 1864, Wilderness, Virginia	Point Lookout, Maryland, transferred to Elmira Prison, NY, August 6, 1864	Oath of Allegiance May 17, 1865
Miller, Samuel Private	Unk	April 16, 1862, Rudes Hill, Virginia	Co. K, 2nd Virginia Infantry	May 12, 1864, Spotsylvania Court House, Virginia	Point Lookout, Maryland, transferred to Elmira Prison, NY, August 2, 1864	Died June 28, 1865 of Chronic Diarrhea, Grave No. 2825
Miller, Theodore Private	18	September 10, 1862, Garysburg, North Carolina	Co. C, 3rd North Carolina Cavalry	May 28, 1864, Madison County, Virginia. Gunshot Wound Left Lung.	Old Capital Prison, Washington, DC transferred to Elmira Prison, NY, August 27, 1864	Exchanged February 20, 1865 at Boulware's or Cox Wharf on the James River, Virginia
Miller, William Private	35	May 27, 1861, New Orleans, Louisiana	Co. G, 14th Louisiana Infantry	May 20, 1864, Spotsylvania Court House, Virginia	Point Lookout, Maryland, transferred to Elmira Prison, NY, July 3, 1864	Exchanged March 10, 1865 at Boulware's Wharf on the James River, Virginia
Miller, William Private	Unk	April 16, 1862, Rudes Hill, Virginia	Co. E, 2nd Virginia Infantry	May 20, 1864, Spotsylvania Court House, Virginia	Point Lookout, Maryland, transferred to Elmira Prison, NY, July 3, 1864	Oath of Allegiance June 30, 1865
Miller, William Marshall Private	25	July 23, 1861, Matthews Court House, Virginia	Co. F, 5th Virginia Cavalry	May 11, 1864, Yellow Tavern, Hanover County, Virginia	Point Lookout, Maryland, transferred to Elmira Prison, NY, August 17, 1864	Oath of Allegiance June 19, 1865
Miller, William P. Corporal	19	October 1, 1862, Zollicoffer, Tennessee	Co. F, 63rd Tennessee Infantry	June 17, 1864, Petersburg, Virginia	Point Lookout, Maryland, transferred to Elmira Prison, NY, July 30, 1864	Exchanged October 29, 1864 at Venus Point, Savannah River, GA.
Miller, Wilson C. Private	18	September 15, 1862, Port Hudson, Louisiana	Captain Youngblood's Confederate States Signal Corps	October 6, 1864, Near Hampton's Ferry, Louisiana	New Orleans, Louisiana transferred to Elmira November 19, 1864.	Exchanged February 20, 1865 at Boulware's or Cox Wharf on the James River, Virginia
Millican, Francis O. Sergeant	26	March 5, 1862, Wilmington, New Hanover County, North Carolina	Co. E, 36th 2nd North Carolina Artillery	January 15, 1865, Fort Fisher, North Carolina	February 1, 1865, Elmira Prison Camp, New York	Died March 16, 1865 of Chronic Diarrhea, Grave No. 1676

Name & Rank	Age	Enlisted	Regiment and State	Where Captured	Prison	Remarks
Millican, Robert A. Private	Unk	February 22, 1862, Subligna, Georgia	Co. J, 35th Georgia Infantry	May 6, 1864, Wilderness, Virginia	Point Lookout, Maryland, transferred to Elmira Prison, NY, August 14, 1864	Oath of Allegiance June 23, 1865
Millican, Sanders Private	Unk	February 2, 1862, Whiteville, North Carolina	Co. H, 51st North Carolina Infantry	June 1, 1864, Cold Harbor, Virginia	Point Lookout, Maryland, transferred to Elmira Prison, NY, July 12, 1864	Died August 1, 1864 of Chronic Diarrhea, Grave No. 145 Name on Headstone S. S. Wilkins.
Milligan, John Sergeant	Unk	October 13, 1861, Mobile, Alabama	Co. A, 21st Alabama Infantry	August 23, 1864, Fort Morgan, Alabama	Steam Press No. 4 New Orleans, Louisiana transferred to Elmira Prison, NY, October 8, 1864.	Exchanged March 14, 1865 at Boulware's Wharf on the James River, Virginia
Milliken, Isaac Sergeant	23	September 12, 1861, Smithville, Brunswick County, North Carolina	Co. C, 30th North Carolina Infantry	May 12, 1864, Near Spotsylvania Court House, Virginia	Point Lookout, Maryland, transferred to Elmira Prison, NY, August 14, 1864	Oath of Allegiance June 23, 1865
Mills, James M. Private	Unk	August 21, 1861, Fredericksburg, Virginia	Captain Cooper's Battery Virginia Light Artillery	September 19, 1863, Taylorsville, Virginia	Old Capital Prison, Washington, DC, transferred to Elmira Prison, NY, August 12, 1864	Oath of Allegiance May 17, 1865
Mills, James N. Corporal	Unk	May 31, 1861, Yellow Branch, Virginia	Co. D, 42nd Virginia Infantry	May 12, 1864, Near Spotsylvania Court House, Virginia	Point Lookout, Maryland, transferred to Elmira Prison, NY, August 6, 1864	Oath of Allegiance June 27, 1865
Mills, John H. Private	41	April 16, 1862, Old Brunswick, North Carolina	Co. G, 36th 2nd North Carolina Artillery	January 15, 1865, Fort Fisher, North Carolina	February 1, 1865, Elmira Prison Camp, New York	Exchanged March 2, 1865 at Boulware's Wharf on the James River, Virginia
Mills, John M. Private	Unk	April 6, 1863, Columbus, Georgia	Co. B, 64th Georgia Infantry	August 18, 1864, New Market, Virginia	Old Capital Prison, Washington, DC transferred to Elmira Prison, NY, August 27, 1864	Died February 13, 1865 of Typhoid Fever, Grave No. 2033

Name & Rank	Age	Enlisted	Regiment and State	Where Captured	Prison	Remarks
Mills, John R. Private	Unk	March 4, 1862, Fort Gaines, Georgia	Co. E, 51st Georgia Infantry	June 3, 1864, Gaines Farm Cold Harbor, Virginia	Point Lookout Prison, Maryland Transferred July 12, 1864 to Elmira, New York	Oath of Allegiance June 23, 1865
Mills, M. J. Private	Unk	March 23, 1863, Camden, Arkansas	Co. E, 3rd Arkansas Infantry	May 12, 1864, Spotsylvania Court House, Virginia	Point Lookout, Maryland, transferred to Elmira Prison, NY, July 30, 1864	Died September 20, 1864 of Pneumonia, Grave No. 349
Mills, Rufus A. Sergeant	21	June 10, 1861, Rowan Mills, Iredell County, North Carolina	Co. B, 4th North Carolina Infantry	July 9, 1864, Harpers Ferry, Virginia	Old Capital Prison, Washington DC. Transferred to Elmira Prison Camp New York July 25, 1864.	Oath of Allegiance May 29, 1865
Mills, Samuel C. Private	Unk	March 11, 1862, Lynchburg, Virginia	Co. D, 42nd Virginia Infantry	May 12, 1864, Near Spotsylvania Court House, Virginia	Point Lookout, Maryland, transferred to Elmira Prison, NY, August 6, 1864	Oath of Allegiance June 27, 1865
Mills, T. B. Corporal	Unk	August 27, 1861, Columbia, South Carolina	Co. F, 13th South Carolina Infantry	July 29, 1864, Petersburg, Virginia	Point Lookout, Maryland, transferred to Elmira Prison, NY, August 12, 1864	Died May 9, 1865 of Chronic Diarrhea, Grave No. 2781. Mills, F. B. & 12th SC on Headstone.
Mills, Timothy W. Private	20	June 1, 1861, Dogwood Grove, North Carolina	Co. K, 3rd North Carolina Infantry	May 12, 1864, Near Spotsylvania County Court House, Virginia	Point Lookout, Maryland, transferred to Elmira Prison, NY, August 14, 1864	Oath of Allegiance June 27, 1865
Millsaps, Jesse Private	24	July 15, 1862, Raleigh, North Carolina	Co. I, 5th North Carolina Infantry	May 12, 1864, Spotsylvania Court House, Virginia	Point Lookout, Maryland, transferred to Elmira Prison, NY, August 6, 1864	Exchanged October 29, 1864 at Venus Point, Savannah River, GA.
Milne, James T. Private	Unk	June 14, 1861, Veldosta, Georgia	Co. I, 12th Georgia Infantry	May 10, 1864, Spotsylvania Court House, Virginia	Point Lookout, Maryland, transferred to Elmira Prison, New York, July 25, 1864	Oath of Allegiance, June 16, 1864

Name & Rank	Age	Enlisted	Regiment and State	Where Captured	Prison	Remarks
Milton, John L. Private	Unk	June 2, 1862, Luray, Virginia	Co. K, 10th Virginia Infantry	May 12, 1864, Spotsylvania Court House, Virginia	Point Lookout, Maryland, transferred to Elmira Prison, NY, August 2, 1864	Died April 12, 1865 of Chronic Diarrhea, Grave No. 2690
Mims, Fletcher Sergeant	Unk	April 11, 1862, Coles Island, South Carolina	Co. G, 27th South Carolina Infantry	June 24, 1864, Near Petersburg, Virginia	Point Lookout, Maryland, transferred to Elmira Prison, NY, August 18, 1864	Oath of Allegiance June 16, 1865
Mims, William H. Private	26	August 11, 1862, Pittsboro, North Carolina	Co. D, 61st North Carolina Infantry	August 27, 1863, Battery Wagner, Morris Island, South Carolina	Point Lookout, Maryland, transferred to Elmira Prison, NY, August 18, 1864	Exchanged October 29, 1864 at Venus Point, Savannah River, GA.
Mince, John H. Private	38	July 15, 1861, Wilmington, North Carolina	Co. C, 8th North Carolina Infantry	June 1, 1864, Cold Harbor, Virginia	Point Lookout Prison Camp, Maryland. Transferred to Elmira Prison, July 17, 1864	Died March 8, 1865 of Diarrhea, Grave No. 2417
Mincey, Jesse Private	19	May 27, 1862, Goldsboro, North Carolina	Co. H, 2nd North Carolina Infantry	July 8, 1864, Harpers Ferry, Virginia	Old Capital Prison, Washington DC. Transferred to Elmira Prison Camp New York July 25, 1864.	Exchanged March 14, 1865 at Boulware's Wharf on the James River, Virginia
Mincy, Patrick Private	Unk	November 17, 1861, Camp Green, James Island, South Carolina	Co. H, 23rd South Carolina Infantry	June 17, 1864, Near Petersburg, Virginia	Point Lookout, Maryland, transferred to Elmira Prison, NY, July 30, 1864	Exchanged March 14, 1865 at Boulware's Wharf on the James River, Virginia
Mine, James T. Private	Unk	June 14, 1861, Valdosta, Georgia	Co. J, 12th Georgia Infantry	May 10, 1864, Spotsylvania Court House, Virginia	Point Lookout, Maryland, transferred to Elmira Prison, NY, July 25, 1864	Oath of Allegiance June 16, 1865
Miner, E. R. Private	Unk	Unknown	Co. F, 58th Virginia Infantry	June 4, 1864, Old Church Cold Harbor, Virginia	Point Lookout, Maryland, transferred to Elmira Prison, NY, July 12, 1864	Oath of Allegiance July 3, 1865

Name & Rank	Age	Enlisted	Regiment and State	Where Captured	Prison	Remarks
Miner, Jesse Private	Unk	November 6, 1863, Mobile, Alabama	Co. E, 1st Battalion Alabama Artillery	August 23, 1864, Fort Morgan, Alabama	Steam Press No. 4, New Orleans, Louisiana transferred to Elmira Prison, NY, October 8, 1864.	Died January 28, 1865 of Variola (Smallpox), Grave No. 1809
Miner, L. M. Sergeant	Unk	July 17, 1863, Carrollton, Alabama	Co. J, 7th Alabama Cavalry	July 23, 1864, Swan's Plantation, Louisiana	New Orleans, LA, Transferred to Elmira Prison, NY, November 19, 1864	Died February 14, 1865 of Chronic Diarrhea, Grave No. 2167
Mink, Colley Private	Unk	Unknown	Co. B, 48th Virginia Infantry	May 12, 1864, Spotsylvania Court House, Virginia	Point Lookout Prison Camp, Maryland. Transferred to Elmira Prison, NY, August 2, 1864	Died March 8, 1865 Remittent Fever, Grave No. 2384
Mink, Wiley P. Private	Unk	February 16, 1862, Scottsville, Alabama	Co. C, 1st Battalion Alabama Artillery	August 23, 1864, Fort Morgan, Alabama	New Orleans, Louisiana transferred to Elmira Prison, December 4, 1864.	Oath of Allegiance June 7, 1865
Minner, Isaac Private	Unk	September 18, 1863, Camp Sam Jones, Virginia	Co. F, 26th Battalion, Virginia Infantry	May 31, 1864, Chickahom-iny, Cold Harbor, Virginia	Point Lookout, Maryland, transferred to Elmira Prison, NY, July 12, 1864	Exchanged October 29, 1864 at Venus Point, Savannah River, GA.
Minnick, James C. Private	Unk	June 25, 1861, Winchester, Virginia	Co. D, 10th Virginia Infantry	May 12, 1864, Spotsylvania Court House, Virginia	Point Lookout, Maryland, transferred to Elmira Prison, NY, August 2, 1864	Transferred for Exchanged 10/29/64 at Venus Point, Savannah River, GA.
Minor, M. Private	19	July 15, 1862, Mocksville, North Carolina	Co. H, 5th North Carolina Cavalry	May 31, 1864, Hanover Court House, Virginia	Point Lookout, Maryland, transferred to Elmira Prison, NY, July 12, 1864	Died November 14, 1864 of Chronic Diarrhea, Grave No. 816
Minor, William Private	Unk	June 11, 1861, Drayton, Georgia	Co. F, 12th Georgia Infantry	May 10, 1864, Spotsylvania Court House, Virginia	Point Lookout, Maryland, transferred to Elmira Prison, NY, July 25, 1864	Oath of Allegiance June 30, 1865

Name & Rank	Age	Enlisted	Regiment and State	Where Captured	Prison	Remarks
Minshew, John Private	Unk	March 4, 1862, Waresboro, Georgia	Co. B, 50th Georgia Infantry	June 1, 1864, Gaines Mill Cold Harbor, Virginia	Point Lookout, Maryland, transferred to Elmira Prison, NY, July 12, 1864	Oath of Allegiance May 19, 1865
Mints, Stephen Private	48	April 16, 1862, Old Brunswick, North Carolina	Co. G, 36th 2nd North Carolina Artillery	January 15, 1865, Fort Fisher, North Carolina	February 1, 1865, Elmira Prison Camp, New York	Exchanged February 20, 1865. Died March 20, 1865 of Unknown Disease at Howard Grove Hospital, Richmond, Va
Mints, William Private	Unk	April 16, 1862, Old Brunswick, North Carolina	Co. G, 36th 2nd North Carolina Artillery	January 15, 1865, Fort Fisher, North Carolina	February 1, 1865, Elmira Prison Camp, New York	Died April 10, 1865 of Typhoid Fever, Grave No. 2605
Mintz, John H. Private	38	July 15, 1861, Wilmington, North Carolina	Co. C, 8th North Carolina Infantry	June 1, 1864, Cold Harbor, Virginia	Point Lookout, Maryland, transferred to Elmira Prison, NY, July 12, 1864	Died March 4, 1865 of Chronic Diarrhea, Grave No. 2427
Mise, William Private	32	Unknown	Co. C, 14th Tennessee Infantry	May 20, 1864, Spotsylvania Court House, Virginia	Point Lookout, Maryland, transferred to Elmira Prison, NY, July 3, 1864	Died November 4, 1864 of Pneumonia, Grave No. 839
Misomer, Henry R. Private	Unk	March 1, 1863, Salisbury, North Carolina	Co. D, 42nd North Carolina Infantry	June 4, 1984, Cold Harbor, Virginia	Point Lookout, Maryland, transferred to Elmira Prison, NY, July 17, 1864	Died December 13, 1864 of Double Pneumonia, Grave No. 1136. Name Misamore on Headstone.
Mitchell, A. Private	Unk	Date Unknown, New Orleans, Louisiana	Co. B, 1st Louisiana Infantry	May 20, 1864, Spotsylvania Court House, Virginia	Point Lookout, Maryland, transferred to Elmira Prison, NY, July 3, 1864	Exchanged February 25, 1865 at Boulware's or Cox Wharf on the James River, Virginia
Mitchell, Adam S. Landsman	Unk	Unknown	Confederate States Navy	May 5, 1864, Albemarle Sound on Steamer CSS Bombshell	Point Lookout, Maryland, transferred to Elmira Prison, NY, August 17, 1864	Transferred For Exchange October 11, 1864 to Point Lookout Prison Camp, MD. Nothing Further.

Name & Rank	Age	Enlisted	Regiment and State	Where Captured	Prison	Remarks
Mitchell, Benjamin F. Private	Unk	April 1, 1861, Lacy's Store, Virginia	Co. B, 44th Virginia Infantry	May 12, 1864, Spotsylvania Court House, Virginia	Point Lookout, Maryland, transferred to Elmira Prison, NY, August 2, 1864	Exchanged March 14, 1865 at Boulware's Wharf on the James River, Virginia
Mitchell, Benjamin T. Private	22	January 27, 1862, Rolesville, North Carolina	Co. I, 1st North Carolina Infantry	May 12, 1864, Spotsylvania, Virginia	Point Lookout Prison Camp, Maryland. Transferred to Elmira Prison, August 6, 1864	Died March 14, 1865 of Diarrhea, Grave No. 1673
Mitchell, C. J. Private	Unk	May 11, 1861, New Orleans, Louisiana	Co. K, 2nd Louisiana Infantry	May 12, 1864, Spotsylvania Court House, Virginia	Point Lookout, Maryland, transferred to Elmira Prison, NY, August 15, 1864	Exchanged February 25, 1865 at Boulware's or Cox Wharf on the James River, Virginia
Mitchell, David H. Private	Unk	April 7, 1864, Talladega, Alabama	Co. A, 12th Alabama Infantry	July 10, 1864, Harpers Ferry, Virginia	Old Capital Prison, Washington DC. Transferred to Elmira Prison Camp New York July 25, 1864.	Oath of Allegiance May 29, 1865
Mitchell, Ephriam Sergeant	56	March 8, 1862, Alamance County, North Carolina	Co. F, 53rd North Carolina Infantry	May 20, 1864, Spotsylvania Court House, Virginia	Point Lookout, Maryland, transferred to Elmira Prison, NY, July 3, 1864	Exchanged October 29, 1864 at Venus Point, Savannah River, GA.
Mitchell, George W. Private	18	July 20, 1861, Camp Pickens, Anderson District, South Carolina	Co, K, Orr's Rifles 1st South Carolina Infantry	May 24, 1864, Hanover Junction, Virginia	Point Lookout, Maryland, transferred to Elmira Prison, NY, July 12, 1864	Died September 8, 1864 of Chronic Diarrhea, Grave No. 213
Mitchell, Harry L. Private	Unk	December 21, 1861, Nashville, Tennessee	Co. J, 44th Tennessee Infantry	June 17, 1864, Petersburg, Virginia	Point Lookout, Maryland, transferred to Elmira Prison, NY, July 30, 1864	Oath of Allegiance May 15, 1865
Mitchell, Henry Private	Unk	Unknown	Co. F, 59th Tennessee Infantry	July 25, 1864, Winchester, Virginia	Old Capital Prison, Washington, DC, transferred to Elmira Prison, NY, August 12, 1864	Oath of Allegiance May 29, 1865

Name & Rank	Age	Enlisted	Regiment and State	Where Captured	Prison	Remarks
Mitchell, James Private	Unk	April 3, 1862, Ascension Parish, Louisiana	Co. E, 28th Louisiana Infantry	October 12, 1864, Near Hampton's Ferry, Louisiana	New Orleans, Louisiana transferred to Elmira November 19, 1864.	Exchanged March 10, 1865 at Boulware's Wharf on the James River, Virginia
Mitchell, James C. Private	20	September 25, 1861, Carricitos, Texas	Co. A, 1st Captain Yeager's Texas Cavalry	August 8, 1864, Simsport, Louisiana	New Orleans, LA, Transferred to Elmira Prison, NY, November 19, 1864	Exchanged February 20, 1865. Died March 24, 1865 at Howard's Grove General Hospital, Richmond, Va.
Mitchell, James H. Private	Unk	July 9, 1861, Camp Trousdale, Tennessee	Co. D, 17th Tennessee Infantry	June 17, 1864, Petersburg, Virginia	Point Lookout, Maryland, transferred to Elmira Prison, NY, July 30, 1864	Exchanged February 13, 1865 at Boulware's wharf on the James River, Virginia
Mitchell, John A. Private	19	May 25, 1861, Madison Court House, Virginia	Co. D, 34th, Virginia Infantry	June 15, 1864, Near Petersburg, Virginia	Point Lookout, Maryland, transferred to Elmira Prison, NY, July 12, 1864	Oath of Allegiance June 19, 1865
Mitchell, John W. Private	19	Unknown	Co. J, 50th Virginia Infantry	May 6, 1864, Wilderness, Virginia	Point Lookout, Maryland, transferred to Elmira Prison, NY, August 14, 1864	Died October 1, 1864 of Chronic Diarrhea, Grave No. 408
Mitchell, Joseph Private	Unk	November 24, 1862, Richmond, Virginia	Co. B, 24th Virginia Cavalry	May 4, 1864, Gloucester Point, Virginia	Transferred From Point Lookout Prison, MD, July 12, 1864. Train Never Arrived at Elmira Prison Camp, NY.	Died July 15, 1864 in Train Wreck at Shohola, Pennsylvania.
Mitchell, Joshua Private	30	February 27, 1862, Reidsville, Rockingham County, North Carolina	Co. G, 45th North Carolina Infantry	May 10, 1864, Spotsylvania Court House, Virginia	Point Lookout, Maryland, transferred to Elmira Prison, NY, August 6, 1864	Exchanged October 29, 1864 at Venus Point, Savannah River, GA.
Mitchell, Lawrence Private	Unk	August 5, 1863, Atlanta, Georgia	Co. A, 64th Georgia Infantry	June 17, 1864, Near Petersburg, Virginia	Point Lookout, Maryland, transferred to Elmira Prison, NY, July 30, 1864	Oath of Allegiance May 29, 1865

Name & Rank	Age	Enlisted	Regiment and State	Where Captured	Prison	Remarks
Mitchell, Richard S. Private	18	June 18, 1863, Raleigh, North Carolina	Co J, 1st North Carolina Infantry	May 12, 1864, Spotsylvania Court House, Virginia	Point Lookout, Maryland, transferred to Elmira Prison, NY, August 6,1864	Oath of Allegiance June 27, 1865
Mitchell, Samuel Private	Unk	March 4, 1862, Pike County, Georgia	Co. H, 44th Georgia Infantry	July 12, 1864, Near Washington, DC	Old Capital Prison, Washington DC. Transferred to Elmira Prison Camp New York July 25, 1864.	Died December 10, 1864 of Pneumonia, Grave No. 1039
Mitchell, Samuel J. Corporal	32	July 25, 1861, Bunker Hill, Bedford County, Virginia	Co. A, 58th Virginia Infantry	May 30, 1864, Cold Harbor, Virginia. Gunshot Wound Right Leg, fracturing bones of the Knee. Leg Amputated.	Old Capital Prison, Washington, DC transferred to Elmira Prison, NY, August 27, 1864	Exchanged February 13, 1865. Died March 11, 1865 at Chimborazo Hospital No. 2, Richmond, Va.
Mitchell, William Private	Unk	March 4, 1861, Selma, Alabama	Co. C, 1st Battalion Alabama Artillery	August 23, 1864, Fort Morgan, Alabama	New Orleans, Louisiana transferred to Elmira Prison, NY, December 4, 1864.	Oath of Allegiance June 21, 1865
Mitchell, William A. Private	Unk	March 31, 1863, Jacksonville, Alabama	Co. G, 10th Alabama Infantry	May 13, 1864, Spotsylvania Court House, Virginia	Point Lookout, Maryland, transferred to Elmira Prison, NY, August 17, 1864	Died March 12, 1865 of Intermittent Fever Grave No. 1850
Mitchen, E. E. Private	Unk	September 26, 1863, Morgan County, Georgia	Co. J, 7th Georgia Cavalry	June 11, 1864, Trevilian Station, Louisa Court House, Virginia	Point Lookout, Maryland, transferred to Elmira Prison, NY, July 25, 1864	Died May 7, 1865 of Variola (Smallpox), Grave No. 2772
Mitchen, Samuel D. Sergeant	25	July 25, 1861, Bunkers Hill, Bedford County, Virginia	Co. A, 58th Virginia Infantry	May 30, 1864, Cold Harbor, Virginia	Old Capital Prison, Washington, DC, transferred to Elmira Prison, NY, December 17, 1864	Died May 17, 1865 of Chronic Diarrhea, Grave No. 2799
Mitchum, John S. Private	21	January 11, 1862, Williamsburg, South Carolina	Co. K, 25th South Carolina Infantry	January 15, 1865, Fort Fisher, North Carolina	January 30, 1865, Elmira Prison Camp, New York	Oath of Allegiance July 11, 1865

Name & Rank	Age	Enlisted	Regiment and State	Where Captured	Prison	Remarks
Mitchum, S. S. Sergeant	45	April 12, 1862, Battery Island, South Carolina	Co. C, 25th South Carolina Infantry	January 15, 1865, Fort Fisher, North Carolina	January 30, 1865, Elmira Prison Camp, New York	Exchanged February 20, 1865 at Boulware's or Cox Wharf on the James River, Virginia
Mitchum, W. E. Corporal	20	May 1, 1862, Gourdin's Depot, Williamsburg, South Carolina	Co. K, 25th South Carolina Infantry	January 15, 1865, Fort Fisher, North Carolina	January 30, 1865, Elmira Prison Camp, New York	Oath of Allegiance July 7, 1865
Mixon, Anthony W. Private	41	January 1, 1862, Camp Harlee, Georgetown, South Carolina	Co. J, 25th South Carolina Infantry	January 15, 1865, Fort Fisher, North Carolina	January 30, 1865, Elmira Prison Camp, New York	Died February 14, 1865 of Chronic Diarrhea, Grave No. 2185
Mixon, Green Private	Unk	April 14, 1864, Fort Morgan, Alabama	Co. A, 1st Battalion Alabama Artillery	August 23, 1864, Fort Morgan, Alabama.	New Orleans, Louisiana transferred to Elmira Prison, NY, December 4, 1864.	Died April 11, 1865 of Chronic Diarrhea, Grave No. 2682
Mixon, Harvey Private	35	March 3, 1862, Bellevue, Louisiana	Co. F, 9th Louisiana Cavalry	July 19, 1864, Rodney, Louisiana	New Orleans, LA, Transferred to Elmira Prison, NY, November 19, 1864	Died November 30, 1864 of Pneumonia, Grave No. 1002
Mixon, Marion C. Corporal	Unk	January 2, 1864, Butler County, Alabama	Co. A, 1st Alabama Artillery	August 23, 1864, Fort Morgan, Alabama.	New Orleans, Louisiana transferred to Elmira Prison, NY, December 4, 1864.	Exchanged March 2, 1865 at Boulware's Wharf on the James River, Virginia
Mixon, W. P. Sergeant	20	January 20, 1862, Darlington, South Carolina	Co. H, 21st South Carolina Infantry	January 15, 1865, Fort Fisher, North Carolina	January 30, 1865, Elmira Prison Camp, New York	Exchanged February 20, 1865 at Boulware's or Cox Wharf on the James River, Virginia
Mize, James A. Private	Unk	May 31, 1861, Atlanta, Georgia	Co. G, 7th Georgia Infantry	August 1, 1864, Turkey Bend, Virginia	Point Lookout, Maryland, transferred to Elmira Prison, NY, August 18, 1864	Exchanged October 29, 1864 at Venus Point, Savannah River, GA.
Mizell, William W. Private	18	June 24, 1861, Williamston, North Carolina	Co. H, 1st North Carolina Infantry	May 12, 1864, Spotsylvania Court House, Virginia	Point Lookout, Maryland, transferred to Elmira Prison, NY, August 6, 1864	Oath of Allegiance June 27, 1865

Name & Rank	Age	Enlisted	Regiment and State	Where Captured	Prison	Remarks
Mizer, Adam Private	Unk	April 14, 1862, Rudes Hill, Virginia	Co. K, 2nd Virginia Infantry	May 12, 1864, Spotsylvania Court House, Virginia	Point Lookout, Maryland, transferred to Elmira Prison, NY, August 2, 1864	Oath of Allegiance June 27, 1865
Mobley, Benjamin L. Private	19	August 8, 1861, Waynesboro, Georgia	Co. D, Cobb's Legion Georgia	May 6, 1864, Wilderness, Virginia	Old Capital Prison, Washington, DC, transferred to Elmira Prison, NY, July 14, 1864	Oath of Allegiance July 3, 1865
Mobley, James H. Private	Unk	January 16, 1864, Danville, Virginia	Co. G, 45th North Carolina Infantry	May 10, 1864, Spotsylvania Court House, Virginia	Point Lookout, Maryland, transferred to Elmira Prison, NY, August 6, 1864	Died March 24, 1865 of Chronic Diarrhea, Grave No. 2451. Name Mably on Headstone.
Mobley, John L. Sergeant	20	June 24, 1861, Williamston, North Carolina	Co. H, 1st North Carolina Infantry	May 12, 1864, Spotsylvania Court House, Virginia	Point Lookout, Maryland, transferred to Elmira Prison, NY, August 6, 1864	Exchanged October 29, 1864 at Venus Point, Savannah River, GA.
Mock, Edward Private	20	November 1, 1863, Orange Court House, Virginia	Co. B, 9th Battalion North Carolina Sharp Shooters	February 6, 1864, Newbern, North Carolina	Point Lookout, Maryland, transferred to Elmira Prison, NY, July 23, 1864	Oath of Allegiance May 12, 1865
Mock, Henry A. Private	30	March 26, 1863, Mocksville, North Carolina	Co. F, 13th North Carolina Infantry	May 23, 1864, North Anna, Virginia	Point Lookout, Maryland, transferred to Elmira Prison, NY, July 25, 1864	Died March 8, 1865 of Chronic Diarrhea, Grave No. 2774
Mock, L. E. Private	Unk	December 16, 1862, Charleston, South Carolina	Co. B, 7th Georgia Cavalry	June 11, 1864, Trevilian Station, Louisa Court House, Virginia	Point Lookout, Maryland, transferred to Elmira Prison, NY, July 25, 1864	Exchanged October 29, 1864 at Venus Point, Savannah River, GA.
Mode, J. T. Private	18	October 18, 1863, Shelby, North Carolina	Co. B, 49th North Carolina Infantry	May 14, 1864, Near Fort Darling, Virginia	Point Lookout, Maryland, transferred to Elmira Prison, NY, August 17, 1864	Oath of Allegiance June 19, 1865

Name & Rank	Age	Enlisted	Regiment and State	Where Captured	Prison	Remarks
Modlin, James A. Private	21	June 24, 1861, Williamston, North Carolina	Co. H, 1st North Carolina Infantry	May 12, 1864, Wilderness, Spotsylvania Court House, Virginia	Point Lookout, Maryland, transferred to Elmira Prison, NY, August 6, 1864	Oath of Allegiance June 27, 1865
Moffit, Zeno Private	34	July 21, 1862, Randolph County, North Carolina	Co. F, 24th North Carolina Infantry	May 16, 1864, Near Drury's Bluff, Virginia	Point Lookout, Maryland, transferred to Elmira Prison, NY, August 18, 1864	Died October 11, 1864 of Chronic Diarrhea, Grave No. 679. Headstone has Veno Moffatt.
Moffitt, Charles W. Private	Unk	March 19, 1862, Franklin County, Virginia	Co. F, 42nd Virginia Infantry	May 12, 1864, Near Spotsylvania Court House, Virginia	Point Lookout, Maryland, transferred to Elmira Prison, NY, August 6, 1864	Oath of Allegiance May 29, 1865
Moffitt, Michael Private	35	June 4, 1861, Camp Moore, Louisiana	Co. J, 6th Louisiana Infantry	May 5, 1864, Wilderness, Virginia	Point Lookout, Maryland, transferred to Elmira Prison, NY, August 17, 1864	Exchanged February 13, 1865 at Boulware's wharf on the James River, Virginia
Moler, D. G. Sergeant	21	March 17, 1862, Shepherds-town, Virginia	Co. D, 12th Virginia Cavalry	April 10, 1865, Fairfax Station, Virginia	Old Capital Prison, Washington, DC, transferred to Elmira Prison, NY, May 2, 1865.	Oath of Allegiance July 3, 1865
Moler, Daniel Corporal	21	April 25, 1861, Harper's Ferry, Virginia	Co. G, 2nd Virginia Infantry	May 20, 1864, Spotsylvania Court House, Virginia	Point Lookout, Maryland, transferred to Elmira Prison, NY, July 3, 1864	Exchanged March 14, 1865 at Boulware's Wharf on the James River, Virginia
Molloy, John G. Sergeant	19	July 29, 1861, Livingston, Tennessee	Co. C, 25th Tennessee Infantry	May 16, 1864, Near Drury's Bluff, Virginia	Point Lookout, Maryland, transferred to Elmira Prison, NY, August 17, 1864	Exchanged October 29, 1864 at Venus Point, Savannah River, GA.
Molloy, Lawrence E. Private	Unk	May 4, 1862, James Island, South Carolina	Co. B, 25th South Carolina Infantry	January 15, 1865, Fort Fisher, North Carolina	January 30, 1865, Elmira Prison Camp, New York	Oath of Allegiance July 7, 1865

Name & Rank	Age	Enlisted	Regiment and State	Where Captured	Prison	Remarks
Molloy, W. P. Private	Unk	February 14, 1863, Charleston, South Carolina	Co. A, 27th South Carolina Infantry	June 24, 1864, Near Petersburg, Virginia	Point Lookout, Maryland, transferred to Elmira Prison, NY, August 18, 1864	Transferred For Exchange 10/11/64 to Point Lookout Prison Camp, MD. Died 11/1/64 of Unknown Causes at Fort Monroe, VA.
Molphurs, William L. Private	17	July 13, 1861, Jacksonville, Florida	Co. B, 2nd Florida Infantry	July 29, 1864, Petersburg, Virginia	Point Lookout, Maryland, transferred to Elmira Prison, NY, August 12, 1864	Oath of Allegiance February 3, 1865. Early Release per Lincoln's Proclamation, 12/8/1863.
Moneymaker, Archibald B. Private	Unk	August 1, 1861, Staunton, Virginia	Co. H, 25th Virginia Infantry	May 12, 1864, Spotsylvania Court House, Virginia	Point Lookout, Maryland, transferred to Elmira Prison, NY, August 12, 1864	Exchanged October 29, 1864 at Venus Point, Savannah River, GA.
Moneymaker, John C. Private	Unk	May 21, 1861, Brownsburg, Virginia	Co. H, 25th Virginia Infantry	May 12, 1864, Spotsylvania Court House, Virginia	Point Lookout, Maryland, transferred to Elmira Prison, NY, August 12, 1864	Died December 18, 1864 of Chronic Diarrhea, Grave No. 1068
Mongle, Abram F. Private	Unk	March 31, 1862, Washington County, Virginia	Co. J, 48th Virginia Infantry	May 12, 1864, Spotsylvania Court House, Virginia	Point Lookout, Maryland, transferred to Elmira Prison, NY, August 2, 1864	Died March 26, 1865 of Pneumonia, Grave No. 2472
Monoc, J. M. Corporal	Unk	Unknown	Co. J, 26th North Carolina Infantry	June 17, 1864, Near Petersburg, Virginia	Point Lookout, Maryland, transferred to Elmira Prison, NY, July 30, 1864	Oath of Allegiance July 3, 1865
Monohan, Patrick Private	35	July 22, 1861, Camp Moore, Louisiana	Co. C, 10th Louisiana Infantry	May 12, 1864, Spotsylvania Court House, Virginia	Point Lookout, Maryland, transferred to Elmira Prison, NY, July 25, 1864	Oath of Allegiance May 19, 1865

Name & Rank	Age	Enlisted	Regiment and State	Where Captured	Prison	Remarks
Monroe, Duncan Private	38	April 9, 1862, Cumberland County, North Carolina	Co. I, 51st North Carolina Infantry	June 1, 1864, Cold Harbor, Virginia	Transferred From Point Lookout Prison, MD, July 12, 1864. Train Never Arrived at Elmira Prison Camp, NY.	Died July 15, 1864 in Train Wreck at Shohola, Pennsylvania.
Monroe, George W. Private	Unk	February 19, 1864, Greenville, Tennessee	Co. B, 1st Tennessee Infantry	May 6, 1864, Wilderness, Virginia	Point Lookout, Maryland, transferred to Elmira Prison, NY, July 23, 1864	Oath of Allegiance January 20, 1865. Early Release per Lincoln's Proclamation, 12/8/1863.
Monroe, Howell Private	Unk	April 24, 1862, Humboldt, Tennessee	Co. A, Jackson's 1st Regiment, Tennessee Heavy Artillery	August 23, 1864, Fort Morgan, Alabama	New Orleans, Louisiana transferred to Elmira Prison, NY, December 4, 1864.	Exchanged March 10, 1865 at Boulware's Wharf on the James River, Virginia
Monroe, James W. Private	Unk	June 2, 1861, Corinth, Mississippi	Co. G, 6th Alabama Infantry	June 10, 1864, Spotsylvania, Virginia	Point Lookout, Maryland, transferred to Elmira Prison, NY, July 25, 1864	Oath of Allegiance June 14, 1865
Monroe, Lewis Corporal	Unk	July 1, 1861, New Orleans, Louisiana	Co. H, 14th Louisiana Infantry	May 12, 1864, Spotsylvania Court House, Virginia	Point Lookout, Maryland, transferred to Elmira Prison, NY, July 25, 1864	Exchanged February 25, 1865 at Boulware's or Cox Wharf on the James River, Virginia
Monteiro, Walter Sergeant	26	April 19, 1861, Fishersville, Albemarle County, Virginia	Co. H, 5th Virginia Infantry	May 20, 1864, Spotsylvania Court House, Virginia	Point Lookout, Maryland, transferred to Elmira Prison, NY, July 6, 1864	Oath of Allegiance October 11, 1864. Early Release per Lincoln's Proclamation, 12/8/1863.
Monteith, A. Private	Unk	Unknown	Co. K, 2nd Louisiana Cavalry	July 31, 1864, Near Morganza, Louisiana	New Orleans, LA, Transferred to Elmira Prison, NY, November 19, 1864	Exchanged February 25, 1865 at Boulware's or Cox Wharf on the James River, Virginia

Name & Rank	Age	Enlisted	Regiment and State	Where Captured	Prison	Remarks
Montgomery, Edward A. Private	25	June 23, 1861, Camp Moore, Louisiana	Co. D, 8th Louisiana Infantry	May 12, 1864, Spotsylvania Court House, Virginia	Point Lookout, Maryland, transferred to Elmira Prison, NY, August 17, 1864	Exchanged February 13, 1865 at Boulware's wharf on the James River, Virginia
Montgomery, Edward P. Private	20	April 12, 1862, Battery Island, South Carolina	Co. C, 25th South Carolina Infantry	January 15, 1865, Fort Fisher, North Carolina	January 30, 1865, Elmira Prison Camp, New York	Oath of Allegiance August 7, 1865
Montgomery, Isaac Sergeant	25	January 1, 1862, Georgetown, South Carolina	Co. C, 25th South Carolina Infantry	January 15, 1865, Fort Fisher, North Carolina	January 30, 1865, Elmira Prison Camp, New York	Oath of Allegiance July 26, 1865
Montgomery, J. A. Private	22	April 12, 1862, Battery Island, South Carolina	Co. C, 25th South Carolina Infantry	January 15, 1865, Fort Fisher, North Carolina	January 30, 1865, Elmira Prison Camp, New York	Oath of Allegiance July 26, 1865
Montgomery, James Private	24	June 20, 1861, Abingdon, Virginia	Co. B, 48th Virginia Infantry	July 8, 1864, Harpers Ferry, Virginia	Old Capital Prison, Washington DC. Transferred to Elmira Prison Camp New York July 25, 1864.	Oath of Allegiance July 3, 1865
Montgomery, James B. Private	29	March 18, 1863, Georgetown, South Carolina	Co. C, 25th South Carolina Infantry	August 21, 1864, Weldon Railroad, Near Petersburg, Virginia. Gunshot Wound Right Leg and Left Arm.	Old Capital Prison, Washington, DC transferred to Elmira Prison, NY, August 27, 1864	Exchanged February 13, 1865 at Boulware's Wharf on the James River, Virginia
Montgomery, John P. C. Private	21	July 4, 1862, Mecklenburg County, North Carolina	Co. H, 35th North Carolina Infantry	June 17, 1864, Petersburg, Virginia	Point Lookout, Maryland, transferred to Elmira Prison, NY, July 30, 1864	Died February 5, 1865 of Pneumonia, Grave No. 1895
Montgomery, John R. Private	19	June 20, 1861, Abingdon, Virginia	Co. B, 48th Virginia Infantry	May 12, 1864, Spotsylvania Court House, Virginia	Point Lookout, Maryland, transferred to Elmira Prison, NY, August 2, 1864	Oath of Allegiance, June 21, 1865
Montgomery, Josiah J. Private	21	August 1, 1862, Knoxville, Tennessee	Co. G, 63rd Tennessee Infantry	June 17, 1864, Petersburg, Virginia	Point Lookout, Maryland, transferred to Elmira Prison, NY, July 30, 1864	Exchanged February 25, 1865 at Boulware's or Cox Wharf on the James River, Virginia

Name & Rank	Age	Enlisted	Regiment and State	Where Captured	Prison	Remarks
Montgomery, Lee A. Private	24	September 3, 1864, Mecklenburg County, North Carolina	Co. H, 35th North Carolina Infantry	May 14, 1864, Near Fort Darling, Virginia	Point Lookout, Maryland, transferred to Elmira Prison, NY, August 17, 1864	Exchanged February 13, 1865 at Boulware's Wharf on the James River, Virginia
Montgomery, P. S. Sergeant	Unk	February 17, 1863, Charleston, South Carolina	Co. K, 27th South Carolina Infantry	June 24, 1864, Near Petersburg, Virginia	Point Lookout, Maryland, transferred to Elmira Prison, NY, August 18, 1864	Transferred for Exchanged 10/29/64 at Venus Point, Savannah River, GA.
Montgomery, S. E. Sergeant	29	April 17, 1862, Georgetown, South Carolina	Co. C, 25th South Carolina Infantry	January 15, 1865, Fort Fisher, North Carolina	January 30, 1865, Elmira Prison Camp, New York	Exchanged March 14, 1865 at Boulware's Wharf on the James River, Virginia
Montgomery, William K. Private	Unk	Unknown	Co. B, 50th Virginia Infantry	May 12, 1864, Spotsylvania Court House, Virginia	Point Lookout, Maryland, transferred to Elmira Prison, NY, August 2, 1864	Died February 19, 1865 of Chronic Diarrhea, Grave No. 2355
Moody, James E. Private	18	February 15, 1862, Newbern, North Carolina	Co. C, 61st North Carolina Infantry	June 16, 1864, Petersburg, Virginia	Point Lookout, Maryland, transferred to Elmira Prison, NY, July 12, 1864	Died October 11, 1864 of Chronic Diarrhea, Grave No. 578
Moody, Samuel S. Private	Unk	September 22, 1862, Waynesville, Georgia	Co. G, 7th Georgia Cavalry	June 11, 1864, Trevilian Station, Louisa Court House, Virginia	Point Lookout, Maryland, transferred to Elmira Prison, NY, July 25, 1864	Transferred for Exchange 10/11/64. Died 10/26/64 of Chronic Diarrhea at Point Lookout, MD.
Moon, John A. Private	26	July 13, 1861, Unionville, Tennessee	Co. C, 23rd Tennessee Infantry	June 17, 1864, Petersburg, Virginia	Point Lookout, Maryland, transferred to Elmira Prison, NY, July 30, 1864	Oath of Allegiance May 17, 1865
Moon, T. C. Private	Unk	July 19, 1861, Montgomery, Alabama	Co. J, 13th Alabama Infantry	May 12, 1864, Spotsylvania Court House, Virginia	Point Lookout, Maryland, transferred to Elmira Prison, NY, July 30, 1864	Oath of Allegiance June 19, 1865

Name & Rank	Age	Enlisted	Regiment and State	Where Captured	Prison	Remarks
Moon, William H. Private	Unk	November 8, 1863, Camp Holmes, North Carolina	Co. F, 22nd North Carolina Infantry	May 6, 1864, Wilderness, Virginia	Point Lookout, Maryland, transferred to Elmira Prison, NY, August 14, 1864	Died November 29, 1864 of Typhoid-Pneumonia, Grave No. 998
Mooney, Francis A. 1st Sergeant	Unk	July 29, 1861, Harrisonburg, Virginia	Co. H, 10th Virginia Cavalry	May 14, 1864, Spotsylvania Court House, Virginia	Point Lookout, Maryland, transferred to Elmira Prison, NY, July 3, 1864	Exchanged March 10, 1865 at Boulware's Wharf on the James River, Virginia
Moore, A. L. Private	18	September 25, 1863, Weldon, North Carolina	Co. E, 35th North Carolina Infantry	June 17, 1864, Petersburg, Virginia	Point Lookout, Maryland, transferred to Elmira Prison, NY, July 30, 1864	Oath of Allegiance July 11, 1865
Moore, A. M. Private	Unk	July 25, 1862, Orange Court House, Virginia	Co. D, 6th Virginia Cavalry	December 9, 1863, Loudoun County, Virginia	Point Lookout, Maryland, transferred to Elmira Prison, NY, August 17, 1864	Transferred For Exchange October 11, 1864 to Point Lookout Prison Camp, MD. Nothing Further.
Moore, Andrew Private	22	March 13, 1862, Fort Fisher, North Carolina	Co. J, 36th 2nd North Carolina Artillery	January 15, 1865, Fort Fisher, North Carolina	February 1, 1865, Elmira Prison Camp, New York	Oath of Allegiance June 12, 1865
Moore, Asa W. Private	18	June 8, 1861, Wilmington, North Carolina	Co. F, 3rd North Carolina Infantry	May 12, 1864, Near Spotsylvania County Court House, Virginia	Point Lookout, Maryland, transferred to Elmira Prison, NY, August 14, 1864	Exchanged October 29, 1864 at Venus Point, Savannah River, GA.
Moore, Benjamin Franklin Private	Unk	May 19, 1862, Darlington, South Carolina	Co. B, 21st South Carolina Infantry	January 15, 1865, Fort Fisher, North Carolina	January 30, 1865, Elmira Prison Camp, New York	Died April 10, 1865 of Chronic Diarrhea, Grave No. 2607
Moore, C. A. J. Private	18	May 1, 1862, Yorktown, Louisiana	Co. F, 2nd Louisiana Infantry	May 12, 1864, Spotsylvania Court House, Virginia	Point Lookout, Maryland, transferred to Elmira Prison, NY, August 17, 1864	Exchanged February 13, 1865 at Boulware's wharf on the James River, Virginia
Moore, Calvin W. Private	Unk	June 1, 1861, Lancaster County Court House, Virginia	Co. F, 47th Virginia Infantry	May 6, 1864, Wilderness, Virginia	Point Lookout, Maryland, transferred to Elmira Prison, NY, August 14, 1864	Died December 31, 1864 of Pneumonia, Grave No. 1325

Name & Rank	Age	Enlisted	Regiment and State	Where Captured	Prison	Remarks
Moore, Carl A. J. Private	18	May 1, 1862, Near Yorktown, Louisiana	Co. G, 2nd Louisiana Infantry	May 12, 1864, Spotsylvania Court House, Virginia	Point Lookout, Maryland, transferred to Elmira Prison, NY, July 11, 1864	Exchanged February 13, 1865 at Boulware's wharf on the James River, Virginia
Moore, Charles H. Corporal	20	February 8, 1862, Piney Woods, North Carolina	Co. A, 51st North Carolina Infantry	June 1, 1864, Gaines Mill Cold Harbor, Virginia	Point Lookout, Maryland, transferred to Elmira Prison, NY, July 12, 1864	Exchanged March 2, 1865 at Akins Landing on the James River, Virginia
Moore, David Private	Unk	March 8, 1862, Ridgeway, Virginia	Co. F, 42nd Virginia Infantry	May 12, 1864, Near Spotsylvania Court House, Virginia	Point Lookout, Maryland, transferred to Elmira Prison, NY, August 6, 1864	Transferred for Exchanged 10/29/64 at Venus Point, Savannah River, GA.
Moore, David H. Private	Unk	May 18, 1861, Lisbon, Virginia	Co. C, 42nd Virginia Infantry	July 18, 1864, Snickers Gap, Virginia	Old Capital Prison, Washington, DC, transferred to Elmira Prison, NY, August 12, 1864	Oath of Allegiance June 27, 1865
Moore, Edward P. Private	19	April 2, 1862, Haynesville, Alabama	Co. K, 5th Alabama Infantry	July 12, 1864, Silver Springs, Virginia. Gunshot Wound Left Thigh, Severe.	Old Capital Prison, Washington, DC transferred to Elmira Prison, NY, August 27, 1864	Exchanged February 13, 1865 at Boulware's or Cox Wharf on the James River, Virginia
Moore, Enoch Private	18	December 8, 1863, Fort Caswell, Brunswick County, North Carolina	Co. F, 36th 2nd North Carolina Artillery	January 15, 1865, Fort Fisher, North Carolina	February 1, 1865, Elmira Prison Camp, New York	Exchanged February 20, 1865 at Boulware's or Cox Wharf on the James River, Virginia
Moore, Enoch Private	29	January 9, 1862, Lynnhaven Beach, Virginia	Co. J, 15th Virginia Cavalry	September 22, 1863, Near Culpepper, Virginia	Point Lookout, Maryland, transferred to Elmira Prison, NY, August 18, 1864	Exchanged March 2, 1865 at Akins Landing on the James River, Virginia
Moore, G. E. Private	Unk	August 9. 1861, Cumberland Gap, Tennessee	Co. D, 17th Tennessee Infantry	June 17, 1864, Petersburg, Virginia	Point Lookout, Maryland, transferred to Elmira Prison, NY, July 30, 1864	Exchanged February 25, 1865 at Boulware's or Cox Wharf on the James River, Virginia

Name & Rank	Age	Enlisted	Regiment and State	Where Captured	Prison	Remarks
Moore, G. W. Private	Unk	May 7, 1861, Loachapoka, Alabama	Co. L, 6th Alabama Infantry	May 8, 1864, Spotsylvania Court House, Virginia	Point Lookout, Maryland, transferred to Elmira Prison, NY, August 17, 1864	Oath of Allegiance June 24, 1865
Moore, George B. Private	20	February 21, 1862, Raleigh, North Carolina	Co. C, 47th North Carolina Infantry	July 14, 1863, Falling Waters, Maryland	Point Lookout, Maryland, transferred to Elmira Prison, NY, August 18, 1864	Transferred for Exchanged 10/29/64 at Venus Point, Savannah River, GA.
Moore, Henry T. Private	Unk	June 9, 1861, Jones County, Georgia	Co. A, 12th Georgia Infantry	May 10, 1864, Spotsylvania Court House, Virginia	Point Lookout, Maryland, transferred to Elmira Prison, NY, July 30, 1864	Exchanged February 20, 1865 at Boulware's or Cox Wharf on the James River, Virginia
Moore, Hiram V. Sergeant	Unk	August 24, 1861, Clayton County, Georgia	Co. E, 24th Georgia Infantry	June 1, 1864, Cold Harbor, Virginia	Point Lookout, Maryland, transferred to Elmira Prison, NY, July 12, 1864	Oath of Allegiance June 14, 1865
Moore, Hix Private	42	February 27, 1862, Reidsville, Rockingham County, North Carolina	Co. E, 45th North Carolina Infantry	May 10, 1864, Spotsylvania Court House, Virginia	Point Lookout, Maryland, transferred to Elmira Prison, NY, August 6, 1864	Exchanged October 29, 1864 at Venus Point, Savannah River, GA.
Moore, Isaac Private	Unk	June 30, 1863, Franklin County, Virginia	Co. B, 36th Virginia Infantry	July 10, 1864, Harper's Ferry, Virginia	Old Capital Prison, Washington, DC, transferred to Elmira Prison Camp, NY, July 25, 1864.	Died August 12, 1864 of Rubeola (Measles), Grave No. 130
Moore, J. F. Private	19	December 23, 1861, Georgetown, South Carolina	Co. B, 21st South Carolina Infantry	January 15, 1865, Fort Fisher, North Carolina	January 30, 1865, Elmira Prison Camp, New York	Oath of Allegiance August 8, 1865
Moore, J. G. Private	Unk	October 9, 1863, Bryan County, Georgia	Co. H, 7th Georgia Cavalry	June 11, 1864, Trevilian Station, Louisa Court House, Virginia	Point Lookout, Maryland, transferred to Elmira Prison, NY, July 25, 1864	Exchanged October 29, 1864 at Venus Point, Savannah River, GA.

Name & Rank	Age	Enlisted	Regiment and State	Where Captured	Prison	Remarks
Moore, J. R. Sergeant	28	December 25, 1861, Bennettsville, South Carolina	Co. F, 21st South Carolina Infantry	January 15, 1865, Fort Fisher, North Carolina	January 30, 1865, Elmira Prison Camp, New York	Died July 18, 1865 of Unknown Disease at US Army Hospital, Elmira, NY. Grave No. 2872. Headstone has 21st NC.
Moore, J. W. Private	Unk	September 18, 1862, Columbus, Mississippi	Co. K, 41st Alabama Infantry	May 16, 1864, Near Drury's Bluff, Virginia	Point Lookout, Maryland, transferred to Elmira Prison, NY, August 17, 1864	Oath of Allegiance July 7, 1865
Moore, Jacob Private	22	August 19, 1861, Pitt County, North Carolina	Co. G, 8th North Carolina Infantry	May 30, 1864, Cold Harbor, Virginia	Point Lookout, Maryland, transferred to Elmira Prison, NY, July 11, 1864	Oath of Allegiance June 30, 1865
Moore, James Private	Unk	October 6, 1863, Dobson, North Carolina	Co. C, 21st North Carolina Infantry	July 10, 1864, Harpers Ferry, Virginia	Old Capital Prison, Washington DC. Transferred to Elmira Prison Camp New York July 25, 1864.	Exchanged March 2, 1865. Died April 15, 1865 of Typhoid Fever at Jackson Hospital, Richmond, Virginia.
Moore, James Private	25	June 10, 1861, Port Republic, Virginia	Co. B, 10th Virginia Infantry	May 12, 1864, Spotsylvania Court House, Virginia	Point Lookout, Maryland, transferred to Elmira Prison, NY, August 2, 1864	Exchanged February 13, 1865 at Boulware's wharf on the James River, Virginia
Moore, James A. Sergeant	Unk	May 12, 1862, Camp Holmes, North Carolina	Co. A, 51st North Carolina Infantry	June 1, 1864, Gaines Mill Cold Harbor, Virginia	Point Lookout, Maryland, transferred to Elmira Prison, NY, July 12, 1864	Transferred for Exchange October 29, 1864. Died October 31st of Unknown Causes at Fort Monroe, Va.
Moore, James R. Private	40	July 24, 1863, Fort Branch, Martin County, North Carolina	Co. G, 40th Regiment, 3rd North Carolina Artillery	January 15, 1865, Fort Fisher, North Carolina	January 30, 1865 Elmira Prison Camp, New York	Exchanged February 20, 1865 at Boulware's or Cox Wharf on the James River, Virginia

Name & Rank	Age	Enlisted	Regiment and State	Where Captured	Prison	Remarks
Moore, John Private	Unk	May 7, 1861, Loachapoka, Alabama	Co. L, 6th Alabama Infantry	May 6, 1864, Wilderness, Virginia	Point Lookout, Maryland, transferred to Elmira Prison, NY, August 17, 1864	Oath of Allegiance July 11, 1865
Moore, John A. Private	Unk	April 3, 1862, Atlanta, Georgia	Co. H, Cobb's Legion Georgia Infantry	June 11, 1864, Trevilian Station, Louisa Court House, Virginia	Point Lookout, Maryland, transferred to Elmira Prison, NY, July 25, 1864	Died January 10, 1865 of Pneumonia, Grave No. 1215
Moore, John C. Private	26	July 6, 1861, Salisbury, North Carolina	Co. H, 8th North Carolina Infantry	May 31, 1864, Cold Harbor, Virginia	Point Lookout, Maryland, transferred to Elmira Prison, NY, July 12,1864	Exchanged October 29, 1864 at Venus Point, Savannah River, GA.
Moore, John H. Private	18	July 22, 1861, Buncombe County, North Carolina	Co. J, 25th North Carolina Infantry	June 18, 1864, Near Petersburg, Virginia,	Point Lookout, Maryland, transferred to Elmira Prison, NY, July 25, 1864	Exchanged March 14, 1865 at Boulware's Wharf on the James River, Virginia
Moore, John J. Private	25	January 1, 1862, Camp Hardee, Georgetown, South Carolina	Co. A, 21st South Carolina Infantry	June 24, 1864, Near Petersburg, Virginia	Point Lookout, Maryland, transferred to Elmira Prison, NY, August 18, 1864	Died February 17, 1865 of Chronic Diarrhea, Grave No. 2213
Moore, John L. Private	21	August 15, 1863, Halifax County, Virginia	Co. C, 59th Virginia Infantry	June 17, 1864, Petersburg, Virginia	Point Lookout, Maryland, transferred to Elmira Prison, NY, July 30, 1864	Oath of Allegiance June 19, 1865
Moore, John M. Private	31	February 28, 1863, Anderson Court House, South Carolina	Co. K, 6th South Carolina Cavalry	August 21, 1864, Petersburg, Virginia. Gunshot Wound Left Hip.	Old Capital Prison, Washington, DC, transferred to Elmira Prison Camp, NY, December 17, 1864	Exchanged February 25, 1865 at Boulware's or Cox Wharf on the James River, Virginia
Moore, John Rufus Private	Unk	November 1, 1863, Tyler County, Virginia	Co. A, 46th Battalion, Virginia Cavalry	July 12, 1864, Hagerstown, Maryland	Point Lookout, Maryland, transferred to Elmira Prison, NY, July 25, 1864. Ward No. 10	Died August 13, 1864 of Typhoid Fever, Grave No. 13. Headstone has James R.

Name & Rank	Age	Enlisted	Regiment and State	Where Captured	Prison	Remarks
Moore, John S. Sergeant	Unk	March 4, 1862, Albany, Georgia	Co. K, 51st Georgia Infantry	June 3, 1864, Gaines Farm Cold Harbor, Virginia	Point Lookout, Maryland, transferred to Elmira Prison, NY, July 12, 1864	Oath of Allegiance June 21, 1865
Moore, John W. Private	Unk	October 15, 1861, Elbert County, Georgia	Co. H, 38th Georgia Infantry	May 20, 1864, Spotsylvania Court House, Virginia	Point Lookout, Maryland, transferred to Elmira Prison, NY, July 3, 1864	Oath of Allegiance June 30, 1865
Moore, John W. Private	18	September 30, 1863, Richmond, Virginia	Co. G, 45th North Carolina Infantry	May 10, 1864, Spotsylvania Court House, Virginia	Point Lookout, Maryland, transferred to Elmira Prison, NY, August 6, 1864	Died August 5, 1864 of Inflammation of the Brain on Passage from Point Lookout, MD. Grave No. 9.
Moore, Jordan Private	Unk	April 23, 1863, Rockbridge County, Virginia	Co. C, Jeff Davis Legion Mississippi Cavalry	June 11, 1864, Trevilian Station, Louisa Court House, Virginia	Point Lookout, Maryland, transferred to Elmira Prison, NY, July 25, 1864	Exchanged October 29, 1864 at Venus Point, Savannah River, GA.
Moore, Levi Private	Unk	May 18, 1861, Huntersville, Virginia	Co. I, 25th Virginia Infantry	May 12, 1864, Spotsylvania Court House, Virginia	Point Lookout, Maryland, transferred to Elmira Prison, NY, August 12, 1864	Died January 30, 1865 of Pneumonia, Grave No. 1803. Headstone has Cavalry.
Moore, Lewis S. Private	Unk	July 11, 1862, Lynchburg, Virginia	Co. I, 42nd Virginia Infantry	May 12, 1864, Near Spotsylvania Court House, Virginia	Point Lookout, Maryland, transferred to Elmira Prison, NY, August 6, 1864	Oath of Allegiance June 27, 1865
Moore, Ollin Sergeant	18	May 13, 1862, Goldsboro, North Carolina	Co. A, 3rd North Carolina Infantry	May 12, 1864, Near Spotsylvania County Court House, Virginia	Point Lookout, Maryland, transferred to Elmira Prison, NY, August 14, 1864	Oath of Allegiance July 11, 1865
Moore, Pettigrew Private	Unk	Unknown	Co. G, 61st North Carolina Infantry	August 27, 1863, Battery Wagner, Morris Island, South Carolina	Point Lookout, Maryland, transferred to Elmira Prison, NY, August 18, 1864	Exchanged March 10, 1865 at Boulware's Wharf on the James River, Virginia

Name & Rank	Age	Enlisted	Regiment and State	Where Captured	Prison	Remarks
Moore, Philo W. Private	17	August 14, 1861, Newton, North Carolina	Co. E, 32nd North Carolina Infantry	May 10, 1864, Wilderness, Virginia	Point Lookout, Maryland, transferred to Elmira Prison, NY, August 6, 1864	Oath of Allegiance June 27, 1865
Moore, R. H. Private	36	January 30, 1863, Halifax County, North Carolina	Co. F, 43rd North Carolina Infantry	May 24, 1864, Hanover Junction, Virginia	Point Lookout, Maryland, transferred to Elmira Prison, NY, July 12, 1864	Oath of Allegiance July 11, 1865
Moore, Richard H. Sergeant	27	February 28, 1862, Lumberton, North Carolina	Co. E, 51st North Carolina Infantry	June 15, 1864, Petersburg, Virginia	Point Lookout, Maryland, transferred to Elmira Prison, NY, July 12, 1864	Exchanged March 10, 1865 at Boulware's Wharf on the James River, Virginia
Moore, Robert W. Private	46	April 2, 1864, Brandon, Mississippi	Co. E, 12th Mississippi Cavalry	August 19, 1864, Weldon Railroad, Near Petersburg, Virginia. Gunshot Wound.	DeCamp General Hospital, David's Island New York Harbor.	Oath of Allegiance May 29, 1865
Moore, Samuel G. Corporal	23	July 15, 1862, Green County, North Carolina	Co. E, 61st North Carolina Infantry	August 27, 1863, Battery Wagner, Morris Island, South Carolina	Point Lookout, Maryland, transferred to Elmira Prison, NY, August 18, 1864	Exchanged March 10, 1865 at Boulware's Wharf on the James River, Virginia
Moore, Thomas B. Private	22	June 7, 1861, Camp Moore, Louisiana	Co. K, 7th Louisiana Infantry	May 5, 1864, Wilderness, Virginia	Point Lookout, Maryland, transferred to Elmira Prison, NY, August 17, 1864	Exchanged February 25, 1865 at Boulware's or Cox Wharf on the James River, Virginia
Moore, Timothy Private	23	June 10, 1861, Burgaw, North Carolina	Co. K, 3rd North Carolina Infantry	May 12, 1864, Near Spotsylvania County Court House, Virginia	Point Lookout, Maryland, transferred to Elmira Prison, NY, August 14, 1864	Oath of Allegiance June 12, 1865
Moore, Warren W. Corporal	Unk	July 11, 1861, Lynchburg, Virginia	Co. I, 42nd Virginia Infantry	May 12, 1864, Spotsylvania Court House, Virginia	Point Lookout, Maryland, transferred to Elmira Prison, NY, August 2, 1864	Oath of Allegiance June 27, 1865

Name & Rank	Age	Enlisted	Regiment and State	Where Captured	Prison	Remarks
Moore, William Private	Unk	November 3, 1863, Butler County, Alabama	Co. E, 61st Alabama Infantry	May 20, 1864, Spotsylvania Court House, Virginia	Point Lookout, Maryland, transferred to Elmira Prison, NY, July 3, 1864	Oath of Allegiance June 19, 1865
Moore, William Private	21	April 27, 1861, Newton, North Carolina	Co. F, 32nd North Carolina Infantry	May 10, 1864, Wilderness, Virginia	Point Lookout, Maryland, transferred to Elmira Prison, NY, August 6, 1864	Oath of Allegiance June 27, 1865
Moore, William C. Private	18	July 15, 1862, Alamance County, North Carolina	Co. B, 1st North Carolina Infantry	May 12, 1864, Near Spotsylvania Court House, Virginia	Point Lookout Prison, Maryland. Transferred to Elmira Prison Camp New York August 6, 1864.	Oath of Allegiance June 14, 1865
Moore, William H. Private	Unk	July 27, 1863, Fort Branch, Martin County, North Carolina	Co. G, 40th Regiment, 3rd North Carolina Artillery	January 15, 1865, Fort Fisher, North Carolina	January 30, 1865 Elmira Prison Camp, New York	Died February 28, 1865 of Remittent Fever, Grave No. 2151
Moore, William H. Private	Unk	July 1, 1861, New Orleans, Louisiana	Co. H, 14th Louisiana Infantry	May 12, 1864, Spotsylvania Court House, Virginia	Point Lookout, Maryland, transferred to Elmira Prison, NY, July 25, 1864	Exchanged February 25, 1865 at Boulware's or Cox Wharf on the James River, Virginia
Moore, William J. Private	Unk	September 16, 1862, Martin County, North Carolina	Co. K, 3rd North Carolina Cavalry	May 28, 1864, Hanover Town, Pamunkey River, Virginia	Point Lookout, Maryland, transferred to Elmira Prison, NY, July 12, 1864	Exchanged February 20, 1865 at Boulware's or Cox Wharf on the James River, Virginia
Moore, William R. Private	28	May 8, 1862, Monroe, Louisiana	Co. A, 28th Louisiana Infantry	May 18, 1864, Yellow Bayou, Louisiana	New Orleans, LA, Transferred to Elmira Prison, NY, November 19, 1864	Oath of Allegiance May 19, 1865
Moore, William T. Private	Unk	March 15, 1862, Marietta, Georgia	Co. G, Phillips Legion, Georgia	June 2, 1864, Gaines Farm Cold Harbor, Virginia	Point Lookout, Maryland, transferred to Elmira Prison, NY, July 12, 1864	Died February 4, 1865 of Variola (Smallpox), Grave No. 1738
Moorman, Fayette Private	Unk	April 18, 1862, Amherst, Virginia	Co. F, 50th Virginia Infantry	May 12, 1864, Spotsylvania Court House, Virginia	Point Lookout, Maryland, transferred to Elmira Prison, NY, August 2, 1864	Oath of Allegiance June 14, 1865

Name & Rank	Age	Enlisted	Regiment and State	Where Captured	Prison	Remarks
Moorman, Zack Private	Unk	April 18, 1862, Amherst, Virginia	Co. F, 50th Virginia Infantry	May 12, 1864, Spotsylvania Court House, Virginia	Point Lookout, Maryland, transferred to Elmira Prison, NY, August 2, 1864	Oath of Allegiance July 3, 1865
Moose, Elcanah A. Private	18	April 27, 1861, Newton, North Carolina	Co. A, 12 North Carolina Infantry	July 14, 1864, Near Washington, DC	Old Capital Prison, Washington DC. Transferred to Elmira Prison Camp New York July 25, 1864.	Exchanged February 13, 1865 at Boulware's wharf on the James River, Virginia
Moragne, Augustus W. Sergeant	Unk	June 4, 1861, Jacksonville, Alabama	Co. G, 10th Alabama Infantry	May 12, 1864, Spotsylvania Court House, Virginia	Point Lookout, Maryland, transferred to Elmira Prison, NY, August 17, 1864	Died October 31, 1864 of Diphtheria, Grave No. 742
Morales, Julian Private	Unk	June 19, 1861, Winchester, Virginia	Co. J, 2nd Virginia Infantry	May 12, 1864, Near Spotsylvania Court House, Virginia	Point Lookout, Maryland, transferred to Elmira Prison, NY, August 6, 1864	Oath of Allegiance June 23, 1865
Moran, Charles Private	19	June 4, 1861, Camp Moore, Louisiana	Co. E, 6th Louisiana Infantry	October 7, 1864, Osyka, Mississippi	New Orleans, Louisiana transferred to Elmira November 19, 1864.	Exchanged February 13, 1865 at Boulware's Wharf on the James River, Virginia
Moran, John Private	35	July 22, 1861, Camp Moore, Louisiana	Co. B, 10th Louisiana Infantry	May 12, 1864, Spotsylvania Court House, Virginia	Point Lookout, Maryland, transferred to Elmira Prison, NY, July 25, 1864	Oath of Allegiance May 14, 1865
Moran, Patrick K. Sergeant	Unk	May 24, 1861, Hillsboro, Alabama	Co. C, 9th Alabama Infantry	May 6, 1864, Wilderness, Virginia	Point Lookout, Maryland, transferred to Elmira Prison, NY, August 17, 1864	Oath of Allegiance May 13, 1865
Moran, William Private	Unk	April 1, 1864, Wytheville, Virginia	Co. A, 21st Virginia Cavalry	July 12, 1864, Beltsville, Virginia	Old Capital Prison, Washington DC. Transferred to Elmira Prison Camp New York July 25, 1864.	Oath of Allegiance May 19, 1865

Name & Rank	Age	Enlisted	Regiment and State	Where Captured	Prison	Remarks
Moreland, H. H. Private	Unk	March 4, 1862, Logansville, Dawson County, South Carolina	Co. F, 38th Georgia Infantry	June 1, 1864, Gaines Mill Cold Harbor, Virginia	Point Lookout, Maryland, transferred to Elmira Prison, NY, July 12, 1864	Oath of Allegiance July 7, 1865
Moreland, J. P. Private	Unk	March 10, 1862, Cahaba, Alabama	Co. F, 5th Alabama Infantry	May 5, 1864, Wilderness, Virginia	Point Lookout, Maryland, transferred to Elmira Prison, NY, August 17, 1864	Oath of Allegiance June 21, 1865
Moreland, John L. Private	Unk	February 25, 1862, Gilmer, Georgia	Co. F, 60th Georgia Infantry	May 6, 1864, Wilderness, Virginia	Old Capital Prison, Washington, DC, transferred to Elmira Prison, NY, July 14, 1864	Oath of Allegiance June 30, 1865
Morgan, Alexander E. Private	Unk	December 30, 1861, Nashville, Tennessee	Co. I, 44th Tennessee Infantry	June 17, 1864, Petersburg, Virginia	Point Lookout, Maryland, transferred to Elmira Prison, NY, July 30, 1864	Exchanged February 25, 1865 at Boulware's or Cox Wharf on the James River, Virginia
Morgan, Charles S. Sergeant	Unk	June 14, 1861, Valdosta, Georgia	Co. J, 12th Georgia Infantry	May 6, 1864, Wilderness, Virginia	Point Lookout, Maryland, transferred to Elmira Prison, NY, August 14, 1864	Oath of Allegiance July 11, 1865
Morgan, Daniel M. Sergeant	Unk	June 14, 1861, Camp McDonald, Georgia	Co. C, 18th Georgia Infantry	June 1, 1864, Cold Harbor, Virginia	Point Lookout, Maryland, transferred to Elmira Prison, NY, July 17, 1864	Died January 29, 1865 of Variola (smallpox), Grave No. 1812
Morgan, E. A. Private	Unk	December 1, 1861, Columbia, South Carolina	Co. G, 6th South Carolina Cavalry	June 11, 1864, Trevilian Station, Louisa Court House, Virginia	Point Lookout, Maryland, transferred to Elmira Prison, NY, July 25, 1864	Exchanged March 2, 1865 at Akins Landing on the James River, Virginia
Morgan, Elwood Private	17	March 3, 1862, Greensboro, North Carolina	Co. B, 45th North Carolina Infantry	July 11, 1864, Harpers Ferry, Virginia	Old Capital Prison, Washington DC. Transferred to Elmira Prison Camp New York July 25, 1864.	Died April 26, 1865 of Chronic Diarrhea, Grave No. 1419

Name & Rank	Age	Enlisted	Regiment and State	Where Captured	Prison	Remarks
Morgan, George H. Private	18	March 4, 1863, Fray, North Carolina	Co. E, 28th North Carolina Infantry	May 12, 1864, Near Spotsylvania Court House, Virginia	Point Lookout, Maryland, transferred to Elmira Prison, NY, August 14, 1864	Oath of Allegiance June 27, 1865
Morgan, James A. Private	39	June 3, 1861, Centre Station, Alabama	Co. G, 9th Alabama Infantry	May 6, 1864, Wilderness, Virginia	Point Lookout, Maryland, transferred to Elmira Prison, NY, August 17, 1864	Exchanged February 20, 1865 at Boulware's or Cox Wharf on the James River, Virginia
Morgan, James M. Corporal	19	December 31, 1861, Springfield, Missouri	Co. G, 1st Missouri Cavalry	May 17, 1863, Big Black Bridge, Champion Hill, Mississippi	Point Lookout, Maryland, transferred to Elmira Prison, NY, August 18, 1864	Exchanged February 25, 1865 at Boulware's wharf on the James River, Virginia
Morgan, John H. Private	Unk	May 29, 1862, Clinton, Louisiana	Co. K, 4th Louisiana Infantry	October 6, 1864, Clinton, Louisiana	New Orleans, Louisiana transferred to Elmira November 19, 1864.	Oath of Allegiance May 29, 1865
Morgan, John M. Private	27	September 3, 1862, Statesville, North Carolina	Co. C, 23rd North Carolina Infantry	May 20, 1864, Spotsylvania Court House, Virginia	Point Lookout, Maryland, transferred to Elmira Prison, NY, July 3, 1864	Oath of Allegiance May 17, 1865
Morgan, John N. Private	Unk	December 15, 1863, Tallahassee, Florida	Co. C, 5th Florida Infantry	May 12, 1864, Spotsylvania Court House, Virginia	Point Lookout, Maryland, transferred to Elmira Prison, NY, July 30, 1864	Died August 20, 1864, of Typhoid Fever, Grave No. 114
Morgan, Joseph N. Private	24	July 15, 1862, Chatham County, North Carolina	Co. E, 5th North Carolina Infantry	May 12, 1864, Spotsylvania Court House, Virginia	Point Lookout, Maryland, transferred to Elmira Prison, NY, August 6, 1864	Died February 21, 1865 of Chronic Diarrhea, Grave No. 2233
Morgan, Lorenzo Private	Unk	February 20, 1864, Greenville, Tennessee	Co. G, 1st Tennessee Infantry	May 6, 1864, Wilderness, Virginia	Point Lookout, Maryland, transferred to Elmira Prison, NY, July 23, 1864	Oath of Allegiance May 15, 1865

Name & Rank	Age	Enlisted	Regiment and State	Where Captured	Prison	Remarks
Morgan, William Private	28	June 19, 1861, Camp Moore, Louisiana	Co. C, 8th Louisiana Infantry	June 2, 1864, Brown's Farm Cold Harbor, Virginia	Point Lookout, Maryland, transferred to Elmira Prison, NY, August 17, 1864	Exchanged October 29, 1864 at Venus Point, Savannah River, GA.
Moring, Richard H. Private	25	May 28, 1861, Meherrin, Virginia	Co. K, 21st Virginia Infantry	May 12, 1864, Spotsylvania Court House, Virginia	Point Lookout, Maryland, transferred to Elmira Prison, NY, August 2, 1864	Exchanged October 29, 1864 on the James River, Virginia
Morning, E. W. Private	Unk	Unknown	Co. A, Captain Norwood's Home Guard Florida	September 27, 1864, Marianna, Florida	New Orleans, Louisiana transferred to Elmira November 19, 1864.	Returned to Fort Columbus, New York Harbor by Order. No further Information Available.
Morrel, Benjamin T. Private	Unk	April 28, 1864, Augusta, Georgia	Co. E, 7th Georgia Cavalry	June 11, 1864, Trevilian Station, Louisa Court House, Virginia	Point Lookout, Maryland, transferred to Elmira Prison, NY, July 12, 1864	Died February 2, 1865 of Variola (Smallpox), Grave No. 1760
Morring, Walter A. Corporal	Unk	Unknown	Co. H, 44th Virginia Infantry	July 8, 1864, Harpers Ferry, Virginia	Old Capital Prison, Washington DC. Transferred to Elmira Prison Camp New York July 25, 1864.	Exchanged March 10, 1865 at Boulware's Wharf on the James River, Virginia
Morris, Andrews J. Private	Unk	February 14, 1863, Catawba, Virginia	Co. K, 26th Virginia Infantry	June 15, 1864, Near Petersburg, Virginia	Point Lookout, Maryland, transferred to Elmira Prison, NY, July 12, 1864	Oath of Allegiance May 17, 1865
Morris, Charles Private	35	April 15, 1862, Asheville, Swannanoa, North Carolina	Co. K, 11th North Carolina Infantry	July 14, 1863, Falling Waters, Maryland	Point Lookout, Maryland, transferred to Elmira Prison, NY, August 18, 1864	Exchanged March 10, 1865 at Boulware's Wharf on the James River, Virginia
Morris, Charles H. Private	Unk	Unknown	Co. D, 5th Virginia Cavalry	July 3, 1864, Leetown, Virginia	Old Capital Prison, Washington DC. Transferred to Elmira Prison Camp New York July 25, 1864.	Exchanged March 14, 1865 at Boulware's Wharf on the James River, Virginia

Name & Rank	Age	Enlisted	Regiment and State	Where Captured	Prison	Remarks
Morris, Columbus W. Private	17	September 15, 1862, Camp Mangum, Raleigh, North Carolina	Co. B, 31st North Carolina Infantry	June 1, 1864, Cold Harbor, Virginia	Point Lookout, Maryland, transferred to Elmira Prison, NY, July 12, 1864	Died September 13, 1864 of Typhoid Fever, Grave No. 176
Morris, Dilmus Private	Unk	February 17, 1862, Yorktown, Virginia	Co. C, 3rd Battalion Georgia Sharp Shooters	August 16, 1864, Front Royal, Virginia	Old Capital Prison, Washington, DC transferred to Elmira Prison, NY, August 29, 1864	Oath of Allegiance July 11, 1865
Morris, E. G. Private	Unk	December 9, 1861, Camp Trousdale, Tennessee	Co. G, 44th Tennessee Infantry	June 17, 1864, Petersburg, Virginia	Point Lookout, Maryland, transferred to Elmira Prison, NY, July 30, 1864	Exchanged February 25, 1865 at Boulware's or Cox Wharf on the James River, Virginia
Morris, Harry Private	29	July 15, 1861, Kimball, North Carolina	Co. D, 8th North Carolina Infantry	May 31, 1864, Cold Harbor, Virginia	Point Lookout, Maryland, transferred to Elmira Prison, NY, July 12, 1864	Oath of Allegiance July 7, 1865
Morris, John Private	Unk	April 1, 1862, Coosa, Alabama	Co. B, 59th Alabama Infantry	June 17, 1864, Petersburg, Virginia	Point Lookout, Maryland, transferred to Elmira Prison, NY, July 30, 1864	Oath of Allegiance July 7, 1865
Morris, John M. Private	Unk	Unknown	Co. B, 2nd Maryland Cavalry	July 10, 1864, Frederick, Maryland	Old Capital Prison, Washington DC. Transferred to Elmira Prison Camp New York July 25, 1864.	Oath of Allegiance May 19, 1865
Morris, John R. Private	35	Unknown	Co. A, 47th North Carolina Infantry	July 14, 1863, Falling Waters, Maryland	Point Lookout, Maryland, transferred to Elmira Prison, NY, August 18, 1864	Oath of Allegiance June 11, 1865
Morris, John T. Sergeant	Unk	July 3, 1861, Lynchburg, Virginia	Co. G, 42nd Virginia Infantry	May 12, 1864, Near Spotsylvania Court House, Virginia	Point Lookout, Maryland, transferred to Elmira Prison, NY, August 6, 1864	Oath of Allegiance June 27, 1865

Name & Rank	Age	Enlisted	Regiment and State	Where Captured	Prison	Remarks
Morris, Martin V. Private	18	August 20, 1862, Cumberland County, North Carolina	Co. F, 8th North Carolina Infantry	June 1, 1864, Cold Harbor, Virginia. Gunshot Wound Left Thigh.	Old Capital Prison, Washington, DC transferred to Elmira Prison, NY, August 27, 1864	Oath of Allegiance June 21, 1865
Morris, Martin V. B. Private	Unk	September 30, 1861, Catawba, Virginia	Co. K, 26th Virginia Infantry	June 15, 1864, Near Petersburg, Virginia	Point Lookout, Maryland, transferred to Elmira Prison, NY, July 12, 1864	Died November 18, 1864 of Chronic Diarrhea, Grave No. 972
Morris, Richard G. Private	Unk	Unknown	Co. D, 44th Virginia Infantry	May 5, 1864, Orange Court House, Virginia	Point Lookout, Maryland, transferred to Elmira Prison, NY, August 2, 1864	Died September 21, 1864 of Chronic Diarrhea, Grave No. 328
Morris, Robert Private	Unk	May 18, 1861, Lisbon, Virginia	Co. C, 42nd Virginia Infantry	May 12, 1864, Spotsylvania Court House, Virginia	Point Lookout, Maryland, transferred to Elmira Prison, NY, August 2,1864	Oath of Allegiance June 27, 1865
Morris, Robert Stockton Private	Unk	August 14, 1861, Atlanta, Georgia	Co. B, Cobb's Legion, Georgia	September 22, 1863, Jack's Shop, Near Madison Court House, Virginia	Point Lookout, Maryland, transferred to Elmira Prison, NY, August 18, 1864	Exchanged March 10, 1865 at Boulware's Wharf on the James River, Virginia
Morris, Samuel A. Private	19	July 15, 1862, Raleigh, North Carolina	Co C, 1st North Carolina Infantry	May 12, 1864, Spotsylvania Court House, Virginia	Point Lookout, Maryland, transferred to Elmira Prison, NY, August 6,1864	Died December 8, 1864 of Chronic Diarrhea, Grave No. 1170
Morris, Thomas Private	Unk	February 6, 1862, Center Hill, Georgia	Co. B, 16th Georgia Infantry	June 1, 1864, Gaines Mill Cold Harbor, Virginia	Point Lookout, Maryland, transferred to Elmira Prison, NY, July 12, 1864	Oath of Allegiance June 14, 1865
Morris, Thomas Private	24	August 13, 1861, Fayetteville, North Carolina	Co. E, 8th North Carolina Infantry	June 1, 1864, Gaines Mill Cold Harbor, Virginia	Point Lookout, Maryland, transferred to Elmira Prison, NY, July 17, 1864	Died November 13, 1864, Chronic Diarrhea, Grave No. 822

Name & Rank	Age	Enlisted	Regiment and State	Where Captured	Prison	Remarks
Morris, W. B. Private	Unk	Unknown	Co. D, 3rd Georgia Infantry	June 17, 1864, Petersburg, Virginia	Point Lookout, Maryland, transferred to Elmira Prison, NY, July 23, 1864	Oath of Allegiance May 13, 1865
Morris, Walter C. Private	Unk	July 17, 1861, Center Hill, Georgia	Co. C, 3rd Battalion Georgia Sharp Shooters	August 16, 1864, Front Royal, Virginia	Old Capital Prison, Washington, DC transferred to Elmira Prison, NY, August 29, 1864	Died February 15, 1865 of Variola (Smallpox), Grave No. 2173
Morris, William J. Private	30	May 21, 1861, Prince Edward Court House, Virginia	Co. J, 23rd Virginia Infantry	May 12, 1864, Spotsylvania, Virginia. Gunshot Wound Left Shoulder Joint, Compound Fracture.	Old Capital Prison, Washington, DC, transferred to Elmira December 17, 1864	Exchanged March 10, 1865 at Boulware's Wharf on the James River, Virginia
Morris, William R. Corporal	18	July 25, 1861, Tullahoma, Tennessee	Co. A, 25th Tennessee Infantry	June 17, 1864, Near Petersburg, Virginia	Point Lookout, Maryland, transferred to Elmira Prison, NY, July 30, 1864	Exchanged February 25, 1865 at Boulware's or Cox Wharf on the James River, Virginia
Morris, Zachariah S. Private	21	September 2, 1863, Marble Valley, Alabama	Co. D, 8th Alabama Infantry	May 12, 1864, Spotsylvania Court House, Virginia. Gunshot Wound Right Hand, Loss of Second Finger.	Old Capital Prison, Washington DC. Transferred to Elmira Prison Camp New York July 25, 1864.	Oath of Allegiance May 29, 1865
Morrison, C. M. Private	Unk	Unknown	Smith's Battalion, Heavy Artillery	June 16, 1864, Petersburg, Virginia	Point Lookout, Maryland, transferred to Elmira Prison, NY, July 12, 1864	Exchanged February 25, 1865 at Boulware's or Cox Wharf on the James River, Virginia
Morrison, James Private	27	October 1, 1862, Snickersville, Virginia	Co. C, 35th Battalion Virginia Cavalry	May 6, 1864, Wilderness, Virginia. Gunshot Wound Left Shoulder.	Old Capital Prison, Washington DC. Transferred to Elmira Prison Camp New York July 25, 1864.	Exchanged March 2, 1865 at Akins Landing on the James River, Virginia

Name & Rank	Age	Enlisted	Regiment and State	Where Captured	Prison	Remarks
Morrison, James S. Private	Unk	March 17, 1862, Richmond, Virginia	2nd Battalion Maryland Artillery	May 11, 1864, Yellow Tavern, Hanover County, Virginia	Point Lookout, Maryland, transferred to Elmira Prison, NY, August 17, 1864	Exchanged October 29, 1864 at Venus Point, Savannah River, GA.
Morrison, John W. Private	22	September 1, 1862, Concorde, North Carolina	Co. A, 52nd North Carolina Infantry	May 12, 1864, Spotsylvania Court House, Virginia	Point Lookout, Maryland, transferred to Elmira Prison, NY, July 30, 1864	Oath of Allegiance June 12, 1865
Morrison, Lewis W. Sergeant	32	November 21, 1861, Alexander County, North Carolina	Co. G, 38th North Carolina Infantry	June 22, 1864, Petersburg, Virginia. Gunshot Wound Right Side of Face.	Old Capital Prison, Washington, DC transferred to Elmira Prison, NY, August 27, 1864	Died November 30, 1864 of Pneumonia, Grave No. 1001
Morrison, Marshall W. Private	Unk	March 1, 1864, Mecklenburg County, North Carolina	Co. H, 35th North Carolina Infantry	June 17, 1864, Petersburg, Virginia	Point Lookout, Maryland, transferred to Elmira Prison, NY, July 30, 1864	Oath of Allegiance June 12, 1865
Morriss, Zachariah T. Private	Unk	February 6, 1862, Halifax County Court House, Virginia	Co. K, 3rd Virginia Infantry	July 27, 1864, Near Petersburg, Virginia	Point Lookout, Maryland, transferred to Elmira Prison, NY, August 18, 1864	Oath of Allegiance May 29, 1865
Morrow, David D. Private	Unk	April 4, 1863, Washington County, Virginia	Co. L, 26th Battalion, Virginia Infantry	June 3, 1864, Gaines Farm Cold Harbor, Virginia	Point Lookout, Maryland, transferred to Elmira Prison, NY, July 17, 1864	Oath of Allegiance July 3, 1865
Morrow, George H. Private	Unk	March 12, 1864, Liberty Mills, Virginia	Co. J, 7th North Carolina Infantry	May 6, 1864, Wilderness, Virginia	Point Lookout, Maryland, transferred to Elmira Prison, NY, August 14, 1864	Died October 3, 1864 of Chronic Diarrhea, Grave No. 620. Headstone has Moore, 37th NC.
Morrow, John A. Private	20	July 30, 1861, Dallas, North Carolina	Co. B, 28th North Carolina Infantry	July 29, 1864, Petersburg, Virginia	Point Lookout, Maryland, transferred to Elmira Prison, NY, August 12, 1864	Exchanged October 29, 1864 at Venus Point, Savannah River, GA.

Name & Rank	Age	Enlisted	Regiment and State	Where Captured	Prison	Remarks
Morrow, Strangeman M. Private	23	March 12, 1864, Liberty Mills, Virginia	Co. J, 7th North Carolina Infantry	May 12, 1864, Spotsylvania Court House, Virginia. Gunshot Wound Right Foot.	Old Capital Prison, Washington, DC, transferred to Elmira Prison, NY, March 3, 1865.	Exchanged March 14, 1865 at Boulware's Wharf on the James River, Virginia
Morrow, W. F. Civilian	Unk	Louisiana	Civilian Quartermaster Department	May 19, 1864, Marksville, Louisiana	New Orleans, LA, Transferred to Elmira Prison, NY, November 19, 1864	Died December 12, 1864 of Pneumonia, Grave No. 1138. Headstone has W. M. Morrow.
Morse, Richard Private	Unk	Unknown	Co. F, 23rd South Carolina Infantry	July 30, 1864, Petersburg, Virginia	Point Lookout, Maryland, transferred to Elmira Prison, NY, August 12, 1864	Transferred to New Haven, Connecticut 1/9/65 per Orders from dated 1/5/65.
Morton, Charles E. Sergeant	21	August 12, 1861, Currituck County, North Carolina	Co. B, 8th North Carolina Infantry	May 31, 1864, Cold Harbor, Virginia	Point Lookout, Maryland, transferred to Elmira Prison, NY, July 11, 1864	Exchanged October 29, 1864 at Venus Point, Savannah River, GA.
Morton, Charles J. Private	Unk	April 1, 1864, Bat Tracy, Tennessee	Co. A, Jackson's 1st Regiment, Tennessee Heavy Artillery	August 23, 1864, Fort Morgan, Alabama	New Orleans, Louisiana transferred to Elmira Prison, NY, December 4, 1864.	Exchanged March 10, 1865 at Boulware's Wharf on the James River, Virginia
Morton, Hardy Owen Private	26	January 28, 1862, Bladen County, North Carolina	Co. B, 36th 2nd North Carolina Artillery	January 15, 1865, Fort Fisher, North Carolina	February 1, 1865, Elmira Prison Camp, New York	Oath of Allegiance July 3, 1865
Morton, Micajah T. Private	26	May 6, 1861, Jacksonville, North Carolina	Co. B, 24th North Carolina Infantry	June 17, 1864, Petersburg, Virginia	Point Lookout, Maryland, transferred to Elmira Prison, NY, July 30, 1864	Oath of Allegiance May 19, 1865
Morton, William G. Private	21	May 10, 1862, Albemarle, North Carolina	Co. K, 28th North Carolina Infantry	May 12, 1864, Near Spotsylvania Court House, Virginia	Point Lookout, Maryland, transferred to Elmira Prison, NY, August 14, 1864	Exchanged March 14, 1865 at Boulware's Wharf on the James River, Virginia
Morton, William H. Private	20	May 6, 1861, Jacksonville, North Carolina	Co. B, 24th North Carolina Infantry	June 17, 1864, Petersburg, Virginia	Point Lookout, Maryland, transferred to Elmira Prison, NY, July 30, 1864	Oath of Allegiance June 21, 1865

Name & Rank	Age	Enlisted	Regiment and State	Where Captured	Prison	Remarks
Morton, William P. Private	24	August 15, 1862, Graham, North Carolina	Co. J, 8th North Carolina Infantry	June 1, 1864, Cold Harbor, Virginia	Point Lookout, Maryland, transferred to Elmira Prison, NY, July 12, 1864	Died December 11, 1864 of Pneumonia, Grave No. 83
Moser, Robert W. Private	21	March 22, 1862, Winston, North Carolina	Co. K, 52nd North Carolina Infantry	May 12, 1864, Spotsylvania Court House, Virginia	Point Lookout, Maryland, transferred to Elmira Prison, NY, July 30, 1864	Oath of Allegiance June 12, 1865
Moses, Martin T. Private	Unk	July 14, 1862, Calhoun, Georgia	Co. K, 61st Georgia Infantry	May 12, 1864, Spotsylvania Court House, Virginia	Point Lookout, Maryland, transferred to Elmira Prison, NY, July 30, 1864	Exchanged March 10, 1865 at Boulware's Wharf on the James River, Virginia
Mosley, David W. Private	29	July 15, 1862, Raleigh, North Carolina	Co. E, 1st North Carolina Infantry	May 12, 1864, Near Spotsylvania Court House, Virginia	Point Lookout Prison, Maryland. Transferred to Elmira Prison Camp New York August 6, 1864.	Oath of Allegiance June 27, 1865
Mosley, J. A. Private	Unk	October 5, 1861, Bowling Green, Kentucky	Co. C, 23rd Tennessee Infantry	June 17, 1864, Petersburg, Virginia	Point Lookout, Maryland, transferred to Elmira Prison, NY, July 30, 1864	Exchanged February 25, 1865 at Boulware's or Cox Wharf on the James River, Virginia
Moss, Andrew Private	29	December 11, 1862, Camp Holmes, North Carolina	Co. C, 26th North Carolina Infantry	May 12, 1864, Spotsylvania Court House, Virginia	Point Lookout, Maryland, transferred to Elmira Prison, NY, July 30, 1864	Oath of Allegiance June 23, 1865
Moss, Florence Private	Unk	February 28, 1862, Louisiana	Co. K, 10th Louisiana Infantry	May 12, 1864, Spotsylvania Court House, Virginia	Point Lookout, Maryland, transferred to Elmira Prison, NY, July 25, 1864	Exchanged October 29, 1864 at Venus Point, Savannah River, GA.
Moss, John M. Private	Unk	November 5, 1862, Franklin, Tennessee	Co. J, 44th Tennessee Infantry	June 17, 1864, Petersburg, Virginia	Point Lookout, Maryland, transferred to Elmira Prison, NY, July 30, 1864	Exchanged February 25, 1865 at Boulware's or Cox Wharf on the James River, Virginia

Name & Rank	Age	Enlisted	Regiment and State	Where Captured	Prison	Remarks
Moss, John P. Private	Unk	April 1, 1863, Wilmington, North Carolina	Co. H, 22nd South Carolina Infantry	July 30, 1864, Petersburg, Virginia	Point Lookout, Maryland, transferred to Elmira Prison, NY, August 12, 1864	Died September 2, 1864 of Typhoid Fever, Grave No. 85. Name Morse on Headstone.
Moss, Noah Private	Unk	December 27, 1861, Yorkville, South Carolina	Co. C, 17th South Carolina Infantry	July 30, 1864, Petersburg, Virginia	Point Lookout, Maryland, transferred to Elmira Prison, NY, August 12, 1864	Oath of Allegiance July 11, 1865
Moss, Robert H. Private	Unk	December 27, 1861, Yorkville, South Carolina	Co. C, 17th South Carolina Infantry	July 30, 1864, Petersburg, Virginia	Point Lookout, Maryland, transferred to Elmira Prison, NY, August 12, 1864	Exchanged October 29, 1864 at Venus Point, Savannah River, GA.
Moss, Wiley I. J. Private	Unk	April 19, 1862, Savannah, Georgia	Co. D, 3rd Battalion Georgia Sharp Shooters	August 16, 1864, Front Royal, Virginia	Old Capital Prison, Washington, DC transferred to Elmira Prison, NY, August 29, 1864	Died December 4, 1864 of Chronic Diarrhea, Grave No. 881
Moss, William S. Private	21	April 23, 1861, Manchester, Virginia	Co. B, 4th Virginia Cavalry	September 19, 1863, Germania Ford, Virginia	Point Lookout, Maryland, transferred to Elmira Prison, NY, August 18, 1864	Exchanged March 10, 1865 at Boulware's Wharf on the James River, Virginia
Motes, Patrick H. Private	Unk	February 22, 1864, Troy, Alabama	Co. E, 1st Battalion Alabama Artillery	August 23, 1864, Fort Morgan, Alabama	Steam Press No. 4, New Orleans, Louisiana transferred to Elmira Prison, NY, October 8, 1864	Died December 23, 1864 of Pneumonia, Grave No. 1100
Motley, Thomas W. Private	Unk	March 4, 1862, Fort Lowry, Virginia	Co. C, 55th Virginia Infantry	June 3, 1864, Near Talapatomoy Creek, Cold Harbor, Virginia	Point Lookout, Maryland, transferred to Elmira Prison, NY, July 17, 1864	Exchanged October 29, 1864 at Venus Point, Savannah River, GA.
Mottsheard, John W. Private	Unk	April 29, 1863, White Sulfur Springs, Virginia	Co. H, 26th Battalion Virginia Infantry	June 3, 1864, Gaines Mill Cold Harbor, Virginia	Point Lookout, Maryland, transferred to Elmira Prison, NY, July 17, 1864	Died October 13, 1864, Chronic Diarrhea, Grave No. 695

Name & Rank	Age	Enlisted	Regiment and State	Where Captured	Prison	Remarks
Moultin, William Private	Unk	July 27, 1864, Big Spain, Virginia	Co. F, 2nd Maryland Cavalry	July 23, 1864, Point of Rocks, Maryland	Old Capital Prison, Washington, DC, transferred to Elmira Prison, NY, August 12, 1864	Oath of Allegiance October 28, 1864. Early Release per Lincoln's Proclamation, 12/8/1863.
Moulton, William Landsman	Unk	Unknown	Confederate States Navy	May 5, 1864, Albemarle Sound on Steamer CSS Bombshell	Point Lookout, Maryland, transferred to Elmira Prison, NY, August 17, 1864	Transferred For Exchange October 11, 1864 to Point Lookout Prison Camp, MD. Nothing Further.
Mounger, George W. Sergeant	32	April 22, 1862, Knoxville, Tennessee	Co. F, 63rd Tennessee Infantry	May 16, 1864, Near Drury's Bluff, Virginia	Point Lookout, Maryland, transferred to Elmira Prison, NY, August 17, 1864	Exchanged February 25, 1865 at Boulware's or Cox Wharf on the James River, Virginia
Mountain, William R. Private	Unk	June 1, 1863, Tallapoosa County, Alabama	Co. C, 61st Alabama Infantry	July 12, 1864, Near Washington, DC	Old Capital Prison, Washington DC. Transferred to Elmira Prison Camp New York July 25, 1864.	Died April 18, 1865 of Epilepsy, Grave No. 1357
Mouzon, S. R. Private	Unk	May 25, 1863, McPherson-ville, South Carolina	Co. J, 4th South Carolina Cavalry	June 11, 1864, Trevilian Station, Louisa Court House, Virginia	Point Lookout, Maryland, transferred to Elmira Prison, NY, July 25, 1864	Exchanged October 29, 1864 at Venus Point, Savannah River, GA.
Mowry, Ephraim Private	Unk	April 15, 1862, Rudes Hill, Virginia	Co. G, 2nd Virginia Infantry	October 28, 1864, Strasburg, Virginia	Old Capital Prison, Washington, DC, transferred to Elmira Prison Camp, NY, December 17, 1864	Died April 4, 1865 of Chronic Diarrhea, Grave No. 2553
Mowry, James Private	Unk	May 23, 1862, New Market, Virginia	Co. A, 11th Virginia Cavalry	August 14, 1864, Strasburg, Virginia	Old Capital Prison, Washington, DC transferred to Elmira Prison, NY, August 29, 1864	Oath of Allegiance June 19, 1865

Name & Rank	Age	Enlisted	Regiment and State	Where Captured	Prison	Remarks
Moye, Joseph Private	Unk	June 17, 1861, Lewisburg, North Carolina	Co. K, 24th North Carolina Infantry	June 17, 1864, Near Petersburg, Virginia	Point Lookout, Maryland, transferred to Elmira Prison, NY, July 30, 1864	Oath of Allegiance July 11, 1865
Moys, Alfred Private	Unk	Unknown	Co. E, 61st North Carolina Infantry	August 27, 1863, Battery Wagner, Morris Island, South Carolina	Point Lookout, Maryland, transferred to Elmira Prison, NY, August 18, 1864	Exchanged March 10, 1865 at Boulware's Wharf on the James River, Virginia
Mozingo, James Private	Unk	April 14, 1863, Fredericks-burg, Virginia	Co. J, 15th Virginia Cavalry	September 13, 1863, Near Culpepper Court House, Virginia	Point Lookout, Maryland, transferred to Elmira Prison, NY, August 18, 1864	Transferred For Exchange October 11, 1864 to Point Lookout Prison Camp, MD. Died October 20, 1864 of Unknown Causes.
Much, B. Private	Unk	Unknown	Co. C, 4th South Carolina Infantry	May 28, 1864, Hall's Shop, Virginia	Point Lookout, Maryland, transferred to Elmira Prison, NY, July 12, 1864	Oath of Allegiance June 30, 1965
Mulholm, Pashail Private	30	July 15, 1862, Chatham County, North Carolina	Co. E, 5th North Carolina Infantry	May 12, 1864, Spotsylvania Court House, Virginia	Point Lookout, Maryland, transferred to Elmira Prison, NY, August 6, 1864	Exchanged March 2, 1865 at Akins Landing on the James River, Virginia
Mulinax, John W. Private	19	March 1, 1864, Shelby, North Carolina	Co. G, 49th North Carolina Infantry	March 25, 1865, Southside Railroad, Petersburg, Virginia,	Old Capital Prison, Washington, DC. Transferred to Elmira Prison Camp, NY, May 23, 1865.	Died May 24, 1865 of Erysipelas, Grave No. 2925. Headstone has G. W. Mullin.
Mulinax, W. B. Private	Unk	May 16, 1863, Pickens, South Carolina	Co. I, Hampton Legion, South Carolina Infantry	July 29, 1864, Petersburg, Virginia	Point Lookout, Maryland, transferred to Elmira Prison, NY, August 12, 1864	Exchanged March 14, 1865 at Boulware's Wharf on the James River, Virginia
Mulkey, Francis M. Private	Unk	September 19, 1861, Dalton, Georgia	Co. D, 60th Georgia Infantry	May 20, 1864, Spotsylvania Court House, Virginia	Point Lookout, Maryland, transferred to Elmira Prison, NY, July 3, 1864	Oath of Allegiance May 29, 1865

Name & Rank	Age	Enlisted	Regiment and State	Where Captured	Prison	Remarks
Mull, John M. Private	32	May 3, 1862, Cleveland County, North Carolina	Co. F, 55th North Carolina Infantry	May 5, 1864, Wilderness, Virginia	Point Lookout Prison Camp, Maryland. Transferred to Elmira Prison Camp, NY, July 30, 1864	Died June 20, 1865 of Chronic Diarrhea, Grave No. 2810
Mullen, Jeremiah Private	35	June 4, 1861, Camp Moore, Louisiana	Co. J, 6th Louisiana Infantry	May 5, 1864, Wilderness, Virginia	Point Lookout, Maryland, transferred to Elmira Prison, NY, August 17, 1864	Oath of Allegiance May 29, 1865
Mullens, John T. Sergeant	34	May 29, 1861, Fayetteville, North Carolina	Co. C, 3rd North Carolina Infantry	May 12, 1864, Near Spotsylvania County Court House, Virginia	Point Lookout, Maryland, transferred to Elmira Prison, NY, August 14, 1864	Exchanged March 2, 1865 at Akins Landing on the James River, Virginia
Mulligan, Adam G. Private	Unk	June 24, 1861, Coosawhatchie, South Carolina	Co. E, 11th South Carolina Infantry	June 24, 1864, Near Petersburg, Virginia	Point Lookout, Maryland, transferred to Elmira Prison, NY, August 18, 1864	Oath of Allegiance June 21, 1865
Mulligan, George B. Private	Unk	July 20, 1863, Bluffton, South Carolina	Co. E, 11th South Carolina Infantry	June 24, 1864, Near Petersburg, Virginia	Point Lookout, Maryland, transferred to Elmira Prison, NY, August 18, 1864	Exchanged February 20, 1865 at Boulware's or Cox Wharf on the James River, Virginia
Mulligan, William H. Private	19	June 24, 1861, Coosawhatchie, South Carolina	Co. E, 11th South Carolina Infantry	June 24, 1864, Near Petersburg, Virginia	Point Lookout, Maryland, transferred to Elmira Prison, NY, August 18, 1864	Died January 27, 1865 of Pleuro Pneumonia, Grave No. 1634
Mullikin, William C. Private	Unk	March 12, 1862, Beaulien, Georgia	Co. G, 61st Georgia Infantry	May 12, 1864, Spotsylvania Court House, Virginia	Point Lookout, Maryland, transferred to Elmira Prison, NY, July 30, 1864	Oath of Allegiance May 29, 1865
Mullins, Martin G. Private	Unk	May 15, 1862, Camp Harris, Tennessee	Co. G, 17th Tennessee Infantry	June 17, 1864, Petersburg, Virginia	Point Lookout, Maryland, transferred to Elmira Prison, NY, July 30, 1864	Died February 26, 1865 of Variola (Smallpox), Grave No. 2146

Name & Rank	Age	Enlisted	Regiment and State	Where Captured	Prison	Remarks
Mullins, William Private	Unk	March 15, 1862, Charleston, South Carolina	Co. C, 27th South Carolina Infantry	June 24, 1864, Near Petersburg, Virginia	Point Lookout, Maryland, transferred to Elmira Prison, NY, July 25, 1864	Oath of Allegiance May 19, 1865
Mullins, William H. Private	Unk	August 26, 1861, Bethel, Tennessee	Co. A, Jackson's 1st Regiment, Tennessee Heavy Artillery	August 23, 1864, Fort Morgan, Alabama	New Orleans, Louisiana transferred to Elmira Prison, NY, December 4, 1864.	Exchanged February 25, 1865 at Boulware's or Cox Wharf on the James River, Virginia
Muncy, J. B. Private	Unk	June 29, 1861, Wytheville, Virginia	Co. B, 50th Virginia Infantry	May 12, 1864, Spotsylvania Court House, Virginia	Point Lookout, Maryland, transferred to Elmira Prison, NY, August 2, 1864	Exchanged October 29, 1864 at Venus Point, Savannah River, GA.
Muncy, William J. C. Corporal	Unk	May 25, 1862, Floyd Court House, Virginia	Co. B, 42nd Virginia Infantry	May 5, 1864, Near Wilderness Tavern, Virginia	Point Lookout, Maryland, transferred to Elmira Prison, NY, August 2, 1864	Oath of Allegiance June 19, 1865
Munday, James A. Private	25	April 19, 1861, Concord, North Carolina	Co. A, 20th North Carolina Infantry	May 20, 1864, Spotsylvania Court House, Virginia	Point Lookout, Maryland, transferred to Elmira Prison, NY, July 3, 1864	Exchanged March 2, 1865 at Akins Landing on the James River, Virginia
Munday, James M. Private	Unk	May 1, 1862, Richmond, Virginia	Sturdivant's Co. A, Virginia Light Artillery	June 15, 1864, Petersburg, Virginia	Point Lookout, Maryland, transferred to Elmira Prison, NY, July 12, 1864	Exchanged March 19, 1865 at Akins Landing on the James River, Virginia
Mundy, James C. Private	Unk	August 13, 1863, Abbeville Court House, South Carolina	Co. F, Holcombe Legion, South Carolina	May 8, 1864, Jarrett's Depot, Virginia	Point Lookout, Maryland, transferred to Elmira Prison, NY, August 17, 1864	Exchanged October 29, 1864. Died July 6, 1865 of Typhoid Fever at 2nd Division Hospital, 23rd A. C.
Munford, Richard W. Private	22	December 5, 1861, Sac River, St. Clair County, Missouri	Co. B, 1st Missouri Cavalry	May 17, 1863, Big Black Bridge, Champion Hill, Mississippi	Point Lookout, Maryland, transferred to Elmira Prison, NY, August 18, 1864	Exchanged February 25, 1865 at Boulware's wharf on the James River, Virginia

Name & Rank	Age	Enlisted	Regiment and State	Where Captured	Prison	Remarks
Mungo, Mack Private	Unk	July 1, 1862, Chesterfield, South Carolina	Co. K, 6th South Carolina Cavalry	June 11, 1864, Trevilian Station, Louisa Court House, Virginia	Point Lookout, Maryland, transferred to Elmira Prison, NY, July 25, 1864	Transferred for Exchange 10/11/64. Died 10/22/64 of Chronic Diarrhea at US Army General Hospital, Baltimore, MD
Munkers, William T. Private	21	April 14, 1862, Arkansas	Co. G, 1st Missouri Cavalry	May 17, 1863, Big Black Bridge, Champion Hill, Mississippi	Point Lookout, Maryland, transferred to Elmira Prison, NY, August 18, 1864	Exchanged February 13, 1865 at Boulware's wharf on the James River, Virginia
Munn, John B. Private	18	August 13, 1863, Brunswick County, North Carolina	Co. G, 40th Regiment, 3rd North Carolina Artillery	January 15, 1865, Fort Fisher, North Carolina	February 1, 1865 Elmira Prison Camp, New York	Died February 26, 1865 of Phthisis Pulmonalis, Grave No. 2157
Munroe, D. J. Private	Unk	Unknown	Co. C, 30th North Carolina Infantry	July 14, 1863, Falling Waters, Maryland	Point Lookout, Maryland, transferred to Elmira Prison, NY, August 18, 1864	Transferred for Exchanged 10/29/64 at Venus Point, Savannah River, GA.
Munt, Henry F. Corporal	Unk	February 14, 1863, Prince George County, Virginia	Co. F, 21st Virginia Infantry	May 12, 1864, Spotsylvania Court House, Virginia	Point Lookout, Maryland, transferred to Elmira Prison, NY, August 2, 1864	Oath of Allegiance June 23, 1865
Murdock, Augustus Private	Unk	September 15, 1863, Urbana, Virginia	Co. A, 1st Maryland Cavalry	July 13, 1864, Montgomery, Maryland	Old Capital Prison, Washington DC. Transferred to Elmira Prison Camp New York July 25, 1864.	Exchanged October 29, 1864 at Venus Point, Savannah River, GA.
Murdock, Edward Private	26	May 29, 1861, New Orleans, Louisiana	Co. E, 6th Louisiana Infantry	May 5, 1864, Wilderness, Virginia	Point Lookout, Maryland, transferred to Elmira Prison, NY, August 17, 1864	Oath of Allegiance May 13, 1865
Murdock, J. Private	Unk	June 29, 1862, Gaines Mill's, Georgia	Co. E, 13th Georgia Infantry	May 20, 1864, Spotsylvania Court House, Virginia	Point Lookout, Maryland, transferred to Elmira Prison, NY, July 3, 1864	Exchanged October 29, 1864 at Venus Point, Savannah River, GA.

Name & Rank	Age	Enlisted	Regiment and State	Where Captured	Prison	Remarks
Murnard, Charles D. Civilian	Unk	Louisiana	Citizen of Louisiana	September 19, 1864, Tensan Parish, Louisiana	New Orleans, LA, Transferred to Elmira Prison, NY, November 19, 1864	Died December 21, 1864 of Pneumonia, Grave No. 1081. Headstone has Murwardy.
Murph, William F. Private	23	July 10, 1861, Fort Johnson, Brunswick County, North Carolina	Co. B, 20th North Carolina Infantry	May 12, 1864, Near Spotsylvania Court House, Virginia	Point Lookout Prison, Maryland. Transferred to Elmira Prison Camp New York August 14, 1864.	Oath of Allegiance June 27, 1865
Murph, John O. W. Private	18	September 29, 1863, Concord, North Carolina	Co. C, 33rd North Carolina Infantry	July 29, 1864, Petersburg, Virginia	Point Lookout, Maryland, transferred to Elmira Prison, NY, August 12, 1864	Died February 21, 1865 of Variola (Smallpox) Grave No. 2235
Murphy, A. W. Private	Unk	Unknown	Co. B, Hood's Battalion, Virginia Reserve Infantry	June 15, 1864, Petersburg, Virginia	Point Lookout, Maryland, transferred to Elmira Prison, NY, July 30, 1864	Oath of Allegiance May 19, 1865
Murphy, David F. Private	Unk	April 30, 1862, Orangeburg, South Carolina	Co. G, 25th South Carolina Infantry	January 15, 1865, Fort Fisher, North Carolina	January 30, 1865, Elmira Prison Camp, New York	Died February 28, 1865 of Diarrhea, Grave No. 2134. Headstone has L. D. Murphy.
Murphy, Dennis Private	46	June 4, 1861, Camp Moore, Louisiana	Co. J, 6th Louisiana Infantry	May 5, 1864, Wilderness, Virginia	Point Lookout, Maryland, transferred to Elmira Prison, NY, August 18, 1864	Exchanged February 20, 1865 at Boulware's or Cox Wharf on the James River, Virginia
Murphy, Doctor F. Private	25	March 24, 1862, Ransom's Bridge, North Carolina	Co. K, 12th North Carolina Infantry	May 12, 1864, Near Spotsylvania, Virginia	Point Lookout, Maryland, transferred to Elmira Prison, NY, August 14, 1864	Oath of Allegiance June 27, 1865
Murphy, G. T. Private	Unk	Unknown	Co. A, 27th Georgia Infantry	June 16, 1864, Near Petersburg, Virginia	Point Lookout, Maryland, transferred to Elmira Prison, NY, July 25, 1864	Oath of Allegiance May 19, 1865

Name & Rank	Age	Enlisted	Regiment and State	Where Captured	Prison	Remarks
Murphy, George Private	18	February 26, 1862, New Orleans, Louisiana	Co. K, 6th Louisiana Infantry	May 5, 1864, Wilderness, Virginia	Point Lookout, Maryland, transferred to Elmira Prison, NY, August 17, 1864	Exchanged February 25, 1865 at Boulware's or Cox Wharf on the James River, Virginia
Murphy, Henry C. Private	Unk	September 23, 1861, Eldorado, Arkansas	Co. E, 3rd Arkansas Infantry	May 12, 1864, Spotsylvania Court House, Virginia	Point Lookout, Maryland, transferred to Elmira Prison, NY, August 12, 1864	Exchanged February 13, 1865 at Boulware's wharf on the James River, Virginia
Murphy, Herbert Private	Unk	May 31, 1862, Phillippi, Virginia	Co. G, 5th Virginia Infantry	May 12, 1864, Spotsylvania Court House, Virginia	Point Lookout, Maryland, transferred to Elmira Prison, NY, August 2, 1864	Oath of Allegiance May 17, 1865
Murphy, J. W. Private	Unk	May 18, 1861, Sutton, Virginia	Co. C, 25th Virginia Infantry	May 6, 1864, Wilderness, Virginia	Old Capital Prison, Washington, DC, transferred to Elmira Prison, NY, July 14, 1864	Oath of Allegiance June 23, 1865
Murphy, James C. Private	Unk	October 17, 1864, Columbia, South Carolina	Co. C, 25th South Carolina Infantry	January 15, 1865, Fort Fisher, North Carolina	January 30, 1865, Elmira Prison Camp, New York	Oath of Allegiance July 11, 1865
Murphy, James W. Private	26	June 25, 1863, Fort Johnson, North Carolina	Co. G, 40th Regiment, 3rd North Carolina Artillery	January 15, 1865, Fort Fisher, North Carolina	February 1, 1865 Elmira Prison Camp, New York	Exchanged February 20, 1865. Died March 16, 1865 of Chronic Diarrhea at Jackson Hospital, Richmond, Virginia
Murphy, Jeremiah K. Private	Unk	June 29, 1861, Abbeville, Alabama	Co. B, 6th Alabama Infantry	May 30, 1864, Mechanics-ville, Virginia	Point Lookout, Maryland, transferred to Elmira Prison, NY, July 12, 1864	Exchanged March 10, 1865 at Boulware's Wharf on the James River, Virginia
Murphy, John Private	Unk	July 22, 1861, Camp Moore, Louisiana	Co. K, 10th Louisiana Infantry	May 5, 1864, Wilderness, Virginia	Point Lookout, Maryland, transferred to Elmira Prison, NY, July 25, 1864	Exchanged February 25, 1865 at Boulware's or Cox Wharf on the James River, Virginia

Name & Rank	Age	Enlisted	Regiment and State	Where Captured	Prison	Remarks
Murphy, John Private	Unk	August 24, 1861, Granada, Tennessee	Co. A, Jackson's 1st Regiment, Tennessee Heavy Artillery	August 23, 1864, Fort Morgan, Alabama	New Orleans, Louisiana transferred to Elmira Prison, NY, December 4, 1864.	No Further Information Available.
Murphy, Joseph Private	Unk	Unknown	Co. G, 5th Louisiana Infantry	May 5, 1865, wilderness, Virginia. Gunshot Wound in Left Leg.	Old Capital Prison, Washington, DC. February 4, 1865 Elmira, Prison Camp, NY	Exchanged February 13, 1865 at Boulware's wharf on the James River, Virginia
Murphy, Lorenzo P. Private	Unk	April 26, 1862, York District, South Carolina	Co. H, 25th South Carolina Infantry	May 9, 1864, Near Petersburg, Virginia	Point Lookout, Maryland, transferred to Elmira Prison, NY, August 17, 1864	Died February 28, 1865 of Chronic Diarrhea, Grave No. 2134
Murphy, Marshal Private	Unk	May 1, 1863, Fetterman, Virginia	Co. A, 25th Virginia Infantry	May 12, 1864, Spotsylvania Court House, Virginia	Point Lookout, Maryland, transferred to Elmira Prison, NY, August 2, 1864	Died October 3, 1864 of Chronic Diarrhea, Grave No. 610
Murphy, Miles Private	Unk	March 29, 1864, Camp Holmes, North Carolina	Co. K, 10th Regiment, 1st North Carolina Artillery	January 15, 1865, Fort Fisher, North Carolina	January 30, 1865, Elmira Prison Camp, New York	Exchanged March 2, 1865 at Boulware's Wharf on the James River, Virginia
Murphy, Owen Private	Unk	June 11, 1861, Perry County, Alabama	Co. K, 11th Alabama Infantry	July 29, 1864, Petersburg, Virginia	Point Lookout, Maryland, transferred to Elmira Prison, NY, August 12, 1864	Oath of Allegiance May 17, 1865
Murphy, Patrick Private	Unk	December 18, 1862, Caroline County, Virginia	Co. F, 44th Virginia Infantry	May 12, 1864, Spotsylvania Court House, Virginia	Point Lookout, Maryland, transferred to Elmira Prison, NY, August 2, 1864	Oath of Allegiance June 19, 1865
Murrah, E. F. Private	Unk	August 17, 1863, Anderson, South Carolina	Co. G, 7th South Carolina Cavalry	May 30, 1864, Old Church, Cold Harbor, Virginia	Point Lookout, Maryland, transferred to Elmira Prison, NY, July 12, 1864	Oath of Allegiance June 17, 1965

Name & Rank	Age	Enlisted	Regiment and State	Where Captured	Prison	Remarks
Murrah, John W. Sergeant	27	May 20, 1861, Camp Martin, Carroll, Louisiana	Co. J, 14th Louisiana Infantry	May 12, 1864, Spotsylvania Court House, Virginia	Point Lookout, Maryland, transferred to Elmira Prison, NY, July 25, 1864	Oath of Allegiance July 7, 1865
Murray, A. D. Private	20	July 26, 1861, George's Station, Hilton Head, South Carolina	Co. H, 11th South Carolina Infantry	June 18, 1864, Petersburg, Virginia	Point Lookout, Maryland, transferred to Elmira Prison, NY, July 30, 1864	Oath of Allegiance July 7, 1865
Murray, Andrew Private	Unk	May 24, 1861, Montgomery, Alabama	Co. B, 1st Battalion Alabama Artillery	August 23, 1864, Fort Morgan, Alabama	New Orleans, Louisiana transferred to Elmira Prison, NY, December 4, 1864.	Oath of Allegiance May 15, 1865
Murray, Henry F. Private	26	July 26, 1861, George's Station, Hilton Head, South Carolina	Co. H, 11th South Carolina Infantry	June 18, 1864, Petersburg, Virginia	Point Lookout, Maryland, transferred to Elmira Prison, NY, July 30, 1864	Died February 2, 1865 of Variola (smallpox), Grave No. 1771
Murray, Henry G. Private	20	September 15, 1862, Raleigh, North Carolina	Co. E, 31st North Carolina Infantry	June 1, 1864, Gaines Farm Cold Harbor, Virginia	Point Lookout, Maryland, transferred to Elmira Prison, NY, July 12, 1864	Died September 18, 1864 of Chronic Diarrhea, Grave No. 510
Murray, J. G. Private	Unk	October 18, 1863, James Island, South Carolina	Co. H, 11th South Carolina Infantry	June 18, 1864, Petersburg, Virginia	Point Lookout, Maryland, transferred to Elmira Prison, NY, July 30, 1864	Exchanged March 14, 1865 at Boulware's Wharf on the James River, Virginia
Murray, James E. Private	Unk	July 30, 1863, McPherson-ville, South Carolina	Co. B, 7th South Carolina Cavalry	May 30, 1864, Crossroads Near Old Church, Virginia. Gunshot Wound Scalp, Severe.	Old Capital Prison, Washington, DC, transferred to Elmira Prison Camp, NY, December 17, 1864	Exchanged March 2, 1865 at Boulware's Wharf on the James River, Virginia
Murray, John W. Private	32	March 7, 1863, Alamance County, North Carolina	Co. J, 8th North Carolina Infantry	June 1, 1864, Cold Harbor, Virginia	Point Lookout, Maryland, transferred to Elmira Prison, NY, July 12, 1864	Died December 1, 1864 of Chronic Diarrhea, Grave No. 1013

Name & Rank	Age	Enlisted	Regiment and State	Where Captured	Prison	Remarks
Murray, Michael Private	36	June 5, 1861, Memphis, Tennessee	Co. L, Jackson's 1st Regiment, Tennessee Heavy Artillery	August 23, 1864, Fort Morgan, Alabama	New Orleans, Louisiana transferred to Elmira Prison, NY, December 4, 1864.	Oath of Allegiance May 15, 1865
Murrell, George W. Private	32	September 5, 1863, Camp Holmes, Near Raleigh, Wake County, North Carolina	Co. B, 36th 2nd North Carolina Artillery	January 15, 1865, Fort Fisher, North Carolina	February 1, 1865, Elmira Prison Camp, New York	Oath of Allegiance July 11, 1865
Murrell, Isaac Private	20	August 9, 1861, Powell's Point, Currituck County, North Carolina	Co. B, 8th North Carolina Infantry	June 1, 1864, Cold Harbor, Virginia	Point Lookout, Maryland, transferred to Elmira Prison, NY, July 12, 1864	Exchanged February 13, 1865 at Boulware's Wharf on the James River, Virginia
Murry, Hugh Private	35	March 15, 1862, Panola County, Mississippi	Co. H, 17th Mississippi Infantry	May 6, 1864, Wilderness, Virginia	Point Lookout, Maryland, transferred to Elmira Prison, NY, August 14, 1864	Oath of Allegiance May 13, 1865
Murry, Silas Private	Unk	December 21, 1862, Grahamville, Georgia	Capt. Slaten's Battery, Co. E, Macon Light Artillery, Georgia Artillery	June 16, 1864, Petersburg, Virginia	Point Lookout, Maryland, transferred to Elmira Prison, NY, July 25, 1864	Oath of Allegiance May 19, 1865
Murtaugh, Michael Private	Unk	March 30, 1863, Macon, Georgia	Co. B, 64th Georgia Infantry	August 18, 1864, New Market, Virginia	Old Capital Prison, Washington, DC transferred to Elmira Prison, NY, August 27, 1864	Oath of Allegiance May 15, 1865
Muse, Comodore G. Corporal	18	September 9, 1861, Carthage, North Carolina	Co. J, 2nd North Carolina Cavalry	September 16, 1863, Near Culpepper Court House, Virginia	Point Lookout, Maryland, transferred to Elmira Prison, NY, August 18, 1864	Died May 11, 1865 of Variola (Smallpox), Grave No. 2794
Muse, Stephen A. Private	18	June 18, 1861, Halifax County, North Carolina	Co. A, 5th North Carolina Infantry	June 10, 1864, Spotsylvania Court House, Virginia	Point Lookout, Maryland, transferred to Elmira Prison, NY, July 25, 1864	Oath of Allegiance June 19, 1865

Name & Rank	Age	Enlisted	Regiment and State	Where Captured	Prison	Remarks
Musgrove, Sampson G. Private	Unk	June 21, 1861, Camp McDonald, Georgia	Co. D, 18th Georgia Infantry	June 1, 1864, Cold Harbor, Virginia	Point Lookout, Maryland, transferred to Elmira Prison, NY, July 17,1864	Exchanged October 29, 1864 at Venus Point, Savannah River, GA.
Musick, Thomas W. Private	Unk	March 31, 1862, Washington County, Virginia	Co. J, 48th Virginia Infantry	May 12, 1864, Spotsylvania Court House, Virginia	Point Lookout, Maryland, transferred to Elmira Prison, NY, August 2, 1864	Oath of Allegiance June 27, 1865
Musselwhite, James T. M. Private	Unk	September 6, 1861, Lumberton, North Carolina	Co. A, 31st North Carolina Infantry	May 31, 1864, Cold Harbor, Virginia	Old Capital Prison, Washington, DC transferred to Elmira Prison, NY, August 29, 1864	Exchanged March 2, 1865 at Akins Landing on the James River, Virginia
Musser, William M. Private	Unk	July 23, 1861, Mount Airy, Wythe County, Virginia	Co. B, 29th Virginia Infantry	June 3, 1864, Cold Harbor, Virginia	Point Lookout, Maryland, transferred to Elmira Prison, NY, July 12, 1864	Oath of Allegiance June 23, 1965
Mustain, Thomas Corporal	Unk	March 15, 1862, Frog Bayou, Arkansas	Co. A, 15th Arkansas Infantry	May 10, 1863, Champion Hill, Mississippi	Point Lookout, Maryland, transferred to Elmira Prison, NY, August 18, 1864	Exchanged October 29, 1864 at Venus Point, Savannah River, GA.
Myers, Cornelius C. Private	20	March 23, 1863, Marion, Virginia	Co. L, 26th Battalion, Virginia Infantry	June 3, 1864, Gaines Farm Cold Harbor, Virginia	Point Lookout, Maryland, transferred to Elmira Prison, NY, July 17, 1864	Died August 2, 1864 of Acute Diarrhea Grave No. 147
Myers, Evan Thomas Private	Unk	April 16, 1862, Near Mount Jackson, Virginia	Co. J, 2nd Virginia Infantry	May 24, 1864, South Anna, Virginia	Point Lookout, Maryland, transferred to Elmira Prison, NY, July 9, 1864	Transferred for Exchange 10/11/64. Died 11/3/64 of Unknown Causes at Fort Monroe, VA.
Myers, Fred M. Private	Unk	October 19, 1863, James Island, South Carolina	Co. G, 25th South Carolina Infantry	January 15, 1865, Fort Fisher, North Carolina	January 30, 1865, Elmira Prison Camp, New York	Oath of Allegiance June 23, 1865

Name & Rank	Age	Enlisted	Regiment and State	Where Captured	Prison	Remarks
Myers, J. B. Private	Unk	July 13, 1861, Hartwell, Georgia	Co. C, 16th Georgia Infantry	August 16, 1864, Front Royal, Virginia	Old Capital Prison, Washington, DC transferred to Elmira Prison, NY, August 29, 1864	Oath of Allegiance June 16, 1865
Myers, Jacob Corporal	Unk	April 1, 1862, Camp Rippen, Pittsylvania County, Virginia	Co. C, 6th Virginia Cavalry	June 11, 1864, Trevilian Station, Louisa Court House, Virginia	Point Lookout, Maryland, transferred to Elmira Prison, NY, July 25, 1864	Exchanged October 29, 1864 at Venus Point, Savannah River, GA.
Myers, James William Private	19	April 18, 1861, Jefferson Court House, Virginia	Co. E, 2nd Virginia Infantry	May 12, 1864, Near Spotsylvania Court House, Virginia	Point Lookout, Maryland, transferred to Elmira Prison, NY, August 6, 1864	Exchanged March 2, 1865 at Akins Landing on the James River, Virginia
Myers, John O. Private	Unk	March 15, 1864, Ashland, Virginia	Co. D, 5th Virginia Cavalry	May 11, 1864, Yellow Tavern, Hanover County, Virginia	Point Lookout, Maryland, transferred to Elmira Prison, NY, August 17, 1864	Exchanged March 10, 1865 at Boulware's Wharf on the James River, Virginia
Myers, Julius Private	Unk	February 26, 1861, Mobile, Alabama	Co. A, 1st Battalion Alabama Artillery	August 23, 1864, Fort Morgan, Alabama	New Orleans, Louisiana transferred to Elmira Prison, NY, December 4, 1864.	Oath of Allegiance May 29, 1865
Myers, Luther Private	Unk	April 11, 1862, Coles Island, South Carolina	Co. G, 25th South Carolina Infantry	January 15, 1865, Fort Fisher, North Carolina	January 30, 1865, Elmira Prison Camp, New York	Oath of Allegiance July 7, 1865
Myers, Sandy L. Sergeant	31	September 7, 1861, Concord, North Carolina	Co. F, 33rd North Carolina Infantry	July 29, 1864, Petersburg, Virginia	Point Lookout, Maryland, transferred to Elmira Prison, NY, August 12, 1864	Exchanged February 13, 1865 at Boulware's Wharf on the James River, Virginia
Myers, Thomas J. Private	Unk	August 28, 1864, Manassas, Virginia	Co. A, 35th Battalion Virginia Cavalry	September 8, 1863, Leesburg, Virginia	Point Lookout, Maryland, transferred to Elmira Prison, NY, August 18, 1864	Exchanged March 10, 1865 at Boulware's Wharf on the James River, Virginia
Myrick, J. F. Private	Unk	Unknown	Captain Norwood's Home Guard, Florida	September 27, 1864, Marianna, Florida	New Orleans, Louisiana transferred to Elmira November 19, 1864.	Oath of Allegiance May 29, 1865

Name & Rank	Age	Enlisted	Regiment and State	Where Captured	Prison	Remarks
Myrick, John F. Corporal	Unk	August 9, 1863 Monroe County, Alabama	Co. E, 61st Alabama Infantry	May 12, 1864, Spotsylvania Court House, Virginia	Point Lookout, Maryland, transferred to Elmira Prison, NY, July 30, 1864	Died February 16, 1865 of Variola (Smallpox), Grave No. 2199
Myrick, Josiah Private	Unk	March 21, 1861, Union Springs, Alabama	Co. A, 1st Battalion Alabama Artillery	August 23, 1864, Fort Morgan, Alabama	Steam Press No. 4 New Orleans, Louisiana Elmira Prison, NY, October 8, 1864.	Died April 18, 1865 of Variola (Smallpox), Grave No. 1349
Myrick, Nathan W. Corporal	27	May 12, 1862, Schlay County, Georgia	Co. A, 27th Georgia Infantry	August 21, 1864, Weldon Railroad, Near Petersburg, VA. Gunshot Wound Fracture Right Thigh, Amputated.	Old Capital Prison, Washington, DC, transferred to Elmira Prison Camp, NY, December 17, 1864	Oath of Allegiance June 19, 1865
Myrick, Nathanial T. Private	Unk	March 15, 1862, Jerusalem, Southampton, Virginia	Co. G, 3rd Virginia Infantry	June 1, 1864, Gaines Farm Cold Harbor, Virginia	Point Lookout, Maryland, transferred to Elmira Prison, NY, July 12, 1864	Died December 5, 1864 of Pneumonia, Grave No. 1027
Myrick, Robert N. Private	19	May 11, 1861, Jerusalem, Southampton, Virginia	Co. G, 3rd Virginia Infantry	June 1, 1864, Gaines Farm Cold Harbor, Virginia	Point Lookout, Maryland, transferred to Elmira Prison, NY, July 12, 1864	Died September 19, 1864 of Pneumonia, Grave No. 496
Myrick, William N. Private	Unk	March 17, 1862, Gloucester Point, Virginia	Co. G, 26th North Carolina Infantry	June 17, 1864, Near Petersburg, Virginia	Point Lookout, Maryland, transferred to Elmira Prison, NY, July 30, 1864	Died April 25, 1865 of Chronic Diarrhea, Grave No. 1416

Name & Rank	Age	Enlisted	Regiment and State	Where Captured	Prison	Remarks
Nabers, Zachariah L. Private	Unk	July 20, 1861, Jefferson, Georgia	Co. G, 16th Georgia Infantry	June 1, 1864, Gaines Farm Cold Harbor, Virginia	Point Lookout, Maryland, transferred to Elmira Prison, NY, July 12, 1864	Oath of Allegiance June 16, 1865

Name & Rank	Age	Enlisted	Regiment and State	Where Captured	Prison	Remarks
Nail, Berrien Private	Unk	September 13, 1861, Whiteville, Georgia	Co. E, 61st Georgia Infantry	August 12, 1864, Newton, Virginia	Old Capital Prison, Washington, DC transferred to Elmira Prison, NY, August 29, 1864	Exchanged March 2, 1865 at Akins Landing on the James River, Virginia
Nall, William B. Private	Unk	March 25, 1864, Chatham County, North Carolina	Co. E, 26th North Carolina Infantry	May 6, 1864, Wilderness, Virginia	Old Capital Prison, Washington DC. Transferred to Elmira Prison Camp New York July 25, 1864.	Exchanged March 2, 1865 at Akins Landing on the James River, Virginia
Nance, Everett Private	28	November 17, 1862, Cerro Gordo, North Carolina	Co. E, 36th Regiment North Carolina, 2nd North Carolina Artillery	January 15, 1865, Fort Fisher, North Carolina	February 1, 1865, Elmira Prison Camp, New York	Oath of Allegiance 7/3/1865
Nance, John T. Private	42	February 27, 1862, Reidsville, Rockingham County, North Carolina	Co. G, 45th North Carolina Infantry	May 10, 1864, Spotsylvania Court House, Virginia	Point Lookout, Maryland, transferred to Elmira Prison, NY, August 6, 1864	Exchanged February 20, 1865 at Boulware's or Cox Wharf on the James River, Virginia
Nance, Joseph W. Corporal	31	June 18, 1861, East Band, North Carolina	Co. F, 28th North Carolina Infantry	July 29, 1864, Petersburg, Virginia	Point Lookout, Maryland, transferred to Elmira Prison, NY, August 12, 1864	Died October 25, 1864 of Pneumonia, Grave No. 851
Nance, Levi Private	32	November 12, 1864, Lincoln County, North Carolina	Co. H, 52nd North Carolina Infantry	May 12, 1864, Spotsylvania Court House, Virginia	Point Lookout, Maryland, transferred to Elmira Prison, NY, August 12, 1864	Exchanged October 29, 1864 at Venus Point, Savannah River, GA.
Naney, P. H. Private	Unk	Unknown	Co. B, 1st Jackson's Tennessee Heavy Artillery	August 23, 1864, Fort Morgan, Alabama.	New Orleans, Louisiana transferred to Elmira Prison, NY, December 4, 1864.	Oath of Allegiance July 7, 1865
Narhstedt, C. Private	29	July 22, 1861, Camp Moore, Louisiana	Co. C, 10th Louisiana Infantry	May 12, 1864, Spotsylvania Court House, Virginia	Point Lookout, Maryland, transferred to Elmira Prison, NY, July 25, 1864	Oath of Allegiance May 15, 1865

Name & Rank	Age	Enlisted	Regiment and State	Where Captured	Prison	Remarks
Nash, Henry C. Private	Unk	July 16, 1861, Lawrenceville, Georgia	Co. J, 16th Georgia Infantry	August 16, 1864, Front Royal, Virginia	Old Capital Prison, Washington, DC transferred to Elmira Prison, NY, August 29, 1864	Oath of Allegiance June 16, 1865
Nash, M. H. Private	Unk	Unknown	Co. D, 38th Georgia Infantry	May 6, 1864, Wilderness, Virginia	Old Capital Prison, Washington D. C. Transferred to Elmira Prison, NY, July 14, 1864	Exchanged February 20, 1865 at Boulware's or Cox Wharf on the James River, Virginia
Naylor, Columbus Private	19	May 9, 1861, Chadbourne, Texas	Co. K, 1st Texas Cavalry	August 8, 1864, Williamsport, Louisiana	New Orleans, LA, Transferred to Elmira Prison, NY, November 19, 1864	Died December 19, 1864 of Pneumonia, Grave No. 1070
Neal, Benjamin R. Corporal	22	September 9, 1861, Middleton, North Carolina	Co. F, 33rd North Carolina Infantry	May 12, 1864, Spotsylvania Court House, Virginia	Point Lookout, Maryland, transferred to Elmira Prison, NY, August 12, 1864	Exchanged February 20, 1865 at Boulware's or Cox Wharf on the James River, Virginia
Neal, George M. Private	18	October 9, 1861, Enfield, Halifax County, North Carolina	Co. F, 36th Regiment, 2nd North Carolina Artillery	January 15, 1865, Fort Fisher, North Carolina	February 1, 1865, Elmira Prison Camp, New York	Exchanged February 20, 1865 at Boulware's or Cox Wharf on the James River, Virginia
Neal, Transly C. Private	21	May 20, 1861, Louisburg, North Carolina	Co. K, 32nd North Carolina Infantry	May 10, 1864, Near Spotsylvania Court House, Virginia	Point Lookout, Maryland, transferred to Elmira Prison, NY, August 6, 1864	Exchanged March 10, 1865 at Boulware's Wharf on the James River, Virginia
Neal, Warren C. Private	Unk	January 14, 1862, Camp Hampton, Columbia, South Carolina	Co. D, 17th South Carolina Infantry	July 30, 1864, Petersburg, Virginia	Point Lookout, Maryland, transferred to Elmira Prison, NY, August 12, 1864	Died April 23, 1865 of Variola (Smallpox), Grave No. 1397
Neally, Datman Private	16	April 26, 1861, Columbus County, North Carolina	Co. D, 20th North Carolina Infantry	May 12, 1864, Near Spotsylvania Court House, Virginia	Point Lookout Prison, Maryland. Transferred to Elmira Prison Camp New York August 14, 1864.	Transferred for Exchanged 10/29/64 at Venus Point, Savannah River, GA.

Name & Rank	Age	Enlisted	Regiment and State	Where Captured	Prison	Remarks
Nealy, Lewis Private	18	April 26, 1861, Columbus County, North Carolina	Co. D, 20th North Carolina Infantry	May 12, 1864, Near Spotsylvania Court House, Virginia	Point Lookout Prison, Maryland. Transferred to Elmira Prison Camp New York August 14, 1864.	Transferred for Exchanged 10/29/64 at Venus Point, Savannah River, GA.
Neathery, Allan S. Private	21	June 4, 1861, Camp Moore, Louisiana	Co. D, 6th Louisiana Infantry	May 5, 1864, Wilderness, Virginia	Point Lookout, Maryland, transferred to Elmira Prison, NY, August 17, 1864	Exchanged 2/25/65. Died 3/1/65 of Phthisis Pulmonalis at Howard's Grove Hospital, Richmond, VA
Neel, A. J. Private	Unk	June 26, 1861, Hixville, Virginia	Co. F, 51st Virginia Infantry	July 12, 1864, Near Washington, DC	Old Capital Prison, Washington DC. Transferred to Elmira Prison Camp New York July 25, 1864.	Oath of Allegiance June 16, 1865
Neel, John Private	Unk	May 8, 1862, Augusta, Georgia	Co. A, 7th Georgia Cavalry	June 11, 1864, Trevilian Station, Louisa Court House, Virginia	Point Lookout, Maryland, transferred to Elmira Prison, NY, July 25, 1864	Exchanged February 13, 1865 at Boulware's wharf on the James River, Virginia
Neese, William H. Private	Unk	March 4, 1864, Hartwell, Georgia	Co. C, 16th Georgia Infantry	May 6, 1864, Wilderness, Virginia	Point Lookout, Maryland, transferred to Elmira Prison, NY, August 14, 1864	Died April 13, 1865 of Typhoid Fever, Grave No. 2706
Neff, Joel M. Private	Unk	April 15, 1862, Richmond, Virginia	Co. D, 5th Virginia Cavalry	June 4, 1864, Chickahominy, Cold Harbor, Virginia	Point Lookout, Maryland, transferred to Elmira Prison, NY, July 12, 1864	Oath of Allegiance May 29, 1865
Neichter, John L. Private	Unk	April 25, 1862, Elk Run, Virginia	Co. D, 10th Virginia Infantry	May 12, 1864, Spotsylvania Court House, Virginia	Point Lookout, Maryland, transferred to Elmira Prison, NY, August 2, 1864	Oath of Allegiance June 19, 1865
Neighbors, William Private	Unk	September 1, 1862, Grahamville, South Carolina	Co. G, 27th South Carolina Infantry	June 24, 1864, Near Petersburg, Virginia	Point Lookout, Maryland, transferred to Elmira Prison, NY, August 17, 1864	Died October 3, 1864 of Chronic Diarrhea, Grave No. 631

Name & Rank	Age	Enlisted	Regiment and State	Where Captured	Prison	Remarks
Neighbours, Joshnay B. Private	Unk	November 27, 1863, Salem, Virginia	Co. E, 42nd Virginia Infantry	May 12, 1864, Near Spotsylvania Court House, Virginia	Point Lookout, Maryland, transferred to Elmira Prison, NY, August 2, 1864	Died November 29, 1864 of Chronic Diarrhea, Grave No. 997
Neil, Henry S. Private	Unk	December 31, 1861, Charlotte, Virginia	Co. B, 22nd Battalion Virginia Infantry	June 4, 1864, Near Talapatomoy Creek, Cold Harbor, Virginia	Point Lookout, Maryland, transferred to Elmira Prison, NY, July 12,1864	Exchanged October 29, 1864 at Venus Point, Savannah River, GA.
Neil, Michael J. Sergeant	Unk	May 1, 1862, Newman, Georgia	Co. A, 12th Georgia Light Artillery	July 15, 1863, Battery Wagner, James Island, South Carolina	Point Lookout, Maryland, transferred to Elmira Prison, NY, August 18, 1864	Exchanged March 10, 1865 at Boulware's Wharf on the James River, Virginia
Neill, John L. Private	Unk	May 15, 1861, Camp Harris, Tennessee	Co. E, 23rd Tennessee Infantry	June 17, 1864, Petersburg, Virginia	Point Lookout, Maryland, transferred to Elmira Prison, NY, July 30, 1864	Died November 25, 1864 of Chronic Diarrhea, Grave No. 918
Nelson, John Private	Unk	Unknown	Co. A, Captain Jones' Home Guard Florida	September 27, 1864, Marianna, Florida	New Orleans, Louisiana transferred to Elmira November 19, 1864.	Oath of Allegiance May 29, 1865
Nelson, John H. Private	Unk	April 10, 1862, Montevallo, Alabama	Co. J, 44th Alabama Infantry	May 6, 1864, Wilderness, Virginia	Point Lookout, Maryland, transferred to Elmira Prison, NY, August 17, 1864	Died November 2, 1864 of Erysipelas, Grave No. 844
Nelson, John H. Corporal	Unk	August 13, 1861, Camp Moore, Louisiana	Co. H, 12th Louisiana Infantry	May 16, 1863, Baker's Creek, Champion Hill, Mississippi	Point Lookout, Maryland, transferred to Elmira Prison, NY, August 18, 1864	Exchanged February 25, 1865 at Boulware's wharf on the James River, Virginia
Nelson, John N. Private	Unk	December 12, 1863, Bon Secour, Alabama	Co. F, 1st Battalion Alabama Artillery	August 23, 1864, Fort Morgan, Alabama	Steam Press No. 4 New Orleans, Louisiana Elmira Prison, NY, October 8, 1864.	Died January 15, 1865 of Chronic Diarrhea, Grave No. 1454

Name & Rank	Age	Enlisted	Regiment and State	Where Captured	Prison	Remarks
Nelson, Ramling W. Private	Unk	May 14, 1862, Richmond, Virginia	Co. 1st Maryland Cavalry	October 27, 1864, Chester's Gap, Virginia	Old Capital Prison, Washington, DC, transferred to Elmira December 17, 1864	Exchanged February 20, 1865 at Boulware's or Cox Wharf on the James River, Virginia
Nelson, Thomas Private	33	May 1, 1862, South Mills, North Carolina	Co. D, 32nd North Carolina Infantry	May 10, 1864, Near Spotsylvania Court House, Virginia	Point Lookout, Maryland, transferred to Elmira Prison, NY, August 6, 1864	Exchanged March 2, 1865 at Akins Landing on the James River, Virginia
Nelson, Thomas J. Private	17	September 3, 1861, Mecklenburg County, North Carolina	Co. H, 35th North Carolina Infantry	June 17, 1864, Petersburg, Virginia	Point Lookout, Maryland, transferred to Elmira Prison, NY, July 30, 1864	Oath of Allegiance June 12, 1865
Nelson, Tillman N. Private	Unk	October 21, 1861, Laurens, South Carolina	Co. G, 27th South Carolina Infantry	June 24, 1864, Near Petersburg, Virginia	Point Lookout, Maryland, transferred to Elmira Prison, NY, August 18, 1864	Exchanged February 20, 1865 at Boulware's or Cox Wharf on the James River, Virginia
Nelson, W. H. Private	Unk	Unknown	Co. A, Jackson's 1st Regiment, Tennessee Heavy Artillery	August 23, 1864, Fort Morgan, Alabama	New Orleans, Louisiana transferred to Elmira Prison, NY, December 4, 1864.	Exchanged February 13, 1865 at Boulware's wharf on the James River, Virginia
Nelson, William A. Private	Unk	March 9, 1864, Richmond, Virginia	Co. E, 25th Battalion Virginia Infantry	July 12, 1864, Cox's Farm, Virginia	Point Lookout Prison Camp, Maryland. Transferred to Elmira Prison Camp New York July 30, 1864	Died August 30, 1864 Of Rubeola (Measles), Grave No. 54
Ness, T. J. Private	Unk	December 5, 1861, Sac River, St. Clair County, Missouri	Co. B, 1st Missouri Cavalry	May 17, 1863, Big Black Bridge, Champion Hill, Mississippi	Point Lookout, Maryland, transferred to Elmira Prison, NY, August 18, 1864	Exchanged October 29, 1864 at Venus Point, Savannah River, GA.
Nesselrhode, Jacob Private	18	April 5, 1862, Camp Shenandoah, Virginia	Co. E, 25th Virginia Infantry	May 6, 1864, Wilderness, Virginia	Old Capital Prison, Washington D. C. Transferred to Elmira Prison, NY, July 14, 1864	Transferred for Exchanged 10/29/64 at Venus Point, Savannah River, GA.

Name & Rank	Age	Enlisted	Regiment and State	Where Captured	Prison	Remarks
Nester, Michael Private	Unk	June 25, 1861, New Orleans, Louisiana	Co. E, 14th Louisiana Infantry	May 5, 1864, Wilderness, Virginia	Point Lookout, Maryland, transferred to Elmira Prison, NY, July 25, 1864	Oath of Allegiance May 19, 1865
Netherton, Charles Private	18	December 31, 1861, Springfield, Missouri	Co. G, 1st Missouri Cavalry	May 17, 1863, Big Black Bridge, Champion Hill, Mississippi	Point Lookout, Maryland, transferred to Elmira Prison, NY, August 18, 1864	Exchanged February 13, 1865 at Boulware's wharf on the James River, Virginia
Nethery, Robert T. Sergeant	40	July 5, 1861, Halifax County, North Carolina	Co. I, 8th, North Carolina Infantry	May 31, 1864, Cold Harbor, Virginia	Point Lookout, Maryland, transferred to Elmira Prison, NY, July 12, 1864	Died October 12, 1864 of Chronic Diarrhea, Grave No. 570
Nettles, John J. Private	Unk	September 22, 1862, Waynesville, Georgia	Co. G, 7th Georgia Cavalry	June 11, 1864, Trevilian Station, Louisa Court House, Virginia	Point Lookout, Maryland, transferred to Elmira Prison, NY, July 25, 1864	Oath of Allegiance June 21, 1865
Nettles, Thomas Private	Unk	March 4, 1862, Homersville, Georgia	Co. K, 26th Georgia Infantry	May 20, 1864, Spotsylvania Court House, Virginia	Point Lookout, Maryland, transferred to Elmira Prison, NY, July 3, 1864	Exchanged October 29, 1864 at Venus Point, Savannah River, GA.
Newell, G. S. Civilian	Unk	Unknown	North Carolina Citizen	January 15, 1865, Fort Fisher, North Carolina	January 31, 1865, Elmira Prison Camp, New York	Died of Variola (Smallpox) April 18, 1865, Grave No. 1352
Nettles, W. Wyatt Private	26	January 13, 1862, Darlington District, South Carolina	Co. G, 21st South Carolina Infantry	July 10, 1863, Morris Island, South Carolina	Point Lookout, Maryland, transferred to Elmira Prison, NY, August 18, 1864	Exchanged March 10, 1865 at Boulware's Wharf on the James River, Virginia
Neville, James H. Private	30	July 15, 1862, Raleigh, North Carolina	Co. K, 1st North Carolina Infantry	May 12, 1864, Spotsylvania, Virginia	Point Lookout Prison Camp, Maryland. Transferred to Elmira Prison, August 6, 1864	Died April 24, 1865 of Variola (Smallpox), Grave No. 1412

Name & Rank	Age	Enlisted	Regiment and State	Where Captured	Prison	Remarks
Neville, Richard H. Private	26	April 25, 1861, Halifax County, North Carolina	Co. G, 12 North Carolina Infantry	July 12, 1864, Near Washington, DC	Old Capital Prison, Washington DC. Transferred to Elmira Prison Camp New York July 25, 1864.	Died March 19, 1865 of Pneumonia, Grave No. 1580
Nevitt, Thomas W. Corporal	Unk	April 20, 1861, Fairfax County, Virginia	Co. F, 6th Virginia Cavalry	June 11, 1864, Trevilian Station, Louisa Court House, Virginia	Point Lookout, Maryland, transferred to Elmira Prison, NY, July 25, 1864	Oath of Allegiance June 8, 1865
Nevitt, William H. Private	27	April 20, 1861, Fairfax County, Virginia	Co. F, 6th Virginia Cavalry	September 14, 1863, Near Culpepper Court House, Virginia	Point Lookout, Maryland, transferred to Elmira Prison, NY, August 18, 1864	Exchanged March 14, 1865 at Boulware's Wharf on the James River, Virginia
Newbern, Henderson A. Private	23	June 1, 1861, Mill Landing, North Carolina	Co. F, 5th North Carolina Infantry	May 20, 1864, Spotsylvania Court House, Virginia	Point Lookout, Maryland, transferred to Elmira Prison, NY, July 12,1864	Oath of Allegiance May 15, 1865
Newbern, W. S. Private	Unk	April 12, 1864, Petersburg, Virginia	Co. B, 8th North Carolina Infantry	May 31, 1864, Cold Harbor, Virginia	Point Lookout, Maryland, transferred to Elmira Prison, NY, July 12,1864	Oath of Allegiance June 30, 1865
Newbill, James A. Private	Unk	February 17, 1864, Richmond, Virginia	Co. K, 14th Virginia Infantry	May 10, 1864, Near Petersburg, Virginia	Point Lookout, Maryland, transferred to Elmira Prison, NY, August 17, 1864	Oath of Allegiance June 19, 1865
Newcomb, J. C. Civilian	Unk	Unknown	Citizen of Gloucester County, Virginia	March 10, 1864, Gloucester County, Virginia	Point Lookout, Maryland, transferred to Elmira Prison, NY, July 12,1864	No Additional Information
Newcomb, James Sergeant	40	July 22, 1861, Camp Moore, New Orleans, Louisiana	Co. F, 10th Louisiana Infantry	May 12, 1864, Spotsylvania Court House, Virginia	Point Lookout, Maryland, transferred to Elmira Prison, NY, July 25, 1864	Oath of Allegiance December 29, 1864. Early Release per Lincoln's Proclamation, 12/8/1863.

Name & Rank	Age	Enlisted	Regiment and State	Where Captured	Prison	Remarks
Newell, Edward R. Private	20	May 29, 1861, Fayetteville, North Carolina	Co. C, 3rd North Carolina Infantry	May 12, 1864, Near Spotsylvania County Court House, Virginia	Point Lookout, Maryland, transferred to Elmira Prison, NY, August 14, 1864	Oath of Allegiance June 16, 1865
Newell, J. G. Civilian	Unk	Unknown	Citizen of North Carolina	January 15, 1865, Fort Fisher, North Carolina	February 1, 1865, Elmira Prison Camp, New York	Died February 18, 1865 of Variola (Smallpox), Grave No. 1352
Newell, James A. Private	22	February 27, 1862, Reidsville, North Carolina	Co. E, 45th North Carolina Infantry	July 12, 1864, Near Washington, DC	Old Capital Prison, Washington, DC. Transferred to Elmira Prison Camp July 25, 1864	Died October 5, 1864 of Chronic Diarrhea, Grave No. 644
Newman, Andrew J. Private	22	June 30, 1862, Rockingham County, North Carolina	Co. G, 45th North Carolina Infantry	May 10, 1864, Spotsylvania Court House, Virginia	Point Lookout, Maryland, transferred to Elmira Prison, NY, August 6, 1864	Oath of Allegiance June 12, 1865
Newman, Archibald W. Private	31	July 15, 1862, Fort Caswell, Brunswick County, North Carolina	Co. A, 36th Regiment, 2nd North Carolina Artillery	January 15, 1865, Fort Fisher, North Carolina	February 1, 1865, Elmira Prison Camp, New York	Oath of Allegiance August 7, 1865
Newman, George Teamster Private	Unk	Unknown	Co. B, 14th Virginia Cavalry	July 16, 1864, Near Harpers Ferry, Loudoun County, Virginia	Old Capital Prison, Washington DC. Transferred to Elmira Prison Camp New York July 25, 1864.	Oath of Allegiance May 15, 1865
Newman, J. H. Private	24	July 25, 1861, Bunker Hill, Virginia	Co. A, 58th Virginia Infantry	May 31, 1864 Mechanics-ville, Virginia	Point Lookout, Maryland, transferred to Elmira Prison, NY, July 12, 1864	Died December 28, 1864 of Pneumonia and Smallpox, Grave No. 1736
Newman, John A. Private	23	May 18, 1861, Lisbon, Virginia	Co. C, 42nd Virginia Infantry	May 12, 1864, Spotsylvania Court House, Virginia	Point Lookout, Maryland, transferred to Elmira Prison, NY, August 2,1864	Exchanged February 13, 1865 at Boulware's wharf on the James River, Virginia

Name & Rank	Age	Enlisted	Regiment and State	Where Captured	Prison	Remarks
Newman, John T. Private	18	April 1, 1862, Amite County, Mississippi	Co. D, 33rd Mississippi Infantry	May 16, 1863, Champion Hill, Mississippi	Point Lookout, Maryland, transferred to Elmira Prison, NY, August 18, 1864	Exchanged March 10, 1865 at Boulware's wharf on the James River, Virginia
Newman, Joseph Private	Unk	June 22, 1861, Wytheville, Virginia	Co. H, 50th Virginia Infantry	May 12, 1864, Spotsylvania Court House, Virginia	Point Lookout, Maryland, transferred to Elmira Prison, NY, August 2, 1864	Died September 12, 1864 of Chronic Diarrhea, Grave No. 191
Newman, Josiah L. Private	22	June 30, 1862, Rockingham County, North Carolina	Co. G, 45th North Carolina Infantry	May 10, 1864, Spotsylvania Court House, Virginia	Point Lookout, Maryland, transferred to Elmira Prison, NY, August 6, 1864	Exchanged March 2, 1865 at Akins Landing on the James River, Virginia
Newman, Terrell N. Private	24	July 24, 1862 Valleytown, Cherokee County, North Carolina	Co. J, Thomas' Legion, North Carolina Infantry	August 10, 1864, Berryville, Virginia	Old Capital Prison, Washington, DC transferred to Elmira Prison, NY, August 29, 1864	Died February 19, 1865 of Chronic Diarrhea, Grave No. 2348
Newman, Thomas Private	24	July 25, 1861, Bunker Hill, Virginia	Co. A, 58th Virginia Infantry	May 31, 1864 Mechanics-ville, Virginia	Point Lookout, Maryland, transferred to Elmira Prison, NY, July 12, 1864	Died May 20, 1865 of Chronic Diarrhea, Grave No. 2942
Newman, William A. Private	Unk	August 12, 1862, Staunton, Virginia	Co. H, 34th Virginia Infantry	June 15, 1864, Near Petersburg, Virginia	Point Lookout, Maryland, transferred to Elmira Prison, NY, July 12, 1864	Oath of Allegiance June 23, 1865
Newmans, Daniel H. Private	Unk	October 21, 1863, Bryan County, Georgia	Co. H, 7th Georgia Cavalry	June 11, 1864, Trevilian Station, Louisa Court House, Virginia	Point Lookout, Maryland, transferred to Elmira Prison, NY, July 25, 1864	Oath of Allegiance June 19, 1865
Newsom, Joab C. Private	33	July 10, 1861, Wilmington, North Carolina	Co. D, 61st North Carolina Infantry	June 16, 1864, Near Petersburg, Virginia	Point Lookout, Maryland, transferred to Elmira Prison, NY, July 12, 1864	Transferred for Exchange October 11, 1864. No Additional Information.

Name & Rank	Age	Enlisted	Regiment and State	Where Captured	Prison	Remarks
Newsom, Nathanial Private	21	June 12, 1861, Weldon, North Carolina	Co. B, 5th North Carolina Infantry	May 12, 1864, Spotsylvania Court House, Virginia	Point Lookout, Maryland, transferred to Elmira Prison, NY, August 6, 1864	Oath of Allegiance June 16, 1865
Newson, N. W. Private	17	March 29, 1864, Bedford County, Virginia	Co. G, 34th Virginia Infantry	June 15, 1864, Near Petersburg, Virginia	Point Lookout, Maryland, transferred to Elmira Prison, NY, July 12,1864	Exchanged October 29, 1864 at Venus Point, Savannah River, GA.
Newton, D. D. Corporal	Unk	November 18, 1862, Bennettsville, Marlboro District, South Carolina	Co. F, 21st South Carolina Infantry	January 15, 1865, Fort Fisher, North Carolina	January 30, 1865 Elmira Prison Camp, New York	Oath of Allegiance July 11, 1865
Newton, George J. Private	Unk	May 6, 1862, Grove Hill, Alabama	Co. I, 5th Alabama Infantry	May 5, 1864, Wilderness, Virginia	Point Lookout, Maryland, transferred to Elmira Prison, NY, August 17, 1864	Exchanged October 29, 1864 at Venus Point, Savannah River, GA.
Newton, John Thomas Private	Unk	March 20, 1862, Pickens Court House, South Carolina	Co. A, 1st South Carolina Infantry	July 14, 1863, Falling Waters, Maryland	Point Lookout, Maryland, transferred to Elmira Prison, NY, August 18, 1864	Transferred for Exchanged 10/29/64 at Venus Point, Savannah River, GA.
Newton, Robert L. Private	Unk	August 1, 1863, Roxboro, North Carolina	Co. E, 35th North Carolina Infantry	June 17, 1864, Petersburg, Virginia	Point Lookout, Maryland, transferred to Elmira Prison, NY, July 30, 1864	Oath of Allegiance June 21, 1865
Niblock, J. C. Private	Unk	Unknown	Co. B, Greg's 7th Texas Infantry	May 12, 1863, Raymond, Mississippi	Point Lookout, Maryland, transferred to Elmira Prison, NY, August 18, 1864	Exchanged February 20, 1865 at Boulware's or Cox Wharf on the James River, Virginia
Nicholes, R. S. Private	Unk	January 20, 1862, Camp Hampton, Grahamville, South Carolina	Co. B, 4th South Carolina Cavalry	May 28, 1864, Hall's Shop, Virginia	Point Lookout, Maryland, transferred to Elmira Prison, NY, July 12,1864	Exchanged October 29, 1864 at Venus Point, Savannah River, GA.

Name & Rank	Age	Enlisted	Regiment and State	Where Captured	Prison	Remarks
Nicholls, John H. Private	28	May 16, 1861, Columbia, North Carolina	Co. F, 32nd North Carolina Infantry	May 10, 1864, Near Spotsylvania Court House, Virginia	Point Lookout, Maryland, transferred to Elmira Prison, NY, August 6, 1864	Oath of Allegiance May 29, 1865
Nicholls, Joseph A. Private	33	September 4, 1862, Camp Hill, Wilkes County, North Carolina	Co. K, 53rd North Carolina Infantry	May 20, 1864, Spotsylvania Court House, Virginia	Point Lookout, Maryland, transferred to Elmira Prison, NY, July 3, 1864	Died August 24, 1864 of Chronic Diarrhea, Grave No. 466
Nicholls, William N. Sergeant	Unk	August 24, 1861, Hiwasse, Towns County, Georgia	Co. D, 24th Georgia Infantry	June 1, 1864, Cold Harbor, Virginia. Gunshot Wound of Throat.	Old Capital Prison, Washington DC. Transferred to Elmira Prison Camp New York July 25, 1864.	Oath of Allegiance June 21, 1865
Nichols, F. F. Civilian	Unk	Unknown	Citizen of Randolph County, North Carolina	April 21, 1864, Near Wilmington, North Carolina	Point Lookout, Maryland, transferred to Elmira Prison, NY, July 25, 1864	Oath of Allegiance June 20, 1865
Nichols, Hazard Private	Unk	March 10, 1862, Fayetteville, North Carolina	Co. K, 10th Regiment, 1st North Carolina Artillery	January 15, 1865, Fort Fisher, North Carolina	February 1, 1865, Elmira Prison Camp, New York	Died March 20, 1865 of Chronic Diarrhea, Grave No. 1579
Nichols, Isaac Private	Unk	Unknown	Co. A, 7th South Carolina Cavalry	August 21, 1864, Petersburg, Virginia	Old Capital Prison, Washington, DC, transferred to Elmira December 17, 1864	Died January 21, 1865 of Pneumonia, Grave No. 1587
Nichols, J. Private	Unk	August 10, 1861, Wake County, North Carolina	Co. K, 30th North Carolina Infantry	May 20, 1864, Spotsylvania Court House, Virginia	Point Lookout, Maryland, transferred to Elmira Prison, NY, July 3, 1864	Exchanged March 14, 1865 at Boulware's Wharf on the James River, Virginia
Nichols, Jasper N. Private	Unk	September 14, 1861, Montgomery, Alabama	Co. F, 1st Battalion Alabama Artillery	August 23, 1864, Fort Morgan, Alabama	Steam Press No. 4 New Orleans, Louisiana transferred to Elmira Prison, NY, October 8, 1864.	Oath of Allegiance May 19, 1865

Name & Rank	Age	Enlisted	Regiment and State	Where Captured	Prison	Remarks
Nichols, William A. Private	Unk	January 28, 1862, Winton, North Carolina	Co. C, 3rd Battalion North Carolina Light Artillery	January 15, 1865, Fort Fisher, North Carolina	February 1, 1865, Elmira Prison Camp, New York	Oath of Allegiance July 11, 1865
Nicholson, James A. Private	Unk	April 19, 1864, Wahalak, Mississippi	Co. C, Jeff Davis Legion Mississippi Cavalry	June 11, 1864, Trevilian Station, Louisa Court House, Virginia	Point Lookout, Maryland, transferred to Elmira Prison, NY, July 25, 1864	Exchanged March 2, 1865 at Akins Landing on the James River, Virginia
Nicholson, John M. Private	21	February 22, 1862, Gramville, North Carolina	Co. A, 44th North Carolina Infantry	June 4, 1864, Gaines Mill Cold Harbor, Virginia	Point Lookout, Maryland, transferred to Elmira Prison, NY, July 12, 1864	Oath of Allegiance June 19, 1865
Nicholson, William George Private	Unk	April 23, 1861, Mobile, Alabama	Co. E, 3rd Alabama Infantry	July 8, 1864, Near Washington, DC	Old Capital Prison, Washington DC. Transferred to Elmira Prison Camp New York July 25, 1864.	Exchanged March 14, 1865 at Boulware's Wharf on the James River, Virginia
Nicholson, William J. Private	16	February 24, 1862, Harrisburg, North Carolina	Co. H, 7th North Carolina Infantry	May 6, 1864, Wilderness, Virginia	Point Lookout, Maryland, transferred to Elmira Prison, NY, August 14, 1864	Oath of Allegiance June 12, 1865
Nicholson, William J. Private	22	June 1, 1861, Stokes County, North Carolina	Co. H, 22nd North Carolina Infantry	May 25, 1864, Hanover Junction, Virginia	Point Lookout, Maryland, transferred to Elmira Prison, NY, July 12, 1864	Died March 9, 1865 of Chronic Diarrhea, Grave No. 1876
Nickens, Sebron Private	Unk	May 15, 1862, Camp Moore, Louisiana	Co. B, 9th Battalion Louisiana Infantry	October 14, 1864, New River, Louisiana	New Orleans, Louisiana transferred to Elmira November 19, 1864.	Oath of Allegiance May 29, 1865
Nifong, Madison Private	33	March 10, 1863, Salem, North Carolina	Co. G, 2nd Battalion North Carolina Infantry	June 2, 1864, Gains Farm, Cold Harbor, Virginia	Point Lookout Prison Camp, Maryland. Transferred to Elmira Prison Camp, New York July 17, 1864	Died September 29, 1864 of Scorbutis (Scurvy), Grave No. 437
Niven, Dougal Private	40	July 24, 1863, Fort Branch, Martin County, North Carolina	Co. G, 40th Regiment, 3rd North Carolina Artillery	January 15, 1865, Fort Fisher, North Carolina	January 30, 1865 Elmira Prison Camp, New York	Oath of Allegiance June 12, 1865

Name & Rank	Age	Enlisted	Regiment and State	Where Captured	Prison	Remarks
Nix, Jesse Private	Unk	May 27, 1862, Charleston, South Carolina	Co. B, 18th South Carolina Infantry	July 29, 1864, Petersburg, Virginia	Point Lookout, Maryland, transferred to Elmira Prison, NY, August 12, 1864	Exchanged March 2, 1865 at Akins Landing on the James River, Virginia
Nix, John G. Private	20	August 2, 1861, Camp Trousdale, Nashville, Tennessee	Co. A, 7th Tennessee Infantry	May 5, 1864, Wilderness, Virginia	Point Lookout, Maryland, transferred to Elmira Prison, NY, August 12, 1864	Oath of Allegiance March 20, 1865 per Commanding General Prisoners March 14, 1865.
Nixon, Harvey Private	27	May 18, 1861, Edenton, North Carolina	Co. A, 1st North Carolina Infantry	May 12, 1864, Spotsylvania Court House, Virginia	Point Lookout, Maryland, transferred to Elmira Prison, NY, August 6, 1864	Died November 23, 1864 of Pneumonia, Grave No. 929
Nixon, Wesley J. Private	21	June 7, 1861, Camp Moore, Louisiana	Co. K, 7th Louisiana Infantry	May 11, 1864, Spotsylvania Court House, Virginia	Point Lookout, Maryland, transferred to Elmira Prison, NY, August 17, 1864	Exchanged February 13, 1865 at Boulware's wharf on the James River, Virginia
Noble, J. E. Private	Unk	August 6, 1861, Brunswick, Georgia	Co. F, 26th Georgia Infantry	May 31, 1864, Chickahominy, Cold Harbor, Virginia	Point Lookout, Maryland, transferred to Elmira Prison, NY, July 12, 1864	Died February 11, 1865 of Variola (Smallpox), Grave No. 2074
Noble, John C. Private	Unk	January 31, 1863, Camp Whiting, Wilmington, North Carolina	Co. G, 51st North Carolina Infantry	June 3, 1864, Gaines Mill Cold Harbor, Virginia	Point Lookout, Maryland, transferred to Elmira Prison, NY, July 12, 1864	Exchanged October 29, 1864 at Venus Point, Savannah River, GA.
Noble, John W. Private	31	June 30, 1862, Edgefield County Court House, South Carolina	Co. C, 6th South Carolina Cavalry	June 11, 1864, Trevilian Station, Louisa Court House, Virginia	Point Lookout, Maryland, transferred to Elmira Prison, NY, July 25, 1864	Exchanged October 29, 1864 at Venus Point, Savannah River, GA.
Noble, R. J. Private	Unk	June 2, 1861, Tuskegee, Macon County, Alabama	Co. L, 12th Alabama Infantry	May 20, 1864, Spotsylvania Court House, Virginia	Point Lookout, Maryland, transferred to Elmira Prison, NY, July 3, 1864	Died March 10, 1865 of Variola (Smallpox), Grave No.1854

Name & Rank	Age	Enlisted	Regiment and State	Where Captured	Prison	Remarks
Nobles, Alexander Private	Unk	July 25, 1864, North Carolina	Co. G, 21st North Carolina Infantry	July 10, 1864, Harpers Ferry, Virginia	Old Capital Prison, Washington DC. Transferred to Elmira Prison Camp New York July 25, 1864.	Oath of Allegiance June 16, 1865
Nobles, John Private	18	March 3, 1862, Cero Gordo, North Carolina	Co. E, 36th Regiment, 2nd North Carolina Artillery	January 15, 1865, Fort Fisher, North Carolina	February 1, 1865, Elmira Prison Camp, New York	Oath of Allegiance July 7, 1865
Noel, John Private	Unk	Unknown	Co. F, 50th Virginia Infantry	May 12, 1864, Spotsylvania Court House, Virginia	Point Lookout, Maryland, transferred to Elmira Prison, NY, August 2, 1864	Died October 14, 1864 of Hospital Gangrene, Grave No. 700. Name Noll on Headstone.
Nolan, J. M. Private	21	June 25, 1863, Randolph, Alabama	Jeff Davis Alabama Artillery	May 5, 1864, Wilderness, Virginia	Point Lookout, Maryland, transferred to Elmira Prison, NY, August 17, 1864	Transferred for Exchange 2/20/65. Died 2/25/65 of Chronic Rheumatism and Inflammation of Lungs at US Army Hospital, Baltimore, MD.
Nolan, John H. Private	Unk	February 16, 1861, Mobile, Alabama	Co. A, 1st Battalion Alabama Artillery	August 23, 1864, Fort Morgan, Alabama	New Orleans, Louisiana transferred to Elmira Prison, NY, December 4, 1864.	Oath of Allegiance May 19, 1865
Nolan, Joseph Private	27	June 6, 1861, New Orleans, Louisiana	Co. C, 14th Louisiana Infantry	May 5, 1864, Wilderness, Virginia	Point Lookout, Maryland, transferred to Elmira Prison, NY, July 25, 1864	Oath of Allegiance May 15, 1865
Noland, George W. Private	24	April 18, 1861, Jefferson Court House, Virginia	Co. A, 2nd Virginia Infantry	May 12, 1864, Near Spotsylvania Court House, Virginia	Point Lookout, Maryland, transferred to Elmira Prison, NY, August 6, 1864	Exchanged March 14, 1865 at Boulware's Wharf on the James River, Virginia

Name & Rank	Age	Enlisted	Regiment and State	Where Captured	Prison	Remarks
Noles, Alfred Private	22	March 4, 1862, Cerogordo, North Carolina	Co. E, 36th Regiment North Carolina Artillery	January 15, 1865, Fort Fisher, North Carolina	February 1, 1865, Elmira Prison Camp, New York	Died May 21, 1865 of Chronic Diarrhea, Grave No. 2937. Headstone has John A. Knowles.
Nolly, Mark B. Private	31	June 5, 1861, Wilson, North Carolina	Co. G, 5th North Carolina Infantry	May 12, 1864, Spotsylvania Court House, Virginia	Point Lookout, Maryland, transferred to Elmira Prison, NY, August 6, 1864	Exchanged October 29, 1864 at Venus Point, Savannah River, GA.
Noriss, Swanney F. Private	27	December 5, 1861, Sac River, St. Clair County, Missouri	Co. G, 1st Missouri Cavalry	May 17, 1863, Big Black Bridge, Champion Hill, Mississippi	Point Lookout, Maryland, transferred to Elmira Prison, NY, August 18, 1864	Exchanged October 29, 1864 at Venus Point, Savannah River, GA.
Norman, James S. Corporal	Unk	April 16, 1862, Washington, North Carolina	Co. K, 10th Regiment, 1st North Carolina Artillery	January 15, 1865, Fort Fisher, North Carolina	January 30, 1865, Elmira Prison Camp, New York	Oath of Allegiance July 11, 1865
Norman, Thomas Private	Unk	February 13, 1862, Camp Holmes, North Carolina	Co. J, 28th North Carolina Infantry	May 12, 1864, Near Spotsylvania Court House, Virginia	Point Lookout, Maryland, transferred to Elmira Prison, NY, August 14, 1864	Oath of Allegiance June 12, 1865
Norman, William Frank Sergeant	Unk	May 7, 1861, Montgomery, Alabama	Co. E, 6th Alabama Infantry	May 5, 1864, Ely's Ford, Wilderness, Virginia	Point Lookout, Maryland, transferred to Elmira Prison, NY, August 17, 1864	Exchanged October 29, 1864 at Venus Point, Savannah River, GA.
Norris, Goldey J. Private	20	April 26, 1861, Columbus County, North Carolina	Co. D, 20th North Carolina Infantry	May 7, 1864, Wilderness, Virginia	Point Lookout, Maryland, transferred to Elmira Prison, NY, August 14, 1864	Oath of Allegiance June 14, 1865
Norris, John Private	21	May 13, 1861, Fetterman, Virginia	Co. A, 25th Virginia Infantry	May 12, 1864, Spotsylvania Court House, Virginia	Point Lookout, Maryland, transferred to Elmira Prison, NY, August 2, 1864	Oath of Allegiance May 29, 1865

Name & Rank	Age	Enlisted	Regiment and State	Where Captured	Prison	Remarks
Norris, John C. Private	Unk	May 8, 1862, Augusta, Georgia	Co. A, 7th Georgia Cavalry	June 11, 1864, Trevilian Station, Louisa Court House, Virginia	Point Lookout, Maryland, transferred to Elmira Prison, NY, July 25, 1864	Died January 6, 1865 of Chronic Diarrhea, Grave No. 1242
Norris, T. L. Private	Unk	February 6, 1864, Columbia, South Carolina	Co. F, 22nd South Carolina Infantry	July 30, 1864, Petersburg, Virginia	Point Lookout, Maryland, transferred to Elmira Prison, NY, August 12, 1864	Exchanged October 29, 1864 at Venus Point, Savannah River, GA.
Norris, William J. Private	Unk	May 12, 1862, Cumberland County, North Carolina	Co. I, 51st North Carolina Infantry	June 1, 1864, Cold Harbor, Virginia	Point Lookout, Maryland, transferred to Elmira Prison, NY, July 12, 1864	Exchanged October 29, 1864 at Venus Point, Savannah River, GA.
North, James P. Private	Unk	March 15, 1864, Cumberland, Virginia	Co. H, 14th Virginia Infantry	May 10, 1864, Near Petersburg, Virginia	Point Lookout, Maryland, transferred to Elmira Prison, NY, August 17, 1864	Died December 24, 1864 of Pneumonia, Grave No. 1109
Northcut, A. N. Private	Unk	January 1, 1864, Darlington District, South Carolina	Co. B, 21st South Carolina Infantry	June 24, 1864, Near Petersburg, Virginia	Point Lookout, Maryland, transferred to Elmira Prison, NY, August 18, 1864	Exchanged October 29, 1864 at Venus Point, Savannah River, GA.
Northcutt, Henry L. Private	Unk	February 29, 1864, Marion, South Carolina	Co. I, 21st South Carolina Volunteers	January 15, 1865, Fort Fisher, North Carolina	January 30, 1865 Elmira Prison Camp, New York	Oath of Allegiance 7/11/1865
Northcutt, John W. Corporal	Unk	November 1, 1863, Darlington, South Carolina	Co. B, 21st South Carolina Infantry	January 15, 1865, Fort Fisher, North Carolina	January 30, 1865 Elmira Prison Camp, New York	Exchanged March 2, 1865 at Boulware's Wharf on the James River, Virginia
Northcutt, S. T. Private	Unk	January 25, 1862, Darlington, South Carolina	Co. B, 21st South Carolina Infantry	January 15, 1865, Fort Fisher, North Carolina	January 30, 1865 Elmira Prison Camp, New York	Oath of Allegiance July 19, 1865
Northern, James B. Private	Unk	March 5, 1862, Fort Lowry, Virginia	Co. F, 55th Virginia Infantry	May 6, 1864, Wilderness, Virginia	Point Lookout, Maryland, transferred to Elmira Prison, NY, August 14, 1864	Exchanged October 29, 1864 at Venus Point, Savannah River, GA.

Name & Rank	Age	Enlisted	Regiment and State	Where Captured	Prison	Remarks
Northington, B. Private	Unk	April 12, 1864, Petersburg, Virginia	Co. G, 8th North Carolina Infantry	May 31, 1864, Cold Harbor, Virginia	Point Lookout, Maryland, transferred to Elmira Prison, NY, July 12, 1864	Oath of Allegiance May 19, 1865
Norton, B. L. Private	Unk	December 9, 1861, Camp Trousdale, Tennessee	Co. D, 44th Tennessee Infantry	June 17, 1864, Petersburg, Virginia	Point Lookout, Maryland, transferred to Elmira Prison, NY, July 30, 1864	Oath of Allegiance June 17, 1865
Norton, H. A. Private	Unk	Unknown	Co. I, 6th North Carolina Infantry	May 30, 1864, Mechanics-ville, Virginia	Point Lookout, Maryland, transferred to Elmira Prison, NY, July 12, 1864	Oath of Allegiance May 19, 1865
Norton, H. J. Private	Unk	Unknown	Co. B, 21st South Carolina Infantry	January 15, 1865, Fort Fisher, North Carolina	January 30, 1865 Elmira Prison Camp, New York	Oath of Allegiance July 11, 1865
Norton, Lorenzo B. Private	Unk	December 9, 1861, Camp Trousdale, Tennessee	Co. D, 44th Tennessee Infantry	June 17, 1864, Petersburg, Virginia	Point Lookout, Maryland, transferred to Elmira Prison, NY, July 30, 1864	Oath of Allegiance June 19, 1865
Norton, Patrick Seaman	Unk	Unknown	Confederate States Steamer Chicora	September 7, 1863, Charleston, South Carolina	Point Lookout, Maryland, transferred to Elmira Prison, NY, July 23, 1864	Oath of Allegiance March 6, 1865
Norton, R. J. Private	Unk	Unknown	Co. D, 44th Tennessee Infantry	June 1, 7, 1864, Petersburg, Virginia	Point Lookout, Maryland, transferred to Elmira Prison, NY, July 30, 1864	Oath of Allegiance May 29, 1865
Norton, William H. Private	Unk	May 15, 1862, Camp Harris, Tennessee	Co. G, 17th Tennessee Infantry	June 17, 1864, Petersburg, Virginia	Point Lookout, Maryland, transferred to Elmira Prison, NY, July 30, 1864	Oath of Allegiance May 17, 1865
Norville, J. S. Private	35	July 17, 1862, Camp Holmes, Raleigh, North Carolina	Co. J, 35th North Carolina Infantry	June 17, 1864, Petersburg, Virginia	Point Lookout, Maryland, transferred to Elmira Prison, NY, July 30, 1864	Died November 22, 1864 of Chronic Diarrhea, Grave No. 927
Norwood, Gilliam Private	20	March 17, 1862, Pittsboro, North Carolina	Co. G, 26th North Carolina Infantry	May 12, 1864, Spotsylvania Court House, Virginia	Point Lookout, Maryland, transferred to Elmira Prison, NY, July 30, 1864	Oath of Allegiance June 16, 1865

Name & Rank	Age	Enlisted	Regiment and State	Where Captured	Prison	Remarks
Nott, Roger Private	Unk	Unknown	Co. A, 10th Virginia Cavalry	October 28, 1864, Snickersville, Virginia	Old Capital Prison, Washington, DC, transferred to Elmira December 17, 1864	Exchanged February 20, 1865 at Boulware's or Cox Wharf on the James River, Virginia
Notts, James G. Private	25	March 21, 1862, Concord, North Carolina	Co. A, 52nd North Carolina Infantry	May 8, 1864, Near Spotsylvania, Virginia	Point Lookout, Maryland, transferred to Elmira Prison, NY, August 14, 1864	Oath of Allegiance June 14, 1865. Probable Spelling Knotts.
Nowell, William N. Private	Unk	September 28, 1863, Eagle Rock, North Carolina	Co. H, 31st North Carolina Infantry	June 1, 1864, Gaines Mill Cold Harbor, Virginia	Point Lookout, Maryland, transferred to Elmira Prison, NY, July 12, 1864	Died August 29, 1864 of Acute Bronchitis, Grave No. 57
Nowlin, Light Private	Unk	May 15, 1862, Camp Harris, Tennessee	Co. C, 17th Tennessee Infantry	June 17, 1864, Petersburg, Virginia	Point Lookout, Maryland, transferred to Elmira Prison, NY, July 30, 1864	Exchanged February 25, 1865 at Boulware's or Cox Wharf on the James River, Virginia
Nowlin, Samuel H. Sergeant	Unk	April 1, 1861, Salem, Virginia	Co. D, 5th Virginia Cavalry	May 11, 1864, Yellow Tavern, Hanover County, Virginia	Point Lookout, Maryland, transferred to Elmira Prison, NY, August 17, 1864	Oath of Allegiance June 15, 1865
Nowlin, Samuel J. Private	Unk	May 28, 1861, Richmond, Georgia	Co. F, 18th Georgia Infantry	June 1, 1864, Cold Harbor, Virginia	Point Lookout, Maryland, transferred to Elmira Prison, NY, July 17, 1864	Oath of Allegiance June 16, 1865
Noyes, John S. Private	Unk	November 3, 1861, Cotton Hill, Virginia	Co. H, 22nd Virginia Infantry	June 3, 1864, Gaines Farm Cold Harbor, Virginia	Point Lookout, Maryland, transferred to Elmira Prison, NY, July 12, 1864	Oath of Allegiance June 16, 1865
Nuckolds, Thomas J. Private	Unk	July 2, 1861, Bethel Am., Virginia	Co. F, 50th Virginia Infantry	May 12, 1864, Spotsylvania Court House, Virginia	Point Lookout, Maryland, transferred to Elmira Prison, NY, August 2, 1864	Died 9/21/64 of Chronic Diarrhea, Grave No. 337. Name J. F. Knuckels on Headstone.

Name & Rank	Age	Enlisted	Regiment and State	Where Captured	Prison	Remarks
Nuckols, Abner C. Private	Unk	May 20, 1861, Manakin, Virginia	Co. F, 23rd Virginia Infantry	July 11, 1864, Near Washington, DC	Old Capital Prison, Washington DC. Transferred to Elmira Prison Camp New York July 25, 1864.	Oath of Allegiance June 14, 1865
Nugent, James Private	29	July 15, 1863, Mobile, Alabama	Co. F, 6th Louisiana Infantry	July 8, 1864, Near Harpers Ferry, Virginia	Old Capital Prison, Washington DC. Transferred to Elmira Prison Camp New York July 25, 1864.	Exchanged March 10, 1865. Died May 17, 1865 of Dysentery at Confederate States General Hospital, Shreveport, Louisiana.
Nunn, Benjamin F. Sergeant	18	October 16, 1861, Lenoir County, North Carolina	Co. G, 40th Regiment, 3rd North Carolina Artillery	January 15, 1865, Fort Fisher, North Carolina	January 30, 1865 Elmira Prison Camp, New York	Exchanged February 20, 1865 at Boulware's or Cox Wharf on the James River, Virginia
Nunnally, J. W. Private	Unk	May 1, 1863, Augusta, Georgia	Co. I, 16th Georgia Infantry	June 1, 1864, Gaines Farm Cold Harbor, Virginia	Point Lookout, Maryland, transferred to Elmira Prison, NY, July 12, 1864	Exchanged February 13, 1865 at Boulware's wharf on the James River, Virginia
Nunnally, Samuel J. Private	24	May 28, 1861, Meherrin, Virginia	Co. K, 21st Virginia Infantry	July 12, 1864, Near Washington, DC	Old Capital Prison, Washington DC. Transferred to Elmira Prison Camp New York July 25, 1864.	Exchanged February 20, 1865 at Boulware's or Cox Wharf on the James River, Virginia
Nunnery, A. L. Sergeant	Unk	November 18, 1861, College Green, Columbia, South Carolina	Co. A, 17th South Carolina Infantry	July 30, 1864, Petersburg, Virginia	Point Lookout, Maryland, transferred to Elmira Prison, NY, August 12, 1864	Oath of Allegiance June 14, 1865
Nunnery, William Private	Unk	May 3, 1862, Cumberland County, North Carolina	Co. J, 51st North Carolina Infantry	June 1, 1864, Cold Harbor, Virginia	Transferred From Point Lookout Prison, MD, July 12, 1864. Train Never Arrived at Elmira Prison Camp, NY.	Died July 15, 1864 in Train Wreck at Shohola, Pennsylvania.

Name & Rank	Age	Enlisted	Regiment and State	Where Captured	Prison	Remarks
Nunnery, William A. Private	22	April 11, 1862, Richmond, Virginia	Co. G, 5th Virginia Cavalry	June 11, 1864, Trevilian Station, Louisa Court House, Virginia	Point Lookout, Maryland, transferred to Elmira Prison, NY, July 25, 1864	Oath of Allegiance June 4, 1865
Nussman, M. J. Private	Unk	March 4, 1864, Gold Hill, North Carolina	Co. H, 8th North Carolina Infantry	May 31, 1864, Cold Harbor, Virginia	Point Lookout, Maryland, transferred to Elmira Prison, NY, July 12, 1864	Died March 29, 1865 of Variola (Smallpox) Grave No. 2494
Nutall, Edward Private	21	April 23, 1861, Gloucester Court House, Virginia	Co. B, 26th Virginia Infantry	June 15, 1864, Near Petersburg, Virginia	Point Lookout, Maryland, transferred to Elmira Prison, NY, July 12, 1864	Exchanged March 14, 1865 at Boulware's Wharf on the James River, Virginia
Nutall, John James Private	18	February 10, 1862, Gloucester Point, Virginia	Co. B, 26th Virginia Infantry	June 15, 1864, Near Petersburg, Virginia	Point Lookout, Maryland, transferred to Elmira Prison, NY, July 12, 1864	Exchanged March 10, 1865 at Boulware's Wharf on the James River, Virginia
Nutt, James M. Private	19	May 22, 1861, Killmasnock, Virginia	Co. H, 40th Virginia Infantry	June 2, 1864, Old Church, Cold Harbor, Virginia	Point Lookout, Maryland, transferred to Elmira Prison, NY, July 12, 1864	Oath of Allegiance May 19, 1865.
Nuttall, Edward M. Private	21	June 2, 1861, Gloucester Point, Virginia	Co. B, 26th Virginia Infantry	June 15, 1864, Near Petersburg, Virginia	Point Lookout, Maryland, transferred to Elmira Prison, NY, July 12,1864	Exchanged February 25, 1865 at Boulware's or Cox Wharf on the James River, Virginia
Nuttall, John James Private	18	February 10, 1862, Gloucester Point, Virginia	Co. B, 26th Virginia Infantry	June 15, 1864, Near Petersburg, Virginia	Point Lookout, Maryland, transferred to Elmira Prison, NY, July 12,1864	Exchanged March 10, 1865 at Boulware's wharf on the James River, Virginia
Nye, John H. Private	Unk	December 16, 1861, Gloucester Point, Virginia	Co. A, 26th Virginia Infantry	June 15, 1864, Near Petersburg, Virginia	Point Lookout, Maryland, transferred to Elmira Prison, NY, July 12, 1864	Oath of Allegiance July 11, 1865

Bibliography

Articles and Periodicals:

Bowden, the Reverend Malachi, *My Life as a Yankee Captive.* Published in the Atlanta Journal and Constitution Magazine.

Byrne, Thomas E., *"Elmira's Civil War Prison Camp: 1864-1865," Chemung Historical Journal, volume 10, No. 1, (September1964)*: page 1287,

Davis, Thaddeus C., *Confederate Veteran* Magazine, February 1899, page 65;

Ewan, R.B., *Reminiscences of Prison Life at Elmira, N.Y.,* January 1908;

Huffman, James, *Prisoner of War, Atlantic Magazine* 163, no. 4, April 1939;

Jones, James P., *A Rebel's Diary of Elmira Prison Camp, Chemung Historical Journal* 20, no. 3, March 1975;

Sherrill, Miles, *A Soldier's Story: Prison Life and Other Incidents,* University of North Carolina at Chapel Hill, 1998;

Stamp, James B., *Ten Months Experience in Northern Prisons, Alabama Historical Quarterly 18,* pages 486-498;

Taylor, G.T., *Prison Experience in Elmira, N.Y., Confederate Veteran* Magazine 20, no. 7, July 1912;

The Treatment of Prisoners during the War Between the States, Southern Historical Society Papers 1, no. 3, March 1876;

The Treatment of Prisoners during the War, Southern Historical Society Papers 1, no. 4, April 1876;

Turner, Henry M. *Civil War Times Illustrated,* 31 (October/November, 1980);

Wade, F.S., *Getting Out of Prison, Confederate Veteran* magazine 34, no. 10, October 1926;

Ward, John Shirley, *Responsibility for the Death of Prisoners, Confederate Veteran* magazine 4, no. 1, January 1896;

Wyeth, John Allan, *Cold Cheer at Camp Morton, Century Magazine* 41 no. 6 (April 1891) 848;

Books:

Benson, Berry, Susan W. Benson, ed., *Berry Benson's Civil War Book: Memoirs of a Confederate Scout and Sharpshooter,* Athens, Ga.: University of Georgia Press, 1962;

Diagnostic and Statistical Manual of Mental Disorders, 5th Edition, *Arlington: American Psychiatric Publishing, pages 160–168,* American Psychiatric Publishing, May 27, 2013;

Gray, Michael P., *The Business of Captivity: Elmira and It's Civil War Prison,* The Kent State University Press, 2001;

Hampson, Helen (Wyeth), My Great-Great Grandfather Was a Prisoner of War . . . Libby Prison, 2002;

Heartsill, W. W., *Fourteen Hundred and 91 Days in the Confederate Army,* Edited by Bell Irvin Wiley, Broadfoot Publishing Co., Wilmington North Carolina, 1987.

Holmes, Clay W., *The Elmira Prison Camp: A History of the Military Prison at Elmira, N.Y. July 6, 1864, to July 10, 1865.* New York: Knickerbocker Press, 1912;

Hopkins, Luther, *Prison life at Point Lookout.*

Horigan, Michael, *Elmira: Death Camp of the North,* Stackpole Books, 2002;

Huffman, James, *Ups and Downs of a Confederate Soldier,* New York: William E. Rudge's Sons, 1940;

Keiley, Anthony M., *In Vinculis; or, The Prisoner of War: Being The Experience Of A Rebel In Two Federal Pens,* Blelock & Co., No. 19 Beekman Street, New York, 1866;

King, John A., *My Experience in the Confederate Army, and in Northern Prisons,* Roanoke, West Virginia, Stonewall Jackson Chapter No. 1333, United Daughters of the Confederacy, Clarksburg, West Virginia, 1917;

Leon, Louis, *Diary of a Tarheel Confederate Prisoner,* Charlotte, N.C.: Stone, 1913;

Malone, Whatley Pierson Jr., *The Diary of Bartlett Yancy Malone,* Published by the University of Chapel Hill, 1919.

Manarin, Louis H. and Weymouth T. Jordan, eds., *North Carolina Troops1861-1865: A Roster,* 13 volumes, Raleigh, North Carolina: Division of Archives and History, 1966-1993;

Miller-Keane, *Encyclopedia & Dictionary of Medicine, Nursing, & Allied Heath, Fifth Edition,* W. B. Saunders Company, Philadelphia.

Opie, John N., *A Rebel Cavalryman with Lee, Stuart, and Jackson,* Morningside Press, Chicago: W.B. Conkey, 1899.

Ottman, Walter H., *A History of the City of Elmira, New York;*

Pickenpaugh, Roger, *Captives In Gray,* The University of Alabama Press, 2009;

Speer, Lonnie R., *Portals To Hell: Military Prisons of the Civil War,* Stackpole Books, 1997;

Speer, Lonnie R., *War of Vengeance: Acts of Retaliation against Civil War POWs,* Stackpole Books, 2002;

Toney, Marcus B., *The Privations of a Private,* Nashville and Dallas: M.E. Church, South, Smith and Lamar, 1907;

Towner, Ausburn, *Our County and Its People - A History of the Valley and County of Chemung From the Closing years of the Eighteenth Century,* D. Mason & Publishers, 1892;

Watkins, Sam R., *Co. Aytch, Maury Grays, First Tennessee Regiment or, A Side Show to the Big Show,* Chattanooga, Tennessee, Times Printing Company, 1900;

Wilkeson, Frank, *Turned Inside Out: Recollections of a Private Soldier in the Army of the Potomac,* New York and London: G.P. Putnam's Sons, 1887;

Williamson, James J., *Prison Life in the Old Capital and Reminiscences of the Civil War,* West Orange, New Jersey, 1911.

Manuscripts:

Greer, William R. Papers, *Recollections of a Private Soldier of the Army of the Confederate States,* Manuscript Department, William R. Perkins Library, Duke University, North Carolina

Papers:

Sanger, Eugene F., *Eugene F. Sanger Papers, Records of the Office of the Adjutant General, Regimental Correspondence, 1861-1865,* Maine State Archives. College of William and Mary, William Lamb Collection;

Official Publications:

Confederate States of America, Congress, *Joint Select Committee to Investigate the Condition and Treatment of Prisoners of War,* March, 1865;

The Medical and Surgical History of the War of the Rebellion, (1861-65), Prepared in Accordance Acts of Congress, Under the Direction of Surgeon General Joseph K. Barnes, United States Army, Washington Government Printing Office, 1870, Volumes I, III, VI.

North Carolina Troops 1861-1865, 22 Volumes, Broadfoot Publishing, edited by Louis H. Marin, and Numerous authors.

War of the Rebellion Official Records of the Union and Confederate Armies, Series II, Volumes IV,

VII, XXVI. Washington, D.C., Government Printing Office, 1870.

Confederate States of America, Congress, *Joint Select Committee to Investigate the Condition and Treatment of Prisoners of War,* March, 1865;

Newspapers:

Daily National Intelligencer, Washington, D. C.,
Elmira Daily Advertiser,
Elmira Daily Gazette,
New York Times,
New York Tribune,